**PEARSON
BACCALAUREATE**

Psychology

DEVELOPED SPECIFICALLY FOR THE
IB DIPLOMA

ALAN LAW • CHRISTOS HALKIOPOULOS • CHRISTIAN BRYAN-ZAYKOV

Pearson Education Limited is a company incorporated in England and Wales, having its registered office at Edinburgh Gate, Harlow, Essex, CM20 2JE. Registered company number: 872828.

www.pearsonbaccalaureate.com

Pearson is a registered trademark of Pearson Education Limited.

Text © Pearson Education Limited 2010

First published 2010

20 19 18 17 16 15 14 13
IMP 10 9 8 7 6

ISBN 978 0 435032 88 3

Copyright notice

Edited by Penelope Lyons
Designed by Tony Richardson
Typeset by Tony Richardson
Original illustrations © Pearson Education Limited 2010
Illustrated by Ian West (Beehive illustration)
Cover design by Tony Richardson
Picture research by Joanne Forrest Smith
Cover photo © Photodisc
Printed in Malaysia, KHL-CTP

Acknowledgements

The authors and publisher would like to thank the following individuals and organizations for permission to reproduce photographs:

(Key: b-bottom; c-centre; l-left; r-right; t-top)

Aaron T Beck: 169t; **Alamy Images:** Custom Medical Stock Photo 177, Image Source 30, Israel images 171, Lebrecht Music and Arts Photo Library 34, North Wind Picture Archives 71, Photofusion Picture Library 144, Rod Edwards 3, Stacy Walsh Rosenstock 93; **Corbis:** Bettmann viiitl, viiitr, viiibl, 36, 169b, Bob Krist 270, Edith Held 187, Farrell Grehan 183, Frank Schnabel 209, Heide Benser 120, JAI / Nigel Pavitt 255, John Van Hasselt 230, Larry Mulvehill 254, Ira Nowinski 102, Reuters / David W Cerny 153, Sunset Boulevard 212, Wolfgang Flamisch 41t; **FLPA Images of Nature:** Inga Spence 210; **Frans van Hoesel/University of Groningen:** 164; **Getty Images:** 208, 213bl, 213br, 236, 240, 284, 298, 307, 310tl, 312, viiibr, AFP 296, 310tr, 325t, Bloomberg 294, Bruce Ayres 179, Commercial Eye 322cr, Digital Zoo 321b, Fuse 221, Gallo Images / Stringer 290, Ghislain & Marie David de Lossy 288, Glow Images 324, Jon Larter 219, Lucas Lenci Photo 27, Mark Harmel 292, NBAE 302, Popperfoto 195, Purestock 89b, Serge Krouglikoff 157, Time & Life Pictures 321t, WireImage 206; **Gregory D. Webster, Daniel Kruger:** 62; **iStockphoto:** 14, 20, 46, 66, 89t, 114, 134tc, 134l, 134c, 134cl, 134cr, 163, 198, 218, 223, 252, 322br; **Pearson Education Ltd:** 4, 5, 22, 39, 45cr, 52, 57, 58, 101, 103cl, 103cr, 132, 147, 184cl, 184cr, 184br, 234, 238, 249, 264, 320bl, 320br, 322tr, 323, 325cl/a, 325bl/b, 326; **Photolibrary.com:** 257br, HuntStock 257bl, John Warburton-Lee Photography 289; **Photoshot Holdings Limited:** Mary Evans Picture Library 327; **Rocket USA:** 121; **Science Photo Library Ltd:** Dr Robert Friedland 43, ISM / Sovereign 42, Jacopin 44, James King–Holmes 86b, Kjell B Sandved viii, Life in View 243, Living Art Enterprises LLC 85, Mark Thomas 41b, MedImage 225, National Cancer Institute / Linda Bartlett 7, NCMIR / Thomas Deerinck 86t, RIA Novosti 190, Roger Harris 45cl, 91, Science Source 200, Wellcome Dept of Cognitive Neurology 159, Will & Deni McIntyre 172; **Simon & Schuster, Free Press:** 65; **Solomon Asch Center for Study of Ethnopolitical Conflict:** 127; **The Advertising Archives:** 227

All other images © Pearson Education Limited

The publisher and authors would also like to thank the following for permission to use © material:

American Psychiatric Association and scientificpsychic.com. Our thanks go to the International Baccalaureate Organization for permission to reproduce its intellectual property.

Every effort has been made to trace the copyright holders and we apologise in advance for any unintentional omissions. We would be pleased to insert the appropriate acknowledgment in any subsequent edition of this publication.

This material has been developed independently by the publisher and the content is in no way connected with nor endorsed by the International Baccalaureate Organization.

Dedications

To my parents, Dorothy and Colin.
    Alan Law

To my dad Ioannis and the memory of my mum Kassiani.
    Christos Halkiopoulos

Moyey lyubimoy zhene Tatyane i moemu prekrasnomu synu Fyodoru.
    Christian Bryan

CONTENTS

INTRODUCTION

 ## What is psychology?

The British Psychological Society defines psychology as the scientific study of people, the mind and behaviour. It is one of the most popular subjects at schools and universities around the world and, because the subject has so many applications, graduates of psychology work in a wide range of fields.

Psychologists develop and test theories scientifically to try to understand how mind and behaviour work, and use their findings to try to create uses outside the laboratory. Their work is applied in such diverse fields as sport, work, advertising, management, the legal system and medicine. What all of this work has traditionally had in common is the attempt to be scientific in trying to establish clear cause-and-effect relationships and thereby come close to establishing good descriptions of what people do in specific situations and explanations as to why.

The subject has developed over time and it is now accepted within the discipline of psychology that there are many different factors involved in how people think and act. This means it is necessary to have a good understanding of internal and external influences on behaviour in order to provide more complete explanations.

 ## History of psychology

People have been interested in studying and explaining their own behaviour for a very long time, and have always attempted to apply the ideas of their time to solving problems. Trephining, for example, is a practice thought to have started in prehistoric times. It involves cutting a hole in the skull, commonly with the intention of releasing from the patient's head some sort of harmful spirit that was causing a change in behaviour.

At various times, explanations for behaviour have varied as explanations of the world based on spirits, gods and demons have become more or less dominant. Hippocrates, in ancient Greece, explained female hysteria in terms of a wandering uterus; across Europe for several hundred years people, usually women, were burned as witches because their actions were assumed to be driven by the influence of devils and demons. In the 19th century in Europe, a shift in thinking inspired a more empirical approach to the study of psychology. In 1879, Wilhelm Wundt opened what is believed to be the first psychological laboratory in Leipzig, Germany, for students to study experimental psychology. Not long after, Sigmund Freud began to have an impact on the scientific and medical worlds with his psychodynamic theories involving the influence of unconscious conflict on human behaviour.

Skull after trephining.

Sigmund Freud argued that unconscious conflict was the cause of much of our anxiety and that most of our personality is formed before the age of 13. One of his most famous propositions was the Oedipus complex, whereby boys fall in love with their mothers.

Wilhelm Wundt (1832–1920) was originally a physiologist.

Sigmund Freud (1856–1939), one of the most famous psychologists of all.

Reactions against Freud's work inspired the birth of a new direction in psychology in the USA. The behaviourist approach was developed most famously by John Watson and B.F. Skinner. This approach focused on the role of previous learning, suggesting that we have an innate predisposition to learn, and the experiences we have during our lives plus the consequences of our behaviour are ultimately responsible for determining our behaviour.

John Watson claimed that it was possible in a controlled environment to influence children so powerfully that he could deliberately direct them to become doctors, lawyers or even thieves.

John Watson (1878–1958).

BF Skinner (1904–90).

Other approaches soon developed, including the humanistic approach and cognitive psychology. Both of these attempted to study a wide range of human experience that is not observable using new methodology that could allow the knowledge gained to be considered scientific.

Positive psychology is a recent new branch of psychology. It is an approach that attempts to focus on how to maximize the positive side of human existence rather than how to correct the negative side. So instead of trying to come up with ways to treat depression, for example, positive psychologists look at ways to improve job satisfaction and teach optimism.

IB Psychology course

The IB Psychology syllabus reflects current thinking in psychology. It is recognized today that there are many different influences on behaviour and mental processes. For this reason, it is important that you understand what the major influences are, and recognize how knowledge from different approaches can be integrated to provide a more holistic or complete explanation of the phenomena being investigated.

Any aspect of human emotion, thinking or behaviour can be looked at using three different levels of analysis, which are like three different lenses of a microscope, each with a different strength (Figure 1).

The biological level of analysis studies an individual in the finest detail. At this level, we consider genetic, chemical and hormonal explanations, and study the role of the brain. One level further out, the cognitive level of analysis, considers the way that the individual processes information. In other words, not looking so much at the biology of the brain, but looking at how patterns of thinking are developed and used in individual interaction with the world. The widest level of analysis is the sociocultural level, which looks beyond the individual to the influence of other people and situations on behaviour. You will study the principles that define these three levels of analysis and learn about the main explanations of behaviour that each level focuses on.

The second component of your course is made up of specific applications of psychological knowledge in a number of possible fields. Here you can use your understanding of the three levels of analysis to explain behaviour and thinking in the contexts of abnormal psychology, human development, health, relationships and sports. You will use your understanding of strengths and limitations in research to evaluate these explanations.

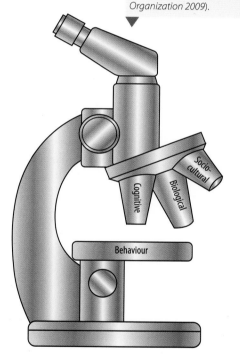

Figure 1
Levels of analysis microscope (*from IB Psychology Guide © International Baccalaureate Organization 2009*).

In all parts of the syllabus, you are expected to evaluate. You will find that you develop a strong understanding of methodological and ethical issues in research using humans and animals. In addition, you should recognize that the material you study is almost always intended to have an application beyond the research setting, so you will learn to criticize and value empirical research that tests the usefulness of theory.

IB Learner Profile and links to TOK and CAS

The IB Psychology course gives you opportunities to be an effective and sensitive learner. You should be a curious inquirer and seek further information about studies and theories

mentioned in this book and independently research topics that interest you. You should use the knowledge you gain to help you in your understanding of other subjects and Theory of Knowledge (TOK). Similarly, you should bring your understanding from other topics to this subject. Psychology is such a broad discipline that almost every other subject contributes to it in some way. Studying psychology and biology together will help you to understand both subjects better. Parts of economics focus on predicting human behaviour in specific situations, and sports and exercise science includes a section on sports psychology.

You will find that psychology is an international subject which encourages the study of cultures other than your own. You should actively seek information about cultures that interest you and consider the role of your own culture in influencing your behaviour, emotions and thoughts. IB psychology fosters intercultural understanding and respect, and you are encouraged to develop empathy for the feelings, needs and customs of others, both within and outside your own culture.

Another aspect of the learner profile particularly relevant for psychology, is the intention for you to develop your critical thinking skills. By studying psychology, you will learn to question in a systematic way, to tolerate ambiguity, and to develop skills in evaluating theory and research. To help you on your critical thinking journey, there are TOK boxes throughout the book which offer you the chance to notice links between subjects and to question knowledge and understanding.

It is hoped that the study of psychology will inspire you to see links with the Creativity, Action and Service component of the IB Diploma. Many of the chapters in this book expose you to information about groups of people who may be in need of help, company, or care, and you are encouraged to seek out organizations in your community that might benefit from your time and assistance.

To learn more about these initiatives, go to pearsonhotlinks.com, enter the title or ISBN of this book and select weblink Int.1a or Int.1b.

In many countries, there are initiatives to help educate young people about mental health issues. You might be interested in bringing them into your school or getting involved with their work in other ways.

For example, *Mind Matters* is an Australian organization, and in Germany, the Czech Republic and Slovakia, a programme called *Crazy? So what!* has been run successfully for several years. Try to find something similar in your country.

How you will be assessed

There are three examinations and an internal assessment (Table 1).

Assessment element	What is it?	% of SL grade	% of HL grade
TABLE 1 THE CONTENTS AND WEIGHTING OF THE FOUR ASSESSMENT ELEMENTS			
Paper 1	Core material: Levels of analysis (Chapters 2–4) One compulsory short answer question about each level of analysis and one essay from a choice of three: one for each level of analysis	50	35
Paper 2	Options material (Chapters 5–9) One essay for SL from one option Two essays from different options for HL	25	25
Paper 3 (HL only)	Qualitative research methodology (Chapter 1) Three questions relating to qualitative methodology		20
Internal Assessment	Simple experimental study	25	20

Learning outcomes

There are four assessment objectives.

1   Knowledge and comprehension of specified content
2   Application and analysis
3   Synthesis and evaluation
4   Selection and use of skills appropriate to psychology

A number of learning outcomes are associated with the first three assesment objectives and these are listed in the relevant sections of each chapter.

Each learning outcome begins with what is called a command term, a word like *analyse* or *discuss*, which gives you an indication of what kind of answer is required. These command terms are placed in a hierarchy as shown in Table 2.

TABLE 2 COMMAND TERMS USED IN LEARNING OUTCOMES

Command terms	What is required
1 Knowledge and comprehension	
Define	Give the precise meaning of a word, phrase, concept or physical quantity.
Describe	Give a detailed account.
Outline	Give a brief account or summary.
State	Give a specific name, value or other brief answer without explanation or calculation.
2 Application and analysis	
Analyse	Break down in order to bring out the essential elements or structure.
Apply	Use an idea, equation, principle, theory or law in relation to a given problem or issue.
Distinguish	Make clear the differences between two or more concepts or items.
Explain	Give a detailed account including reasons or causes.
3 Synthesis and evaluation	
Compare	Give an account of the similarities between two (or more) items or situations, referring to both (all) of them throughout.
Compare and contrast	Give an account of similarities and differences between two (or more) items or situations, referring to both (all) of them throughout.
Contrast	Give an account of the differences between two (or more) items or situations, referring to both (all) of them throughout.
Discuss	Offer a considered and balanced review that includes a range of arguments, factors or hypotheses. Opinions or conclusions should be presented clearly and supported by appropriate evidence.
Evaluate	Make an appraisal by weighing up the strengths and limitations.
Examine	Consider an argument or concept in a way that uncovers the assumptions and interrelationships of the issue.
To what extent ...	Consider the merits or otherwise of an argument or concept. Opinions and conclusions should be presented clearly and supported with appropriate evidence and sound argument.

From IB Psychology Guide © International Baccalaureate Organization 2009

The command terms associated with synthesis and evaluation ask for more complicated work. You will only be asked questions like this for the essay questions in part 2 of Paper 1 and in Paper 2. The short answer questions in Paper 1 will begin with command terms associated with knowledge and comprehension, and application and analysis (Table 2).

You should not learn material exclusively in the context of the command term stated in the learning objectives as any command term from within the same assessment objective group could be used. Moreover, a command term from a less demanding group could be used

instead. So, for example, in Chapter 2 you will find the learning outcome 'Discuss the use of brain-imaging technologies in investigating the relationship between biological factors and behaviour'. You need to be sure that you can also describe and compare brain-imaging technologies, because *describe* is listed before discuss in Table 2 and *compare* is in the same assessment objective group. More guidance on this is given in each chapter.

Internal Assessment and Extended Essays

Every student of psychology must complete a single piece of experimental work that is marked by their teacher first, with a sample of students' work moderated externally. The Internal Assessment for psychology is a simple experimental study, an opportunity for you to complete a practical investigation in an area that interests you. Full details of this and a practical guide to planning, conducting, and writing up your research are given on pages 328–339.

Psychology is a very popular choice among IB candidates when it comes time to select a subject for their Extended Essay. There are very clear guidelines for how this should be done, and full details and advice about these are given on pages 340–349. The core task of the Extended Essay in psychology is to conduct an independent research investigation into a research question that invites some level of debate. Note that it does not include a practical component: it is a systematic review of literature that develops an argument to answer the question set.

Information boxes

Throughout the book you will see a number of coloured boxes interspersed through each chapter. They may be in the margins or in the main text area. Each of these boxes provides different information and stimulus as follows.

> **Learning outcomes**
> - Outline principles that define the biological level of analysis.
> - Explain how principles that define the biological level of analysis may be demonstrated in research.

You will find a box like this at the start of each section in each chapter. They are the learning outcomes for the section you are about to read and they set out what content and aspects of learning are covered in that section.

In addition to the Theory of Knowledge chapter, there are TOK boxes throughout the book. These boxes are there to stimulate thought and consideration of any TOK issues as they arise and in context. Often they will just contain a question to stimulate your own thoughts and discussion.

In what sense precisely can the study of cognition be viewed as scientific? Should we in psychology seek understanding in terms of reasons rather than explanations in terms of causes?

Research by Gosling (2009) uses the FFM to show how your music preferences, the way you keep your room or office, or the look of your Facebook pages reveal quite a few things about your personality.

The yellow interesting fact boxes contain interesting information which will add to your wider knowledge but which does not fit within the main body of the text.

The green key facts boxes contain key facts which are drawn out of the main text and highlighted. This makes them easily identifiable for quick reference. The boxes also enable you to identify the core learning points within a section.

Cognitive therapy tries to restructure negative information-processing styles.

EMPIRICAL RESEARCH

Yoga and well-being (Hartfiel et al., 2010)

These researchers organized a randomized controlled trial in the UK. In the trial, 48 employees were placed in either a yoga group or a wait-list control group. The yoga group was offered six weeks (January through to March 2008) of dru yoga, comprising one hour-long lunchtime class per week with a certified dru yoga instructor. The wait-list control group received no intervention during this six-week study. Participants were administered psychological tests measuring mood and well-being before and after the six-week period. Results showed the yoga group reported significant improvements in feelings of clear-mindedness, composure, elation, energy, and confidence. In addition, the yoga group reported increased life purpose and satisfaction, and feelings of greater self-confidence during stressful situations.

Empirical research boxes are self-contained examples that you can use to answer questions on specific points. They are usually longer than this example.

Examiner's hints provide insight into how to answer a question in order to achieve the highest marks in an examination. They also identify common pitfalls when answering such questions and suggest approaches that examiners like to see.

● **Examiner's hint**
The command term *discuss* in relation to the effects of violence means you need to refer to both short-term and long-term effects and to address problems of research in this area, particularly focusing on methodological issues highlighted in the text. You should be sure to include reference to the studies in the empirical research boxes and remember to be critical about them too.

Dr Martin Perry, a sport psychologist in the UK, keeps a blog relating to sport psychology. To learn more about the variety of contexts sport psychology can be applied to, go to www. pearsonhotlinks.com, enter the title or ISBN of this book and select weblink 9.1.

Hotlinks boxes direct you to the Pearson hotlinks site which in turn will take you to the relevant website(s). On the web pages there you will find additional information to support the topic, video simulations, and the like.

Blue online resources boxes indicate that online resources are available that relate to this section of the book. These resources might be extension exercises, additional practice questions, interactive material, suggestions for IA, EE and revision, or other sources of information.

To access Additional information 6.1 on Anthropology and Margaret Mead, please visit www.pearsonbacconline.com and follow the on-screen instructions.

RESEARCH METHODOLOGY

Learning outcomes

SL and HL

- Evaluate research studies.

HL only

Theory and practice in qualitative research

- Distinguish between qualitative and quantitative data.
- Explain strengths and limitations of a qualitative approach to research.
- To what extent can findings be generalized from qualitative studies?
- Discuss ethical considerations in qualitative research.
- Discuss sampling techniques appropriate to qualitative research (for example, purposive sampling, snowball sampling).
- Explain effects of participant expectations and researcher bias in qualitative research.
- Explain the importance of credibility in qualitative research.
- Explain the effect of triangulation on the credibility / trustworthiness of qualitative research.
- Explain reflexivity in qualitative research.

Interviews

- Evaluate semi-structured, focus group and narrative interviews.
- Discuss considerations involved before, during and after an interview (for example, sampling methods, data recording, traditional versus postmodern transcription, debriefing).
- Explain how researchers use inductive content analysis (thematic analysis) on interview transcripts.

Observations

- Evaluate participant, non-participant, naturalistic, overt and covert observations.
- Discuss considerations involved in setting up and carrying out an observation (for example, audience effect, Hawthorne effect, disclosure).
- Discuss how researchers analyse data obtained in observational research.

Case studies

- Evaluate the use of case studies in research.
- Explain how a case study could be used to investigate a problem in an organization or group (for example, a football team, a school, a family).
- Discuss the extent to which findings can be generalized from a single case study.

1.1 HL vs SL: What you need to know

The IB Psychology syllabus expects all students to develop a good understanding of the most common methods used in psychological research. There are two ways to achieve this:

- requiring students to describe, explain and evaluate published research
- requiring students to carry out their own research for the Internal Assessment.

In addition to this, Higher Level students are also required to complete a separate examination paper relating to qualitative methods.

1.2 What is good research? Reliability and validity

Researchers in psychology have traditionally attempted to adopt a scientific approach, whether trying to add to understanding of mind and behaviour through the creation and testing of theories, or trying to answer a practical question like how to increase motivation at work or in sport. Efforts to follow a scientific approach have helped the academic community to accept findings made by psychological researchers as a valid form of knowledge, or in other words, as 'true'.

Empiricism and objectivity

Empirical evidence is evidence gathered using our own senses.

For psychological research to be considered scientific, several key ideas need to be embraced. Perhaps the most fundamental of these is empiricism: an approach to the acquisition of knowledge that places high value on direct sensory information. It is not enough for psychologists to make knowledge claims based solely on their own thoughts or beliefs; there must be **empirical evidence** for their ideas. The evidence is gathered using the methods outlined in this chapter. One of the greatest challenges for psychology has been to explore and describe the human mind when it is not, in itself, a thing that can be directly observed. In recent times, technology has helped us observe the brain in action, and this has unquestionably aided psychologists in their attempts to be empirical.

Following the **scientific method** requires both an empirical approach and an attempt to be as **objective** as possible. Being objective requires the researcher to be **unbiased**. This means that his or her thoughts about the topic should have no influence on the evidence gathered or the interpretation of it. In this way, we hope that the conclusions reached by researchers are trustworthy; that if others did the same research, they would observe similar results; and that they would draw similar conclusions.

Operational definitions are descriptions of variables that are specific and quantifiable.

In order to achieve this, good scientific research needs to have several characteristics. First, the topics being studied – the behaviours or the aspects of mind under investigation – must be clearly defined. Researchers use **operational definitions** to explain what they are measuring. For example, it is not enough to say that you are measuring 'aggression' in children; it is necessary to have an explanation of specific aggressive behaviours that will be recorded.

When we understand exactly what is being measured, we also need to be convinced of two things: that the data obtained by the researcher is **reliable** and that the method used was a **valid** way to obtain the data.

Reliability

Reliability (similar to accuracy) can be established by considering the following questions.

1   Did more than one person record and interpret the data, and do they agree?

The answer to this question relates to the idea of **inter-rater** reliability. This can be very important in psychological research where people might disagree about whether the behaviour they have observed, even in a highly controlled environment, does in fact constitute an occurrence of the behaviour they are interested in recording. For example, if two people were recording the number of laughs made by an individual while watching a television comedy, they might easily disagree.

How easy is it to measure how much people laugh?

2   If you use the method again in the same situation, do you get the same results?

An acceptable answer to this question depends on two things. First, that the research can be repeated. This is referred to as the **replicability** of a study and is, in turn, dependent on the researcher giving clear details of the method used, and in particular providing operational definitions. Secondly, ideally the study has been replicated and similar results found. If we use a reliable test with the same participant, for example, we should get the same result. This is called **test–retest** reliability.

 Ideally, all research needs to be replicable so that findings can be confirmed by others.

Validity

Validity can seem a complex idea. It can be broken down into two types: internal validity and external validity. Internal validity is concerned with the quality of the research itself, particularly in experiments when the researcher wants to make cause–effect claims. Researchers should be studying what they claim to be studying, and measuring what they claim to be measuring. Is counting a viewer's laughter a valid way of measuring how funny a television comedy is? The independent and dependent variables specified by the researcher must be clearly defined and be a fair reflection of the phenomenon being investigated. When the study is carried out, extraneous variables such as noise or changes in behaviour because of the experimental situation should be eliminated or their effects minimized. External validity is concerned with how appropriate it is to apply the results of the study to the intended population.

Again, there are several questions we should consider before deciding whether researchers' methodology and conclusions are valid or not. Some of the most important questions are examined in the following pages.

Internal validity issues

1   What is the researcher trying to manipulate (in experiments) and measure? Is this really what they measured? Does it seem to be what they are measuring?

This kind of validity is probably the most important, and it is another reason that operational definitions of variables are so important. Many psychologists argue that IQ tests, for example, are measuring something, but not exactly what people mean when they are talking about intelligence. If research at a very superficial level seems to have been done well, then it can be said to have good **face validity**.

2   Did the location or nature of the research somehow make the participants act in a certain way?

Sometimes participants try to guess the nature of the research they are participating in and then act accordingly, which is one reason why psychologists sometimes prefer to keep it secret. **Demand characteristics** are the effects that occur because of this. The **Hawthorne effect** occurs when participants try to perform in a way that they think meets the expectations of the researcher. A lesser known opposite of this is the **screw-you effect**, where participants act in a way that might sabotage the researcher's aims. If research is done in a more natural setting, or if participants know little about the research or their participation in it, demand characteristics are less of a problem.

> Research has face validity if it appears to be investigating the phenomenon the researchers intend to examine. A lot of intelligence and personality research uses tasks that measure *something* but it is not clear that they measure these complicated phenomena.

> Children often try hard to please the experimenter.

3   Has the researcher maintained objectivity in their interpretation of the results?

Reading the conclusions of researchers after reading through their results can occasionally be confusing or even disappointing. Sometimes it is clear that the researcher wanted to be able to draw certain conclusions, and the data have been misinterpreted, variables poorly defined, or the researcher has relied only on their own judgement through the whole process of research. It is particularly difficult to maintain objectivity when researchers have hopes and expectations about the conclusions they might be able to draw from their research.

External validity issues

1 Was the research done in an artificial environment, or were the tasks performed artificial?

Sometimes this is referred to as the artificiality of a study, at other times it might be referred to as the **ecological validity**. The latter term focuses mostly on the environment in which the work was carried out. Experiments in laboratories enable the researcher to control the conditions and eliminate many variables that might interfere with his or her work. However, this can create an environment so unrealistic that it becomes impossible to generalize from the artificial environment to the real-life environment to which the results should apply. Also, when researchers attempt to measure psychological processes, they often ask participants to perform tasks that are not like their normal activities. Brain-imaging technology, for example, is giving us a better understanding of how the brain works, but researchers are very limited in what kind of activities they can ask participants to perform as they must often lie inside a large machine.

Many experiments lack ecological validity because they are carried out in an unnaturally pure environment, free from the influence of unwanted variables and need to be replicated in a more natural setting before we can consider the findings valid.

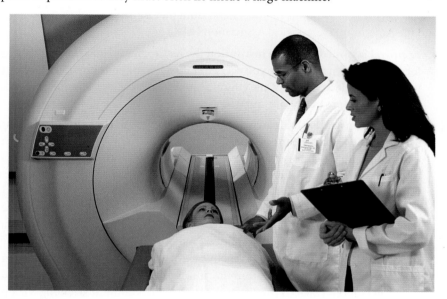

It is difficult to move inside an MRI machine, which limits how much we can learn from MRI studies.

2 Can we generalize from the participants in the sample to the wider population?

There are two very simple examples that illustrate this point. First, a lot of research has been done on animals because it is considered unethical to do the same research on humans. One of the reasons it has been possible to do this kind of research, is the assertion that animals and humans are fundamentally different in terms of consciousness or ability to feel pain. If it is accepted that animals are different from humans in this way and therefore it is ethically acceptable to do the research, is it valid to generalize from animals to humans?

The second example concerns sampling in psychological research carried out at universities. An estimated 75% of research has used undergraduate students as participants, with psychology students making up around a third of all research samples (McCray et al., 2005). Are psychology students representative of the general population? In some ways they are, but it is usually better to find a more varied sample if you plan to generalize.

● **Examiner's hint**
Whenever you are asked to *evaluate, discuss* or *compare* research, you can start by considering reliability and validity in general. Each method has typical strengths and weaknesses and these are discussed in this section.

There are a number of other factors that can render the conclusions a researcher draws invalid, and examples of these will be addressed when you look at individual studies and theories.

1.3 What is good research? General ethical issues

Good research needs to be **ethical** for several reasons. One reason is to preserve the reputation of psychology in the academic world and among the public – particularly to ensure that people will continue to come forward to participate in research. There are several important historical examples of research that was done without the consent of participants, or that caused significant psychological or physical harm. In the USA and later in the UK, guidelines were drawn up to try to ensure that all research done within the discipline is not damaging to institutions carrying out research or to the individuals who participate.

Guidelines for research involving people

The following are key points to understand from the British Psychological Society (BPS) and the American Psychological Association (APA).

- **Approval is gained from the institution the researcher is working for**. This is relevant for IB students in that before you carry out research for your internal assessment, you need a full understanding of the ethical requirements and you should not proceed without the approval of your teacher.

- **Informed consent is obtained from all those who will participate**. *Consent* indicates agreement. *Informed* means that participants have been made aware of the purpose, duration and procedures of the research; and of their rights, benefits and any possible negative consequences of participation. Of course, sometimes it is not possible to give full information about the research, and it is acceptable not to obtain informed consent if no harm is expected and only anonymous questionnaires or naturalistic observation are used as methods. The BPS also stresses that records of informed consent should be kept and that naturalistic observations should be done without consent only if the behaviour observed would normally be expected to be observed by strangers. This is usually understood to mean that it must occur in a public place. Additionally, researchers should take cultural considerations into account in deciding what behaviours might be acceptably observed or recorded. The BPS also specifies that children under the age of 16 years, and adults not competent to understand the nature and purpose of the research should not be allowed to consent alone: a guardian or family member should also consent.

- **Deception is to be avoided** unless it is justified by the potential significant contribution that the research will make, and the impossibility of avoiding deception. If psychological harm or physical pain are expected, deception is explicitly not allowed. When participants are deceived, they should be informed about this at the earliest possible opportunity. Clarifications in the BPS guidelines emphasize that there is a difference between falsely informing participants about the nature of the study and the more ethical withholding of information that might affect the participant's behaviour while being researched. Researchers should use their judgement to avoid doing research if participants would be upset when they find out the true nature of the research.

- **Debriefing must take place**. This means that the nature, results and conclusions of research need to be made available to participants as soon as possible. Any harm the participant experiences and of which the researcher becomes aware is then minimized. In addition, where research has effected a change in physical or psychological state,

these effects are undone. The BPS refers, for example, to research that induces a negative mood state. It would be wrong to cause a bad mood in participants and allow them to leave still in a bad mood.

- **Participants' rights include the right to confidentiality and the right to withdraw.** The right to withdraw is usually upheld at all points during the research process, including the point after data has been collected and the participant has been debriefed. In addition, the BPS guidelines stress that if any inducements to participate were offered, such as academic credit or payment, these should not be affected by a participant's decision to withdraw.
- **Fabrication of data is unacceptable**, and any errors should be later corrected.

Guidelines for research involving animals

Both the BPS and the APA provide guidelines for doing research with animals. There is a great deal of controversy surrounding the use of animals for research in a number of fields, and it is important that guidelines are followed to prevent clearly unjustified harm or ill-treatment to animals. The guidelines suggest the following key points.

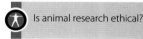
Is animal research ethical?

- There must be a clear scientific purpose that will increase knowledge of processes relating to the evolution, development, maintenance, alteration, control or biological significance of behaviour; the research should also benefit the health or welfare of humans or other animals.

- If the procedure would cause pain in humans, it should be assumed that it will also cause pain in animals, and should therefore have very strong justification. If any aversive stimuli are used, these should be set at the lowest possible levels. The APA recommends that psychologists test all painful stimuli on themselves.

- Animal welfare should be monitored throughout the research. Animals should be treated humanely inside and outside the context of research.

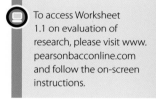
To access Worksheet 1.1 on evaluation of research, please visit www.pearsonbacconline.com and follow the on-screen instructions.

- When serious or long-term harm is caused to animals, they should be euthanized (killed) as soon as possible. Although this may seem harsh, it is considered the ethical thing to do if the research has caused damage to the animal that will affect its ability to live a relatively normal, pain-free life.

Animals used in research laboratories must be treated humanely.

EMPIRICAL RESEARCH

Personal space invasion (Middlemist et al. 1976)

This research took place in a men's toilet in which men normally had free choice about which of three individual urinals they used. In order to test the effects of having another person close to a man while he urinates, the researchers randomly assigned visitors to the toilet to one of three conditions. Participants entering the first condition were forced to use the urinal closest to the toilet stalls because the furthest urinal bore a sign saying 'Don't use, washing urinal', while a confederate occupied the middle urinal, pretending to be urinating. In the second condition, the confederate and the sign were switched so that the out-of-order urinal was between them, increasing the personal space between the men. The third condition involved no confederate.

A student measured onset and persistence of urination in the unknowing participant using a stopwatch and a periscopic prism that allowed him to witness the signs that it had begun from inside the toilet stall next to the urinal, but did not allow him to see the participant's face. The researchers found that having a man standing at the nearest urinal increased the time taken for urination to begin and decreased its persistence. Participants were not informed that they had been involved in an experiment.

● **Examiner's hint**
Most of the research in this book is considered to be ethical, but you should consider what ethical problems researchers might have had to overcome and how breaches of ethical guidelines might have been justified.

EXERCISE

1 The research study above has been criticized on ethical grounds. Evaluate it in terms of validity, reliability and ethics.

1.4 Sampling techniques

In order for researchers to be able to state with complete confidence that they have accurate results that apply to the entire human population, the research would need to be carried out on the entire human population. This is clearly impossible, and therefore researchers take a sample of the population under investigation that they expect to be representative of that population.

In order to be sure that they have a representative sample, several considerations need to be taken into account. First, a **target population** needs to be identified. While researchers often hope the target population would include all humans, it is more likely that they will acknowledge that differences such as culture and gender mean that they cannot apply their results to everyone. It is more appropriate, therefore, that the target population is more narrowly defined. Such a population could be, for example, all registered users of a website, or students from your school, or customers of a telecommunications company. Ideally, **random sampling** is then done from the target population in order to avoid **sampling bias**. For example, research carried out on students at the beginning of a university lecture will fail to include those students who arrive late for class. This is important if it can be demonstrated that there are differences between those who are included in the sample and those who were excluded. Some techniques commonly used by researchers to obtain their sample are outlined below.

 Although random sampling is the ideal, it is not often possible in psychology.

1 Random sampling – If a list of all members of the target population is available, the researcher can then ensure that every member has an equal chance of being invited to participate, for example by numbering members and selecting them using a random number generator, or by pulling names out of a hat. Clearly, the more people in the target population, the more time-consuming this will be. In addition, there is still the risk that, because not all people who are invited to participate will agree, there could be a bias in the sample if there are important differences between those who are willing

to participate and those who are not. This is particularly important when dealing with sensitive topics or in personality measurement. Thus, it could be argued that it is not possible to obtain a truly random sample, so it is important for researchers to attempt to randomize as much as possible.

2 Opportunity or convenience sampling – A lot of psychological research done on non-clinical populations (therefore assuming a target population of 'normal' adults) has been carried out using undergraduate psychology students. While this clearly has its drawbacks, the rationale behind it is clear. Psychology students represent an easily available and usually sympathetic pool of potential participants and it is often considered a necessary part of the learning process for them to participate in research while learning how to best conduct it. This is typical use of an opportunity or convenience sample: using a group of participants not randomly selected from the target population, but invited to participate because they are easily contactable. The major drawback of this method is simply that there may be differences between the group that is easy to contact and the other members of the target population. Psychology students may be different in some important ways from the rest of the undergraduate student population.

If such a large amount of psychological research has been carried out using a population of psychology students, and psychology students are known to be significantly different in some key characteristics, does this mean that knowledge claims made by psychological researchers should be considered invalid?

3 Stratified sampling and quota sampling – If a researcher looks carefully at the target population, it will be clear that this group can be broken down into smaller categories. For example, the student population at a school can be grouped according to age, year or grade, ethnicity, or gender. If a researcher knows that there are more females than males in the target population, it may seem wise to ensure that the same proportion is maintained in the sample. The required number from each of the strata (or layers) is set as a quota. So, if participants are randomly selected and the quota for a particular category is filled, then individuals in that category will no longer be invited to participate. In practice, this could mean that a researcher standing on a street corner inviting passers-by to participate in a short survey might stop approaching male passers-by after the appropriate number of males has completed the survey. This is useful in preventing one group becoming over-represented in the sample and biasing it. It is a useful consideration to make if time of day, for example, affects who is invited to participate, as would be the case if a researcher surveyed opinions on a street during school hours when many teenagers are in school and therefore unable to participate.

4 Cluster sampling – Sometimes it is easier to randomly select just one section of the target population. Members of this cluster are then invited to participate. This could be effective in gauging political opinions, for example, as it might be impractical to conduct telephone interviews with every registered voter in a country or state, so just one region might be selected and individuals within that region invited to become the representative sample. The obvious drawback to this is that the cluster selected might somehow be different from other sections of the target population. For example, a region with a high proportion of high-income earners might not represent the distribution of political views throughout the entire target population.

5 Purposive sampling – Although it seems easy to criticize this technique for allowing too much subjectivity into the research process, it is sometimes the most effective way of obtaining research data, especially in qualitative research (page 11). According to this technique, individuals who are expected to offer the most detailed or otherwise most appropriate information for the study will be approached and invited to participate. Clearly the researcher's prejudices are an important factor that might bias the sample, but this does not always invalidate the research if the use of the technique has been acknowledged and justified by the researcher.

Purposive sampling and snowball sampling are more typical of qualitative research where the focus is not on having a representative sample, but obtaining a sample that will provide rich data.

6   Snowball sampling – Researchers using the snowball technique ask participants to invite other people they know to participate. So, in the way that a snowball increases in size as it rolls down a slope, the sample grows larger and larger. Again, this is a technique that can be criticized for being biased, but it is popularly used in qualitative research, particularly when a researcher is investigating a topic without an easy means of getting in touch with potential participants. For example, when investigating motivating factors involved in illegal drug use, it may be more effective to ask participants to encourage others to join in because (a) it could be difficult to find people and (b) the personal recommendation of a friend or acquaintance might increase the number of people willing to participate.

EXERCISE

2   Propose suitable sampling techniques for the following research ideas. Explain your choices.

   a   You want to investigate student opinions about the school moving to another site.

   b   You want to investigate the relationship between caffeine use and Alzheimer's disease in older people.

   c   You want to investigate the possible effects of drug use on student performance at school.

   d   You want to know who the most popular sportsperson in your country is.

Obtaining data: Quantitative vs qualitative methodology (HL only)

There are a number of different ways to collect and analyse data, and the researcher's intentions and assumptions about the nature of the topic being researched will affect what methods they use. One of the most important distinctions to understand is the difference between quantitative and qualitative methodology.

Quantitative methods, such as the experiment, have been used partly in order to maintain the appearance of psychology as a scientific discipline with valid knowledge claims. However, during the 20th century there was a shift in emphasis away from quantitative methodology as the only valid way to gain information. It is generally considered worthwhile to have a good understanding of the use of both quantitative and qualitative data, to recognize their relative strengths and weaknesses, and to use the most appropriate method for a particular research project.

While methods can roughly be grouped as quantitative or qualitative, the differences can be seen in terms of data collection and data analysis and the distinction is not always simply made. However, for the HL exam, you need to distinguish between the two areas of research. The following are some of the key features of quantitative and qualitative data collection methods.

Quantitative methods

These methods assume that variables can be identified and the relationships between them measured using statistics, with the aim of inferring a cause–effect relationship. For this reason, quantitative methods require operational definitions (page 2), and the measurement of the dependent variable must be reliable and objective, with as few complicating factors

or extraneous variables as possible. This means that a laboratory environment is often most appropriate. It is an important assumption that objectivity is possible and that this is the only way to reach a valid conclusion about human behaviour that can be generalized beyond the study and used to explain and predict human behaviour.

The decision to use a quantitative method usually comes after consideration of theories that allow the researcher to construct hypotheses to be tested in the research situation. This is because an important focus is to test whether a theory is correct or not according to analysis of numerical data using, for example, tests of statistical significance. The main methods used within this type of approach are **experiments** and **correlational studies**. However, it is also common to use observations to obtain quantitative data, for example in counting the number of previously defined occurrences of 'aggressive behaviour' in a children's playground or classroom. Similarly, questionnaires, surveys and inventories (such as personality tests) are often quantitative in terms of their collection of numerical information in order to make generalizations and comparisons.

Evaluation of quantitative research focuses on the reliability and validity of the research design and the conclusions made and the degree to which the results can then be generalized beyond the sample used in the research.

Qualitative methods

Researchers engaging in qualitative research are less interested in employing measurement instruments to obtain numerical data in a sterile environment. They are more interested in trying to describe human behaviour by investigating the subjective meaning that people attach to their experience so it can be described (but not necessarily explained in causal terms), without necessarily removing participants from the real context within which they live and act. Although this may sound too subjective, qualitative researchers argue that if the subjectivity is acknowledged and the research conducted appropriately, it is just as valuable as (sometimes more valuable than) quantitative research. The researcher becomes the main instrument for data collection and analysis.

There is less need to obtain a large, random, representative sample from a target population because qualitative research is not usually intended to be generalized beyond the group of people studied. In fact, groups and individuals might be chosen for research *because of* their special interest or experience in a particular area, and it is acceptable to have small numbers of participants. Similarly, rather than trying to assume an air of neutrality, it is not uncommon for researchers to acknowledge their own biases and employ them to help increase the descriptive power of their research.

In addition, in contrast to quantitative methodology, qualitative methods are often used to help construct theory rather than to test existing theory. In this way, the researcher is less likely to impose their own subjective thoughts about the world on the research process under the guise of scientific neutrality.

Methods that allow the researcher to gain this kind of depth and detail include **interviews**, **case studies** and **observations**, and a number of designs that are less easy to categorize, such as asking participants to describe and explain photographs or videos of themselves or others. Evaluation of these methods does not always focus on reliability and validity, and recognizes that interpreting behaviour can be a very ambiguous process. Eisner (1991) suggests that instead, qualitative research should be judged based on whether it is coherent and detailed, whether the results can be corroborated, for example through triangulation, and whether the results are meaningful and useful to the reading audience.

● **Examiner's hint**
The learning outcomes listed below are particularly relevant to this section.
● Discuss ethical considerations in qualitative research.
● Explain effects of participant expectations and researcher bias in qualitative research.
● Explain the importance of credibility in qualitative research.
● Explain the effect of triangulation on the credibility / trustworthiness of qualitative research.
● Explain reflexivity in qualitative research.

● **Examiner's hint**
Qualitative methodology rests on certain assumptions. First, true objectivity is almost impossible to achieve as so many factors in research design can introduce bias. For example, when defining aggression, the researcher's own judgement may exclude certain forms of aggression which will then be ignored in the research. Or the laboratory environment used in the study may elicit a set of unnatural behaviours that do not reflect the participants' normal set of behaviours. In addition, it is **reductionist** to believe that something as complex and multi-faceted as human behaviour can be explained in terms of the causal relationships between single variables. Qualitative research will usually involve fieldwork and direct contact with participants.

Lincoln and Guba (1985) go even further than this and provide a set of criteria by which to judge the value of qualitative research. The criteria correspond to similar criteria used for evaluation of quantitative information (Table 1.1)

TABLE 1.1 CRITERIA FOR JUDGING QUANTITATIVE AND QUALITATIVE RESEARCH

Criterion	Quantitative or qualitative	What it means
internal validity	quantitative	Conclusions made are a correct interpretation, and the variables defined were accurately and appropriately manipulated and measured in a representative sample.
credibility	qualitative	As it is impossible to remove all ambiguity from the research process, it is important instead to consider the breadth and depth of information gathered and how well the researcher appears to have analysed it. In short, how believable are the researcher's conclusions? This can only be judged if the researcher has given very detailed description of context and methods and has acknowledged potential sources of bias
external validity or generalizability	quantitative	The research conclusions can be applied to different settings because the sample is representative and the research context has had a controlled and minimal impact on the findings.
transferability	qualitative	As it is unlikely that a research environment will have no impact on the findings, it is important to focus on to what extent the research context is similar to another specific situation. This can only be determined if the researcher has provided detailed contextual information and if the reader has adequate information about another situation to which they would like to transfer the results.
reliability	quantitative	Repeated use of the instruments used provides stable measurements and researchers using them find similar results.
dependability	qualitative	Data obtained cannot be expected to be the same every time. Instead, dependability relies on the researcher having described all the factors in the research context that might have influenced the data obtained.
objectivity	quantitative	As many sources of bias from opinion are eliminated from the research process.
confirmability	qualitative	Subjectivity is not only unavoidable; it is valued. Researchers should give details of the procedures used in their work and those doing similar research should be able to re-use the methodology and attempt to find examples that contradict the findings. Without detailed information about the procedures used, research findings cannot be confirmed.

Quantitative and qualitative research have different assumptions and aims so they should be evaluated differently.

How quantitative and qualitative methodologies can work together

Triangulation

Triangulation involves the use of different approaches to the gathering of data in a single study in order to improve the trustworthiness of the conclusions. There are several different ways to achieve this, all sharing the same fundamental objective.

Data triangulation

This involves the use of different data, which could mean using data collected from different sources; for example, two different schools or a single school at two different times. Clearly, this means that claims based on the research will be more trustworthy because they are not based on data collected at a single site or at a single time.

Researcher triangulation

This involves using different people as researchers; for example, the use of two or three observers, which increases the confirmability and credibility of conclusions made in analysing the data. Without confirmation from others, data collection and analysis may be affected by researcher bias. In using content analysis, for example, it is quite common to consult a colleague to confirm that the thematic categorizing process is credible and free from excessive subjectivity on the researcher's part.

Theoretical triangulation

This involves using different theoretical approaches to address a single situation. This is advantageous in that it requires the researcher to look at the data analysis from different viewpoints. In undertaking this process, the researcher is forced to justify why they consider a particular theory to be relevant in explaining the phenomena observed. From the reader's perspective, this justification and explanation will enhance the credibility of the conclusions made.

Methodological triangulation

This involves using different methods to research a single topic. At this point, it becomes clear how qualitative and quantitative methods can be used to complement each other. For example a researcher might choose to send a questionnaire into a company and conduct interviews afterwards. A school changing from one exam programme to another might choose to correlate exam results from the two different systems and also to conduct interviews, and may attempt to construct a case study from this. Clearly, the different approaches to the collection of data will help to construct a fuller picture of the phenomena under investigation, which will increase the credibility of any conclusions made, and thereby improve the trustworthiness of the study.

Triangulation: conclusion

However, triangulation is not always guaranteed to increase credibility. When the decisions about how to triangulate are made by researchers, there is just as much risk of subjectivity as when the researchers are not triangulating. If there is a systematic bias, for example in terms of researcher expectancies, judgements made at different times, using different methods, or employing different theoretical perspectives could all be affected. This would mean that the conclusions of research using triangulation are not made more credible, but have the illusion of credibility. For this reason, researchers need to be careful that their biases and motivations are clear. In addition, qualitative methodology assumes that the data obtained from any single gathering procedure are representative only of that single event. This means that we don't need to expect responses to a questionnaire to agree with what people say in an interview, so combining the two methods does not bring us closer to an objective truth; it simply gives us two different sets of data with different meanings.

● **Examiner's hint**
The learning outcomes listed below are particularly relevant to this section.
- Distinguish between qualitative and quantitative data.
- Explain strengths and limitations of a qualitative approach to research.
- To what extent can findings be generalized from qualitative studies?

● **Examiner's hints**
To answer a question about the value of reflexivity in qualitative research, you should make reference to the different opportunities for reflexivity provided by interviews, case studies and observations. These are addressed in section 1.6.

Reflecting on research decisions is an important part of the research process.

Reflexivity

Reflexivity refers to the researcher's need to constantly be aware of how and why they are conducting the research, and to recognize at what points their own beliefs and opinions about the topic under investigation might have influenced data collection or analysis. Reflexivity should not just be an issue addressed internally so that biases can be reduced; it should be a topic for discussion in the final report, as this can help readers to make the important decisions about whether or not the researcher's conclusions are credible and trustworthy. To help them to be reflexive, many researchers using qualitative methodology undergo an interview with a colleague to try and expose any biases they have.

1.6 Methods of collecting and analysing data: Experiments

The experiment is probably the best known method of scientific investigation. A true experiment occurs when a researcher manipulates an **independent variable** and measures a **dependent variable** while attempting to minimize the effects of any possible **confounding variables**. A statistical analysis of the results obtained enables a conclusion to be drawn about the relationship between the variables based on rejecting either the **research hypothesis** or the **null hypothesis**.

The hypothesis is the researcher's statement regarding the expected outcome of the study. It usually suggests that the independent variable will have an effect on the dependent variable. An example of this would be the experimental hypothesis that drinking coffee will make participants feel more stressed. In this case, the independent variable would be the amount of caffeine in the drink, and the dependent variable would be participants' stress levels. In order for the hypothesis to be clearly tested, the variables must be defined very accurately, because this allows the experimenter to construct a more valid experiment. In this example, the amount of caffeine would be clearly specified, and the researcher would have to ensure that this independent variable has genuinely been manipulated in the experiment

by preventing all participants from ingesting caffeine before the experiment. Similarly, the dependent variable (stress level) would need to be very clearly defined so that it can reliably be measured. It may be necessary in this case to define stress in terms of anxiety measured physiologically using appropriate instrumentation, or to define it according to scores on a questionnaire asking participants to rate their stress. You will remember that these definitions are referred to as operational definitions. This kind of experiment would normally take place in a laboratory so the experimenter would be able to maintain control over extraneous variables, such as noise levels and temperature or any other factors that might affect levels of stress. The details of this experiment are summarized in Table 1.2.

TABLE 1.2 DETAILS OF AN EXPERIMENT TO MEASURE THE EFFECTS OF CAFFEINE ON STRESS LEVELS	
Independent variable	amount of caffeine present in coffee given to participants
Dependent variable	scores on a stress questionnaire
Research hypothesis	participants who are given a high dose of caffeine in a coffee drink will report higher levels of stress
Null hypothesis	there will be no difference in the amount of stress reported by participants who receive a high dose and those who receive no dose of caffeine
Possible confounding variables	• caffeine in drinks that participant has drunk before the experiment • feelings of stress from the experimental situation

Coffee – does it help or hinder?

Clearly, if there were other factors interfering with the participants' levels of stress, the researcher could not be sure that any effects observed in the experiment were really due to the caffeine, as the hypothesis states. To be sure that stress levels had increased, the experimenter would need to have at least two conditions of the independent variable to compare. In this case, the experiment would require a group of participants who drink some coffee, a group of participants who do not drink any coffee, and a group of participants who drink something like decaffeinated coffee. These three groups could be referred to as the **treatment group**, the **control group**, and the **placebo control group** respectively. By including two groups who do not ingest caffeine, we can compare the results and see if we observe an effect. By including the placebo control, we are attempting to eliminate the effects of any participant expectations, and this is extremely important in experimental drug trials, for example.

The **placebo effect** in medical research occurs when participants show some kind of change although they have not received an active treatment, perhaps receiving a sugar pill while another group receive a pill with a genuine active ingredient. In research that simply compares taking the active pill with taking no pill, the participants might show change because they have received a pill and expect an effect, and therefore we would struggle to argue for a cause–effect relationship between the pill and the change.

A final key feature of a true experiment is the random assignment of participants to the different conditions of the independent variable so that the only difference between the groups is the one intended by the researcher.

The experimenter also needs to provide a null hypothesis as a contradiction to the experimental hypothesis. This will be a statement that the independent variable will not affect the dependent variable; for example, that drinking coffee will not increase stress levels. Following an analysis of the data obtained, the experimenter can then reject one of the two hypotheses. So, if stress levels do indeed increase in the experimental group, we can reject the null hypothesis and assume that stress levels increased because of the effect of the coffee. In this way, we have been able to establish a cause–effect relationship between coffee and stress.

Clearly, if any extraneous variables such as time or the unnatural laboratory environment affect our ability to accurately measure the dependent variable, this cause–effect relationship will be more questionable. Those variables that might influence our results in such a way are referred to as confounding variables. The expectations of the participants, the placebo effect and previous experience can all be confounding variables. There is an enormous range of other possible factors that researchers need to try to control for that are specific to any experiment.

Whenever people participate in an experiment, there is a risk that demand characteristics (page 4) will confound the experiment because people are usually made aware that they are participating. For this reason, it is common for the researcher to attempt to prevent participants from knowing whether they are in the control group or the experimental group. This is called a single-blind procedure. Medical research often uses a placebo to achieve this, as it is difficult for a person to know whether the pill they receive has an active ingredient or not, so the effect of their expectations is minimized. A double-blind procedure involves also preventing the researcher from knowing which group a participant is in. The reason for this is that researcher expectancies can also be a confounding variable and systematically bias the results.

In experiments, expectations of researchers and participants can interfere with the results, so it is wise to use a single- or double-blind procedure.

Types of experiment

There are three main types of experiment to be aware of, each with slightly different strengths and limitations:

- the laboratory experiment
- the field experiment
- the natural or quasi experiment.

Laboratory experiments

The caffeine experiment described above is a laboratory experiment. The key feature of this kind of experiment is that it takes place in an environment designed to maximize control over extraneous variables to help ensure the validity of the study.

This gives the experiment its two major strengths:

- it is usually the method with the highest levels of reliability
- it allows valid cause–effect conclusions in terms of the variables measured because of the certainty gained by control over extraneous variables.

This kind of precision allows for easy replication of the experiment, which increases the chances of the results being checked and confirmed by other researchers.

The main limitation of laboratory experiments is that the high level of control over variables means that the environment or the tasks completed by participants can become artificial or unrealistic. Thus, we have achieved high levels of reliability but ecological validity is low and we cannot generalize our results beyond the experimental situation (page 5)

A further limitation of experiments is that participant expectations and demand characteristics can become problems as people in an artificial environment begin to act differently from how they might normally act (the Hawthorne effect and the screw-you effect, page 4).

Field experiments

To decrease the artificiality of an experiment, it may be necessary to conduct it in the natural environment where the behaviours of interest normally occur. If, for example, we were interested in levels of stress experienced by office workers during work time, the natural environment would be the participants' normal workplace. It is still necessary to compare the results obtained for an experimental group and a control group in order to be certain about the cause–effect relationship. Thus, the field experiment is a way to improve ecological validity, but in doing this, we open the experiment to the influence of extraneous variables that might prevent us from confidently establishing a cause–effect relationship between our independent and dependent variables.

Natural or quasi experiments

One of the key components of a true experiment is the manipulation of an independent variable. Sometimes, the variable of interest is naturally occurring outside the control of the researcher, making the study a natural experiment. One topic of interest studied several times is the change that occurs in an area when television is introduced for the first time. In these cases, researchers study changes in individuals or society after the event occurs, but they themselves are not responsible for the manipulation of the independent variable. Without this responsibility, clearly the researcher has very little control over any of the variables and it will be nearly impossible to replicate the experiment with precisely the same conditions. On the other hand, because of minimal experimenter influence, the experiment is likely to be less artificial, and although replication might be impossible, the method allows researchers to take advantage of relatively rare events that would be financially or ethically impossible to study otherwise.

Quasi experiments involve naturally occurring independent variables such as gender or age. In other words, they usually involve characteristics of participants that clearly cannot be changed in the context of an experiment to see what effect it might have on a dependent variable. The inability to randomly assign participants to groups reduces the validity of the experiment, but clearly it would be unusual to try to manipulate such participant characteristics experimentally.

1.7 Methods of collecting and analysing data: Correlational studies

Correlational studies use a statistical technique of analysing data. The technique tests the relationship between two variables of interest, such as age and the number of hours sleep per day. By obtaining numerical data on both variables for a number of participants, researchers can then run a correlation between the two data sets and obtain a correlation coefficient, which is a number between −1 and +1 (or 1). This number represents the degree of interrelationship between the two variables, such that 1 is a perfect positive correlation, meaning that as one variable increases, so does the other one. In the example mentioned above, such a correlation would mean that the youngest people sleep the least and older people sleep the most. A −1 correlation would mean that as one variable increases, the other decreases. So in our example, this would mean that the older the person is, the less sleep they get. A score close to 0, whether positive or negative, indicates that there is no relationship between the two variables. For the example given above, this would mean that there is no linear relationship between the age of people and the number of hours they sleep (Figure 1.1).

Figure 1.1
Graphs showing three different correlations.

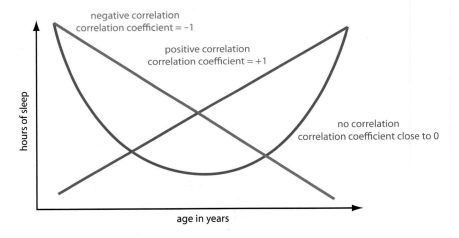

The main advantages of correlational studies are:
- they are relatively simple and provide a numerical representation of the relationship that can be easily understood and compared
- they allow the study of a number of variables that cannot be manipulated experimentally.

The main disadvantage of these studies is that it is impossible to make cause–effect conclusions. Much correlational research is reported in the media as indicating that one of the variables in a study caused an effect on the other variable, but without the setup of an experiment, such conclusions are completely invalid. A positive relationship like the example given above could be explained in several different ways, and we cannot be sure which is the correct way. Obviously, it could be the case that age causes people to sleep more, but the result could also be explained with the unlikely scenario that sleeping more causes people to grow older.

The problem of the third variable is a major limitation in correlational studies. This means that although two variables were measured and correlated, their relationship can be explained by a third variable that causes both of them. For example, we could consider

the number of fashion magazines read and dissatisfaction with body shape. It could be concluded that reading fashion magazines causes dissatisfaction with body shape, or that being dissatisfied with your body somehow causes people to read fashion magazine. Or, it might be that a third variable such as parental influence causes both dissatisfaction with body shape *and* interest in reading fashion magazines.

A final problem with correlational studies is that sometimes it is clear when the data is presented graphically that there is a pattern to the results that is not as simple as a straight line (i.e. that variables increase together or that one increases while the other decreases). For example, the graph might have a U-shape, as in our example of age and sleep. In practice, we might find that both younger and older people sleep more and that the lowest amount of sleep is for young to middle-aged adults. Visually we can see this relationship clearly, but the correlation coefficient cannot describe this relationship and it is likely that we will obtain a number close to 0 (Figure 1.1).

 # Methods of collecting data: Observations (with HL extension)

Observation as a method of collecting data is different from the experiment mostly in that there is no manipulation of an independent variable, and researchers are therefore unable to draw conclusions regarding the causes of what they are observing. Observers should usually specify at least one **target behaviour** and provide clear operational definitions of any behaviours they are trying to observe.

● **Examiner's hint**
For HL students, the learning outcomes listed below are particularly relevant to this section.
● Evaluate participant, non-participant, naturalistic, overt and covert observations
● Discuss considerations involved in setting up and carrying out an observation
● Discuss how researchers analyse data obtained in observational research.

Types of observation

Observations can be categorized in a number of ways.

Covert and overt observations

The first distinction to note is between **covert** and **overt** observations. In a covert observation, the participants do not know they are being observed. This could be because the researcher is hidden or is using audio or visual recording devices. The advantage of doing the observation this way is that the participants should act more naturally. Overt observations occur when the participants know that their behaviour is being observed and may even be able to see the observer.

Participant and non-participant observations

A second distinction is between **participant** and **non-participant** observations. There are many reasons why a researcher might want to observe the behaviour of a group of people from within the group. For example, a researcher might wish to gain a deeper understanding of the behaviour of participants; in other words, to obtain richer data. In such cases, participant observation may be the most appropriate option. This requires becoming part of the group of people being observed, which may require deception to achieve. For example, in organizational research, it is quite common for a researcher to appear to join the staff in order to understand their behaviour as well as recording and analysing it. On the other hand, the researcher may not be able to become part of the group, for example when studying small children. Non-participant observations occur when the researcher remains outside the group being studied, even though they may be in the same room.

The key difference lies in the perception of the participants that the researcher is one of them or not. It is quite predictable that people will behave differently depending on whether they are being observed by a member of their group or by a stranger, regardless of whether the observation is overt or covert. Although participant observations can improve the validity of conclusions made about the behaviours observed, they may also encourage the observer to be too subjective. 'Going native' is a term taken from anthropological research, and means a researcher has become so heavily involved with the group they have joined that their objectivity might be completely lost.

Naturalistic and controlled observations

The third way to classify observations is by the environment in which they occur. As with experiments, observations can be carried out in a location that is natural for the participants or in an artificially created one. A **naturalistic observation** is one that takes place in the environment in which the target behaviour normally occurs. This could be the participants' workplace or a child's home. The intention of this approach is to ensure that the observations made are based on a valid sample of participants' behaviour. A **controlled observation** can occur in any environment, whether a laboratory or a more natural one, but involves an artificially constructed situation devised by the researcher in order to observe the behaviour under a given set of circumstances. Because of the researcher's involvement in altering the environment, conclusions made about the behaviour of the participants may be less generalizable to a naturally occurring situation. These observations might also take place in a laboratory.

Strengths and weaknesses of observations

The major strength of observations is that they allow researchers to capture the behaviour of individuals as it really happens, generally with little artificiality. Information can be recorded as the behaviour occurs, and thus allow researchers to study behaviour that people might find difficult to describe or discuss.

There are significant weaknesses, however, including the high probability that when participants know they are being observed, demand characteristics may be a problem and render the results invalid. The Hawthorne effect (page 4) refers to alterations in behaviour

People often act differently when they know they are being watched.

according to participants' expectations about what is being studied. **Audience effects** occur more often during observations and refer to exaggerations or concealment of behaviour simply because of being watched. An example of this is the finding that children's facial expressions indicate more pain when their parents are present during medical examinations (Vervoort et al., 2008).

A different problem lies on the side of the researcher. In defining the target behaviour and interpreting whether the behaviour has been performed or not, there is the possibility for researcher bias to affect results. For example, a researcher may be biased in the selection of target behaviours or the perceived frequency of these behaviours in the observations. Researcher expectations might best be prevented from affecting the recording of data by using neutral or uninformed observers who do not need to understand the research topic or the researcher's intentions.

 Both researcher and participant expectations can affect the value of observation data.

Another major limitation of observation is related to ethics. While it is generally acceptable for researchers to study behaviour that would normally be observed by others without gaining informed consent, in specific cases it is not always easy to determine whether or not people would be upset at knowing that their behaviour has been observed. This limits researchers' freedom in obtaining genuinely unbiased samples of normal behaviour.

Ethics in observational research

As explained in the section on general ethical guidelines (page 6), observational research has received special attention. While it remains the case that in most research, the context of the observation will be a relatively public place where participants would normally expect to be seen by others, important decisions need to be made about disclosure of the research aims. Some people will resent having their behaviour studied, and the researcher needs to find a balance between disclosing the fact that they will be observed, in the interests of obtaining informed consent, or that they already have been observed, in the form of a debriefing, against the potential psychological harm or negative emotional states that disclosing this information might cause. This relates mostly to covert research, when participants will probably not work out for themselves that they are being observed.

There is also the difficult balance with overt observations whereby participants know that they are being observed, but informing them as to the nature and purpose of the study might have seriously damaging consequences for the validity or credibility of conclusions made from the research. The question of how much information to give participants is a very difficult one and, in qualitative research in particular, is probably best made in consultation with colleagues or other interested parties. Thus there is a delicate balance between methodological and ethical interests, and researchers should be able to justify the decisions they make.

● **Examiner's hints**
The decision about how much to disclose is an example of the importance of reflexivity in research.

Recording and analysing observational data
Recording data

Recording data from observations often involves constructing a grid, the design of which depends on the nature and purpose of the study, the number of participants, and the number of observers. Bales (1950) designed a grid useful for studying small group interaction. In this design, expected behaviour is categorized and observers tick the appropriate cell of the grid when a behaviour is observed. For example, a researcher observing one child in a group of children playing in a room with many different toys, games and books, might construct a grid like Figure 1.2 (overleaf).

Figure 1.2
Bales grid for observing child playing in a group.

solitary activity	reads a book	plays with one other child	group activity
	plays alone	plays with a small group	
	watches others playing	plays with a large group	
positive social actions	shares a toy	physically attacks another child	negative social actions
	invites another child to play	takes something away from another child	
	helps another child with a toy or game	says something rude or insulting to another child	

A grid like this makes it easy for the observer to record target behaviour, but the result is of mixed value. A rich display of behaviour is reduced to a set of frequencies, which may be used as numerical information to compare children. The problem is that the grid was designed in advance by the researcher and reflects their assumptions and expectations, rather than what was actually observed. This may be referred to as a structured observation.

Can the behaviour of these children be reduced to numbers?

There is no single way to carry out an observation. Methods vary according to the situation and the aims of the researcher.

To capture a more holistic view of the situation under observation, qualitative researchers sometimes use a vaguely defined protocol to complete their recording of data. An example of this might be to use a single page divided in half, and to record descriptive notes about what is observed on one side, while recording the researcher's thoughts relating to the observed behaviour on the other side. This reflects the assumptions of qualitative research in that the researcher's subjectivity should both be acknowledged *and* form a part of the researcher's interpretation of the data. It is also necessary for the researcher to make notes about the context in order to help readers of the final research report come to decisions about how trustworthy the researcher's conclusions are.

The concept of reflexivity was discussed on page 14. You may recognize that, in order to provide honest and informative accounts of interactions with participants and any problems that arise during the study, it is useful for the researcher to make notes or keep a diary. When this information is presented in the final research paper, the reader is able to make judgements regarding the trustworthiness and credibility of the study.

Analysing data

The analysis of observational data clearly depends on what approach to recording the data has been taken. Where the data obtained can be counted, traditional quantitative analysis can be used, such as the comparison of mean or mode values.

Where the researcher has made notes in a more unstructured way, the task can be more complicated. A huge amount of information might have been obtained. The aim of analysis is to reduce this data to more manageable chunks and then use the reduced version of the data to make sense of the behaviour and context observed. There are several ways to reduce the data, and one of the most common is to look for themes in the data and code the observations according to those. For example, if the observation of children's play described above were done in a more qualitative way, some of the behaviours inside the grid might have been observed at various times and could each be considered a theme. If it emerges that these themes can be grouped in some way which can be given a superordinate label that describes the set of themes (behaviours) contained inside it, then the behaviours observed can be considered subordinate themes. This information is often presented graphically, in a table or list. It is extremely important that the researcher keeps notes to explain how this was done, as it involves some subjectivity. In order for readers to feel that the research is credible, a full account of the process must be available.

The final step is to use the superordinate themes (labels) to reconstruct the 'story' of the observation. This should be a descriptive account of what was observed that integrates multiple sources of information: the themes identified, the researcher's notes made during observation and the researcher's interpretation of these.

You should now be able to clearly see a difference between qualitative and quantitative research:

- quantitative research makes a large number of *a priori* assumptions and imposes the researcher's interpretation of reality on research design and analysis procedures
- qualitative analysis allows an interpretation of reality to emerge from the observations made during the research.

 A priori assumptions are assumptions made before the research was started.

HL EXERCISES

3 Construct a table to summarize the strengths and limitations of the different types of observation.

4 Imagine you are going to observe shopper behaviour in a supermarket to assist the supermarket in making decisions about possible changes to layout. Answer the following questions and justify your answers.

   a What type of observation will you carry out?

   b What ethical concerns are associated with your observation?

   c How will you deal with these?

   d What target behaviours will you look for? Define them carefully.

   e How might the behaviour of your participants differ from normal?

   f Can you deal with this in any way?

   g Discuss a sampling technique which would be appropriate for this study.

   h To what extent could you generalize the findings of this study to the behaviour of people in general?

   i Suggest how you would record and analyse data obtained in this naturalistic observation.

   j Discuss how researchers analyse data obtained in observational research.

   Design and carry out your own observation.

5 Write a report that demonstrates the considerations made before you carried out the observation and summarizes your findings. The final part of your report should explain how and why you analysed your data.

1.9 Methods of collecting data: Case studies (with HL extension)

The case study is often considered not a method in itself, but rather a way of describing research that has been done using several different methods to gain detailed information about a particular individual or group of people. Examples of this can frequently be found in medical and therapeutic contexts, where a single patient has undergone treatment or diagnostic procedures and the researcher reports the conclusions gathered from all of the different techniques used to obtain data. The case study of HM described in Chapter 2 (page 44) is a very good example of this.

There are a number of other fairly high-profile case studies that have contributed to our understanding of human behaviour, including the case study of Genie – a girl found at the age of 13 with severe language deficiencies, probably as a result of extreme childhood deprivation.

The case study lends itself easily to individual cases where the researcher is a medical professional gathering information as it is required for diagnosis or treatment decisions. However, the method is also used in situations such as when an organization is undergoing some kind of widespread change – for example, the introduction of new technology that changes the way people work. As with the observational method, in good qualitative research, it is necessary for the researcher to try to describe the context of the research in as much detail as possible in order to enhance the study's credibility.

Types of case study

To learn more about Genie, go to pearsonhotlinks.com, enter the title or ISBN of this book and select weblink 1.1a.
To learn more about other similar case studies, go to www.pearsonhotlinks.com, enter the title or ISBN of this book and select weblink 1.1b.

The most important distinction is between **intrinsic** and **instrumental** case studies. Stake (1994) describes intrinsic case studies as being those of interest purely for their own sake, where there is no need to generalize beyond the case researched or to attempt to build theory based on the conclusions. In contrast, the instrumental case study (sometimes called extrinsic) is carried out in order to describe, explain or build theory around a phenomenon that occurs with some frequency. Findings from an instrumental case study are expected to have relevance to other cases.

The examples of HM and Genie are best understood as intrinsic case studies – they were studied because of their uniqueness. It is not the purpose of the research to find general rules to apply to others with similar experience because such people are rare.

In contrast, Buchanan (2001) describes an instrumental case study of a hospital that has undergone changes to the way patients move through the hospital. His findings are of relevance to readers considering changes in a similar context.

Strengths and limitations of case studies

The main strength of this approach is its ability to construct a full and detailed description of the individual, group or organization under investigation. Such studies frequently combine multiple forms of data from different collection methods, and often yield **rich data**. This means that the validity of conclusions drawn from this information is higher than might be gained from any one of those sources individually. However, obtaining such depth of information can make the case study costly in terms of both time and money. It can also be the case that researchers doing case studies over a period of time develop

more personal relationships with the participants, which may result in subjective decisions about research design or the reporting of findings or may change the behaviour of the participants.

However, because the cases studied are often unique or of special interest, the results and conclusions might not be generalizable beyond the participants in the case study. It is also often assumed that the sampling methods used for qualitative research are exaggerated in case studies, as they frequently involve a small sample that was not randomly selected but was, for example, a purposive sample. This means that case studies are very useful in constructing and challenging theory, but cannot usually be used to establish general cause–effect relationships for application to the general population. This does not mean there is no possibility of transferring the findings, but several factors must be considered.

According to the criteria for evaluating qualitative research (page 12), a decision about how relevant results are beyond the case studied is the responsibility of those who read and attempt to apply the research. The responsibility of the researcher is to provide enough detailed information to allow readers to establish for themselves whether or not the findings can be transferred to another context in which the reader is interested. Findings from a case study *without* adequate description cannot be transferred to another person or context.

 It is not always possible to generalize from a case study, but this is not always the intention of the research.

It is possible that future instrumental case studies with adequate description of the background and context of the study and participants will confirm the findings of an earlier case study. When this happens, the generalizability of the earlier study is increased. It should be noted that an enormous amount of medical knowledge has been gained from the case study method. These histories often start with a single unusual case such as a person with an unusual combination of symptoms which, when fully understood and described in detail, help doctors and researchers understand a similar case that occurs later.

With enough cases, more concrete conclusions can be made. This is explained by Yin (1989, 1994), who suggests that the applicability of a case study beyond the single case is dependent on the quality of the methodology used in the case and the adequacy of its description. Yin refers to this as **theoretical generalization**. What is meant by this is that researchers are attempting to expand the quality and applicability of theory by generalizing the findings of the study to existing *theory* rather than to *other cases* in the general population, which would be called **statistical generalization**.

Ethical issues in case studies

Some ethical issues are specific to case studies. Perhaps the most important of these is that a case study involving only one person (particularly when the person has been studied because they are unique) risks the possibility that readers might identify the participant. Such loss of anonymity is usually avoided by the use of initials or pseudonyms and sometimes the alteration of personal details. Case studies can also be damaging to participants because of the intensity of data collection. While this varies according to the research aims, it can be the case that a researcher continually asking participants to carry out tasks results in the participants resenting the amount of time taken up. Or, as frequently happens in exploratory case studies where the researcher is trying to investigate the extent of brain damage, the participant might become upset or frustrated at the implications of the data being collected. The researcher needs to manage this, trying to minimize harm and to ensure that support is offered to the participant if they become uncomfortable because of the research.

How a case study could be used to investigate a problem in an organization

Having identified that there is a problem in their organization, an employer could ask an organizational psychologist to investigate the problem and make recommendations about how to solve it. **Absenteeism** is a common problem in organizations. That is, employees are not at work when they are supposed to be, whether the alleged reason is sickness, lateness, dentist appointments, etc.

A case study in this situation could start with the analysis of interview data gathered from various members of staff in management and non-management positions. A focus group discussing causes of absence would be a particularly good way to elicit data, but employees may be uncomfortable admitting to bad behaviour and it would be important to have arranged with the employer that the interviewees remain completely anonymous. The use of diaries would also provide good data for this study: employees could make a note any time they were not where they should be and why they were not there.

After data from these sources has been analysed, it may be possible to identify changes that address the problem. Such changes might involve flexitime systems that allow employees to work at times more convenient for them, reducing employer expectations about how many hours employees should work, offering an on-site medical service, introducing fines for lateness, or making the workplace a nicer environment in any number of ways.

If the case study were to continue, an experimental approach could be taken: one or more of the possible solutions could be trialled, each with one group of employees, and after a month or two, the collection of qualitative data could be repeated to determine whether or not there has been a change.

HL EXERCISES

6 Construct a table to summarize strengths and limitations of case studies. Use your table to evaluate one case study from elsewhere in this book.

7 Discuss the extent to which findings can be generalized from a single case study. Make reference to one case study from elsewhere in this book.

1.10 Methods of collecting data: Interviews (HL only)

As with all qualitative research, it is a good idea for the researcher to keep a diary while preparing for an interview so that aspects of the decision-making process can be reported in the final research paper. This helps the researcher maintain their reflexivity and will assist the reader in making conclusions about the credibility of the researcher's conclusions.

Types of interview

There are several ways to categorize interviews based on distinctions in the communication medium, the number of participants and the structure.

Means of communication between researcher and participants

While face-to-face interviews are typical, it is also possible to carry out telephone interviews, e-mail interviews, and internet interviews through messaging or chat applications.

Number of participants

An individual interview allows the researcher to directly ask questions of a participant without the possible embarrassment or conflict involved in sharing ideas in front of other people. A group interview (sometimes called a **focus group**) offers the researcher the possibility of gathering data from more people than individual interviews in the limited time available for most research.

The interviewer's role in a group interview is usually quite different. Rather than taking turns to speak in the interview, the interviewer acts as a facilitator of discussion, introducing topics or stimuli like photographs, encouraging quieter members of the group to speak and respond to each other's ideas, and trying to ensure that conversation does not drift away from the focus of the interview. Weiner (2005) ran focus groups in her study of Czech female factory workers as a way to gather initial information to help her construct an interview schedule for individual interviews. She also used the focus group as a way to gather potential participants for her future sample.

Although there is a risk that being in a group might discourage some people from speaking (out of fear of being judged), there is also the possibility that being with other people talking about the same topic might trigger memories or opinions that an individual might not have offered alone. Focus groups are frequently used in market research as it has been noted that a lot of useful information comes out of participants' discussions with peers – such discussions allow for a simulation of normal conversation around topics, including questions between participants that the interviewer might not have considered important. In most focus groups, as with most groups of people talking, there will be some who talk more than others and there is a risk that those who are more confident might dominate. Other limitations of the focus group include the possibility that participants will conform to the opinions of others, rendering the process pointless, and the possibility that participants will not feel comfortable discussing more sensitive topics or revealing personal information that is of interest.

A common 1-to-1 interview is the typical job interview in which the interviewer asks questions which the interviewee answers. But how accurate is the information gained?

Interview structure

Sometimes a researcher will have a very specific set of questions to ask and no deviation can be allowed from those questions as that will increase the amount of time taken to complete the interview. It will also increase the amount of data obtained, perhaps unnecessarily if the questions specified are known to target the issues of greatest interest to the researcher. This is a structured interview. An interview can also be described as semi-structured, unstructured and conversational, or narrative.

Semi-structured interviews contain a basic structure, but the interviewer allows for the possibility that the set questions will not necessarily capture all the potential data that can come from the interview. Therefore, deviation from the interview schedule is allowed, which is particularly useful in asking for clarifications and exploring beyond the first answer given by participants. Semi-structured interviews appear to be a good compromise between the rigidity of a structured interview and the looseness of an unstructured

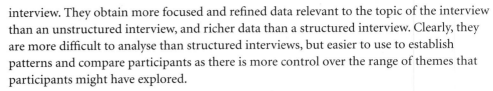

Semi-structured interviews provide a balance between obtaining too little and too much information and allow the researcher to keep the participant on-topic.

interview. They obtain more focused and refined data relevant to the topic of the interview than an unstructured interview, and richer data than a structured interview. Clearly, they are more difficult to analyse than structured interviews, but easier to use to establish patterns and compare participants as there is more control over the range of themes that participants might have explored.

Unstructured interviews and conversational interviews still require some preparation on the part of the interviewer, but they allow for a freer discussion of a topic and can be very useful in theory building where not enough research has been done to justify particular questions being chosen.

Narrative interviews are a more recent phenomenon. One of the main intentions of this approach is to minimize the influence of the interviewer on the data obtained. When asking questions during a traditional interview, the interviewer directs the flow of the interview. Even if this is done conversationally, it is possible that the interview captures only a reconstructed and edited version of the participant's ideas about the topic being studied. The narrative interview tends to use fewer questions, sometimes only a single instruction like 'Tell me about your childhood'. This allows the participant to proceed with the interviewer as an active listener who does not alter or redirect the flow of the interview. The researcher can return to the interview situation and seek clarification if necessary, but the original narrative remains intact for analysis.

Burnell et al. (2009) developed a model of analysis to study the reports of people with traumatic war memories from World War II and more recent wars. Using this model, they analysed such content as main characters, the way the episodes described are structured and integrated, and emotional evaluation of the events they related. They found that generally there was a difference in the extent to which participants had come to terms with difficult memories of war and that where participants described coming to terms with those memories, they usually preceded this in their stories with explanations of how important the social support of family and fellow veterans had been.

The primary advantage of this type of interview lies in its attempt to capture an unadulterated version of reality from the participant. This reflects the fact that much of our lives revolves around stories, which are used by people to make sense of experiences (Burnell et al., 2009). It could be argued that every interview question essentially elicits a narrative with plot and characters constructed by the participant as they speak. The most obvious problem is that some participants may not feel comfortable speaking in this manner and may offer less data for the researcher to deal with. Narrative accounts of human experience vary wildly in terms of content and according to the verbal abilities of the participants; some interviews will yield richer data than others. When there is rich, detailed and extensive data, the researcher may find that so much data has been obtained that the analysis of it will take an extremely long time.

Conducting an interview

As with other methods, there are a number of considerations that need to be made before a researcher embarks on an interview.

The sample

The first consideration should be how to obtain the sample of people to be interviewed and how large this should be. Given that interviews yield a large amount of data, it is unlikely that a researcher will want to interview a large sample of people. The larger the sample, the more likely it is that the researcher will choose to use a more structured approach to the

interview to try and make the data obtained more manageable. The sampling technique chosen is likely to be one of those more appropriate to qualitative research, like purposive sampling or the snowball technique, because the participants most likely to offer the richest data are those who have the most to say about a topic and they cannot be found randomly. In addition, interviews often deal with sensitive or specialist topics and it is perfectly acceptable to sacrifice the randomness of the sampling method for a deliberate and ethically careful approach.

Sensitive topics

There are other ethical issues to consider. Interviewers dealing with sensitive topics need to ensure that the questions they are asking are questions that participants will not mind answering. When dealing with topics such as criminal behaviour, interviewers may find themselves in the difficult position of obtaining information that they have a responsibility to pass on to relevant authorities – therefore, the limited extent of confidentiality needs to be made clear to participants beforehand.

Although participants should always be told that they have the right not to answer a question, it can be difficult during an interview for the participant to express their reluctance to an interviewer. Similarly, some participants will find it easier to talk to someone who is like them in terms of gender, ethnicity or age, among other variables. So, careful planning needs to be done regarding whether the researcher or someone else will interview the participants. Rosenthal (1966) suggests that the gender of the interviewer and participants will have important effects. For example, female interviewees are treated more attentively and warmly by both genders of interviewer; female interviewers tend to smile more; and interviewees rate male researchers as more friendly. Walker (2005) interviewed black South African men to investigate changes in notions of masculinity since the end of apartheid. Concerned that as a white woman she was an outsider to the group of men interviewed, she trained a black male research assistant and then compared the type of information they both were able to obtain. Contrary to her expectations, her difference from the participants actually seemed to increase the richness of the data obtained as participants were more enthusiastic to tell their stories to an outsider. Thus, while it cannot be accurately predicted what effects the choice of interviewer will have, researchers should consider them and take steps to reduce any influence that might damage the richness of the data.

● **Examiner's hints**
The decision about who will conduct the interview is another example of the importance of reflexivity in qualitative research.

Type of questions

Another planning consideration is the type of questions to be used. Although structure was discussed earlier, there are a number of other considerations relating to how questions are asked. Short, closed questions such as 'Do you feel happy with your current doctor?' are unlikely to yield much data unless there is a good rapport between the interviewer and participant. Spradley (1979) outlines different types of question that researchers can ask to achieve different results.

Descriptive questions can be used to obtain a large amount of information about an event or place and include 'Grand tour' and 'Mini-tour' questions that are, respectively, more general and more specific in terms of what is asked of the participants. Examples could include 'Could you describe your hospital ward for me?' or 'Tell me what normally happens at lunchtime in your school'.

Structural questions are used to try and establish the meaning of important concepts. For example, Burnell et al. (2009) wanted to investigate what flying meant for veteran pilots who have flown in war, so the interviewer simply asked a participant if he enjoyed flying.

Different question types will provide different data so the researcher needs to choose the most appropriate.

Another approach might be to use pilot interviews to gather a set of words that can be used in the context under investigation and ask the participant to sort them. For example, a school student might be asked to consider different causes and symptoms of stress and then sort them into groups. While participants carry out the sorting tasks, they can explain their actions.

Contrast questions are used to establish how words or ideas mentioned by participants are different from each other. For example, students might be asked to explain the difference between homework and schoolwork, or between homework and studying.

Recording the interview

Another consideration during the interview process is how and what to record. For ethical reasons, participants should always be told if the interview is being recorded and what will happen to the recording later. Unfortunately, when participants are informed about this, it can make them feel uncomfortable and quite reticent. It is therefore important to work on establishing a trusting rapport with participants, possibly beginning with more informal conversation at the beginning to put them at ease. At times, participants or the interviewer might want the recording device to be switched off, so that something more personal can be said. Hussey and Hussey (1997) suggest that ostentatiously turning off the recorder can be a way to elicit richer data from the participant, and it is usually wise for the interviewer to make notes for eventualities such as this.

Voice recording during an interview.

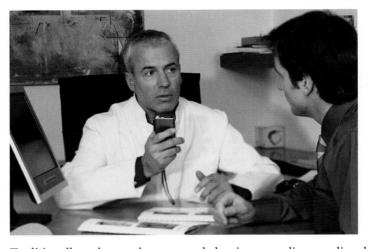

Traditionally, only speech was recorded, using an audio recording device. While this accurately records what participants say, other features of the social interaction in the interview might be lost between the interview and later analysis. For this reason, **postmodern transcription techniques** are increasingly used. This involves making either notes or an accompanying video so that non-verbal components of the interview (such as laughter, reluctant or disgusted facial expressions, non-facial body language such as sitting back or leaning forward) can be recorded.

Postmodern transcription can increase the credibility of research but also can be difficult to analyse.

It can be difficult to decide how best to analyse this sort of information, and it is often simply noted in the presentation of the final research as an accompaniment to quotes in an attempt to give more credibility to the conclusions the researcher has made.

A practical consideration here is whether the equipment is working or not. A great deal of data has been lost because researchers have failed to check batteries and the positioning of recording devices. This can be devastating after so much preparation. Therefore, equipment should be checked before the interview, and it pays to check again during the interview to ensure that the participant(s) can be heard.

Interviewer training

The interviewer should have had training before the interview. Skilled interviewers notice when a participant is struggling to answer a question and are able to provide guidance. Novice interviewers might find that they are so focused on asking questions and trying to understand the answers that they lose focus on the participant. This can leave the participant feeling more uncomfortable as the situation becomes slightly more unnatural than a qualitative interview is intended to be.

The rapport established should also involve clear understanding of what is and is not expected in terms of content. If the researcher is attempting to carry out a neutral analysis, they should have no expectations of what participants will say, but participants are not always able to sense this. As with other research, the interview situation may cause changes in the behaviour of both people. The interviewer may unintentionally focus on statements they are most interested in obtaining for their future analysis, while participants might try to predict what is expected and focus on saying what they think the interviewer wants to hear. These expectancies can only be reduced by open discussion before the interview and a full explanation of how the research process is to be carried out. **Active listening skills**, such as are used in a therapy context, are helpful in showing the participant that the interviewer is paying attention to what they are saying. This includes using body language and checking understanding by restating what the participant has said without trying to interpret and certainly not trying to change or correct their answers.

 Interviewer training is especially important when more than one person is interviewing so that interviews are standardized.

Debriefing

Participants need to be debriefed for ethical reasons, as they should be in all research. A full debriefing after an interview involves restating much of the information that should have been given beforehand, such as how the recorded information will be used, who will have access to it, and both when and how the participant will receive feedback about the researcher's findings from the interviews. It is also extremely beneficial for the researcher to talk to the participant again during the analysis process in order to check if the participant agrees with the researcher's interpretations. This is sometimes known as **member checking**. It is another way to increase the credibility of the researcher's conclusions.

● **Examiner's hint**
If you are asked about considerations in setting up and carrying out an observation, remember to make reference to ethical and practical considerations.

Analysis of interview data

There are a number of ways to approach the analysis of interview data including discourse analysis, template analysis and content analysis. For the HL IB examination, only the use of **inductive content analysis**, sometimes also called **thematic content analysis**, is needed.

Inductive content analysis involves allowing themes to emerge from the data. This process is similar to the qualitative analysis suggested for observational data (pages 22–23) but needs more detail as the interpretation of other people's words, the meanings they attach to ideas, and the non-verbal information gathered to accompany the verbal data, can be a difficult and complicated process.

To begin with, the researcher takes the transcript of each interview and identifies **raw themes** within it. Themes are usually simple statements participants have made, such as 'I enjoy working at home.'

Some researchers like to write each theme on a small card indicating which participant the theme comes from. After doing this with transcripts from even a single participant, it is possible to begin grouping themes and coding them according to their similarity. For example, it may emerge that a participant has talked a lot about work as a positive social experience, and therefore themes that contribute to this category can be coded as such.

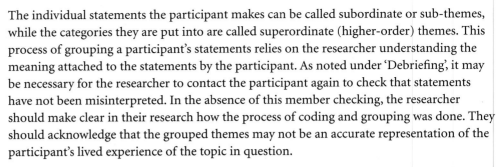

Inductive content analysis begins with raw themes that are grouped into superordinate or higher level themes, which are then grouped into dimensions.

The individual statements the participant makes can be called subordinate or sub-themes, while the categories they are put into are called superordinate (higher-order) themes. This process of grouping a participant's statements relies on the researcher understanding the meaning attached to the statements by the participant. As noted under 'Debriefing', it may be necessary for the researcher to contact the participant again to check that statements have not been misinterpreted. In the absence of this member checking, the researcher should make clear in their research how the process of coding and grouping was done. They should acknowledge that the grouped themes may not be an accurate representation of the participant's lived experience of the topic in question.

Another approach is for the researcher to make notes on the transcript as they notice each theme and then construct a summary list or table of the themes that have emerged. (This technique could be applied to the analysis of any form of written material, such as newspaper articles or diary entries.)

In order to make conclusions that represent the interpretations of the whole sample, not just individual participants, the next step is to attempt to revisit the data with a complete list of subordinate and superordinate themes and work out how they can be grouped to account for all of the data. This should result in a set of **dimensions** that can be paired with evidence in the form of quotations from several participants to be presented in the final paper.

Again, in the interests of reflexivity, it is useful for the researcher to carry out a content analysis in consultation with peers, and to keep a diary with thoughts on the process so that decisions can be assessed at a later point and described in the final research paper. By checking with peers, the researcher can expose any systematic bias in the way they have grouped themes, for example, and a discussion about any differences in opinion about how data should be grouped can be very helpful in improving the credibility of the final product.

● **Examiner's hints**
Reflexivity is again evidenced here; researchers should check with peers to see that their grouping of themes is reasonable.

HL EXERCISES

8   Construct a table to summarize strengths and limitations of semi-structured, focus group and narrative interviews. Use your table to evaluate a study using interviews as a method from elsewhere in this book.

9   Choose a study that uses interviews as a method from elsewhere in this book. Write a discussion of how the considerations outlined in this chapter apply to the research scenario.

10 Explain how researchers use inductive content analysis (thematic analysis).

PRACTICE QUESTIONS

The stimulus material below is based on a research article.

1   One of the key concerns in the health system is how users of services adapt to life after being discharged from an institution. The researcher in this study wanted to investigate the lifestyles of 50 people who were discharged from 'mental handicap' hospitals in Somerset in the UK. Several methods were used,

5   including interviews with social workers and the former patients, and participant observations in their own homes. The participant observation was conducted in part to check the accuracy of social workers' knowledge of their clients' ordinary lives and to establish the credibility of participant observation in participants' homes as a research method.

10 Eleven people were selected from the larger group of 50 people who were included in the study. In order to be included, they had to live in minimum support groups (more than one or two people living in the home) and know the researcher primarily as a social worker rather than as a researcher. She felt that it would be too intrusive to send an observer in to a one- or two-person home
15 and may disrupt their ordinary life too much. An undergraduate university student was the participant observer and she had no prior knowledge of 'mental handicap'. The observer was given a checklist of activities and contexts she needed to gather information about by making detailed notes during two visits to each group home, one in the evening and one on a weekend day.

20 The observer described realising the necessity to stay a certain distance from the members of the group home to minimise the influence of her presence, and yet a need to join in activities and conversation so that they were relaxed enough to go about their routines as normal. She paid particular attention to meal times as these yielded a lot of data about household relationships and the division of
25 labour and the conflicts that arose from these activities.

The following is an example of the notes the observer took at 5.30 p.m. one evening:

Stuart carries the teapot into the living room, Melanie calls upstairs for Nicholas and he comes down. Melanie places my sandwiches down and draws
30 *up another seat. She pours out the tea. Stuart asks me, 'How do you like your tea, black or with milk? Sugar?' ... Melanie and Nicholas stand up and begin to clear the tea things away. Stuart a little slower, begins to help. They work in silence, each knowing what is to be done. Nicholas washes the pots, Stuart dries them and puts them away. They continue to work in silence. Melanie tidies up.*
35 *The silence lasts for five minutes.*

It was concluded that participant observation in the home is an acceptable research method because it was not overly intrusive or upsetting to participants and there was little difference between social workers' reports and observation findings. It was noted that a separate participant observation of former patients
40 outside the home was less successful because it appeared to involve far greater distress for the participants.

Atkinson, D. 1985. The use of participant observation and respondent diaries in a study of ordinary living. *Brit J Ment Subnorm* 31(1):33–40

Answer all of the following three questions.

1 This study attempts to establish the credibility of participant observation as a research method. Explain the importance of credibility in qualitative research. *[10 marks]*

2 Evaluate the use of participant observation as a research method in the context of this study. *[10 marks]*

3 This study used a checklist to guide the observer in making detailed notes about behaviour she observed. Distinguish between qualitative and quantitative data that could be obtained in a study such as this. *[10 marks]*

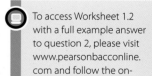
To access Worksheet 1.2 with a full example answer to question 2, please visit www.pearsonbacconline.com and follow the on-screen instructions.

To access Worksheet 1.3 with additional practice questions relating to this chapter, please visit www.pearsonbacconline.com and follow the on-screen instructions.

THE BIOLOGICAL LEVEL OF ANALYSIS

2.1 Introduction: Historical and cultural development

For thousands of years, philosophers, medical specialists and others have attempted to find the causes of behaviour inside the human body, attaching significance to biological characteristics and processes according to information available at the time. An early example is the work of Hippocrates (470–360 BC), who described humorism, a theory that personality is affected by the balance of four bodily liquids (humours): blood, phlegm, black bile and yellow bile.

Darwin was a young man in his twenties when he began to develop his theory of evolution although he didn't publish *On the Origin of Species* until he was much older.

In Europe and the USA, biological explanations for behaviour, cognition and emotion have changed in popularity as theorists have explored such ideas as a soul existing outside the body, or have attributed behaviour to the intervention of gods and demons. Key changes that focused psychology towards the principles that now define the biological level of analysis were (a) the discovery that the brain (and the neurons it is composed of) influenced behaviour, and (b) the publication of Charles Darwin's *On the Origin of Species* (1859). This hugely important book proposed the revolutionary new, comprehensive theory that all species, including humans, developed over time through the processes of evolutionary adaptation.

Medicine and the natural sciences grew enormously in popularity during the 19th century. With the dominance of theories of learning and interest in the experimental study of animals, the focus of psychology began to move away from the study of an unobservable mind towards working with medical and biological researchers to discover how physiological processes and behaviour might interact. Sometimes extreme claims are made on both sides of what is known as the nature–nurture debate; for example, offering a purely genetic or hormonal explanation for love or murder. However, it is now increasingly recognized that biological factors are extremely important in affecting our behaviour, thoughts and emotions and, moreover, that the inverse is true: our behaviour, thoughts and emotions can affect our physiology.

This chapter shows you the most important concepts in studying psychology at this level of analysis and the research that supports their use in interpreting behaviour.

2.2 Principles of the biological level of analysis

Learning outcomes
- Outline principles that define the biological level of analysis.
- Explain how principles that define the biological level of analysis may be demonstrated in research.

● **Examiner's hint**
These learning outcomes may be tested as short-answer questions. For each piece of research described at this level of analysis, you should make a note of the principles it demonstrates to help you organize material for later study.

● **Examiner's hint**
You should be able to provide a brief description of the principles that define the biological level of analysis

These principles are the main ideas that have driven research to focus on specific areas of human behaviour and physiology in order to achieve an understanding of how behaviour can be caused or influenced by biological factors.

There are three key principles that define the biological level of analysis:
- emotions and behaviour are products of the anatomy and physiology of the nervous and endocrine systems
- patterns of behaviour can be inherited
- animal research may inform our understanding of behaviour.

Emotions and behaviour are products of the anatomy and physiology of the nervous and endocrine systems

This principle suggests that all observable behaviour, as well as the internal mental activity of an individual (e.g. emotions and cognitions), can be traced back to physiological events. This is encouraged by research findings that there are biological correlates of behaviour. Links have been found between psychological events and physiological activity in three main areas:
- the effect of neurotransmitters
- the effect of hormones
- the effect of brain localization.

Emotions, for example, are seen to be produced by activity in the brain and by the activity of hormones. Some examples with supporting research at the biological level of analysis are given on pages 54–58. This principle reflects a desire to find the causes of behaviour, emotion, and thought within the human body. It has specifically required the development of an understanding of relevant components of the nervous system (particularly the way the brain interacts with the body) and the endocrine system (which is responsible for the secretion of hormones that also affect behaviour). However, psychologists working at the biological level of analysis do not necessarily deny the influence of environmental factors on human behaviour. In fact, many of them are working to develop an understanding of the interaction of social and cognitive factors with physiological and genetic factors to inform a more comprehensive picture of how humans work.

The endocrine system is responsible for the secretion of hormones.

Much of this chapter is dedicated to developing your understanding of how the brain and endocrine system have been the focus of theory and research, and you are expected to be able to use the research presented in this chapter to explain principles such as this one.

Patterns of behaviour can be inherited

This principle reflects the line of thought inspired by the work of Darwin. Two particular branches of scientific inquiry demonstrate this principle very well: evolutionary psychology and the study of genetics. Both rely on our understanding of evolution (page 62) which shows us that humans have changed physically and behaviourally according to the demands of the environment. Genetic information is transmitted from parents to children and, over time, physical characteristics and behaviours that are helpful to an individual or social group in terms of surviving and reproducing can be passed on. Thus, patterns of behaviour that we see today are theorized to have been of evolutionary benefit. Some examples with supporting research at the biological level of analysis are given on pages 62–63.

Although a great deal of research has sought to find causes of behaviour in our genes, modern researchers acknowledge it is unlikely that single genes are responsible for any of the complex behaviour psychologists are interested in. Research into possible causes of homosexuality, differences in intelligence, criminal behaviour and psychological disorders such as schizophrenia, has been motivated by the hope that finding a genetic component will help us understand human experience better. More and more, researchers are finding that what is inherited may be a predisposition for certain behaviour that requires particular environmental stimuli before the behaviour will become manifest. For example, the diathesis–stress model of abnormal behaviour suggests that a genetic vulnerability to disorders like depression can be inherited, but that an environmental trigger like childhood separation or a traumatic divorce is required for the person to actually become depressed.

Animal research may inform our understanding of behaviour

Pavlov's research with dogs helped us to understand human learning processes.

One of the key assumptions of a biological approach, based initially on Darwin's work, is the idea that humans and the many types of animal are different species now because of thousands of years of evolutionary adaptation to environmental demands. This suggests that we share an earlier common ancestral species and, in many ways are fundamentally the same; the human being is a type of animal. When it comes to studying physiology and behaviour, therefore, it is valid to try to make inferences about human behaviour based on animal research, because the mechanisms that underlie behaviour are the core similarity we share with animals. Brains can be studied in animals that appear to be quite closely related to humans, such as monkeys and apes. It is also possible to make generalizations from

studies that manipulate levels of specific neurotransmitters in the brain of other mammals –rats, for example. It has also been extremely useful to observe evolution in manageable contexts with animals that have much shorter lifespans than humans (e.g. fruit flies and foxes) and to assume that the same processes apply to humans. Details of such research are given throughout this chapter and, again, you should be able to explain how that research demonstrates this principle.

There is significant controversy about the use of animals in research and it is important to understand the advantages and disadvantages of this type of research.

 ## 2.3 Biological research methods and ethics

Learning outcomes
- Discuss how and why particular research methods are used at the biological level of analysis.
- Discuss ethical considerations related to research studies at the biological level of analysis.

The biological level of analysis, according to the principles outlined above, tends to use three main research methods:
- laboratory experiments
- case studies
- correlational studies.

Laboratory experiments

At the biological level of analysis, these experiments are commonly used to establish cause–effect relationships between the variables studied.

A key point to note at this level of analysis is the use of animal experiments as well as human experiments. When researchers want to test the effect of changes to physiology (e.g. by an injection of hormones) or to test the effectiveness of a new medication (e.g. for schizophrenia), it is unlikely that it will be ethically possible to carry out the experiment with human participants if there is any possibility that participants could be harmed. While participants can give their informed consent, there is a limited number of people willing to undergo such experimentation.

There is also the risk that receiving full information about the nature of the experiment might lead to changes in the participants' behaviour. For example, a **placebo effect** can occur when participants believe they are receiving a treatment – their body reacts to simply to being treated, rather than to the specific treatment they receive. And in particular, when researchers want to find out what effect can be observed when specific parts of the brain are damaged, it would clearly be impossible to carry out the research with human subjects.

 The placebo effect occurs, for example, when a person takes a neutral pill but it has an effect.

This is one of the most important arguments in favour of animal experiments: such research cannot be done on humans. Research departments often maintain a population of animals such as rats, pigeons and fruit flies for use in research. An advantage of fruit flies in particular, is that their lifespan is very short and researchers can control their environment. This makes it possible for researchers to make changes to the environment and observe a form of evolution in a fairly short timeframe.

 Does it matter that laboratory experiments are more common than field experiments at the biological level of analysis?

Sometimes, it is assumed that animals have a lesser experience of pain or have less conscious awareness of their suffering than humans would in the same situation. There are guidelines for the treatment of animals in laboratories, and adherence to these is usually monitored closely.

On the other hand, there is a strong argument that animal experimentation is morally wrong. For many people, the difference between animal and human suffering is not large enough to justify what can seem like very cruel treatment. And, if animals are so different from people that we feel ethically excused from wrong-doing, it must be asked whether it is still valid to do the experiments on them and generalize the results to humans.

How can we know if animals experience pain and suffering? Is it possible to resolve this issue logically?

Case studies

The case study is another way to deal with the ethical problem of carrying out research on human participants. Instead of causing some kind of change to a person's physiology, researchers can take advantage of naturally occurring irregularities (e.g. brain damage or long-term drug use) by obtaining detailed information about the participant's condition. This has frequently been a very useful source of information in a medical context. As this approach is mostly descriptive, there is relatively little harm that can be done to participants. The most important ethical risk is that the depth of information obtained and the possible uniqueness of the case make it more likely that there is a threat to participants' anonymity, so the researcher may need to take extra steps to protect the identities of those involved.

Correlational studies

As with the case study, the correlational study does not usually necessitate the manipulation of an independent variable that might cause damage to the participant; instead it takes scores on two or more measures and works out the relationship between them. This approach is often at the core of twin studies and adoption studies (pages 60–61), which are important sources of information about the link between genetics and behaviour.

In both cases, the correlation represents the frequency of a second family member having a particular characteristic when we already know that one member of the family has it. In addition, many of the techniques used to observe brain activity such as fMRI and PET (page 42) are essentially correlating brain activity with behaviour, cognition or emotion. This means that although a relationship can be established, we cannot infer causation. In other words, although we might find that a particular part of the brain is active while a participant experiences a particular emotion, we cannot be sure that the brain activity is the cause of the emotion.

EXERCISE
1   Keep a diary of ethical issues relating to the research studies you come across in this chapter. When you are at the end of the chapter, be prepared to write a summary.

2.4 Physiology and behaviour: Localization of function

Learning outcomes
- Explain one study related to localization of function in the brain.
- Examine one interaction between cognition and physiology in terms of behaviour. Evaluate two relevant studies.
- Discuss the use of brain imaging technologies in investigating the relationship between biological factors and behaviour.
- Discuss two effects of the environment on physiological processes.

In this section, we look at the main ways researchers have investigated brain function and evaluate these methods. In your exam, you may be asked to explain a study that uses one of these methods.

Early investigations of localization of function

Early attempts to locate the cause of behaviour in the brain sometimes appear to us now to be rather unusual or even ridiculous. This is partly because of our shared confidence that we understand the brain so much better now because science has developed more accurate ways of investigating the brain. Until more recent times, research suffered from the central problem that it was not possible to directly study the brain in living humans. Thus, it was rather difficult to prove early theories correct or incorrect.

Phrenology is a good early example of brain-related research that now appears inaccurate. Phrenologist Franz Joseph Gall (1758–1828) assumed that certain parts of the brain were responsible for specific facets of personality and behaviour. He believed that by manually searching for bumps and depressions on the skull, one could detect the influence of the brain. Expert phrenologists attempted to make inferences about an individual's personality from this procedure, reaching conclusions regarding, for example, an individual's intelligence and tendency towards murder.

This is a phrenology head. It shows the attempt to map certain functions to certain areas of the brain located by feeling for bumps on the skull.

▼

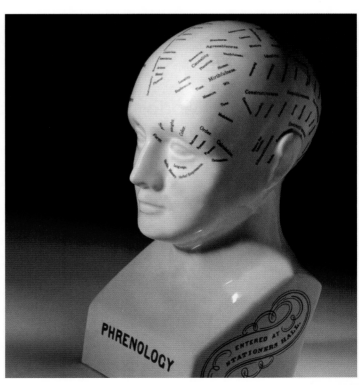

While phrenology is largely discredited today and many find it ridiculous, it is clear that some of its basic assumptions are still valid. In particular, it is clear that different parts of the brain do indeed have different functions, and that it is possible to study the relationship between brain and behaviour. Research from the 19th and 20th centuries has guided us towards a much better understanding of how we should do such research and how functions of the brain are localized. Localization of function refers to the idea that behaviour, emotions and thoughts originate in the brain in specific locations.

Case studies of people with naturally occurring brain damage

Scientific research into brain function was, until the 20th century, largely limited to case studies of individuals who were known to have suffered some kind of brain damage or head injury. This type of research, not being experimental, could never clearly establish a cause–effect relationship between the behaviour of the person before death and the location of the brain damage. However, it would clearly be unethical to conduct the kind of experiment required, for example, to test what the effect on behaviour might be after a volunteer had a portion of their brain removed.

Probably the most famous example of this type of research is the case study of Phineas Gage (page 44). Gage was a railway worker in the 19th century who survived the passing of an iron rod through his head. He is documented as having undergone dramatic changes in personality after the injury, changes that his doctor blamed on the damage to his brain.

Two further studies from the 19th century revealed important new information about the function of specific areas of the brain. Paul Broca (1824–80) studied a new patient, soon to be known as 'Tan' because this was one of few sounds the patient could make with any frequency. After Tan died, Broca announced that from conducting a post-mortem autopsy on this patient (and several others), he now had evidence that damage to a specific area of the brain was responsible for the loss of the ability to produce coherent speech. This became known as **Broca's area**. The effects of damage to this part of the brain can most easily be observed in the speech of stroke victims, many of whom are temporarily or permanently unable to produce language, a condition known as **Broca's aphasia**.

Another type of aphasia is **Wernicke's aphasia**. This is also a speech disorder, but involving a different part of the brain which seems to be responsible for the comprehension of speech. Individuals with this type of aphasia might have problems understanding the speech of others or might substitute wrong words into planned phrases. Carl Wernicke worked in a similar fashion to Broca, by noting behaviour and conducting post-mortem autopsies to locate brain damage after patients had died.

Thus it was becoming clear that specific parts of the brain were responsible for specific human activities, but it was still very difficult to find ways to investigate this further.

To learn more about Broca's aphasia, go to pearsonhotlinks.com, enter the title or ISBN of this book and select weblinks 2.1a and 2.1b.

● **Examiner's hint**
You need to be able to explain these technologies, what they are used for, and their relative strengths and limitations. You also need to give examples of research that uses these technologies to demonstrate your points.

Modern technology and localization of function

Advances in technology have allowed us to build a more accurate understanding of how the brain works. These technologies include the electroencephalogram (EEG), computer tomography (CT), magnetic resonance imaging (MRI), functional magnetic resonance imaging (fMRI), positron emission tomography (PET).

Electroencephalogram (EEG)

This technology was developed around the beginning of the 20th century and given its name by Hans Berger in 1929. In its present form, electrodes are placed on the outside of a person's head in specific locations. This is often done using a special cap or helmet so that the electrodes are fitted to standardized places on the skull. The electrodes detect changes in electrical activity below them. When areas of the brain are active, the EEG produces a graphical representation of the activity from each electrode.

The best known use of this technology is for sleep research, which requires a person to spend a night 'wired up' to the machine. The researcher or doctor can look at the set of lines printed by the machine and compare them to the graphs usually produced during

sleep. Research has established that brain activity changes in specific ways during sleep. For example, there is a clearly distinct pattern of activity during rapid eye movement (REM) sleep when a person is dreaming. Although it is very useful in this context, the EEG is not sufficiently accurate for most research into localization of function. The reason for this inaccuracy is that the electrodes are outside the skull, and detect the activity of an uncountable number of neurons on the surface on the brain. Thus, we are given a vague idea of what parts of the brain were active, but this is not enough to make strong conclusions in relation to localization of function, so more accurate means of detecting brain activity have been developed

Computed tomography (CT)

The CT scanner combines computer and X-ray technology. A traditional X-ray image shows human bones extremely well, but not soft tissue such as the brain. Computer technology has allowed us to see the brain. The images acquired from a CT scan can be taken from the top, bottom, back, front or sides of the head and can show the brain at any depth. The images look like slices of brain. This technology used to be called computed axial tomography (CAT), where *axial* indicated that it was limited to scans from only one angle.

CT scans are extremely useful for showing structural changes in the brain. For example, structural changes due to a brain tumour or brain damage are very evident on a CAT scan. However, this technology has its limitations. The main one is that a structural image is the only kind of image this technology can produce. Other technologies are needed to provide images of brain activity. The case study of Janet (page 45) provides an example of how this scanning technology is used.

Magnetic resonance imaging (MRI)

This technology is based on the discovery that when the body is exposed to a strong magnetic field, the protons in the water inside the body change their alignment. When a magnetic field is used in conjunction with radio frequency fields, the alignment of the hydrogen atoms is changed in such a way as to be detectable by a scanner. The signal from the scanner can be transformed into a visual representation of the area of the part of the body being studied. The exposure to magnetism can be dangerous for some individuals, such as those with metal screws used after surgery for broken bones. But for most people, MRI is believed to be safe, and is often preferred over the CT scan for tumours where exposure to X-ray radiation might cause concern. The image that is produced can represent a slice of the brain taken from any angle, and can now also be used to create a three-dimensional image of the brain. MRI technology is still being enhanced, allowing specialists to obtain more precise images of the structure of a brain.

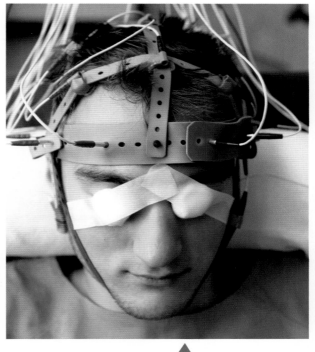

This person is undergoing an EEG in a sleep clinic.

Radiologist examining a CAT scan.

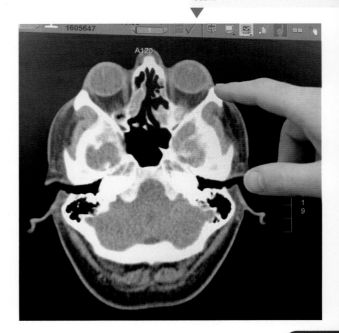

Functional MRI (fMRI)

This is a modification of the regular MRI technique. It takes advantage of the fact that when neurons in a particular region are active, more blood is sent to that region. The fMRI machine can map metabolic changes that indicate brain activity to provide us with a picture that shows with increasing precision which parts of the brain are active while certain activities are being performed or certain thoughts or emotions occur. This clearly allows for a wide range of human behaviours, thoughts and emotions to be correlated with brain activity as they happen, to help us understand the role of certain parts of the brain. It is more flexible than regular MRI in its ability to provide dynamic rather than static information. It is also more precise than positron emission tomography (PET), another method of studying dynamic function.

The study of meditating monks (pages 46–47) is an example of fMRI use in research.

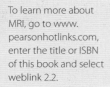

To learn more about MRI, go to www.pearsonhotlinks.com, enter the title or ISBN of this book and select weblink 2.2.

This fMRI scan shows activity in the right hemisphere of the brain.

Cognitive brain-imaging researchers are increasingly able to use technology to show what people's brains are doing. Showing participants static images or video footage and using a computer to find similarities in brain activation has also allowed researchers to do the reverse: look at brain activation in an individual and use it to predict what the person is visually imagining – with increasing accuracy.

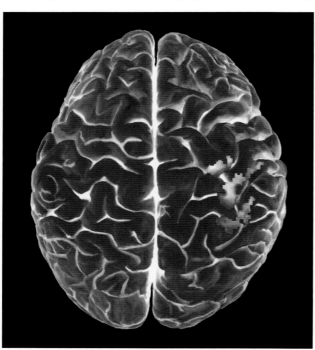

Positron emission tomography (PET)

This technology requires the injection of a radioactive substance into the participant. Usually, this is a form of sugar that produces gamma rays as it is metabolized by the brain. Like the fMRI, this technology relies on the knowledge that parts of the brain will metabolize the sugar at different rates according to whether they are more or less active. The gamma rays produced can be detected by the machine in which the person is placed. Eventually the signal is turned into a computer image that displays a colourful map of activity in the different parts of the brain.

PET is good for showing a dynamic image of activity, but it is much less precise than the fMRI. Its use seems most appropriate now for conditions that do not show structural changes early enough to be detected by MRI or CT scans. For example, a patient with Alzheimer's disease will show some quite dramatic differences in brain structure and activity when the disease has progressed and the amount of brain tissue has decreased in certain areas. However, an earlier PET scan can be a helpful diagnostic tool showing abnormalities in activity levels. As with CT scans, a specialist might have some concerns about carrying out a PET scan depending on specific individual health problems.

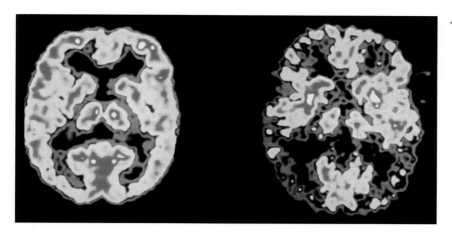

This PET scan shows a normal brain (left) and the brain of a patient with Alzheimer's disease (right). Brain activity (red and yellow areas) is much reduced in the brain on the right.

Studies of individuals who have undergone brain surgery

HM

One of the most famous personalities in psychology died in December 2008. Known as HM, he was studied regularly for many years after brain surgery in 1953 to correct his epilepsy. An important part of his hippocampus was removed and when he recovered from the surgery, it was noted that he had now had significant memory problems as detailed (page 44). This allowed researchers to make inferences about the role of the hippocampus in memory, although of course there are a number of factors that made it difficult to be sure about cause and effect here. For example, it was not clear until 1997 exactly what the extent of damage to the hippocampus was. Moreover, HM was using anti-epileptic drugs after the operation, some of which are suspected to have caused further damage to his brain.

To learn more about HM and read his obituary, go to www.pearsonhotlinks.com, enter the title or ISBN of this book and select weblink 2.3.

Sperry and the split brain

The work of Roger Sperry (page 45) was very influential in helping neuroscientists to understand the way brain functions appear to be not only localized in specific regions, but also lateralized –that is, the left and right hemispheres seem to be more or less responsible for certain activities. The participants in Sperry's work had all undergone an operation to reduce the severity of their epilepsy by severing the corpus callosum. The corpus callosum is a part of the brain that joins the two hemispheres and it appears to be responsible for communication between them. Without this communication and under the right experimental conditions, the two hemispheres could be studied separately and their sometimes subtle differences identified.

EXERCISES

2 Read the studies in the following Empirical research boxes.

   a Which one provides the most reliable information about the functions of the brain?

   b Which one is the most useful?

   You may like to refer to sections 1.2 and 1.3 (pages 2–8) for guidance.

3 Sperry's work is sometimes considered a natural experiment although others argue it is a case study. What do you think? Can you generalize the findings of this research to the rest of the human population? Explain your answer.

Disinhibition is quite common following head injury. When the brain moves forward inside the skull, the prefrontal cortex is often damaged by the bones around the eye. Disinhibition results in a loss of resistance to carrying out impulses; angry outbursts, for example, are not stopped as they might be in people without this kind of damage.

A reconstruction of the injury to Gage's brain. ▶

The case of Phineas Gage

Phineas Gage was a liked and respected foreman for a team of railway workers. In 1848, while he was using a tamping iron to press explosives into a hole, an explosion sent the rod through his head. It entered below his left cheek and exited through the top of his skull. Under the care of his physician, J.M. Harlow, he was nursed to recovery but significant changes in his personality were noted. Harlow described him as having little restraint, using extremely rude language, and making grand plans for the future which would be instantly replaced with others.

It is common for people with frontal lobe brain damage to become disinhibited. This means that they start doing things they might normally have stopped themselves from doing, and it appears that this is what had happened to Gage. Although he wanted to continue working, his impulsive and rude behaviour was not conducive to working with other people and he could not therefore continue. It is suggested that he kept the tamping iron with him even when he went on to work in a circus. After his death, his skull was kept and later discovered by researchers who decided to use modern technology to work out what the likely damage to Gage's brain was.

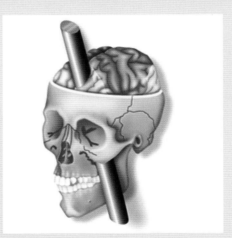

Opposite, you can see a reconstruction of Gage's injury based on the work of Damasio, et al. (1994). It shows the likely path of the rod through Gage's brain. From this, we can expect that Gage's frontal lobes were indeed damaged in the left pre-frontal region. This would account for his disinhibited behaviour.

The case of HM

At the age of 27, HM underwent surgery to remove the medial temporal lobes in order to reduce the frequency of his epileptic seizures. This operation was not expected to result in the problems that occurred, partly because at the time (1953) it was not clear what role the temporal lobes might have in memory. HM's operation resulted in the removal of more of his brain than was intended – removal of the hippocampus was a particular concern – and had profound effects on his memory. MRI brain scans were carried out in 1996 and showed the surprising extent of damage: besides damage to the temporal lobes, other parts of the brain had been damaged, and it is supposed that this was caused by a bad reaction to the epileptic medication HM was taking.

HM's memory problems most famously included an inability to create long-term memories. This means that he could hold information in his working memory, but when distracted, HM would 'forget'. He was able remember some of his childhood, but very little from the 11 years prior to his surgery. This kind of amnesia is known as retrograde amnesia – loss of memory from before an event (surgery in HM's case). Ogden (2005) describes him as unable to detect that time has passed, probably because he is not forming new memories. This form of amnesia is called anterograde amnesia – an inability to remember relating to the time since his operation. It is clear that he picked up a few facts after the operation as he had some idea who Elvis Presley and John F. Kennedy were. His mood is reported by Ogden to be generally calm, perhaps because years of medication have dulled his mood or because of damage to the emotional amygdalae caused by the operation – such damage might prevent the kind of anger that others have felt at being unable to exist beyond a single moment in time. She adds that HM may also be genuinely content and good natured.

The case of Janet

Ogden (2005) describes her study of a woman who died after developing a brain tumour. The case demonstrates the curious phenomenon known as hemineglect. This is a condition that results from damage to one side of the brain and causes various forms of inattention to the opposite side of space.

Janet, for example, was found to have a brain tumour in the parietal lobe of her right hemisphere, detected by CT. Her problems first manifested themselves at a birthday party where she blew out the candles only on the right side of the cake. When reading aloud, she tended to omit words from the left side of the page, and when writing, she would often use only the right side of the page. When asked to fill in the numbers on the face of clock, she wrote on only the right half of the clock, squeezing all the numbers into half the available space. She would also ignore parts of her own body on the left side, even claiming that her left arm belonged to someone else and had been mistakenly left in her bed.

Ogden suggests that this is not from an inability to see or sense, but rather an apparently willing neglect by the half of the brain that is affected. Seemingly errors in performance during neuropsychological assessment can often be accompanied by justifications, rationalizations and jokes that show that patients have some awareness of their own tendencies (although this is more likely when the damage is to the right hemisphere!).

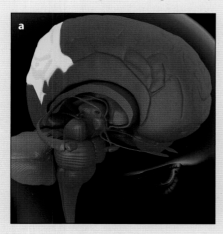

a The yellow area in this image of the brain indicates the parietal lobe. Damage to this area can result in hemineglect. **b** Drawings by a hemineglect patient with damage to right parietal lobe.

Roger Sperry's work with split-brain patients

Prior to his most famous work with human participants (1968), Roger Sperry had already established that when the corpus callosum was severed in cats, it prevented the transfer of information from one side to the other. Myers and Sperry (1953) allowed split-brain cats to learn their way through a maze with one eye blindfolded and found that when the blindfold was removed and put on the other eye, the cats appeared unable to repeat the learned behaviour. They did not detect any other difficulties.

When a group of 10 patients who had undergone a split-brain operation to relieve severe epilepsy became available for research, Sperry and his colleagues began testing the capabilities of each of the two hemispheres to establish what functions might be lateralized in the human brain. Experiments included showing images to only one hemisphere by asking patients to focus on a central point and flashing the image to the far left or right too quickly to allow the eyes to move.

Understanding Sperry's experiments requires the knowledge that *both* eyes send information to the brain about *both* halves of the visual field. Information from the left half of the visual field is sent to the right half of the brain by the optic nerves and information about the right half of the visual field is sent to the left half of the brain. It is necessary to understand that movement of the left half of the body is controlled by the right half of the brain, and of the right half of the body by the left half of the brain. We know from the work of Paul Broca that speech production is a function of the left hemisphere.

continued

To learn more about the work of Sperry and his colleagues, go to www.pearsonhotlinks.com, enter the title or ISBN of this book and select weblink 2.4.

● **Examiner's hint**
Short-answer questions may require you to write an explanation of a study connected with localization of function. Any of the studies in the boxes above are appropriate but note that lateralization of function is not the same as localization of function, so answers using Sperry need to focus on the function of the corpus callosum, not on differences between left and right hemispheres of the brain. In order to write a good answer, you need to describe the study and clearly indicate how it shows that brain functions are localized. For practice, write a one-page explanation of one study, detailing what part of the brain was affected, how the researcher found out, and what the effect on behaviour, cognition or emotion was.

A typical example of the tasks asked of Sperry's participants involved the presentation of a single face consisting of the left half of one person's face and the right half of another's. Participants were asked to describe the face, but their descriptions usually related only to the half-face presented on the right half of space. When shown the full faces and asked to point to the face they had seen with their left hand, participants usually selected the complete version of the half-face that had been presented on the left half of space. Sperry's findings won him the Nobel Prize in medicine in 1981.

The conclusions drawn by Sperry and his colleagues about lateralization of function include the assertion that the right half of the brain is dominant for visuo-spatial ability (demonstrated in tasks like reading maps or recognizing faces), as well as musical abilities and understanding intonation in speech. The left half of the brain seems to be more positive than the right and is dominant for language and logical or mathematical abilities.

Neuroplasticity

Neuroplasticity is the concept that, although localization of function occurs, the specific location of a function is not necessarily fixed for all individuals, and the area of brain dedicated to certain functions can be redistributed according to environmental demands. This is best illustrated through examples. It seems that the more a person performs a particular activity, the more neuronal connections are formed in the area of the brain responsible, and this creates a physical change in the brain.

EMPIRICAL RESEARCH

The effects of meditation on the brain (Brefczynski–Lewis et al., 2007)

The purpose of this study was to examine differences in brain activity that might have resulted from having engaged in meditation over a long period of time. The main hypotheses were that meditating activates specific parts of the brain that are not active while a person is at rest, and that those with the most experience meditating would show less activity in those regions than less-experienced meditators because experience has reduced the amount of effort required to sustain attention.

Tibetan monk meditating.

● **Examiner's hint**
The main learning outcomes associated with this section of the syllabus require you to show an understanding of how cognition and physiology can interact and how the environment and experience can affect the brain through neuroplasticity. Besides the empirical research in the boxes here, other studies in this chapter that can help you in this area include the case studies of H.M. and Janet. In some cases, it seems that brain damage has effects on cognition, and in others, cognition has effects on brain structure. Be clear about what each study shows.

The independent variable was experience meditating and the experimenters compared newly trained meditators with people with between 10 000 and 54 000 hours of meditation practice in a Tibetan Buddhist method. Seven of the 12 experienced meditators were Asian, and they were compared with untrained Caucasian participants with an interest in learning to meditate. To be sure that this interest was not a confounding variable, a third group of participants were promised a financial incentive if their attention regions were most active. Participants' brains were scanned using fMRI while they concentrated on a dot on a screen in front of them and while at rest with no concentration. While they did this, researchers played various noises in an attempt to distract participants from their meditation and force them to work harder to sustain attention. Noises included a woman screaming, a baby cooing and restaurant background noise.

It was expected that attention-related networks in the brain and the visual cortex would be more active during meditation than during rest periods, and novice meditators would find it more difficult than experts to sustain their concentration, so this effort would be observed on the fMRI. In addition, it was expected that experienced meditators would show less activation in areas of the brain associated with daydreams, emotional processing and other thoughts not relating to the task.

The results confirmed these expectations. The researchers noted the interesting finding that experienced meditators showed a response to the disturbing stimuli, not in terms of a change in attention away from the target of their concentration meditation, but in terms of some kind of adjustment of concentration, perhaps an active resistance to being disrupted.

The researchers believe that the differences observed are not related to age differences or possible brain differences relating to ethnicity or culture because they conducted statistical tests to eliminate these possibilities. Instead, they conclude that the differences are probably due to neuroplasticity, some kind of changes in the brain that have occurred over time as a result of periods of sustained meditation.

EXERCISE

4 **a** Briefly summarize this study under the headings *Aim*, *Method* and *Findings*.

   b Is this a true experiment? How else could you describe the study?

   c Are the conclusions valid?

EMPIRICAL RESEARCH

Changes in the brain after juggling training (Draganski et al. 2004)

These researchers were interested in determining whether both functional and structural changes could be detected in the human brain (using brain-imaging technologies) as a result of learning a new motor skill.

Twenty-one females and three males participated in the study, which required half of the participants to spend three months learning to perform a basic juggling routine for a minimum of 60 seconds. Structural MRI scans were done before and after the three months of practice, and a third scan was made three months later, during which time participants were not supposed to practise their new skills.

While there were no significant group differences in brain structure in the first scan (before training), two areas of the brain were significantly different in size after training. The difference became smaller in the third scan, when practice had ceased for three months. These differences were apparently due to an increase in volume in the two regions of the jugglers' brains, which are associated with the retention of visually detected movement information rather than physical co-ordination. Thus, the practice of watching balls moving through the air repetitively and learning to move in response to this has strengthened the connections between neurons in the parts of the brain responsible for this activity.

EXERCISE

5 **a** Briefly summarize this study under the headings *Aim*, *Method* and *Findings*.

   b The researchers compared differences in the two groups before and after, rather than differences in individuals.

   Can you think of any different ways they could have analysed their data?

   c Do you think there are any problems with generalizing the results of this study?

EMPIRICAL RESEARCH

Changes in the brains of experienced London taxi drivers (Maguire et al. 2000)

It is known that animals which employ spatial memory seem to show morphological changes in the hippocampus (Figure 2.1). London taxi drivers must undertake special training that takes about two years to complete during which time they must learn the roads and routes to the extent that they can reliably navigate their way around the central area without the aid of a map. This learning period is referred to as being 'on the knowledge'. On the basis of all this information, Maguire et al. predicted that fully licensed London taxi drivers will have structural differences in their hippocampi as a result of this learning experience.

Figure 2.1
The location of the hippocampus within the brain.

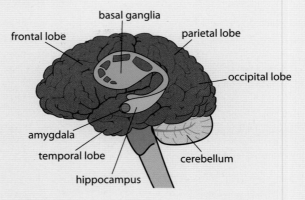

basal ganglia
frontal lobe
parietal lobe
occipital lobe
amygdala
temporal lobe
cerebellum
hippocampus

To investigate this idea, the researchers used structural MRI scans of fully licensed male taxi drivers with a range of years' experience driving, and compared them with control subjects. The control subjects were not actual participants, but existing scans of healthy males who did not drive taxis.

They found that both the left and right hippocampi were significantly higher in volume in taxi drivers' brains, although there were some parts of the hippocampi that were smaller in taxi drivers. In addition, the researchers ran a correlation between volume of hippocampi and time spent as a taxi driver, and found a positive correlation that could not be accounted for by age differences. Maguire et al. conclude that there has probably been a redistribution of grey matter in the hippocampi as a result of intense development and use of spatial memory skills, specifically those relating to learning and remembering routes through the city. Again, this is likely to be a strengthening of connections between neurons in a well-used part of the brain.

EXERCISES

6   **a**   Is this a true experiment? Why/why not?

      b   How trustworthy are the results of this study?

7   Maguire did further research on this topic. What kind of research is necessary to illustrate that the differences are genuinely caused by 'the knowledge'?

EMPIRICAL RESEARCH

PET evaluation of bilingual language compensation following early childhood brain damage (Tierney et al. 2001)

It has long been known that Broca's area in the left hemisphere of the frontal cortex plays an important role in speech production in the majority of healthy adults. Tierney et al. report the case of a 37-year-old man (MA) with normal speech function who was participating as a volunteer in a speech study when it was discovered that he had a lesion in his left frontal lobe, probably as a result of encephalitis he had suffered at the age of 6 weeks that had had no long-term, clinically significant consequences.

Both of his parents were deaf and he had used sign language at home from a young age. The researchers were curious to know if this might have had something to do with his ability to speak despite brain damage that should have prevented him from doing so..

The researchers compared MA and 12 control participants, who were also fluent in sign language, using PET scans while the participants produced narrative speech or signs. In addition, a set of motor control tasks were completed so that researchers could contrast movements required for sign language and speech with movement of the corresponding parts of the body without speech.

The researchers found that MA's right hemisphere was more active than control subjects' during the production of both speech and sign language. They also noted that he seemed more anxious and agitated, with more anger than the majority of participants. He was otherwise judged normal by independent observers of speech and sign language production, and according to scores on various neuropsychological tests. These findings suggest that language function seems to have developed in the right hemisphere instead of the left hemisphere as a form of adaptation following his early brain damage. This demonstrates the plasticity of the brain, especially during early childhood.

Further points of interest were that although the regions of the left hemisphere used by the controls during production of sign language were actually intact in MA, his right hemisphere still seemed to be responsible. At the same time, his visuo-spatial abilities were slightly below normal. These findings suggest that his language abilities may have developed in the right hemisphere at the expense of visuo-spatial ability.

 Sign language requires the use of different parts of the brain: most deaf users of sign language use both sides of the brain: the language centres in the left and the visuospatial areas in the right.

EXERCISE

8 **a** How would you describe the method used in this study? What are the strengths and limitations of the study?

b Are there any practical implications of this study?

Environment and brain function

The studies in this section focus on how the brain changes in response to the way we use it. For example, highly practised meditating monks appear to have different levels of brain functioning because of the time they have spent meditating. The case study of MA shows how the brain can change in response to brain damage and new areas can take over the function of language if there is enough practice. The taxi drivers used their hippocampi to store more visual information than most people, so their brains appear to have adapted to their cognitive behaviour. And exercising the parts of the brain responsible for visual processing of movement is associated with changes in relevant regions of the brain. Remember, however, that you have identified strengths and limitations of the studies in this section, and it is important to question whether we can draw conclusions about causes and effects in terms of the interaction between cognition and physiology. MA's exposure to sign language is an example, and you will meet more examples throughout the book. This shows how important the environment is in shaping the structure of the brain and helps account for individual differences in brain structure and function.

2.5 Physiology and behaviour: Neurotransmission

Learning outcomes
- Using one or more examples, explain effects of neurotransmission on human behaviour.

How nerve cells communicate

One of the most important discoveries that have influenced psychology is the role of neurotransmission in behaviour, thought and emotion. Here, you will find that an understanding of how chemistry and biology work will improve your understanding of how humans think and act.

The brain is made up of an enormous number of neurons or nerve cells (Figure 2.2). Recent estimates suggest there may be as many as 100 billion in the human brain. The most important thing for you to understand about neuron structure is that they receive information from other neurons through their dendrites and transmit it (by electrical impulse) across the cell body and along the axon to the terminal buttons at the end. Most of what you need to know for the purposes of this course relates to the synapse, the gap between two neurons, which is where communication from one neuron to the next occurs.

Figure 2.2
Structure of a neuron.

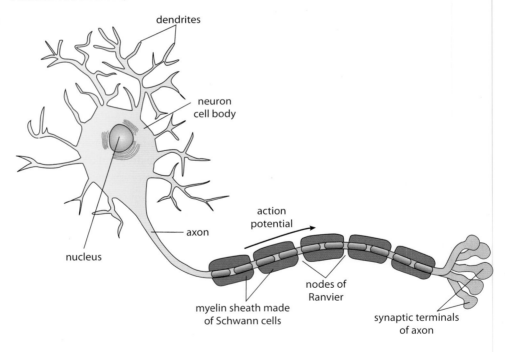

Communication *between* neurons is a chemical process; one neuron sends out chemicals known as neurotransmitters, and other neurons pick up the chemicals and may or may not send the message on. *Voluntary* movement of any muscle in the human body first requires the transmission of an 'instruction' to move through the appropriate parts of the brain and then to the muscle. The 'instructions' for *reflex* movements can be transmitted more rapidly because they usually involve the spinal chord and not the brain. Examples are the knee jerk test (when a doctor taps your knee) and the rapid removal of your hand from a

very hot object. At the biological level of analysis, *voluntary* movement can be viewed as the release of neurotransmitters in the primary motor cortex of the brain, triggering further communication through nerve cells until the appropriate muscles are activated to perform the movement.

Neurons are specific in which neurotransmitters they can release and receive. Neurons working with certain neurotransmitters can be found in greater or lesser concentration in certain parts of the brain. The primary motor cortex is populated by neurons that use dopamine and acetylcholine to communicate; the 'pleasure circuit' in the limbic system of the brain is populated by neurons using dopamine; neurons in the areas of the brain thought to be responsible for mood tend to use a chemical called serotonin.

To understand the effect of many of the drugs that have an effect on neurotransmission, it is important to note that there are three main parts to the transmission process at the synapse (Figure 2.3).

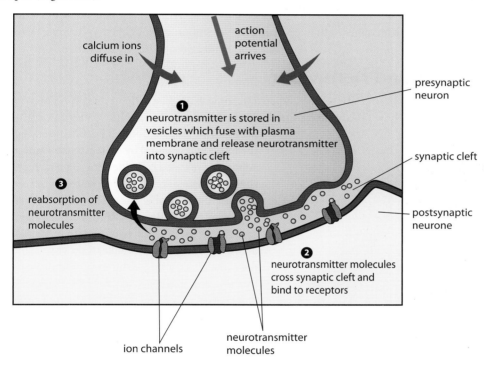

◄ **Figure 2.3**
Chemical transmission at a synapse.

1 Neurotransmitters are stored in vesicles inside the terminal button of the axon; the vesicles are transported to the edge of the button and the neurotransmitters released into the synaptic gap.

2 In the synapse, neurotransmitters can bind with a receptor site on the next neuron if the receptor site is the right type of receptor and is vacant. This is often described by a lock-and-key analogy, in that the neurotransmitters are like keys, and can only fit into certain receptor sites in the same way that only the right key should open a lock. If enough of the neurotransmitter binds to the receiving neuron's receptor sites, the neuron will 'fire' – this means it transmits the information across its cell body electrically. When the information arrives at the end of the axon of this neuron, the chemical process is repeated.

3 Any unused neurotransmitter is eventually absorbed back into the neuron it came from (otherwise, enzymes will remove it from the synaptic cleft). This process is called reuptake. The neurotransmitter can then be used again.

Any of these three parts can be altered by drugs.

 To learn more about synaptic transmission, go to www. pearsonhotlinks. com, enter the title or ISBN of this book and select weblinks 2.5a and 2.5b.

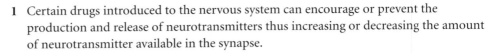

1 Certain drugs introduced to the nervous system can encourage or prevent the production and release of neurotransmitters thus increasing or decreasing the amount of neurotransmitter available in the synapse.

2 Certain drugs can occupy receptor sites that would normally receive a neurotransmitter. When a drug does this, it has its own effect on the receiving neuron as well as preventing the naturally occurring neurotransmitter from completing the intended communication.

3 Certain drugs can prevent the reuptake of neurotransmitters, which allows them more time to bind to receiving neurons.

Many people are familiar with the action of caffeine on the brain. Caffeine follows the second of the processes outlined above. When a person begins to feel sleepy, a neurotransmitter called adenosine is being released into the synaptic gap in a specific part of the brain. Adenosine acts to inhibit activity and prepare the body for sleep. When caffeine enters the synaptic gap, it binds with the receptor sites that adenosine normally uses, and prevents the normal inhibition of activity. In addition, caffeine actually stimulates brain activity, which means that a person's movements and thoughts may become faster.

Drugs and behaviour

Over time, the brain can become addicted to some drugs like caffeine, and it is important to understand how this is reflected in the brain. It is likely that if a heavy user of caffeine prevents the transmission of adenosine enough, the brain will respond by increasing the amount of adenosine released or by developing new receptor sites for adenosine. Both of these responses should increase the chance of successful transmission of the sleepy feeling through the body. This is why many drug users find it necessary to increase the amount of the drug they take in order to achieve the same effect – their drug use is compensated for by the brain. It also accounts for the feeling that coffee users may know, whereby a cup of coffee can prevent you from feeling sleepy for a limited time, but when this effect wears off, the sleepy feeling that arrives immediately afterwards can be quite overwhelming.

Biological researchers have investigated the effect of neurotransmitters on behaviour, and while some of their conclusions are only theoretical, others are based on having found a causal relationship through experimentation with animals and humans (Table 2.1).

◄ Sometimes, you fall asleep as soon as the caffeine effect wears off.

TABLE 2.1 EFFECTS OF SOME DRUGS ON NEUROTRANSMISSION AND BEHAVIOUR

Neurotransmitter / drug	Result	Explanation (action on neurotransmission)
Acetylcholine (Ach)		
black widow venom	convulsions and death through exhaustion	over-stimulation of motor neurons resulting in uncontrollable excess movement
curare (a poison traditionally used in South America)	paralysis	inhibition of acetylcholine transmission, preventing muscle movement
Dopamine		
L-dopa	reduction of symptoms of Parkinson's disease*	triggers release of dopamine in areas of the brain that lack it, such as the motor cortex
anti-psychotic medication e.g. chlorpromazine	reduction of symptoms of schizophrenia**	reduces the amount of dopamine in the brain
cocaine	intense feelings of pleasure and faster cognitive activity	prevents re-uptake of dopamine, increasing the amount available in the synapse
Serotonin		
Prozac	improved mood in depressed people	prevents re-uptake of serotonin in the brain, allowing more successful regulation of mood
LSD	vivid hallucinations and a positive mood	theoretically, may bind with serotonin receptors and block the normal inhibition of dreams while the person is awake, allowing dreams to occur while the person is fully conscious

* such as resting tremor and difficulty initiating movement
** such as hallucinations and delusions

There are a number of other neurotransmitters at work in the brain and we will deal with some of them in other chapters.

You should notice from Table 2.1 that some of the drugs included act in apparently opposite ways. For example, L-dopa and chlorpromazine act by respectively increasing and decreasing the amount of dopamine present at the synapse.

Dopamine levels

L-dopa was a breakthrough in treatment for Parkinson's disease, a degenerative condition that usually involves a resting tremor, a difficulty initiating movement, and difficulty in controlling directed movement such as picking up a spoon or a cup. The drug was designed to relieve these symptoms because it was believed that increasing the amount of dopamine available would have a positive effect. It was initially very effective, but the effects do not usually last as the brain adapts to the presence of the drug. Other treatments have been developed more recently, such as the implantation into the brain of a device that can stimulate the release of dopamine in relevant areas, according to a patient's individual needs. This results in fewer side effects.

Some evidence for the dopamine theory of schizophrenia comes from the discovery that patients who were overmedicated for Parkinson's disease started to develop some of the positive symptoms of schizophrenia, such as hallucinations and delusions. It had also been noted that individuals who were being medicated with tranquillizers that reduced the amount of dopamine available were less likely to experience these symptoms. In turn, overmedication with antipsychotic drugs was often found to lead to a condition known as tardive dyskinesia, which describes the same kind of movement problems found in Parkinson's disease. Thus it appears that there is a balance of dopamine required in individuals, and on one hand, too much dopamine can lead to symptoms of schizophrenia, while on the other hand, too little can lead to difficulties with movement.

 To learn more about implantation to control tremors, go to www.pearsonhotlinks.com, enter the title or ISBN of this book and select weblink 2.6.

 Schizophrenia has been associated with high levels of dopamine; Parkinson's disease is associated with low levels of dopamine.

Serotonin levels

A similar relationship can be seen between Prozac and LSD. Prozac was found to be effective in reducing symptoms of depression, theoretically because depression is associated with low levels of serotonin in specific regions of the brain responsible for mood regulation. Prozac's action of blocking serotonin reuptake is able to increase the amount of serotonin available and therefore facilitate the transmission of mood regulation messages in the brain.

The action of LSD has not been definitively established, but one theory is that it works against serotonin activity by blocking serotonin receptors. It seems that one of the main functions of serotonin is to inhibit dreaming while we are not sleeping. Bonson et al. (1996) used a questionnaire to discover that users of LSD who enjoyed its hallucinogenic effects but were diagnosed with depression and received antidepressants tended to find that although the depressive symptoms were reduced when the antidepressants began to take effect, a normal dose of LSD was no longer enough to give the same effect as it used to. The roles of serotonin and dopamine in abnormal psychological behaviour, cognition and emotion are discussed further in Chapter 5.

2.6 Physiology and behaviour: Hormones

Learning outcomes
- Using one or more examples, explain functions of two hormones in human behaviour.

Hormones are chemical messengers that are secreted by glands and can have a widespread effect on both physiology and psychology in humans. The system of glands that releases hormones into the bloodstream is called the endocrine system.

Adrenaline

When this hormone is secreted, it has a number of effects on the human body. One general description of its effects is the **fight or flight response**; adrenaline prepares the body for action to help the organism deal with a threat, either by fighting it or by running away from it. Although we might associate adrenaline mostly with negative emotions such as fear, those who take part in 'extreme sports' know that exposing themselves to danger is thrilling, and the release of adrenaline in such situations appears to be associated with positive feelings.

In general, adrenaline increases the flow of oxygen and blood to the brain by increasing the activity of the heart and dilating blood vessels. It is sometimes used medically when a person has had a heart attack or a severe allergic or asthmatic reaction that prevents breathing. Other specific effects include an increase in heart rate and blood pressure, dilation of pupils in the eyes, and the transfer of key resources like oxygen and glucose away from internal organs towards the extremities of the body. Functions like digestion are less important in a stressful situation than being able to think and move quickly. Adrenaline is released from the adrenal medulla of the adrenal gland and increases alertness. It has been suggested that adrenaline might be responsible for the creation of emotion, and various studies have attempted to investigate the effect of this hormone on behaviour.

EMPIRICAL RESEARCH

Adrenaline and emotion (Schachter and Singer, 1962)

In this study, the researchers intended to challenge several theories of emotion. There has been a lot of debate regarding the origin of emotion, and this centred specifically on whether, on recognizing a threat:

- the brain automatically initiated the fight or flight response by releasing adrenaline, and the emotion of fear was a consequence of this increase in adrenaline

or

- the emotional state and the release of adrenaline were independent of each other, both caused by the brain at approximately the same time.

Schachter and Singer proposed that while adrenaline was able to cause emotion, the nature of the emotion caused was dependent on contextual factors. Moreover, they proposed that different emotions might be essentially the same set of physiological changes in the body that are labelled by the brain according to cognitive processing of the context.

To test this idea, they recruited volunteers to receive a vitamin injection and informed them that they would be participating in vision experiments. None of the 184 male participants received the injection they believed they were getting: three groups received an injection of adrenaline, and a fourth group received a placebo injection of saline solution. The three groups receiving the adrenaline injection were given different types of information about possible side-effects. One group were told that they might experience an increased heart rate and shaky hands (the actual effects of receiving an adrenaline injection). The second group were not given any information about possible side-effects. The third group were told that some people experienced a headache and numbness or itchiness in the feet as side-effects.

Thus, the first adrenaline group understood how their body would react and had an explanation of its cause, the other two adrenaline groups would inevitably experience the same physiological changes, but without explanation.

In order to manipulate the nature of the emotion experienced by participants, the researchers constructed two contexts:

- euphoria, in which a confederate of the experimenter encouraged the participant to join in games with office equipment in a waiting room

- anger, in which a confederate filled out a mock questionnaire at the same pace as the participant, but getting increasingly outraged by the increasingly personal nature of the questions.

The researchers used observational data based on structured observation of participants in each condition and then asked them to complete a self-report form that assessed their mood in terms of anger and happiness when they were finished.

In the euphoria condition, it was clear that the groups who had received an adrenaline injection without the correct information about its physiological effects showed more of the euphoric behaviours, and also reported more happiness on the self-report form.

Although the anger context did not elicit the corresponding pattern of reporting, the researchers suggested this might have resulted from discomfort in reporting anger compared to reporting happiness. They relied instead on behavioural data, which did show that participants who were aware of the real expected physiological changes performed less of the angry behaviours than the groups who had no explanation for their physiological arousal.

The researchers concluded that emotion occurs by a process of cognitive labelling: the interpretation of physiological cues is combined with contextual cues to construct a person's subjective experience of emotion.

Melatonin

Melatonin is a hormone with a role in the cycle of sleep. It is secreted from the pineal gland at the base of the brain. This gland is sometimes referred to as the third eye because of its ability to sense changes in light, a function more important in non-human animals.

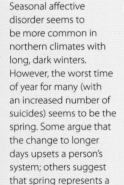

Melatonin is secreted when we are in the dark. It helps us to sleep.

In humans, the pineal gland relies on signals from the eyes and other sense organs relating to light and temperature for information about the time of day. It responds by secreting melatonin during darkness but not in light. One of the major actions of melatonin is to communicate with the pituitary gland, which then inhibits the secretion of many other hormones in the body that relate to states of wakefulness. Thus melatonin's role in sleep is to 'turn off' the body.

Researchers have suggested that the phenomenon of seasonal affective disorder (SAD), may be related to melatonin levels. SAD is a type of depression related to the beginning and end of winter. In countries that experience a very short day when winter arrives, people have reduced exposure to daylight and may therefore have high levels of melatonin.

Seasonal affective disorder seems to be more common in northern climates with long, dark winters. However, the worst time of year for many (with an increased number of suicides) seems to be the spring. Some argue that the change to longer days upsets a person's system; others suggest that spring represents a new beginning, which reminds sufferers that the cycle is about to repeat itself.

Avery et al. (2001) randomly assigned 95 SAD patients to three groups:
- one to receive dawn simulation (timed to begin at 4:30 a.m.)
- one to receive a more traditional bright-light therapy
- one to receive a placebo of a dim red light at dawn.

Using a structured interview that results in a depression-rating specific to this disorder, Avery et al. found that those who received traditional bright-light therapy or the placebo showed less improvement and more side-effects than the group who experienced dawn simulation. Members of the placebo group complained of insomnia significantly more than the other groups after four weeks of the study. This added to the conclusion that indeed the symptoms were related to a shift in the participants' sleep patterns: they found themselves in winter getting up before they were ready to wake because of a lack of light at their normal waking time. Bright-light therapy and dawn simulation were both able to help realign the sleep patterns with participants' lifestyles by encouraging the inhibition of melatonin secretion at an appropriate time, but dawn simulation was more likely to have positive therapeutic benefits and less likely to cause the side-effects of nausea and headache than bright-light therapy.

Lewy et al. (2006) note that the brain is sensitive to changes in the length of time that melatonin is released, so that as days become shorter and melatonin is released more, this is a signal to the brain to trigger other activity. Animals, for example, might enter hibernation or their breeding season in response to changes in the length of the night. Thus, SAD could be the result of an incompatibility between biological instincts and lifestyle. Lewy et al. tested their ideas in a similar way to Avery et al. (2001), but also administered low doses of melatonin to another group of participants in the evening. They found that sleep patterns and mood improved in participants who received this treatment, but that the improvements in mood were not as great as those experienced by those who received bright-light therapy in the morning.

Our understanding of the relationship between melatonin and the sleep–wake cycle has been useful when applied to help explain the phenomenon of jet lag. Jet lag occurs when

a person travelling in an aeroplane, usually from west to east across time zones, later experiences some of the same symptoms as SAD. These include feeling tired during the day, being unable to sleep at night, having low level of concentration, and disturbances in digestion and appetite. Again, this seems to result from an incompatibility between the information about time we receive from the environment (through exposure to light) and the information we have in our brain about what stage in our sleep–wake cycle we should be in. It seems that melatonin is not released in our brains at a time appropriate for the new location and we are, therefore, unable to sleep. Thus, we become tired at approximately the same time we would have been tired had we stayed in our original location. Over time, we do adapt to the new location. Our understanding of the sleep–wake cycle has provided two main aids to help us adapt:

- melatonin can be taken in pill form during the flight and on arrival at the destination to help reprogramme the brain to fit with our new location
- we can train ourselves to adapt to the new location by allowing ourselves to sleep only at specific times and for a limited amount of time while flying so that we are already prepared for our new destination when we get there.

● **Examiner's hint**
This section helps explain the function of melatonin in the body and also, in terms of the relationship between light and the release of melatonin, deals with an effect of the environment on physiology.

Oxytocin

Oxytocin is sometimes known as the 'love hormone' or the 'trust hormone'. This refers to an early finding that oxytocin is released as a trigger for contractions in the uterus when a woman is giving birth. It is also released when a woman's nipples are physically stimulated, for example during breastfeeding. Before it was recognized that oxytocin might have a role in human social bonding, studies of animals indicated that it was involved in several forms of social attachment in mammal mothers. For example, in rats, oxytocin appears to lead to a shift in the mother's focus from grooming herself to grooming the rat pup (Pedersen and Boccia, 2003).

 Oxytocin is sometimes thought to be the 'love hormone'.

In the case of animals and humans, it has been suggested that the function of this oxytocin is not only one of bonding, but also one of stress reduction. This makes good sense in light of the finding by Holt–Lunstad et al. (2008) that after an increase in positive physical contact between husband and wife, oxytocin levels rose and the husband's blood pressure decreased, which predicts other positive health outcomes.

Does massage affect oxytocin levels?

In another study, Morhenn et al. (2008) randomly assigned 96 students to a massage-and-trust, rest-and-trust, or massage-only group. The massage conditions consisted of 15-minute Swedish massages (a light massage which was shown to increase oxytocin levels in many people by Turner et al., 1999) while the rest condition required participants to rest for the same amount of time in the same room.

Participants then played a trust game that asked them to make a decision about how much money to give to another participant, knowing that this money would be tripled and there was a possibility that the other participant might share the profit. Sending a large amount of money was taken to indicate a high level of trust. Blood samples were taken twice, once at the beginning of their participation, and again close to their decision in the trust game, so that oxytocin levels could be measured.

The group that received only the massage were tested immediately following it. There was no significant change in their levels of oxytocin overall, although women were more likely to show increased levels.

Participants in the massage-and-trust group who made the decision about sending money to another participant sent $6.30 on average, only slightly more than the group who had simply rested without the massage.

However, the amount that the other participant sent back to the decision-maker was significantly different. Those who had been massaged sent back an average of $6.85. In addition, a positive correlation was found in participants who were sent money and the change in their oxytocin level, according to whether they had received a massage or simply rested.

The researchers concluded that while one episode of touch in the form of massage was not enough to raise oxytocin levels, the massage seemed to prime participants to sacrifice money when a stranger displayed trust towards them by sending them an amount of money – an act that they did not need to reciprocate, and an act accompanied by an increase in oxytocin. Thus, oxytocin levels are able to predict the amount of sacrifice the participants made in the trust game, suggesting that oxytocin's effect on behaviour is to increase generosity and cooperation among adults.

To learn more about oxytocin, go to www.pearsonhotlinks.com, enter the title or ISBN of this book and select weblink 2.7.

If raised oxytocin levels increase trust, cooperation and bonding, is it wrong to attempt to use oxytocin for personal benefit?

EXERCISE

11 Make a table summarizing the effects on behaviour of the three hormones examined using the column titles: *Hormone name*, *Behaviour affected*, *Example*.

2.7 Genetics and behaviour

Learning outcomes
- With reference to relevant research studies, to what extent does genetic inheritance influence behaviour?

Model of the double helix formed by the DNA molecule

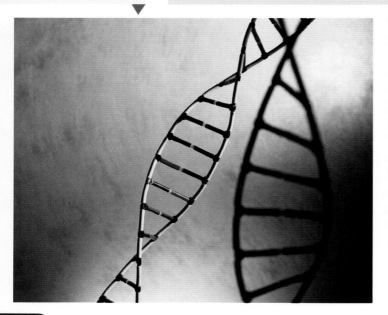

The human being is one of many species that reproduce sexually. Sexual reproduction brings together genetic information from two parents in a fertilized egg. This accounts for a large number of inherited characteristics each new organism has. Knowledge of this mechanism existed before the discovery of the DNA molecule by Watson and Crick in 1953. It was perhaps most obviously observed in the breeding of dogs and horses, where breeders have for centuries been attempting to encourage stronger, faster, or more attractive animals to reproduce, in the knowledge that some of these characteristics would be passed on to their offspring.

Genetic information is contained in chromosomes, which are tightly wound strings of DNA present in every cell of the human body. What we call genes are groupings within the DNA of any chromosome. There are 23 pairs of chromosomes in every human cell (except egg cells and sperm). Each chromosome pair consists of one chromosome from each parent. Therefore there are two different sets of DNA, and therefore two different sets of genetic information. This means that genes also come in pairs, one gene on each chromosome of a chromosome pair.

Genes are thought to be responsible for the development of physical and behavioural characteristics. We refer to the genetic make-up of an individual as their genotype.

However, it has also been known for a long time that the genotype does not exclusively dictate the characteristics of any individual organism. There are a number of environmental influences such as diet and habitat that also influence the way an organism develops. The observable characteristics of an organism are known as the phenotype. Phenotype is the result of genotype and environment interacting.

You may have noticed that some fruit trees bear more fruit than others, sometimes because of access to sunlight. In 1948, Clausen et al. carried out a famous experiment that involved planting genetically identical yarrow plants at different altitudes. They found that the resulting phenotypes were quite different because of differences in the environmental conditions the plants were growing in.

Thus, when making conclusions about the role of genes in determining human behaviour and physical characteristics, it is essential to bear in mind that although some characteristics are strongly affected by genetic inheritance, it is not a simple causal relationship. There are a number of very broad, exaggerated and reductionist claims made in the media about the role of genes in human behaviour and you need to be able to think critically about these, in particular about the interaction between genotype and environment that occurs before we observe many human characteristics.

What does genetic information do?

One of the most famous examples of successful genetic research that has helped us understand human behaviour relates to a genetic condition called phenylketonuria (PKU).

 In many countries, prenatal tests for PKU are the norm. The condition can be managed and its effects avoided.

If you check the ingredients on a packet of chewing gum or a diet soft drink, you might notice a warning that it contains phenylalanine, an amino acid present in artificial sweeteners. If you suffered from phenylketonuria, this would be important to you because you would not be able to produce the enzyme that metabolizes phenylalanine. Unlike most people who consume artificial sweeteners, those who have PKU build up a level of phenylalanine that eventually causes brain damage.

This is a good example of findings from genetic research for a number of reasons. First, the gene has been identified. Secondly, the role of the gene is clear. Thirdly, an intervention follows: in this case, abstinence from artificial sweeteners is recommended. Unfortunately, a lot of genetic research falls short of this example. A lot of such research is reported poorly in the media, resulting in a tendency for people to feel that genetic information has a stronger influence on their behavioural and physical characteristics than there is evidence for.

Examples of empirical research involving genes at the biological level of analysis are presented in the boxes overleaf.

EMPIRICAL RESEARCH

Is schizophrenia genetic? (Heston, 1966)

This was an adoption study. Adoption studies assume that if offspring are separated from their biological parents, we can conclude that any physical and behavioural similarities observed later between parent and child are largely caused by genetic factors.

Heston looked at the incidence of schizophrenia in children who lived in foster homes. He correlated this incidence with the diagnosis of schizophrenia in their biological mothers. The specific interest in this study was whether schizophrenia is genetic or not. If the condition were genetic, it would be expected that adoption would not affect the number of children who were later diagnosed with schizophrenia. But because of biological inheritance, a higher incidence of schizophrenia would be expected among the adopted children of schizophrenic mothers than among adoptees whose mothers did not have a diagnosis of schizophrenia. If nurture were more important, it might be hoped that adoption would reduce the number of children who were later diagnosed with schizophrenia, and the incidence would be approximately the same as among the other adoptees.

The incidence of schizophrenia in the general population is about 1%, and it was similar for those people who were adopted with no family history of schizophrenia. Heston found that over 10% of the adopted children with a family history of schizophrenia were later diagnosed with it. This is considered strong evidence that schizophrenia has a genetic component.

EXERCISE

12 **a** What problems are there with this type of research (adoption studies)?

  b Are there any plausible alternative explanations for these results?

EMPIRICAL RESEARCH

Twin studies

Twin studies are a common research method at the biological level of analysis. For example, Bailey and Pillard (1991) studied monozygotic (MZ) twins and dizygotic (DZ) twins; they found a difference in concordance for homosexuality, measuring how often, when one twin was homosexual, the other one was also homosexual. DZ twins had a concordance rate of 22%, while MZ twins had a rate of 52%. These results indicate that although there must be some environmental influence to explain why the MZ twins did not have 100% concordance, there must also be a strong genetic component to explain why MZ twins have more than double the rate of concordance of DZ twins.

Santtila et al. (2008) carried out an enormous twin study in Finland using 6001 female and 3152 male twins and their siblings between the ages of 18 and 33. The researchers wanted to test the idea that reported rates of homosexuality might underestimate the frequency of homosexual attraction, and that it is more appropriate to study potential for homosexual response. This would allow for circumstantial changes in behaviour such as occur in prisons, in the military, and for profit in pornography.

The researchers asked twins to answer a questionnaire to establish sexual orientation, based on frequency of same-sex sexual contact during the preceding year. The participants were also asked to rate how likely it would be for them to agree to sexual intercourse with a handsome person of the same sex who suggested it, if nobody would know and it could be done on the participant's own terms.

Reported incidences of homosexual behaviour were 3.1% for men and 1.2% for women, but the potential for homosexual response was much larger, with 32.8% of men and 65.4% of women

suggesting there was some chance that they would agree in the situation described. Concordance rates for both the potential for homosexual response and overt homosexual behaviour indicated that there is probably a genetic component, with MZ twins more than twice as likely to answer the questions in the same way (Table 2.2).

TABLE 2.2 CONCORDANCE RATES FOR POTENTIAL FOR HOMOSEXUAL RESPONSE AND OVERT HOMOSEXUAL BEHAVIOUR AMONG MZ AND DZ TWINS

	Concordance rate for	
	Potential for homosexual response	**Overt homosexual behaviour**
Monozygotic male	0.534	0.380
Monozygotic female	0.526	0.594
Dizygotic male	0.234	0.000
Dizygotic female	0.264	0.000

The researchers considered that these results indicate that genes have a role in determining homosexual behaviour (even when they accounted for possible effects of a shared environment) and also that previous research into homosexuality has probably too narrowly defined homosexuality by focusing on overt behaviour rather than the potential for it.

Concordance rates can be expressed as a percentage (e.g. 52%) or as a number between 0 and 1 (e.g. 0.52).

EXERCISE

13 **a** Evaluate this research using your knowledge from the research methodology section.

b Are there plausible alternatives to the conclusion?

One of the problems with research like these examples is that it does not actually locate the gene or genes responsible, as occurred in the example of PKU given earlier. The more research is done into behavioural genetics, the clearer the picture is becoming: although genes have some role in influencing behaviour, they do not work in isolation from each other, nor in isolation from environmental factors. It appears in the case of behaviour that a set of genetic markers can be located and their biological function identified, but that environmental triggers are required for the behaviour to occur. This seems to be the case for a number of patterns of behaviour and disorders, including Alzheimer's disease, dyslexia, schizophrenia, and antisocial behaviour.

So what conclusions can we make so far about the genetic influence on behaviour? It is fair to say that we know a lot more than we used to, and that we have a long way to go before we can make confident claims that our genetic inheritance determines our behaviour. Because research is not yet able to satisfactorily explain which genes are responsible for which behaviours and how this happens, we rely heavily on twin studies, adoption studies, animal models, and theoretical explanations of how and why behaviour might be inherited.

At the same time, however, it has become more and more important to understand the role of the environmental triggers. The diathesis–stress model is used in abnormal psychology (Chapter 5). It follows this basic principle: inherited factors can provide a vulnerability and environmental stimuli (like difficult life events) can interact to result in a disorder like depression.

For example, there appears to be a relationship between physical or sexual abuse in childhood and the development of antisocial behaviour and schizophrenia (Read et al., 2004). It is possible that differences in genetic vulnerability can explain why only some people are affected in this way. However, some argue that pursuing the causes of vulnerability should take a lower priority than addressing the triggers that we are increasingly certain about. Knowledge of only genetic vulnerability or only environmental triggers is usually insufficient.

To learn more about genetic factors and behaviour, go to pearsonhotlinks.com, enter the title or ISBN of this book and select weblink 2.8.

● **Examiner's hint**
There are many genetic explanations for behaviour in the options chapters (Chapters 5–9). Use them to help you address the learning outcomes for this section.

2.8 Evolutionary psychology

Learning outcomes
- Examine one evolutionary explanation of behaviour.

This branch of psychology is based on some of the key principles of the biological level of analysis. If we assume (a) that a predisposition for certain behaviours is inherited and (b) that the principles of evolution dictate that genetically based behaviours of an individual who has reproduced are passed on (while genetically based behaviours of unsuccessful individuals are lost over time), then behaviours we observe today should have evolutionary explanations. In essence: if a behaviour exists in humans today, then it must in the past have helped human survival and reproduction. Behaviour that has helped a species survive and reproduce is described as adaptive. The key assumption of all evolutionary psychology research is that human behaviour must have been adaptive under some circumstances in the past.

While recorded history allows us to look back and make conclusions about similarities between behaviour now and in the past, it is clear that many evolutionary psychology offerings are guesswork at best. However, such arguments can help clarify many of the questions we ask.

The most popular topics of research in the journal *Evolution and Human Behaviour* are represented in this word-frequency cloud.

To access Worksheet 2.1 on an experiment in evolution with the silver fox, please visit www.pearsonbacconline.com and follow the on-screen instructions.

How could homosexuality be adaptive behaviour?

One of the potentially confusing issues with the twin studies into homosexuality outlined on page 60 is the question: How can homosexuality be genetically transmitted when it seems more likely to prevent reproduction?

Zietsch et al. (2008) provide a possible answer to this from an evolutionary psychology perspective. They consider several existing explanations; for example, that the presence of an individual homosexual person in the family offers some kind of reproductive advantage to others in the family – perhaps by sharing resources and care of others, thus increasing the reproductive fitness of the family, while not reproducing themselves.

Instead of such theories, however, Zietsch et al. investigate the idea that the genes which incline a man towards homosexuality are advantageous in a heterosexual man – perhaps somehow increasing his attractiveness to women. This idea is linked to other research which shows that women are more attracted to men with more feminine faces at certain times during their menstrual cycle.

To investigate this idea, the researchers mailed questionnaires to 4904 identical twins, asking them about sexual orientation, number of opposite-sex partners and gender identity. They found that sex-atypical gender identity (e.g. when a male feels he is more like a woman) is associated with having more heterosexual sex partners than others, and that this was exaggerated in a twin pair when one twin was homosexual – that is, the heterosexual twin brothers of homosexual men had a large number of sex partners. This is in line with the researchers' theory that when we inherit some of the genetic predisposition for homosexuality, but do not consider ourselves homosexual, we have inherited some characteristics normally associated with the opposite sex, and these somehow make us more attractive to members of the opposite sex. Men may, therefore, be attracted to women who have the stereotypically masculine features of competitiveness and sexual willingness.

Identical (monozygotic) twins share 100% of their genes.

Could homicide be adaptive behaviour?

Another example of an evolutionary psychology theory is the homicide adaptation theory (HAT). This theory suggests that humans today have evolved with some psychological adaptations for killing. It is logical that to be able to kill is a possible psychological advantage in an environment or context where killing is required (e.g. hunting) or is more likely to increase one's own chances of reproductive success (e.g. killing potential rivals or step-children, defending resources, or protecting one's own children from being killed).

Comparative psychology research has indicated that other species engage in killing behaviour within their species. This is considered to be an adaptation based on increasing their own or their offspring's chances of survival. It is therefore possible that humans carry a specific capacity for this behaviour, one that is reflected in the frequency of homicidal fantasies that occur in situations where murder might actually increase an individual's chances of reproducing, or their children's chances of surviving.

Durrant (2009) suggests that a possible weakness of this theory is the idea that some behaviours which have evolved over time are not adaptations to increase survival or reproductive success, but are by-products of evolution. So, perhaps homicide has no advantage.

To test a theory of evolutionary psychology, it is sometimes necessary to carry out a cost–benefit analysis. In this case, the advantages and disadvantages of killing are weighed against each other. If there are more costs than benefits, it seems unlikely that the behaviour is the result of successful adaptation. It has been argued, for example, that rape cannot be an adaptive behaviour as the costs outweigh the benefits. Durrant gives the example that attempting to kill will expose an individual to potential harm that might result in their own death, which is hardly adaptive, nor is the risk of being ostracized by a social group. He concludes that the HAT is unlikely to be correct.

To learn more about evolutionary explanations of behaviour, go to www.pearsonhotlinks.com, enter the title or ISBN of this book and select weblink 2.9.

This example of evolutionary psychology in action illustrates many of the problems with this branch of psychology. It is difficult to come close to proving that an evolutionary explanation is accurate, and that alternative explanations are not. Without being able to conduct experiments, it is impossible to establish cause–effect relationships, and it is therefore necessary to settle for the kind of correlational evidence used by Zietsch et al. (2008) above.

EXERCISE

14   **a**   Browse the journal found through the Hotlinks box above and choose an explanation of behaviour. Summarize it and think about how convincing the explanation is.

       b   Is there any evidence for the claims made, and are there plausible alternatives?

Is there any way we can know if an evolutionary psychology explanation for behaviour is accurate?

2.9   Ethical considerations in research into genetic influences on behaviour

Learning outcomes
*   Discuss ethical considerations in research into genetic influences on behaviour.

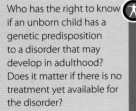

To learn more about Huntington's disease, go to www. pearsonhotlinks. com, enter the title or ISBN of this book and select weblink 2.10.

Who has the right to know if an unborn child has a genetic predisposition to a disorder that may develop in adulthood? Does it matter if there is no treatment yet available for the disorder?

Genetic testing

In many countries in the world, certain genetic tests are considered normal and appropriate during pregnancy – this has helped to prevent many potential problems. For example, a test can be done during pregnancy to see if a baby has PKU; if it is positive, parents can be prepared to follow the special diet the baby needs right from the start so brain damage is prevented. It is also now possible to test for Huntington's disease, but there is no treatment.

But as we discover more about the role of genes in determining our behaviour and identify specific genes associated with risk for diseases and disorders, certain dangers emerge. Access to information about genetic heritage is at the core of ethical issues in this field. There are consequences for any individual who finds out that they have a genetic predisposition to a disorder or behaviour that they might consider unpleasant or harmful. There are additional problems if other parties are allowed to know, such as insurance companies who might prevent a person from receiving life insurance, or employers, who might refuse employment. For these reasons, genetic testing requires consent from the person involved or from the family members who are responsible for them. And everyone concerned should have access to counselling to deal with the consequences.

Research findings

In the context of research, any information obtained about a participant should be accessible to the participant. This means that when a person participates in a study investigating the role of genes in any kind of behaviour, there is a risk that the person will learn something about themselves they are not prepared to deal with. Again, counselling should be offered as part of a full debriefing. In addition, it is often necessary to repeat the test to confirm the result as reporting inaccurate information could lead to a range of negative consequences.

An alternative is to ensure that any data will be anonymously coded so that neither the researcher nor the participant knows which results match which specific DNA sample.

A further ethical issue is in the interpretation of research findings. When Richard Herrnstein and Charles Murray published a book called *The Bell Curve* in 1994, it caused widespread controversy. Their interpretation of research that demonstrated a difference in IQ scores between black and white Americans and between socio-economic groups led to a conclusion – widely reported and exaggerated in the media – that state money was being wasted on encouraging reproduction among low IQ groups and that investing money in education programmes for those with low access would not yield useful results as the differences in IQ are genetic.

Should governments invest in programmes to help increase IQ if it is genetic?

While the assumption that intelligence is partly genetic seems to have good support, none of the available research has sidelined the role of environmental factors.

This is an example of how researchers need to be careful that the conclusions they reach and report are valid and reliably demonstrated in the available research. In the case of genetic research, we are profoundly lacking in causal evidence due to a lack of the possibility to experiment for ethical reasons, and a lack of longitudinal research. The Human Genome Project completed a map of the human genome in 2000, and it can be expected that we will be treated to more and better-informed longitudinal studies based on the knowledge gained from the project in future. It is unlikely that it will ever become ethically possible to conduct genetic experiments with humans, so we will likely need to rely on data obtained from twin studies, adoption studies and longitudinal studies. The majority of these are correlational in nature, and therefore we are unlikely to have 100% certainty that genes in combination are entirely responsible for any human behaviour.

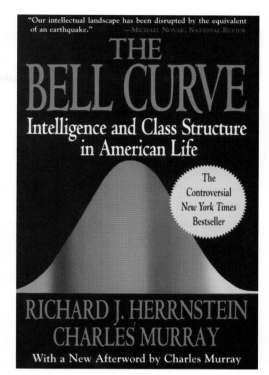

"Our intellectual landscape has been disrupted by the equivalent of an earthquake."
—MICHAEL NOVAK, NATIONAL REVIEW

THE BELL CURVE

Intelligence and Class Structure in American Life

The Controversial New York Times Bestseller

RICHARD J. HERRNSTEIN
CHARLES MURRAY

With a New Afterword by Charles Murray

A highly controversial book: its title is derived from the bell-shaped normal distribution curve of IQ scores.

To learn more about the human genome project and advice on many ethical issues, go to www.pearsonhotlinks.com, enter the title or ISBN of this book and select weblink 2.11.

To access Worksheet 2.2 on methods used in the biological level of analysis, please visit www.pearsonbacconline.com and follow the on-screen instructions.

EXERCISE

15 Consider the material in this section and add any examples from the Human Genome Project website that demonstrate ethical issues.

PRACTICE QUESTIONS

Short answer questions

1 Identify **two** hormones and, using examples, explain their function in human behaviour.

2 Describe **one** evolutionary psychology explanation of behaviour.

3 Explain **one** interaction between cognition and physiology.

4 Explain **one** study related to localization of function in the brain.

Essay questions

1 Discuss the use of brain imaging technologies in investigating the relationship between biological factors and behaviour.

2 Discuss ethical considerations related to research studies at the biological level of analysis.

To access Worksheet 2.3 with a full example answer to short answer question 4, please visit www.pearsonbacconline.com and follow the on-screen instructions.

To access Worksheet 2.4 with a full example answer to essay question 2, please visit www.pearsonbacconline.com and follow the on-screen instructions.

3

THE COGNITIVE LEVEL OF ANALYSIS

3.1 Introduction: Historical and cultural development

The cognitive level of analysis studies **cognition**. The term *cognition* refers to all the mental structures and processes involved in the reception, storage and use of knowledge. It involves the study of phenomena such as attention, perception, memory, decision-making, problem solving and language. So, in a sense, what is studied at the cognitive level of analysis is the mind.

The term *mind* is rather ambiguous and psychologists, starting from the 1950s, prefer to view mental processes in terms of **information-processing**. The mind, according to this approach, is an information-processing system which functions much like a computer: the brain corresponds to the computer's hardware whereas the mind corresponds to the programs (software) run by the computer. Both brains and computers receive information (input), process it in a number of stages and deliver some output. Processing means change, or transformation, and a main objective in cognitive psychology is to study how information changes as it advances through the various information processing stages.

The study of information-processing in psychology, based on the use of scientific methods (e.g. experiments), is widely believed to be scientific. A definition of modern cognitive psychology could, therefore, be: cognitive psychology studies cognition, viewed in terms of information-processing, by means of established scientific methods.

Yet most of what cognitive psychology studies is not directly observable from the outside. I cannot observe your mind, and you cannot observe mine. Questions, therefore, arise as to the extent one can study something so well hidden from the investigator's gaze.

Like a computer, the brain processes information.

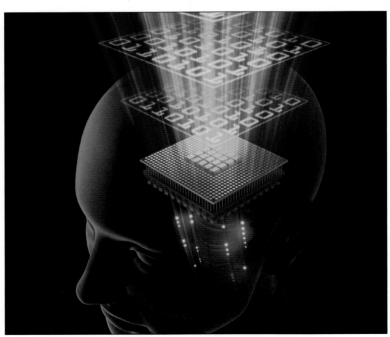

Behaviourism

The study of cognition was not always popular with psychologists. A very influential 20th century movement in psychology was based on the premise that mental processes could not be studied scientifically. Supporters of this movement contended that such processes should be ignored by a scientific psychology because they believed that you cannot study scientifically what you cannot observe directly or measure accurately. It can be doubted you can do either when studying the mind, but many psychologists felt you could do both while studying behaviour. Thus, psychologists who concentrated on the scientific study of external behaviour are known as **behaviourists** and their brand of psychology is called **behaviourism**. They were very influential from the mid-1910s to the 1950s, especially in the USA.

The beginning of psychology as a separate discipline was helped considerably by the work, towards the end of the 19th century, of Wundt and his colleagues (pages vii–viii). Although using experimental methodology, Wundt's data collection relied all too often on his participants' introspective reports about how they were carrying out the various tasks he was asking them to perform. The subjective nature of the data collected in this way gave rise to disputes about several issues relating to the mind. Many psychologists felt these disputes could not be resolved from within introspectionistic psychology.

Watson (1913), the founder of behaviourism in the USA, reacted to this state of affairs by rejecting not only introspectionism but also the study of the mind in general as a legitimate subject matter for scientific psychology. According to him, only external behaviour should be studied. He was influenced by the work of the Russian physiologist Pavlov who, in the early decades of the 20th century, was studying in dogs a basic form of learning now called **classical conditioning** (Pavlov, 1928).

One of the disputes arising during the introspectionistic era in psychology centred on the question: Can we think without forming any images (imageless thought)? Despite many attempts, it proved very difficult to settle this issue relying on introspectionistic methods.

Later, another form of conditioning (**operant conditioning**) was added by Skinner, based on his studies of learning in rats and pigeons (Skinner, 1938). What should be emphasized here is that, according to the behaviourists, one can predict and control an organism's behaviour simply by observing and measuring what is observable from the outside. There is no need to speculate about what (if anything) goes on inside the mind. They attempted to base an entire psychology on the premise that psychology should make no reference to anything that could not be observed.

Both forms of conditioning are simple types of **associative learning**. This is learning based on the gradual building up of associations between stimuli (classical conditioning) or behaviour and its consequences (operant conditioning).

In one of Pavlov's experiments studying classical conditioning, a dog learns to salivate to the sound of a bell by being presented for around a dozen times with the following contingency: the sound of the bell is followed shortly by food. Pairing the two stimuli (bell and food) for around a dozen times results in the bell producing salivation when presented on its own. The pairing of two stimuli in this way is called **reinforcement** and it is this that forms the basis of classical conditioning.

In a demonstration of Skinner's **operant conditioning**, a hungry rat is trapped in a box containing a bar which, when pressed, operates a mechanism that delivers some food. With time, the rat presses the bar with increasing frequency revealing the learning of a behaviour (bar-pressing)–consequence (food) association. The animal's learning of this association has been reinforced by the food.

In both types of conditioning the learning is direct, as is the reinforcement (which could be reward or punishment). In operant conditioning, for instance, it is the animal that behaves and the animal that receives the reward or the punishment. This distinguishes traditional

learning theory from a more recent development, the investigation by Bandura (1977) of **observational learning**. In this case, learning is by observing and imitating others. This more cognitive form of learning is discussed in Chapter 4 (pages 119–123).

Despite considerable early successes in the study of basic forms of learning, it eventually became clear that behaviourism was far too limited to address many substantial psychological phenomena. It ran into problems explaining findings from several learning experiments and, more importantly, entire phenomena that were widely considered especially important were either being ignored or addressed in a very unsatisfactory way. When Skinner attempted to explain language from a behaviouristic perspective (Skinner, 1957), a well-known linguist was quick to demonstrate that behaviourism could not possibly explain the complexity of language (Chomsky, 1959).

Many psychologists (e.g. Bartlett, 1932), especially outside the USA, never espoused behaviourism (page 71).

Cognitive psychology

Developments during and after World War II also helped bring about the demise of behaviourism and the advent of cognitive psychology. Psychologists realized that behaviouristic training had not prepared them well for the types of problem they were invited to investigate during the war (e.g. teaching radar equipment operators, helping in the design of proper aircraft controls). The war situation also brought them into contact with specialists from other fields, most importantly communication engineers. Soon psychologists started viewing human psychological apparatus as a communication channel with limited capacity (Broadbent, 1958). The discovery of the digital computer at around the same time provided psychologists with a powerful way to describe and analyse what the human mind was doing. The computer metaphor became the new source of inspiration for psychologists and cognitive psychology as an information-processing discipline was born.

The mind could be studied once more, but with a difference. Behaviourism had set high standards of objectivity for psychology, so a return to introspectionism was not an option. Cognitive psychologists started to study behaviour in ways that enabled them, with the help of information-processing models, to infer the internal workings of the mind.

While Watson was arguing in favour of a behaviouristic psychology in the 1910s, physicists were embarking on the study of atoms and subatomic particles. Nobody ever saw an atom, and certainly not a subatomic particle. But by studying some of the more visible consequences of the atom's and subatomic particles' behaviour, and using theories to make testable predictions about such behavioural consequences, physicists have been able to say a lot about them. Couldn't psychologists do the same with the mind? Couldn't they study the behavioural manifestations of the mind by deriving testable hypotheses about them from information-processing theories? Couldn't they use scientific methods (e.g. experiments) to test such hypotheses? Many thought the answers to these questions were all positive.

Can Kuhn's notion of paradigmatic shift help us explain the demise of behaviourism and the emergence of cognitive psychology during the so-called cognitive revolution?

In the last couple of decades or so, the objectivity with which internal mental processes can be studied has increased substantially because of the rapid development of **cognitive neuroscience**. Technological advances, such as powerful brain-scanning techniques (e.g. MRI, fMRI) have made it possible to study the biological substrates of cognition in ways that are undoubtedly scientific.

Do you think there is a difference between the ways in which mental phenomena are unobservable and the ways in which natural phenomena (like atoms, etc.) are unobservable? Was Watson right, after all?

3.2 Principles of the cognitive level of analysis

Learning outcomes
- Outline principles that define the cognitive level of analysis.
- Explain how principles that define the cognitive level of analysis may be demonstrated in research

● **Examiner's hint**
While studying this chapter, make it a habit to relate studies you read about to these two principles. This will result in an excellent list of studies relevant to answering exam questions on the principles underlying the cognitive level of analysis.

A number of general assumptions or principles seem to be widely accepted by those working at the cognitive level of analysis. Here are two of them:
- mental processes can and should be studied scientifically
- mental representations guide behaviour.

Mental processes can and should be studied scientifically

This principle is based on the following claims.
- Viewing mental processes in terms of information-processing has made it possible to formulate testable theories about unobservable cognitive structures and processes.
- Such models or theories can be tested by conventional scientific methods (e.g. laboratory experiments, brain-imaging studies) without having to rely on introspection for data collection.
- The study of mental processes has enabled psychologists to address important psychological phenomena which behaviourism found difficult, or even impossible, to address.
- The flourishing state of modern cognitive psychology, cognitive neuroscience and other related fields, bear witness to the success of addressing psychological phenomena at the cognitive level of analysis.
- The study of phenomena at the cognitive level of analysis can often be integrated with the study of these same phenomena at the biological and sociocultural levels thus leading to more comprehensive explanations.

The rest of this chapter contains many studies and models or theories which demonstrate this principle.

Mental representations guide behaviour

What guided behaviour for the behaviourists were the mechanical associations created by classical and operant conditioning. In their way of thinking, nothing intervened between the stimuli and the responses. Not so in cognitive psychology. There are cognitive mediators between what happens in the environment (the input) and what is delivered as output. The processing that intervenes is based to a very great extent on the way the world is represented in our memory. Examples of such mental representations are the **schemas** (cognitive structures) which organize our knowledge of objects, events, ourselves and others.

We never confront reality full on. Rather, we interpret and perceive it on the basis of our stored knowledge about it. Schemas are primary examples of such mental representations. Any of the studies discussed in sections 3.3 and 3.4 (pages 70–77) and several of the studies on stereotypes (pages 113–118) demonstrate the principle that mental representations guide behaviour.

 In what sense precisely can the study of cognition be viewed as scientific? Should we in psychology seek understanding in terms of reasons rather than explanations in terms of causes?

3.3 ## Schema theory

> **Learning outcomes**
> • Evaluate schema theory with reference to research studies.

● **Examiner's hint**
For applications of schema theory in abnormal psychology see pp. 160–161.

Schema theory is also extensively discussed in section 3.4 (pages 73–77) where the reliability of memory is addressed. It is further discussed in Chapter 5, where stereotype formation and the effects of stereotypes on behaviour are covered (pages 113–118).

Knowledge stored in our memory is to a very great extent organized. There are many theories of knowledge organization – **schema theory** is just one of them. The main idea underlying this theory is that new encounters with the world are rarely, if ever, completely new. Rather, the way we process information at any particular moment, or the way we act in specific settings, is determined to a very significant extent by relevant previous knowledge stored in our memory and organized in the form of schemas.

Bartlett was carrying out research on memory, a cognitive process, during the behaviouristic era in psychology. He published most of his research in 1932.

A schema is a cognitive structure that provides a framework for organizing information about the world, events, people and actions. This is consistent with the views of Bartlett (1932). In his pioneering work on the effects of schemas on memory, some of which is discussed below, he viewed schemas as organizations of past experience.

Different terms are often used to refer to schemas relevant to different aspects of our world.
• **Scripts** are schemas which provide information about the sequence of events that occur in a more-or-less unchanging order in particular contexts such as going to a restaurant, visiting the dentist, or attending a class.
• **Self-schemas** organize information we have about ourselves; for example, information stored in our memory about our strengths and weaknesses and how we feel about them.
• **Social schemas** (e.g. stereotypes) represent information about groups of people; for example, Americans, Egyptians, women, accountants, etc.

Over the years, theorists in many areas of psychology have used the schema notion to explain a huge variety of phenomena. Most of the discussion in this chapter relates to the effects schemas have on memory. The discussion owes a lot to the work of Bartlett (1932) on the effects of previous knowledge on the comprehension and remembering of texts.

An outline of schema theory

The term *schema theory* is used to refer to a number of interrelated ideas, proposed over the years by several theorists to account for the influence of stored knowledge on current information-processing and behaviour. Schema theory has benefited particularly from the work of Bartlett (1932), Rumelhart (1975) and Schank and Abelson (1977). According to these theorists, schemas perform many interrelated functions:
• they organize information in memory
• they can be activated to increase information-processing efficiency
• they enable the generation of expectations about objects, events and people
• they regulate behaviour
• they are relatively stable and usually very resistant to change thus ensuring continuity in the ways we process information and the ways we act.

Try and imagine how life would be without schemas or similar cognitive structures.

Schemas can also lead to distortions and mistakes when:
• settings are unfamiliar (and thus require novel approaches)
• the wrong schemas become activated.

Experimental studies of the effects of schemas on memory

EMPIRICAL RESEARCH

The effect of schemas on memory (Bartlett, 1932)

Bartlett asked his English participants to read *The War of the Ghosts*, a Native American folk tale. The first part of this story is reproduced below.

> One night two young men from Egulac went down to the river to hunt seals and while they were there it became foggy and calm. They heard war cries, and they thought, 'maybe this is a war party.' They escaped to the shore and hid behind a log. Now, canoes came up, and they heard the noises of paddles and saw one canoe coming up to them. There were five men in the canoe, and they said, 'What do you think? We wish to take you along. We are going up the river to make war on the people.'
>
> One of the young men said, 'I have no arrows.'
>
> 'Arrows are in the canoe', they said.

Native American hunters in traditional canoes.

The participants' memory for this story was tested by Bartlett by using two techniques, **serial reproduction** and **repeated reproduction**. In serial reproduction, the first participant reads the original story and then reproduces it on paper. The first participant's reproduction is read by the second participant who also reproduces it for a third participant. This procedure continues until six or seven reproductions are completed by an equal number of participants. In repeated reproduction, the same participant contributes all six or seven reproductions. This takes place in a number of attempts separated by intervals of from 15 minutes to as long as several years, from reading the original story. In Bartlett's studies these two methods led to very similar findings.

Unsurprisingly, with successive reproductions the story became increasingly shorter. However, the most important findings related to the distortions the participants introduced in their recall of the story. Several of these distortions were in the direction of making the story more understandable from within the participants' experiences and cultural background. Thus, activities which were culturally unfamiliar (e.g. hunting seals) were changed into more familiar ones (e.g. fishing). On several occasions, 'canoes' became 'boats'. The combined effect of these changes was to transform what started as a very strange tale into a conventional English story.

According to Bartlett, the way the participants recalled the story came under the influence of relevant schematic knowledge in their memory. Such knowledge consisted of schemas acquired in, and reflecting, the participants' own culture. Bartlett used the term **rationalization** to refer to the process of making the story conform to the cultural expectations of the participants.

Memory is an active reconstructive process rather than a passive reproductive one.

The picture of memory emerging from Bartlett's work is that of an active reconstructive process, rather than a passive reproductive one. Bartlett's views on schemas and his portrayal of memory as a reconstructive process have exerted a very significant influence in modern psychology. His work has, however, been criticized on methodological grounds. Bartlett did not explicitly ask his participants to be as accurate as possible in their recollection of the story, nor did he use standardized instructions or care much about the exact environments in which he was carrying out his studies.

In their replication of Bartlett's study, Gauld and Stephenson (1967) did emphasize the importance of accurate recall in a better-controlled experiment. Around half of the errors expected (on the basis of Bartlett's findings) were eliminated, but many errors of the types Bartlett had detected remained. Although Bartlett's procedures were not as strict as one would expect in more recent times, confirmation for his major findings has come from several well-controlled studies (Eysenck and Keane, 2010).

Bartlett (1932) argued that schematic influences were exerted mostly during retrieval. Research by Bransford and Johnson (1972) attempted to identify more precisely the processing stage or stages at which schemas are likely to exert their influence. Bransford and Johnson's study involved participants hearing quite a long speech (partially reproduced below) under three different experimental conditions:

> The procedure is actually quite simple. First, you arrange things into different groups. Of course, one pile may be sufficient depending on how much there is to do. If you have to go somewhere else due to lack of facilities, that is the next step; otherwise you are pretty well set. It is important not to overdo things …

The three experimental conditions were:
- the 'no title' condition, in which participants heard only the paragraph
- the 'title before' condition, in which participants heard the same paragraph after being told, 'The paragraph you will hear will be about washing clothes'
- the 'title after' condition, in which participants were told that the paragraph had been about washing clothes after they had listened to it.

After hearing the paragraph, participants indicated how easy they found it to understand and tried to recall as much from it as they could.

Participants in the 'no title' and 'title after' conditions found the paragraph much more difficult to comprehend than participants in the 'title before' condition. Of the 18 ideas the paragraph contained, participants recalled an average of 2.8 ideas in the 'no title' condition, 5.8 ideas in the 'title before' condition and 2.6 ideas in the 'title after' condition.

How can this pattern of findings be explained? The what-the-paragraph-is-about information given in the 'title before' condition seems to have activated schematic knowledge about what is involved in washing clothes. This information helped disambiguate the paragraph. When hearing the sentence 'The procedure is actually quite

simple', for example, participants knew that the procedure in question was washing clothes. Words like *items* were encoded in this context as *items of clothing*. Perceiving the passage within the context defined by the relevant schemas improved understanding.

In the 'title after' condition, the information came too late to provide the necessary context. By the time participants heard the title, there was simply not much to comprehend as the relevant material had already been forgotten.

The final study in this section does not address memory in any direct way but it clearly demonstrates a basic property of schemas: that they simplify information-processing and function, to use Macrae et al.'s expression, as *energy-saving devices*.

Macrae et al. (1994) asked participants to carry out two tasks at the same time. In the first task, participants had to form impressions of a number of target persons described by their name and 10 personality characteristics. While carrying out this task, they were also participating in a comprehension test for which there were two conditions: half of the participants were told the jobs of the target persons, half were not.

It was assumed that, when forming their impressions, those who had been informed of the targets' jobs would be able to use their stereotypical knowledge of the professions to simplify the processing demands of the impression-formation task. Participants who relied on the job stereotypes did perform better at both tasks. Thus, for example, knowing that Nigel is a doctor makes the task of processing personality characteristics like caring, reliable, intelligent or hard-working, easier.

To access Additional information 3.1 on an experiment by Bower et al. (1979) on scripts, please visit www.pearsonbacconline.com and follow the on-screen instructions.

3.4 Reliability of memory

Learning outcomes
- Discuss, with reference to relevant research studies, the extent to which one cognitive process is reliable.

Several of the studies discussed in this section are relevant to schema theory.

Studies of eyewitness memory

The criminal justice system relies heavily on eyewitness testimony. Judges, jurors and the police tend to often treat eyewitness testimony as very reliable. And yet, as evidence from various sources shows, eyewitness memory can be disturbingly inaccurate. An organization was founded in the USA in the 1990s (The Innocence Project), which provided assistance to wrongly convicted persons to overturn their convictions on the basis of DNA evidence. By the end of 2008, this organization helped 220 individuals prove their innocence. What is of importance in the present context is that the guilt of over 75% of these people had been established through mistaken eyewitness identification.

Much of the psychological research on eyewitness testimony has been based on Bartlett's account of memory as a reconstructive process. The idea that eyewitnesses do not reproduce what they witness but, rather, reconstruct their memories on the basis of relevant schematic information has provided the basis of much of the pioneering work on eyewitness testimony by Loftus and her colleagues (Loftus, 1979). What follows is a description of one of their more characteristic experiments.

Eyewitness testimony can be highly unreliable

EMPIRICAL RESEARCH

Schemas and eyewitness testimony (Loftus and Palmer, 1974)

Participants in this study watched seven film clips of different car accidents. After each clip, participants described what they saw and answered a number of questions about it. One of the questions, the **critical question**, asked about the speed of the cars in the accident. The experiment involved five experimental conditions which were defined by the verb used to ask the question about the cars' speed. The critical question in one of the conditions was: About how fast were the cars going when they hit each other? For the other conditions the verb *hit* was replaced with *contacted, collided, bumped* and *smashed into*. Loftus and Palmer found that the speed estimates were influenced by the wording used. The average estimates in each of the five conditions are reported below:

- contacted – 31.8 mph
- hit – 34 mph
- bumped – 38.1 mph
- collided – 39.3 mph
- smashed into – 40.8 mph.

Loftus and Palmer's findings can be explained by Bartlett's view of memory as an active reconstructive process. It can be argued that the verbs used in the various conditions activated slightly different schemas which influenced the speed estimates. Typical schemas of cars smashing into one another contain, in all likelihood, the assumption that the cars are moving faster than cars just hitting each other.

In Loftus and Palmer's study, information was received after witnessing the accident. The information took the form of a **leading question**. This is a question that contains hints about what the right answer to it may be. The accident seems to have been reconstructed in the participants' minds in ways reflecting schematic influences, a finding easily accountable by Bartlett's views on how reconstructive memory works.

Further support for this explanation comes from Loftus and Palmer's findings in a second, similar, experiment. Once more, after participants were presented with a one-minute film depicting a multiple car accident, they were asked questions about it, including a critical question about the speeds of the cars involved. Three conditions were used: two groups were asked questions about the speed by using either *smashed* or *hit*. Participants in the third group, the control group, were asked no questions about the speed of the cars. One week later, all participants were asked: Did you see any broken glass? There was no broken glass in the film. Still, 32% of those who had been asked about the cars' speed with the verb *smash* claimed they had seen broken glass compared to only 14% of the participants in the *hit* group. The schema activated by the verb *smashed* must have aroused a stronger expectation of broken glass than that activated by the verb *hit*. Of those in the control group, 12% claimed to have seen broken glass.

EXERCISES

3 Identify the independent and dependent variables in the two studies.

4 Comment on the ecological validity of these studies.

Another important aspect of Loftus's research on eye witness testimony is the demonstration of the **weapons effect**. In a study by Loftus et al. (1987), participants heard a discussion going in the room next to the one they were in. There were two conditions:

- no-weapons condition – a man with greasy hands emerged from the next room holding a pen
- weapons condition – a man came out of the next room holding a paperknife covered in blood.

All participants were later asked to identify the man from a selection of 50 photographs. Participants in the no-weapons condition were more accurate. Loftus et al. explained this finding in terms of the different ways in which participants in the two conditions allocated their attention. The weapon drew more attention to itself than the pen, so less attention was paid to the man's face. This explanation was supported by an analysis of the participants' eye movements. Of course, weapons may also exert their influence by raising the eyewitness's anxiety level. It is to the effects of anxiety on the reliability of eyewitness testimony that we now turn.

Deffenbacher et al. (2004) conducted meta-analyses of studies investigating the role of emotion on eyewitness testimony. They found that anxiety and stress reduces the reliable recall of crime details including information about the behaviour of the main characters.

There have been studies, however, where anxiety and stress seem to improve eyewitness accuracy. Deffenbacher et al. deal with such exceptions by suggesting that increases of anxiety up to a certain level increase accuracy but further increases may produce the opposite effect.

Evaluation of research on eyewitness memory

Many of the studies discussed above were laboratory experiments. This raises questions about their ecological validity. Eysenck and Keane (2010), for example, discuss the following differences between eyewitness reports obtained in laboratory studies and those provided by eyewitnesses in real-life situations.

- The reports of real accidents or crimes, unlike those in experimental studies, are very often provided by the victims themselves.
- Watching a video of an accident or crime is far less stressful than observing one in real life.
- Cases of mistaken eyewitness identification in real life (e.g. a court case) have real and often serious consequences.
- Most of the memory distortions demonstrated seem to involve peripheral or minor details (e.g. the presence of broken glass) rather than central aspects of the scene (e.g. features of a criminal).

Although the differences between experimental demonstrations and real-life cases of eye witness testimony are real, they should not be overstated. An experiment relevant to this issue is reported below.

Ihlebaek et al. (2003) staged a robbery involving two robbers armed with handguns. There were two conditions: a live condition in which participants were involved in the staged robbery, and a video condition in which participants viewed a video of the robbery in the live condition. It was found that memory for the robbery tended to be better in the video condition. As Eysenck and Keane (2010) note, such findings suggest that the distortions in eyewitness memory obtained under laboratory conditions may underestimate the unreliability of real-life eyewitness testimony.

There is little doubt that eyewitness testimony can be unreliable. In fact, even when participants are warned about the presence of misleading information they are still vulnerable to it (Eakin et al., 2003). But there are also studies which show that eyewitness testimony can be reliable.

In an archival study of eyewitness memory of the sinking of the *Titanic*, Riniolo et al. (2003) found that, in general, survivors recalled the events accurately. Yuille and Cutshall (1986) followed up 13 witnesses to an armed robbery in Canada. These eyewitnesses were interviewed around five months after the crime. Their recollections of the crime were

 To learn more about Loftus and her work, go to www. pearsonhotlinks. com, enter the title or ISBN of this book and select weblink 3.1.

 Meta-analysis is a statistical procedure, often used in psychology, which combines the results of several studies addressing the same hypothesis. The outcome is an average measure of the effects obtained in the individual studies. Usually it is a weighted average: the better studies (e.g. those with the bigger sample sizes) are allowed to influence the outcome to a greater extent.

 Although the most confident and consistent eyewitnesses are the most persuasive, all eyewitnesses (whether right or wrong) express more or less the same level of confidence in their reports (Bothwell et al., 1987). Moreover, confidence does not predict the accuracy of eyewitness testimony (Colby and Weaver, 2006).

compared with the initial detailed reports they had given to the police. Despite the fact that the interviews intentionally included misleading questions, the recollections of the eyewitnesses very closely matched the original reports.

Conclusions: To what extent is memory reliable?

The discussion in the last two sections is based on the premise that memory is an active reconstructive process. Our memory system is not a passive container of information. To a very great extent, every time we use it, stored information is altered. We live in a world which bombards us with far more information than we can handle and, moreover, imperfect information that is full of ambiguities. We are forced to simplify it by relying on our prior knowledge which, at least according to the theoretical views expressed in this section, is organized in the form of schemas.

Experiments like the one by Bransford and Johnson (1972) establish schemas as great facilitators in the comprehension and memorization of information. Macrae et al. (1994) demonstrated how schemas (in this case, stereotypes) assist ongoing information processing by simplifying it and thus enabling more effortless and efficient processing. Thus, reconstruction does not necessarily, perhaps not even typically, mean distortion. Life is full of repetitive patterns and by capturing essential regularities, schemas help us predict future occurrences and fill up gaps.

Of course, schematic processing can lead to error and distortion. Mere forgetting, which of course can lead to extremely unreliable reports, is not the focus of this discussion. Rather, we concentrated on the effects on memory reliability of schematic processing mostly in the area of eyewitness testimony where it has been most systematically investigated.

What ethical issues are raised by the research studies on eyewitness testimony discussed in this section?

Several studies point to the unreliability of eyewitness testimony, including Loftus and Palmer's (1974) laboratory experiment and Ihlebaek et al.'s (2003) study involving a more realistic setting. Yuille and Cutshall's (1986) findings, on the other hand, showed that eyewitness testimony in real-life settings can be very accurate. Research addressing specific factors or processes can no doubt help us predict the circumstances in which eyewitness testimony will be reliable or unreliable. Representative of such streams of research were the studies by Loftus et al. (1987) on how attention may underlie the weapons effect. Similarly, research on the role of stress and emotion on eyewitness testimony provides additional information about the settings in which eyewitness testimony may be expected to be unreliable.

The reconstructive nature of memory does not necessarily make it unreliable.

Some concluding comments on schema theory

Schemas help us organize and process information efficiently. This, along with the fact that schemas are usually activated automatically and effortlessly, makes them energy-saving devices. Just imagine having to perceive and remember all the details of each new object, person or event we encounter, or having to plan the actions we regularly carry out from scratch. In a sense, schemas function as our theories about how the world is and how best we can act upon it. They enable us to approach the world with expectations that determine how we attend to, interpret, perceive, store and retrieve information. They also direct to a very great extent our actions. Finally, they are relatively stable and usually very resistant to change, thus ensuring continuity in the ways we process information and act.

In situations where new encounters require a genuinely novel approach, when schema-based expectations conflict with reality, or simply the wrong schemas become activated, errors and distortions in the way we perceive, remember and think can be all but inevitable.

Research on the unreliability of eyewitness testimony poses serious questions about the possibility of reaching certainty when making knowledge claims about directly perceived events

EXERCISE
5 Think of examples where schemas conflict with reality, or situations where the wrong schemas become activated. How do such occurrences affect information processing?

By identifying and exploring the functions performed by schemas, and by elucidating both their positive and negative effects on information processing and behaviour, schema theory has made a most important contribution to several areas in psychology. References to schemas are made throughout this book. For example, in Chapter 4 we discuss how social schemas like stereotypes lie at the heart of our perceptions and misperceptions of entire groups of people. Moreover, schema theory is one of the major contributors to attempts to explain stereotype formation and the effects stereotypes have on behaviour. In conclusion, most of the studies discussed in this chapter, along with those in Chapter 4, provide an impressive base of empirical support for schema theory.

As Eysenck (2009) remarks, 'Schema theories have proved generally successful. Of particular importance, they have identified some of the main reasons why our memories are sometimes distorted.' However, many researchers have complained that schema-based theories tend to be vague in that they do not specify the precise nature of schemas. Schema theory is a cognitive theory relying on the notion of the schema. Schemas are not, of course, directly observable. Like any other cognitive structure they are inferred from behavioural evidence. Identifying and exploring the properties of such inferred cognitive structures, even with the tools provided by the computer metaphor and sophisticated experimental techniques, was never meant to be easy.

As discussed earlier (page 68), psychologists are trying to arrive at the best possible explanation of the findings obtained in their empirical studies. The schema notion has served them well in that it offers plausible explanations for the structuring, and often distorting, effects previous knowledge can have on the ways perception, memory, and other cognitive processes work. Whereas general theoretical claims about such effects are unlikely to be revised significantly in the coming years, more specific claims about the internal structure of schemas and the precise manner in which schemas operate are bound to show considerable development.

● **Examiner's hint**
Do not finalize your notes on schemas before you study stereotype formation and activation in Chapter 4. This will lead to a richer understanding of schema theory and its applications.

3.5 Models or theories of memory

Learning outcomes
• Evaluate two models or theories of one cognitive process.

The multistore model of memory

In the 1960s it became increasingly popular to claim that there is no single memory system. Models started to appear with two, three, or even more memory stores. An influential version, the **multistore model** (**MSM**,) was proposed by Atkinson and Shiffrin (1968). It is a typical early example of the information-processing approach.

According to the MSM, memory consists of the three types of **memory stores**:
• sensory stores
• short-term store (STS)
• long-term store (LTS).

Altkinson and Shiffrin's (1968) multistore model of memory was also known as the **modal model** because it was representative of many similar models proposed by various theorists in the 1960s.

Figure 3.1 shows the stores are arranged in a linear fashion. Information received by the senses registers in the sensory stores. Some of it is passed on to the STS. Information in the STS may then be transferred to the LTS. The flow of information between the memory stores is managed by a number of **control processes**. As information gets moved between the stores it undergoes significant changes.

Figure 3.1
The multistore model of memory – clearly an information-processing model.

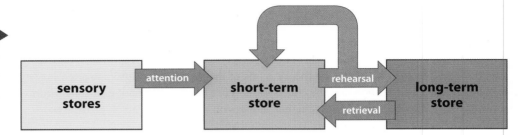

The three types of memory stores differ from one another in some important respects:
- duration – how long information can be stored
- capacity – how much information can be stored
- coding – in what form information can be stored.

The sensory stores are of unlimited capacity. All the information picked up by our senses enters its corresponding sensory store and registers in a code reflecting its initial form. Thus, visual information enters the visual sensory store, called **iconic memory**, and is stored in visual form (images). Auditory information is handled by the auditory sensory store, called **echoic memory**, and registers in an acoustic, that is sound-based code (sounds). These stores are, therefore, modality specific and there is one sensory store for each one of the senses.

Although sensory stores have unlimited capacity, information in them decays rapidly and is soon lost. Iconic memory, for example, lasts from a fraction of a second to 1 second; echoic memory lasts a bit longer (2–4 seconds). **Attention** is the control process responsible for the transfer of information from the sensory stores to the STS. Only information that is attended to while it is in the sensory store is transferred to the next stage of processing, the STS.

Unlike the sensory store, the STS has an extremely limited capacity. It can store only around seven units of information at any one time (Miller (1956) came up with the so-called magical number 7 plus or minus 2 units; this is often taken as an estimate of STS capacity). The duration of information in the STS is anything from several seconds to half a minute. After this, it is lost unless it is maintained in the store by **rehearsal** (repetition).

But rehearsal does more than simply hold information in the STS. Items that are rehearsed enough get transferred to the LTS. The LTS is of unlimited capacity and information there can last up to a lifetime. LTS uses a semantic code, a code based on meaning so what is stored in LTS is the meaning of the information processed.

Information is recalled from the LTS by the process of **retrieval**, which brings information back to the STS.

So, the main theoretical claims of the MSM can be summarized thus:
- memory is not unitary but comprises three different memory stores – sensory stores, STS and LTS
- these stores differ from one another in a number of respects including duration, capacity and coding
- information flows between these stores in ways controlled by control processes such as attention, rehearsal and retrieval.

Experimental studies relevant to the MSM

Duration of short-term memory

In an experiment carried out by Peterson and Peterson (1959) participants were presented with consonant triplets (e.g. KDF, CLS) to memorize. The triplets were presented one at a time and had to be recalled after an interval during which the participants had to count backwards in threes from a given number (e.g. 468, 465, 462, etc.). The counting task lasted for 3, 6, 9, 12, 15 or 18 seconds, after which the participants had to recall the triplet. As the time interval increased, recall of the triplets became progressively worse. After a 3-second interval participants could recall around 80% of the triplets. After 18 seconds, recall fell to less than 10%. Peterson and Peterson concluded that when rehearsal is prevented, information is very rapidly lost from the STS.

Free recall studies and the serial position curve

A task that psychologists have used extensively in studies of the MSM is **free recall**. Participants study a list of items, usually unrelated words, presented one at a time and then attempt to recall these words in any order (free recall). The typical finding is that words at the beginning and at the end of the list are better recalled than those in the middle (Murdock, 1962). The better recall of the first few items, compared to the middle ones, is called the **primacy effect**. The better recall of the last few items is called the **recency effect**. The pattern that emerges when recall is plotted against the position of the words in the list is called the **serial position curve**. Several theorists view findings like these as supporting the distinction between an STS and an LTS.

However, a behaviouristic explanation of such effects has proved elusive. Moreover, it was soon realized that the explanation of findings like Murdock's made it necessary to claim that the information we memorize goes through a number of processing stages and involves more than one memory system. This is further elaborated in what follows.

EXERCISE

6   Try to explain the serial position curve without reference to internal mental structures and processes.

EMPIRICAL RESEARCH

Serial position curves with immediate and delayed free recall (Glanzer and Cunitz, 1966)

These researchers presented participants with a list of 15 words which the participants knew they had to memorize. Half of the participants recalled the words immediately after presentation (immediate free recall condition, IFR). The other half recalled them after a delay of 30 seconds (delayed free recall condition, DFR). To prevent further rehearsal of the list words during the delay, participants in this second condition had to count backwards in threes from a three-digit number.

In the IFR condition, Glanzer and Cunitz obtained the expected serial position curve with pronounced primacy and recency effects. They explained the recency effect by claiming that the last few words were still in the STS when recall commenced. It was from this store that the participants recalled these items. The primacy effect, on the other hand, reflected recall from the LTS. The first few items attracted attention. This ensured that when these words entered the STS, they were rehearsed more than subsequent words. Thus, findings for the IFR were consistent with the MSM.

(Remember that in the MSM, rehearsal is the control process that transfers information from the STS to the LTS and the more an item is rehearsed the more likely it becomes that it will be transferred to the LTS.)

continued

But what does the MSM predict for the DFR condition? A delay of 30 seconds should not affect recall from the LTS. Therefore, the primacy effect should not be affected by the delay. Given that the STS lasts no longer than 30 seconds, the recency effect should disappear. This is exactly what Glanzer and Cunitz found (Figure 3.2).

Figure 3.2
Graph showing Glanzer and Cunitz's (1966) findings.

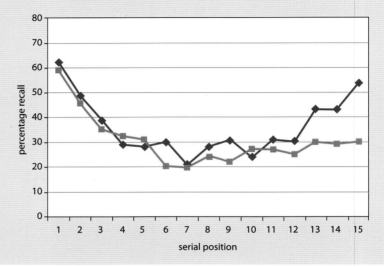

EXERCISES

7 Can you think of an explanation for the pattern of findings obtained in this study that does not make it necessary to distinguish between an STS and an LTS?

8 Comment on the ecological validity of this study.

9 Relate this experiment to the notion proposed earlier (page 68) that psychologists can use combinations of behavioural data and theory to make claims about the structure and functioning of an unobservable mind.

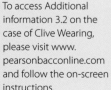 Not everybody agrees with the explanation of the primacy and recency effects offered here. More complex explanations, some not requiring the STS/LTS distinction have been proposed (e.g. Davelaar et al., 2005).

To access Additional information 3.2 on the case of Clive Wearing, please visit www. pearsonbacconline.com and follow the on-screen instructions.

 To learn more about the Clive Wearing case, go to pearsonhotlinks.com, enter the title or ISBN of this book and select weblink 3.2.

The explanation of primacy and recency effects offered by Glanzer and Cunitz is further supported by findings from experiments investigating how variables other than delay can affect these two effects differently. What would happen, for example, if the words were presented at a faster rate? As there would be less time for rehearsal to transfer the first few items to the LTS, the primacy effect should decrease with increasing presentation rate. The recency effect, on the other hand should not be affected as words recalled from STS do not depend on rehearsal. This is precisely the pattern of results that Glanzer (1972) report with increased presentation rate.

Neuropsychological evidence for the MSM

The case of HM (Milner, 1966) is discussed on pages 43 and 44. The surgery performed on HM affected his hippocampus, an area closely associated with memory (see also Alzheimer's disease, pages 84–87). HM's STS was relatively normal. But he could not transfer new information from his STS to his LTS.

Clive Wearing, a musician in London, suffered a similar impairment after a viral infection caused damage to his hippocampus.

The combination of a largely intact STS and a severely damaged LTS is usually taken as strong evidence of the claim that we have different memory systems. The logic is rather simple: if STS and LTS are distinct memory stores, then some types of brain damage to one store should leave the other unaffected (Baddeley, 2009).

An evaluation of the MSM

It is clear that major aspects of the MSM are well-supported by relevant experimental and neuropsychological studies. Its main claim that there are different types of memory stores is almost universally accepted in modern psychology. However, since inception of the model in the 1960s, it has become increasingly clear that the MSM offers a rather simplistic view of how memory works. Some of the model's shortcomings are listed below.

- The importance of rehearsal (viewed as mere repetition of information in STS) for the long-term storage of information has been doubted (Craik and Watkins, 1973).
- It is now known that both the STS and LTS rely on several different codes to represent information. Thus, semantic processing takes place in the STS, whereas the LTS uses a variety of codes including visual, acoustic and semantic codes (Eysenck and Keane, 2010).
- The linear order, according to which information flows from a sensory store to STS and then to the LTS, proved far too simplistic to account for the multiple ways in which different memory stores communicate and influence one another.
- The STS has been subdivided into a number of distinct and interacting short-term memory components. This has led to a number of different multi-component models of short-term memory, including Baddeley and Hitch's (1974) **working memory model**. Such models view the STS as a far more active and important system than a mere relay station for information on its way to the LTS.
- The LTS has also been subdivided into a number of different components specializing in the storage of different types of information (page 84). Important subdivisions include the distinction between **declarative memory** and **procedural memory**. Declarative memory is further divided into two components: one for storing facts and concepts (**semantic memory**) and one for storing information about events (**episodic memory**). Procedural memory, on the other hand, stores information about the skills we have on how to do things.
- An early criticism of the MSM was its emphasis on structures (the stores) at the expense of investigating processing in any detail. Although the MSM did make reference to a number of control processes, including attention and rehearsal, it did not address processing to the extent required.

All the criticisms outlined above are certainly valid. However, what should not be forgotten is that most of the developments in memory research followed the introduction of the MSM and owe a lot to it. In fact, they reinforce its main claim that there are multiple memory systems. So much so, that it is not always clear whether more recent models should be viewed as different models entirely, or simply as elaborations on the MSM.

 Although in its original form the MSM is largely wrong on several specific points, its main ideas remain valid.

● **Examiner's hints**
Although neuropsychological evidence is only briefly discussed here, it is very important to answering questions on the multistore model. Make sure you refer to pages 43, 44 and 84–87 for further information.

EXERCISE
10 Research further Baddeley's working memory model. This model is usually viewed as a separate model from the MSM. Is this justified? Is it not using the same logic and research techniques to address the question of whether STS is unitary or whether we should better view it as a multi-component system?

Levels of processing

Craik and Lockhart (1972) were very critical of models like the MSM. The emphasis in such models, they argued, was on distinguishing between different memory stores. To the extent the models referred to control processes at all, they did so only to explain the flow of information between the memory stores identified. Craik and Lockhart did more than aim at a more balanced consideration of structural and processing requirements. In a radical

move, they ignored completely the idea that we may have different memory stores. They did not explicitly deny the existence of different memory stores. They felt more substantial progress in memory research could be made by investigating in detail how information was processed early on, in particular, during its initial encoding.

Before explaining Craik and Lockhart's thinking, you need to have a clear idea of what they mean by **levels of processing** (**LOP**). Consider the information in Table 3.1.

TABLE 3.1 HOW DO YOU ANSWER THESE QUESTIONS?			
Question	**Answer: Yes**	**Answer: No**	**Level of processing**
Is this word in upper case?	TABLE	table	structural
Does this word rhyme with 'fad'?	mad	train	phonological
Is salmon a fish?	The answer here is *yes*		semantic

Three different types of questions are shown in the table above. The first is a structural question and relates to the appearance of the target word (TABLE). In order to answer it, the target word has to be processed at the **structural level of processing** – a level that encodes the physical features (structure) of the relevant stimulus. Answering the question about rhyming, on the other hand, requires processing at the **phonological level of processing** – a level which delivers information about how the words (fad, mad) sound. Finally, answering the question about whether salmon is an example of fish requires processing at the **semantic level of processing** – a level that extracts the meaning of the word *salmon*.

Craik and Lockhart also introduced the notion of **depth of processing**. According to them, as one moves from the structural, through the phonological to the semantic levels of analysis, the depth of processing increases. Information can be processed at any of these three levels.

So far, this is a descriptive account of a number of levels at which incoming information may be initially processed or perceived. What is interesting about Craik and Lockhart's theory is the very simple way in which they turn these uncontroversial claims about perception into a framework within which important memory phenomena can be addressed. According to Craik and Lockhart, memory is a by-product of perception. What this means is that memory is a direct consequence of the way information is perceived or encoded. And now for the central claim of the LOP approach: the deeper the level at which information is processed during encoding, the longer-lasting the memory trace it creates in memory.

Craik and Tulving (1975) put this idea to the experimental test. They asked their participants to answer a number of structural, phonological and semantic questions much like those in Table 3.1. The participants were not told to memorize the target words. Following the initial task, participants were tested to see if they had learned the target words. They were surprised with a list of words containing words already presented to them and new words. The participants had to recognize the items already shown to them (this is called a **memory recognition test**).

As predicted by the LOP, theory words processed at the semantic level were the best remembered, followed by the phonologically processed words. Words processed at the structural level were the least well remembered.

The pattern of findings obtained by Craik and Tulving supports the main idea of LOP theory – namely that the deeper the processing received by the items, the better the memory for these items. Craik and Tulving obtained the same pattern of findings when using a recall, rather than a recognition, test.

Evaluation of LOP

The idea that deeper processing leads to better memory has been supported in a large number of experiments. As Baddeley (2009) remarks, 'as a basic generalization or rule of thumb, the principle that deeper … processing leads to better retention is arguably our most useful generalization about human memory'. Despite these positive findings, many have criticized the LOP theory (e.g. Eysenck, 1978).

A serious problem is that, despite several attempts, there is no convincing measure of processing depth. A second shortcoming is that the LOP approach is more a description of what happens than an explanatory theory. Why, for instance, is the semantic level better for memory than the others? In the years following the introduction of the LOP approach, several attempts were made to rectify this shortcoming. Thus, according to Craik and Tulving (1975) semantic encoding leads to richer and more elaborate memory codes. Related to this, Anderson and Reder (1979) found that elaboration is easier at the semantic than the phonological or structural levels.

All these criticisms regard theoretical issues. At a more practical level, the LOP approach has also been criticized on empirical grounds. The simple ordering on which the approach is based (semantic better than phonological better than structural) has not always been supported in empirical research. In fact, several studies have demonstrated that there are situations in which deeper processing does not guarantee better memory. This may occur, for example, when encoding happens at the semantic level and memory for it is accessed at the phonological level. For example, a learner encodes the word *table* semantically but during recall we provide him or her with a phonological reminder by saying that the word rhymes with *cable*. Had the word been encoded phonologically, then the phonological reminder would easily bring it to mind (Fisher and Craik, 1977). This shortcoming relates to the fact that LOP theory does not address the retrieval stage of the memory process.

In conclusion, much like the MSM, the LOP theory has been supported by a large number of empirical studies. Again, like the MSM, in its original form it has been subjected to several critiques. Although problems remain, the LOP approach has given rise to further developments which address some of its earlier shortcomings (e.g. using the notion of elaboration to become more explanatory).

In their update of their theory, Lockhart and Craik (1990) accepted the original LOP theory was over simplistic and that they had not adequately taken into consideration retrieval processes. Moreover, they acknowledged that deeper processing is not invariably better for memory than shallower processing. The main emphasis on semantic processing, however, remained. In plain English: if you want to memorize something effectively, for most intents and purposes, try to understand it.

Despite differences between the MSM and LOP theory, their seminal notions and the ideas they helped to bring about, often continue together in modern accounts of memory. While addressing structural questions (i.e. trying to explore an increasing number of different memory stores) modern models also incorporate highly sophisticated and complexly interacting processes at both the encoding and the retrieval stages of memory.

 Memory depends on both what happens to information during encoding and what happens at retrieval time.

● **Examiner's hint**
In order to evaluate models or theories of memory you need a good understanding of their respective strengths and weaknesses. Make systematic notes in which you explicitly list the strengths and weaknesses of models or theories. Can you compare and contrast the two?

EXERCISES
11 What are the main similarities and differences between the multistore and the LOP models?
12 What do you understand by the sentence: *Although both the multistore and the LOP models have been subjected to substantial critiques, they have both made very important contributions because they helped generate a lot of empirical research.*
13 Research Tulving's encoding specificity principle. How does this principle relate to the LOP model?

3.6 Biology and cognition

Learning outcomes
- Explain how biological factors affect one cognitive process.

Alzheimer's disease

Alzheimer's disease (**AD**) is a serious degenerative brain disease. As in many other degenerative diseases, the onset of symptoms is gradual but its progression is continuous and irreversible. The main symptoms of AD relate to memory impairment. However, for AD to be diagnosed, the person must also experience serious problems in at least one other area. For example, symptoms such as difficulty speaking and understanding language, problems with focusing attention, impaired movement or altered personality are all pertinent to AD.

AD progresses to ever more serious memory loss. In addition, patients experience confusion, depression, hallucinations, delusions, sleeplessness and loss of appetite. It takes 2–15 years for AD to run its course. Drugs may slow down progress, but as there is no cure AD inevitably leads to death. AD occurs in about 10% of the population over the age of 65. Between 30% and 50% of adults over 70 exhibit Alzheimer's symptoms; over 80, more than 50% develop the disease.

AD does not influence every memory system equally; episodic memory is the most severely affected. Disruptions of episodic memory are the earliest symptom of AD and episodic memory deficits continue to be one of the most significant problems throughout progression of the disease. An analysis by Salthouse and Becker (1998) of data from 180 AD patients and over 1000 normal elderly individuals, found that AD was primarily a disorder of episodic memory.

Episodic memory is memory for events and personal experiences (autobiographical memory) that occurred in a given place at a particular time (page 81). Typical episodic memory problems (when frequent and worsening) that are indicative of the onset of AD include misplaced keys, missed appointments and the like. As AD progresses, memory of events that occurred around the time its onset get forgotten. Memories of events from the more distant past are less affected, especially in the initial stages of the disease.

AD affects semantic memory as well. Semantic memory stores general knowledge about the world, concepts and language (page 81). Hodges et al. (1994) measured semantic memory in AD patients with such tasks as naming pictures of objects or animals, or picking the appropriate picture given its name. They found a steady decline in semantic memory.

Procedural memory (page 81) is less affected. In fact, most of it is spared for most of the course of the disease. Thus, AD patients retain their knowledge of motor and cognitive skills such as playing the piano, riding a bicycle or holding a conversation. In fact, they retain for a considerable time the capacity to learn new skills (Ilse et al., 2007).

To learn more about Alzheimer's disease, go to www. pearsonhotlinks. com, enter the title or ISBN of this book and select weblink 3.3.

The brain and AD

Brain structure
The main areas of the brain are shown in Figure 3.3; Figure 2.1 (page 48) shows the position of the hippocampus.

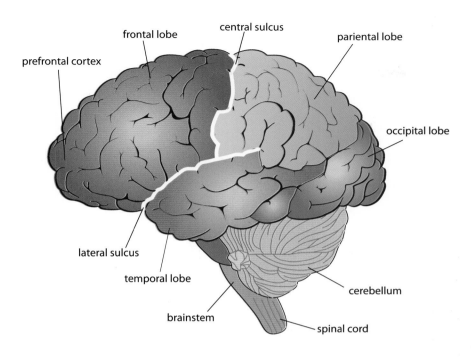

Many studies have investigated the role of the medial temporal lobe (MTL) in AD; there are two main reasons for this. Its role in episodic memory is well established, and it is the first area of the brain to show pathological changes in AD. In a recent meta-analysis of functional magnetic resonance imaging (fMRI) studies of episodic memory in AD, Schwindt and Black (2009) concluded that it was well-established that, compared to normal controls, AD patients show decreased activation of the MTL.

AD develops through a series of stages. First, the MTLs are affected, in particular the hippocampus, then the parietal lobes and other brain regions. The symptoms of AD seem to be caused by the loss of brain cells and the deterioration of neurons involved in the production of acetylcholine. Acetylcholine is particularly prevalent in the hippocampus.

The hippocampus is very much involved in the formation of new memories (Eichenbaum, 2000). You will recall that the hippocampus was destroyed in HM and several other well-known amnesia cases. The hippocampus of normal people contains high concentrations of acetylcholine (Squire, 1987). Low concentrations are found in people with AD. This is the outcome of severe brain tissue loss in areas of the forebrain which are known to secrete acetylcholine.

MRI scan showing signs of AD in the medial temporal lobes (pink, bottom of scan) and parietal lobes (purple, top of scan).

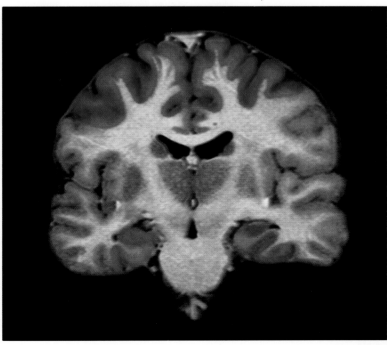

Autopsies reveal two characteristic abnormalities in these acetylcholine-producing neurons. The brains of AD patients show abnormal levels of **amyloid plaques** and **neurofibrillary tangles**.

Amyloid plaques

Amyloid plaques.

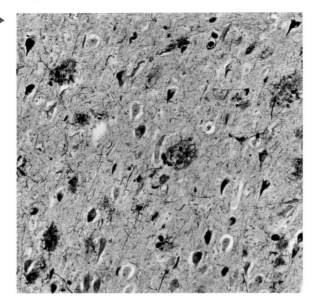

These are caused by deposits in the brain of a sticky protein called **amyloid-β protein**. This protein results from the faulty breakdown of its precursor. Amyloid-β protein accumulates and damages the membranes of axons and dendrites (Lorenzo et al., 2000). The amyloid plaques are formed from the degenerating axons and dendrites and contain a dense core of amyloid-β protein. These plaques accumulate in the spaces between neurons. There is a lot of evidence for the involvement of amyloid-β protein in the onset of AD. In fact, most AD patients accumulate amyloid plaques before the onset of disease (Selco, 1990).

Neurofibrillary tangles

Neurofibrillary tangles.

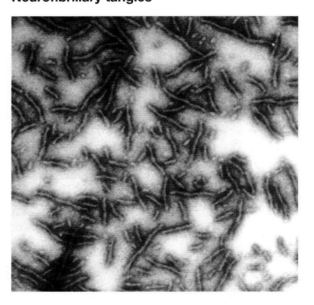

The brains of AD patients also show the accumulation of an abnormal form of the **tau protein**. This protein normally forms part of the support structure of neurons. In Alzheimer's disease, the tau protein is abnormal and, as a result, the structural support of neurons collapses. The abnormal protein produces neurofibrillary tangles – tangles in which microtubules (tiny rods) are twisted around each other. They are found in the cell body and dendrites of neurons (Kensinger and Corkin, 2003).

The formation of amyloid plaques and neurofibrillary tangles are thought to contribute to the degradation of the neurons in the brain and the subsequent symptoms of Alzheimer's disease. As a result of this degradation, the cerebral cortex and the hippocampus, as well as additional areas, suffer from widespread atrophy (shrinking).

The cognitive and the biological levels of analysis in AD

This discussion of AD demonstrates the close connection between the cognitive and the biological levels of analysis. A distinctly psychological (cognitive) process, memory, is determined to a very great extent by the state of identifiable brain structures like the MTL and the forebrain. With the advent of powerful imaging techniques such as fMRI, investigators have started unravelling the biological underpinning of AD. Of course, the studies are not without their problems: the technical challenges of imaging the brain of AD patients are often significant (Schwindt and Black, 2009).

While investigating brain involvement in AD, we gain precious insights about the functioning of the memory system. The claim that we have different long-term memory systems, gains considerable support from such imaging studies. Such knowledge as we gain will hopefully help in the development of better treatments for a serious and sadly very common medical condition.

 3.7 ## The interaction of cognitive and biological factors in emotion

 The fact that brain damage can affect one's sense of identity poses problems to attempts to hold humans morally responsible. After all, our sense of self seems to depend on the functioning of an organ we hardly control.

Learning outcomes
- Discuss to what extent cognitive and biological factors interact in emotion.

Two-factor theory of emotion

According to James and Lange (e.g. James, 1890) the state of our body determines the emotions we experience. However, as Cannon (1929) argued, emotions are not easy to distinguish at the physiological level. More recent research has not much altered these early views. Different emotions are, of course, experienced differently. However, researchers have found it difficult to detect clear physiological differences between them (Barrett, 2006). Thus, very similar patterns of autonomic arousal seem to underlie emotions as distinct as fear, joy and anger. There are some physiological differences between emotions. The hormone secretions associated with fear and rage, for example, differ (Levenson, 1992). But the differences between different emotions in general are neither large nor consistent. Some theorists have claimed, therefore, that an additional factor is needed to transform ambiguous physiological states into specific emotions.

For Schachter and Singer (1962), the requisite additional factor is cognition. According to their **two-factor theory** (**TFT**), two factors interact to determine specific emotions:
- physiological arousal
- an emotional interpretation and labelling of the physiological arousal.

According to the TFT, experiencing distinct emotions in specific settings requires the interaction between physiological arousal and an interpretation of what has caused the arousal in that setting. While the *strength* of the physiological arousal determines the *intensity* of the emotional experience, its *interpretation* determines *which particular* emotion is experienced.

Schachter and Singer (1962) put these ideas to the experimental test (page 55). You will recall that their main finding in that study was that the same arousal state (produced by the adrenaline injection), could be experienced as either of two emotions (anger or elation), depending on how the participants interpreted and labelled their arousal state.

Although Schachter and Singer's study is a classic in psychology, it has been subjected to several criticisms (Reisenzein, 1983). Methodological criticisms include the fact that physiological arousal was measured in a rather rudimentary way by measuring only pulse rate. Importantly, according to subsequent research (e.g. Marshall and Zimbardo, 1979) the arousal produced by adrenaline injections is unpleasant rather than neutral. Finally, there have been replication failures (Mezzacappa et al., 1999).

Critics have also doubted the ecological validity of the study or, in general, the extent to which Schachter's theory can be used to explain how emotions are experienced in real-life situations. We usually know what is causing our physiological arousal (Fiske, 2004). On the positive side, Schachter's work has generated a lot of research and has drawn attention to the cognitive component of emotional states (Reisenzein, 1983). Although Schachter emphasized the role of cognition in emotional states he did not, in any systematic way, link specific types of cognitions to specific emotional states. But Lazarus (1982, 1991) did.

Appraisal theory of emotion

Lazarus (1982, 1991) proposed a theory of emotion based on the notion of **appraisal**. This refers to the evaluation of situations according to the significance they have for us. More precisely, we experience emotions when, in our interaction with our environment, we appraise events as beneficial or harmful to our well-being. For Lazarus, as for Schachter, cognition is an essential part of all emotional states.

Initially Lazarus distinguished between two types of appraisal, **primary appraisal** and **secondary appraisal** (Lazarus, 1982). In later work, Lazarus and his colleagues (e.g. Smith and Lazarus, 1993) identified six appraisal components, three for each type of appraisal.

- Primary appraisal – This relates to deciding whether a situation is personally relevant. There are three components of primary appraisal.
  - Motivational relevance – Is the situation relevant to my goals? An emotion will only be experienced if the answer is positive.
  - Motivational congruence – Is the situation favourable to my goals? Positive and negative emotions will follow yes and no answers, respectively.
  - Accountability – Who is responsible for what is happening?
    The outcome of primary appraisal is not full blown emotion but a basic positive and negative approach and avoidance responses towards or away from the situation that gave rise to them. Experiencing more specific emotions requires secondary appraisal.
- Secondary appraisal – The aim of secondary appraisal is to provide information about the individual's coping options in a situation. It has three components.
  - Problem-focused coping – Can I cope with the situation by changing it to make it less threatening?
  - Emotion-focused coping – Can I change the situation by changing the way I feel about it; for instance, by reinterpreting it so as to reduce its emotional impact?
  - Future expectancy – To what extent can I expect that the situation will change?

Which emotion is experienced in a particular situation is determined by the pattern of answers individuals give to the questions relating to these six appraisal components. Lazarus uses the term **core relational theme** (CRT) to refer to a summary of all the appraisal judgements that define specific emotions. CRTs determine the personal meanings that result from particular patterns of appraisal about specific person–environment relationships.

To give just two examples: We feel angry when the situation is relevant and unfavourable to our goals, and we think someone else is responsible for it. We feel relief when an earlier judgement that a situation was incompatible with goal attainment has now been revised to indicate a more favourable outcome.

We usually consider emotion to be distinct from thinking. Lazarus's theory emphasizes the close interrelationships between thinking and the emotions. This theme is elaborated further in Chapter 5 where cognitive theories of various psychological disorders are discussed.

Several studies have supported Lazarus's appraisal theory. Smith and Lazarus (1993) asked participants to identify with the central character of stories they were reading. In one of the stories, the character is appraising his very poor performance in an important course. Accountability was manipulated by either describing the situation as one that involved an unhelpful teacher or the character's bad working habits. Manipulations of appraisal components led to the participants reporting emotional states that were largely consistent with appraisal theory.

How we feel depends on the way we think.

Although many studies do support appraisal theory, it should be noted that some studies fail to get results that are entirely consistent with Lazarus's theory (e.g. Kuppens et al., 2003). Moreover, is identifying with characters in stories equivalent to personal appraisals and more genuine emotions?

Herrald and Tomaka (2002) investigated the relationships between different emotions (anger, shame and pride), patterns of cognitive appraisal, and cardiovascular reactivity during real emotional episodes. Participants were asked to express their opinion on a variety of college-related topics in the presence of a confederate behaving in such a way as to make them feel anger, shame, or pride. The confederate did this by using behaviour based on the CRTs outlined by Lazarus. The shame manipulation, for instance, involved the confederate expressing disappointment in the participant and commenting that he or she should do better. Physiological arousal was measured throughout the study by monitoring the participants' cardiac activity and blood pressure. The results were largely consistent with Lazarus's theory. Discrete emotions were closely associated with specific appraisal patterns. Moreover, anger and shame (both negative emotions) were associated with greater physiological arousal than pride (a positive emotion).

Negative emotions such as anger are associated with physiological arousal.

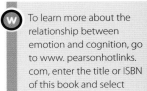

To learn more about the relationship between emotion and cognition, go to www. pearsonhotlinks. com, enter the title or ISBN of this book and select weblink 3.4.

Conscious/unconscious appraisals and the body

The effects of appraisal on autonomic arousal (Speisman et al., 1964)

An early study by these researchers clearly illustrates the way cognitive appraisals affect the body's responses to stressful situations. Speisman et al. showed their participants a stressful film depicting aboriginal boys undergoing circumcision in the context of a puberty rite. The film was accompanied by a soundtrack and by manipulating this soundtrack the investigators defined four experimental conditions:

- trauma condition – the pain experienced by the boys and the use of a sharp knife were emphasized
- denial – the boys' anticipation of entering manhood was pointed out thus de-emphasizing the negative aspects of the film
- intellectualization – the soundtrack ignored the emotional aspects of the situation and emphasized instead the traditions of aboriginal culture
- silent – there was no soundtrack in this condition.

Arousal state was measured by galvanic skin response (GSR) – a measure of the electrical conductivity of the skin and an indicator of autonomic arousal – and heart rate. It was highest in the trauma condition and lowest in the intellectualization and silent conditions. The denial condition occupied an intermediary position. Clearly, the way participants appraised what they were seeing in the circumcision film affected their physiological reaction to it.

EXERCISES

14   Discuss ethical issues relevant to this study.

15   Think of instances you have used cognitive reappraisal to cope with the emotional impact of an unpleasant event or situation.

More recent studies, relying on fMRI technology, offer further support for the view that appraisals correlate with biological responses. Moreover, such research has started to reveal the brain structures and circuits that are involved in the cognitive processing related to emotion and emotion regulation. Some of these very important studies are discussed on pages 96–98.

Are appraisals always conscious, thus involving rather slow, controlled, deliberate and novel processing? Or, can they also occur unconsciously, on the basis of rapid automatic processing that draws on information already stored in memory? Lazarus claimed that all emotional responses are based on cognitive processing. However, he did not suggest that processing is always conscious. Others (e.g. Zajonc, 1980) argue that, at least in some settings, emotional responses may be directly triggered without the prior involvement of cognition.

Most contemporary theories agree with Lazarus and claim that cognitive appraisals can indeed occur automatically outside conscious awareness. A popular view is that basic appraisals (e.g. Is the situation good or bad for me?) can take place unconsciously. More complex appraisals (e.g. those attributing responsibility) depend on more conscious information processing (Robinson, 1998). The two studies briefly outlined below support the view that appraisals can take place unconsciously.

Öhman (2000) presented pictures of spiders or snakes to participants who feared spiders, participants who feared snakes and participants who had no fears of either. One of the experimental conditions involved the presentation of the stimuli at durations that enabled

the participants to consciously recognize them. In a second condition, the pictures were shown for 30 milliseconds and followed by a neutral stimulus, an arrangement that resulted in the participants not becoming aware of the content of the stimuli presented. Phobic participants showed nearly identical physiological responses (increased sweat gland activity) to pictures of their phobic animals, regardless of whether or not they had consciously seen the spiders or snakes presented. These findings seem to indicate that appraisals can occur at unconscious levels.

Whalen et al. (1998) used the same technique to show participants photos of faces with fearful expressions for about 30 milliseconds. These photos were closely followed by photos of the same faces in a neutral expression. Although the participants reported no conscious awareness of the fearful faces, imaging data showed activation within the amygdala. This brain structure is closely involved in emotional responding; its position within the brain is shown below and on pages 48 and 159. Whalen et al.'s findings suggest that the amygdala can monitor emotional stimuli at an unconscious level.

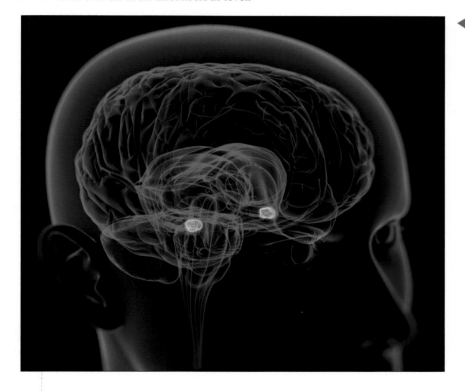

The amygdala responds to fearful stimuli. In this image, the activated amygdalae are shown in yellow.

Concluding comments

The two theories discussed above argue that cognitive and biological factors are both essential to emotion. Emotional states are determined, according to these theories, by the interaction of cognitive and biological factors in a way that emotion cannot arise in the absence of cognition. Those who claim that some emotional states are possible without any cognitive involvement (e.g. Zajonc, 1980) seem to be using rather idiosyncratic definitions for the term cognition. They seem reluctant to view as cognitive basic automatic and largely unconscious perceptual processes.

As the studies by Ohman and Whalen et al. show, recognition and similar processes can occur at unconscious levels. Of course, the more elaborate the emotion, or the less frequently one has encountered an emotionally arousing situation, the higher the involvement of deliberate conscious processing.

Relate the research covered in this section to the view that emotion is a way of knowing.

3.8   # How does emotion affect cognition?

Learning outcomes
- Evaluate one theory of how emotion may affect one cognitive process.

Flashbulb memory

Do you remember where you were when you first heard news of Michael Jackson's death? How did you feel about this unexpected event? How did you come to hear about the death? Were others present, or were you on your own? What else was going on at the moment you received the news? To the extent you can answer these questions about the circumstances surrounding your reception of the news with confidence and in vivid detail you have formed what is called a **flashbulb memory** (**FBM**) of the event of Michael Jackson's death.

Brown and Kulik (1977) who were the first modern psychologists to study FBMs, defined them as 'memories of the circumstances in which one first learned of a very surprising and consequential (or emotionally arousing) event'. The defining feature an FBM is *not* the memory of the event, but memory of its reception context – the circumstances of the news' reception.

Brown and Kulik proposed a theory of the formation and maintenance of FBMs. According to their theory, FBMs:
- form in situations where we encounter surprising and highly emotional information
- are maintained by means of overt rehearsal (involving discussion with others) and covert rehearsal (private rehearsing or ruminating)
- differ from other memories in that they more vivid, last longer, and are more consistent and accurate
- require for their creation the involvement of a specialized neural mechanism which stores information permanently in a unique memory system.

EMPIRICAL RESEARCH

A study of flashbulb memory (Brown and Kulik, 1977)

Brown and Kulik (1977) asked 80 American participants (40 white and 40 black) to answer questions about 10 events. Nine of the events were mostly assassinations or attempted assassinations of well-known American personalities (e.g. J. F. Kennedy, Martin Luther King). The tenth was a self-selected event of personal relevance and involving unexpected shock. Examples included the death of a friend or relative or a serious accident. Participants were asked to recall the circumstances they found themselves in when they first heard the news about the 10 events. They were also asked to indicate how often they had rehearsed (overtly or covertly) information about each event.

The events were unexpected and for many were also of personal relevance. They were expected, therefore, to cause FBMs. The assassination of J. F. Kennedy in 1963 (over a decade before the study) led to the highest number of FBMs with 90% of the participants recalling its reception context in vivid detail. African Americans reported more FBMs for leaders of civil rights movements (e.g. the assassination of Martin Luther King) than Caucasian Americans. Most participants recalled a personal FBM which tended to be related to learning about the death of a parent.

EXERCISES
16 Give two examples of what you think are FBMs of your own. Use Brown and Kulik's theory to explain why you formed these FBMs.
17 What research method was used in Brown and Kulik's study?
18 What criticisms would you apply to this study's methodology?

Findings from this study are clearly consistent with Brown and Kulik's theory. Additional support comes from a study by Conway et al. (1994). These researchers used both UK and non-UK citizens to study FBMs caused by the unexpected resignation of the British Prime Minister Margaret Thatcher in 1990. There were several data collection points in this study including a few days after the resignation and after 11 months. Conway et al. found that 85.6% of UK citizens, and considerably fewer non-UK citizens, had a flashbulb memory after 11 months.

Despite numerous studies supporting Brown and Kulik's theory, most of its claims have been criticized (Winograd and Neisser, 1992). Several studies, some discussed below, suggest that FBMs may not be as accurate or permanent as the theory states. Moreover, it has proved difficult to find consistent evidence for Brown and Kulik's view that a special neural mechanism, or indeed any type of special mechanism, is needed to explain how FBMs are formed.

To learn more about flashbulb memory, go to www. pearsonhotlinks. com, enter the title or ISBN of this book and select weblink 3.5.

Neisser and Harsch (1992) asked their participants to report on the circumstances of their learning about the *Challenger* space disaster. Participants reported on this event twice. The first time was one day after the disaster and the second two and a half years later. One day after the disaster, 21% of the participants reported that they had heard about the disaster on TV. However, two-and-a-half years later, this rose to 45%. Clearly, their memories of how they learned the news about *Challenger* changed over time. Assuming participants were more accurate one day after the disaster, it can be concluded that their memories about how they had heard the news deteriorated significantly during the subsequent two-and-a-half years. This suggests that FBMs are not very reliable. Neisser and Harsch claimed that such findings suggest FBMs may be ordinary memories.

How reliable are FBMs of key events?

The studies discussed so far suffer from a serious methodological shortcoming: they do not include a control condition to allow for a comparison between normal memories and flashbulb memories. They simply assume that flashbulb memories are better remembered than other kinds of memories.

Talarico and Rubin (2003) asked participants to recall the events of 11 September 2001 on four occasions: 1, 7, 42 and 224 days after the attack. They also tested the participants' memory for an everyday event that had happened at around the same time with the attack. Once more, memory was tested four times, following the same time arrangements used for the recall of the attack. Talarico and Rubin found the FBMs remained very vivid throughout the study. Moreover, participants were very confident about their accuracy. However, they were not any more consistent than the participants' corresponding memories for the everyday event.

What is the current status of Brown and Kulik's theory?

Brown and Kulik overestimated the durability and consistency of FBMs.

The studies discussed above, and additional research, demonstrate that FBMs:

- are long lasting but not permanent
- may not be any longer lasting than important everyday memories
- are more vivid than most ordinary memories
- are recalled with a higher degree of confidence than other memories.

As to the causes of FBMs, we now have a better idea than Brown and Kulik did when formulating their theory. Luminet and Curci conducted a study with the goal of comparing four theoretical models accounting for FBM formation, including Brown and Kulik's model (Luminet, 2009). The data involved US and non-US participants and related to the terrorist attacks of 11 September in the USA. According to their analysis, high importance/ consequences and strong emotional feelings are the only two conditions that are required for the formation of an FBM. Surprise, on the other hand, has produced mixed findings. It is noteworthy that FBMs have been found for expected events such as the first moon landing (Winograd and Killinger, 1983).

So what can we conclude about Brown and Kulik's theory? Williams et al. (2008) conclude their discussion of FBM by noting that Brown and Kulik identified two important determinants of FBMs: event importance and event emotionality. The third factor, surprise, is not so well supported by relevant research. Some of the properties Brown and Kulik ascribe to FBMs, like permanence and consistency, are disputed, whereas others, like confidence and vividness, are better supported by the relevant research. The claim that has faired least well is their assumption that flashbulb memory is a special memory system based on a dedicated neural mechanism. Few nowadays would accept this aspect of Brown and Kulik's theory. What is certain, though, is that their pioneering work has generated a lot of research about the relation between emotion and cognition.

But how does emotionality affect the formation and maintenance of FBMs? Despite what Brown and Kulik believed, there is little evidence that emotionality has much of an impact during the initial encoding of the event. Rather, emotionality seems to exert its effects at a later stage by affecting rehearsal and social sharing. This is further discussed below.

3.9   The effects of social or cultural factors on cognitive processes

Learning outcomes
- Discuss how social or cultural factors affect one cognitive process.

Bartlett's work (1932) demonstrating how schemas originating in one particular culture can affect how text from another culture is recalled is directly relevant to this learning outcome. His participants relied on schematic knowledge, acquired within their culture, to understand and later recall a story from a very different culture. Bartlett's work showed that our past is, to a significant extent, a construction; moreover, one that relies heavily on the ideas and knowledge we develop in the cultural settings we inhabit. The role of social or cultural factors in memory is further discussed by examining how one particular cultural dimension (individualism/collectivism) affects FBM.

Individualism/collectivism and flashbulb memory

There is evidence that the emotionality of a public news event is a good predictor of whether it will cause FBMs (Julian et al., 2009). According to several researchers, what emotion does in such contexts is to influence the extent to which the memory is rehearsed and shared. It is known that individuals tend to share their emotional experiences with others and to seek more information about what happened. Moreover, the more intense the emotional experience, the more often social sharing is elicited (Luminet et al., 2000).

A number of researchers (e.g. Paez et al., 2009; Wang and Aydin, 2009) have recently discussed the possibility that cultural factors, including individualism/collectivism, may affect the determinants of FBM. Such cultural factors would, therefore, influence FBM formation and maintenance. Individualism/collectivism, along with other cultural dimensions, is discussed in detail in Chapter 4 (pages 135–137).

In individualistic cultures (e.g. USA, UK, Australia and the Netherlands) persons are viewed as unique and autonomous with distinctive qualities and individual autonomy. In such societies, somebody's emotions are part of his or her uniqueness. Expressing emotions and sharing them with others is acceptable and encouraged (Wang and Aydin, 2008).

In more collectivistic cultures (e.g. China, Japan, Venezuela and Pakistan) identity is defined more by the characteristics of the collective groups to which one belongs. Individual autonomy and self-expression, are inhibited. In some collectivist societies (e.g. China, Japan) expressing emotion, especially negative emotion, is usually viewed as dangerous and is not encouraged. Furthermore, collectivist societies do not encourage individuals to focus on their internal states or reflect (ruminate) on their emotional states (Wang and Aydin, 2008).

● **Examiner's hints**
Remember to study further the individualism/collectivism distinction on pages 135–137. Not all collectivistic societies are reserved regarding emotional expression. Some South American cultures countries score highly on collectivism (e.g. Brazil, Venezuela) but are very emotionally expressive, unlike some Asian collectivistic cultures (e.g. China, Japan).

EXERCISE
19 Can you think of possible methodological problems of the cross-cultural studies referred to in this section?

Consistent with this, Basabe and Ros (2005) have found that, compared to people in individualist societies, those in several collectivist societies report:
- lower levels of emotions
- lower levels of mental ruminations
- less social sharing of emotion.

Furthermore, sharing memories with others is considered a valuable social practice in Western cultures but not so much in Asian societies (Pasupathi, 2001).

Such findings on the effects of culture on factors underlying FBM lead to the prediction that, in individualistic cultures, people will form more FBMs. As Wang and Aydin (2008) argue, given the social nature of the emotion expression and sharing 'it is obvious that the facilitative effect of emotion on FBM cannot be reduced to a state of arousal or a mere subjective feeling state, but must be situated in a cultural context'.

Recent cross-cultural findings of FBM recollection are consistent with Wang and Aydin's views. Wang and Aydin (2008) discuss studies which have found that when Chinese participants were asked to recall memories of public events, they managed to recall fewer FBM details than participants from the USA, UK, Germany and Turkey. Otani et al. (2005) found that only a small percentage of Japanese participants formed FBMs of a nuclear accident.

It is clear that culture and the social practices associated with it affect FBMs. Research demonstrates that those living in individualist cultures are more likely to form FBMs, and reveals some of the relevant mediating processes. That is, research has contributed to an analysis of precisely how these differences come about as a result of differences in such processes as the experience and the communication of emotion.

To what extent does research showing that culture can affect cognition support the postmodernist view that reality is a social construction?

The use of technology in investigating cognitive processes

3.10

Learning outcomes
- Discuss the use of technology in investigating cognitive processes.

● **Examiner's hint**
You need to study this section along with relevant material from Chapter 2, especially pages 40–46.

In this chapter, you have looked at many studies relying on modern technologies to investigate aspects of memory (e.g. fMRI studies of Alzheimer's disease). Moreover, MRI and fMRI studies discussed in Chapter 2 (pages 46–48) address the relationship between physiology and cognition. All such studies are directly relevant to addressing this learning outcome. You are now going to examine studies using fMRI scanning to investigate cognitive processes in decision-making and cognitive reappraisal. The latter studies are relevant to Lazarus's theory.

fMRI studies of decision-making

Several studies have identified brain regions involved in decision-making. In general, the activation of areas in the prefrontal cortex and the parietal cortex (Figure 3.3) increases during decision-making (Platt, 2002). Moreover, the activation is stronger when the decisions studied involve risk (Paulus et al., 2001).

Psychologists often distinguish between two forms of decision involving uncertainty.
- Risky decisions – These decisions have several possible outcomes, the probabilities of which are known. Betting on red or black in roulette, or on the throw of a dice, are examples of risky decisions.
- Ambiguous decisions – These decisions have several outcomes the probabilities of which are not known. An example would be deciding to go for a beach holiday without any idea about what the weather will be like.

Theorists differ in whether they view decisions involving risk and decisions involving ambiguity as similar or different types of decision-making. Huettel et al. (2006) used fMRI scanning to explore these two possibilities.

EMPIRICAL RESEARCH

The physiology of ambiguous and risky decisions (Huettel et al., 2006)

These researchers presented participants with pairs of monetary gambles. The gambles included both ambiguous and risky decisions and the participants had to choose among them. The study confirmed earlier findings about brain regions that are activated in decision-making tasks (both the prefrontal cortex and parietal cortex showed increased levels of activation). More importantly, Huettel et al. were able to identify selective increases in areas of activation to decision-making under ambiguity and decision-making under risk.

- Preference for ambiguity increased activation in the lateral prefrontal cortex.
- Preference for risk was associated with increased activity in the posterior parietal cortex.

Another interesting finding was that impulsiveness in decision-making was associated with activity in the prefrontal cortex. The researchers found that activation of the prefrontal cortex was associated with less impulsivity in decision-making under uncertainty. This confirms earlier findings about the crucial role of the prefrontal cortex in the inhibition of impulsive or automatic behaviour (Parrott, 2000).

Huettel et al.'s (2006) study illustrates the beneficial use of advanced scanning technologies in the investigation of cognitive processes. Such studies contribute to the integrated study of psychological phenomena involving more than one level of analysis, and they help to resolve theoretical disputes at the psychological level. In Huettel et al.'s study, we see how fMRI scanning can help decide whether or not decision-making in risky settings is substantially different from decision-making in ambiguous settings, or if they are simply different examples of the same process. This distinction had proved rather elusive in conventional studies involving only behavioural measures.

fMRI studies of cognitive reappraisal

Cognitive reappraisal involves cognitively reinterpreting the meaning of emotional stimuli in ways that change their emotional value. Several fMRI studies have shown that when participants are asked to use cognitive reappraisal in this way, a number of changes in the activation levels of identifiable brain areas can be detected (Ochsner and Gross, 2008). The main findings are listed below.

- Activation increases in the prefrontal cortex (Figure 3.4). The more active the prefrontal cortex, the more successful the reappraisal.
- Activation decreases in the amygdalae (Figure 3.4), which are associated with negative emotions.
- Activation increases in the nucleus accumbens (Figure 3.4), which is associated with positive emotions.

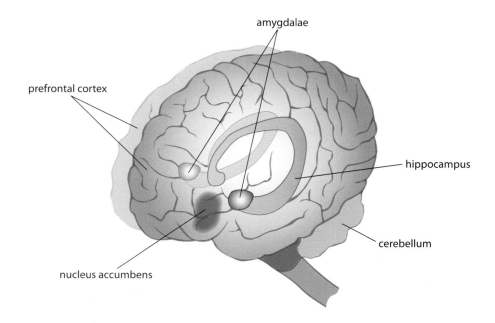

Figure 3.4
Section through the brain showing the position of the prefrontal cortex, the amygdalae and the nucleus accumbens.

EMPIRICAL RESEARCH

The physiology of emotion regulation (Wager et al. 2008)

These researches carried out a study involving three conditions. All participants took part in all three conditions. In all conditions, participants viewed images presented during fMRI scanning.

In the look/neutral condition, participants viewed neutral images. In the look/negative condition, they viewed negative images. In both of these conditions, participants were asked to look at the images and experience whatever emotional response they might elicit.

In the reappraise/negative condition, participants viewed negative images and were asked to generate positive reinterpretations of those images so as to reduce their negative emotional impact. Following presentation of each image, participants were asked to rate their emotional reaction.

Wager et al.'s findings were consistent with previous research. To start with, the reappraisal was successful in lowering the emotional impact of the negative images. Engaging in reappraisal resulted in increased activation in the prefrontal cortex. The reappraisal strategies also reduced activity in the amygdala. Moreover, the reduction of activity in the amygdala seemed to be associated with increased activity in the nucleus accumbens. Importantly, the researchers' analyses led them to the conclusion that the prefrontal cortex affects emotional regulation by means of dampening the activity in the prefrontal cortex–amygdala pathway and by increasing the activity in the prefrontal cortex–nucleus accumbens pathway.

Wager et al.'s study provides an elegant demonstration of fMRI use to chart in some detail what happens in the brain while somebody engages in a cognitive process such as cognitive reappraisal.

Wager et al. are careful to note that several other brain areas may be involved in emotion regulation. Moreover, they note that their complex findings are also consistent with additional models of precisely how the prefrontal cortex affects the amygdala and the nucleus accumbens.

Discuss the view that all fMRI studies can do is detect correlations between phenomena at the psychological and the physiological levels. This hardly qualifies as genuine knowledge about the nature of psychological phenomena.

3.11 Methods used in the cognitive level of analysis and the ethical concerns they raise

Learning outcomes
- Discuss how and why particular research methods are used at the cognitive level of analysis.
- Discuss ethical considerations related to research studies at the cognitive level of analysis.

● **Examiner's hints**
Some studies considered in this chapter were evaluated, others not. A few further examples in this section illustrate some essential points. You should use your knowledge of methodological and ethical issues to reflect on and evaluate the unevaluated empirical studies that were discussed in enough detail.

Research at the cognitive level of analysis relies on a variety of research methods. Mainstream cognitive psychology uses mostly **experimental methods**. Cognitive neuroscience combines the experimental methodology of cognitive psychology with **neurophysiological techniques** such as brain imaging. Several other methods are also used including the **computer modelling** of cognitive theories.

EXERCISES

17   What is meant by *cognitive modelling*? Research this notion and find two relevant examples.

Experimental methods

The experiment is as necessary in the cognitive level of analysis as it is in any context where explanatory theories are being tested. With its ability to detect cause-and-effect relationships between variables, the well-controlled experiment is the method of choice when we need to establish the causes of the cognitive phenomena we investigate. Experiments do not make much sense unless they are considered in the context defined by the theoretical ideas (hypotheses about causal relationships) they address.

Glanzer and Cunitz's (1966) laboratory experiment, a typical example of a cognitive experimental study, used an independent groups design to explore the effects of the independent variable (recall type) on such dependent variables as the strength of the primacy and recency effects. The logic of the experiment was such as to allow an inference to be drawn about the distinction between STS and LTS (unobservable cognitive structures) from the pattern of the objective behavioural data obtained. As a laboratory experiment, this study was high on internal validity with questions arising about its ecological validity – How often do we have to memorize lists of unrelated items?

Ethical concerns in studies like Glanzer and Cunitz's are minimal but informed consent should always be sought from the participants. Other experimental studies raise more serious ethical issues; for example, some of the experiments on eye witness testimony where criminal scenes (potentially upsetting for participants) are staged (Ihlebaek et al., 2003), or experiments where the weapons effect is investigated (Loftus et al., 1987).

Field experimental studies may increase ecological validity but this is usually at the expense of internal validity. **Cross-cultural studies**, like those investigating cultural influences on FBMs, are, in effect, natural experiments with very little, if any, control over extraneous variables. Their value derives from their high ecological validity and the meaningfulness of their findings.

Neurophysiological techniques

Neurophysiological studies are usually carried out as experiments or correlational studies. Wager et al.'s (2008) study is a good example here. The power of fMRI technology to identify the neural pathways involved in cognitive reappraisal is amazing. However, it should not be forgotten that what is established by such studies are correlations between phenomena at the psychological level and some neural activation patterns.

Despite their methodological sophistication, the fMRI studies discussed in this chapter make their contributions within the usual constraints posed by the nature of the technology used: fMRI scans are not direct photos of what is happening in the brain. The construction of the colourful images we habitually see is often based on the averaged activity of several individuals. Moreover, it is based on computer models that make complex, and often disputed, assumptions (Purves et al., 2008). Such provisos notwithstanding, there can be no doubt that fMRI technology has hugely expanded the ways we can approach the study of cognition and has already, in the hands of cognitive neuroscientists, led to considerable breakthroughs. Neurophysiological techniques are covered in more detail in Chapter 2.

Regarding ethical issues, it should be noted that scanning procedures are time-consuming and many individuals find them very uncomfortable. Potential participants should always be fully briefed and their wishes always respected.

 Although neurophysiological findings are very useful and the enthusiasm surrounding cognitive neuroscience is justified, you should not forget that moving from the biological level to consider the nature of the psychological is fraught with problems. You may wish to do some research on what, in the philosophy of mind, is called the **mind–brain problem**.

Case studies

Case studies, like the neuropsychological case studies discussed in Chapter 2 (e.g. HM), have made substantial contributions by providing in-depth information about phenomena that cannot be studied experimentally. It is not always easy to generalize from case studies, but as more and more case studies relevant to the same phenomenon accumulate and point to the same conclusions, so our confidence in those conclusions increases. Needless to say, the eagerness of scientists to investigate individuals with unusual characteristics should never lead to a situation where liberties are taken with the studied individuals' time and comfort. Finally, confidentiality and anonymity, more perhaps than in other studies, should always be promised and delivered.

Interviews

Several of the studies covered in this chapter made use of interviewing procedures. The fact that we rely on interviews in the cognitive level of analysis should not come as a surprise. The subjective data collected are not the type of introspectionistic data that led to the demise of introspectionism. Participants are not asked about the minutiae of the workings of their mind; they are asked to report on subjective experiences (e.g. FBMs) that are readily accessible and to a great extent easy to communicate to others. The value of the data collected by interviews does, of course, depend on the type of interview used, the sensitivity of the issues addressed, and the validity of the data analysis techniques employed. Likely ethical issues relate to the immediacy and power relations inherent in the types of social interaction interviewing requires, the sensitivity of what is being discussed and confidentiality issues.

In conclusion

Different methods have their respective strengths and weaknesses. It is, therefore, necessary to use triangulation – that is, apply a variety of methods to the study of the same cognitive phenomenon.

To access Worksheet 3.1 with a full example answer to short answer question 3, please visit www.pearsonbacconline.com and follow the on-screen instructions.

To access Worksheet 3.2 with a full example answer to essay question 1, please visit www.pearsonbacconline.com and follow the on-screen instructions.

PRACTICE QUESTIONS

Short answer questions

1   Outline **one** model of one cognitive process.

2   Describe **one** theory of how emotion may affect **one** cognitive process.

3   Explain how technology can be used to investigate cognitive processes.

4   Analyse how social or cultural factors affect **one** cognitive process.

Essay questions

1   Evaluate schema theory with reference to research studies.

2   Discuss the extent to which cognitive and biological factors interact in emotion.

THE SOCIOCULTURAL LEVEL OF ANALYSIS

4.1 Introduction: Historical and cultural development

Not long after Wundt and other like-minded researchers established psychology as an independent field of study towards the end of the 19th century, psychologists started addressing questions about how social influences affect thinking and action. Such questions define the field of **social psychology**. Soon after the introspectionists started studying the mind, behaviourism became the dominant force and interest in the study of mental processes waned, especially in US psychology. However, many social psychologists deviated from this general trend and went on to investigate the role of mental states (e.g. thoughts and feelings) on behaviour. Since almost the very beginning of the discipline, psychologists were studying how attitudes, personality, impressions of others and group identifications affected behaviour (Smith and Mackie, 2007).

◀ A social group.

World War II significantly influenced the emergence and development of the cognitive orientation in psychology. It also had an impact on social psychology. Many European social psychologists, acutely aware of social influences on behaviour and trained mostly in ways that still addressed internal processes and cognition, emigrated to the USA. They became involved in research exploring social influences in the regulation of behaviour. Soon, several researchers were carrying out groundbreaking studies on conformity and other social influence processes.

Another influence was an interest in explaining Nazi atrocities in terms of the prejudiced attitudes that had fuelled and supported the war. Research programmes were initiated in the USA by such interests and led to original work on prejudice, discrimination, stereotypes and, more directly, obedience As Europe recovered from the war, European psychologists started making significant contributions in many areas, including the study of how social identities form and how they affect behaviour.

The main entrance gate at Auschwitz concentration and extermination camp. How to explain what happened in Europe during World War II became an influential driver of social psychological research after the war.

Social psychology never needed a cognitive revolution. However, in the 1970s and 1980s many social psychologists started systematic use of research techniques from cognitive psychology to explore in detail how cognitive processes affect the ways individuals perceive, influence and relate to one another. The result was the birth of **social cognition** – a new approach in which cognitive theories and research techniques are used to investigate social psychological phenomena.

Other recent developments in social psychology include the increasing influence of **cultural psychology** in the last 20 years or so and, more recently, **social neuroscience**. Cultural psychologists have shown how cultural experiences are central and closely linked with social psychological functioning. Social neuroscientists address questions of how the state of the brain (for example, as captured in brain scans) relates to social thought and action.

The beginning of the 21st century finds a vibrant social psychology. One that is confident in its growing knowledge base, that influences and is influenced by both cognitive and biological orientations in psychology, and that reflects the increasing relevance of a multicultural perspective. There is a growing realization that studying psychological phenomena at the sociocultural level of analysis (i.e. addressing both their social and cultural determinants and manifestations) is both necessary and rewarding.

4.2 Principles of the sociocultural level of analysis

Learning outcomes
- Outline principles that define the sociocultural level of analysis.
- Explain how principles that define the sociocultural level of analysis may be demonstrated in research.

● **Examiner's hint**
Throughout your reading of this chapter, keep a record of all the theories and studies that are relevant to these two principles. This will enable you to achieve all relevant learning outcomes.

By far the most basic principle of social psychology is what Smith and Mackie (2007) call the 'pervasiveness of social influence'. Several other principles can follow from this, depending on what aspect of behaviour one chooses to focus on. Two important interrelated principles are:
- the social and cultural environment influences individual behaviour
- we construct our conceptions of the individual and social self.

Influence of the social and cultural environment on behaviour

Whether physically present or not, other people exert profound influences on the ways we think, feel and behave. The influences may be direct or indirect but they are always there. An example of a direct influence is when somebody makes a direct request that you behave in a particular way (e.g. a request that you participate in an energy-saving plan). We are often influenced in surprising ways by direct requests coming from others. The discussion of conformity research will familiarize you with the notion of social norms and how, in the form of internalized standards of behaviour, norms regulate our social lives. You will also see how desire to be accepted by others is so strong that, all too often, it makes us behave in ways that surprise or shock us. Moreover, our personalities are frequently set aside by the strong situational influences emanating from our social world.

Our thinking about others, especially groups of others, is almost continuously influenced by the stereotypes that our social learning has instilled in us. Not only do these socially derived structures affect us, we are often unaware that we have them.

● **Examiner's hint**
Material relevant to answering questions about the principles that define the sociocultural level of analysis appears throughout this chapter.

a

b

What processes are at work in the formation of social identities?

Concepts of the individual and social self

Our sense of self depends on the types of group we belong to and identify with. Once we categorize our social world in terms of a basic us-and-them dimension, we place ourselves at the mercy of a host of exceptionally powerful social and cognitive processes. These processes result in the formation of our social identities. These identities reflect the influence of the social on us and extensively determine our behaviour.

Some theorists distinguish between our social and personal identities. For the moment, you should note that our personal identities largely derive from social comparison processes. Moreover, as documented by social psychologists, the way we attribute success and failure and explain our behaviour in general, is often biased. This inevitably influences the ways we construct our sense of self and self-worth.

Many of the social norms that regulate our behaviour have their origin in the culture we inhabit. Growing up in the USA or the UK is not the same as growing up in China or Japan. You will look at several studies which show that anything from basic behaviours (e.g. how fast people walk in the streets) to entire life philosophies depend to a great extent on culture. In fact, several of the phenomena of social influence manifest themselves differently in different cultures. The same applies to our sense of self. The extent to which the self is defined in terms of personal characteristics or group membership is significantly affected by culture.

The rest of this chapter provides examples that can be used to show how these principles may be demonstrated in relevant research.

4.3   Sociocultural cognition

● **Examiner's hint**
Additional material relevant to the first of these learning outcomes is covered throughout this chapter.

Learning outcomes
- Describe the role of situational and dispositional factors in explaining behaviour.
- Discuss two errors in attributions.
- Evaluate social identity theory, making reference to relevant studies.
- Explain the formation of stereotypes and their effects on behaviour.

Situational and dispositional factors in the explanation of behaviour

When people go to parties what determines the extent to which they will socialize with others? Is it the kind of person they are, or the situation they find themselves in? If you think the answer is *both*, you're probably right. But psychologists differ in the importance they attribute to the two causes of behaviour.

- Dispositional causes – When attributing the cause of people's behaviour to their internal characteristics, we are making a **dispositional attribution**. The term *disposition* refers to somebody's beliefs, attitudes, and personality.
- Situational causes – When we attribute people's behaviour to external factors such as the immediate rewards and punishments in a social setting or social pressure, we are making a **situational attribution**.

In general, personality researchers tend to emphasize dispositional explanations whereas social psychologists show a preference for situational explanations.

Cross-situational consistency, behaviour stability and traits

To learn more about your own personality as assessed by the highly regarded IPIP-NEO questionnaire, go to www. pearsonhotlinks. com, enter the title or ISBN of this book and select weblink 4.1.

Personality is often defined in terms of **traits**. These are dispositions to behave in a particular way over a range of similar situations. If you are high on the trait of anxiety, for example, you will behave in an anxious manner in a variety of related settings such as exams, interviews, or when meeting new people. Thus, your anxiety exhibits **cross-situational consistency**, and it will also show **stability** over time. If you are an anxious person today, you will be an anxious person next year, the year after and, possibly, well beyond that. But is behaviour as consistent and as stable as personality theories relying on traits seem to suggest?

Mischel (1968) argued that there was far less evidence of consistency in behaviour than claimed by trait theories. According to him, behaviour depends very much on the situation in which it occurs and, therefore, its causes should be sought in the (external) situation rather than in (internal) traits. In making these claims, Mischel relies on studies that show behaviour is not consistent across situations. He cites the classic study by Hartshorne and May (1928) which showed that school children who behaved dishonestly in one school setting were not necessarily likely to be dishonest in other settings. Similarly, Mischel's own studies of student conscientiousness (Mischel, 1968) revealed a very modest correlation between students being conscientious on one occasion (e.g. attending classes on time) and being conscientious on another occasion (submitting homework on time).

Evidence of the kind reviewed by Mischel may not be as damaging to trait approaches as it would at first appear. Trait theorists do not claim that trait theory can predict behaviour

in single situations. As Epstein showed, traits should be viewed as referring to classes of behaviours over a range of different situations, not to specific behaviours in specific situations.

Epstein (1983) studied the behaviour of college students for about a month. His findings showed a lot of behavioural variability. How the participants behaved in a particular situation on one day could not predict their behaviour in similar circumstances on another day. However, when the participants' behaviour was aggregated over a 2-week interval it was highly predictive of their behaviour in similar circumstances over another 2-week interval. Such data support the existence of traits provided the appropriate time perspective is adopted. Thus, I can be happy meeting new people at work today and rather apprehensive about meeting new people at work tomorrow. But if there is a general tendency for me to be happy meeting new people at work this week, in all likelihood the same tendency will manifest itself next week. Several other studies have replicated Epstein's findings (e.g. Moskowitz, 1986).

But what about trait stability? In their meta-analysis of 152 long-term longitudinal studies, Roberts and DelVecchio (2000) found a high correlation between personality measures obtained for groups of participants at a particular point in time and the measures obtained from the same individuals seven years later. Moreover, there is plenty of evidence to suggest that significant personality changes beyond early adulthood are rare (McCrae and Costa, 2003).

The five-factor model of personality

The five-factor model (FFM) of personality (McCrae and Costa, 1999) is very popular. It claims that much of what we need to know about somebody's personality is captured by his or her standing on five measurable personality factors or traits (Table 4.1). The FFM is based on an impressive number of empirical studies and is widely accepted as a valid portrayal of personality (Chamorro–Premuzic, 2007).

● **Examiner's hint**
The five-factor model provides concrete examples of dispositions (traits) that are believed by most personality psychologists to determine behaviour.

TABLE 4.1 THE FIVE FACTORS AND SOME OF THE CHARACTERISTICS OF LOW AND HIGH SCORERS		
FFM factor	**Low scorers are:**	**High scorers are:**
Neuroticism	relaxed, even-tempered	emotional, moody, impulsive
Extraversion	reserved, serious, passive	outgoing, active, sociable
Openness to experience	down-to-earth, practical	imaginative, creative
Agreeableness	hostile, selfish, cold	kind, trusting, warm, altruistic
Conscientiousness	easygoing, unreliable, sloppy	organized, tidy, striving

There are several measures of the five factors of the FFM, including the 300-item NEO-PI (R) devised by Costa and McCrae (1992).

The FFM offers the basis of valid predictions both in research settings (McCrae and Costa, 1999) and in everyday life settings. In a recent review of the available research on real-life important outcomes, Ozer and Benet–Martinez (2006) report that personality, as captured by the FFM, relates to several real-life outcomes. These include level of happiness, physical and psychological health, and quality of relationships with peers, family, and romantic partners. Personality is also associated with occupational choice, work satisfaction, and work performance. Therefore, dispositions in the forms of personality factors emerge as significant determinants of behaviour and should be taken into consideration when trying to explain behaviour.

Although highly influential, the five-factor model has also been criticized. Some people think there may be additional factors (e.g. religiousness; Almagor et al., 1995). Others, going in the opposite direction, suggest there may not be more than three major personality factors (e.g. Eysenck, 1992).

The claim is not that personality is in general the most important determinant of behaviour, much less that we can predict with great accuracy how a particular individual

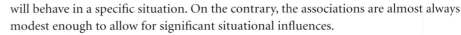

Research by Gosling (2008) uses the FFM to show how your music preferences, the way you keep your room or office, or the look of your Facebook pages reveal quite a few things about your personality.

To learn more about Gosling's research, go to www. pearsonhotlinks. com, enter the title or ISBN of this book and select weblink 4.2.

Personality matters more than most situationists believe.

In what sense is our personality 'ours'? Do we choose our personality? To the extent that we do not, can we be held morally responsible for actions (co)determined by our personality?

will behave in a specific situation. On the contrary, the associations are almost always modest enough to allow for significant situational influences.

Bandura's social-cognitive perspective on personality emphasizes the interaction of traits and situations. Bandura (1986, 2006) views the person–environment relationship in terms of **reciprocal determinism**. Traits and situations interact in several ways, including the following.

- People often choose their environment under the influence of their disposition; for instance when we choose where to live or who our friends are.
- Our personalities shape both our interpretation of events and the ways we react to them. Thus, anxious people are sensitive to potentially threatening events and tend to overreact to them (Eysenck, 1992).

So, personality and the environment interact in ways that often determine each other. In a sense, we are both influenced by and design the environments we inhabit. Most psychologists nowadays espouse some form or other of interactionism and accept that dispositions and situations co-determine behaviour. Our task, Pervin (2003) reminds us 'is not to ignore one and focus on the other, but to appreciate and understand the interplay between the two'.

Mischel (1973) had allowed for personality to play some role in the causation of behaviour. He drew a distinction between **strong situations** and **weak situations** with the latter allowing for more personality influences on behaviour. Strong situations are powerful enough to suppress individual differences. For example: when a teacher is relaxed about deadlines, a student's personality will determine to a significant extent the level of adherence to the deadlines; with a stricter teacher, personality will have less of an impact on this behaviour.

EXERCISE

1   Use examples to illustrate Bandura's notion of reciprocal determinism.

Disposition and situation in a famous social psychological study

Sabini et al. (2001) remark that if one were to ask social psychologists what has been the most important finding in social psychology since the 1940s, most would say the same thing: the finding that *situations* are much more important determinants of behaviour than is usually assumed. Two sets of studies, both addressing how different types of social influence can lead to high levels of control by situational factors, are usually discussed in this context:

- Milgram's studies of obedience to authority (Milgram, 1974)
- Asch's studies of conformity (Asch, 1951, 1956).

This section discusses Milgram's studies; conformity is discussed in detail on pages 126–133. Many of the studies discussed in this chapter refer to the importance of situations as determinants of behaviour.

EXERCISE

2   While you study the rest of this chapter, make a note of studies that demonstrate the effect of situational manipulations on behaviour.

Milgram (1963, 1974) carried out a series of 21 studies (most of them at Yale University) to investigate the extent to which participants, in the role of a teacher, would obey an

authority figure (the experimenter) to administer a series of increasingly severe, and eventually potentially lethal, electric shocks to an innocent learner. The shocks were the punishment learners were supposed to receive each time they made a mistake in a memory task. The learner was actually a confederate of the experimenter and never received any genuine shocks, but behaved as if he did.

Before carrying out his first study, Milgram described it to lay people, Yale psychiatrists and Yale psychology students. He asked them all to predict the percentage of participants they thought would obey throughout and administer the maximum punishment of 450 volts. The overall average prediction was that less than 1% of the participants would obey. Yet, the actual percentage in Milgram's first study was a disturbing 65%. One can safely assume, Milgram notes, that those asked to predict what would happen did not even suspect the real causes of the obedience behaviour in his study.

The usual social psychological explanation for Milgram's findings (e.g. Milgram, 1974) is that the participants' behaviour was under situational control (e.g. a legitimate authority's orders), rather than dispositional control (e.g. the participants' conscience). Indeed, some view Milgram's research on obedience as the most striking example of the power of situations on behaviour (Benjamin and Simpson, 2009).

Milgram himself never denied the importance of dispositional determinants of obedience. He just commented that he had not managed to identify them in his research. In a sense, this is self-evident. As Blass (1991) notes, in most obedience studies, given the same situation, one finds both obedience and disobedience taking place. Blass reviews several studies showing that individuals high on authoritarianism, for example, are more likely to obey in Milgram's experiment than those low on this personality dimension. This is hardly surprising as those with an authoritarian personality are hostile towards others and show submissiveness towards those in authority.

Sabini et al. (2001) are even more extreme in their rejection of simple situationalist explanations of Milgram's findings. They argue that virtually all the situational explanations used to account for Milgram's findings can easily be turned into dispositional explanations. Unless somebody has the disposition to obey, no obedience will occur. What happened in Milgram's experiment, from this point of view, was that the dispositions to obey, cooperate with, or be liked by the experimenter proved stronger than rival dispositions to be compassionate towards the victim or act according to one's conscience.

Be that all as it may, it is clear that Milgram's experimental setting is an example of what Mischel (1973) called a strong situation. Strong situational forces are in operation the strength of which people do not seem capable of imagining until they experience them.

The BBC replicated Milgram's experiments in 2009 with much the same results.

Attribution errors
Fundamental attribution error

Laypeople, like some psychologists, favour explanations of behaviour in terms of dispositional, rather than situational, factors. So, if people behave kindly towards us (i.e. they greet us with a smile) we conclude they have a kind personality. And if they behave in ways that seem impolite to us (i.e. they do not greet us at all) we tend to think of them as rude. Instead of acknowledging the important role played by situational determinants, we assume that other people's behaviour reflects their dispositions. To the extent that we do so, we commit the **fundamental attribution error** (**FAE**). This term refers to a bias to attribute other's behaviour to stable internal causes rather than external circumstances.

To learn more about the BBC's 2009 replication of Milgram's study, go to www. pearsonhotlinks. com, enter the title or ISBN of this book and select weblink 4.3.

Was Milgram ethically justified in carrying out his experiments on obedience? Would it be ethically justified not to carry out such research given the contribution it makes to our understanding of such an important phenomenon?

Part of the explanation of the FAE in at least some settings must be the fact that some situational influences are subtle and difficult to detect.

EMPIRICAL RESEARCH

A demonstration of the FAE (Jones and Harris, 1967)

These researchers asked their participants to read essays written by fellow students. The essays were about Fidel Castro's rule in Cuba and were either supportive or critical of Castro. The participants' task was to guess what attitude the writers of the essays really held towards Castro and his government. Half the participants were told that the essayists were free to choose whether to take a positive or a negative view about Castro in their essay (choice condition). The other half were told that the essayists did not have any choice: the experimenter had assigned them in the pro-Castro or anti-Castro role (no choice condition).

As expected, participants in the choice condition assumed that the essays reflected the genuine attitudes of their writers. However, participants' ratings seemed to indicate that those in the no choice condition also thought that the essays reflected the genuine views of their authors. So, despite the fact that it was made clear that the essayists' behaviour was severely constrained by the situation, observers still opted for an internal attribution.

EXERCISES

3   Is it likely that participants in this study simply responded to its demand characteristics?

4   How do you think you would have behaved as a participant in the no choice condition?

An experiment by Gilbert and Jones (1986) went further by demonstrating that participants would still hold speakers responsible for the views they express even when it was the participants themselves who had determined which side of the argument the speakers were allowed to argue.

The FAE has been demonstrated in many studies (Jones, 1979). Yet there is evidence to suggest that dispositional attributions are far from inevitable.

In a study by Fein et al. (1990), US students read an essay about a character called Rob Taylor. In one of the conditions, the participants were told that Rob had been assigned to write either in favour or against some view. In this condition, the expected FAE was obtained. In a second condition, participants were led to believe that Rob's essay expressed views which were very similar to those held by his professor and which, therefore, would be found pleasing by his professor. In this condition, no FAE was demonstrated. Commenting on this and other similar studies, Fein (2001) argues that we resist making dispositional attributions in situations where we suspect actors may have ulterior motives for their behaviours.

In their explanation of the FAE, Gilbert and Malone (1995) argue that it involves a two-step attribution process. When we observe some behaviour, we draw an inference, based on largely automatic and often unconscious processing, that the behaviour has been caused by some disposition. The second step is based on more controlled and conscious processing. During this step, we enquire into whether or not situational factors may have had an influence on the behaviour. We make the FAE as often as we do, Gilbert and Malone explain, for a simple reason: the first step always forms part of the attribution process, but we proceed only occasionally to the second step. In effect, the FAE happens either because we are involved in other tasks (not enough cognitive resources to think deeply about how best to explain some behaviour) or because we believe that for the behaviour under consideration the initial automatic step alone can result in the right explanation. Gilbert and Malone's two-step explanation of the FAE has received considerable experimental support.

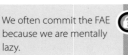

We often commit the FAE because we are mentally lazy.

Self-serving bias

Our attributions exhibit the **self-serving bias** (**SSB**) when we explain our successes on the basis of internal, dispositional factors and blame our failures to external, situational factors. Such biased attributions are viewed by many as serving the interests of preserving or increasing self-esteem.

Consider professional sport. As Lau and Russell (1980) showed, professional athletes and coaches attribute 80% of their wins to internal factors (e.g. ability, skill, professionalism). Losses are far more likely to be attributed to external factors (e.g. bad luck, unfair refereeing). Studies with students have obtained very similar findings. Bernstein et al. (1979) found that students tended to attribute their good grades to their intelligence and hard work, whereas bad grades tended to be attributed to bad teaching or bad luck.

EMPIRICAL RESEARCH

A demonstration of SSB (Johnson et al., 1964)

In this study, participants (psychology students) taught two children how to multiply numbers by 10 and by 20. The teaching was done in two phases via a one-way intercom. The first phase involved teaching the children how to multiply by 10; the second phase, how to multiply by 20. After each phase, the children's worksheets were made available to the participants to assess the learning progress of the children.

In fact, the worksheets had been marked in such a way that in both conditions, pupil A gave the right answers to all the questions on both worksheets. Depending on condition, pupil B either did badly on both tasks, or did badly on the first worksheet but improved on the second. The participants, therefore, had either failed or succeeded in teaching pupil B the two tasks.

What Johnson et al. found was that in the condition where pupil B's performance improved, participants explained the improvement as a success based on their abilities as teachers. When pupil B failed to improve, they attributed this to the pupil's lack of ability.

Although SSB is widespread, there are exceptions. We are more likely to rely on self-serving attributions when we fail in a domain *in which we cannot improve*. However, as Duval and Silvia (2002) demonstrated, we are more likely to attribute our failure to internal causes if we believe we can do something to improve the situation in the future.

The emotional state we are in also affects our reliance on SSB: being in a bad mood may reverse the attributional pattern that characterizes self-serving attributions. Furthermore, Abramson et al. (1989) demonstrated that depressed people often rely on an attributional style that attributes success to external, and failure to internal, causes.

How can the attributional style that defines SSB be explained? Zuckerman (1979) reviewed a number of studies of SSB and confirmed that the effect depends on a desire to maintain self-esteem. Evidence from cross-cultural studies is consistent with this interpretation. Heine et al. (1999), for example, found that members of collectivistic cultures (e.g. Japan) are far less likely to strive for positive self-esteem than individuals from individualistic cultures (e.g. USA). Consequently, the Japanese were found to be less likely to make self-serving attributions than Americans.

Miller and Ross (1975) proposed that several uses of self-serving attributions are rational and not based on the need to enhance self-esteem. They argue that what seem to be self-serving biases often arise because effort changes with success but not with failure. If trying harder does not improve performance, then it is reasonable to conclude that something about the task is presenting the obstacle. However, if trying harder does improve performance, then success is logically attributable to your trying.

 If we can be so wrong about ourselves how can we have any confidence when making knowledge claims in other domains?

Social identity theory

Social identity theory (SIT) was developed by Tajfel and his colleagues (e.g. Tajfel and Turner, 1979) and is based on four interrelated concepts:

- social categorization
- social identity
- social comparison
- positive distinctiveness.

Social categorization

Social categorization divides the social environment into **ingroups**, to which an individual belongs (*us*) and **outgroups**, to which the individual does not belong (*them*). Social categorization:

- reduces perceived variability within the ingroup (*we* are similar to one another)
- reduces perceived variability in the outgroup (*they* are all the same)
- increases perceived variability between the ingroup and the outgroup (*we* are different from *them*).

This exaggeration of group differences and intragroup similarities is called the **category accentuation effect**.

Social identity

Social identity is that part of our self-concept that is based on knowledge of our membership of one or more social groups. It is separate from personal identity, which is the part of the self-concept that derives from the way we perceive our personality traits and the personal relationships we have with other people (Turner, 1982). Personal identity is associated with interpersonal behaviours. Social identity is related to **intergroup behaviours**. When I relate to you interpersonally, my individual characteristics determine my behaviour. When we relate towards one another as members of separate groups, our social identities determine our behaviours. Consider competition: a pair of individuals can compete as individuals or as members of rival teams (Fiske and Taylor, 2008).

People can have several social and personal identities, reflecting the groups they identify with and the close relationships and personal characteristics that define them as individuals.

Interpersonal behaviour is different from intergroup behaviour.

Social comparison and positive distinctiveness

According to SIT, we strive for a positive self-concept. Our social identity contributes to how we feel about ourselves, so we seek positive social identities to maintain and enhance our self-esteem. Positive social identities may result from the process of **social comparison**. We continuously compare our ingroups with relevant outgroups. This social comparison process is fuelled by our need for **positive distinctiveness** (the motivation to show that our ingroup is preferable to an outgroup). By establishing the superiority of our ingroup over relevant outgroups, we make sure that our social identities, and therefore our self-esteem, are positive enough.

Intergroup behaviours based on social identities exhibit several general characteristics including the following.

- Ethnocentrism – This can be defined as an ingroup-serving bias. It is the group equivalent of SSB. It involves:
  - positive behaviours by ingroup members being attributed to dispositions
  - negative behaviours of ingroup members being attributed to situational factors
  - positive behaviours of outgroup members being attributed to situational factors
  - negative behaviours by outgroup members being attributed to dispositions.
  So, if *we* do good things it is because we are good and if we misbehave that is due to external factors. The reverse applies to *them*.
- Ingroup favouritism – Behaviour that favours one's ingroup over outgroups.
- Intergroup differentiation – Behaviour that emphasizes differences between our ingroup and outgroups.
- Stereotypical thinking – Ingroupers and outgroupers are perceived according to relevant stereotypes (pages 116–117).
- Conformity to ingroup norms – Acting in accordance to standards of behaviour defined by the ingroup (page 129).

EXERCISE

8   Use examples from everyday life to illustrate all the terms outlined above.

Studies relevant to SIT: The minimal group paradigm

SIT has been supported by many experiments using the **minimal group paradigm** introduced by Tajfel (e.g. Tajfel et al., 1971). This technique defines ingroups and outgroups on arbitrary criteria such as tossing a coin. Group members never meet or in any other way interact with one another. In fact, group members do not even know who else belongs to either their ingroup or the outgroup. That SIT is largely supported by such experiments is hardly surprising as the theory was initially developed by Tajfel and his colleagues to explain the findings from studies using the minimal group paradigm.

EMPIRICAL RESEARCH

The minimal group paradigm (Tajfel et al., 1971)

Tajfel and colleagues divided a number of British schoolboys into two groups. Although the experimenters allocated the participants randomly to the two groups, the boys were led to believe that the groups were defined on the basis of a preference for paintings by Klee or Kandinsky. The boys, working individually, had to distribute points to ingroup and outgroup members. They were not allowed to give points to themselves. The researchers were interested to see how the participants distributed the points.

continued

The boys showed a strong tendency to favour members of their ingroup over members of the outgroup, thus manifesting ingroup favouritism.

Interestingly, the boys' strategies also provided evidence for SIT's notion of positive distinctiveness. On many occasions, the boys would sacrifice gain for their ingroup in order to maximize the difference between their ingroup and outgroup. For example, when using the matrix below, participants would often give an ingroup member 7 points and an outgroup member 1, rather than giving them both 13 points as they could have done.

Points you can give to your ingroup										
7	8	9	10	11	12	13	14	15	16	17
Corresponding points you must give to the outgroup										
1	3	5	7	9	11	13	15	17	19	21

The categorization into ingroup and outgroup members was even more arbitrary and meaningless in an experiment by Billig and Tajfel (1973). Participants in this study were explicitly told that they have been assigned to either group X or group Y completely randomly. The experimental task was very similar to that used by Tajfel et al. (1971) and findings closely resembled the findings of the earlier study.

What can we conclude from these studies? In accordance with SIT, it seems that however arbitrary the categorization of participants into ingroups and outgroups, it produces:

- identification with the ingroup
- ingroup favouritism
- outgroup discrimination
- positive distinctiveness.

There are several hundred studies, including a number of cross-cultural studies, using the minimal group paradigm. Most of these support the major tenets of SIT (Hogg and Vaughan, 2008).

The minimal group effect research, however, has also been criticized. Hogg and Vaughan (2008) discussed whether it could be that the effects obtained are the result of the participants responding to demand characteristics. This is unlikely as the minimal group effect can be obtained even when the participants do not know they are being observed (Grieve and Hogg, 1999). Moreover, ingroup favouritism and outgroup discrimination have been repeatedly demonstrated in natural settings with real-life groups. Brown (1978), for example, carried out a field study of wage negotiations in a British aircraft engineering factory. He found that trade union representatives from one department sacrificed around £2 a week in order to increase their relative advantage over a competing outgroup to £1. This finding, reminiscent of Tajfel et al. (1971), clearly demonstrates positive distinctiveness.

The strength of the minimal group effect varies depending on a number of factors. Mummendey and Otten (1998) found that the effect is more powerful when participants distribute positive resources (e.g. money, points) and weaker (if present at all) with negative resources (e.g. punishment). The strength of the minimal group effect can also be reduced when participants have to justify their allocation of resources to ingroup and outgroup members (Dobbs and Crano, 2001).

Tajfel's original goal was to find what is minimally required for humans to experience that they belong to a group. He planned to then add more and more group characteristics until ingroup–outgroup biases occurred. Tajfel was very surprised to discover that arbitrary groups (e.g. groups based on meaningless categorization) already had the potential to generate the ingroup–outgroup bias.

An evaluation of SIT

Here are some of SIT's strengths.

- Starting with Tajfel's pioneering minimal group studies, SIT has been supported by hundreds of relevant empirical studies.
- SIT demonstrated the crucial role of social categorization in intergroup behaviour.
- SIT drew the distinction between personal identity and social identity and explored the ways our basic need to belong affects social interaction.
- SIT has contributed very significantly to the explanation of an impressive list of social psychological phenomena. In addition to what is discussed here, SIT has provided the theoretical basis for explanations in several other areas of social psychology such as stereotypes and stereotyping (pages 116–117) and explanations of conformity, groupthink and group polarization (pages 130–133). Importantly, it helped to explain intergroup conflict in settings where there was no realistic basis for conflict (e.g. no competition for resources).
- The original SIT theory has been expanding over the years and continues to generate a lot of research.

Here are some weaknesses of SIT.

- The self-esteem hypothesis, which figured extensively in the original statement of the theory, is no longer viewed as central to SIT. Some studies have shown that the increase in self-esteem associated with outgroup discrimination is too short-lived to have long-lasting effects on how ingroup members view themselves (Rubin and Hewstone, 1998).
- One of the expressed aims of SIT was to favour situational explanations over dispositional ones. Yet there is at least some evidence suggesting that individual differences do affect SIT processes. Platow et al. (1990), for example, found that competitive participants showed greater ingroup favouritism than cooperative participants.

Despite its shortcomings, SIT has stood the test of time and continues to make substantial contributions to our understanding of intergroup behaviour. As Hogg and Vaughan (2008) observe, the simple idea underlying SIT, namely that social categorization has extensive consequences, 'has developed and evolved over the years to become perhaps the pre-eminent contemporary social psychological analysis of group processes, intergroup relations and the collective self'.

● **Examiner's hint**
Material (theoretical ideas and studies) relevant to SIT can be found throughout this chapter.

Stereotypes

For Aronson et al. (2007), stereotypes are widely held evaluative generalizations about a group of people. Stereotypes assign similar characteristics to all members of a group, despite the fact that group members may vary widely from one another. The way stereotypes are usually defined makes them very similar to the schemas we discussed in the previous chapter. In fact, many psychologists explicitly view stereotypes as schemas. According to Augoustinos et al. (2006), 'a stereotype is a schema, with all the properties of schemas'.

Typical stereotypes are based on such obvious characteristics as gender, race or age. Sex stereotypes, for instance, are especially widespread. Fiske (1998) notes that extensive research has shown that both men and women perceive women as nice but not very competent, and men as competent but not very nice. Moreover, Williams and Best (1982) regard these stereotypes as having some cross-cultural generality as they have been detected throughout Europe, the Americas, Australia and parts of the Middle East.

Stereotypes can turn up in all sorts of places – even road signs.

Additional examples of extensively held stereotypes include age stereotypes (e.g. elderly people are slow and forgetful), ethnic stereotypes (e.g. Germans are methodical and Italians are passionate) and occupational stereotypes (e.g. accountants are conformists and artists are eccentric).

EXERCISE

9   List three stereotypes you think are prevalent in your society and relate them to the way stereotypes are defined above.

By some estimates, only 10% of the population of Western democracies hold extreme, blatantly negative stereotypes (Fiske and Taylor, 2008). However, many more are thought to harbour implicit (i.e. unconscious) racist, sexist, ageist or homophobic attitudes.

Theories of stereotype formation

Following Augoustinos et al. (2006), we discuss the following approaches to stereotype formation:

- social-cognitive theories
- social identity theory
- systems-justification theory and social-representations theory.

Social-cognitive theories

Social-cognitive theories of stereotype formation are based on the following reasoning:

- our social world is very complex and presents us with too much information
- since our capacity to process information is limited there is a need to simplify our social world
- one of the ways in which we avoid information overload is social categorization
- the categories used in social categorization are stereotypes
- stereotypes are schemas and have the following characteristics:
  - they are energy-saving devices
  - they can be automatically activated
  - they are stable and resistant to change
  - they affect behaviour.

To learn more about whether, or to what extend, you hold racist, sexist, ageist etc. attitudes, go to www.pearsonhotlinks.com, enter the title or ISBN of this book and select weblink 4.4.

Stereotypes as energy-saving devices which simplify information processing in social perception is discussed on page 73. Additional evidence of their schematic nature comes from the study by Cohen (1981) on the effects of stereotypes on memory.

Cohen presented participants with a videotape showing a woman having dinner with her husband. Half the participants were told that the woman was a waitress and the rest that she was a librarian. At a later memory test, participants showed better recall for stereotype-consistent information. Those who thought she was a waitress remembered her beer drinking. Participants who thought she was a librarian were more likely to remember that she was wearing glasses and was listening to classical music. Like the studies on the effects of schemas, Cohen's study shows that we are likely to notice and subsequently remember information which is consistent with our stereotypes.

Like all schemas, stereotypes are formed over time on the basis of relevant experiences. For Fiske and Dyer (1985), stereotype formation begins with the learning of independent schema elements. For example, the formation of a gender schema for 'female' begins with isolated elements such as 'girls dress in pink' and 'girls play with dolls' whereas, 'boys dress in blue and play with cars'. With advancing age additional elements are added, such as information about gender-appropriate behaviours and work-related preferences. Eventually, strong associations form between all the various elements and a single schema emerges. Fiske and Dyer's account is very similar to the gender-schematic processing theory of gender development (Bem, 1985) which has been supported by several studies. Once formed, repeated practice in the use of the schema may lead to such levels of integration that it can be activated automatically and unconsciously

> Fiske and Neuberg (1990) emphasize that most person impressions are primarily and initially based on categories, including stereotypes. We are likely to rely on stereotypes when we do not have time for systematic processing and we lack the cognitive resources or the motivation to think carefully and accurately. However, we are capable of more systematic and less stereotypical thinking when the situation requires it.
> Note the similarity between this theory and Gilbert and Malone's explanation of the FAE (page 108).

EMPIRICAL RESEARCH

Automatic stereotype activation (Bargh et al., 1996)

Participants in this experiment were asked to complete a test involving 30 items. This task was presented to the participants as a language proficiency task. Each of the 30 items consisted of five unrelated words. For each item participants had to use four of the five words to form, as fast as possible, a grammatically correct sentence. There were two conditions in this experiment. In one, the task contained words related to and intending to activate the elderly stereotype (e.g. grey, retired, wise). In the other condition, the words used were unrelated to the elderly stereotype (e.g. thirsty, clean, private). After completing the experimental tasks, participants were directed towards the elevator. A confederate, sitting in the corridor, timed how long the participants took to walk from the experimental room to the elevator.

Bargh et al. found that participants who had their elderly stereotype activated walked significantly more slowly towards the elevator than the rest of the participants. Priming of this stereotype must have taken place unconsciously. As Bargh et al. note, the task words did not directly relate to time or speed and no conscious awareness of the elderly stereotype was ever in evidence for the duration of the study.

 Stereotypes can be activated automatically and influence behaviour.

EXERCISES

10 Describe this study as one demonstrating some properties of schemas.

11 Does this study raise any significant ethical issues?

Several proponents of cognitive approaches to stereotypes have tried to identify the specific cognitive processes that underlie their formation.

Negative stereotypes of minority groups may be based on **illusory correlation** (the phenomenon whereby observers conclude that two factors are associated despite the lack of any real association between them). Illusory correlation was first demonstrated experimentally by Hamilton and Gifford in 1976.

EMPIRICAL RESEARCH

Illusory correlation (Hamilton and Gifford, 1976)

These researchers asked participants to read descriptions about two made-up groups (Group A and Group B). The descriptions were based on a number of positive and negative behaviours. Group A (the majority group) had twice as many members than Group B (the minority group).

In the descriptions, Group A members performed 18 positive and 8 negative behaviours. Group B members performed 9 positive and 4 negative behaviours. So, for both groups, twice as much of the information involved positive, rather than negative, behaviours. Clearly, there was no correlation between group membership and the types of behaviours exhibited by the groups. However, when asked later, participants did seem to have perceived an illusory correlation. More of the undesirable behaviours were attributed to the minority Group B, than the majority Group A.

Hamilton and Gifford's explanation of their findings is based on the idea that distinctive information draws attention. Group B members and negative behaviours are both numerically fewer and therefore more distinct than Group A members and negative behaviours. The combination of Group B members performing negative behaviours, therefore, stands out more than the combination of Group A members performing such behaviours. This causes the illusory correlation.

Members of minority groups are, of course, numerically distinctive. So are the negative behaviours (e.g. criminal acts) often attributed to them. Reviewing over 30 years of research on the link between illusory correlation and stereotype formation, Stroessner and Plaks (2001) confirmed the importance of illusory correlation in the formation of stereotypes of minority groups.

SIT theories

According to SIT, stereotype formation is based on the category accentuation effect and positive distinctiveness (pages 110–111).

Sherman et al. (2009) discuss evidence which supports one of the ways stereotypes can form according to SIT. According to such research, we pay more attention to those ingroup and outgroup members who maximize positive distinctiveness. Thus, conforming accountants will draw more attention than independently minded ones in the minds of the members of an artistically inclined group. This process is facilitated by the biased way in which ethnocentrism affects the ways we attribute positive and negative behaviours to ingroup and outgroup members. Thus, you may attribute the conformist outlook of your artistic friend to the fact that he is forced to behave like that by his job, whereas you may explain away an accountant's flamboyant dressing as his complying with directions from a domineering wife.

> You will recall that category accentuation, an outcome of social categorization, refers to the exaggeration of within-group similarities and between-group differences. Positive distinctiveness refers to the motivation to show the superiority of one's ingroup over some outgroup.

EXERCISE

12 Compare your group of friends to a relevant outgroup in ways that create as much positive distinctiveness as possible. Relate the way you carry out this task to the Sherman et al.'s SIT account of stereotype formation. Is there evidence of ethnocentricity in your comparison?

Although both are based on the notion of social categorization, there are important differences between the schema perspective and the SIT perspective. As Augoustinos et al. (2006) observe, stereotypes and stereotyping are given a whole new meaning within the SIT perspective. Some of the differences between social-cognitive and SIT views on stereotypes are listed below.

- For social-cognitive models, social categorization simplifies social perception; in SIT, it enriches social perception. Even in minimal group experiments, participants try to

make some sense of whatever trivial categories are introduced by the experimenter by elaborating on what being an ingroup or an outgroup member means in that situation (Hogg and Vaughan, 2008).

- Unlike social-cognitive accounts, SIT theorists do not think that stereotypes have a biasing effect on social perception, or that perceiving humans as individuals, rather than as members of groups, is necessarily more accurate (Oakes and Haslam, 2001). However, not all social identity theorists share such positive views about stereotypes (Abrams et al., 2005).
- Whereas social-cognitive accounts conceptualize stereotypes as stored mental schemas with a fixed content waiting to be activated, SIT predicts that stereotypes are flexible and context-dependent.

Viewing schemas as static structures awaiting activation, is not obligatory for those wishing to view stereotypes as schemas. Schemas can be dynamic and their activation can certainly reflect the context within which they are activated (Smith and Semin, 2004).

Haslam and Turner (1992) asked Australian participants to report their perceptions of Americans in contexts that encouraged comparisons either with the Soviet Union or with Iraq. When compared to the Soviets, Americans were seen as aggressive. When the comparison was with the Iraqis, they were viewed as less aggressive. It is easier to interpret such findings if one views stereotypes as flexible and changeable than as fixed pictures held by groups about each other.

EXERCISE

13 To what extent do you agree with the SIT view that viewing persons as individuals is not necessarily more accurate than perceiving them as members of a stereotype group?

The system-justification theory and the social-representations theory

For some theorists, stereotyping cannot be fully explained unless we move beyond the individual or intergroup level to address more collective societal influences on stereotype formation. For example, according to Jost and Banaji's (1994) system-justification theory (SJT), stereotypes are used to justify social and power relations in society. Examples include the distinction between the rich and the poor, the powerful and the powerless, etc.

SJT claims that social-cognitive and SIT approaches cannot explain **negative self-stereotyping** (the phenomenon of disadvantaged groups tending to internalize the negative stereotypes of themselves held by others).

EXERCISE

14 In what ways does negative stereotyping pose problems for social-cognitive and SIT explanations of stereotypes?

The **social-representations theory** (**SRT**) of Moscovici (1984) holds that social representations are the shared beliefs of the society we live in or the group to which we belong. Although social representations are social categories they are not the outcome of individual cognitive functioning (unlike the schemas of the social-cognitive theory). Rather, they are widely shared and emerge from the social and cultural life of the individual.

Moscovici argues that biases (often associated with stereotypes) are not just the result of ineffective information processing, as the social-cognitive model claims. They are based on social representations which reflect dominant preconceptions shared by extensive social groups. Moscovici (1984) puts it thus: 'When we classify a person among the neurotics, the

Jews and the poor, we are obviously not simply stating a fact but assessing and labelling him, and in so doing, we reveal our "theory" of society and of human nature.'

Both SJT and SRT are helpful in that they reinstate a feature of stereotypes that psychologists have tended to underemphasize in recent years: their negative connotations (Augoustinos et al., 2006). This is appropriate as most group stereotypes are predominantly negative (Fiske and Taylor, 2008). Recent work on stereotypes has focused more on the process of stereotyping than on their content, but several theorists continue to link stereotypes with prejudice and discrimination.

Conclusions

There can be little doubt that all the theories of stereotype formation discussed in this section have contributed significantly to our understanding of stereotype formation and the effects stereotypes have on behaviour.

Despite the often partisan way in which social-cognitive and SIT accounts of stereotype formation are discussed, these theories can be reconciled to a certain extent. Automatic stereotype activation and several of its effects on information processing and overt behaviour can be comfortably explained by the social-cognitive perspective. Moreover, this perspective is consistent with the search for specific cognitive mechanisms (e.g. illusory correlation) underlying stereotype formation. Viewing stereotypes as schemas should not necessarily lead to the conclusion that they bias social cognition in a negative manner. In fact, like other types of schematic structures stereotypes, viewed as schemas, may well contain valid representations of at least some aspects of the social groups to which they relate.

The fact that stereotypes can be flexibly involved in everyday social cognition is comfortably handled by recent SIT perspectives that view them as dynamic, rather as stable and static structures. And as we have seen, schema theory can be adapted to handle such flexibility. There can be little doubt that the SJT and the SRT act as strong reminders of the wider social, political and ideological contributions to stereotype formation and use. It should not be forgotten, however, that the writings of at least some major proponents of SIT show great awareness of some of the wider sociopolitical determinants and consequences of stereotypes (e.g. Abrams et al. 2005).

Stereotype threat: A cautionary note for everybody

Considerable interest has been shown in recent research on the effects of negative stereotype activation on performance. An example of this is research on the **stereotype threat effect** (i.e. the performance impairment that results when individuals asked to carry out a task are made aware of a negative stereotype held against them regarding their group's ability to perform well in that task). Sadly, it is very easy to obtain this effect with even the simplest of manipulations.

Spencer et al. (1999) found that simply informing female participants, before they undertook a maths test, that males usually do better in maths led to a deterioration of female performance in the test. Steele and Aronson (1995) found that the performance of African Americans in a difficult verbal task is impaired if they are asked to indicate their race before taking the test. Presumably, concern that they may be judged in the light of a negative stereotype affected their performance, possibly by increasing anxiety (Osborne, 2001).

EXERCISE
15 List all the examples of the effects of stereotypes on behaviour mentioned in this section. Note that the term *behaviour* includes overt behaviour as well as cognitive functioning (attention, perception, memory, etc.).

4.4 Social norms

● **Examiner's hint**
Research relevant to this
learning objective continues in
the next section.

Learning outcomes
- Explain social learning theory, making reference to two relevant studies.
- Discuss the use of compliance techniques.
- Evaluate research on conformity to group norms.
- Discuss factors influencing conformity.

A social norm 'is a generally accepted way of thinking, feeling, or behaving that most people in a group agree on and endorse as right and proper' (Smith and Mackie, 2007). Thus, norms provide for a group's appraisal of what is to be viewed as:
- true or false
- appropriate or inappropriate.

Given that the majority of people tend to follow norms most of the time, they are very important regulators of behaviour (Baron et al., 2008). Furthermore, by generating expectations about people's behaviour, norms make social life fairly predictable. True insights into the nature of norms are gained by reflecting on such expressions as 'a well-known fact', 'public opinion' or 'the way things are' – which are so often used in everyday speech. What people are talking about when using such expressions are social norms (Smith and Mackie, 2007).

Several social psychologists distinguish between written laws and regulations (e.g. speed limits) and social norms. They point out that deviations from social norms are punished from within relevant social groups, not the legal system (Hewstone and Martin, 2008).

Many social norms are implicit (e.g. don't stare at others for long periods of time) whereas others are explicit (e.g. the dress code in a traditional organization). Often, we may not be aware of the norms regulating our behaviour and the behaviour of others. Norms also differ with respect to how restrictive they are. Thus, norms relevant to group loyalty (e.g. talking badly about one's ingroup to others) tend to be more restrictive than norms relating to less important aspects of the group (e.g. how many hours of sleep on average group members can get at night).

EXERCISE

16 Provide examples from your everyday life of different types of norms.

Let us consider how norms are formed and transmitted and how, by setting normative standards, they affect important aspects of our social lives.

Social learning theory

Behaviouristic theories of learning are essentially theories of conditioning and emphasize the role of reinforcement in learning (page 67). Moreover, conditioning is viewed as a direct form of learning based on direct forms of reinforcement. Thus, we learn as a result of what we do and the consequences our actions have on ourselves and our environment. While acknowledging the importance of direct forms of learning, **social learning theory** (**SLT**) (Bandura, 1977, 1986) extended behaviouristic accounts of learning to allow for indirect forms of learning (**vicarious learning**) and indirect forms of reinforcement (**vicarious reinforcement**).

One form of vicarious learning is **observational learning**. In observational learning, we learn by observing and imitating others. We observe the behaviour of others (called **models**) and notice the consequences it has on them and their environments. By so doing, we learn without the need to perform the observed behaviours ourselves.

Observational learning. ▶

Bandura's views on reinforcement differ in important ways from those expressed by the behaviourists. In behaviouristic models of learning, the effects of reinforcement and punishment are automatic. In operant conditioning, as viewed by Skinner, reinforcement increases and punishment decreases (in an entirely mechanical manner) the likelihood that some behaviour will be performed again in the future. Nothing cognitive is involved. But in SLT, reinforcement is distinctly cognitive. For Bandura, reinforcement increases the ability to predict the future. We observe the relationship between actions (our own as well as those of others) and their consequences, and we form expectations which we use to control our behaviour. Finally, in a dramatic departure from behaviouristic learning theory, SLT claims that reinforcement is not necessary for learning. It is necessary for the performance of what has been learned. We return to this later.

Thus, it is clear that SLT is based on a cognitive theory of motivation and involves several distinct cognitive processes.

- Motivation – Our present behaviours are largely governed by internalized outcome expectancies.
- Attention – The model's behaviour and its consequences must be attended to by the learner. Research shows that more attractive, distinctive and powerful models are better attended to.
- Coding and memory – The behaviour of the model needs to be properly encoded and stored in the learner's memory in ways that allow both for immediate imitation or imitation that is delayed (**deferred imitation**).

In the 1980s, Bandura renamed SLT as **social cognitive theory** (**SCT**) to accommodate the ever increasing importance in his thinking of cognitive factors (Bandura, 1986). In addition to the cognitive features of SLT discussed above, SCT claims that learning extends beyond the imitation of others' behaviours to include the learning of more abstract skills, a type of learning called **abstract modelling**. Thus, we may learn the rule on which a model's behaviour is based without the rule itself being made explicit in the model's behaviour.

In addition to becoming increasingly more cognitive over the years, SLT has also been enriched by Bandura with his views about the effects of **self-efficacy** on behaviour (Bandura, 1997). This term refers to a person's belief in their own effectiveness in specific situations. If we believe in our ability to perform an action, we are more motivated to do so. Moreover, we are more likely to imitate a model performing in areas in which our sense of self-efficacy is high (Durkin, 1995).

Bandura's views on how reinforcement operates make it possible to understand how **normative standards** (i.e. criteria for acceptable behaviour in our society) become internalized. It would be impossible to learn what counts as acceptable behaviour solely by direct forms of learning. Rather, we learn the social norms that define normative standards largely by indirect learning. Moreover, the regulation of our behaviour does not require the direct presence of a reinforcing (or punishing) environment. Our knowledge of what is expected and what is appropriate is mentally represented. Such mental representations of relevant normative standards regulate our behaviour even in the absence of external reinforcement or punishment. Thus, our behaviour is largely regulated by our beliefs and expectancies rather than, as the behaviourists believed, by the external environment. Bandura does not deny the importance of the environment. After all, it is the environment which affords us the learning opportunities on which observational learning is based. His notion of reciprocal determinism (pages 105–106) points to a close interaction between persons and environments in determining behaviour.

● **Examiner's hint**
Bandura's self-efficacy notion is discussed further on pp. 246 and 288–290.

Two experimental studies of SLT

EMPIRICAL RESEARCH

Social learning of aggression (Bandura, 1965)

Bandura (1965) showed young children a film of an adult behaving aggressively towards an inflatable Bobo doll. These dolls are based on the image of Bozo the clown and always bounce back when knocked down.

The aggressive acts performed by the adult model included throwing the Bobo doll in the air, kicking it across the room and hitting it in the head with a wooden mallet. There were three experimental conditions under which the film was shown.

- Control condition – The children were shown the film with the adult behaving aggressively towards the Bobo doll.

- Model-rewarded condition – Children saw the same film used in the control condition but after the aggression was over, a second adult appeared in the film to reward the aggressor with sweets and a soft drink.

- Model-punished condition – As the model-rewarded condition, but the second adult scolded and spanked the model for behaving aggressively.

Bobo dolls are clown-like dolls with a weight in the bottom.

continued

After viewing the film, all the children were taken individually into a playroom with several toys which included a Bobo doll and a mallet. While in the playroom, the children's behaviour was observed for a period of 10 minutes and any acts of aggression similar to those performed by the model were recorded.

The control and the model-rewarded groups showed an equal level of aggressiveness towards the Bobo doll (2.5 acts). The model-punished condition was associated with significantly fewer aggressive acts (1.5 acts). However, when at a later stage the children were asked to reproduce the behaviour of the model and were rewarded for each act of aggression they displayed, they all (regardless of which original condition they were in) produced the same number of aggressive acts (3.5 acts).

EXERCISES

17   Were the children responding perhaps to the demand characteristics of the study?

18   What ethical issues are raised by this study?

Bandura's study exemplified and supported the following features of SLT.

- Vicarious (observational) learning – The children clearly learned specific aggressive behaviours by observing the adult model.
- The learning manifested during the second part of the study was based on vicarious reinforcement or punishment as the children were never rewarded or punished themselves.
- Reinforcement or punishment was necessary for performance not learning: All children behaved in an equally aggressive manner towards the Bobo doll when rewarded to do so.

Methodologically speaking, the study was a well-controlled experiment. Because the models performed aggressive acts unlikely to be part of the children's repertoire, Bandura could clearly identify acts of imitative aggression. Bandura's findings supported his theory that aggression is a learned, rather than instinctive, type of behaviour.

Despite its strengths and importance, however, Bandura's study can be criticized on a number of grounds. Questions easily arise as to the extent to which the aggression documented was real aggression. Many people would doubt that hitting an inanimate doll, especially one that bounces back with a smile after every hit, qualifies as real aggression. Were the children, perhaps, responding to the study's demand characteristics? Some of the children did say they thought they were expected to show aggression. Moreover, the fact that some aspects of aggression can be learned does not mean that all aggressive behaviour is learned behaviour.

Could mirror neurons provide a neural basis for observational learning? di Pellegrinio et al. (1992) were recording cortical activation in macaque monkeys while grasping objects from a box. As expected, the recordings, which were made by using a single neuron recording technique, showed that areas in the premotor cortex became active. To their surprise, however, the researchers noticed that the prefrontal cortex was also activated when the monkeys simply observed the experimenters grasping the objects. Direct recordings from single neurons have not been made with humans, but evidence from brain-imaging studies seem to indicate that the human motor system may be performing a mirroring function. It is not only activated when humans perform motor actions, but also when they merely observe motor actions performed by others (Rizzolatti and Craighero, 2004). Thus, research on motor neurons can help investigate possible brain mechanisms involved in observational learning.

EMPIRICAL RESEARCH

Selective imitation in 14-month-old infants (Gergely et al., 2002)

This experiment used 14-month-old infants as participants and involved two conditions.

- Hands-free condition – In this condition, the infants observed an adult place her hands on a table. Following this, she used a strange action to illuminate a light box: she bent over and pressed the box with her forehead. One week later, the same infants were given the opportunity to play with the box; 69% of them used their head to illuminate the light.

- Hands-occupied condition – Infants in this condition observed the adult perform the same strange action to illuminate the box. In this condition, however, the model was using her hands to hold a blanket around her shoulders. This rendered the hands unavailable for other actions. When given the opportunity one week later to play with the box, only 21% of the infants illuminated the light by using their head. The rest used their hands to press the light.

Discussing their findings, Gergely et al. note that in the hands-occupied condition infants seem to have assumed that the adult used her head because she had to. But this constraint did not apply to the infants. In the hands-free condition, the adult could have chosen to use her hands. She did not. The children seem to have assumed there must have been a reason for this choice, so they copied it.

Gergely et al.'s findings, which have been replicated with 12-month-old infants (Schwier et al., 2006), demonstrate that very young infants have the ability to observe a model's behaviour and infer his or her intentions and constraints on his or her behaviour. The infants then use such information to decide precisely what parts of the models' behaviour are possible or desirable to imitate. So, not only are 14- (even 12-) month-old children capable of observational learning, they also combine their basic ability to imitate with more abstract and complex forms of reasoning, much as would be expected from Bandura's increasingly cognitive SCT.

Compliance

Suppose I want to borrow your notes on brain localization. I can ask you and hope you will comply with my request. Aronson et al. (2007) define **compliance** as 'a form of social influence involving direct requests from one person to another'. Psychologists have studied several compliance techniques (i.e. tactics humans use to persuade others to comply with their appeals) (Cialdini, 2009).

Compliance techniques

The foot-in-the-door technique

If I want to persuade you to give me access to all of your psychology notes, I may start by asking if I could have a brief look at your notes on brain localization. This is an example of the foot-in-the-door (FITD) technique, a widely used compliance tactic. The FITD technique aims at increasing compliance with a large request by first asking people to go along with a smaller request. Some experimental studies of the FITD technique are discussed below.

EMPIRICAL RESEARCH

A demonstration of the FITD technique (Freedman and Fraser, 1966)

These researchers arranged for a researcher, posing as a volunteer worker, to ask a number of householders in California to allow a big ugly public-service sign reading 'Drive Carefully' to be placed in their front gardens. Only 17% of the householders complied with this request. A different set of homeowners was asked whether they would display a small 'Be a Safe Driver' sign. Nearly all of those asked agreed with this request. Two weeks later these same homeowners were asked, by

---

Observational learning, even in one-year-old infants can be an amazingly sophisticated process.

● Examiner's hints

SLT can be used to explain at least some aspects of stereotype formation (pages 113–117). Think about the role of the media, family and peers as providers of models of stereotypical thinking and behaviour. Reflect on the ways stereotype formation may be based on such models.

continued

a 'volunteer worker', whether they would display the much bigger and ugly 'Drive Carefully' sign in their front gardens. 76% of them complied with this second request, a far higher percentage than the 17% who had complied in the first condition.

In a second study, Freedman and Fraser (1966) first asked a number of householders to sign a petition in favour of keeping California beautiful, something nearly everybody agreed to do. After two weeks, they send a new 'volunteer worker' who asked these homeowners whether they would allow the big and ugly 'Drive Carefully' sign of the previous study to be displayed in their front gardens. Note that the two requests relate to completely different topics, but nearly half of the homeowners agreed with the second request. Again, this is significantly higher than the 17% of homeowners who agreed to display the sign in the absence of any prior contact.

EXERCISES

19 Comment on the internal validity of this field-experimental study.

20 Is the study high on ecological validity?

How could such findings be explained? The answer, according to Cialdini (2009), lies in the twin notions of **consistency** and **commitment**. Many psychologists have commented on our desire to be consistent with our beliefs, attitudes, and actions. It is crucial in the case of compliance to secure an initial commitment because people are more willing to agree to requests that are consistent with a prior commitment (Cialdini, 2009).

But, how could the findings of the second experiment be explained? According to Freedman and Fraser (1966), signing the petition changed the view the homeowners had about themselves. As a result, they saw themselves as unselfish citizens with well-developed civic principles. Agreeing, two weeks later, to display the 'Drive Carefully' sign reflected their need to comply with their newly-formed self-image. Not only do commitments change us but also, to use Gialdini's own expression, they 'grow their own legs'.

Be careful with commitments – they grow their own legs.

Several studies have replicated and extended Freedman and Fraser's original studies of the FITD technique. Some of the relevant findings are outlined below as they demonstrate how FITD has, or can be, used to bring about compliance.
- Initial requests should not be so large that people will refuse them (Burger, 1999).
- FITD requires a delay between the initial request and the later larger one (Burger, 1999).
- When the same person makes both requests, it is difficult to get compliance (Chartrand et al., 1999).
- People with a high degree of consistency show bigger FITD effects (Cialdini et al., 1999).

As Cialdini (2009) notes, the FITD technique is particularly helpful to those trying to solicit donations of time, money, effort, and even body parts. The studies discussed below testify to its extensive use by both charitable and business organizations.

Sherman (1980) called residents in Indiana (USA) and asked them if, hypothetically, they would volunteer to spend 3 hours collecting for the American Cancer Society. Three days later, a second experimenter called the same people and actually requested help for this organization. Of those responding to the earlier request, 31% agreed to help. This is much higher than the 4% of a similar group of people who volunteered to help when approached directly.

Dolin and Booth–Butterfield (1995) found that an FITD manipulation during a health fair at a shopping mall increased compliance with a request to schedule a gynaecological examination. Using the FITD technique has also been shown to increase blood donations (Lipsitz et al., 1989) and the willingness to be an organ donor (Girandola, 2002).

Meineri and Gueguen (2008) used an FITD technique to motivate people in France to take part in a demanding energy-conservation project. For a randomly selected half of the participating households, the request was preceded by a telephone call asking them to answer a short questionnaire on environmental issues. A higher percentage of households receiving the telephone call before the request agreed to participate in the energy-saving project.

Lowballing

Consider the following example. A car salesman offers a customer a good deal. After the customer accepts it, the salesperson finds an excuse to change the deal and make it less attractive to the customer. Very often customers in such situations agree to the new, less desirable deal. The compliance technique used in this example is called lowballing. It involves changing an offer to make it less attractive to the target person after this person has agreed to it.

EMPIRICAL RESEARCH

A demonstration of lowballing (Burger and Cornelius, 2003)

In this study, students were contacted by phone by a female caller and asked whether they would be prepared to donate five dollars to a scholarship fund for underprivileged students. There were three experimental conditions.

- The lowball condition – Students were told that those who contributed would receive a coupon for a free smoothie at a local juice bar. Students who agreed were then informed that the investigator realized she had run out of coupons. The students were asked if they would still be willing to contribute. 77.6% agreed to make a donation in this condition.

- The interrupt condition – The caller made the same initial request as in the lowball condition. However, before the participants had a chance to give their answer, the caller interrupted them to let them know that there were no more coupons left. Only 16% of the participants made a donation in this condition.

- The control condition – Participants were simply asked to donate the five dollars without any mention of coupons. 42% made a donation in the control condition.

The results support the view that the lowball technique is based on the principle of commitment. The technique is effective only when individuals make an initial public commitment. Once they have made this commitment, individuals feel obliged to act in accordance with it even when the conditions that led to them making the commitment have changed (Cialdini, 2009).

An impressive study by Palak et al. (1980) shows how lowballing can be used in an important real-life setting. These investigators first asked Iowa (USA) householders to conserve energy by providing them with energy-conservation tips and encouraging them to try to save fuel (natural gas). This did not achieve any savings. Following this, a different sample of householders was contacted by the interviewer. This time, in addition to the request as made to the first group, homeowners were told that those who agreed to save energy would have their names published in newspaper articles describing them as good, fuel-conserving citizens. One month later, this manipulation resulted in an average saving of 12.2% of natural gas. At this stage, the homeowners received a letter informing them that it would not be possible to publish their names in the local press after all. For the remaining winter months, these families saved 15.5% of natural gas – more than when they thought they would have their names published in the local press.

The homeowners went on saving because the commitment had 'grown its own legs'. When the offer of publicity was withdrawn, they were able to take fuller ownership for their commitment and view themselves as fully committed to energy-saving. Cialdini (2009)

claims this new self-image increased their resolve to go on saving and may explain the increased savings after receipt of the letter telling them there would be no publicity.

Which is the more effective technique?

Hornik et al. (1990) compared the effectiveness of the FITD technique and lowballing in increasing the response rate of randomly selected Israelis to telephone interviews on public health issues. Their results showed that whereas both techniques were effective, lowballing was significantly more effective in inducing compliance among the participants. Interestingly, a technique combining both the FITD and the lowballing techniques emerged as even more effective than either applied alone.

EXERCISES
21 List various uses of the FITD and the lowballing techniques and indicate the psychological principles on which they are based.
22 What ethical issues are raised by the use of compliance techniques like FITD and lowballing?

Conformity

Most definitions of conformity refer to social norms. According to Baron et al. (2008), conformity is 'a type of social influence in which individuals change their attitudes or behaviour to adhere to existing social norms'. A distinction is usually drawn between **private conformity**, which is the private acceptance of social norms, and **public conformity,** which is overt behaviour consistent with social norms that are not privately accepted (Smith and Mackie, 2007).

Studies of conformity

The following empirical research boxes describe three characteristic experimental studies of conformity each reflecting a different type of influence.

EMPIRICAL RESEARCH
Norm-formation and conformity in an ambiguous situation (Sherif, 1935)
This study relies on the autokinetic effect – an optical illusion that makes a stationary light appear to move when seen in complete darkness. Participants were led to believe that the experiment was investigating visual perception and told the experimenter was going to move the light, something that was never done. They had to make 100 judgements as to how far the light, placed on the far wall of a darkened room, seemed to have moved.
To start with, participants made their judgements alone. Their estimates fluctuated for some time before converging towards a standard estimate, a **personal norm**. Such personal norms varied considerably between participants. In further sessions of 100 trials on subsequent days, the participants were joined by two other participants. They took turns in a random order to call out their estimates about the light's movement. In this group condition, participants' estimates soon reflected the influence of estimates from the others in the group. Eventually, a common group norm emerged, a **social norm**, which was the average of the individual estimates. Different groups formed different group norms. Interestingly, the participants denied that their estimates were influenced by the other group members. During a third phase of the study, participants performed the task alone again; their estimates showed a continued adherence to the social norm established during the group session.

EXERCISES

23 In what sense do participants in the group condition constitute a real group?

24 What is the importance of the finding that the participants continued following the social norm well after the other group members had been removed?

Sherif demonstrated conformity in a setting where the stimulus was ambiguous. But could conformity be demonstrated with an easy task using completely unambiguous stimuli? This is the question addressed in a series of famous experiments by Asch.

EMPIRICAL RESEARCH

Conformity in a non-ambiguous situation (Asch, 1951)

In his conformity studies, Asch made extensive use of an experimental technique which has come to be known as the Asch paradigm. Participants, who think they are taking part in a study of visual perception, are asked to indicate which one of three comparison lines is equal in length to a standard line. This task is repeated 18 times. On each one of these times (called trials) different cards, showing lines of different lengths, are used but the logic of the task remains the same. This task is so easy that when participants perform it alone (the control condition) they are nearly always right.

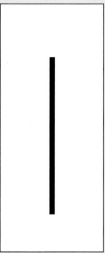
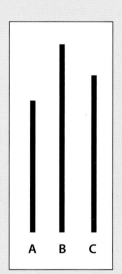

A B C

Solomon Eliot Asch (1907–96) and some trial cards from his experiment.

In the main condition of the study, the participants state their answers aloud in the presence of people they think are six other participants. However, the others are confederates of the experimenter and they behave in a way prearranged by the experimenter. Confederates gave the wrong answer on 12 out of the 18 trials. The genuine participants were always the last but one to answer. The set of 18 trials was repeated many times, each time testing a different genuine participant.

Participants conformed. They went along with the wrong answer given by the majority on nearly 37% of the critical trials; 76% of participants conformed on at least one critical trial ; only 24% of participants remained independent throughout the experiment.

After the experiment, Asch asked participants to explain their conformity; most said they had conformed in order to avoid criticism and social disapproval.

EXERCISES

25 Is this a good demonstration of the power of situational determinants on behaviour?

26 What ethical issues does this experiment raise?

Do ingroups cause more conformity than outgroups? This is the question addressed in a series of studies by Abrams et al.

EMPIRICAL RESEARCH

Ingroups cause more conformity than outgroups (Abrams et al., 1990)

These researchers replicated Asch's experiment with psychology students using three confederates. Depending on condition, genuine participants were either led to believe that the confederates were, like themselves, psychology students from a neighbouring university (ingroup condition), or ancient history students from the same neighbouring university.

The 18-trial sequence consisted of 9 correct and 9 incorrect responses by the confederates, presented in a random order. For the part of the experiment reported here, all four group members responded publicly. 100% of the participants conformed at least once when they thought the confederates belonged to their ingroup. The corresponding percentage for those participants who thought the confederates belonged to an outgroup was only 50%.

Abrams et al.'s study shows that we are far more influenced by groups we feel we belong to than by groups we consider as outgroups.

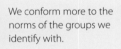

To access Additional information 4.1 on a real-life conformity study by Salganik et al. (2006), please visit www. pearsonbacconline.com and follow the on-screen instructions.

Explanations of conformity

Three social influence processes have been postulated to explain conformity:

We conform more to the norms of the groups we identify with.

- informational influence
- normative influence
- referent informational influence.

Informational influence

We are subjected to **informational influence** when we accept the views and attitudes of others as valid evidence about how things are in a particular situation. Having an accurate perception of reality is, of course, essential for our efficient functioning in our environment. Others are often viewed as valid sources of information, especially in settings where we cannot on our own test the validity of our perceptions, beliefs and feelings.

Informational influence seems to be the most likely explanation for Sherif's (1935) findings. Because reality was ambiguous, participants used other people's estimates as information to remove the ambiguity. Informational influence tends to produce genuine change in people's beliefs thus leading to private conformity. Sherif's work is important because it demonstrates how, at least in ambiguous settings, social norms can develop and become internalized (that is, function without the need of the actual presence of others).

Normative influence

Normative influence underlies our conformity to the expectations of others. This type of influence is based on our need to be liked and be accepted by others. In fear of social disapproval and rejection, we often behave in ways that conform to what others expect of us with little concern about the accuracy of the beliefs we express or the soundness of our actions.

Normative influence was the most likely cause of conformity in Asch's experiment (Asch, 1951). The stimuli used in that experiment were unambiguous and there was no need

for disambiguating information. Moreover, the participants' behaviour was, at all times, public and under the surveillance of the group. Finally, most participants explained their conformity in terms of the desire to be accepted by the rest of the group.

Dual-process models

Explanations of conformity based on informational and normative types of social influence have been popular since the 1950s (e.g. Deutsch and Gerrard, 1955). Models of conformity based on these two types of influence have been called **dual-process models**. In simple terms, according to the dual-process model, people conform because they want to be right and they want to be liked. This model has received support from a very large number of conformity studies including the experiments by Sherif and Asch discussed earlier. Such models have been criticized, however, especially by those trying to explain conformity from within a SIT perspective.

Referent informational influence

The notion of **referent informational influence**, introduced by social identity theorists (e.g. Turner, 1981), forms the basis of SIT explanations of conformity. From an SIT perspective, conformity is not simply a matter of adhering to just any social norms; it has more to do with adhering to a person's ingroup norms. We conform out of a sense of belongingness and by so doing we form and maintain desired social identities. It follows from this that we are far more likely to conform to the norms of groups we believe we belong to and identify with.

Referent informational influence differs from normative and informational influence in a number of ways, including the following two identified by Hogg (2010).

- People conform because they are group members, not to validate physical reality or avoid social disapproval as dual-process models suggest.
- People conform not to other people but to a norm. They use other people simply as a source of information about what the appropriate ingroup norm is in a particular setting.

The study by Abrams et al. (1990), based on Asch's experimental procedures, provides clear support for the SIT explanation of conformity. The researchers clearly demonstrated that the impact of confederates on norm formation and conformity depended on the extent to which they were viewed by the genuine participants as ingroup members.

Dispositional and situational explanations of conformity

Hogg and Vaughan (2008) suggest that studies by several investigators have identified several dispositional characteristics associated with increased conformity:

- low self-esteem
- high need for social support and approval
- high anxiety
- feelings of low status in the group.

While acknowledging the role of dispositional factors, most social psychologists emphasize what they think is of even greater importance: the situational determinants of conformity.

We have already seen that high levels of conformity are obtained even in settings involving no ambiguity and involving tasks of an exceedingly easy nature. Asch's conformity studies are viewed by many as exemplary cases of situational control of behaviour (Sabini et al., 2001). It is certainly surprising that as many as 76% of participants in the Asch study showed some conformity in a situation involving a completely unambiguous and easy task. Additional support for the situational perspective is provided by studies that show how easy it is to vary conformity levels by manipulating situational variables like group size and social support.

To access Additional information 4.2 on using fMRI technology to identify neural correlates of conformity, please visit www.pearsonbacconline.com and follow the on-screen instructions.

 To learn more about how all three levels of analysis can be integrated in research (paper by Berns et al., 2005), go to www.pearsonhotlinks.com, enter the title or ISBN of this book and select weblink 4.5.

● **Examiner's hints**
The examples of dispositional and situational determinants of conformity outlined here supplement those discussed on pages 104–107).

 To what extent do scientists conform to what their colleagues are saying and doing rather than independently arriving at their own conclusions?

EXERCISES

27   Research the role of group size and social support in conformity.

28   Can you make the case for a dispositional explanation of Asch's conformity findings based on Sabini et. al.'s (2003) similar treatment of Milgram's findings (page 107)?

Additional factors affecting conformity

This section discusses risky shift and group polarization, and groupthink. Culture as an influence on conformity is discussed on pages 135–137.

Risky shift and group polarization

Do individuals working as a group and asked to reach consensus make riskier decisions than the same individuals working on their own?

EMPIRICAL RESEARCH

A study of the risky shift (Wallach et al., 1962)

These researchers asked their participants to complete the Choice Dilemmas Questionnaire. This involves a series of 12 stories in each of which the main character faces a dilemma with two options, one riskier than the other. An example of such a dilemma is illustrated below.

> A low-ranked participant in a national chess tournament, playing an early match against a highly favoured opponent, has a choice of attempting or not attempting a deceptive but risky manoeuvre that might lead to quick victory if it is successful or almost certain defeat if it fails. Indicate the lowest probability of success that you would accept before recommending that the chess player play the risky move.
>
> _____ 1 chance in 10 of succeeding
>
> _____ 3 chances in 10 of succeeding
>
> _____ 5 chances in 10 of succeeding
>
> _____ 7 chances in 10 of succeeding
>
> _____ 9 chances in 10 of succeeding
>
> _____ I would not recommend the alternative no matter how high its likelihood of success.

During the first phase of the experiment participants worked individually. In a second phase they worked as a group and were asked to arrive at a unanimous decision for each of the dilemmas. Wallach et al.'s findings indicated that the options chosen in the group condition were riskier than those chosen by the individuals working alone.

The phenomenon demonstrated by the Wallach et al. study was initially called the **risky shift** – a term that refers to the tendency for group discussions to produce riskier decisions than those reached by group members working on their own. However, later research demonstrated that group decisions are not inevitably riskier. The risky shift is only an example of the wider phenomenon of **group polarization**. This term refers to the tendency for groups to make decisions that are *more extreme* than the decisions members make on their own. This means riskier group decisions if the members' initial tendency is to be risky, or more cautious group decisions in those cases where the members' initial tendency is to be cautious. So, group decisions tend to be polarized in the direction favoured by the individual members' initial positions. Myers and Bishop (1970), for example, found that groups of racial liberals became more liberal on race-related issues following discussion. Groups of racial conservatives, on the other hand, polarized in the opposite direction.

Groups often adopt more extreme positions than those of their members.

Several theories have been proposed to explain group polarization.

Social comparison theory

According to the **social comparison theory** (Jellison and Arkin, 1977), group discussions make public the prevailing social norms, including norms indicating whether the group favours risky or cautious decisions. As a result of normative influences, group members seeking acceptance by the group, shift their initial views in the direction of the group social norms. Group polarization seems to be an outcome in settings where, in addition to satisfying their conformity needs, some individuals also attempt to satisfy their need to stand out. Support for the overall direction of the group's position ensures that such individuals are accepted by the group. At the same time, they register their individuality by exaggerating in the direction of the emerging consensus position. Given time, the outcome will be a group norm that is more extreme than the average of the group members' initial positions.

Several studies support this explanation but it should be noted that polarization effects have been obtained in settings where the absence of surveillance removes the type of normative influence required by the social comparison theory (Goethals and Zanna, 1979).

Social identity theory

The social identity theory of polarization (Turner and Oakes, 1989) treats polarization as a regular conformity phenomenon. The ingroup–outgroup distinction, an outcome of social categorization, is crucial here. According to SIT, relevant group norms are not arrived at in a vacuum; they are constructed from the positions held by ingroup members in relation to positions assumed to be held by outgroup members. In accordance with the category accentuation effect, the emerging norms minimize variability in the ingroup and maximize the distinction between the ingroup and outgroups. Norms will, therefore, be polarized away from target outgroups. Research supports this perspective in confirming that norms can be polarized in the interests of securing positive distinctiveness (Hogg et al., 1990).

● **Examiner's hint**
Make sure you add this explanation to your coverage of SIT.

Relevance of group polarization to discussions of conformity

The factors involved in group polarization include:
- a strong, and often explicit, need to reach consensus
- a preference, within the group, for the same side of an argument.

Baron (2005) claims (and is supported by relevant studies such as David and Turner, 1996) that given these two preconditions, both informational and normative influences will be intensified. If social identity factors also become involved, then social identification processes further strengthen the chances and magnitude of group polarization. So, a third factor, linking group polarization to conformity is:
- an ingroup social identity defined in relation to an outgroup.

In a nutshell, the factors that contribute to group polarization act as conformity magnifiers.

Groupthink

Reflecting on the 1961 ill-fated plan to invade Cuba with 1000 Cuban exiles, President John F. Kennedy wondered: *How could we have been so stupid?* Janis (1972) thought he had the answer to the President's question. He used an archival method to study retrospective accounts provided by those close to the decision-making process in the case of the Cuban invasion and a number of other US foreign policy decisions. It did not take him long to claim that stupidity was not the explanation.

According to Janis, the cases that had disastrous outcomes had certain features in common including:

- high group cohesiveness – group members were closely bonded
- decisional urgency – groups were under pressure to make fast decisions
- need for consensus – there was such an overriding need to reach a consensus that groups cared more about reaching one than how they did it.

Janis (1972) used the term **groupthink** to describe the defective group decision-making process that led to the poor decisions. Groupthink refers to a thinking style in highly cohesive groups where the desire to reach unanimous agreement is so strong that it overrides the motivation to use appropriate decision-making procedures. Typical groupthink outcomes include:

Groupthink does not lead to good decision-making.

- a strong tendency to maintain group cohesion and force conformity by suppressing independent thinking and downplaying disagreements
- exaggeration of the prospects of success and belittling of any talk of serious risks to the group
- a perception of the group as superior and invulnerable and perception of outgroups in negative and stereotypical ways.

Janis's account of groupthink has been very influential. Moreover, few if any, doubt that groupthink is a real and quite common phenomenon (Baron, 2005). However, evidence from relevant studies, especially experimental studies, is not always consistent with Janis's own portrayal of groupthink phenomena.

Case studies and content analyses of naturalistic group decision-making studies of groupthink tend to be supportive of at least some aspects of the Janis model. Consider the space shuttle accident in which *Challenger* exploded in 1986, 73 seconds after launch. Esser and Lindoerfer (1989) analysed 88 statements clearly indicative of groupthink processes which they identified in the report of the Presidential Commission on the Space Shuttle Challenger Accident. They discovered little evidence for the importance of group cohesion as defined by mutual attraction among the group members. They did, however, find evidence for the importance of stress and did detect a number of groupthink symptoms including illusion of invulnerability, illusion of unanimity and pressure on dissenters.

Janis's account of groupthink has not received unequivocal support from experimental studies (Baron, 2005). Importantly, studies of cohesiveness have produced mixed results with only some of the relevant studies obtaining the expected positive relationship between cohesiveness and groupthink. However, working from within a SIT perspective, Turner et al. (1992) claim cohesion should not be conceptualized in terms of how group members, as individuals, feel about one another. It should be defined at the group-level. Hogg and Hains (1998) have provided experimental support for this analysis. In a study of four-person discussion groups, they found that groupthink was associated with cohesiveness based on group-based liking but not cohesiveness based on interpersonal attraction.

Turner et al. (1992) view groupthink as a process by which ingroup members attempt to maintain a positive view of their group in the face of threat. In groupthink situations, we find group members sharing information in accordance with their social (not personal) identities. This is another way to say they conform to prevailing group norms. The need to reach and maintain consensus can be very strongly expressed in such settings. Again, social identification strengthens the impact of both informational and normative influence (Baron, 2005) thus intensifying whatever conformity pressures may be present.

Relevance of groupthink to discussions of conformity

This discussion of groupthink has identified a number of factors that can affect conformity in group-decision settings:
- strong need to reach consensus
- decisional urgency
- high group cohesiveness especially when defined in terms of social identification, rather than interpersonal liking.

These factors are not that different from those involved in group polarization. In fact, according to Baron (2005), the two phenomena are not that different from one another. However, they have typically been studied in situations involving rather different situational determinants. In groupthink, for example, high levels of social identification are more often than not the case. In typical case studies, this is also accompanied by decisional urgency.

In fact, if one formed genuine groups, allowed for discussion and insisted on consensus in typical conformity studies, one would get very close to the types of conformity involved in group polarization and groupthink.

Highly cohesive groups under pressure often rely on very defective decision-making tactics.

4.5 Cultural norms

Learning outcomes
- Define the terms *culture* and *cultural norms*.
- Examine the role of two cultural dimensions on behaviour.

Definitions of culture and cultural norms

There is no single generally accepted definition of culture. The two definitions quoted below seem to capture most of what is meant by this term.
- 'A set of attitudes, behaviours and symbols shared by a large group of people and usually communicated from one generation to the next' (Shiraev and Levy, 2004).
- 'A unique meaning and information system, shared by a group and transmitted across generations, that allows the group to meet basic needs of survival, pursue happiness and well-being, and derive meaning from life' (Matsumoto and Juang, 2008).

Both definitions state that culture is transmitted from generation to generation.

Shiraev and Levy's definition refers to (cultural) attitudes, behaviours and symbols, terms which they explain as follows.
- Attitudes include beliefs (for example, political, religious and moral beliefs), values, superstitions, and stereotypes.
- Behaviours include norms, customs, traditions and fashions.
- Symbols can be words, gestures, pictures, or objects that carry a meaning which is recognized only by those who share a particular culture.

29   Illustrate important aspects of your culture by giving examples of characteristic cultural attitudes, behaviours and symbols.

Matsumoto and Juang's definition makes reference to some of the essential functions of culture.

- Culture makes it possible for people to interact with other people to produce food, procreate and develop the knowledge, skills and tools needed to protect themselves from their environment.
- Culture provides for the formation of complex social networks and relationships. It enables the production, appreciation and use of art, science and mathematics.

Different cultures produce different expressions in art and architecture around the world. ▶

Triandis (2002) distinguishes between **objective culture** and **subjective culture**. Objective culture involves visible characteristics such as dress styles, use of various technologies and cuisine. Subjective culture, on the other hand, refers to the beliefs, norms and values groups consider important enough to pass on to future generations. They include moral codes, religious beliefs and social etiquette.

Drawing from definitions of social norms and definitions of culture, we can define **cultural norms** as the norms of an established group which are transmitted across generations and regulate behaviour in accordance with the group's beliefs about acceptable and unacceptable ways of thinking, feeling and behaving.

It thus becomes clear that cultural norms are a special kind of social norm. In cultural norms, the social dimension extends to cover wider social groups (e.g. entire ethnic groups) compared to other types of social norm (e.g. one's peer group). Cultural norms, more than non-cultural social norms, often contribute to what for many is a more fundamental and longer lasting sense of social identity (e.g. ethnic identity). One may wish to also define **(sub)cultural** norms to refer to cultural subunits such as the tribes, social classes and castes one finds within the same nation. Other (sub)cultural norms may regulate behaviour in such (sub)cultures as particular organizations, naturists, hippies, cults, criminal gangs, etc. The discussion that follows does not address culture at this lower level of generality.

Cultural dimensions of behaviour

● **Examiner's hints**
This discussion is relevant to the discussions of compliance (pages 123–126) and conformity (pages 126–133).

The discussion below on how individualism/collectivism influences conformity and compliance is also relevant to earlier discussions of these topics.

Hofstede's pioneering research of the work-related attitudes and values of IBM employees in 40 different countries has been used extensively to understand national culture in general (Hofstede, 1984). By 2001, Hofstede had data on 72 countries (Hofstede, 2001).

His analysis of this impressive bulk of cross-cultural information over the years led to the identification by 1984 of four major work-related values. In 2001, Hofstede added a fifth.

- Individualism/collectivism – In individualistic cultures identity is defined by personal characteristics (e.g. individual choices and achievements). In more collectivistic societies identity is defined more by the characteristics of the collective groups to which one belongs.
- Power distance – This refers to the extent to which different cultures promote and legitimize power and status differences between individuals. In high power distance cultures, less-powerful members learn to accept inequalities in the distribution of power as natural.
- Uncertainty avoidance – Members of cultures high on this dimension feel more threatened and anxious by the unknown or ambiguous situations than those coming from low uncertainty avoidance cultures.
- Masculinity/femininity – High masculinity cultures are characterized by an emphasis on achievement, success and possessions. High femininity cultures emphasize interpersonal harmony, taking care of others and quality of life. The dimension also refers to the extent to which cultures promote differences between the sexes.
- Long-term or short-term orientation or Confucian dynamism – This is the dimension Hofstede added in 2001. It reflects the extent to which a culture has a dynamic future-orientated mentality and refers to the degree to which a culture encourages delayed gratification of material, social and emotional needs among its members.

Individualism/collectivism

We have already defined the terms individualism and collectivism as used by Hofstede. Cultures differ with respect to how they socialize their members to develop identities that are either individually or collectively based. In individualistic cultures:
- the personal is emphasized more than the social
- persons are viewed as unique
- individual autonomy and self-expression are valued
- competitiveness and self-sufficiency are highly regarded.

Societies high on collectivism are characterized by giving priority to the goals of important groups (e.g. extended family, work group) and define one's identity on the basis of one's membership of such groups. So, in collectivist cultures:
- the social is emphasized more than the personal
- the self is defined by long-standing relationships and obligations
- individual autonomy and self-expression are not encouraged
- there is more of an emphasis on achieving group harmony rather than on individual achievement.

It is not that members of individualistic societies do not have the need to belong or that their identities are exclusively personal identities. SIT was after all developed in individualistic counties (e.g. UK, Australia) to explain primarily the behaviour of members of those societies. However, they are *less focused* on group harmony or doing their duty for the types of mostly traditional groups (e.g. family) that collectivist societies are based on (Brewer and Chen, 2007).

To learn more about your country's standing on Hofstede's dimensions, go to www. pearsonhotlinks. com, enter the title or ISBN of this book and select weblink 4.6.
You can also find the three highest- and three lowest-scoring countries on each of Hofstede's dimensions.

● **Examiner's hint**
Additional material on individualism/collectivism can be found in Chapter 3, page 95).

Examples of cultures usually classified as individualist include north American countries (USA, Canada), western European countries (e.g. UK, Germany), Australia and New Zealand. Collectivist cultures include several Asian countries, for example, China and Japan. Several authors are at great pains to emphasize that the individualist/collectivist culture distinction is one of degree, with countries tending to adopt more or less extreme positions on these dimensions. Moreover, there is diversity within the same culture. There are many individuals with collectivist values in places like the USA, and there are substantial numbers of individualists in Japan.

Individualism/collectivism and compliance

Research has shown that in collectivistic cultures, people are less likely than those in individualist cultures to behave consistently with their personal choices and earlier commitments (Heine and Lehman, 1997). When viewed in the context of Cialdini's explanation of the foot-in-the-door (FITD) technique (page 123), such findings lead to the hypothesis that collectivists show lower levels of compliance than individualists when this technique is used.

EXERCISE

30   Explain in some detail the reasoning that leads from Cialdini's consistency-based explanation of the FITD technique to the prediction that collectivists will be less likely to show the FITD effect.

EMPIRICAL RESEARCH

Collectivists show lower levels of compliance than individualists when the FITD technique is used (Petrova et al., 2007)

This hypothesis was tested in a field experiment–experimental study by Petrova et al. (2007). Their study involved over 3000 students at a US university. Nearly half were native US students and the rest were Asian students at the same university. All were sent an e-mail asking them to participate in a survey. A month later, the students received a second e-mail asking them whether they would agree to take part in an online survey.

The researchers found that the proportion of students agreeing to the first request was higher among the Asian students than it was among the US students. However, compliance with the first request had a stronger impact on compliance with the second request among the US students than among the Asian students. In fact, the proportion of US students who agreed to the second request (having previously agreed to the first) was twice as high as it was among the Asian students. This is a positive example of the FITD effect among the US students (i.e. students from an individualist culture).

EXERCISE

31   Discuss possible methodological problems of Petrova et al.'s study.

Cialdini et al. (1999), however, suggested that individuals from collectivist cultures may be more sensitive to information about the compliance histories of other members of their groups rather than their own compliance history. It follows from this that in collectivistic cultures, one would perhaps be more successful in gaining compliance by presenting participants with information that others, belonging to the same group as themselves, have complied in the past.

Individualism/collectivism and conformity

Bond and Smith (1996) carried out a meta-analysis of 133 conformity studies all using the Asch paradigm. The studies were carried out in 17 countries. The meta-analysis showed that more conformity was obtained in collectivistic countries like the Fiji Islands, Hong Kong and Brazil than in individualistic countries like the USA, the UK or France (Table 4.2).

 For a definition of meta-analysis, see key fact box on page 75.

TABLE 4.2 BOND AND SMITH'S META-ANALYSIS OF CONFORMITY STUDIES

Ranked size of conformity effects (rank 1 relates to the highest effect)		Number of studies
1	Fiji	2
2	Hong Kong	1
3	Zimbabwe, Ghana, DR Congo	3
6	Brazil	3
7	Japan	5
8	Canada	1
9	Kuwait, Lebanon	2
11	USA (Asch's studies)	18
12	Belgium	4
13	Germany	1
14	USA (excluding Asch's studies)	79
15	UK	10
16	Netherlands	1
17	Portugal	1
17	France	2

Bond and Smith's findings are consistent with the way that the individualism/collectivism dimension was portrayed earlier (pages 135–136). Members of collectivistic countries value conformity because it promotes supportive group relationships and reduces conflicts. Thus, agreeing with others in collectivist societies is more likely to be viewed as a sign of sensitivity than one of submission to somebody else's will, which is the way it is often perceived in individualistic cultures (Hodges and Geyer, 2006).

 Individualism/collectivism affect both cognitive processes and social behaviour.

EXERCISE

32 What methodological and other problems may reduce the validity of cross-cultural studies of the type meta-analysed by Smith and Bond (1996)? What additional critical points are possible from an inspection of Table 4.2?

It should not be concluded from this discussion that members of collectivist societies always conform to group views. As Earley (1993) has demonstrated, the level of conformity they show depends on the exact nature of the group. Thus, collectivists may be more likely to conform to members of a group they are tied to (e.g. family, classmates, fellow workers) than they are to groups to which they are not attached. Consistent with this analysis, Williams and Sogon (1984) found significantly higher levels of conformity among Japanese groups who already knew one another than among groups lacking pre-acquaintance.

 As Matsumoto and Juang (2008) remark regarding conformity, 'cultures construct different meanings about it.'

Time orientation (Confucian dynamism)

Many have argued that time is not defined and perceived in the same way everywhere. To a significant extent, the way humans experience time is influenced by their culture (Hall, 1959). In 2001, Hofstede proposed a classification of cultures based on their time orientation.

In the mid-80s, Bond asked a number of Chinese social scientists to create a list of what Chinese people viewed as their basic values (Hofstede and Bond, 1988). A questionnaire, based on this list, was then administered to people in 23 countries. The outcome of this project was the emergence of a fifth cultural dimension, not related to the other four originally identified by Hofstede (page 135). The additional dimension was called **Confucian dynamism** because it reflected Confucius's ideas about the importance of perseverance, patience, social hierarchy, thrift and having a sense of shame. The new dimension was later renamed **long-term vs short-term orientation**.

Cultures scoring high on this dimension show a dynamic, future-oriented mentality. These are cultures that value long-standing, as opposed to short-term, traditions and values. Individuals in such cultures strive to fulfil their own long-term social obligations and avoid *loss of face*. Cultures with a short-term view are not as concerned with past traditions. They are rather impatient, are present-oriented and strive for immediate results. In practical terms, the long-term versus short-term orientation refers to the degree to which cultures encourage delayed gratification of material, social, and emotional needs among their members (Matsumoto and Juang, 2008).

Seven of the ten highest ranking countries on Hofstede's time orientation dimension were in Asia. Western countries tended to be more short-term oriented.

EMPIRICAL RESEARCH

Time orientation in bicultural participants (Chen et al., 2005)

In Eastern countries, characterized by a long-time orientation, patience is valued more than in Western countries. Based on this, Chen et al. predicted that part of the Western mentality is to place a higher value on immediate consumption than an Eastern mentality. They investigated this idea in an experimental study using 147 Singaporean 'bicultural participants'. This technique uses participants who have been exposed extensively to two different cultures (in this case, Singaporean and American) and assumes that both can affect behaviour depending on which is more actively represented in the mind at any particular moment.

Chen et al. selectively activated one or the other of the two cultures by presenting half the participants with a collage of easily recognizable photos which were relevant to Singaporean culture and the other half with a collage of photos relevant to US culture. Impatience was tested by having the participants perform an online shopping scenario in order to purchase a novel. The book could be delivered either within four working days for a standard fee or next day for an additional charge. The extra money participants were willing to pay for faster delivery of the book was used as a measure of impatience. Chen et al. found that US-primed participants valued immediate consumption more than the Singaporean-primed participants.

● **Examiner's hint**
Research that has not gone through the peer-review process should be treated with caution. Like with most books, and unlike published journal articles, such research has not been appraised by a panel of anonymous specialists in the relevent field.

Strong support of cultural differences in time orientation comes from a recent impressive study by Wang et al. (not published in a peer-reviewed journal). They surveyed over 5000 university students in 45 countries and compared them on time orientation. They found, for instance, that students coming from long-term orientation cultures were also more likely to postpone immediate satisfaction and wait for bigger rewards later.

Ayoun and Moreo (2009) used a survey method to investigate the influence of time orientation on the strategic behaviour of hotel managers. A questionnaire was posted to top-level hotel managers in the USA and Thailand. Compared to US managers, Thai managers were found to place a stronger emphasis on longer-term strategic plans and a stronger reliance on long-term evaluation of strategy.

Cultural differences in time orientation also seem to relate to everyday behaviours. Levine and Norenzayan (1999) measured how fast people walked a 60-foot distance in downtown areas in major cities, the speed of a visit to a post office, and the accuracy of clocks in 31 countries. They found that life pace, as indicated by the activities they measured, was fastest in countries like Switzerland, Ireland and Germany and slowest in Mexico, Indonesia, Brazil and Syria.

The last three studies are natural experiments and, in effect, observational studies. Their findings should, therefore, be interpreted with caution as no confident causal statements can be made in the absence of adequate control over extraneous variables.

 To learn more about the standing of at least some of the countries involved in Levine and Nozerayan's study on the time orientation dimension, go to www. pearsonhotlinks. com, enter the title or ISBN of this book and select weblink 4.7.
Are the study's findings consistent with what you would expect from the countries' rankings?

EXERCISE

33 List at least two extraneous variables that are relevant to these three studies.

In conclusion, it is clear that Confucian dynamism or time orientation has significant effects on behaviour.

 ## 4.6 Emic and etic concepts

Learning outcomes
• Use examples to explain the emic and etic concepts.

The terms **etic** and **emic**, first introduced by linguist Pike (1954), are based on the distinction between **phonetics** and **phonemics**. Phonetics is the study of universal sounds used in all human languages. Phonemics is the study of sounds that are particular to a specific language. Pike thought that the etic–emic distinction could be generalized beyond linguistics to define two different approaches to research in the social sciences. In effect, the distinction relates to the extent to which research aims to establish what is common to all humans and what is unique to specific cultures.

Etic approaches aim to discover what all humans have in common. It addresses the universals (or etics) of human behaviour. Etic approaches have been used extensively in cross-cultural studies. In such studies theories developed in one particular culture (usually Western) are tested cross-culturally. As the researchers rely on theories and techniques developed in their own culture to study some other culture, such studies are often said to use the **imposed etic approach** (Berry, 1969).

Emic approaches are not interested in cross-cultural comparisons but rather in culture-specific phenomena. A culture's uniqueness is explored by such studies through the discovery of its distinctive behaviours (or emics). Emic studies do not import theoretical frameworks from another culture. It is assumed that the meaning of behaviour can only be defined from within the culture studied.

EXERCISE

34 Was Hofstede's research on cultural dimensions of the etic or emic type? Were all five of his dimensions identified with the same type of research?

Etic and emic perspectives in mental health research

Tanaka–Matsumi (2001) distinguishes between two major strands in the research addressing cultural influences on the study of the causes and nature of psychological disorders (psychopathology). The first, an etic approach, assumes that the underlying psychological mechanisms and the ways psychological disorders are subjectively experienced are very similar, if not universal, across cultures. All culture can do is influence the way abnormal behaviour manifests itself. Etic approaches have generated research on the cross-cultural validity and reliability of psychiatric diagnosis (Chapter 5).

The second approach is an emic approach and is based on the idea that abnormal behaviours can be understood only in the context provided by the culture within which they occur. It studies abnormal behaviour as it occurs in specific cultures and shows no interest in cross-cultural comparisons. Since there are cross-cultural differences in the values and norms regulating behaviour, what is considered normal or abnormal may well differ in different cultures.

EXERCISE

35   Look in Chapter 5 for examples relevant to the claim that what is viewed as normal and abnormal differs between cultures.

Etic approaches to the study of depression

An example of the etic approach is a study sponsored by the World Health Organization (WHO, 1983) on the diagnosis and classification of depression in Switzerland, Canada, Japan and Iran. The investigators used a standard diagnostic scheme to investigate the symptoms of depression of 573 patients in these four countries. It was found that most patients experienced several symptoms that were the same in all four countries. Thus 76% of patients reported sadness, joylessness, anxiety, and a sense of insufficiency. Additional studies, for example studies comparing Hungarians with Americans and Canadians (Keitner et al., 1991) and studies involving children in six countries (Yamamoto et al., 1987) also obtained a common pattern of symptoms with depressed patients.

Importantly, 40% of patients in the WHO project displayed symptoms such as somatic complaints and obsessions that were not part of the symptoms measured by the diagnostic scheme used. Marsella et al. (1985) interpreted these findings as a strong demonstration of cultural factors. Other studies have also found variations in the way depressive symptoms are experienced in different cultures. Thus, patients in some cultures (e.g. Nigerians) are not at all likely to report feelings of worthlessness or guilt-related symptoms and the Chinese often report somatic symptoms such as body pains and upsets (Draguns and Tanaka–Matsumi, 2003).

Emic approaches to the study of depression

An example of an emic approach to the study of depression is the research by Manson et al. (1985) on the development of the American Indian Depression Scale. Through interviews with native informants, the authors derived the following five (translated) Hopi illness categories relevant to depression:

- worry sickness
- unhappiness
- heartbroken
- drunken-like craziness
- disappointment.

Most Hopi participants said they could not identify a Hopi word that was equivalent to the term depression. But they were all familiar with all five of the Hopi illness categories.

Some of the characteristics identified by Manson et al. (e.g. unhappiness) were similar to Western ways of looking at depression. Others were entirely different. The category of heartbroken, for example, included the following symptoms: weight loss, disrupted sleep, fatigue, psychomotor retardation and agitation, loss of libido, a sense of sinfulness, shame, not being likeable, and trouble thinking clearly. As a pattern, this set of symptoms does not form part of any Western diagnostic scheme.

Combining etic and emic approaches

Research seems to converge towards the conclusion that although depression is a universal disease, the way it expresses itself is culturally determined. Similar conclusions have been drawn about anxiety and other disorders (Kleinman, 1988). It would seem the best approach would involve both etic and emic components. In the **derived etic approach**, for example, it is assumed that although the phenomenon under study is the same across cultures, its development and expression may well show cultural influences.

Marsella et al. (2002) point out, for example, that the way depression expresses itself in a particular culture depends, among other things, on the culture's standing on the individualism/collectivism dimension. Thus, in individualistic cultures, feelings of loneliness and isolation are prevalent, whereas in collectivistic cultures, somatic symptoms such as headaches are more often reported.

 Does emic research support the view that what we call 'reality' is a social construction?

There are both etics and emics to be studied by social scientists.

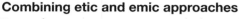

● **Examiner's hint**
Chapter 5 has a very useful discussion of cultural influences on psychopathology (pages 152–155).

 4.7

Methods used in the sociocultural level of analysis and the ethical concerns they raise

Learning outcomes
- Discuss how and why particular research methods are used at the sociocultural level of analysis.
- Discuss ethical considerations related to research studies at the sociocultural level of analysis.

As with the other levels of analysis, the sociocultural level of analysis makes use of several research methods. Some examples from the studies discussed in this chapter can be used to demonstrate the methodological choices at this level and to consider some of the ethical issues they may raise.

Experiments

Most of the research you have read about in this chapter aims to be scientific. Many studies address causal hypotheses based on explanatory theories. The method of choice when causal hypotheses are tested is, of course, the **experimental method**.

Several *laboratory experiments* were discussed, including Jones and Harris's experimental study of the FAE, Bargh et al.'s experiment on automatic stereotype activation and Bandura's Bobo doll study on observational learning. High on internal validity, most of these experiments can be questioned on the grounds that their artificiality poses a threat to their ecological validity. It should be noted, however, that modern psychology, including social psychology, does not place much confidence on individual studies.

EXERCISE
36   Relate the claim that modern psychology does not place much confidence in individual studies to the notions of meta-analysis and triangulation.

Several of the laboratory experiments we covered in this chapter are *field experiments* addressing the same hypotheses, thus allaying anxieties about the weaknesses of individual laboratory studies. Good examples of field experimental studies include Palak et al.'s study of lowballing and several other studies of compliance.

For most of the field experimental studies in compliance research, there are several laboratory experiments which obtained more or less the same findings.

One would wish for similar triangulation in settings where cross-cultural studies are used. For obvious reasons, experimental studies are not possible in this area of research, although Chen et al.'s study with 'bicultural participants' comes close to it. In effect, such studies are *natural experiments*, essentially observational studies, for the findings of which no confident causal statements can be made.

Correlational studies

Other studies relied on large-scale surveys – these are correlational studies (e.g. Hofstede's research on cultural dimensions). Although his findings have been at least partially replicated, there is something about such large-scale studies that arouses suspicions in many minds. The complexities of the mathematical models used to identify relevant factors (factor analysis) and the fact that individuality is completely crushed in the interests of arriving at general dimensions are concerns that have repeatedly been voiced. Perhaps we should see Hofstede's dimensions as general guides to cultural background that allow more specific claims to be made about individual cultures. Takano and Sogon (2008), for example, objects to viewing Japan in the collectivistic manner many researchers are accustomed to.

Case studies

Case studies based on **interviews** or **archival research** were discussed when looking at studies of groupthink (e.g. Janis, 1972; Esser and Lindoerfer, 1989). Important as sources of rich data, case studies can hardly be generalized and their preferred data collection methods often raise doubts about their objectivity.

While reflecting on the studies you come across, you may wish to challenge the view that they really study what they purport to study. Take Sherif and Asch's conformity studies for example. One cannot help objecting to calling the aggregates of participants used genuine groups. In Sherif's study, the experimental room was so dark that participants could not even see each other. Commenting on Asch's study, Eysenck (2009) writes: 'Asch's research on conformity is among the most famous in the whole of social psychology. Oddly, however, there was nothing very social about his research because he used groups of strangers!' Another way to view these studies, of course, is to claim that even the slightest hint of a group can have dramatic effects on behaviour.

EXERCISE
37   Research observational studies used in the sociocultural level of analysis.

Ethics

Several of the studies covered raise very serious ethical issues. Milgram's study is a classical example of a study where participants experienced unacceptable levels of stress; it perhaps should never have been carried out. To a lesser extent, the Asch paradigm generates internal conflict, whereas many of the studies use deception. The extent to which deceiving participants is justified depends on one's value system and the seriousness of the deception involved. Informed consent is rarely sought in such studies as explaining the nature of the experiment would, in most settings, destroy the possibility of carrying it out. Imagine telling Milgram's participants at the very beginning of the study that the electric shocks were not real.

Some of the studies on stereotyping raise ethical concerns. Is it ethical to activate stereotypes without the participants' consent and knowledge as happened in Bargh et al.'s study? Is it acceptable to evoke stereotype threat?

Studies of compliance also have their problems. Should investigators involve unsuspecting participants in long and possibly stressful energy-saving schemes for the sake of a scientific study as happened in Palak et al.'s study?

What about the cross-cultural studies discussed? The etic studies of Hofstede can easily lead to the stereotyping of entire nations. More emic studies, based on observational and interviewing techniques, may sound better but one has to respect the culture one studies and never offend or in any way inconvenience the native informants. Moreover, when the findings from such studies are made public, the same concerns about culture stereotyping apply.

One must obviously be alert to the ethical issues studies at the sociocultural level of analysis. But also one must always address the following questions as well.
- Can we afford *not* to study these phenomena?
- Can we do without the precious knowledge they deliver, often about the most disturbing aspects of the way we think about and behave towards one another?

At what point, if any, do ethical considerations become unjustifiably restrictive of the processes that generate knowledge in psychology?

● **Examiner's hint**
Use your knowledge of methodology to find and evaluate further examples of the various research methods you have looked at.

To access Worksheet 4.1 with a full example answer to short answer question 3, please visit www.pearsonbacconline.com and follow the on-screen instructions.

To access Worksheet 4.2 with a full example answer to essay question 1, please visit www.pearsonbacconline.com and follow the on-screen instructions.

PRACTICE QUESTIONS

Short answer questions

1   Outline **two** principles that define the sociocultural level of analysis.
2   Explain **one** error in attribution.
3   Describe the role of **one** factor influencing conformity.
4   Explain the terms *etic* and *emic*.

Essay questions

1   Evaluate social identity theory, making reference to relevant studies.
2   Discuss research on conformity to social norms.

5 ABNORMAL PSYCHOLOGY

5.1 Introduction: What is abnormal psychology?

Learning outcomes
● Discuss to what extent biological, cognitive and sociocultural factors influence abnormal behaviour.
● Evaluate psychological research (that is, theories and/or studies) relevant to the study of abnormal behaviour.

Abnormal psychology is the branch of psychology that deals with studying, explaining and treating 'abnormal' behaviour. Although there is obviously a great deal of behaviour that could be considered abnormal, this branch of psychology deals mostly with that which is addressed in a clinical context. In effect, this means a range of behaviours, emotions and thinking that tend to result in an individual seeing a mental health professional, such as a psychiatrist or a clinical psychologist.

Abnormal psychology attracts researchers who investigate the causes of abnormal behaviour and try to find the most effective treatments for them, whether these involve medication or a talking cure or a combination. There are also practitioners, psychologists who use their knowledge of theory and research to deliver treatment to people in a therapeutic setting.

A large number of conditions occur commonly enough to be categorized systematically within various cultures and, in some cases, across the world. The IB Psychology syllabus deals with only three groups:
● anxiety disorders
● affective disorders
● eating disorders.

Defining these groups of disorders is straightforward because of the diagnostic systems available, but there is considerable disagreement about the validity of the distinctions between normal and abnormal behaviour.

◀ Therapist and client in individual therapy

5.2 Concepts and diagnosis

Learning outcomes
- Examine the concepts of normality and abnormality.
- Discuss validity and reliability of diagnosis.
- Discuss cultural and ethical considerations in diagnosis.

Normality and abnormality

The word normal usually refers to conformity to standard or regular patterns of behaviour. The concept of abnormality is essentially a label applied to behaviour that does not conform. Unfortunately, this explanation is not very precise and it remains difficult for mental health professionals to agree on who is abnormal enough to require or deserve treatment.

Looking at different common interpretations of abnormality highlights this problem.

Statistical abnormality

An interpretation of normality that depends on literal meaning assumes there is such a thing as average behaviour, or behaviour that most frequently occurs in particular situations. Thus, behaviour that does not occur very often in a given context can be considered to be abnormal. This is a particularly useful approach when dealing with numbers, such as IQ scores for measuring intelligence, or scores on personality measures like extroversion. When using numbers, we can obtain means; the majority of people scoring around the middle of the scale, with very few people scoring extremes.

It is much harder to be sure about what the average is when we are not dealing with numbers. For example, how much hunger is normal or abnormal? Hunger is not often expressed numerically, and it is very difficult to compare such a subjective experience between two people.

It may be better to consider what is normal for the individual in a particular situation, rather than what others would do. Research into helping behaviour among humans, for example, suggests that those working in helping professions (e.g. nurses and doctors) are more likely than others to help a stranger who seems to be in need. Also, those who have previously helped a stranger are more likely to intervene. With this in mind, it seems that we need to know quite a lot about a person before we can begin to claim that their behaviour is normal or abnormal based on comparison with the behaviour of 'the average person'.

Statistically unusual behaviour is often attributed to mental illness, perhaps because assuming that people are suffering from some sort of psychiatric condition helps us understand the strangeness of their behaviour. However, it must be noted that not all statistically infrequent behaviour is considered a sign of madness or mental incompetence. For example, low intelligence is frequently labelled in various ways and education programmes attempt to help individuals at the extreme low end of the intelligence scale, but the same is not often true at the other end of the scale, where high intelligence is usually valued, and even if it is considered abnormally high, it is not stigmatized or compensated for in the same way. There are no special schools that try to *reduce* genius IQ.

Think about behaviour you have seen in another culture that you think is strange. Then think about behaviour that is normal in your culture that might be considered strange in another. Why is it important to understand the influence of culture and history on the way we view behaviour?

Deviation from social norms

Social norms are not necessarily related to statistical norms. Instead of referring to what is frequent in a particular context, the idea of deviation from social norms assumes that in any situation there is an expected behaviour. The expected behaviour is that which the rules of society and culture dictate is appropriate for that context. Using this definition, we can say that although it is acceptable to talk loudly to friends in a noisy cafe, it is abnormal to talk at the same volume in a library or a cinema. Many teachers might also find it abnormal for a student to be asleep during class, not simply because it is an infrequent event, but because it seems to be socially inappropriate.

When people violate such social rules, we have a tendency to assume there is something wrong with them, and it is easy to attribute this to some kind of madness. This approach to defining abnormality has been with us for a long time, but there are three key problems with it.

- First, social norms vary enormously across cultures and social situations. For example, the appropriate response to dealing with a running nose ranges from using a tissue to blow your nose, spitting the mucus out from the mouth or, if you are a sportsman, blowing your nose without a tissue. Any of these options would seem strange if carried out in the wrong situation.
- The second key problem is historical variation. In *Models of Madness* (2004), Read et al. detail a number of examples of behaviour that were considered symptomatic of mental illness in the past but would now be acceptable in many cultures and social situations. Examples include sexual interest in people of the same gender and a slave's desire to run away.
- The third key problem is controversial. In many cases, what is considered socially acceptable or unacceptable has been established by groups with social power. Judging normality according to conformity to expectation has led to cruel treatment of many individuals who engage in behaviours that threaten the interests of the powerful group(s). One of the most pervasive examples of this has been the existence of double-standards for men and women: in many cultures, men have reserved certain activities for themselves. Smoking and drinking are typical examples of this, and it is often still considered more abnormal for a woman to drink too much alcohol than it is for a man. In some cultures, for a woman to have more than one sexual partner can result in legal execution. In Western culture, it was previously considered wrong for a married woman to protest at her husband forcing her to have sexual intercourse and abnormal for a woman to live an unmarried life.

Spousal rape was made a crime in Sweden in 1965, in Australia in 1981 and in all of the USA by 1993. Many countries close to these leaders made changes soon after, but there are still a number of countries where this action remains exempt from rape definitions, often for religious reasons.

It is, therefore extremely important for mental health practitioners to understand the diversity of behaviour across cultures, times, and even genders, if they are to treat their clients well.

Maladaptiveness and adequate functioning

Another way to decide what is abnormal is to assume that all humans perform behaviours that are good for them in their particular environmental context. We might expect people to develop an understanding of social expectations, regardless of whether they agree with them or not, and to be able to function within their social group. Behaviours that threaten one's ability to function well within that social context can be considered maladaptive.

To learn more about countries where homosexuality is illegal, go to www. pearsonhotlinks.com, enter the title or ISBN of this book and select weblink 5.1.

This approach works well when we consider such conditions as alcoholism and anorexia, where it is clear that a person's health is in danger because of the way he or she is behaving. People who spend so much time on the internet that they lose contact with their peers might also be seen to be engaging in maladaptive behaviour – internet addiction is a fairly recent addition to the range of abnormal behaviour practitioners might deal with.

The most frequently cited problem with this approach is that people whose motivation is clearly *not* indicative of a serious disorder will sometimes engage in maladaptive or dangerous behaviour. Examples include extreme sports people and political protestors such as Guillermo Farinas, who went on a hunger strike in Cuba to protest at internet censorship.

W To learn more about the hunger strike of Guillermo Farinas, go to www.pearsonhotlinks.com, enter the title or ISBN of this book and select weblink 5.2.

Suffering and distress

If it is insufficient to define behaviour that is bad for a person as an indicator of abnormality, perhaps it is better to ask whether the person is suffering or not, or if they are experiencing distress. This conveniently ignores the problems of most of the other criteria above and can allow those who feel that they need some kind of medical or psychological attention to gain it. However, it carries with it the assumption that individuals engaging in this kind of abnormal behaviour will have enough insight to experience distress. This is not always the case.

For example, irritability is a common symptom of depression among men, but it is not the kind of symptom that would encourage a man to seek help. Another example occurs when a person begins drinking a lot of alcohol – their behaviour may be unhealthy for them, but until there is damage to their physical health or changes in relationships with family or friends, there may be no suffering. Users of illegal drugs may be unaware of the problems they are causing themselves or they simply may not experience any significant distress – but this does not mean they don't need help. In addition, some degree of suffering and distress must be considered a normal response to challenging life events such as the death of a loved one or divorce, and nobody should consider this a sign of mental illness – it is rather a sign of mental health.

Jahoda's positive mental health

Marie Jahoda (1958) took a different approach in that instead of defining what is abnormal, she tried to define what is normal. If a definition of normal in a mental health context could be established, it should be logical and straight-forward to consider behaviour that deviates from the ideal to be indicative of the kind of abnormality that mental health practitioners might feel needs treating. Jahoda identified six components of ideal mental health based on a review of literature:
- positive attitude toward own self
- growth, development, and self-actualization
- integration
- autonomy
- accurate perception of reality
- environmental mastery.

▲ Internet addiction or a positive approach to modern society?

Her approach suggests that the state of ideal mental health is achieved when a person has a realistic and positive acceptance of who they are, and is able to resist stress (so they maintain a lack of symptoms of psychological disorders) while they act voluntarily in the interests of their own growth in the physical and social environments they inhabit.

While this is an attractive approach in many ways, it appears that the more intensely one analyses it, the fewer people we might be able to say are in such a state of ideal mental health. Some research, for example, has found that those with depression are more accurate in their perception of reality, and that for most of us, functioning adequately requires an element of self-delusion (Taylor and Brown, 1988). Unreasonable optimism seems to be beneficial for many people.

Thus, it is extremely difficult to explain exactly what abnormal behaviour in a population is. But perhaps it is a goal that is unnecessary to achieve. There are diagnostic symptoms available to mental health practitioners that attempt to remove some of the problems of subjectivity and help us deal with the large numbers of exceptions to all of the criteria outlined above.

EXERCISE

1   Summarize the main approaches to defining abnormality and use bullet points to identify problems with each one. Try to think of your own examples of behaviour that is abnormal or normal and cannot be accounted for by each of the approaches detailed above.

Diagnostic systems and the validity and reliability of diagnosis

Worldwide, there are several major systems of diagnosis.

The *Diagnostic and Statistical Manual of Mental Disorders* (DSM)

The DSM is revised regularly by a panel of psychiatrists in the USA to keep it in line with current thinking.

This publication by the American Psychiatric Association is probably the most famous system of diagnosis. It was first published in 1952 and has been revised several times; it is now in its revised fourth edition (DSM-IV-TR), and the fifth edition is scheduled for release in 2013. Revisions are intended to make the diagnosis of mental disorders a more reliable process and a more valid reflection of general wisdom at the time. For example, the manual attempts to describe any disorder in such terms that two clinicians referring to the system would probably agree with the diagnosis it suggests. Disorders are added and removed as time goes on. Homosexuality was removed from the DSM as a disorder in 1980, and alterations have been made to the class of eating disorders several times since then.

The DSM groups disorders into categories and then offers specific guidance to psychiatrists by listing the symptoms required for a diagnosis to be given. An improvement made in 1987 was the creation of a multiaxial approach, whereby a diagnosing clinician should consider the individual under investigation not only in terms of whether they qualify for diagnosis, but also whether they have medical conditions, psychosocial and environmental problems, and how well they are functioning generally. This approach has encouraged psychiatrists using the system to take a more holistic approach to understanding the person who has presented with some problems. This reflects a widely held belief among mental health practitioners today that the origin of each person's problems should be analysed according to a bio-psycho-social framework.

To learn more about DSM-V, scheduled for release in 2013, go to www. pearsonhotlinks. com, enter the title or ISBN of this book and select weblink 5.3.

Modern diagnosis is often able to take advantage of medical breakthroughs. For example, Alzheimer's disease and attention-deficit-hyperactivity disorder (ADHD) are disorders that can sometimes be diagnosed using brain-imaging technology thanks to our understanding of changes in brain structure or functioning.

The *International Classification of Diseases* (ICD)

The ICD is now in its tenth edition (ICD-10) and is more commonly used internationally than the DSM (Mezzich, 2002). It was originally intended by the World Health Organization to be a means of standardizing recording of cause of death. It therefore covers a wide range of diseases and conditions for the sake of classification rather than diagnosis. One chapter categorizes mental disorders and it looks very similar to the DSM-IV system because the authoring teams worked in consultation with each other. With each revision, differences between the ICD and the DSM are becoming fewer.

The *Chinese Classification of Mental Disorders* (CCMD)

This system has not yet generalized far outside Chinese territory. It is currently in its third edition (CCMD-3). It has not attempted to capture the full range of human diagnoses but maintains a focus on issues that are of interest in Chinese culture. For this reason, some disorders identified in the ICD-10 and DSM-IV-TR that are not common in China are left out, and others are included that appear to be culture-bound disorders found only within Chinese culture. Examples include koro – a kind of anxiety or depression, and mental disorder due to Qigong – a form of meditative exercise – which is also now included in the DSM. Ego-dystonic homosexuality is also included in the CCMD; this disorder is characterized by homosexual urges that are unwanted. Although at first glance, some of these disorders may appear strange, it is interesting to consider how unusual some of the Western disorders we take for granted are. Some researchers consider anorexia nervosa to be a culture-bound disorder, for example. This is discussed in more detail later.

 Culture-bound disorders are those disorders occurring only within a specific culture.

Some ethical considerations

There are strong arguments that these systems are not reliable and, more fundamentally, that it is not valid to take such a medical approach to the treatment of psychological problems. In addition, many people have expressed fundamental objections to the way in which the systems have been used. In many countries where ego-dystonic homosexuality is considered a disorder, treatments are available and used to remove the source of the problem. In the Soviet Union, the diagnosis of schizophrenia was applied much more liberally than in the USA at the time. It lead to the incarceration and compulsory treatment of many individuals who might have been better understood under a more specific diagnostic system.

However, while examples like these may appear to lend ethical superiority to the ICD and DSM systems, it is by no means certain that ethnic minorities and women are treated equally with others in terms of their likelihood of receiving a diagnosis, level of understanding offered by practitioners, and the type of treatment offered.

Reliability issues

Receiving a diagnosis can be a difficult experience for some and a huge relief for others. In either case, it seems important to ask whether the systems used are in fact reliable. Two key forms of reliability, as outlined on page 3, are relevant here: inter-rater reliability and test–retest reliability. Inter-rater reliability can be assessed by asking more than one practitioner to observe the same person and, using the same diagnostic system, attempt to make a diagnosis. If practitioners make the same decision, the system is reliable. Test–retest reliability is concerned with whether the same person will receive the same diagnosis if they are assessed more than once (e.g. on two different days).

One of the most commonly cited studies of inter-rater reliability across several diagnostic systems was carried out by Nicholls et al. (2000) and asked two practitioners to use either DSM-IV, ICD-10 or the Great Ormond Street Hospital's own diagnostic system (GOS) to

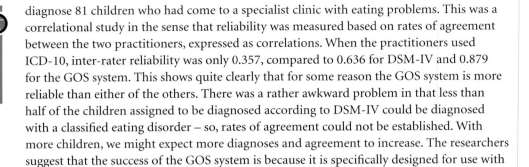

Dasha Nicholls, who conducted the study, works at Great Ormond Street Hospital. Does this mean we should not trust the results of this study?

diagnose 81 children who had come to a specialist clinic with eating problems. This was a correlational study in the sense that reliability was measured based on rates of agreement between the two practitioners, expressed as correlations. When the practitioners used ICD-10, inter-rater reliability was only 0.357, compared to 0.636 for DSM-IV and 0.879 for the GOS system. This shows quite clearly that for some reason the GOS system is more reliable than either of the others. There was a rather awkward problem in that less than half of the children assigned to be diagnosed according to DSM-IV could be diagnosed with a classified eating disorder – so, rates of agreement could not be established. With more children, we might expect more diagnoses and agreement to increase. The researchers suggest that the success of the GOS system is because it is specifically designed for use with young children.

Mary Seeman (2007) completed a literature review examining evidence relating to the reliability of diagnosis over time. She found that initial diagnoses of schizophrenia, especially in women, were susceptible to change as clinicians found out more information about their patients. It was common for a number of other conditions to cause the symptoms for which women were receiving the diagnosis of schizophrenia. This indicates the problem of test–retest reliability with schizophrenia diagnoses.

Validity issues

Several forms of validity are discussed on page 4. The key concern for diagnostic systems is whether they correctly diagnose people who really have particular disorders and do not give a diagnosis to people who do not. Unfortunately, there is a circular logic involved here – it is difficult to establish whether a person truly has a disorder without using a diagnostic system. This means that the only people we can be fairly sure about are those who have already been diagnosed, although many will argue this is also insufficient.

Thomas Szasz and R.D. Laing are famous critics of the diagnostic biomedical approach.

R.D. Laing

Laing's work suggests that although diagnosis is made within a medical model, the diagnosis is more of a social fact than a medical one. Psychiatrists do not diagnose because of a set of biological facts; this is because (as you will see), there are no reliable biological tests for diagnosing most psychological disorders, only guidance about categorizing behaviour, thoughts and emotions. The process of diagnosing is full of financial, political and legal implications. It is also frequently a bureaucratic step of secondary importance to treatment, which (within the medical model), often consists of medication, hospitalization, and limited attempts to see the presenting symptoms as an understandable reaction to life difficulties.

To learn more about links between psychiatry and pharmaceutical companies, go to www.pearsonhotlinks.com, enter the title or ISBN of this book and select weblink 5.4.

The pharmaceutical industry has been heavily criticized for its influence over the medical profession and it is of interest to note that a large number of those serving on advisory panels for revisions in the fourth edition of the DSM had financial ties to the pharmaceutical industry, mostly in terms of research funding (Cosgrove et al., 2006).

Thomas Szasz

Thomas Szasz also suggested that it is wrong to use a mental illness metaphor to describe behaviour that does not conform to our expectations. It is clear that there are biological correlates of behaviour (page 15), but it is reductionist to assume that conditions like depression and schizophrenia are diseases like any other, especially as biological causes have not yet been established for most psychological disorders. In particular, it is important to note that the terms 'depression' and 'schizophrenia' are essentially labels given to a set of behaviours, emotions, or thoughts. Can a person really have depression in the same way

that they can have influenza? It is somehow more attractive for many of us to imagine that an underlying condition called depression is the cause of a person's severe unhappiness, but there is no underlying condition tested for. The depression *is* the unhappiness (along with other symptoms), rather than the *cause* of it. Anorexia nervosa does not *cause* eating problems, it *is* the problem.

The DSM symptoms for major depressive disorder have been reviewed several times, and a concession that sometimes life events (rather than an underlying medical condition) might make a person feel bad was included. The specific allowance in DSM-IV-TR is for the death of a loved one although symptoms should only continue for two months.

Wakefield et al. (2007) conducted a study which suggests that a wide range of other life events can account for symptoms of depression and therefore the exclusion is inappropriately narrow. This lack of clarity about when the symptoms of depression really indicate a medical condition and when they indicate an understandable response to life events is only one example of the problems with validity.

Other problems

EMPIRICAL RESEARCH

Labelling theory (Caetano, 1973)

Caetano conducted an experiment in which he videoed a male psychiatrist carrying out separate, standardized interviews with a paid university student and with a hospitalized mental patient. Two groups of people were shown these interviews – a group of 77 students of psychology and a group of 36 psychiatrists attending a meeting. They were asked to diagnose the interviewees and rate their degree of mental illness. Within each sample of viewers, there was random assignment to two different groups, each of which received different information about the interviewees: either that both were volunteers who were paid to participate, or that both were patients in a state mental hospital.

Caetano acknowledged that it was possible to argue that the student selected could have had an undiagnosed psychiatric disorder and that the patient selected was close to normal (with the appearance, manner and attitudes of a hippie whose drug use was explainable). The results indicated that psychiatrists with clinical experience were more likely to be persuaded by the information given about the two interviewees and label them both as mentally ill (if they were described as patients) or both not mentally ill (if they were described as volunteers).

This study demonstrates labelling theory: the theory that the behaviour of the person being diagnosed is not the most important component of diagnosis and, in the ambiguous situation of a diagnostic interview, any suggestion that the subject is or has been mentally ill will be a powerful influence on any decision.

EMPIRICAL RESEARCH

What is normal behaviour (Rosenhan et al., 1973)

Rosenhan and a group of colleagues and acquaintances (including a housewife, a painter and a student) presented themselves at 12 different hospitals across the USA complaining of hearing voices, but otherwise presenting their life history and present state as normal. All but one were admitted with a diagnosis of schizophrenia.

On admission to the hospital, their instructions were to cease complaining of any symptoms (although they were generally rather nervous because of the situation). Their goal was to get out.

They did all achieve this, but with a diagnosis of schizophrenia in remission. Thus, their (apparent) normality was never detected although descriptions from nursing staff show that there was no further evidence of difficult or psychotic behaviour.

continued

In fact, 35 of the 118 patients in the wards to which the Rosenhan's pseudopatients were admitted expressed some kind of concern about their presence, assuming in many cases that they had an alternative purpose such as journalism or checking on the hospital in some way. It took between 7 and 52 days for the pseudopatients to be released, with an average of 19 days. This time was used by the pseudopatients to conduct a participant observation of life in the hospital, which involved them making notes about the interactions between staff and patients. Although their writing was noticed by staff in some cases, this was seen as a symptom of their illness, perhaps because it is not something that patients normally do. They were not asked what they were writing about. It is clear then, that with some significant symptoms, an apparently normal person can receive a diagnosis.

Conversely, Rosenhan found that 'abnormal' people can be mistakenly assumed to be healthy. He followed his first study with a second, in which staff at a hospital who had claimed that they would not have been fooled by Rosenhan's pseudopatients were invited to estimate how many times Rosenhan attempted to trick them in this way during a 3-month period. With great confidence, at least one staff member estimated that 41 out of the 193 people who were admitted during the test period were pseudopatients. This time, Rosenhan had sent none: all were genuine patients. Which people should really have been admitted and which ones are actually normal? Of the patients admitted in this time, 19 were thought to be normal by a psychiatrist and at least one other staff member. Although this study was conducted in 1973, it provides some important evidence for a general inability to tell the difference between normal and abnormal behaviour.

EXERCISE

2   Write a short paragraph to summarize the problems of validity illustrated by the Caetano and Rosenhan studies.

Criterion-related validity

Criterion-related validity is a form of validity based on whether a new system agrees with existing measures of the phenomenon in question. Gavin Andrews has published research on using DSM and ICD-10 systems, particularly in the diagnosis of anxiety disorders. He has generally found only moderate agreement between them. When a person has been diagnosed according to one system but cannot be diagnosed according to another system by the same practitioner or group of practitioners, this indicates poor validity.

In one study, Peters et al. (1999) found only moderate agreement between the two systems because the DSM-IV requires the presence of distress or impairment to functioning in the person being diagnosed. Andrews has been working on constructing more systematic diagnostic interviews and refinements to the criteria from both systems to help them converge. This should help improve their criterion-related validity, even if we risk over-diagnosis of people who in fact are functioning quite well.

It is still the case that certain groups of people are more likely to receive a diagnosis, and it is very difficult to remove the subjectivity of practitioners from the diagnostic process. Some of these problems are outlined in the following section.

Personality tests are often compared to check criterion-related validity. If existing tests show a person is an extrovert, new tests of the same person should also show the same finding.

Culture, gender and ethical considerations in diagnosis and treatment

Labelling theory (described above and demonstrated by the studies of Caetano and Rosenhan) indicates that once a diagnosis has been made, it tends to stick. The two key problems with this are:

- we are not convinced that such diagnosis is reliable or valid, even if this situation is improving
- there are significant negative effects of such a diagnosis on a person's subsequent treatment by other people.

Many employers require job applicants to declare any mental illnesses or medication they are taking when they apply for a job, and although discrimination is often prevented by law, fear of being treated differently can be a significant cause of discouragement among those who have been diagnosed. Recent research suggests that 92% of people in the UK would be afraid of admitting they had a mental illness because it would damage their career. More than half of those surveyed would rather not hire someone if they knew they had a mental illness.

Read (2007) summarized a large amount of research relating to stigma. The findings showed that attitudes towards those diagnosed in a medical context tend to be characterized by fears, especially regarding dangerousness and unpredictability; also that knowing someone has a diagnosis of mental illness increases reluctance to enter into romantic relationships with them. Sato (2006) discusses how schizophrenia (formerly, seishin bunretsu byo, split-mind disease) has been renamed in Japan because there was such stigma attached to it that less than 40% of patients who had been diagnosed with it had actually been informed of the diagnosis.

There is also a concern that treatment after diagnosis may worsen or create symptoms. Iatrogenesis is the phenomenon whereby treatment for a condition causes other complications. It has been used to describe the process by which adaptation to life in an institution causes mental patients to develop new behaviours which are then considered symptoms of their condition. Rosenhan's (1973) study (page 151) gives an indication of how this can occur, particularly in the sense that a lot of the social interactions observed by the pseudopatients were lacking in care and concern.

Similar concerns have been raised about life in prisons, where conditions can be cruel and dehumanizing in a way that makes a return to the community difficult. Additionally, diagnoses can be part of a self-fulfilling prophecy. An example might be a person diagnosed with depression who takes time off work, finds it difficult to return and ends up losing their job. The consequential unemployment can increase the person's sense of isolation and feelings of worthlessness, and compound the symptoms that they originally presented with.

This is in line with the argument that psychiatry functions to exclude those who are perceived as different or difficult in some way, or at least uses diagnosis and institutionalization instead of attempting to understand differences. This is reflected in rates of diagnosis for conditions like schizophrenia and depression, which are wildly different between ethnic groups and between men and women. Types of treatment offered are also quite different.

For example, Morgan et al. (2006) found that in the UK, the incidence of schizophrenia is nine times higher for Afro-Caribbeans and six times higher for those of black African descent, than for white British people. The researchers argue that genetic differences cannot account for this and it is more likely that diagnostic biases account for it. Migrants and

To access Worksheet 5.1 on the causes and effects of stigma, please visit www.pearsonbacconline.com and follow the on-screen instructions.

Stigma towards those with mental illnesses can cause problems after diagnosis.

Institutions are often difficult environments to be in. JK Rowling, author of the Harry Potter books, raised concern about the use of caged beds in hospitals.

Ethnic minorities are often over-represented among patients in mental institutions who have diagnoses of schizophrenia.

ethnic minorities in many European countries and the Anglo-American world are over-represented in mental hospital populations (Read et al., 2004).

Women are more likely to be diagnosed with depression. While one vein of research investigates the unique biological reasons why this might be the case, another argument suggests that diagnostic criteria for depression are a description of normal female responses to social pressures, and as such should not be pathologized but be understood better and treated on a social rather than individual level.

The reverse side of this is the potential denial of treatment to people who need it. The possibility that an individual with suicidal thoughts might go through a diagnostic interview, not be diagnosed with depression and offered treatment, and then carry out a suicide attempt, is a very powerful incentive for a clinician to make a diagnosis as a precaution. The immediate safety of the interviewee is a higher priority than any potential long-term negative effects of stigma related to the diagnosis. In many cases, medication and institutionalization are favoured options as they are frequently very successful in preventing harm to the patient or to other people. It could be argued that medical diagnosis is not the most efficient way to achieve this, but there is a lack of well-funded alternatives and the public has a high level of respect for and trust in the medical establishment.

Behaviour and interpretation across cultures

In Chapter 4 (page 139), you considered emic and etic approaches to psychological research. You might wish to review this material before reading on.

Culture-bound syndromes were referred to earlier (page 149). Different parts of the world and different ethnic groups have different ways of explaining the kind of strange behaviour that is dealt with by psychology and psychiatry in the Western world.

EXERCISE
3   Conduct further research about two of the culture-bound syndromes found on weblink 5.5, looking for causes and treatments and write a paragraph to explain both.

Where there is such a huge variety of labels for behaviour that shares as its basis either dangerousness or violation of social norms, it must be asked whether the DSM criteria are valid beyond the culture they were created in. In particular, it is a problem that the existence of labels for disorders may affect the likelihood of a person developing the symptoms for one of those disorders, and there are significant implications for treatment.

An interesting example of the possible role of culture was noted in a statistical analysis of data from two cities in the United States by Levav et al. (1997). Rates of alcoholism and depression were compared across various religious groups and it was found that Jewish males were much more likely to have a diagnosis of depression, and less likely to have a diagnosis of alcoholism.

One implication of this is that there is some kind of underlying issue that manifests itself differently depending on cultural traditions and expectations. This becomes very important in a clinical setting where relatively few practitioners are members of ethnic minorities and might be able to offer greater insight into patients' problems.

A second possibility is that the diagnosing clinician's cultural stereotypes influence his or her clinical judgement, for example in terms of what constitutes a symptom. Read et al. (2004) note that in New Zealand, where Maori people are over-represented in psychiatric institutions, psychiatrists do not feel it is inappropriate to use European diagnostic systems with non-European patients. This may lead to misunderstandings and misdiagnosis.

To learn more about culture-bound syndromes, go to www.pearsonhotlinks.com, enter the title or ISBN of this book and select weblink 5.5.

If knowledge is gained using the scientific method, should it apply to all cultures?

In New Zealand

Studies here show that there are differences in what is considered a mental health issue among the Maori and Pacific Island population and other ethnic groups. Thus, affective disorders such as depression account for only 16% of diagnoses given to Maori mental health service users compared with 30% for Europeans; the majority of diagnoses were for schizophrenia – 60% of diagnoses compared to 40% for Europeans. Maori mental health service users also report more experience of hallucinations, and have more records of aggression and problems of living (Tapsell and Mellsop, 2007). Other research also indicates that Maori are less likely to be medicated for depression than Europeans in New Zealand (Arroll et al., 2002).

Such observations can be useful in helping practitioners realise that they may misunderstand service users on a cultural level, if not on an individual one. For example, the concept of Mate Maori refers to ill health or strange behaviour related to breaking tribal law, especially that connected with what is sacred – so contact with a tohunga (a person with a role similar to that of a priest) is usually recommended. A further example is the description from The Best Practice Advocacy Centre of New Zealand (2008) giving details of Whakama, a set of behaviours arising from a sense of disadvantage or loss of standing that can show as 'marked slowness of movement and lack of responsiveness to questioning, … of avoidance of any engagement with the questioner … [and] a pained, worried look … suggestive of depression or even a catatonic state'. Moreover, it is not uncommon for Maori to report seeing or hearing deceased relatives. So, it is not always appropriate to consider these manifestations as symptoms of psychological disorders. Knowledge of the culture of patients is extremely important.

In the UK

Other research relating to ethnic minorities shows that many factors affect mental health and the way users of mental health services should be treated whether they are aboriginal people, immigrants, long-established residents or newly arrived refugees. Palmer and Ward (2006) found in a content analysis of interviews that those who experienced trauma in their previous location are affected by difficulties in their new environment as well as memories of the old. For example, among immigrants to London from Somalia, Rwanda and Iran, experiences of violence or persecution in their home country mix with new problems like bad housing or homelessness, and loss of identity without hope of quickly finding an appropriate job. In addition, degrees of stigma towards those with mental health problems and language interpretation problems can limit people's access to psychologists – who may not always understand them or their background.

Kirov and Murray (1999) studied a group of patients taking lithium prophylaxis (lithium is a drug sometimes used for depression and bipolar disorder). They found that there were clear differences in the symptoms and diagnoses that had resulted in patients being medicated: black patients were less likely than white patients to have suicidal ideas or to have attempted suicide and generally had more manic symptoms, resulting in a diagnosis of bipolar disorder. The authors suggest that because of this difference in the manifestation of the underlying problem, many black patients in the UK may be diagnosed with schizophrenia rather than with an affective disorder. This may contribute to the finding by Riordan et al. (2004) that compulsory hospitalization orders are more likely to be applied to black than to white patients.

 Compulsory hospitalization orders can be made if a person is considered to be a danger to themselves or others.

Conclusion

From these examples, we can see that there are a number of important cultural and ethical considerations when diagnosing psychiatric and psychological disorders. Further investigation into this area will show you how political and full of controversy the literature is.

5.3   Psychological disorders

Learning outcomes

- Describe symptoms and prevalence of one disorder from two of the following groups:
  - anxiety disorders (page 156)
  - affective disorders (page 165)
  - eating disorders (page 174).
- Analyse etiologies (in terms of biological, cognitive and/or sociocultural factors) of one disorder from two of the above groups.
- Discuss cultural and gender variations in prevalence of disorders.
- Examine biomedical, individual and group approaches to treatment.
- Evaluate the use of biomedical, individual and group approaches to the treatment of one disorder.
- Discuss the use of eclectic approaches in treatment.

● **Examiner's hint**

For an essay question asking about cultural and gender variations in prevalence, you may need to deal with more than one disorder. Review your notes on this chapter so far and use bullet points to record gender and cultural variations. Add to your notes as you read about specific disorders.

Prevalence is an estimate of how many people in a population have the disorder.

The abnormal psychology option in the IB Psychology exam requires you to be familiar with at least two specific disorders from two different groups of disorder. You need to describe the disorder, analyse the range of possible causes, and discuss treatment for one disorder in more depth. You also need to be aware of the prevalence of the disorders you choose, to discuss them in general and to evaluate research relating to them.

The prevalence of a disorder refers to the number of people in the population who have the disorder (as opposed to the incidence rate, which is the number of new diagnoses each year). It is impossible to know how many people actually have a specific phobia, for example, because many people who have a phobia will be undiagnosed, so the figures are estimates. Prevalence rates are sometimes also expressed as lifetime risk estimates, indicating the percentage of the population who are likely to be diagnosed with a disorder.

Anxiety disorders
Definitions and diagnosis

This category of disorders includes a range of conditions characterized by the experience of anxiety or fear. In ICD-10 they are referred to as neurotic, stress-related and somatoform disorders. This is a broader category and includes phobias, post-traumatic stress disorder, panic disorder and obsessive–compulsive disorder, as well as conditions where there appear to be physical symptoms (such as intense pain) because of the anxiety. You only need to know about one of these disorders. Here we consider specific phobia.

Diagnostic criteria for specific phobia

Reprinted with permission from the *Diagnostic and Statistical Manual of Mental Disorders*, 4th Edn, Text Revision (Copyright 2000). American Psychiatric Association.

  A   Marked and persistent fear that is excessive or unreasonable, cued by the presence or anticipation of a specific object or situation (e.g. flying, heights, animals, receiving an injection, seeing blood).

  B   Exposure to the phobic stimulus almost invariably provokes an immediate anxiety response, which may take the form of a situationally bound or situationally predisposed panic attack.

Note: In children, the anxiety may be expressed by crying, tantrums, freezing, or clinging.

C The person recognizes that the fear is excessive or unreasonable.
Note: In children, this feature may be absent.

D The phobic situation is avoided or else is endured with intense anxiety or distress.

E The avoidance, anxious anticipation, or distress in the feared situation interferes significantly with the person's normal routine, occupational (or academic) functioning, or social activities or relationships, or there is marked distress about having the phobia.

F In individuals under age 18 years, the duration is at least 6 months.

G The anxiety, panic attacks, or phobic avoidance associated with the specific object or situation are not better accounted for by another mental disorder, such as obsessive–compulsive disorder (e.g. fear of dirt in someone with an obsession about contamination), post-traumatic stress disorder (e.g. avoidance of stimuli associated with a severe stressor), separation anxiety disorder (e.g. avoidance of school), social phobia (e.g. avoidance of social situations because of fear of embarrassment), panic disorder with agoraphobia, or agoraphobia without history of panic disorder.

Types:
- animal type
- natural environment type (e.g. heights, storms, water)
- blood–injection–injury type
- situational type (e.g. airplanes, elevators, enclosed places)
- other type (e.g. phobic avoidance of situations that may lead to choking, vomiting, or contracting an illness; in children, avoidance of loud sounds or costumed characters)

We can break the symptoms described in the DSM-IV definition into four types:
- affective (related to mood or emotion)
- behavioural
- cognitive
- somatic (related to the body).

Although the experience of anxiety is different for everybody, it is typical for people to experience feelings of terror or dread and a loss of control, the persistent and salient thought that they are going to faint, vomit or even die, to feel dizzy, to have trouble breathing and to start sweating. The behavioural symptoms of phobias are concentrated around avoiding the thing that the person is afraid of. It is this urge to avoid the fear stimulus that causes the problems of daily function that might bring a person to the attention of a psychologist or psychiatrist. For many people, avoiding something they are afraid of does not require daily effort. For example, many people are afraid of flying in aeroplanes, but rarely need to do so. Others have a specific phobia of stairs, which are experienced more often. Others have a phobia of loud noises, which could occur at any time and are not within the person's control – it is clearly more difficult to find strategies to avoid this.

Common phobias include arachnophobia, social phobia and brontophobia.

Specific phobia is the most commonly diagnosed of the anxiety disorders in the USA. It is overall third among all disorders, behind major depression and substance abuse disorders, with a lifetime prevalence of 12.5% (Kessler and Merikangas, 2004). Prevalence rates are lower in other countries; as little as 0.63% reported in Florence, Italy (Faravelli et al., 1989).

Women usually make up a far greater part of these statistics, and symptoms usually begin during childhood, around the age of 7 (Kessler and Merikangas, 2004). When looking at reasons for the different prevalence of phobias in men and women, it is important to remember that diagnosis requires significant impairment of functioning. Because it is possible to manage one's life around avoiding the situation, animal or item that causes anxiety, it is clear that some types of phobia are more likely than others to be diagnosed, even if they are not the most common phobias. Situational phobias appear to be dealt with in a clinical context more than others, and a further reason for this might be that a person's expectation of a positive outcome from therapy is higher.

Etiology: Biological level of analysis

According to the biological level of analysis, specific phobias should be explainable in terms of evolutionary adaptation, genetic susceptibility, the action of neurotransmitters in specific regions of the brain, and the role of hormones. Recent research even suggests that there is a possibility that anxiety disorders are caused by breathing problems and an excessive intake of carbon dioxide (Wilhelm et al., 2001).

The fight or flight response

The fight or flight response (page 54) is generally considered to be the basis of the anxiety reaction. It seems to prepare the human body for action to deal with a threatening situation through activating the sympathetic nervous system. Researchers have investigated the hormone adrenaline, which is known to be involved in this system, and the neurotransmitter GABA, which is known to be involved in the parasympathetic nervous system which returns the body to its normal state when a threat has passed. The biological level of analysis predicts that overactivity in the sympathetic nervous system, or underactivity in the parasympathetic nervous system, is responsible for the phobia.

Merckelbach et al. (1996) indicate that increased levels of adrenocorticotropic hormone (ACTH) enhance the acquisition of new fears and that phobic individuals (both humans and primates) do tend to have elevated levels of this hormone. There is research showing that women learn fears more slowly while menstruating and this may be related to hormone levels. There is also much research relating to the role of GABA in preventing the anxiety reaction, but this comes mostly from animal studies. Evidence from studies of treatment effectiveness show that anxiety can be successfully reduced in humans by increasing the availability of GABA in the brain (Cryan and Kaupmann, 2005).

While research into hormones and neurotransmitters assists in establishing the biological correlates of the fear reaction, they are not yet able to offer a causal explanation. Clearly, we are limited in what we can do experimentally with humans for ethical reasons.

Drugs that increase levels of GABA often reduce a person's experience of anxiety.

EXERCISE

4 What ethical and practical problems are there in experimental research into specific phobias in humans? Write a short paragraph to describe them.

Figure 5.1 shows two structures deep in the centre of the brain (one in each temporal lobe) called the amygdalae (singular, amygdala). See also Figure 2.1 (page 48).

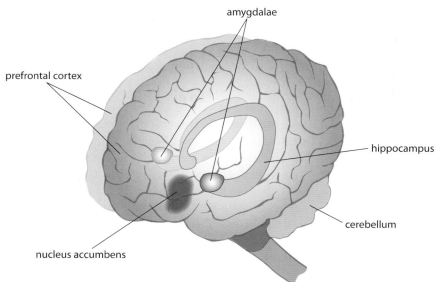

amygdalae

prefrontal cortex

hippocampus

cerebellum

nucleus accumbens

Figure 5.1
The location of the amygdalae.

Åhs et al. (2009) studied the role of the amygdalae by exposing 16 female volunteers with either snake or spider phobias to pictures of both, so that reactions to the fear stimulus could be compared with reactions to the animal they were not afraid of. To ensure participants were genuinely afraid of the animals, the Snake Anxiety and Spider Anxiety Questionnaires were used.

PET scans (page 42) were carried out to obtain images of brain activity during exposure. The PET scans were compared with participants' estimates of distress. The researchers found that there was a strong correlation between amygdala activity in the right hemisphere of the brain and ratings of distress. Their conclusion was that the amygdala is activated after object-recognition areas in the brain indicate that the object is threatening. The amygdala then works to activate other regions of the brain to support the activation of a fight or flight response to the stimulus. They suggest that a process of classical conditioning has biologically predisposed individual humans to have this biological reaction to some stimuli but not to others.

The role of the amygdala in activating this response may be countered by a regulatory system in the prefrontal cortex, as Hermann et al. (2009) found that women with a spider phobia showed lower than normal prefrontal activity in an fMRI study when trying to manage their emotional reaction to pictures of spiders.

PET scan showing an an amygdala and the fear response.

Classical conditioning

Other research has already suggested that classical conditioning is a biological process involving the unconscious strengthening of neural connections in the brain according to experience (e.g. Öhman et al., 1975). Öhman experimented on human participants, testing whether he could create fear reactions to pictures of prepared stimuli like snakes and unprepared stimuli like flowers. It was easier for him to create the fear response for the prepared items and these responses were more likely to last than others. These results suggest that humans are biologically predisposed through an evolutionary process to fear some objects more than others.

Bennett–Levy and Marteau (1984) come some way to explaining this in a correlational study that measured fear of animals and asked participants to rate them on certain

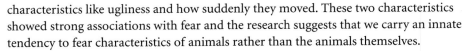

characteristics like ugliness and how suddenly they moved. These two characteristics showed strong associations with fear and the research suggests that we carry an innate tendency to fear characteristics of animals rather than the animals themselves.

More recent research by Davey et al. (1998) suggests that what has been selected for in human evolution is fear elicited by stimuli associated with disease rather than direct predatory attack. These researchers conducted a cross-cultural study in the USA, the UK, India, Japan, Hong Kong, Korea and the Netherlands. They found that ratings of fear were strongest for disgust-relevant animals (e.g. slugs and spiders) although India's ratings were lowest for these and Japan's were highest. The results suggest that animals which trigger a disgust reaction (an adaptive response to help humans avoid disease) will trigger the brain mechanisms that activate the sympathetic nervous system and thereby the fight or flight response. This study clearly offers directions for both cognitive and sociocultural explanations that are explored below. It also found gender differences, which was not surprising given that females generally have a stronger disgust reaction than males, again possibly an adaptation favoured by natural selection because a failure to recognize disease would threaten a female's own life and the lives of her children.

Twin studies

One of the problems with evolutionary explanations is that they lack concrete evidence, and it is the ultimate aim at a biological level of analysis to find a genuine genetic basis for specific phobias. Twin studies offer some support for a genetic cause. Skre et al. (2000) found that specific phobias were shared by identical twins much more often than by non-identical twins. Merckelbach et al. (1996) suggest that although twin studies usually show some support for genetic inheritance, what is inherited is not the specific phobia, but a general tendency for neurotic responses, and this usually manifests itself as specific phobias. The exception is a phobia of blood, which does seem to be inherited more specifically than other phobias.

Weaknesses

This highlights the main weakness of biological explanations for phobias. Despite increasing understanding of the biological mechanisms involved (e.g. activation in some areas of the brain and reduced activity in others), researchers tend to study animal phobias, whereas situational phobias are more common. Inheritance of a disgust reaction may work to explain animal phobias, but it is a poor explanation for a fear of flying. More research is needed to discover if there are biological similarities among different phobic types.

Etiology: Cognitive level of analysis

Bandura's self-efficacy theory (page 121) has been used to account for the causes of phobias (Bandura, 1982), focusing on an individual's expectations about their ability to perform a particular task relating to the source of their phobia. For example, many people might have a fear of flying, but a person who cannot imagine they will successfully get onto an aeroplane and survive the flight will suffer greater anxiety than others. However, there is limited support for this as a causal explanation of specific phobias, and the work of Beck and Emery appears to be more relevant (Armfield, 2006).

Cognitive schemas

The Beck and Emery model explains that cognitive schemas are responsible for an increased and maladaptive perception of threat, a misinterpretation of environmental stimuli that triggers the fear response. Typical cognitive patterns are also responsible for this (e.g. magnification and personalization), which can make the person focus too much on themselves and the likelihood that they are facing a serious threat. This sense

---

To access Worksheet 5.2 on the Bennett–Levy and Marteau (1984) study, please visit www.pearsonbacconline.com and follow the on-screen instructions.

A lot of phobias seem to be connected to the emotional disgust reaction.

The thought processes of people with phobias can be quite similar when they are exposed to the phobic object, regardless of the type of phobia. This generally includes catastrophizing the situation, with racing thoughts telling sufferers that something terrible is going to happen.

of vulnerability combines with low self-efficacy and appraisal theory, such that when a possible threat is encountered (primary appraisal), the person makes a secondary appraisal about whether they can cope with it. If either part of the appraisal is biased in a maladaptive direction, the chances of a strong anxiety reaction increase. Learned avoidance strategies are then employed to remove the person from the fear situation.

There is some empirical support for this idea, such as a study by Thorpe and Salkovskis (1995). However, it appears that thoughts specifically relating to suffering harm are relatively infrequent before people with phobias encounter the phobic stimulus. This suggests that phobias are held by normally rational people with relatively correct interpretations of the level of danger and their ability to deal with it, but that this rationality is overcome

by the kind of thinking Beck and Emery discuss during the experience of phobia. This limits its value as a causal explanation.

Flying: a relaxation for some, a horror for others.

Armfield (2006) lists a number of cognitive factors (e.g. negative self-focused attention, memory bias and attentional bias) that have been shown to be associated with anxiety generally and phobia specifically. However, he concludes that there is a deficit in cause–effect relationships in every case. It seems that we are left unsure if the phobia causes the problems in thinking, or if the problems in thinking cause the phobia. He focuses on perceived unpredictability of the stimulus and perceived uncontrollability of both stimulus and situation, such as when a person sees a dog and believes they cannot predict or control the behaviour of the animal or escape from it. This is supported by experimental evidence that when participants are able to turn off unpleasant stimuli being presented to them, they show a smaller physiological reaction to the stimuli than participants who cannot (Sartory and Daum, 1992). Further supporting evidence is that when asked about their beliefs about spiders, phobic individuals tend to refer more to unpredictability and lack of control over their behaviour than to negative thoughts such as dirtiness or disgust (Arntz et al., 1993).

Armfield's (2006) conclusion is a cognitive model based on schema theory: a person with a specific phobia has a vulnerability schema for the phobic stimulus which combines uncontrollability, unpredictability, danger and disgust; this schema is automatically employed to interpret the situation when a person is presented with their phobic stimulus. Armfield assumes that individual personality traits and biological dispositions (e.g. genetic susceptibility) and previous experience are all contributors to the schema. The activation of the schema triggers evaluative processes leading to the somatic, behavioural and cognitive components of the specific phobia.

Cognitive models like this are adequate in explaining the mechanisms involved in triggering a phobia in response to a specific stimulus, and appear to fit quite comfortably next to the descriptions of the biological correlates of the phobic response. However, we are still lacking a full explanation of how such a schema develops, and we are still faced with the difficulty that experimental evidence of a cause–effect relationship is almost impossible to obtain.

Etiology: Sociocultural level of analysis

There is much less research available about sociocultural influences in the development of specific phobias, but there is research that indicates there are differences across cultures that must be accounted for somehow. Research by Davey et al. (1998) indicates, for example, that ratings of disgust and fear for some animals were much lower in India than Japan (page 160). In Japan, there is also a specific phobia related to the disgustingness of one's own body that does not tend to be reported in Western cultures.

The masculinity of a country appears to influence the prevalence of phobias.

Iancu et al. (2007) investigated the prevalence of specific phobias among 850 Israeli youths of both genders recruited into schools for military medicine or mechanics. They found that phobic symptoms were more present among males, those in the school for mechanics, those who had not graduated from high school, those not in a romantic relationship and those with fewer than two good friends. The researchers suggest that Israeli youths live in a masculine and high-stress psychological atmosphere. Both these characteristics are suggested by Arrindell et al. (2003) as causing a higher prevalence of **agoraphobia** among young people. This 2003 study found that the prevalence of agoraphobia was much higher in countries such as Japan and Hungary that scored high on Hofstede's masculinity/femininity index (page 135) than in low scorers such as Sweden and Spain.

Members of different cultural groups tend to have different phobias.

Athough Iancu et al. cannot show exactly how this engenders the development of specific phobias, some suggestions are offered by Chapman et al. (2008). These researchers offer explanations based on their findings when they compared African and Caucasian Americans with regard to the types of specific phobia experienced. They found that African Americans held more fears, with the greatest number grouped in the natural environment category (e.g. fear of deep water or storms) whereas Caucasian Americans tended to hold most fear over situations (e.g. public speaking or flying). Earlier studies finding similar results have been explained in terms of a generally higher level of anxiety among African Americans because of overt racism, but Chapman et al. prefer to explain that specific phobias are transmitted inter-generationally and socially. This can also account for a larger number of phobias relating to spirits and demons in cultures where these are an accepted part of the culture. In addition, they note that African Americans tend to score lower on standardized measures of anxiety. This could be either because the tests fail to pick up some kind of culture-specific anxiety, or because there actually is less anxiety.

It is clear that, at each level of analysis, we are forced to consider the other levels of analysis. It appears that an interaction between environmental influences such as cultural climate and social expectations as well as individual personality and biological factors can contribute to the kind of cognitive and behavioural symptoms of specific phobias, and it is better to consider them in a more holistic way than to attempt to apply a blanket explanation for the etiology of this disorder.

● **Examiner's hint**
You can be asked to what extent the biological, cognitive and socio-cultural levels of analysis influence abnormal behaviour. This means you need to compare the levels of analysis and discuss their relative strengths and weaknesses.

EXERCISE

5   Write a table summarizing strengths and limitations of each level of analysis in explaining specific phobias.

Treatment for specific phobias

There is a range of successful treatments for specific phobias, and many psychologists and psychiatrists these days describe themselves as eclectic. This means they draw on many different theoretical approaches to guide their treatment. An eclectic approach has intuitive appeal but requires therapists to undergo training in a variety of areas.

Psychologists are unable to prescribe drugs but should be aware of how medication

affects patients. Psychiatrists can prescribe drugs, but they should also be able to perform several different therapeutic techniques to help solve a variety of problems. This approach acknowledges that the causes of problems are not always clear. Moreover, different therapeutic techniques will be appropriate according to the needs of clients in terms of class, status, gender, previous experience of therapy, expectations, thinking styles, the urgency of their situation and so on. Several examples of how therapies can work together are given below; you will need to refer to these to answer questions about eclectic treatment. More advice is given at the end of the chapter.

Biomedical therapy

Biomedical approaches to treating specific phobias focus on medication to alleviate anxiety symptoms and biofeedback training to help the individual manage their own physiological arousal. Neither of these tend to be used in isolation, but will be addressed separately here.

Going to the dentist is frightening for many people. Dentists try hard to help calm fears.

The use of medication is reviewed by Choy et al. (2007), and mostly consists of the use of benzodiazepines (e.g. alprazolam) which enhance the effectiveness of GABA although there is some strong evidence that paroxetine, a selective serotonin reuptake inhibitor (SSRI), is effective (Benjamin et al., 2000). In a study into the use of medication by people with a fear of flying, less anxiety was reported during a flight by patients using alprazolam. However, as is typical of studies using medication, the researchers found that the effects did not last into another event a week later, and in fact symptoms were worse than in a group who had taken a placebo the week before.

For dental anxiety, similar results were found for midazolam (another benzodiazepine): after three months, symptoms were back to their original levels. This study compared the effectiveness of a single dose of the drug with a single individual psychotherapy session, and found longer-lasting benefits for the latter.

The use of benzodiazepines has been criticized for two main reasons.
- They can have significant side-effects and patients can easily develop physical tolerance to them, rendering the drug ineffective. Side-effects can include drowsiness and sexual difficulties, and sometimes an increase in aggression and irritability.
- They do not tackle the cause of the problem. They maximize the effectiveness of GABA, the key neurotransmitter involved in the parasympathetic nervous system that calms a person down, but fail to solve the problem of the initial reaction, whether this is a biologically, cognitively or socioculturally caused phenomenon, and individual psychotherapy is therefore usually favoured.

 Dentists often need to use medication with immediate but short-lived effects because the dental situation is very frightening for many people.

Sedatives like nitrous oxide have been found to be effective for dental phobia, perhaps because of the context in which the phobia manifests. Going to the dentist is not a daily activity for most people, and there is little risk of an unexpected encounter with a dentist's chair, so the immediate calming effects in the presence of a trained professional are effective. Long-term studies show that even where there is not physical tolerance to the drug, the benefits of medication do not last.

Individual therapy

The two most successful treatments are behavioural and cognitive. Behavioural treatment is based on classical conditioning theory, which suggests that the fear is a learned response to a stimulus, and that this association can be broken through various different approaches in therapy.

Systematic desensitization is probably the best known of these approaches. It consists of the construction of a hierarchical set of fear situations relating to the phobic stimulus, training in muscle relaxation, and then exposure to the stimulus through imagination. Ideally, as the person undergoing desensitization imagines progressively worse situations as they learn to relax, they replace the response of fear and anxiety with a relaxation response. Initially, for example, a person might be asked to imagine being outside an airport; after they can relax at the thought of this, they then imagine going into the airport. Eventually, they will imagine getting on the plane. Ideally, by the time they try to do this in reality, their anxiety response will have been extinguished.

Systematic desensitization has longer-lasting effects than drugs for many people.

Choy et al. (2007) suggest that studies into systematic desensitization have shown that it is good at reducing anxiety levels, but not so good at reducing avoidance behaviours. Thus, people will feel less anxiety, but still have the problems of functioning that are likely to have brought them to the attention of practitioners initially. Choy et al. also show that when systematic desensitization has been beneficial, the effects are long lasting – up to 3.5 years in one study without further treatment. Individual therapy like this is preferable to medication because of its effectiveness, and also because it appears to be correcting the problem rather than alleviating the symptoms. It is a better long-term solution without side-effects.

In vivo exposure seems to be the most immediately effective individual treatment. This involves real life exposure to the phobic stimulus, such as a real flight on a plane, or actually touching a spider. This approach was founded on behaviourist principles and expects to extinguish the fear response by targeting the worst possible scenario the person can imagine. Generally, since by definition phobias involve fear disproportionate to the actual threat involved in the situation, this is not as dangerous as it sounds, and it is a very effective treatment for people who have problems with flying and heights in particular. With animal phobias, it is unclear how effective the treatment is but a study of dog phobics (Rentz et al., 2003) suggests that real exposure was no better than imagined exposure.

Virtual reality exposure for a fear of flying.

Virtual reality therapy is now used for the same purpose as in vivo exposure and has been shown to be quite effective but perhaps more expensive than necessary in some situations. Choy et al. (2007) give the example of treatment for spider phobia being something of a waste of money. It is obviously more sensible to apply this technology to more expensive situations like flying.

Cognitive therapies are also used to treat specific phobias. They attempt to correct some of the faulty thinking that is assumed to be causing the problem. This means that irrational or exaggerated thoughts need to be restructured, often with the presentation of factual evidence that challenges a person's beliefs about the likelihood of danger. Shafran et al. (1993) found this type of therapy to be successful by itself and when combined with in vivo exposure for claustrophobia. The effects tend to last longer, although this seems to be more the case for claustrophobia than dental phobia (Choy et al., 2007), possibly due to the genuine likelihood of discomfort and pain in a dental situation.

An eclectic approach can be used in individual therapy by combining medication with therapy or by choosing an appropriate psychotherapy from the range available. One of the most difficult problems a person faces when they have a phobia is the combination of anxiety and the desire to avoid therapy. If medication can help to reduce the effects of this, then it is possible that exposure therapies will be more successful.

 Eclectic approaches combining more than one treatment are very effective for phobia sufferers.

Beutler et al. (1991) give guidance for psychotherapists interested in taking a truly eclectic approach by suggesting a number of questions that need to be addressed before therapy. In the specific example of a woman who has a phobia of automobiles, the initial questions are non-directive or non-confrontational to build rapport and relax the patient. Behavioural therapy then begins with homework exercises and later includes the husband to work on her interpersonal communication skills as well.

Group therapy

Group therapies are also used in treating specific phobias. Öst et al. (1998) tested the effectiveness of treatment carried out in groups of eight people with spider phobia. One group received direct treatment with modelling from the therapist, each participant having their own set of four spiders of increasing sizes that they needed to learn to touch; a second group observed one person receiving this treatment; and a third group watched a video of this type of treatment. Anxiety levels were reduced much more in the first group, who all touched the spiders, than in either of the other groups. Öst et al. explain that this is probably due to the increase in self-efficacy that having gone through such a procedure gives participants. Group therapy is cheaper and more efficient in terms of time than individual therapies. However, it can be difficult to predict how long it is going to take if individual outcomes are set, as in this case of group systematic desensitization where the aim was for all participants to complete their tasks.

Group cognitive behaviour therapy has also been used for children with a mix of different anxiety disorders and seems to have good long-term outcomes, partly because of the advantage of seeing peers develop new skills in dealing with their anxiety. In Lumpkin et al. (2002), all children showed improvement, except one. Although this child was not one of those with a specific phobia, it highlights one of the problems of group therapies: they are good for those who are showing improvement, but they can compound problems by reducing self-efficacy for those who are not showing improvement.

Affective disorders
Definitions and diagnosis

Affective disorders are disorders related to mood. There are several disorders included within this category, and again, for the purposes of the IB examination, you need to focus on only one of these. Here we consider major depressive disorder.

The DSM-IV-TR criteria for diagnosing this condition are outlined overleaf.

Relevant criteria for major depressive episode

Reprinted with permission from the *Diagnostic and Statistical Manual of Mental Disorders*, 4th Edn, Text Revision (Copyright 2000). American Psychiatric Association.

A   Five (or more) of the following symptoms have been present during the same 2-week period and represent a change from previous functioning; at least one of the symptoms is either:

- depressed mood or
- loss of interest or pleasure.

   Note: Do not include symptoms that are clearly due to a general medical condition, or mood-incongruent delusions or hallucinations.

   1   Depressed mood most of the day, nearly every day, as indicated by either subjective report (e.g. feels sad or empty) or observation made by others (e.g. appears tearful).
      Note: In children and adolescents, can be irritable mood.
   2   Markedly diminished interest or pleasure in all, or almost all, activities most of the day, nearly every day (as indicated by either subjective account or observation made by others).
   3   Significant weight loss when not dieting or weight gain (e.g. a change of more than 5% of body weight in a month), or decrease or increase in appetite nearly every day.
      Note: In children, consider failure to make expected weight gains.
   4   Insomnia or hypersomnia nearly every day.
   5   Psychomotor agitation or retardation nearly every day (observable by others, not merely subjective feelings of restlessness or being slowed down).
   6   Fatigue or loss of energy nearly every day.
   7   Feelings of worthlessness or excessive or inappropriate guilt (which may be delusional) nearly every day (not merely self-reproach or guilt about being sick).
   8   Diminished ability to think or concentrate, or indecisiveness, nearly every day (either by subjective account or as observed by others).
   9   Recurrent thoughts of death (not just fear of dying), recurrent suicidal ideation without a specific plan, or a suicide attempt or a specific plan for committing suicide.

B   The symptoms do not meet criteria for a mixed episode (including mania as well).

C   The symptoms cause clinically significant distress or impairment in social, occupational, or other important areas of functioning.

D   The symptoms are not due to the direct physiological effects of a substance (e.g. a drug of abuse, a medication) or a general medical condition (e.g. hypothyroidism).

E   The symptoms are not better accounted for by bereavement (i.e. after the loss of a loved one) the symptoms persist for longer than 2 months or are characterized by marked functional impairment, morbid preoccupation with worthlessness, suicidal ideation, psychotic symptoms, or psychomotor retardation.

The United States National Institute of Mental Health claims that major depressive disorder is the leading cause of disability in the USA between the ages of 15 and 44 with a lifetime prevalence of 16.6% (Kessler and Merikangas, 2004). It affects women more than men. This difference appears to start around the age of 13, and results in up to three times more women than men having a diagnosis of depression. Several recent studies have compared the prevalence of depression in various countries, and there is significant variation. Polish men, for example, had a prevalence rate of 20.4%, and both Polish and Russian women were high at 32.9% and 33.7% respectively (Nicholson et al., 2008). However, this particular

study used self-report data and may reflect a reporting bias rather than genuinely higher rates of depression.

Differences can be difficult to account for as there is no experimental way to address the problem. Explanations include the tendency for psychiatrists to be male and from the dominant culture, which results in over-diagnosis for groups that they fail to understand or have stereotyped beliefs about (i.e. women and minorities). Otherwise, there may be genuine differences that are either biological or sociocultural in origin, as shown by Levav et al.'s 1997 study indicating a higher prevalence of depression among Jewish males with relatively low alcoholism. This same study also offers the possibility that some groups are more likely than others to seek help for depression and, in some cultures, going to see a medical doctor when there are mood problems is not the expected path of action. A barman, a priest, a shaman or a friend might all be more appropriate. Etic and emic approaches to the cross-cultural study of depression are discussed on page 140.

EXERCISE

6   Under the headings *Affective, Cognitive, Behavioural* and *Somatic*, group together the symptoms of depression.

Etiology: Biological level of analysis

Hagen et al. (2004) offer an evolutionary perspective on major depressive disorder, suggesting that it is a psychological adaptation favoured by natural selection and serves two main purposes: to signal need and to elicit help from others in the social group. This is an interesting approach with powerful logical argument (including, for example, the point that most suicides by depressed individuals are preceded by the threat of suicide, which therefore signals a need for help and attention). However, like all evolutionary explanations, it is impossible to test experimentally. In addition, we would still need to find the genetic basis of this evolved behaviour.

 Although evolutionary arguments are hard to prove, they do make disorders more like normal human behaviour rather than inexplicable variations on normal.

The search for genes for depression has involved a large number of twin studies and, more recently, molecular genetic research has attempted to identify genes with a role in depression. A very large Swedish twin study with over 42 000 participants used telephone interviews to diagnose depression on the basis of (a) the presence of most of the DSM-IV symptoms or (b) having had a prescription for antidepressants. The researchers found concordance rates among monozygotic twins of 0.44% for female and 0.31% for male, compared with 0.16% and 0.11% for female and male dizygotic twins respectively. If the disorder were purely genetic, we might expect the monozygotic concordance rates to be much higher. But the difference between monozygotic and dizygotic concordance rates is enough to indicate a strong genetic component (Kendler et al., 2006).

EXERCISE

7   What ethical and methodological problems are there with a study like this?

Some convincing research suggests that short alleles of a gene known as 5-HTT affect the transmission and reuptake of serotonin to increase the chances of a person suffering from depression. People with the long allele seem less likely to suffer depression.

Drugs that prevent serotonin reuptake (e.g. Prozac) are known to improve the symptoms of depression but Levinson (2005) notes that the short allele on 5-HTT acts in a similar way; it hinders reuptake of serotonin. This means that a hypothesized genetic cause of depression and a medical treatment for depression have the same physiological effect. This confusing

picture needs further research. Levinson (2005) also notes that rather than causing depression, the gene is more likely to make individuals more sensitive to stressful life events.

The catecholamine theory of depression was proposed in 1965 after researchers found that reserpine, a drug used for hypertension, was apparently able to cause a depression-like state, and that iproniazid, a drug used to treat tuberculosis, was able to improve mood (Rivas–Vazquez and Blais, 1997).

These drugs are no longer in use but they affected the release and break-down of catecholamine neurotransmitters, which include noradrenaline, dopamine and serotonin. This led to the rather reductionist theory that depression is caused by deficiencies in the availability of these neurotransmitters, with serotonin becoming the primary target of research and theory in more recent times. This theory was supported by the large amount of research demonstrating the effectiveness of the new drug fluoxetine (marketed as Prozac), timed around its introduction in 1988.

To learn more about the Lacasse and Leo (2005) paper, go to www. pearsonhotlinks.com, enter the title or ISBN of this book and select weblink 5.6.

Problems with the serotonin hypothesis are summarized by Lacasse and Leo (2005). The central problem is a lack of evidence that any depressed person has low levels of serotonin. In fact, there is no baseline balanced level of serotonin to measure against. The authors cite a common analogy for what is wrong with using the effectiveness of a treatment as support for a causal explanation: headaches are successfully treated by aspirin, but we do not have any theory suggesting that headaches are caused by a lack of aspirin. In addition, tianeptine, a drug commonly used in Europe and South America to treat depression, has precisely the opposite action to fluoxetine (Sarek, 2006). Its effectiveness lies in the prevention of neuronal damage due to stress, which brings us to the role of hormones in depression.

Researchers are interested in the role of cortisol in a number of areas of human behaviour. It seems that exposure to stressful events increases levels of cortisol, and this in turn has damaging effects on the brain, particularly when it is not yet fully developed.

The hormone that has received the most attention from researchers in depression in recent times is cortisol. It is seen as particularly relevant because of its role in stress. A meta-analysis of studies connecting this hormone with depression found that there seems to be a difference in reactivity to stress between depressed and non-depressed people: when non-depressed people are put under stress, cortisol levels rise and fall rapidly; depressed people have a more blunt reaction and remain under stress for longer (Burke et al., 2005).

A study of homeless children between the ages of 4 and 7 found a significant correlation between high levels of cortisol and a history of many negative life events (Cutuli et al., 2010). Higher levels of cortisol were found in children whose families were unable to participate in a poverty alleviation programme in Mexico. The most important group differences within the sample were between children whose mothers were depressed – the results indicated that participating in the programme, which included advice about good mothering, helped to reduce stress levels in children who might otherwise have been likely to also develop depression (Fernald and Gunnar, 2009).

Unfortunately, we are still left without a clear understanding of how depression might develop biologically, despite a number of physiological correlates of the disorder having been identified. At best, it seems that this information indicates a need for more research about the interactions between stressful life events, genes, hormones and neurotransmitters.

Etiology: Cognitive level of analysis

Cognitive psychologists have suggested a cognitive vulnerability model for depression. According to this model, people who have certain cognitive characteristics are more likely to become depressed. This is not because depression is caused by these characteristics, but that they make an individual more vulnerable.

Underlying beliefs about ourselves can affect the way we interpret the world.

Aaron Beck (1976) suggests that a cognitive triad underlies the information-processing style of depressed individuals. The cognitive triad is a cluster of negative thoughts grouped into three categories: the self, the world, and the future. A person develops and

maintains these negative core beliefs through a set of cognitive biases such as over-generalization (e.g. I always fail tests), selective abstraction (usually focusing on the negative parts of something), and polar reasoning (not being able to appreciate ambiguity in interpretations of life). These thinking styles combine to give the person a negative self schema – a fundamentally pessimistic attitude about themselves which can be contributed to by parents or peers early on in life, and makes it very, very difficult for a person to see anything positive in life. One of the problems with Beck's work is that, although it is descriptively very powerful, it remains unclear whether this information processing is really a cause of depression, or if these models are simply a good description of disordered thinking.

Hankin and Abramson (2001) extend the model to try and correct for this weakness and also to improve its ability to explain gender differences in the prevalence of depression. Core to their extension is the occurrence of a negative life event that creates negative effect (e.g. a sad or angry mood) before the thinking styles described by Beck come into play. Their model helps explain how traumatic experiences like sexual abuse or separation from close relatives can contribute to the construction of negative self schemata and provides targets for therapy.

▲ Aaron Beck (1921–).

Another well-known theorist, Albert Ellis (1962), offers a similar explanation, focusing on negative cognitive style as the basis of depression. Specifically, irrational and self-defeating beliefs affect an individual's interpretation of antecedent or activating events, leading

to negative emotional consequences. For example, if all members of a class received a low score for a test, some would be content and others would be upset. The activating event was precisely the same, but the consequences are different, and it is underlying beliefs that are responsible for this, beliefs like 'I am stupid' or 'the teacher hates me' being possible culprits.

◄ Albert Ellis (1913–2007).

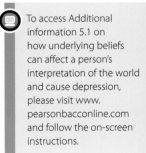

These explanations resonate with most people, and there is some empirical support suggesting that depressed people do indeed have negative thinking styles (Robins and Block, 1989). However, you should bear in mind the work of Taylor and Brown (1988) which suggests that depressed people are actually more realistic in their interpretations of activating events (page 148).

To access Additional information 5.1 on how underlying beliefs can affect a person's interpretation of the world and cause depression, please visit www.pearsonbacconline.com and follow the on-screen instructions.

Etiology: Sociocultural level of analysis

At this level of analysis, we focus on social and cultural factors that seem to increase risk or vulnerability. There is a large amount of research on this area, much of it sparked by the work of Brown and Harris (1978), who provided a vulnerability model based on the interaction of vulnerability factors and provoking agents. Their original vulnerability factors were:

- losing one's mother at an early age
- lack of a confiding relationship
- more than three young children at home
- unemployment.

Levels of mental illness and stress in the UK have tended to be higher when there is a greater disparity between 'the haves' and 'the have-nots' – in other words, when there is a big difference in economic security between rich people and poor people.

Unemployment and poverty, in particular, are factors that have been associated with depression, but in themselves seem unlikely to be responsible for creating feelings of extreme sadness. They must be understood within the context of cultures where work and material wealth provide meaning, status and identity to people's lives. In the same way, some cultures place more social value than others on the existence of an intimate relationship with one other person, and family members have very different roles in terms of social support.

Nicholson et al. (2008) found that men in the most socially disadvantaged groups in Poland, Russia and the Czech Republic were five times more likely to report depressive symptoms than their compatriots in higher socio-economic groups. In the USA, there appears to be lower prevalence of depression in Hispanic communities (Wu and Anthony, 2000), supposedly because levels of social support are higher and act as a preventative against depression. Similarly, Gabilondo et al. (2010) found that depression occurs less frequently in Spain than in northern European countries, and that there is a lower rate of suicide. Stronger traditional roles of family and higher religiosity were proposed as sociocultural variables that might explain lower prevalence in this study.

Deeper analysis suggests that in countries and historical periods where social inequalities are more pronounced, rates of depression seem to be higher (Cohen, 2002). This is possibly because of feelings of powerlessness and worthlessness that, in some cases, have a physical basis through the experience of physical stress or undernourishment. In other cases, these feelings are a more subjective product of socialization within individualist, materialist cultures; such feelings lead to perceptions of inequality, unfairness and inability to participate in the 'ideal' society enjoyed and advertised by those in higher socio-economic groups.

Does the desire for material wealth encourage feelings of depression?

Various commentators have suggested that depression did not exist in cultures outside the West, but others have found that with increasing Westernization, rates of depression increase. This may not simply reflect the influence of new social pressures or some sort of cultural channelling of unhappiness into a specific set of symptoms; it may reflect changes in diagnostic patterns as mental health practitioners become more Western in their methods. Researchers have noted in Africa and Asia, for example, that depression is accompanied by somatic symptoms, but certain core symptoms are shared across cultures; these core symptoms should be the focus of attention (Okulate et al., 2004). The core symptom most often shared is the affective component of depression, with somatic symptoms secondary in Africa, while suicidal thoughts and guilt are more common secondary symptoms in European patients (Binitie, 1975).

A final set of explanations for depression at a sociocultural level of analysis comes from studies employing Hofstede's cultural dimensions (page 135). Arrindell et al. (2003) found a high correlation between prevalence of depression and scores on the Masculinity–Femininity Index in a sample of European countries.

Individualism has also been found to be associated with high rates of depression. In a recent study that integrated biological and sociocultural levels of analysis, Chiao and Blizinsky (2010) found that depression was associated with individualism and that this dimension had a negative correlation with the frequency of the short allele relating to serotonin transporters (page 167). Rather than suggest that a lack of social support causes depression, the researchers suggest that cultural norms, such as increased social support, have developed to protect the more biologically vulnerable groups; thus, collectivism is evidence of biological vulnerability. More research will be needed to confirm these findings as the data required are not readily available for many of the collectivist countries around the world.

Does collective living prevent depression?

Treatments for major depressive disorder

Biomedical therapy

Drugs are widely used to treat depression because we are aware of some of the neurochemical activity associated with the disorder. The serotonin hypothesis suggests that there is an inadequate amount of serotonin available in the synaptic gap between neurons for effective transmission to occur. Many medications aim to increase the amount of serotonin available. Most of these work by preventing the reuptake of serotonin, making it stay in the synaptic gap longer, and thereby increasing the efficiency of the serotonin already present. Such drugs are called selective serotonin reuptake inhibitors (SSRIs), and include fluoxetine (first marketed as Prozac). It is now produced by many drug companies under different brand names. The two main criticisms of fluoxetine are that it treats the symptoms but does not cure the disorder, and that there are significant side-effects. Side-effects include sexual problems, dry mouth, insomnia, and even an increase in suicidal thoughts. For many people, these side-effects outweigh the benefits of the medication, and it seems that the drug is more helpful for more serious cases of depression. Because only the symptoms are treated and because depressive episodes usually recur, it is necessary for patients to continue taking the medication. Unless the medication is used with therapy, it is unlikely that the disorder will disappear permanently.

We can look at two main tests of how well these drugs work. One way is to compare the drug with a placebo when prescribed to patients with depression, and the other is to compare it with other forms of therapy. One difficulty in looking at this research is that many of the studies which show that medication is no better than placebos have gone unpublished. A large meta-analysis by Kirsch et al. (2008) showed that there is at best only a small difference in efficacy between placebo and medication.

 Not all research is published, and sometimes unwanted findings are not reported.

The European Committee for Medicinal Products for Human Use has addressed these concerns and claims that the design of many outcome studies is flawed: instead of measuring only change in severity of symptoms, an absolute criterion should be set, and the proportion of patients on the drug who reach this criterion should form an additional

● **Examiner's hint**
The Cuijpers (2009) study
indicates the benefit of
an eclectic approach to
treatment. Make a note of this
as you will want to refer to it.

measure of efficacy (Broich, 2009). Antidepressants do better in this kind of research. The debate is a very political one, and the potential consequences of regulatory bodies accepting Kirsch's conclusion that antidepressants are not effective would include a massive loss of income for a number of pharmaceutical companies, so it is not taken lightly. There is also an ethical problem with research, in that lying to patients about the kind of treatment they receive is not only deceptive, but also possibly dangerous if the patient is having frequent suicidal thoughts.

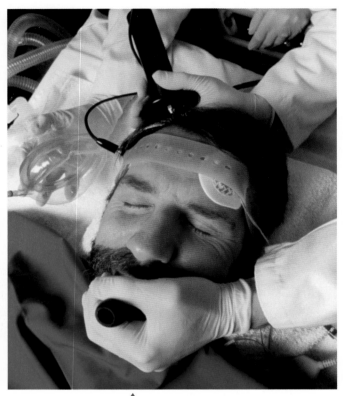

A meta-analysis of studies comparing the effectiveness of various treatments for depression (Cuijpers et al., 2009) found that psychotherapy groups do significantly better than control groups (which sometimes include discussions as a placebo). Medication was found to be more effective than psychotherapy in improving symptoms, especially when SSRIs were used. But the best results were found in studies that used a combination of medication and psychotherapy. The authors of this study note that although psychotherapy appears to be effective in alleviating symptoms and may have good long-term effects, this is more true for patients with milder forms of depression.

One further biomedical treatment should be considered here: electroconvulsive therapy (ECT). This is a very controversial treatment that has significant restrictions on its use in most countries. It is generally claimed that this form of treatment is only appropriate for individuals for whom other forms of treatment have failed. Its use is in decline, but it is interesting to note that almost half of the people who receive ECT are over the age of 65, and by far the majority are female, up to 76% in Finland (Read et al., 2004).

Patient ready for ECT.

Individual therapy

The most well-known individual therapy for depression is cognitive-behavioural therapy (CBT). It was initiated by several psychologists in the 1950s and 1960s, the most famous among them being Aaron Beck. The therapy consists of identifying the automatic, negative thoughts assumed to underlie the depression and helping the depressed person see and understand the connection between these thoughts and their emotional state. By addressing these thoughts together, and through individual homework exercises like keeping a mood diary, the person in therapy and the therapist can gradually change the negative self-schema and find more positive ways to interpret life events. This clearly accounts for the cognitive name in this approach to therapy, but there is also a behavioural side. This involves identifying behaviours that are rewarding for the individual and encouraging him or her to engage in them. One of the key symptoms of depression is a loss of interest in activities that used to give pleasure, and it is an aim of therapy to regain these levels of interest. At first, this may be a difficult and effortful process, but it should provide enough positive reinforcement for the client to continue participating in the world in a positive way.

Cognitive therapy tries
to restructure negative
information-processing
styles.

Another form of therapy emerged accidentally when it was found repeatedly that tests of efficacy of psychotherapy using a control group saw improvements in the control group as well as the patient group. The control groups often consisted of a sympathetic person discussing past experiences but without any theoretical guidance, and yet this proved to be

effective. Interpersonal therapy (IPT) was developed based on this finding. It concentrates on helping the client develop and use any positive social support networks they have in their life with improved communication skills. At times, IPT adjusts clients' expectations to be more realistic.

A review of the effectiveness of CBT and IPT indicates that IPT alone is not as quick as medication in relieving symptoms, but does provide substantial improvement at a slightly later point (Parker et al., 2006). The review highlighted an interesting finding: patients who receive medication in addition to IPT do better than patients who receive IPT in addition to medication. This is perhaps a reflection of patient expectation in terms of a preference for medication to solve problems. Studies comparing the effectiveness of IPT and CBT by assigning participants randomly to treatment groups have found no significant differences between IPT and CBT treatments, but Parker et al. (2006) suggest that this may be because psychotherapies are not necessarily delivered according to a pure theoretical format.

Butler et al. (2006) reviewed several meta-analyses of efficacy studies for CBT and concluded that CBT is extremely effective for depression, although the effect is not usually greater than medication alone, and outcomes are usually better when CBT is combined with medication.

Although individual therapies like this might appear to be inappropriate for use in other cultures with more collectivist tendencies, an interesting review by Hodges and Oei (2007) considers the likely applicability of CBT to Chinese culture. Their conclusion is that because of the power distance between therapist and client, CBT may actually be more effective in Chinese culture because clients are likely to accept the therapist's interpretations and advice about faulty information-processing. An expected disadvantage would be that for many clients, successful CBT requires an element of argument, and the therapist needs to be persuasive. Thus, although for Chinese clients the therapist's word would be taken, without the process of argument and justification, the true nature of the thoughts at the heart of depression might never be identified.

The most common form of eclecticism in treatment for major depressive disorder combines the use of medication with psychotherapy. In many cases, a person has come to the attention of the health system because they have become a danger to themselves or others. In these circumstances, medication is often the fastest way to see the kind of results that mean psychotherapy can begin. It is sometimes considered irresponsible to use either medication without therapy or therapy without medication. In the former case, this is because it makes the person dependent on the medication and they are likely to relapse if they stop taking it. In the latter, it is because when a person's thinking is disordered, appealing to them on a rational basis can be very difficult. When CBT is successful, it teaches people the kind of skills they need in order to function without further use of medication.

Group therapy

Group therapy is another option for people with depression. The rationale here is that people who may not hear or share when they are alone with a therapist may be encouraged to participate in discussion when they are surrounded by others. There is a chance that they can learn vicariously through the experience of others and become more optimistic about their own chances for recovery if they meet others who have improved.

Group CBT is commonly carried out and has been shown to be effective in several countries, including South Korea, where Hyun et al. (2005) randomly assigned depressed adolescents at a shelter for runaways to group CBT or a group receiving no treatment. They found group CBT to be extremely effective at relieving symptoms of depression. This is not an isolated result. Meta-analyses by McDermut et al. (2001) and Toseland and Siporin (1986) indicated that group therapy is at least as useful for patients as individual therapy.

What possible reasons are there for the clear gender and age bias in the treatment of depression? Consider the validity issues in diagnosing abnormality discussed earlier in this chapter (page 150).

● **Examiner's hint**
The Butler et al. (2006) study indicates the benefit of an eclectic approach to treatment. Make a note of this as you will want to refer to it.

Why is CBT likely to be more effective in China when it was devised in the West?

Truax (2001) considers group therapy to be well validated empirically as a treatment for depression but qualifies this by saying that most of the studies included in meta-analyses excluded the more severely depressed patients. This means that we do not know if group CBT is effective for all depressed people.

Clearly one of the disadvantages of group therapy is that dissatisfaction with the group or any of its members might lead to drop-out, and Truax (2001) cites this as the main reason why people drop out from studies like this. Clearly if optimism is to be improved among individuals suffering from depression, it could be counter-productive to populate the group with severely depressed people, especially if they have been undergoing treatment longer.

Eating disorders
Definitions and diagnosis

Eating disorders are known to affect females much more than males: only an estimated 5–15% of people with anorexia or bulimia are male. The National Institute of Mental Health in the United States suggests that females with anorexia have a death rate 12 times higher than the general female population. This clearly contributes to the status of anorexia as the psychiatric disorder with the highest mortality rate (van Kuyck et al., 2009). The disorder affects those from households with above-average income to a greater extent, and affects around 0.3% of the population (Zandian et al., 2007). It usually begins between the ages of 14 and 19. Symptoms can include performing rituals at mealtimes like cutting food into small pieces, and excessive exercise.

The condition is far more common in Western and individualist cultures, and it is not clear why this is so. Possible explanations include a greater focus on dieting since the 20th century in Europe and Anglo-American societies, exposure to unreasonably thin models in television, film and magazines, and social pressures to conform to a particular body weight, all of which appear to affect females more than males. While a biological explanation for this might be possible, it may be that males with body-image issues tend to perform different behaviours rather than self-starving.

It is interesting to compare the prevalence of eating-related problems in different cultures. Although eating disorders appear to be more uncommon in less industrialized countries and countries where there are more limitations on women's behaviour, it is also possible that cases of anorexia are more concealed in some cultures and therefore never diagnosed. Within the USA, Roland (1970) found that class and ethnicity were both important contributors – the vast majority of anorexia patients were Caucasian, with people of Italian and Jewish origin being over-represented in the statistics. Rates of anorexia seem to have increased during more affluent periods and in cultures where food is valued and in abundance.

 Anorexia used to be uncommon outside the developed world, but its prevalence is increasing.

Diagnostic criteria for anorexia nervosa

Reprinted with permission from the *Diagnostic and Statistical Manual of Mental Disorders*, 4th Edn, Text Revision (Copyright 2000). American Psychiatric Association.

A Refusal to maintain body weight at or above a minimally normal weight for age and height (e.g. weight loss leading to maintenance of body weight less than 85% of that expected; or failure to make expected weight gain during period of growth, leading to body weight less than 85% of that expected).

B Intense fear of gaining weight or becoming fat, even though underweight.

C Disturbance in the way in which one's body weight or shape is experienced, undue influence of body weight or shape on self-evaluation, or denial of the seriousness of the current low body weight.

D In postmenarcheal females, amenorrhea (i.e. the absence of at least three consecutive menstrual cycles). (A woman is considered to have amenorrhea if her periods occur only following hormone (e.g. estrogen) administration.)

Specify type:

restricting type: during the current episode of anorexia nervosa, the person has not regularly engaged in binge-eating or purging behavior (i.e. self-induced vomiting or the misuse of laxatives, diuretics, or enemas)

binge-eating/purging type: during the current episode of anorexia nervosa, the person has regularly engaged in binge-eating or purging behavior (i.e. self-induced vomiting or the misuse of laxatives, diuretics, or enemas)

EXERCISE

8 Under the headings *Affective, Cognitive, Behavioural* and *Somatic,* group together the symptoms of depression.

Etiology: Biological level of analysis

An evolutionary explanation for anorexia nervosa has been offered by Surbey (1987). Based on the findings that the weight loss usually comes after the amenorrhea (cessation of menstruation) and that anorexia often occurs in girls who are maturing early, the reproductive suppression model suggests that starvation is an adaptive response to stress that deliberately delays the onset of reproductive capabilities until a more appropriate time. The obvious weakness of this idea is that it excludes males; this is a weakness even if males are a very small sub-group of anorexics. However, the model does offer a possibility for longitudinal research in that it predicts that females who delay the onset of menstruation (or halt it after it has started) should enjoy greater reproductive success later. It also helps explain the obsession with food that many anorexic patients have; adaptive behaviour in times of food shortage and starvation is to shift attention to the acquisition of food.

 Anorexia may be an adaptive behaviour that delays reproduction until the female is better prepared to carry a baby.

Zandian et al. (2007) suggest that anorexia is an expression of an underlying obsessive–compulsive disorder (OCD, an anxiety disorder) as these disorders frequently precede anorexia. There is a hypothesized genetic basis to the disorder: in males, the OCD does not usually manifest itself as anorexia, but female biology interacts with the OCD to transform it into an eating disorder. Twin studies have provided varying estimates of how heritable anorexia is. A Swedish study that considered shared environment as a confounding variable and attempted to correct for it gave a heritability estimate of 56%, suggesting that there is a strong genetic component (Bulik et al., 2006). Striegel–Moore and Bulik (2007) indicate that molecular genetic studies have isolated potential genes, particularly related to the development of serotonin receptors, that may be responsible for mood issues among anorexic patients. However, the relationship between these genes and the disorder remains unclear.

Serotonin levels have been found to be low in many anorexic patients, and this has therefore been proposed as a possible cause of the disorder. However Zandian et al. (2007) point out that the studies which measure serotonin levels are not usually longitudinal – they do not have a 'before' measure as this is almost impossible to obtain. When an 'after' measure is included, it appears that the resumption of normal eating habits and return to healthy weight are accompanied by a return to normal serotonin levels. Given that serotonin is known to inhibit eating, it seems likely that decreased serotonin levels do not cause anorexia, but instead are a consequence of reduced food intake (Zandian et al., 2007).

 There may be a genetic component to anorexia, but environmental factors play an important role.

van Kuyck et al. (2007) summarize brain-imaging studies with anorexic patients, and show that the parietal cortex is frequently underactive. Decreased activity in this part of the brain could relate to anorexic patients' symptoms of overestimating their own weight and shape,

and to a kind of anosognosia – lack of knowledge and insight into their disorder. This part of the brain is sexually dimorphic (i.e. it is different in size in males and females) and this may explain the large difference in prevalence of the disorder between the sexes. Again, however, there is a problem of identifying cause here. Differences in neurocircuitry may be responsible for the development of the disorder, but it is also possible that poor diet changes the brain in these areas.

A model that integrates much of our knowledge about hormones, neurotransmitters and the brain is offered by Zandian et al. (2007). According to this model, there are two risk factors for the development of anorexia: reduced food intake and physical activity. In combination, these factors encourage the release of corticotrophin-releasing factor and cortisol, which in turn activate the dopamine reward pathways in the limbic system. This gives anorexic patients a reward when they begin dieting and increases the chances of repeated diet-and-exercise behaviour, thus locking the patient into a cycle of addiction-like behaviour.

Etiology: Cognitive level of analysis

At this level of analysis, the focus is on how disordered thinking or faulty perception might cause the disorder. Fairburn et al. (1999) provide a detailed account of how low self-esteem and an extreme need for self-control are at the core of the disorder. These researchers suggest that for most people with anorexia, the need for control is quite easily met through mastery in the eating domain in a way that is harder to achieve through work, school or sport.

The idea that dieting and control go together is a schema commonly built and encouraged in Western societies. The disordered eating patterns are maintained because the person's sense of control is increased to the point where control over eating becomes a measure of self-worth. In addition, constant checking of body shape to obtain objective information about the success of dieting is made unreliable by distorted perception, caused by negative mood and the presence of thin women in media. In addition, there is an attentional bias towards negative information about body shape. This can compel some patients to stop looking, thus eliminating any chance they might have of finding out just how much weight they have lost (Fairburn et al., 1999).

Bruch's body-image distortion hypotheses (1962) was an early recognition of this type of cognitive element to anorexia, suggesting that anorexic people overestimate their body size. However, this may be normal among women anyway, as a study by Fallon and Rozin (1988) found that when families were asked to compare their body shape to their ideal body shape, only the sons reported that their body shape was acceptable. Both mothers and daughters in the sample believe that men prefer thinner women than they actually do. Other psychologists have applied Beck's ideas (page 160) to anorexia, and suggest that the same tendencies to overgeneralize, personalize and polarize thinking exist for anorexic people as well.

Etiology: Sociocultural level of analysis

It is often thought that eating disorders like anorexia and bulimia are culture-bound disorders restricted to the Western world and are encouraged by conceptions of beauty and attractiveness that tell females to be thin and males to be athletic. Lee et al. (1996) suggest that a social fat phobia may underlie anorexia, and that this phobia is beginning to thrive in many other parts of the world. Where anorexia has developed most intensely, there is considerable mass media influence, and large amounts of information about both dieting and eating disorders. Girls who become anorexic are more likely to accept the messages about beauty and thinness in the media. However, it is not clear whether the anorexia has caused this receptiveness, or if acceptance of the message led to anorexia, or if an alternative

To learn more about the dramatic increase in dieting and eating disorders in Fijian girls after the introduction of television in 1995, go to www. pearsonhotlinks. com, enter the title or ISBN of this book and select weblink 5.7.

explanation is better. Lee et al. also point out that the increase in anorexia in other countries could be an artefact of increased use of Western diagnostic systems that pathologize behaviours. Moreover, body weight is not necessarily indicative of psychiatric problems – an estimated 16% of healthy but slim Chinese women would meet Western diagnostic criteria for anorectic weight. In line with this idea, anorexia was four times more prevalent in Japan in 1998 than in 1993, probably reflecting changes in social support networks and moral values in Japan (Yasuhara et al., 2002).

Strahan et al. (2007) offer the possibility that the influence of media is not so much that it causes women to believe that they are the wrong shape, as that it encourages them to think that everyone else accepts thin models and actresses as normal and attractive. It is then conformity to the perceived expectations of others that leads to excessive dieting. This influence may be playing a part in our development from a very young age for both males and females; research has shown that toy action figures are increasingly lean and muscular, yet the probability of finding a woman with Barbie's body shape is less than 1 in 100 000 (Norton et al., 1996). Models for magazine centrefolds and Miss America beauty contestants have been becoming smaller at the same time as advertising for dieting and exercise products has increased (Sypeck et al., 2006).

Anorexia is usually accompanied by a distorted perception of body shape.

As compelling as sociocultural arguments are, it is still something of a mystery that only some people are affected by these influences in a way that brings them to the attention of clinical staff. It is likely that an understanding of the interaction between biology, cognition, and the sociocultural context of a person's life is needed in order to fully understand how anorexia develops.

Treatments for anorexia nervosa

Biomedical therapy

SSRIs are frequently used to treat anorexia, although there is limited evidence that this is effective on its own, even though some research has found these drugs can help prevent relapse (Holtkamp et al., 2005). A double-blind study by Kaye et al. (2001) showed that patients given a placebo over a one-year period were much more likely to drop out, indicating that there is some benefit. It seems likely, however, that this medication targets symptoms of anorexia that are not causing the disorder, and provides an argument against the idea that negative mood or depression play a causal role in the development of anorexia, even if they frequently occur together.

 If we can misperceive our own shape, what else might we perceive wrongly? How much can we trust that other people see what we see when we view ourselves in the mirror?

Instead of focusing on medication, the biomedical approach tends to ensure that weight gains are made in the first instance, which can mean attaching the patient to a drip. Following this, the patient needs to be encouraged to eat normally again, and this is more likely to be achieved through the use of individual therapies. It is sometimes suggested that anorexia is a form of anxiety disorder or depression, and for some individuals, ongoing use of medication can help prevent the kind of emotional state that precedes relapses. However, it is very uncommon for a person to be given purely biomedical treatment with no access to therapy: treatment for anorexia is almost always eclectic.

Individual therapy

Bowers (2002) details a form of CBT that is recommended for use in a multidisciplinary team, recognizing that neither a physician, a psychotherapist nor a dietician is likely to be able to deal with an anorexia patient alone. The ultimate aim of CBT here is to help the individual to understand that their thought processes and belief systems are causing problems, and to help change them. The CBT aims to change (a) negative self-statements like, 'I'll never be thin enough' and (b) basic assumptions that are generally fixed and resistant to change, often in the form of high personal expectations. Changes are also needed to cognitive schemata to do with weight, food and control, so it is first essential to spend time talking with the patient to establish what the content of these schemata are. It may require some practice for patients to identify their own moods and thoughts about these areas. They can then be challenged to produce evidence for these ideas and encouraged to come up with logical thoughts as alternatives to what are generally negative or self-defeating but persistent thoughts. This type of therapy generally has good outcomes and as it attempts to address the thoughts at the core of the problem, relapse is relatively unusual.

There are also behaviourist treatments available for anorexia. Usually, an operant conditioning approach is taken, whereby certain target behaviours are to be reinforced with a reward personalized to the patient. Token economies are not uncommon in hospital wards dealing with anorexic inpatients, and these offer staff a way to observe and reward small improvements in behaviour. Rewards like watching television or spending time socializing with others can be made conditional on completion of a meal. Sometimes, patients are asked to eat a meal placed on a kitchen scale, so that they can see the weight of the food disappearing. The intention here is to form immediate feedback about success in learning new eating habits. While these behaviourist treatments are often quite successful at helping anorexic patients get back to a normal weight, relapse is more likely than with CBT, for two main reasons. First, the reasons behind the disorder have not been addressed, whether these are biological, cognitive, or sociocultural. Secondly, when the person leaves the hospital, they need to have internalized the reward process, or have strong support from family or friends, as the reward system is likely to be neglected.

Token economies work well inside institutions but lose their effectiveness when nobody is monitoring the patient's progress.

It is for these reasons that family therapy is often offered. Family therapy bridges the gap between individual and group therapy: sometimes, the family is trained to provide support to the sufferer; sometimes, the whole family benefits from therapy to change their communication styles. Some models of causation assume that interactions, particularly between mother and daughter, are contributing factors to the development of the disorder, and learning more effective ways to communicate is beneficial for many family members, not just for the person with anorexia.

Harris and Kuba (1997) dealt specifically with the treatment of eating disorders among black women in the USA. They noted that there are more individuals with eating problems than are being diagnosed, and that treatment for minority groups requires special attention. They recommend that therapy involve not just the individual patient and therapist, but family, community, and even other practitioners of more cultural relevance, such as a shaman.

Group therapy

Group therapy is very common for anorexia patients – both as inpatients, as part of treatment to help them get better, and as outpatients, to help prevent relapse. A study by Woodside and Kaplan (1994) put males and females together in group therapy that specifically targeted negative and destructive attitudes towards food and eating, using a CBT approach similar to that outlined above for individuals. Both males and females showed improvement on the eating attitudes test.

Group therapy is more cost-effective than individual therapy and offers the opportunity for group members to interact with others who are at different stages in dealing with the disorder. This provides hope for those in the early stages, and confirmation of progress for those who are successful, along with increased self-esteem as they have the opportunity to help others.

Polivy (1981) identifies two significant problems with group therapy, however. The first is that being in a group of other anorectic patients lends legitimacy to the development of a new identity based on group membership; the patient then requires individual therapy to help carve out an independent identity. The second problem is that members of the group often teach each other, not always intentionally, strategies to avoid weight gain or hide weight loss. This means group therapy can actually undermine individual progress.

 Sometimes, group therapy teaches anorexic people strategies to avoid eating.

Treatment review

Learning outcomes
- Examine biomedical, individual and group approaches to treatment.
- Discuss the use of eclectic approaches to treatment.
- Discuss the relationship between etiology and therapeutic approach in relation to one disorder.

Evaluating treatment

For the first learning outcome above, you should look at treatment for more than one disorder. This chapter systematically deals with the treatments for each disorder under the discussions of each disorder. You therefore need to organise your own notes to bring together information on treatment options.

EXERCISE

9 Using the information in this chapter, make notes in bullet-point form under the headings *Biomedical*, *Individual* and *Group* on:
- types and examples of treatments used to treat disorders
- strengths and limitations
- gender and culture issues in treatment
- research: key examples and methodological problems.

Use these notes to construct an essay plan that describes the treatments offered and evaluates them, and uses research to back up any claims that you make.

● **Examiner's hint**
Given that there is such a wide range of possible causes of anorexia and a similarly wide range of treatment options, an eclectic approach seems particularly appropriate for this disorder, so it is wise to use anorexia in an essay asking you to discuss eclectic approaches to treatment.

The second of the learning outcomes listed above is concerned with eclectic approaches. In some countries, a general practitioner is able to prescribe psychiatric medication, so sometimes a biomedical approach may be taken by itself; on the other hand, a patient might enter group or individual therapy without being medicated. However, it is rarely the case that a person who is suffering significant problems of living because of one of the disorders in this chapter, will be offered just one treatment. Usually, a multidisciplinary team involving at least one therapist and one medical professional (e.g. a psychiatrist, doctor or a prescribing nurse), will work together to combine their skills and aid the patient's progress. This eclectic approach is referred to in this chapter several times and there is research demonstrating its effectiveness.

EXERCISE

10 Review the chapter and add to your notes from exercise 9 by noting references to combinations of treatment and record whether they are successful or not.
- Use these notes to construct an essay plan to answer the question *Discuss the use of eclectic approaches to treatment.*
- You need to explain why treatments are not always used in isolation and what the benefits of an eclectic approach are. Remember to link your ideas to research from this chapter (make use of the examiner's hint boxes indicating studies or information that will be useful).

The relationship between etiology and treatment

The final learning outcome listed above requires you to choose one disorder and consider the reasons why a particular approach is used.

Biomedical treatment usually focuses on the biological level of analysis, using medication to alleviate the symptoms of a disorder without necessarily attempting to cure the person. Individual psychotherapy focuses on the psychological and social features of the disorder and helps the client to develop strategies to function well on a daily basis. Group therapy is similar, but takes advantage of the benefits of being with other people to assist in building social competence as well as individual competence.

To access Revision notes 5.1 on the three disorders covered in this chapter, please visit www.pearsonbacconline.com and follow the on-screen instructions.

EXERCISE

11 Choose one disorder from this chapter and make notes under the headings *Biomedical*, *Individual* and *Group* on:
- proposed cause
- possible treatment
- whether or not the treatment addresses the cause
- gender and culture issues
- research: key examples and methodological problems

Using this information, you can write an essay plan to answer the question *Discuss the relationship between etiology and therapeutic approach in relation to one disorder.* Remember, you need to consider the strengths and limitations of treatment for this disorder and present a balanced argument that includes both evaluation and reference to research.

PRACTICE QUESTIONS

1 Discuss how biological factors influence **one** psychological disorder.

2 Evaluate **two** studies related to abnormal psychology.

3 Evaluate the use of biomedical or individual or group approaches to treatment for **one** psychological disorder.

To access Worksheet 5.3 with a full example answer to question 1, please visit www.pearsonbacconline.com and follow the on-screen instructions.

To access Worksheet 5.4 with additional practice questions and answer guidelines, please visit www.pearsonbacconline.com and follow the on-screen instructions.

DEVELOPMENTAL PSYCHOLOGY

6.1 Introduction: What is developmental psychology?

Learning outcomes
- Discuss to what extent biological, cognitive and sociocultural factors influence human development.
- Evaluate psychological research (that is, theories and/or studies) relevant to developmental psychology.

Developmental psychology deals with the lifelong process of change and is the study of how and why people change over time in the way they behave, think, and relate to others. Developmental psychology focuses on developmental areas such as identity, attachment and adolescence. Psychologists assume it is important to understand the extent to which early experience may influence later life, and if there are critical periods for acquiring certain behaviours during the process of development. Knowledge about the influence of biological, social and cultural factors in people's lives is helpful for families and also in professional childcare and education. There are areas of controversy in developmental psychology. For example, the impact of environmental or biological influences on the development of the child and the extent to which these influences interact; the notion of resilience and why different children react differently to stressors in the environment; the origins of gender identity and the interaction between culture and biology in the formation of gender roles.

To access Revision notes 6.1 on Section 6.1, please visit www. pearsonbacconline.com and follow the on-screen instructions.

6.2 Cognitive development

Learning outcomes
- Evaluate theories of cognitive development.
- Discuss how social and environmental variables may affect cognitive development.

Cognitive developmental psychology focuses on how cognitive processes (such as reasoning, perception, memory, intellectual development) change over time. Researchers in this area question how these changes can account for behaviour shown at different ages. The main area of debate is *why* these changes occur over time – what are the main deterministic forces behind them? The nature side of the debate looks at the effects of **maturation** – the unfolding of behaviours under the influence of genetic predisposition. The nurture side of the debate looks at the effects of the **environment** such as diet, parenting styles, culture and education.

It is assumed the major changes occur during childhood and developmental psychologists look at how these impact individuals as they move through their lives. Recently, there has been a renewed interest on the later end of life as researchers focus on the effects of old age on cognitive abilities.

Piaget

One of the main theorists in cognitive developmental psychology is Jean Piaget. He was born in the French-speaking part of Switzerland into a middle-class family whose father was a professor of medieval literature. From an early age, he was interested in the natural world and developed a keen interest in biology as well as philosophy. In later life, he combined these interests and described himself as an epistemologist. Epistemology is the study of the scope and limitations of knowledge and deals with questions such as:

- What is knowledge?
- How is knowledge acquired?
- What do people know and how do they know what they know?

Epistemology also focuses on notions such as truth and belief. Piaget believed these questions could be answered, or at least more appropriately framed, if researchers focused on the genetic context behind them. As a result, his theories of cognitive development and his epistemological views are known collectively as genetic epistemology.

Jean Piaget (1896–1980).

While working as a teacher in Paris, Piaget was helping to grade responses to an intelligence test when he noticed that children consistently gave the wrong answers to certain questions. More specifically, younger children made the same pattern of mistakes that older children and adults did not. This, as well as his intense studies with his own children in the 1920s led him to the following assumptions (which he spent the rest of his career testing).

- Intelligence is under genetic control and develops in the form of predetermined stages.
- Children do not passively receive their knowledge; they are curious, self-motivated and seek out information to construct their own understanding of the environment.
- Children think qualitatively differently from adults. Previous thought dictated that children were the same as adults but 'less than' – that is, they had the same thought processes but were not as advanced or as sophisticated. Piaget argued that children are completely different and their mental processes cannot be viewed in the same way.
- Individuals construct their view of the world through mental frameworks of understanding.

 Piaget used his own children to test his own theories. This has been criticized for lacking scientific rigour but it allowed him to study long-term changes firsthand in a loving and supportive environment.

Piaget's theory of cognitive development

Piaget argued that knowledge developed through cognitive structures known as schemas. Schemas are mental representations of the world and how the individual interacts with it. The word has Greek roots meaning shape or plan. Mental schemas help order our thinking and act as mental shortcuts. They influence perception and attention and can be as diverse as mental maps for ease of navigation around a familiar building or a set of expectations for dealing with a person.

As a child develops, his or her schemas develop as a result of his or her interaction with the world. All children are born with an innate range of schemas, such as a schema for sucking, reaching, and gripping. These are in turn modified as a result of experience; Piaget called this process of modification **adaptation**. He also argued children actively *construct* knowledge themselves as a result of their interaction with new objects and experiences. For this reason Piaget is also known as a constructivist. The child's interaction with new events and objects as well as the intermingling of these with existing knowledge cause him or her to develop cognitively.

 Piaget saw himself as an epistemologist. Epistemology is the study of the scope and limitations of knowledge and deals with questions such as: What is knowledge? How is knowledge acquired? What do people know? How do they know what they know?

There are two types of adaptation.

- **Assimilation** – This process occurs when new events (such as objects, experiences, ideas and situations) can be fitted into existing schemas of what the child already understands about the world. For example, a child may call the family German Shepherd a 'doggie'; when he or she also points at the neighbours' Labrador and calls it a 'doggie', we can see that the child has understood the parameters of his existing schema (furry, playful, four legs) and fitted the image into it. Assimilation is a consolidation of existing knowledge; existing schemas receive support and reinforcement.
- **Accommodation** – This process occurs when new events do not fit existing schemas. Either a schema has to be modified to allow the new world view, or a new one schema has to be created. For example, consider a young boy pointing at a small horse and calling it a 'doggie'. He would be corrected and told it is a 'horse' and he would have to create a new schema (with new parameters) in order to understand all future encounters with horses. Accommodation is the creation of new knowledge and the rejection or adaptation of existing schemas.

How does a child know only two of these animals are dogs?

Piaget saw children as little scientists who are always engaged in creating and then testing hypotheses. Piaget forwarded the notion of constructivism, whereby children are actively engaged with constructing their knowledge of the world rather than acting as passive receivers of information.

These two hypothetical processes clearly demonstrate the Piagetian child. He or she is an active learner who is constantly engaged with the world, testing and retesting ideas. Piaget saw children as little scientists who are always engaged in creating and then testing hypotheses.

Piaget proposed four stages each child moves through in sequential order during cognitive development. Each stage is more sophisticated than the last and is the result of biological maturation and an active interaction with the environment. Piaget saw each stage as radically or qualitatively different from the others.

The four stages are:

- the sensorimotor stage
- the pre-operational stage
- the concrete operational stage
- the formal operational stage.

The sensorimotor stage (0–2 years)

This stage is characterized by the infant having no formal schema for the world or itself. It can only know the world via its immediate senses and the motor or movement actions it performs. This stage is illustrated by the following.

- Profound egocentrism – The infant cannot distinguish between itself and the environment as has no real knowledge of the world around it.
- A lack of object permanence – When an infant cannot see or act on an object then the object effectively ceases to exist for the infant. Piaget argued object permanence develops at around 8 months – a 4-month-old will not look for an object it has been introduced to whereas an 8-month-old will. This shows the 8-month-old infant understands the object exists even though it cannot be seen. However, object permanence is still not complete; the 8-month-old will only look for an object in the place where it was found the last time he or she interacted with it. Even if the infant is shown the object being hidden somewhere else, he or she will still seek the object in the place where they found it last. It is only between the ages of 18 and 24 months that toddlers develop full object permanence.

Piaget's claims have been contradicted by other researchers. Bower (1982) constructed a simple experiment whereby a child was shown an object and then a screen was placed between object and infant. The object was removed and the screen taken away. Bower claimed the children showed enough surprise at the disappearance of the object to argue that object permanence was a much more flexible phenomenon than Piaget had envisaged.

The pre-operational stage (2–7 years)

Operations are logical mental rules and Piaget argued that, at this age, the child cannot internalize these disciplines and therefore still relies on external appearances rather than consistent internal logic (hence the label, pre-operational).

This stage begins with the establishment of object permanence and ends with the emergence of concrete operations. It is still dominated by the cognitive limiting effects of egocentrism as the child has a limited ability, or in some cases no ability, to see, think, feel or imagine the world from another's point of view. The child is also still obsessed by the appearance of objects (which Piaget also saw as a cognitive limitation) but shows **centration** – the tendency to focus on only one aspect of an object or situation at any one time. Because of this, pre-operational stage children have a lack of **conservation** – the realization objects can remain the same despite a change in appearance.

Piaget demonstrated this with glasses of water. A child is presented with two glasses containing the same quantity of water and then witnesses the contents of one of the glasses being poured into a taller, thinner container. Children at this stage will argue the taller, thinner container contains more water. This shows the child does not understand how objects can remain the same (in this case, the quantity of water is fixed) despite a change in appearance.

Piaget also argued that this stage is characterized by a third cognitive inhibitor, **classification limitation**. This refers to the early pre-operational child's inability to classify similar objects into the same groups. This ability begins around the age of four and appears in basic form, such as characterizing objects based on shape or colour.

EXERCISE

1   Design theoretical methods to demonstrate: egocentrism, a lack of object permanence, and lack of conservation. To comply with IB ethical guidelines for conducting research on young children, you should not actually carry out the experiments.

EMPIRICAL RESEARCH

Egocentrism (Piaget and Inhelder, 1956; Hughes, 1975)

These researchers demonstrated the egocentrism of the pre-operational child through their 'three mountain experiment'. When 4-year-olds were shown a mountain scene, they tended to be unable to describe the same scene from the point of view of a doll on the other side. Six-year-olds showed more awareness of the different viewpoints but still tended to choose the wrong one when asked to specifically identify a scene from the doll's perspective.

The mountain scene apparatus and the methodology have been criticized as being too far from the normal operating world of the child – children are not used to seeing such scenes. They may have been confused by the layout, by adult objects placed on the scenes and by the need to identify the doll's position through a photograph (Hughes, 1975).

Hughes devised his own experiment known as 'the policeman doll' study where children had to hide a boy doll from two policeman dolls who were arranged around a piece of cardboard apparatus (Figure 6.1). The children had to consider the viewpoint of the two policeman dolls before making a decision as to where to place the boy doll so it was hidden from the policeman dolls.

Figure 6.1
The policeman doll experiment.

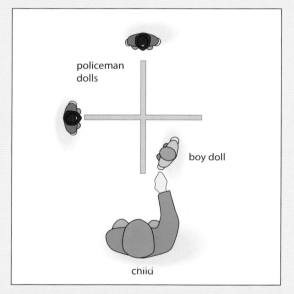

Hughes' sample consisted of children aged between three-and-a-half and five. Of these, 90% gave correct answers suggesting they had overcome the egocentrism that characterizes the pre-operational stage. It should be noted that when a child made a mistake, the mistake was explained and the child allowed to try again. However, Hughes states that very few mistakes were made. Even when he devised a more complex situation, with more walls and a third policeman, 90% of 4-year-olds were successful. This demonstrates egocentrism in the Piagetian sense can be overcome if the task is made more age appropriate.

Piaget can be criticized for approaching the issue of egocentrism through the adult gaze – that is, he approached it as an abstract mental problem and his methods can be seen as indicative of his thinking. The use of the photograph and the mountain scene itself, were far from normal expectations of children and it is difficult to imagine any young child being at ease with this. The Hughes' approach is more commonsensical. Also, his correction of the children and encouragement for them to have more tries is a more realistic reflection of what would happen in the 'real world' with parents/caregivers stepping in to correct faulty thinking.

There are criticisms of the Piagetian view of this stage. Piaget himself was interested in the pre-operational characteristic of **symbol use** in play: children often use a single object (e.g. a broom handle) for many different roles (e.g. a horse, a sword). This suggests a more

sophisticated understanding of objects than the simple lack of conservation ability can portray. Another criticism is the negative tone Piaget uses to describe this stage. By calling it 'pre-operational', he focuses on what children cannot do (their cognitive limitations) rather than what they can achieve.

Children at this stage have been shown to have active imaginations. Field et al. (1982a) found 4–5-year-old children can spend as much as 20% of their playtime constructing sophisticated roles for different objects above and beyond their intended use (e.g. blocks become trucks, brooms become horses). At this stage, children also construct complicated role plays for themselves and others (games of 'mummies and daddies', 'cowboys and Indians', etc.). They issue explicit instructions for each member of the group on how to fulfil these roles in sometimes lengthy monologues before play begins (Howes and Matheson, 1992).

Children at this stage can also develop imaginary companions with complex character nuances and with whom they engage in conversation. This used to be seen as a sign

Children have complex games usually made up between them. Lengthy monologues are often delivered before they begin.

of disturbance but it is now seen as a product of a rich imagination and a normal part of the development of pretence for children (Taylor et al., 1993a). Imaginary friends are a significant phenomena in childhood. They act as guardians or protectors and represent, according to some, a child's inner anxieties, goals and perceptions. A small minority of children are unable to distinguish them from real people, but most do understand the difference and use the imaginary friend as an exercise in creative thinking. It has been theorized that children with imaginary friends are able to develop linguistic and mental skills earlier than children who do not have such friends as the former are practising such skills, albeit in a non-real universe. Most children report having an imaginary friend at some point in their early life but, as they reach school age and acquire real friends, imaginary ones are quickly abandoned. These elaborate fantasies demonstrate the advanced skills children possesses in re-imagining the world for their own use; they provide a more complete picture of the child at this age than the pre-operational stage does.

Children design complex role-playing games showing active imaginations and an understanding of the adult world.

The concrete operational stage (7–11 years)

During this stage, the child develops definitive rules or schemas for ordering the world. These rules are termed **operations**, but they can only be applied to real objects in the real 'concrete' world. Piaget claimed the mental agility needed for carrying out logical operations without a real world object to aid them had not yet been developed.

An example of an operation the child has developed by this stage is conservation – the realization objects can remain the same despite a change in appearance. The pre-operational child lacks conservation (page 185). Piaget demonstrated the development of conservation in this age group using two rows of beads (Figure 6.2a). When the green row is spread out (Figure 6.2b), the concrete operational child realizes the number remains the same even though the appearance has changed.

However, McGarrigle and Donaldson (1974) questioned whether Piaget's methods were suitable for such young children. They used a glove puppet, known as Naughty Teddy, to 'accidentally' transform the beads (Figure 6.2c). Under this condition, they found 63% of 4–6-year-old children could successfully conserve as they recognized the number of beads remained the same.

Figure 6.2
a Equal numbers of yellow and green beads, equally spaced. **b** The green beads have been spread out. **c** Naughty Teddy has moved the green beads.

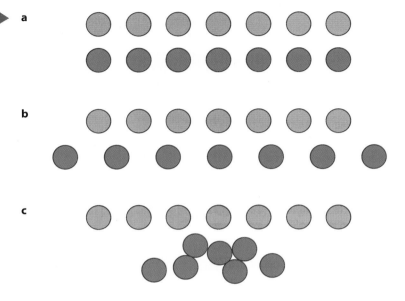

The formal operational stage (11 years onwards)

At this stage, the child's mental structures are so well developed that ideas and problems can be manipulated mentally without the need for physical objects. Children can think about possible occurrences and imagine themselves in different roles without the need for dolls or play acting. They can also think about hypothetical problems and abstract concepts they have never encountered before, such as:

if $A > B > C$, then $A > C$ (where $>$ means 'is greater than').

Piaget believed everyone reached this stage by the age of 20.

EXERCISE
2   Outline the key assumptions of Piaget's theory.

Evaluation of Piaget's theory

Piaget produced the first comprehensive theory of child cognitive development. He modified the theory to take account of criticism and envisaged it constantly changing as new evidence came to light. A great deal of criticism has been levelled at the 'ages and stages' part of his theory but it is important to remember the theory is biologically based and demonstrates the child as a determined, dynamic thinker, anxious to achieve coherence and test theories. Piaget was the first to investigate whether biological maturation drove cognitive development and his vision of a child having cognitive changes regulated by biology is now widely accepted and supported by cross-cultural research. He also developed the notion of **constructivism** – he argued children are actively engaged with constructing their knowledge of the world rather than acting as passive receivers of information. This now widely accepted idea changed the view of childhood and significantly influenced the education profession.

Piaget was the first to investigate the role biological maturation played in cognitive development. His vision of a child as having cognitive changes regulated by biology is now widely accepted and supported by cross-cultural research.

However, there are some well-grounded negative criticisms which should be considered.

- Piaget's methods have been criticized as too formal for children. When the methods are changed to show more 'human sense', children often understand what is being asked of them and show cognitive ability outside of their age-appropriate stage. The small sample sizes also mean caution should be used when generalizing to large groups and cultures.

- Piaget failed to distinguish between competence (what a child is capable of doing) and performance (what a child can show when given a particular task). When tasks were altered, performance (and therefore competence) was affected.

- The notion of biological readiness has also been questioned. If a child's cognitive development is driven solely by innate factors, then training would not be able to propel the child onto the next stage. However, many studies have been carried out whereby children have been taught skills they would not be able to develop according to the Piagetian view. Piaget did go some way to account for this as he argued children will experience uneven cognitive development due to personalized learning styles.

- Piaget has been criticized for under-estimating the role of language in cognitive development.

- Piaget has also been criticized for under-estimating the role of social development in cognitive development. The 'three mountain experiment' is a presentation of a social scene and yet Piaget focused on it solely as an abstract mental problem. When the approach was changed to a more age-appropriate paradigm (the use of a policeman doll), more children were able to understand the different views. Children may also have been anxious to provide what they considered to be the more socially desirable answer.

- He has also been criticized for under-estimating children's cognitive abilities in general as many children show more abilities at younger ages than Piaget outlined.

- Piaget over-estimated people's formal operational ability. Some research has suggested only around one-third of the population reach this late stage of cognitive development.

- The theory is very descriptive but it does not provide a detailed explanation for the stages. Piaget's supporters would suggest that, given his broad genetic explanations, the technology did not exist for him to research his assumptions in depth.

- The model can be seen as too rigid and inflexible. However, its supporters argue that Piaget never intended it to be seen in such a light, and it should be seen more as a metaphor and a guiding principle for teaching and learning.

How might development be seen subjectively? To what extent is it a definitive biological process? To what extent is it a social construction?

EXERCISE
3   Evaluate Piaget's theory. Make sure you use positive and negative evaluations in your answer.

Vygotsky

Lev Semyonovich Vygotsky was born in the Russian empire in what is today Belarus. He was heavily influenced by his cousin David Vygodsky, a poet, teacher, translator and literary critic. In 1938, David was killed as part of Stalin's purges of the intelligentsia class. At the time, the authorities took a great of interest in the work of scholars, looking for anything which might be considered subversive. This was very different from conditions academics worked under in the West. In the Soviet Union at that time, repression, imprisonment and murder were a daily reality.

Although Lev Vygotsky died from tuberculosis when he was 37, his impact on psychology has been immense. He studied ferociously through his lifetime and covered many philosophical as well as psychological areas that are still discussed today. He focused on how children play and socialize as well as their language development in the context of their understanding of the world.

Lev's descendents became directors of the Psychological Institute of Vygotsky, in Moscow and he is widely regarded as one of the few genuine pioneers of the cognitive approach.

Lev Semyonovich Vygotsky (1896–1934).

Vygotsky and his followers founded the school of **cultural–historical psychology** which looks at how cognition can develop in specific times and places. The key assumption is human cognition develops as a response to the knowledge and cultural constructions left by the generation before.

Vygotsky focused on social interaction, culture and language in a child's cognitive development. The Vygotskian child makes sense of the world through shared meaning with others.

Vygotsky's theory of cognitive development

Vygotsky's main contribution is his focus on the importance of social interaction, culture and language in a child's cognitive development. The Vygotskian child makes sense of the world through shared meaning with others whereas the Piagetian child makes sense of the world as the result of an innate maturation process that drives cognitive development.

Vygotsky divided the intellect into basic innate capabilities which he termed elementary functions (e.g. attention and sensation) and higher mental functions. Vygotsky argued elementary functions can only develop into higher functions via the input of culture. Vygotsky thought of culture as a body of knowledge held by persons of greater knowledge or in books – ideas transmitted through language – hence the importance he placed on language development as part of overall cognitive development. Thus, cultural knowledge is the means by which cognitive development takes place.

Vygotsky hypothesized that the child begins to interact with the world through its actions but society places meaning on those actions through social interaction. A typical example of this is pointing. A child may try and reach for an object but fail to actually grasp it. The adult will then hand the object to the child. Therefore, the original movement by the child will take on a new meaning: from simply trying to reach an object to communicating with an adult by pointing to an object.

The primary way we communicate with the world is by language not physical gestures. Language for children is primarily a way to produce change in others. However, when language becomes internalized, it converges with thought, and eventually we are able to

direct and control our thinking with the use of language. We develop an inner voice for thinking and a more complex, vocabulary-rich voice for communication with others.

Vygotsky envisaged language progressing in three stages.

- Pre-intellectual social speech (0–3 years) – Thought is not constructed using language and speech is only used to enact social change (e.g. receiving objects from a parent).
- Egocentric speech (3–7 years) – Language helps to control the child's own behaviour and is spoken out loud (e.g. when children play games they often verbalize their actions).
- Inner speech (7+ years) – The child uses speech silently to develop their thinking and publicly for social communication.

Vygotsky articulated the importance of culture through the zone of proximal development (ZPD). A more useful translation is the zone of potential development as the ZPD is seen as the distance between the child's current and potential abilities under adult supervision. Instruction from an expert wakens a whole series of embryonic functions that can be extended under supervision from an expert (usually an adult).

These abilities would lie dormant and unused if they were left untutored. This precisely illustrates the difference between the Piagetian individual construction approach and the importance of social construction put forward by Vygotsky. Wood et al. (1976) introduced the notion of scaffolding as development of Vygotsky's ZPD theory, in which the disorganized and spontaneous thoughts presented by the child are responded to with the more systematic, logical and rational concepts of a more knowledgeable (usually adult) helper.

To learn more about Vygotsky, go to www.pearsonhotlinks.com, enter the title or ISBN of this book and select weblink 6.1.

EXERCISE
3 Outline the key assumptions of Vygotsky's approach.

Evaluation of Vygotsky's theory

The concept of scaffolding has been useful from a teaching perspective. Conner et al. (1997) argued that the quality of the scaffolding provided by a mother and father could predict the success of the child in the classroom. This can be applied to reading and mathematical problems in early development: Those children who are supported at home will be more confident in the classroom. The value Vygotsky placed on inner speech has also received support. He argued the inner voice was a key part of learning and cognitive development; Behrend et al. (1992) quantified inner speech by observing the amount of whispering and lip movement children engaged in when given a task. They found children who used the greatest amount of inner speech tended to perform better on tasks.

Vygotsky makes an important contribution to developmental psychology as he emphasizes the importance of social interaction on cognitive development – an area lacking in Piaget's approach.

Vygotsky's approach has been criticized for placing too much emphasis on the social environment and he can also be criticized for being too vague in his outline of social influence. However, it should be noted that Vygotsky died at the age of 38, so his work as a cognitive developmental researcher was still in its infancy. Had he lived longer, he would have advanced his theories and been able to respond to peer review.

Vygotsky and Piaget's ideas should not be seen as diametrically opposed to each other. In many ways they complement each other and an integration of both views might be a productive way forward. However, there is a lack of empirical support for Vygotsky's ideas – this is largely explained by his emphasis on processes rather than outcomes (processes are harder to test for).

● **Examiner's hint**
When evaluating, be considered and balanced. Many studies and theories have been constructed over many years by experienced psychologists; dismissing them in one sentence is a not a sophisticated response.

● **Examiner's hint**
Never present Vygotsky and Piaget's ideas as diametrically opposed to each other; in many ways, they complement each other.

● **Examiner's hint**
Be considered and balanced
when discussing variables.

Social and environmental variables

For ease of learning and presentation, we here examine various social and environmental variables individually. However, to understand how they affect cognitive development in the real world, you need to see that such factors all interact. For example, economic issues may influence the standard of school a child attends; such issues may themselves be the result of the education level of the parent whose job is dependent on their education. A parent's education may also affect the child's diet, which influences their grades as well as how others perceive them. The social environment can influence the peer group the child becomes attached to as he or she grows up, and this may in turn influence their outlook and aspirations as it provides norms and routines that may limit or enhance the child's cognitive growth.

Diet

Processed food is fast becoming a social issue as obesity rates increase in the USA and in Europe. There are many grass roots campaigns to fight the effects of poor food and improve education; there are political incentives to improve the diet of those in the developed world. One area where the debate is particularly well researched is the effect of junk food on children's behaviour and cognitive development. Junk food is a controversial term that usually refers to food with little or no nutritional value, or food where the nutritional content is offset by the unhealthy nature of the food or some ingredient(s).

A child's diet begins before they are born. Mother's have to eat healthily and seafood is the primary source of omega-3 fatty acids which are essential for neural development.

The effect of diet begins before the child is born; for example, seafood is the primary source of omega-3 fatty acids which are essential for neural development. Hibbeln et al. (2007) compared two groups of women (those consuming high levels of omega- 3 fatty acids and those consuming low levels of the same). They found the children of those mothers who had a low seafood intake during pregnancy had lower motor (movement and coordination) skills and lower social development and communication skills than the children of mothers who consumed high levels of seafood. Raloff (1989) studied 1023 6th-grade children over the course of one year and found those who were given free school breakfasts improved their maths and science scores.

EMPIRICAL RESEARCH

The benefits of breakfast (Food Research Action Centre, 2010)

Breakfast has wide cognitive–behavioural benefits. A meta-analysis of breakfast programme studies by the Food Research Action Centre (FRAC) in the USA came to the following conclusions.

Children given free school breakfasts improved their maths and science scores. Those experiencing hunger are more likely to be hyperactive, absent and tardy, in addition to having behavioural and attention problems more often than other children.

- Children who skip breakfast are less able to distinguish among similar images, show increased errors, and have slower memory recall.
- Children experiencing hunger have lower math scores and are more likely to have to repeat work – or even an academic year.
- Behavioural, emotional and academic problems are more prevalent among children with hunger.
- Children experiencing hunger are more likely to be hyperactive, absent and tardy, in addition to having behavioural and attention problems more often than other children.
- Children who are undernourished score lower on cognitive tests when they miss breakfast.
- Teens experiencing hunger are more likely to have been suspended from school, have difficulty getting along with other children, and have no friends.
- Children with hunger are more likely to have repeated a grade, received special education services, or received mental health counselling, than low-income children who do not experience hunger.

Caution should be used when attributing improved cognitive functioning to a healthy diet. A healthy diet can have less quantifiably measurable affects on a child such as increased self-esteem, improved personal discipline and a greater sense of responsibility all of which would have an effect on school grades.

Cook et al. (1996) found children who participate in universal school breakfast programmes have lower rates of absence and tardiness, which would inevitably improve their cognitive development simply because they are in school more. This is supported by McLaughlin et al. (2002) who found that schools which provide universal school breakfast have higher breakfast participation, especially when breakfast is served in the classroom, and students who significantly increase their breakfast participation are more frequently in attendance and on time.

How do you measure self-esteem and feelings of self-worth?

To learn more about how diet affects children, go to www. pearsonhotlinks. com, enter the title or ISBN of this book and select weblink 6.2.

EXERCISE

4 Outline the key influences of diet on cognitive development.

Parenting

In this context, parenting refers to the act(s) of supporting a child physically, emotionally, socially and intellectually; it does refer to any biological relationship between the adult and child. The duties of parents differ according to cultural variations and expectations: some cultures (e.g. Japan) give some parenting duties to siblings to promote responsibility and family cohesion. In the USA, the Michigan Department of Education (MDE, 2002) in 2001 argued that the most consistent predictors of a child's academic achievement and social adjustment were parent expectations: parents of high-achieving students set higher standards for their children's educational activities than parents of low-achieving students and this drove educational achievement and therefore cognitive development. The MDE stated that when parents are involved, students have:

- higher grades, test scores and graduation rates
- increased motivation and better self-esteem
- better school attendance
- lower rates of suspension
- decreased use of drugs and alcohol
- fewer instances of violent behaviour.

Family participation in education was twice as predictive of students' academic success as family socio-economic status; the more intensely parents were involved, the more beneficial the achievement effects. For example, children who practise reading at home with their parents, make significant gains in reading achievement compared to those who practise only at school (Tizard et al., 1982). But this has wider implications, as parents who read to their children are also more likely to have more books available, take trips together as family, monitor TV watching, and provide stimulating experiences which together contribute to cognitive development.

Overall, the MDE found families whose children are doing well in school exhibit the following characteristics.

- They have an established daily family routine such as providing time and a quiet place to study, assigning responsibility for household chores, being firm about bedtime and having dinner together.
- They monitor out-of-school activities such as setting limits on TV-watching, checking up on children when parents are not home, arranging for after-school activities and supervised care.

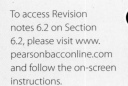

Isolating one variable (e.g. diet or parenting) and attributing to it a relative level of cognitive development lacks some degree of ecological validity and is more useful in academic debate rather than real world analysis.

What is effective parenting? Is it definitive? Are there universals all parents should subscribe to?

To access Revision notes 6.2 on Section 6.2, please visit www.pearsonbacconline.com and follow the on-screen instructions.

● **Examiner's hint**
The command term *discuss* means you should present a range of theories in a balanced and considered way. Do not dismiss entire theories, all have some merit and an eclectic approach is often the most appropriate way to address complex human phenomena.

- They model the value of learning, self-discipline, and hard work, such as communicating through questioning and conversation, demonstrating that achievement comes from working hard.
- They encourage children's development and progress in school by maintaining a warm and supportive home, showing interest in children's progress at school, helping with homework, discussing the value of a good education and possible career options, staying in touch with teachers and school staff.
- They encourage reading, writing, and discussions among family members such as reading, listening to children read and talking about what is being read.

Moscovici (1993) encourages social scientists to always lay claim to the higher wisdom of common sense and this applies in this instance: children who are loved and cared for will be disciplined, given healthy food and encouraged to be reflective and set high goals for themselves. As a result, they will have higher self-esteem and will do better in school and in personal relationships and will therefore succeed more in their chosen area of employment. Isolating one variable (e.g. diet or parenting) and attributing to it a relative level of cognitive development lacks some degree of ecological validity and is more useful in academic debate rather than real world analysis.

Vygotsky's ZPD theory provided Wood et al. (1976) with the idea to develop the notion of scaffolding (page 191). The parental strategies above can be seen in the Vygotskian scaffolding sense.

EXERCISE

5   Outline the key influences of parenting on cognitive development.

 ## 6.3 Social development

Learning outcomes
- Examine attachment in childhood and its role in the subsequent formation of relationships.
- Discuss potential effects of deprivation or trauma in childhood on later development.
- Define resilience.
- Discuss strategies to build resilience.

Attachment

Attachment is a long-lasting, strong and close emotional bond between two people; when separation occurs, the result is distress. First attachments in infancy are of particular interest to psychologists as they appear to have significant consequences for the later development of the individual – especially in terms of relationships. There is strong evolutionary support for a biological explanation of attachment: babies who are attached to a loving care-giver are more likely to survive and be better adjusted. Attachment, particularly between mother and baby, is seen by many psychologists as an innate, predetermined drive and manifests during its initial stages as biologically controlled signals such as smiling, grasping, babbling and crying. In turn, these behaviours elicit caring acts from the parent (feeding, protection and giving affection) necessary for healthy growth.

Bowlby

John Bowlby (1907–90) is a key theorist for the developmental concept of **attachment**. He was born to an upper-middle class family in London and was the fourth of six children. Due to the fashions of the time, he rarely saw his parents. Giving a lot of maternal affection was seen as spoiling the child, so children from elite socio-economic backgrounds were raised by teams of nannies and sent to boarding school from a young age. Bowlby studied psychology at Cambridge University and later qualified as a psychoanalyst but it was World War II that acted as a catalyst for many of his ideas.

In England at that time, a number of wartime activities were seen by Bowlby as having significant effects on the later development of young children. These activities included:

- the rescue of Jewish children (many of whom were orphans) from Nazi Europe
- the evacuation of children from London and other metropolitan areas to more rural areas to keep them safe from air raids
- the use of group nurseries to allow mothers of young children to contribute to the war effort by working in factories and as nurses.

Bowlby became interested in attachment as a result of the scenes he witnessed in war-torn London.

Bowlby's attachment theory

Bowlby's attachment theory was first published in 1951 but has been adapted and improved many times over the years by Bowlby himself and by other researchers. Like Piaget, Bowlby's theories have been heavily criticized and adapted but like all good social scientists, he provided a solid theoretical footprint to stimulate debate and further research.

The basic assumptions are of Bowlby's theory are as follows.

1 Between 6 and about 30 months, children are likely to form emotional attachments to familiar care-givers – usually the mother, especially if the adults are sensitive and responsive to child communications such as facial expressions and hand gestures, crying, laughing and so on.

2 The emotional attachments of children manifest themselves in their preferences for familiar people; they seek proximity to those people, especially in times of distress, and then use the familiar adults as a secure base from which to explore the environment.

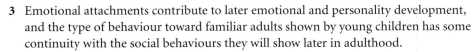

Bowlby's views on attachment were influenced by the scenes he witnessed in war-torn London, especially the effects of separation on Jewish refugees and the child evacuees.

3   Emotional attachments contribute to later emotional and personality development, and the type of behaviour toward familiar adults shown by young children has some continuity with the social behaviours they will show later in adulthood.

4   Events that interfere with attachment, such as abrupt separation or the inability of carers to be responsive, sensitive or consistent in their interactions, have short-term and long-term consequences for the child.

5   Attachment schemas guide early attachment and later relationships. Bowlby argues that a developing child forms a mental representation of their first attachment relationship – known as the internal working model. This schema as acts as a model for expectations of behaviour and care-giving from others. While the motivation to form attachment is biologically predetermined, the schema is modified by ongoing experience.

The model has important implications for the development of the self. If a child receives consistent love and affection from their care-giver, they develop a schema in which they – the self – is worthy of love and affection. Bowlby argued such children will develop confidence and be able to provide love and affection to others in the future. Similarly, if a child is given hostile experiences, they will develop an internal working schema in which they are worthy of such treatment and will repeat the pattern of abuse when they reach adulthood.

EMPIRICAL RESEARCH

'A strange situation' (based on Ainsworth et al., 1978; Main and Solomon, 1990)

During the 1970s, Mary Ainsworth aimed to provide empirical support for Bowlby's theories. She developed a procedure, called 'A strange situation', to observe attachment between care-giver and child.

The procedure involves observing a child playing for 20 minutes while care-givers and strangers enter and then leave the room, creating a flow of familiar and unfamiliar situations that mirror the real life of a child. The situations vary in stressfulness and the child's responses are observed. The situations are as follows.

- Parent and infant are introduced to the experimental room.
- Parent and infant are alone – Parent does not participate while infant explores.
- Stranger enters, converses with parent, then approaches infant. Parent leaves inconspicuously.
- First separation episode – Stranger's behaviour is geared to that of infant.
- First reunion episode – Parent greets and comforts infant, then leaves again.
- Second separation episode – Infant is alone.
- Continuation of second separation episode – Stranger enters and gears behaviour to that of infant.
- Second reunion episode – Parent enters, greets infant, and picks up infant; stranger leaves inconspicuously.

Four aspects of the infant's behaviour are observed.

- The amount of exploration (e.g. playing with new toys) the infant engages in.
- The infant's reactions to the departure of the care-giver.
- The level of anxiety displayed when the infant is alone with the stranger.
- The infant's behaviour during and after their reunion with the care-giver.

On the basis of their responses, Ainsworth categorized the infants into three groups.

- Type A: Avoidant or detached (shown by approximately 20% of the children) – The child shows apparent indifference when the mother leaves the room, and avoids contact with her when she returns. Also, the child is apparently unafraid of strangers. Ainsworth argued that the mothers of type A children tend to be insensitive and do not seem interested in their child's play.

- Type B: Securely attached (shown by approximately 70% of the children) – The child is upset when the mother leaves and is happy to see her again. The child is easily comforted by the mother. The mother is very interested in the child's play and actively supports play and communication.

- Type C: Ambivalent or anxious resistant (shown by approximately 10% of the children) – The child is discontented and can be very upset when the mother leaves the room. When she returns, the child is not easily soothed and may not always seek comfort from the mother. Ainsworth argued that mothers of type C children tend to be inconsistent in their reactions to their children.

Main and Solomon (1990) later added a fourth type.

- Type D: Insecure/disorganized/disorientated attachment – A child with this attachment type shows no discerning reaction when the mother leaves or returns. This attachment type has been associated with child abuse and depressed mothers.

'A strange situation' is a methodological procedure and can be criticized for lacking ecological validity. In some ways, all theoretical research procedures lack realism as their goal is to produce quantifiable results in a controlled environment.

Other criticisms include the following.

- The procedure lacks cross-cultural applicability as separation of parent and infant varies. In Japan and Russia, children are rarely separated from their mother in the early stages of life.

- The technique relies on brief separations and reunions of 20 minutes. This is a highly standardized and constructed approach, designed to increase the reliability of the method not mimic real life.

- It should be noted that only 20 minutes of interaction are used to draw broad conclusions about a complex human process.

'A strange situation' is methodological procedure designed to induce different levels of stress in an infant.

Temperament has a biological basis.

Animal breeders regularly breed for certain types of temperament in the offspring. Dog breeds are often identified by their innate temperament and yet academic research into innate human temperaments is still in its infancy.

Attachment patterns differ from one family to the next, and even between siblings. The following list contains some of the factors thought to influence the process.

- Parental sensitivity – Ainsworth argued secure attachment is particularly dependent on emotionally responsive mothers. Sensitive and responsive mothers tend to have securely attached babies, while insensitive mothers have insecurely attached babies.

- Child temperament – Kagan (1982) states innate differences in children's temperaments influence how the children and the environment interact. He argues a child's temperament is stable over time and is therefore predictive of future behaviour. Kagan claims temperament rather than actual attachment is being measured in the 'strange situation' research procedure as each child will respond differently to different situations as a result of their innate personality. He was also critical of the rigidity of much of the debate surrounding attachment, arguing it was a complex human phenomenon and not well understood by the psychological establishment.

- Family circumstances – A family is not always a stable, unchanging unit over time and setting. Events such as poverty and bereavement intervene, and the child may not receive the consistent support. This will affect attachment development – a stable, loving home is still the best predictor for a well-adjusted adult, competent in navigating their own as well as others' emotional worlds.

The role of attachment in future relationships

Research on adult attachment is guided by the assumption that the same motivational systems which give rise to emotional bonds between care-givers and their children are responsible for the bond that develops between adults in emotionally intimate relationships. This has been challenged by some researchers but overall it is accepted that adult attachment is influenced by childhood attachment patterns.

Baby-talk, infant-directed talk (IDT) or care-taker speech is a non-standard form of speech adults use to communicate with babies. It is usually delivered in a sing-song intonating style and has soothing as well as communicative properties. It has been shown to increase cognitive development and language understanding in particular. It is found in many cultures but not all – some cultures do not speak to their infants. IDT is also used between adults and is often directed at domestic animals. It is far more effective at receiving and maintaining infant attention than regular speech patterns.

To learn more about how Bowlby's ideas have been applied to adulthood, go to www. pearsonhotlinks. com, enter the title or ISBN of this book and select weblink 6.3.

Hazan and Shaver (1987) studied parent–child relationships and romantic couplings. They asked people to recall their childhood experiences and argued that adults who were secure in their romantic relationships were more likely to recall their childhood relationships with parents as being affectionate, caring, and accepting. They also note infant-and-care-giver relationships and adult romantic partners share the following features:

- both feel safe when the other is nearby and responsive
- both engage in close, intimate, bodily contact
- both feel insecure when the other is inaccessible
- both share discoveries with one another
- both play with one another's facial features and exhibit a mutual fascination and preoccupation with one another
- both engage in 'baby-talk'.

On the basis of these parallels, Hazan and Shaver argued that adult romantic love is a property of the attachment behavioural system, as well as the motivational systems that give rise to care-giving and sexuality.

According to Fraley and Shaver (2000), secure infants tend to become the most well-adjusted adults, to get along with their peers and are well liked. Generally, secure adults tend to be more satisfied in their relationships than insecure adults. Their relationships are characterized by greater longevity, trust, commitment, and interdependence and they are more likely to use romantic partners as a secure base from which to explore the world. In addition, secure adults are more likely than insecure adults to seek support from their partners when distressed and they are more likely to provide support to their distressed partners.

Segal and Jaffre (2007) emphasize that the non-verbal skills learned in childhood are essential for adult attachment relationships. Newborn infants cannot talk, reason or plan, yet they are able to communicate with a care-giver who understands and meets their physical and emotional needs. Segal and Jaffre argue that the learning and practice of non-verbal cues deeply impact our later love relationships.

Loving parents have long-lasting effects on their child's emotional skills.

Cultural differences in attachment (Miyake et al., 1985)

According to these researchers, Japanese mothers place great value on developing close relationships with young infants and are rarely separated from them. They also place prominence on allowing children to develop their own identity and to solve problems within a wider social group. Essentially, children are raised in a close relationship with the mother but as conscious members of the wider social milieu. Miyake contrasts this style with American parenting in which children are encouraged to be independent from a young age and adults intervene to solve problems within a group setting. As a result, American children show greater avoidant attachment than Japanese children – which can be interpreted as showing greater independence – whereas Japanese children show higher rates of secure attachment – leading to greater sensitivity to group needs as adults.

Deprivation and trauma

Early development and adult disease prevalence

There has been a great deal of research in early developmental experiences and later adult behaviour patterns. The Adverse Childhood Experiences study (Felliti et al., 1998) examined exposure to seven categories of adverse events during childhood (e.g. sexual abuse, physical abuse, witnessing domestic violence). This study found a clear correlation between the number of adverse events in childhood and adult health and the prevalence rates of diseases such as heart disease, cancer, chronic lung disease, and various risk behaviours). In addition, with four or more adverse childhood events, the risk for various medical conditions significantly increased.

Early development and adult behaviour

The pit of despair (Harlow and Suomi, 1971)

Harlow aimed to produce clinical depression in Rhesus monkeys and then monitor their behaviour as they developed. He designed a device to isolate monkeys and so cause them to be depressed. Technically, it was called a vertical chamber apparatus. However, Harlow wanted a more dramatic name and insisted on calling it the 'pit of despair' to stimulate debate and gain notoriety. He had at first wanted to call it the 'dungeon of despair' and also used terms like 'well of despair, and 'well of loneliness.' It was simply a steel cage that denied the monkey any connection with the outside world or any other living organism: an animal form of a prison isolation wing. Baby monkeys were placed in these steel boxes soon after birth; four were left for 30 days, four for six months, and four for an entire year.

After 30 days, the 'total isolates' were found to be enormously disturbed. After being isolated for a year, they barely moved, did not explore or play, and were incapable of having sexual relations. Two of them refused to eat and eventually starved to death.

Harlow also wanted to test how isolation would affect parenting skills, but the isolates were so badly damaged they were unable to mate. At that stage, artificial insemination had not been developed and so Harlow devised what he called a 'rape rack', to which the female isolates were tied in normal monkey mating posture and forcibly impregnated by a male monkey. When they became parents, he found they were actually unable to parent their offspring, either abusing or neglecting them. Having no social experience themselves, they were incapable of engaging in appropriate social interaction with others – including their own young: one mother held her baby's face to the floor and chewed off his feet and fingers while another crushed her baby's head and many others simply ignored their offspring.

continued

This young monkey is showing the effects of prolonged isolation.

Monkeys who were completely isolated from other monkeys emerged enormously disturbed. They would not procreate or socialize and some starved themselves to death.

The main outcome of Harlow's experiments is to demonstrate the importance of love and nurturing on later life. At that time, it was commonplace to advise parents to limit bodily contact to avoid excessive amounts of emotional stimulation of the child – seen as a form of spoiling or over-indulgence. However, Harlow's experiments have been heavily criticized for violating ethical standards in psychological methods. He has also been criticized for deliberately designing the apparatus to cause shock and revulsion in his colleagues, ostensibly to generate controversy – naming his apparatus the way he did and avoiding technical language is an example of this.

However, the most damning criticism comes from Deborah Blum, who argues that the studies simply produce results that are common sense: monkeys are very social animals, when placed in isolation, they emerge badly damaged (Blum, 2002). Generalizing animal findings to humans should always be carried out cautiously, but it seems reasonable to argue that depriving human youngsters of a loving, nurturing environment will produce adults who are less well adjusted emotionally and socially.

Examples of the results of childhood trauma and deprivation can be seen in the Jamie Bulger case and the Edlington torture case, both of which occurred in the UK. Jamie Bulger was a 2-year-old from Kirkby in Merseyside. He was abducted, tortured and murdered by Robert Thompson and Jon Venables who were both 10 years old at the time of the killing. In the Edlington torture case, two brothers aged 10 and 11, subjected two other boys to sadistic and brutal violence over a 90-minute period which they also partially filmed. In both cases, the crimes were planned and coordinated by children still at primary school.

The criminal psychologist Paul Britton argues that disturbed children nearly always come from disturbed backgrounds, with violence and neglect as the norm and where the parents have not given emotional space for their children to develop. Robert Thompson and Jon Venables were found guilty and sentenced to 10 years in a young offenders' institution. This sentence was subsequently reduced to 8 years after the Lord Chief Justice argued that such places were corrosive for young people – an implicit acknowledgement of the toxic effect of abusive backgrounds. The Edlington brothers were sentenced to indefinite detention with a minimum of 5 years to serve but it was noted at their trial they had been removed from their biological parents by social services as they had grown up in an environment characterized by poverty, extreme violence, emotional neglect and general chaos.

Britton (1997) argues such environments produce a strong urge to exert power and control over others to compensate for the high levels of emotional unpredictability, constant

feelings of humiliation and general lack of control in their own lives. Being in control over a victim outweighs any moral constraint or knowledge of wrong doing. Such inhibitors of behaviour are nearly always weak in children raised in abusive environments; violence and degradation are norms rather than exceptions.

However, Jamie Bulger's parents argued one of the killers, Robert Thompson, showed clear signs of being an undiagnosed psychopath, a personality disorder characterized by an extreme lack of empathy and morality despite the ability to appear normal. This is a disorder in which an individual uses charisma, violence, sex and manipulation to control others to fulfil his or her own needs. Such people violate social norms but feel no remorse. Thompson, in contrast to Venables, was reported as not showing any remorse during the trial. Such behaviour has been shown to have genetic causes and it seems likely that the emotional sensitivity which impacts moral frameworks is under the influence of biological mechanisms.

Genetics and parenting

Recently, there has been debate over the interaction between genetic predisposition and rearing styles, and the subsequent effects on adult behaviour. According to Dobbs (2009), most of us have genes that make us able to thrive in challenging environments. He uses a flower metaphor, describing such people as dandelions: able to take root and survive almost anywhere. However, Dobbs argues some people are more like the orchid: fragile and fickle, but capable of blooming if given attentive greenhouse care. Dobbs calls this approach the orchid hypothesis: with a poor environment and poor parenting, orchid children can end up depressed, drug-addicted, or in jail – but with the right environment and good parenting, they can grow up to be society's most creative, successful, and happy people. In other words, there is a genetic predisposition to vulnerability and this can be acted on positively or negatively by the environment the child is raised in.

Criminal psychologist Paul Britton argues that children who suffer serious abuse and neglect often have strong desires to wield power and control and this can lead to criminal and immoral behaviour. To what extent should society hold children responsible for their actions if they come from abusive backgrounds?

EMPIRICAL RESEARCH

Rearing styles and adult behaviour (Suomi, 2005)

Rearing styles have been shown to have long-lasting biological effects on non-human animals. For example, Suomi (2005) studied wild rhesus monkeys (considered to be genetically close to humans). In one study, he found high levels of serotonin in the least aggressive adult animals and low levels in the most aggressive. Two groups were studied: one group was reared in a nurturing, supportive environment and the other in a less supportive, non-nurturing environment where they were left to fend for themselves with their siblings. As expected, the non-nurtured group had low levels of serotonin and high levels of aggression and the opposite was true of those reared with a close relationship with their mothers.

In another study, Suomi found clear links between rearing styles and adult behaviour. He identified two types of adult monkey with trouble managing complex adult relations. One type, which he called depressed or neurotic, accounted for about 20% of each generation. These monkeys are slow to leave their mothers' sides when young, even when pushed away by the parent. As adults they are tentative, withdrawn and anxious, and they form fewer bonds and alliances than other monkeys.

The other type, generally male, Suomi called bullies; they do not know how to calibrate their aggression and read signs from other monkeys to moderate their behaviour. They account for approximately 10% of each generation.

Suomi tested the monkeys with a 'cocktail hour' procedure whereby they were given unrestricted access to an alcoholic drink for an hour. Most monkeys have three or four drinks and then stop. However, according to Suomi, bullies do not know how to stop. In this way, he was able to demonstrate their predisposition to extreme behaviour.

● **Examiner's hint**
Caution should be used when generalizing the findings of animal studies to humans. However, this does not mean they should be dismissed in their entirety. Researchers use animals because of the ethical restraints imposed on them with human subjects – such studies can give insight into phenomena that would otherwise be left without thorough research.

continued

In adult life, the neurotics and the bullies meet different fates. The neurotics mature late and stay within their mothers' family circles an unusually long time allowing them to acquire the social and diplomatic skills necessary for communal living. They don't mate prolifically as they do not rise high enough in their new troops to acquire significant status but they usually survive and pass on their genes.

The bullies fare much worse: they seldom make friends, their aggression and risk-taking leads to social rejection and, therefore, isolation. Most die before reaching adulthood and few mate.

Suomi argues bullies are genetically predisposed to engage in risk-taking and anti-social behaviour but they also came from harsh, disciplinarian mothers who deprived their offspring of opportunities to form attachments through socializing. Thus, genetic predisposition coupled with harsh parenting technique produced offspring which exhibited extreme behaviour detrimental to themselves and their ability to pass their genes onto the next generation.

Again it should be noted that this is an animal-based study. Caution should always be used when generalizing the results to humans but it has the value of common sense that can be found in what Ellis and Boyce (2005) label as folk wisdom: individuals with a close attachment to a care-giver have less need to develop aggressive behaviour as their needs are met through nurturing.

To what extent does academic psychology teach us more than folk wisdom or common sense?

Suomi argues that his results mirror real world studies on humans. For example, a longitudinal study conducted over 26 years followed 1037 children born in 1972 in Dunedin, New Zealand (Caspi et al, 2002). The researchers found that children were much more likely to grow up to be aggressive and antisocial if they had inherited a 'short' version of a gene called MAOA. The gene codes for monoamine oxidase A, an enzyme which helps to break down neurotransmitters such as serotonin. Monoamine oxidase A production is less efficient in the individuals with the 'short' version of the gene. However, these individuals became antisocial only if they had experienced an abusive upbringing. Individuals with the short version of the gene and good mothering were usually completely normal. Suomi replicated these findings in monkeys, showing that carriers of the 'short' MAOA gene only turned bad when denied good mothering.

To learn more about how childhood trauma affects later development, go to www. pearsonhotlinks.com, enter the title or ISBN of this book and select weblink 6.4.

EXERCISE

6   Discuss the potential effects of deprivation in childhood on later development.

Resilience

Resilience refers to the process of avoiding adverse outcomes or doing better than expected when confronted with major assaults on the developmental process.

According to Schoon and Bartley (2008), there is consistent evidence to suggest serious harm can be caused by the experience of poverty and adverse life events. Factors such as socio-economic disadvantage, material hardship and family breakdown greatly increase the risk of developing later problems such as educational failure, behavioural problems, psychological distress or poor health. However, there is also evidence that not everyone is affected in the same way. Schoon and Bartley argue that some people seem to be more able to 'beat the odds', to do well despite the experience of adversity. They talk of capability (the ability to do or to achieve certain desired functionings). They also cite Luthar et al. (2000) to define **resilience** as the process of avoiding adverse outcomes or doing better than expected when confronted with major assaults on the developmental process.

Strategies to build resilience

● **Examiner's hint**

If a question asks you to discuss strategies to build resilience, your first task is to define resilience even though it has not been explicitly asked for.

Schools are the fulcrum of many communities and a place where children learn academic subjects as well as socialization skills, meet role models and have their aspirations and

feelings challenged and shaped. Schools, therefore, have a duty of delivery beyond the explicit curriculum of academic subjects but within the hidden curriculum of the school environment. This represents an active acceptance that schools teach values, build emotional worlds and create expectations in children beyond the classroom.

According to Sagor (1996) and Wang et al. (1994), schools can provide support to students, particularly those at risk, through resilience-building experiences that focus on five themes:

- competency (feeling successful)
- belonging (feeling valued)
- usefulness (feeling needed)
- potency (feeling empowered)
- optimism (feeling encouraged and hopeful).

Ackerman (1997) argues schools can also be more explicit in developing resilience in children, particularly those who have been hit by unexpected adversity such as divorce. He outlines how group therapy, peer therapy, classroom meetings, individual counselling, and play therapy all build resilience if delivered consistently.

The New York Center for Children noted in 2004 that 872 000 children were abused or neglected in America. They also stated that 81% of all deaths from child abuse comprised those of infants and toddlers. They propose the following strategies for building resilience and preventing further abuse.

- Home-visit programmes – Such programmes have been shown to be effective in reducing child abuse particularly in low-income families. They serve a practical purpose in increasing access to healthcare and also provide a psychological boost, lowering rates of maternal depression and thus enhancing the formation of attachment between mother and baby. They serve to remind the mother of her obligations to care for the child and demonstrate a wider social interest in her parenting skills.
- Teen-mother parent education – Britner and Reppucci (1997) found groups for adolescent mothers were effective in providing peer support and reducing social isolation and depression. The programme also involved the extended family in the baby's care providing a wider social support network for new mothers.
- Head Start and Early Head Start programmes – Love et al. (2005) found parents who participated in Early head start programmes became more emotionally supportive, better at stimulating language development, and used less corporal punishment.
- After-school programmes in all high-risk communities – Mahoney et al. (2005) carried out a longitudinal study of the effect of after-school programmes on the development of academic performance and motivation for disadvantaged children. They found participants who participated in a full year's after-school programme achieved better test scores, reading achievement, and over all motivation.

 According to the New York Center for Children, 872 000 children were abused or neglected in America in 2004.

 To learn more about the New York Center for Children, go to www.pearsonhotlinks.com, enter the title or ISBN of this book and select weblink 6.5.

EMPIRICAL RESEARCH

Sources of resilience (Schoon and Bartley, 2008)

These researchers conducted a meta-analysis of a number of studies covering decades of research. The studies included: the 1958 National Child Development Study, the 1970 British Cohort Study, the 2000 Millennium Cohort, the British Household Panel Study, the Boyd-Orr Cohort, the English Longitudinal Study on Ageing, the Whitehall II Study and censuses. In total, their findings were based on information covering the lives of some 40 000 individuals.

Initially, they identified the following sources of adversity.

- Poverty and disadvantage – Growing up in poverty gives people less opportunity to build up strengths and capabilities to maintain good physical and mental health and well-being. This is

continued

because low income and poor housing are all associated with increased levels of family distress, less effective parenting, and higher risk of separation and divorce.

- Social exclusion – Living in poverty does not just mean not having enough money; it also means being excluded from normal social interactions. Poorer families are more likely to live in places where facilities and services are in a poor state of repair and may even be unable to access essential services such as healthcare and education.

- Unemployment or low-quality work – This leads to low self-esteem: someone who is unemployed or in low-quality employment may feel they lack control over their life. This impacts family life including aspirations for the children and how they might view opportunities in society such as education. It should be noted that having a job and strong family ties greatly improves self-esteem because work and family are spaces where people can engage in social interaction and build strong supportive relationships.

Schoon and Bartley then put forward the following sources of resilience.

- Academic competence – Resilience was most prevalent in individuals who demonstrated and maintained early academic competence and who had self-belief in their own capabilities. These children had an active life outside of the classroom – they were more likely to participate in extracurricular activities and social networks. They were motivated and showed positive aspirations for the future.

- An effective and supportive family life – Individuals manifesting resilience in the face of adversity (e.g. thriving academically despite growing up in relatively disadvantaged families, with parents employed in unskilled jobs, living in rented and overcrowded conditions) were more likely to have experienced a supportive family environment, and to have parents who showed an interest in their education. A supportive family environment was further characterized by parents who read to their child, who took an active interest and involvement in their education and career planning, and who took the children out for family activities such as holidays and days out. Another important factor was a supportive father figure who helped the mother with the household chores. A warm relationship with both the mother and father is associated with more secure attachments in adulthood and this in turn is been associated with greater career success in those without the advantage of higher levels of education.

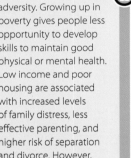

Poverty is a main source of adversity. Growing up in poverty gives people less opportunity to develop skills to maintain good physical or mental health. Low income and poor housing are associated with increased levels of family distress, less effective parenting, and higher risk of separation and divorce. However, these ills are not a direct cause of lack of resilience since many poor families produce well-adapted children who go on to be highly constructive members of society.

- An effective social environment – Schoon and Bartley note that the chances of developing into a healthy, happy and successful adult, despite growing up in poverty, can be improved by the provision of high-quality and affordable childcare because this is key both to children's early development and to releasing parents' time to participate in learning and employment opportunities. Teachers play a role as they smooth the progress of young people, giving them confidence in their own abilities and encouraging positive aspirations for their educational and occupational futures. Government initiatives such as apprenticeship schemes, day-release from work, and evening and adult education classes all contribute to an effective thriving community.

- Employment is a key part of family and social cohesion but Schoon and Bartley note efforts to secure employment should not be enforced at the expense of activities which help people build self-esteem and the social interactions that will help them fulfil their capabilities.

Elder and Conger (2000) examined data from several Iowa counties to see how the farm crisis of the 1980s and 1990s affected children growing up in rural parts of the USA. They found a large number of young people had been protected from the worst social aspects of the crisis and were on paths to successful development and long-term achievement. They also noted that many of the children grew up to be academically successful and law-abiding.

They were able to identify five resource mechanisms:
- strong intergenerational bonds, joint activity between parents and children
- being socialized into productive roles in work and social leadership; stressing non-material goals

- a network of positive engagement in church, school, and community life
- close ties with grandparents, support from grandparents
- strong family connections with the community.

Therefore, in resiliency research it seems there are three factors that are important when it comes to building resilience:
- the child should have a close relationship with at least one parent; even children who suffer from extreme early deprivation can be resilient as long as the rearing environment is loving and supportive
- the temperament of the child and its ability be self-critical and to seek support when needed
- access for the child to a well-rounded social and educational support network in the community.

To access Revision notes 6.3 on Section 6.3, please visit www.pearsonbacconline.com and follow the on-screen instructions.

EXERCISE

7 Define resilience and discuss strategies to build it.

6.4 Identity development

Learning outcomes
- Discuss the formation and development of gender roles.
- Explain cultural variations in gender roles.
- Describe adolescence.
- Discuss the relationship between physical change and development of identity during adolescence.
- Examine psychological research into adolescence.

What is gender?

There are a number of ways to categorize human beings: *biological sex* refers to the sexual characteristics a person possesses, *sexuality* refers to the people a person finds sexually attractive and *gender* refers to the identity a person adopts as a result of developmental processes. Gender identity is usually linked to biological sex organs but this is not always the case. Some women adopt a masculine identity, some men adopt a feminine identity, and there is a great deal of nuanced gradation in between. Identity formation is an active cognitive process and is therefore open to influence from innate physiological processes as well as from social forces (such as media, cultures, parenting and so on). This is why it is of such interest to psychologists. Gender role refers to the sets of behaviours, rights, duties and obligations of being male or female (Bee, 1995). It is therefore a schema, a mental guide for action, steering an individual towards a socially agreed construction of gender expression.

Nearly all cultures expect the two different genders to behave differently but many cultures do not expect gender roles to be distinctive and binary.
- Some Native American and Canadian First Nation indigenous groups allow for multiple genders to exist at the same time in a person via the *two-spirit* concept. This concept recognizes that an individual may possess both male and female identities.

Gender role refers to a schema or a set of behaviours, rights, duties and obligations of being male or female.

● **Examiner's hint**
In a question asking you to *discuss* the formation and development of gender roles or *explain* cultural variations in gender roles, your first task should be to *define* gender roles.

- In Oman, the Xanith form an accepted *third gender* in a strictly gender-segregated society. They are usually male homosexual prostitutes who dress as males but have female mannerisms. Xanith mingle with women but they also run their own households, performing all tasks of both male and female gender roles (Lorber, 1994).
- Western cultures have a notion known as androgyny (Bem, 1974). Androgynous individuals have a mixture of feminine and masculine characteristics and Bem argued these people are freer – less constrained by social impositions – and better adjusted. Pop culture figures such as David Beckham, David Bowie and Eddie Izzard have challenged traditional notions of masculinity displaying many characteristics associated with the opposite gender. It is worth noting that in Western cultures it is arguably more acceptable for men to display female characteristics than for women to display masculine characteristics; this inequality often goes unchallenged by cultural commentators.

Eddie Izzard with make-up and nail varnish.

Most psychologists agree that, by the age of 3, most children have an understanding of gender; by the age of 7, they know that a person's biological characteristics are fixed and the person will remain a male or a female – this is known as gender constancy. However, there is some evidence that the genders differ in their enthusiasm for gender role identity. Huston (1983) found children become less rigid in their gender stereotyping as they mature. Carter and Patterson (1982) noted that, as they move through childhood, boys have an increasing preference for male stereotyped activities but girls have less enthusiasm for female stereotyped activities.

There are a number of approaches to explain gender role formation and development:
- social learning theory
- cognitive developmental theory
- biology-based theories.

Despite the terminology, these are not unitary theories – they are approaches that have been adapted over years of research. They should be evaluated in the context of each other as they represent competing approaches to explaining gender role formation. Rarely can any one theory or approach explain complex human phenomena.

Social learning theory

Social learning theory assumes children learn gender-appropriate and gender-inappropriate behaviour via processes present in the environment/culture such as modelling and conditioning through reward and punishment.

Reinforcement can be direct and explicit:
- 'You look like a girl in that hat' (said to a boy)
- 'Girls don't wear jeans' (said to a girl).

Or it can be more subtle in the form of media images and expectations in peer groups.

Archer and Lloyd (2002) report on women observed playing with a 4-month-old baby. The baby was either dressed as a boy or as a girl. They were given a choice of toys to play with. Lloyd found they chose gender-appropriate toys depending on how the baby was dressed. This study has some flaws, most notably the demand characteristics placed on the women (they may have behaved this way to 'please' the experimenter).

Lamb and Roopnarine (1979) observed nursery-age children at play and found they reinforced each other for gender-appropriate play. They also noted reinforcement was more potent if it came from the same gender as the child being reinforced.

Leary et al. (1982) found children who were frequent television watchers are more likely to hold stereotyped ideas about gender and conform more to gender role preferences – suggesting the potency of modelling behaviour from media. Lewis (1972) observed parent–child interaction and found boys were encouraged to be active and independent and girls were encouraged to be passive and dependent. It should be noted, these Western-centric studies have a degree of ecological validity as they were conducted as observations but they were also in a time when gender roles were more clearly defined and caution must be used when contemporizing the results either to current Western society or to other cultures.

Even nursery-age children reinforce gender-appropriate play suggesting a cognitive and sophisticated understanding of gender roles. Reinforcement is more potent if it comes from the same gender as the child being reinforced.

EMPIRICAL RESEARCH

Gender role differences reflect cultural diversity (Mead, 1935)

Mead's classic study from 1935 is used widely to illustrate the socially constructed nature of gender roles. She studied different tribes in New Guinea to illustrate gender relativism (gender roles are specific to culture and place) and gender determinism (the notion of underlying gender constancy). Mead found the following differences.

- The Mundugumour tribe – Both males and females adopted what Western individuals might describe as traditional masculine behaviour – aggressively sexual, ruthless and bold.
- The Arapesh tribe – Both males and females adopted traditional Western feminine behaviour – warm, emotional and non-aggressive.
- The Tchambuli tribe – Gender roles were completely inverted from their Western counterparts.

Social learning theory and Mead's work offer the best explanation for cultural variation in gender role formation. They clearly demonstrate gender as the result of social constructionist forces present within individual cultures. However, although Mead's results showing gender relativity are well known, it must be stressed that she also found cross-cultural similarities in gender roles. This is less widely reported. She found that men were always more aggressive than women, regardless of the culture. This strongly suggests a biological link to gender roles – an idea which is discussed further below.

 Mead found cross-cultural differences as well as fixed definitives in gender roles. Her findings therefore suggest underlying biological drives in determining gender identity. For example: men were always more aggressive than women regardless of culture.

Mead's cross-cultural consistencies are supported by Williams and Best (1990) who found gender expectations in children as young as 5 years old; these expectations become firmer and more pronounced by the age of 8. They also found that the male characteristics of aggression, strength and cruelty, *and* the female characteristics of gentleness and

appreciativeness showed remarkable uniformity across cultures. However, they found this uniformity was stronger in collectivistic societies and weaker in individualist societies. These findings again support the social learning theory approach to gender role construction because the differences were due to culture.

To access Additional information 6.1 on Anthropology and Margaret Mead, please visit www. pearsonbacconline.com and follow the on-screen instructions.

Sexuality has an influence on gender role identity. Some lesbians identify with male role models/ heroes and some gay men identify with female role models/ heroes. However, this is far from always the case and few generalizations can be made. What is certain is the interaction between sexuality and gender is a highly complex and personal area and it is difficult to draw broad conclusions. However, both sexuality and gender have clear biological as well as societal influences.

Many gay men see Kylie Minogue as an icon but that doesn't mean they would want to emulate her gender-specific behaviour.

The social learning theory has traditionally seen children as passive receivers of the effects of conditioning and modelling. However, recent revisions by Bussey and Bandura (1992) have modified the theory to take account of the child's active participation in gender role development. Cognitive factors such as motivation and perception affect how a child sees and responds to the processes present in the environment. If a girl is told that wearing jeans is a masculine behaviour *and she wants to look masculine* (because this is the gender role she identifies with), then she may not want to stop wearing the jeans. She will be aware of female gender role expectations but decide not to conform to them. She may well perceive jeans as attractive and therefore be more motivated to wear them more than other girls. Perception and motivation are cognitive processes and are not fully explained by social learning theory.

To learn more about how social learning theory can be applied, go to www. pearsonhotlinks.com, enter the title or ISBN of this book and select weblink 6.6.

Cognitive development theory

This approach focuses on the mental events which lead to gender identity and then role enactment. Kohlberg (1966) argued children acquire greater understanding of gender as cognition matures – this means children can only acquire gender identity and enact appropriate role behaviours when they are mentally ready. Initially, children acquire a gender concept and then actively seek information from members of the same gender for clues on how to behave. Once they understand gender is fixed and they are to be a boy or a girl forever, they become increasingly motivated to find information on appropriate behaviours.

Cognitive factors such as motivation and perception affect how a child sees and responds to the processes present in the environment and may override negative conditioning.

Kohlberg thought gender identity was acquired between the ages of 2 and 3. Between the ages of 3 and 7, the child understands gender is largely fixed but can still change if there is a change in appearance such as hair or clothing. Gender constancy occurs between 4½ and 7 years old. This represents a form of the Piagetian notion of conservation as the child understands gender as immovable regardless of superficial changes.

There is empirical support for the Kohlbergian approach: Marcus and Overton (1978) report gender conservation occurs at the same time as other forms of conservation suggesting the process has clear cognitive developmental origins. Kohlberg argued children actively construct their gender role knowledge and this is supported by Slaby and Frey (1975) who divided 2–5-year-olds into two groups: one group they considered to have high gender constancy, and the other group considered to have low gender constancy. They showed a film with a split screen; one side had male models performing a task, the other side had female models performing a task. Children with high gender constancy had more same-sex bias in their attention. This shows children actively seek and then respond to appropriate gender models.

However, Kohlberg's theory does not address how most children come to prefer gender-appropriate toys and garments long before they have gender constancy (Bee, 1995). This is addressed with gender schema theory. Gender schema theory proposes that children form mental guides for action linked around concept clusters that radiate information on how to behave appropriate to gender. The key assumption is that clusters develop before the children have an understanding of gender constancy. This would explain why toys and clothing have different levels of potency for different genders in pre-school age children.

How much of our gender identity is innate and how much is learned from the environment?

Liben and Signorella (1993) found that children who were shown pictures of adults engaged in perceived gender inversion behaviour (e.g. a male nurse) disregarded the information and forgot it – suggesting children are actively engaged in constructing their world view and only select information that supports their vision of gender-appropriate behaviour. However, this emphasis on cognition does not account for biological drives which play a role in perception formation and behaviour manifestation.

Fagot (1985) found that parents and teachers – and perhaps schools in general – positively reinforce the feminine behaviour stereotype (sedentary, quiet, calm behaviour) and negatively reinforce masculine behaviour (impulsive, physical). Yet boys still display masculine behaviour characteristics. Fagot argues this is due to the strength of the male schema the boys have constructed. However, it will also be due to basic biological differences in boys and girls and these are discussed in greater detail below.

Children are actively engaged in constructing their world view and only select information that supports their vision. This applies to gender and to those they wish to identify with. Therefore, gender construction must be seen as an active cognitive, biological as well as a sociocultural process.

Biology-based theories

The biological approach assumes behaviour is the result of physiological mechanisms. There is strong evidence that much of our gender role identity is linked to innate natural

processes but a biologically deterministic position to explain a complex cognitive and social construction such as gender role behaviour is probably unrealistic.

Rough and tumble play

Rough and tumble (R&T) play is a key area for gender psychologists. It is widely accepted that R&T play is the result of hormonal changes in young male mammals, in particular an increase in testosterone in early infanthood (priming or organizing effect) and at puberty (activating effect).

R&T play is prevalent in the males of most mammals, in particular in chimpanzees, orang-utans and humans (Braggio et al., 1978) and even squirrels (Biben, 1998).

According to Jarvis (2006), R&T play was first academically named by Karl Groos in his books *Play of Animals* (1898) and *Play of Man* (1901). Jarvis states most research carried out into R&T play of young humans and non-human primates indicates that R&T play creates valuable practice for the complex social interactions creatures need to undertake in order to become competent, socially mature adults. Jarvis notes that over the past 25 years in Western society there has been an increasing reduction of the time and space allocated for children to engage in such play while over the same period, concerns about poor socialization of young people (particularly young men) have been increasingly raised.

Michael Thompson, author of *Raising Cain: Protecting the Emotional Life of Boys*, has written extensively about the unique world of boys and how schools and modern society frequently prevent boys from expressing themselves the way they are naturally inclined to. He has argued many teachers overreact to boys' behaviour in classrooms, corridors and play grounds since most R&T play is non-violent and will not lead to violence. He argues for a recalibration of how we see boys at work and play, and points to other cultures (e.g. Japan) where rules and appropriate behaviour guidelines for socializing and play are left in the hands of the children, not the adults.

To learn more about Michael Thompson and his focus on male psychology, go to www.pearsonhotlinks.com, enter the title or ISBN of this book and select weblink 6.7.
To learn more about Michael Thompson's documentary, go to www.pearsonhotlinks.com, enter the title or ISBN of this book and select weblink 6.8.

R&T play occurs primarily in males. It is found cross-culturally and across species suggesting a clear link between biology and behaviour.

O'Donnell and Sharpe (2004) argue that R&T play situations in which boys explore a sense of nationalism and territory show human similarity to other mammalian species which also use physical and expressive play to explore dominance hierarchies. Jarvis (2006) observed children in a primary school in northern England and concluded that boys show a clear preference for R&T play in terms of amount, pace and intensity, as well as showing gender differences and awareness in R&T play-based fantasy narratives. She puts forward an evolutionary argument to explain the prevalence of this behaviour in young males: boys need to learn how to compete with other boys for resources and access to female mates and those who are more practiced are more likely to be successful. Females occupy a primarily nurturing role in primate societies and do not need to engage in R&T play as it does not serve an evolutionary purpose. Girls predominantly engage in complex social and emotional interactions as well as grooming activity, which is also prevalent in primate societies.

Other evidence

Congenital adrenal hyperplasia (CAH) is a condition resulting from pre-natal exposure to male androgens. Berenbaum and Snyder (1995) found that girls with the condition showed a significantly greater preference for boys' toys and activities, while boys with the condition did not differ significantly from a non-CAH control group in any way. This clearly shows the impact of hormones on behaviour. Beach (1974) found female dogs exposed to male hormones were more likely to urinate like male dogs and this is supported by Young et al. (1964) who found female monkeys exposed to male hormones were more likely to engage in R&T play.

Taking an entirely biological position on gender-specific behaviour and ignoring social and cognitive factors will not present a nuanced view of a complex phenomenon. However, the evidence does suggest gender roles are under significant physiological influence. This may affect cognitive strategies for coping with the world as well as influencing the choices boys and girls make about who they socialize with and imitate.

Male hormones produce male behaviour in monkeys and dogs. Again, this suggests a clear link between gender and physiological processes.

EXERCISE
8 Define gender roles and explain cultural variations in how they develop.

R&T play is primarily a male activity. To what extent should schools allow it to happen? Schools promote calmness, verbal communication and ask children to sit for long periods to learn information. To what extent are they feminine places?

Adolescence

Adolescence is typically defined as the transitional period between childhood and adulthood.

Cognitive approach

From a cognitive developmental perspective, adolescence can be defined as the period when the Piagetian notion of formal operational thought develops. This allows for the consideration of new beliefs and possibilities.

Sociocultural approach

Adolescence can also be defined through a political or socially constructed paradigm. The World Health Organization (WHO) defines it as the period between 10 and 20 years of age. However, this does not take into account the varying social roles undertaken in many cultures as a consequence of adolescence. In the West, 18 or 19-year-olds may still be seen as adolescents, but in other cultures, 14-year-olds may be expected to marry and perform adult functions in the community. The culture of **the teenager** developed in post-World War II America and teenagers quickly became a clearly demarcated group for social researchers and for corporations manufacturing specific products (e.g. films, jeans, cars, hair products) to sell to them. A modern equivalent of this trend is the recent increase in interest in the pre-teens from market researchers and companies. They have discovered that many young children in the West have a degree of disposable income and can be persuaded to spend it on tailored food, ring-tones, toys and games, if properly targeted.

Adolescence is typically defined as the transitional period between childhood and adulthood. It can also be defined from a Piagetian perspective as the period in which formal operational thought develops. This allows for the consideration within the individual of new beliefs and possibilities.

EXERCISE
9 Discuss how advertisements are aimed at children. You can choose from magazines, bill boards, the TV or radio. Address the following: How do they target children? What methods do they use? How do they portray gender, age-appropriate play, parenting? Consider the ethical implications for these practices. Find out what regulatory bodies are in place to monitor corporate messages to children and research instances where there have been serious transgressions.

James Dean helped to establish the concept of the teenager –a concept not shared by all cultures.

To what extent is adolescence a social construction? To what extent is it the result of biological processes?

James Dean was 24 when he played his iconic role in *Rebel Without A Cause*. The film is an attempt to explore teenage angst and is credited with helping to construct the concept of the teenager in the American mindset. It also influenced how youthful masculinity was portrayed on-screen. The film opened one month after Dean's death in a car accident and he never saw his ascent to icon status.

Biological approach

Adolescence can be defined from a purely biological perspective as the period when there is a rapid increase in growth (known as the growth spurt) and the redistribution of muscle tissue and body fat. The pituitary gland acts to increase the amount of sex hormones entering the bloodstream (oestrogen in girls and testosterone in boys). The individual becomes biologically capable of producing and nurturing children.

Boys start producing sperm around the age of 15; girls start their menstrual cycle somewhat earlier. This transition is typically known as puberty. The body changes shape – girls become heavier with broader hips and the development of breasts; boys develop greater muscle mass and their shoulders widen.

This biological approach does not standardize how we view adolescence as there is increasing evidence that puberty in Western countries is being induced sooner because of environmental toxins (either food additives or the myriad of other chemicals in everyday life). This is particularly true in some girls who, in certain cultural groups, are menstruating at a much younger age than previous generations.

The physical changes of the body can cause problems for teenagers as they develop. Some of these problems centre on the notion of **body image**. According to Croll (2005), body image is the dynamic perception of one's body – how it looks, feels, and moves. The notion of it being dynamic suggests it is constantly under review and is not fixed. It is therefore open to influence.

The physical changes taking place during puberty represent constant challenges to a teenagers' self-image. Body image is shaped by perception, emotion, physical sensation, mood, physical experience, and environment. It is influenced strongly by self-esteem and self-evaluation, more so than by external evaluation by others. It is also influenced by cultural messages, norms and societal standards of appearance and attractiveness. A great deal of research supports the view of a gender difference in how teenagers respond to physical changes in adolescence and Croll cites the following research findings to support her claims.

- 50–88% of adolescent girls feel negatively about their body shape or size.
- 49% of teenage girls say they know someone with an eating disorder.
- Only 33% of girls say they are at the right weight for their body, while 58% want to lose weight and 9% want to gain weight.
- 66% of females think their current size is too large; 21% of males feel this way.
- Over 33% of males think their current size is too small; 10% of women feel this way.
- Strikingly, while only 30% of older adolescents consider their current size acceptable to themselves, 85% of females and 95% of males considered their current size socially acceptable for others.
- 85% of young women worry 'a lot' about how they look and twice as many males as females say they are satisfied with their appearance.

- A report by the American Association of University Women indicated that for girls, 'the way I look' is the most important indicator of self-worth. For boys, self-worth is based on ability rather than looks.

Croll (2005) argues that puberty for boys brings characteristics typically admired by society – height, speed, broadness, and strength. On the other hand, puberty for girls brings characteristics often perceived as less desirable; girls generally get rounder and have increased body fat. These changes can serve to further enhance dissatisfaction among girls going through puberty.

Challenges to perception over physical change come from a variety of sources but the media and television in particular are major sources of those challenges.

The following information comes from the TV-Turnoff Network (2005) in the USA.
- Adolescents watch an average of 28 hours of television per week.
- American youth spend, on average, 900 hours a year in school and an average of 1023 hours a year watching television.
- The average American consumes 11.8 hours per day of media of all kinds.
- Children view more than 20 000 commercials per year.
- 75% of all adolescents spend at least 6 hours a week watching music videos.
- Eight million children at 12 000 schools across America watch television at school each day via Channel One, an in-school broadcast current events programme provided (including TV and VCR equipment) free of charge to schools. The programme includes 10 minutes of broadcast news and current events coverage and 2 minutes of advertisements for products such as chips, candy, and beauty-aids.

Brownell and Napolitano (1995) illustrate how the body-image expectations of pre-teens can be distorted with their 'If Barbie and Ken Were Real' study. Barbie's neck would be too long and thin to support the weight of her head, and her upper body proportions would make it difficult for her walk upright. In Ken's case, his huge barrel chest and enormously thick neck would nearly preclude him from wearing a shirt. Rather bizarrely, Ken would be 7 feet 2 inches tall while Barbie would be 5 feet 2 inches.

Body image is the dynamic perception of one's body – how it looks, feels, and moves. The notion of it being dynamic suggests it is constantly under review and is not fixed. It is therefore open to influence.

What would people really look like if their proportions were based on these dolls?

10 Define adolescence and discuss the relationship between physical change and the development of identity during this period.

Psychological research

Erikson's approach

Erikson put forward an assumption in the 1950s that adolescence is a period of stress and uncertainty brought about by intense physical change which causes a crisis in identity. This view was developed when he worked with emotionally and behaviourally disturbed (EBD) youngsters as a therapist and he can be credited with coining the phrase **identity crisis**. He argued that a typical adolescent thinks: 'I ain't what I ought to be, I ain't what I'm gonna be, but I ain't what I was' (Erikson, 1950). Despite the colloquial language, this statement suggests teenagers cannot achieve a sense of identity because of the intense biological changes taking place in their bodies. He also argued that the crisis was normal and an essential part of identity construction for later adulthood. Erikson's theory has four main components which represent areas an adolescent has trouble processing.

- Intimacy – Adolescents fear a commitment to others as it may involve a loss of identity.
- Time – Erikson argued that teenagers have an inherent disbelief that the passage of time may bring about the possibility of change – while simultaneously being afraid that it might. He called this time diffusion.
- Industry – This involves an inability to concentrate or enormous energy being expended in a singular area. Erikson called this a diffusion of industry.
- Negative identity – Erikson argued teenagers show scornful and snobbish behaviour towards the role offered either by their family and/or society.

He also put forward the notion of a psychosocial moratorium. This refers to a temporary suspension of activity during the period of identity formation when the adolescent is moving between childhood (when identity is clearer) and adulthood (when a new identity has to emerge). Erikson notes this is often recognized by those around teenagers, when society and family members allow adolescents to 'find themselves' and try on different identities in an effort to find one that suits them best. This is seen as the dominant task of this age group and its eventual resolution forms the basis of the adult identity.

Evaluation of Erikson

Erikson intimates adolescence is associated with low self-esteem and low productivity when this is not always the case. Adolescence is more likely to be associated with positive identity formation (Marsh, 1989) and can be a time of community projects and productive charity work. Offer et al. (1981 cited in Eysenck 2000) conducted a meta-analysis of adolescence literature and concluded that most American teenagers can be characterized as being confident, happy and self-satisfied – a contradiction of the Erikson view as the teenager in constant, negative turmoil.

Erikson did not conduct any empirical research to support his view. He based his theory on non-rigorous observations of teenagers undergoing therapy in the 1940s and 50s. This represents a biased sample and also has scientific shortcomings in method. This does not mean academics should reject his notions completely, but it does mean caution should be used when generalizing to a larger group.

Erikson argued females develop their sense of identity later than males as part of their identity and social status is heavily dependent on the type of men they will marry. He

published this view in 1969. It can now be seen as largely outmoded in Western society, although it may still be applied to non-Western cultures.

In the West, identity demarcation was clearer in the 1950s than it is today: Erikson's notion of identity construction was formed at a time when a job-for-life was accepted as the norm and he centred his notion of identity on a career and a marriage partner. It was also a time when people could be easily identified via socio-economic class, geographic and ethnic background, and music preference. Arguably, modern culture and technology, globalization and contemporary economic reality has made identity less fixed and more fluid – open to buffeting from market conditions and the myriad of identities available to construct.

Marcia's approach

Marcia reformulated much of Erikson's work so it could be tested empirically. His basic approach is centred on the notions of crisis and commitment. Crisis occurs through having to re-evaluate previous choices and values; commitment occurs after this re-evaluation and the individual must take on a set of roles and ideologies.

After developing a semi-structured interview for identity research, Marcia proposed identity statuses as psychological identity development:

- Identity diffusion – The status in which the adolescent does not have a sense of having choices; he or she has not yet made (nor is attempting/willing to make) a commitment.
- Identity foreclosure – The status in which the adolescent seems willing to commit to some relevant roles, values, or gaols for the future. Adolescents in this stage have not experienced an identity crisis. They tend to conform to the expectations of others regarding their future (e. g. allowing a parent to determine a career direction) As such, these individuals have not explored a range of options.
- Identity moratorium – The status in which the adolescent is currently in a crisis, exploring various commitments and is ready to make choices, but has not made a commitment to these choices yet.
- Identity achievement – The status in which adolescent has gone through an identity crisis and has made a commitment to a sense of identity (i.e. certain role or value) that he or she has chosen.

Based on Marcia (1966).

These statuses are not *stages* and should not be viewed as a sequential process.

The core idea is that a person's sense of identity is determined largely by the choices and commitments made regarding certain personal and social traits. The work done in this paradigm considers how much a person has made certain choices, and how much he or she displays a commitment to those choices.

 According to Marcia, identity is determined largely by the choices and commitments made regarding certain personal and social traits.

Evaluation of Marcia

Marcia's approach was an extension of Erikson's original work and was an attempt to make it more empirically robust and therefore more useful. Research does suggest confusion and crisis decline as adolescence progresses. For example, Meilman (1979) looked at 12–24-year-old males and found identity achievers rose steadily post-15 years old. There is also an intimation of active, dynamic identity construction which sits well with what we know about teenagers and their predisposition to try out different identities in sometimes very explicit ways. However, Marcia used mainly middle-class, white male American fathers and sons in his sample and conducted his interviews in the 1960s and 70s. Caution should therefore be used when generalizing to wider cultures in a contemporary setting.

Waterman and Waterman (1975) suggested Marcia's theory suffers from cohort effects – that is, the statuses are dependent on particular groups (cohorts) in society. Cohorts are linked to age and culture, and Waterman and Waterman argue many of the fathers in Marcia's sample matured in the pre-World War II period, when adulthood was achieved earlier. The sons in the sample reached adolescence in the 1950s and 1960s when attitudes towards adolescence and young people in particular, had shifted. There is also an assumption in Marcia's work that adolescents have either formed an identity or they have not; this suggests a binary, all-or-nothing approach. This is an oversimplification of a complex human process.

Archer (1982) tested the identity statuses in areas such as occupational choice, gender roles, religious values and political ideologies and found only 5% had the same identity statuses in all four areas. This suggests that people are at different stages towards identity formation in different areas of their lives. There is also a great deal of cultural relativity in identity formation. Condon (1988) studied Inuit in the Canadian Arctic circle: he found that individuals who would be seen as adolescents in Western culture were treated as adults from the onset of puberty. They simply had no time or an appropriate environment in which to ponder their inner identity in the same way that Marcia's middle-class, college-bound sample might in 1960s and 1970s America.

Gender differences in identity development

Recent studies have shown gender differences in identity development and these can be linked to biological processes. Lenroot et al. (2007) examined evidence from 829 MRI scans taken from 387 subjects, aged between 3 and 27 years. They argued that brain development differences between males and females are much larger than height differences. The evidence from MRI scans suggest young women reach full brain developmental maturity between 21 and 22 years of age while young men do not achieve this until nearly 30 years of age. Such differences are rarely noted in educational literature but Lenroot et al. do note that what is developmentally appropriate for a 6-year-old girl may not be developmentally appropriate for a 6-year-old boy. Killgore and Yurgelun–Todd (2004) support these findings. They conducted fMRI scans during a test requiring participants to respond to images of fearful faces. They argued emotional development occurs at different rates in males and females and this is linked to brain development.

Examiner's hint
Psychological research refers to empirical studies as well as theory construction. Erikson did not produce a great deal of empirical research but he did construct an influential theory.

Evidence from MRI scans suggests brain development differences between males and females are much larger than the more obvious differences such as height.

To access Revision notes 6.4 on Section 6.4, please visit www.pearsonbacconline.com and follow the on-screen instructions.

To access worksheet 6.1 with a full example answer to question 2, please visit www.pearsonbacconline.com and follow the on-screen instructions.

PRACTICE QUESTIONS
1 To what extent do biological, cognitive and sociocultural factors influence human development?
2 Evaluate one psychological theory relevant to developmental psychology.
3 Discuss how social and environmental variables may affect cognitive development. Use empirical research to support your answer.
4 Examine attachment in childhood and its role in the subsequent formation of relationships. Use empirical research to support your answer.

To access Worksheet 6.2 with additional practice questions and answer guidelines, please visit www.pearsonbacconline.com and follow the on-screen instructions.

HEALTH PSYCHOLOGY

7.1 Introduction: What is health psychology?

Learning outcomes
- Discuss to what extent biological, cognitive and sociocultural factors influence health-related behaviour.
- Evaluate psychological research (that is, theories and/or studies) relevant to health psychology.

Over the past century, the relationship between behaviour and individual health has attracted attention because of an increase in diseases caused by personal habits. In the modern Western world, it is generally acknowledged many personal ailments are caused by personal behaviours and so the focus has been on prevention – not cure. Health psychology is concerned with how different factors, such as lifestyle and social context, may influence illness and the well being of the entire person. One of the key aims of health psychology is to promote understanding of appropriate behaviour that leads to a healthier lifestyle.

Health psychologists have investigated causes of health problems such as stress, substance abuse, addiction, overeating and obesity in order to find ways to counter their damaging consequences and prevent their occurrence. One of the benefits of this research is an improved understanding of the relationship between environmental and biological factors as well as cognition in determining individual behaviour. This helps in the development of prevention and treatment strategies, and public health campaigns.

There are differences in attitudes towards health-related behaviour among different cultures, as well as variations in the incidence of health problems such as stress, eating disorders and substance abuse. There are also socio-economic and political factors to consider (the influence of family norms on eating habits, alcohol intake and exercise, the influence of corporations on government policy, and campaign groups). There are physiological factors to consider (appetite control centres in the brain, metabolic rate), and cognitive factors (health beliefs). It is always important for health psychologists to take these wider factors into account when addressing human behaviour because caution should always be used when attributing complex human phenomena to single causes.

To access Revision notes 7.1 on Section 7.1, please visit www.pearsonbacconline.com and follow the on-screen instructions.

7.2 Stress

Learning outcomes
- Describe stressors.
- Discuss physiological, psychological and social aspects of stress.
- Evaluate strategies for coping with stress.

● **Examiner's hint**
The command term *discuss* means you should present a range of causes in a balanced and considered way.

Stress and stressors

According to Selye (1956) stress refers to a failure to respond appropriately to emotional or physical threats. The key aspect of Selye's definition is that the threats can be real or imagined but would usually be accompanied by physiological, cognitive and behavioural changes. Any challenging event can cause stress and, therefore, stress can be the result of imagined realities.

It is important to consider the impact of individual differences in the creation of stress because we all have different definitions of what we consider to be a **stressor** – a cause of a stress. Stressors vary for different people (e.g. dogs are warm and friendly for some, for others they are a source of anxiety) but the body can also respond to stress of which it is not conscious (e.g. suppressed memories).

In summary:
- stress is a deeply personal experience
- shares with emotion the three components of subjective interpretative experience (physiological reaction, cognitive reaction and behavioural expression)
- stressors can be defined as any event, real or imagined, cognitive, environmental or biological that leads to stress.

Physiological aspects of stress

Men generally engage in individual pursuits to work of stress. Women tend to socialize to relieve stress.

The different genders have different physiological aspects of stress. Women often have to take responsibility for the home as well as working full time in a workplace. Men, who tend to be more competitive and impulsive, feel pressures to work harder and longer in their chosen career. Frankenhauser et al. (1976) reported boys have adrenaline rushes in exams that take longer to return to normal, whereas girls had a gentler, lower increase and returned to normal much quicker.

The term **psychoneuroimmunology** is used to describe the interactions between psychology and the physiological systems. Most psychologists agree stress has a negative outcome on physical health. Powell et al. (1967) found that children who had been exposed to significant stress in their home life (e.g. marital discord, alcoholism and child abuse), had

According to Selye, stress refers to a failure to respond appropriately to emotional or physical threats whether these threats be real or imagined.

● **Examiner's hint**
When asked about stressors, you should also provide a definition for stress.

impaired growth due to a lowering of the production of growth hormone in the pituitary gland. Stone et al. (1987) correlated negative life experiences with respiratory illness while also arguing positive life experiences decline in the run up to serious illness. Stone et al. also report a correlation between a change in mood and a change in antibody concentration in bodily fluids – suggesting good moods contribute to a healthy immune system.

Gross (1996) argues people often catch colds soon after periods of high stress (e.g. exams) and cites Goetsch and Fuller (1995) who refer to studies that show decreases in the activity of lymphocytes (white blood cells that fight viruses) among medical students during their final exams. Cohen et al. (1991) gave participants nasal drops containing a mild cold virus and found that those who had experienced negative life events in the preceding weeks were twice as likely to develop colds than those who reported lower levels of stress. Stress often increases the secretion of hydrochloric acid while at the same time weakening the ability of the gastrointestinal tract to protect against its negative effects – this leads to gastric ulcers (Pinel, 1993). Tache et al. (1979) report cancer was more common among those who were divorced, widowed or separated from their partners.

 Psychological states lead to physiological changes. Children who have been exposed to significant stress in their home life can have impaired growth due to a reduction of the production of growth hormone in the pituitary gland.

Psychological aspects of stress

Lazarus (1966) argued that, for a situation to be stressful, it must be considered or appraised as such by the person concerned. Therefore, there is a clear cognitive component to stress because any event or phenomenon, real or imagined, can be considered or perceived as stressful. Kagan (2007) outlines how humans have complex semantic concepts for imagined events and creatures that do not exist (e.g. elves or trolls) and perceptual representations for experiences that do not have a consensual semantic label (e.g. the smell of a wet golden retriever).

Fantasy can produce emotions (and bodily reactions) considered to be within the realm of the real by the individual feeling them, and can cause fear and anxiety and lead to stress. Fear is usually a response to a known, external source whereas anxiety is a response to an unknown or imprecise internal source (Kaplan and Sadock, 1998).

Anxiety is a response to a construction from within the individual and is therefore open to interpretation through language. For example, a feeling of anxiety can be translated into language (which becomes a semantic concept) and this itself becomes a construct to be interpreted by the individual and the audience. Therefore, psychologists must consider individual interpretations and the personal value people place on what they consider to be stressors.

We can be stressed by imagined realities as much as real ones.

Expectations of physical health have been shown to have an impact on health outcomes. According to Reed (1999), HIV-positive men who are bereaved stay healthier longer if they remain optimistic about their own future. These researchers argue that hope serves as a vital asset for the long-term survival of infected men who have lost a partner to AIDS.

Social aspects of stress

Humans are social animals and as such we are acutely sensitive to changes in our social environment. Holmes and Rahe (1967) suggest a major cause of stress is some form of change. They compiled the Social Readjustment Rating Scale (SRRS) to rate social events out of 100 for their potential to lead to stress. For example, the death of a spouse was given a rating of 100; change of school was given a rating of 20. People who scored over 300 were viewed as high risk for stress-related health problems. However, this can be seen as a reductionistic approach to a complex and personal problem; caution should be used when quantifying personal and social events in this manner.

A large part of our lives is spent working. Therefore, many areas of psychology are given over to studying the workplace and, in particular, areas where aspects of the workplace can lead to stress. According to The National Institute for Occupational Safety and Health (NIOSH) (1999), workplace stress can be defined as the harmful physical and emotional responses that occur when there is a poor match between job demands and the skills and resources, or personal needs, of the worker. Personality types and general coping skills are the main predictor of whether an individual will experience workplace stress – some people are not suited to the job they have chosen, or been forced to accept.

EMPIRICAL RESEARCH

Emotional labour (Hochschild, 1983)

Hochschild coined the term **emotional labour** in her book The *Managed Heart: The commercialization of human feeling* to refer to the type of work taking place in the modern work environment. She argues there has been a shift away from physical toil of the industrial labourer towards a workplace where we are expected to enhance, suppress and even fake our emotions to meet the needs of employers – and this can lead to stress.

Each time we interact with someone it takes the form of a mini-government with rules and taxes to pay in the form of expected behaviour to maintain the social order. Hochschild argued that the mere pressure of needing to conform to these expectations can lead to negative effects such as emotional dissonance. This occurs when the person feels false and hypocritical and leads to stress and anxiety. **Alienation** occurs as a result of conforming to emotional expectations that are not genuine in the service of an employer – there is lack of **emotional autonomy.**

There is also a degree of **exploitation** as the employee does not own or control the source of profit generation – emotional regulation is in the hands of the employer and employees are expected to conform. In the USA this has led to lawsuits. Grandey (2000) reports a court case where a major retail outlet chain is being sued by their customer service employees as a result of the policy of asking workers to smile and talk to customers. This allegedly caused sexual harassment because customers were unsure of how to respond to what they assumed were genuine expressions of emotion.

To learn more about emotions in the workplace, go to www.pearsonhotlinks.com, enter the title or ISBN of this book and select weblink 7.1.

Another aspect of the modern workplace is **de-individuation** – people losing their identity when working for large corporations which demand that employees express themselves in a certain way (Ovisignkina, 1976; Perrow, 1984). This prompted Foegen (1988) to call for hypocrisy pay for those service agents who are expected to display emotions they do not actually feel as part of their work. The production of negative effects on the employee is supported by Rutter and Fielding (1988) who positively correlated the suppression of emotions in the workplace with stress, and negatively correlated the suppression with job satisfaction.

However, Menzies (1975) describes how procedures and routines (e.g. rotational shifts and wearing uniforms) are implemented unconsciously as ways to reduce stress in the

Where do emotions come from? If they have a basis in biology, what does this mean for concepts of morality?

workplace. He labelled these activities **organizational rituals** and argued they are the most effective way to reduce work-related stress.

Job autonomy in a managerial sense can also affect stress levels – workers with less job autonomy, and therefore less facility to make decisions about their work lives, have been shown to experience greater levels of stress. Marmot et al. (1997) found clerical and office-support employees in the civil service were four times more likely to die of a heart attack than those in the most senior grades. Theorell et al. (1985) found greater blood pressure in high demand–low control occupations such as waiters and cooks.

We experience stress in the modern workplace because we are frequently asked to show emotions we do not feel.

 Increased job autonomy can lead to a decrease in stress.

EXERCISE

1   **a**   Describe stressors.

     b   Make a table of physiological, psychological and social aspects of stress.

Strategies for coping with stress
Stress inoculation training (SIT)

This technique was developed by Meichenbaum in the 1970s and has been gradually improved since. It takes a cognitive approach to treatment with the underlying aim of changing thought processes to combat the effects of stress. Meichenbaum saw the therapy in the same light as medical inoculation and therefore believed training should come *before* the onset of extreme anxiety, not after a stressful event, if it is to be most effective.

According to Meichenbaum (1996), there are three distinct phases to SIT.

- Conceptualization phase – A collaborative relationship is established between the client and the therapist using Socratic-type exchanges with the aim of educating clients about the nature and impact of stress. Clients are encouraged to view perceived threats and provocations as problems-to-be-solved and to identify which aspects of their situation and reactions are potentially changeable as well as those aspects that are not. Clients are then taught how to breakdown global stressors into specific short-term, intermediate and long-term coping goals. Re-conceptualization then takes place: the specific re-conceptualization is individually tailored to the client's specific problem but it may involve identifying the sources of anxiety and ways to combat them – a new model must be agreed on, one that lends itself to specific intervention and is characterized as hopeful and helpful for the client.
- Skills acquisition and rehearsal phase – Skills for coping with the stress are offered and rehearsed. Examples of such skills include emotional self-regulation, self-soothing and acceptance, relaxation, self-instruction, cognitive restructuring, problem-solving, interpersonal communication skills, attention diversion procedures, using social support systems and fostering meaning-related activities.

- Application and follow through phase – This provides opportunities for the clients to imagine stressful events and apply the variety of coping skills across increasing levels of stress. Such techniques involve imagery and behavioural rehearsal, modelling, role playing.

Evaluation of SIT

● **Examiner's hint**
When evaluating coping strategies for stress, you should first define stress to show the examiner you have a good grasp of the topic. Evaluation means balance. You should provide both negative and positive evaluations.

SIT is designed to be individually tailored to the needs of the person suffering stress and comes under the banner of cognitive–behavioural therapy because it changes both thought and behaviour. The key advantage of SIT is that it accepts the stress an individual can experience is often unavoidable –as in a work environment. It tailors the therapy to the needs of the client with the active cooperation of the client. The client-centred approach inherent within SIT promotes equality between client and therapist and empowers the individual to take control of their stress management. It also posits emotional and cognitive awareness at the forefront of the therapeutic environment thereby increasing the chances of long-term success.

To what extent is stress a social construction? Do Western office workers experience more stress than trash-heap scavengers in the developing world? How can we investigate stress objectively?

However, individuals will always vary in how they respond to treatment and some may not be able to cope with the stressors present in their environment regardless of the training they undertake. SIT takes time and money, and is not suited to all lifestyles. If carried out properly, it is a rigorous programme requiring high levels of commitment and motivation. Some cultures (e.g. North American cultures) promote self-betterment and empowerment as a matter of routine thereby rendering those people more suitable to the SIT approach. The requirement to discuss feelings and private thoughts renders the therapy more suitable to some cultures than others.

Yoga

In the broad sense, yoga refers to a range of mental and physical disciplines originating in India approximately 5000 years ago. The practice derives from Hinduism, Buddhism and Jainism but the branches of yoga most commonly known originate in Hindu philosophy and include raja yoga, karma yoga, jnana yoga, bhakti yoga, and hatha yoga.

Yoga has been around for approximately 5000 years. The practice derives from Hinduism, Buddhism and Jainism. 'Yoga' means to yoke, or to join two things together.

'Yoga' means to yoke, or to join two things together and 'hatha' means sun (masculine, active) and moon (feminine, receptive) energy. Therefore, hatha yoga means to join these two powerful forces together. Hatha can also mean forceful, therefore hatha yoga intimates the notion that powerful work must be carried out to purify the mind and body. Hatha yoga is the form of yoga most commonly practised for mental and physical health.

A significant portion of hatha yoga derives from the teachings of Yogi Swatmarama, a 15–16th century yogic sage from India.

He promoted the concepts of:
- asana – the positions or postures to promote physical flexibility and allow meditation. The cross-legged seating position is the most commonly known but there are many more
- pranayama – subtle energy control usually associated with breathing
- nadis – channels or flows of consciousness through the body
- kundalini – coiled instincts or pure desire that yoga can awaken to allow the individual to be more in touch with the world and give it unadulterated expression.

To learn more about yoga, go to www.pearsonhotlinks.com, enter the title or ISBN of this book and select weblink 7.2.

Yoga represents a holistic approach to stress reduction and incorporates physical, cognitive and spiritual concepts with the aim of making the individual more self-aware and more aware of the universe around them. Cosmic awareness in this way is thought to reduce stress and promotes physical and mental well being.

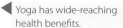

Yoga has wide-reaching health benefits.

Evaluation of yoga

Yoga is an expansive term and so it is difficult to give precise evaluations for the whole practice. However, some generalizations can be made.

- Yoga can be said to improve quality of life (Cohen, 2006). It provides exercise, relaxation and self-awareness as well as putting the individual in touch with like-minded people with regular social interaction. Most yoga classes consist of a combination of physical exercises, breathing routines, and meditation. These activities make yoga beneficial for people with certain health conditions such as hypertension, asthma, and back problems.

- Lasater (1995) in her book, *Relax and Renew: Restful Yoga for Stressful Times*, argues that restorative yoga poses help relieve the effects of chronic stress in several ways.

  - First, the use of props provides a completely supportive environment for total relaxation.

  - Second, each restorative sequence is designed to move the spine in all directions improving the health and flexibility of the back.

  - Third, a well-sequenced restorative practice also includes an inverted pose, which reverses the effects of gravity on the body. Lasater argues we stand or sit most of the day, and therefore blood and lymph fluid accumulate in the lower extremities. By changing the relationship of the legs to gravity, fluids are returned to the upper body and heart function is enhanced. She also argues yoga dramatically alters hormone levels, thus reducing brain arousal, blood pressure and fluid retention, and can counter sleeping problems. Lasater attributes these benefits to a slowing of the heart rate and dilation of the blood vessels in the upper body that comes from reversing the effects of gravity.

  - Fourth, restorative yoga alternately stimulates and soothes the organs. For example, by closing the abdomen with a forward bend and then opening it with a backbend, the abdominal organs are squeezed, forcing the blood out, and then opened so that fresh blood flows in to the organs. With this movement of blood comes the enhanced exchange of oxygen and waste products across the cell membrane (Lasater, 1995).

● **Examiner's hint**
When evaluating, be reasonable and considered. Many studies and theories have been constructed over many years by experienced psychologists; dismissing them in one sentence is a not a sophisticated response.

EMPIRICAL RESEARCH

Yoga and well-being (Hartfiel et al., 2010)

These researchers organized a randomized controlled trial in the UK. In the trial, 48 employees were placed in either a yoga group or a wait-list control group. The yoga group was offered six weeks (January through to March 2008) of dru yoga, comprising one hour-long lunchtime class per week with a certified dru yoga instructor. The wait-list control group received no intervention during this six-week study. Participants were administered psychological tests measuring mood and well-being before and after the six-week period. Results showed the yoga group reported significant improvements in feelings of clear-mindedness, composure, elation, energy, and confidence. In addition, the yoga group reported increased life purpose and satisfaction, and feelings of greater self-confidence during stressful situations.

There is no doubt yoga has many positive benefits but as a targeted stress reduction therapy it may be limited. Stress often has a very specific source relative to the individual (e.g. marital, occupational) that may need specialist counselling or therapy. Yoga is often a holistic lifestyle choice for its practitioners and incorporates many sensible ways to take control of one's life and live a more peaceful and healthy existence. It also provides a social outlet and physical exercise, education about the body and natural world and promotes a calmer, less anxiety-driven existence. However, it is only of benefit to those individuals who truly internalize the teachings and adopt the practices in their entirety; this may have cultural and personal limitations for some.

To access Revision notes 7.2 on Section 7.2, please visit www. pearsonbacconline.com and follow the on-screen instructions.

To learn more about health-related issues for teenagers, go to pearsonhotlinks.com, enter the title or ISBN of this book and select weblink 7.3.

EXERCISE

2 Outline two strategies for coping with stress and list the advantages and disadvantages of each.

7.3 Substance abuse and addictive behaviour

● **Examiner's hints**
The command term *explain* means to give a detailed account, including causes. The command term *examine* asks you to consider the underlying assumptions of a model or theory.

Learning outcomes
- Explain factors related to the development of substance abuse or addictive behaviour.
- Examine prevention strategies and treatments for substance abuse and addictive behaviour.

What is substance abuse?

A substance is anything an individual ingests to alter their cognition (thought processes), behaviour or affective state (mood). This broad definition allows substances such as coffee or food to be seen as potentially addictive substances. Substance abuse can be defined as: the over-indulgence or dependence on a drug or other chemical leading to effects which are detrimental to the individual's physical and mental health, or the welfare of others (Nutt et al., 2007). There is a social paradigm for substance abuse as a person is said to be addicted when their behaviour leads to a significant impairment of their ability to meet their obligations in employment, relationships or the community.

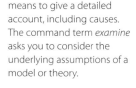

A substance is anything an individual ingests to alter their cognition, behaviour or affective state.

Alcoholism

In this section, we discuss substance abuse in the context of alcoholism.

Alcoholism can be defined as a disabling addictive disorder characterized by a compulsive need for alcohol that leads to negative effects on the drinker's physical, emotional and social health. As with other drug addictions, alcoholism is seen by Western medical establishments as a treatable disease. It is characterized by an incremental physiological tolerance for the drug. This leads to an uncontrolled increase in consumption that has severe consequences for the alcoholic and the people around them. Alcoholism leads to a myriad of mental, social and physical dysfunctions including:

- brain shrinkage
- liver disease and strokes
- tremors, sleep disruption and amnesia,
- anti-social, aggressive and irrational behaviour,
- depression, anxiety, hallucinations and ultimately death.

According to UK Medical Research Council, more than half of all the deaths in Russia between the ages of 15 and 54 are caused by excessive use of alcohol. In the UK, 9000 people die from alcohol-related diseases every year (Lister, 2009).

Physiological factors contributing to alcoholism

Recent research into biological predispositions for alcoholism has usually focused on trying to identify an addictive gene. However, research findings indicate the following.

- Alcoholism does run in families and is particularly prevalent within male bloodlines. According to the US Centers for Disease Control, about 17% of men and 8% of women in the USA become alcoholics at some point in their lives.
- Addiction is linked to risk-taking behaviour, low inhibition, resistance to punishment and a tendency to favour short-term over long-term rewards. This may explain why addiction is more prevalent in men than women.
- Alcoholism is more likely to develop in those exposed to the drug early. This suggests alcohol can influence the development of the adolescent brain.
- There are significant differences in rates of alcoholism across cultures and racial lines but it is currently unclear as to why this is so. However, a great deal of research is being conducted into the relationship between genetic make-up and alcohol dependency.

Overstreet (2000) argues that despite different life experiences, twin brothers show remarkable consistency in alcohol preference. According to Prescott et al. (2005), genetic contributions to alcoholism in males of white, north European descent are well established and researchers should turn their attention to women and other ancestral lines. Cross

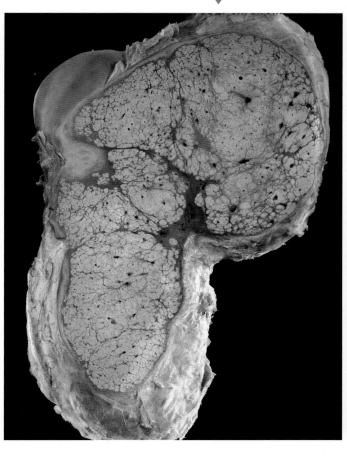

This liver is badly damaged by cirrhosis caused by alcoholism. Healthy liver tissue looks dark red and smooth.

Alcoholism is approximately twice as common in men as in women.

To learn more about research into alcoholism in the USA and UK, go to www. pearsonhotlinks. com, enter the title or ISBN of this book and select weblinks 7.4a and 7.4b.

Should all racial groups be treated the same in the context of alcoholism if biological differences are found between them? To what extent does biology determine a person's identity?

(2004) cites Enoch who speculates genetic predisposition manifests itself in different ways in different racial and cultural groups.

For example, Enoch found some members of a native American tribe who are exposed to environmental stresses such as poverty, trauma and deprivation, and have the genotype COMT Met158Met seem to be protected against alcoholism. But the same genotype expressed in European men is associated with late-onset alcoholism and increased alcohol consumption. She speculates that this genotype leads to an anxious personality and that Europeans who have this type of personality may drink to relieve anxiety as is the norm in this culture. However, in native Americans, a more cautious temperament may actually protect against drinking excesses as the individual will be more sensitive to the effects of alcoholism and seek to avoid them. Cross goes on to state that alcoholism is often associated with other disorders such as nicotine addiction, depression and anti-social personality disorders and there may be a cocktail of susceptibility genes common to all of them.

The evidence is far from unequivocal in identifying an 'alcoholic' gene. To date, the only genes known conclusively to affect drinking habits are those that code for proteins involved in alcohol metabolism: 40% of Asians have gene variants that code for inactive forms of alcohol dehydrogenase (ADH) or aldehyde dehydrogenase (ALDH2). Consequently, they cannot break down alcohol efficiently. Those with ALDH2 deficiency turn red and feel sick as soon as they consume alcohol.

Cross (2004) also cites Lingford–Hughes' use of brain-imaging techniques to look at the number of GABA receptors in the brains of alcoholics. He found fewer receptors in the frontal lobes of alcoholics' brains compared to non-alcoholics. GABA is thought to be involved in calming the body; fewer GABA receptors would suggest a greater susceptibility to anxiety and therefore an increased likelihood of alcohol consumption in certain cultural groups. However, it is not clear if the brain differences are a cause or consequence of alcohol susceptibility.

It should be noted that genetic predisposition does not determine behavioural destiny. In other words, having the biological architecture does not automatically mean an individual will become an alcoholic. At the same time, families without a history of alcoholism can still produce alcoholics. As ever, a complex human phenomenon such as alcoholism should be addressed with a comprehensive and eclectic approach; it is unlikely a single causal factor will be identified.

Cognitive and sociocultural factors contributing to alcoholism

Alcohol has been fermented for around 12 000 years. It is deeply engrained in many human cultures as a way to alter states of consciousness. Social learning theory assumes behaviour is the result of reinforcement, punishment or observational learning. In the modern Western world, manufacturers of alcoholic drinks spend a great deal of money convincing people that alcohol is cool, desirable and an appropriate lifestyle choice from which the user will receive positive consequences. For many adults, it would be very difficult to imagine socializing without drinks being available.

The normalization of drug consumption is deeply engrained in many cultures: coffee provides an acceptable caffeine rush almost everywhere and smoking is popular in many parts of the world. In the UK, the concept of the 'pub' is central to many peoples' lives and is the focal point of many communities. Films, books and plays are filled with characters who drink as a norm, sometimes adversely. It would be very difficult to grow up in Western culture and not be aware of alcohol as a normal part of existence. The socialization of

alcohol affects the way people perceive it. In this way cognitive and sociocultural factors play an important part in onset of alcoholism.

Chen et al. (2005) found children and teenagers respond particularly positively to TV advertisements featuring animals, humour, music and celebrities. They suggest alcohol advertisers should use only content which is less appealing to children and teenagers.

Hill and Casswell (2001) outline how underage drinking is more likely to lead to alcohol problems in later life because young people are expecting positive consequences from alcohol use – precisely the expectations the advertising is designed to encourage. Saffer and Dave (2003) found heavy advertising by the alcohol industry in the USA has such a considerable influence on adolescents that its removal would lower underage drinking. Their analysis suggests that eliminating alcohol advertising in a local setting could reduce monthly drinking by adolescents from about 25% to about 21%, and binge drinking from 12% to around 7%.

Snyder et al. (2006) found that youths who saw more alcohol advertisements drank more, on average. They also found young people from markets with more alcohol advertisements showed increased drinking levels into their late 20s whereas drinking reached a plateau in the early 20s for young people from markets with fewer advertisements.

Many ancient works of art – including cave drawings – are thought to have been created under altered states of consciousness.

Alcohol advertising that is not specifically aimed at adolescents still increases alcohol consumption in that age group.

TOTAL FIRST PINT REFRESHMENT
drinkaware.co.uk

Corporations which manufacturer alcoholic drinks market them aggressively.

There is a common sense element to this data and to the social learning theory approach to alcohol consumption in particular. The aim of a corporation is to use positive advertising (involving product placement, sponsorship and celebrity endorsement) to recruit new consumers and maintain existing ones. If alcohol advertising did not lead to increased consumption, then it would not be used by corporations to sell their products.

This is best illustrated by Dring and Hope (2001) who studied the impact of alcohol advertising in Ireland and found the following.

To learn more about how children are affected by advertising, go to www. pearsonhotlinks.com, enter the title or ISBN of this book and select weblink 7.5.

- Alcohol advertisements were identified as their favourites by the majority of teenagers surveyed.

Drinks known as alcopops are often criticized for appealing to a younger consumer. They have been blamed for the increase in teenaged binge drinking and the subsequent health and social problems.

According to the National Health Service (NHS) in the UK, in 2005–06, there were 187 640 NHS hospital admissions among adults aged 16 and over with either a primary or secondary diagnosis specifically related to alcohol. This has more than doubled from 89 280 in 1995–96. In 2006, alcohol was 65% more affordable than it was in 1980 and in 2004, the UK Government estimated alcohol misuse cost the health service between £1.4 and £1.7 billion per year (cited in Cole and Kmietowicz, 2007).

To learn more about effects of alcohol abuse on the NHS, go to www.pearsonhotlinks.com, enter the title or ISBN of this book and select weblink 7.6.

● **Examiner's hint**
Clearly define your area of substance abuse or addictive behaviour before you begin your answer. In the case of the information above, we have looked at alcohol and alcoholism.

- Most of the teenagers believed the majority of the alcohol advertisements were targeted at young people. This was because the advertisements depicted scenes – dancing, clubbing, lively music, wild activities – identified with young people.
- The teenagers interpreted alcohol advertisements as suggesting that alcohol is a gateway to social and sexual success. This is contrary to the code governing alcohol advertising. They also thought the advertisements suggested that alcohol has mood altering and therapeutic properties (cited in the Institute of Alcohol Studies fact sheet).

In the UK, the Advertising Standards Authority (ASA) has strict guidelines for the advertising of alcohol.

- Advertisers are not allowed to promote alcohol to under-18s and this includes any context, medium or content which the ASA thinks might appeal to under-18s (e.g. text messages).
- No medium can be used to promote alcohol if more than 25% of its regular audience is under 18. This refers to children's networks, some magazines and teen shows on the TV.
- In adverts promoting alcohol, none of the models should look under 25. They cannot be seen acting a way that could be termed 'adolescent'. People who are younger may be seen onscreen during family celebrations – but not in a way that suggests they have consumed alcohol.
- Adverts cannot reflect the culture of people who are under-18 in a way that would promote drinking. For example, pop stars who appeal to children cannot be used to sell alcohol, even to an adult audience.

(Cited from KidsAndAdvertising (2010)).

Despite these policies, the data suggests young people are still influenced by alcohol advertising. The question is whether this leads to alcoholism. There is recognition that alcohol advertising and the normalization of alcohol consumption has pernicious effects. The World Health Organization's European Charter on Alcohol states: 'All children and adolescents have the right to grow up in an environment protected from the negative consequences of alcohol consumption and, to the extent possible, from the promotion of alcoholic beverages.' As part of a strategy for alcohol action, the charter suggests that each Member State should 'implement strict controls, recognizing existing limitations or bans in some countries, on direct and indirect advertising of alcoholic beverages and ensure that no form of advertising is specifically addressed to young people, for instance, through the linking of alcohol to sports.' The charter has been signed by all the member states of the EU, including the UK (studies cited from Institute of Alcohol Studies, UK).

EXERCISE
3   Produce a leaflet to explain how substance abuse or addictive behaviour may develop.

Prevention strategies and treatments for substance abuse and addictive behaviour

Alcohol is a **sedative–hypnotic** drug. Sedative–hypnotics act in a calming way on the body, reducing irritability, slowing reflexes and, usually, controlling anxiety. Therefore, alcoholics are likely to be attracted to these effects and some addicts may well be using other sedative–hypnotics as part of their addiction. However, an alcoholic has to be clearly defined as a person addicted to alcohol, not addicted to the effects of alcohol, because this will affect treatment.

There is a high probability some alcoholics will be cross-using alcohol with other sedatives

as part of their need to self-medicate. Failure to investigate a user's full drug repertoire could result in serious harm if addictions are not uncovered and treated properly. For example, many alcoholics cross-use with benzodiazepine, a drug with very similar effects to alcohol. Benzodiazepine addiction can lead to cravings for and consumption of alcohol and, if not managed properly, it can lead to serious health problems (Poulos and Zack, 2004).

Dual addictions should always be considered by healthcare professionals. However, the discussion that follows deals with users who are addicted only to alcohol

Alcoholics Anonymous

Alcoholics Anonymous (AA) was founded in Ohio (USA) during the 1930s by Bill Wilson and Dr Bob Smith. These two are known to AA members as Bill W. and Dr Bob. At the time, alcoholism was seen as a moral failing and attempts to cure addicts acquired a religious significance. The key contribution of Wilson and Smith was their assertion that alcoholics were in a state of insanity, not in a state of sin. This new medical paradigm paved the way for alcoholism to be treated as a disease rather than as a personal or moral failing.

AA is centred around 'the twelve steps and twelve traditions'. The twelve steps are guidelines for self-improvement (Alcoholics Anonymous, 2001).

1   We admitted we were powerless over alcohol – that our lives had become unmanageable.

2   We came to believe that a power greater than ourselves could restore us to sanity.

3   We made a decision to turn our will and our lives over to the care of God as we understood Him.

4   We made a searching and fearless moral inventory of ourselves.

5   We admitted to God, to ourselves, and to another human being the exact nature of our wrongs.

6   We were entirely ready to have God remove all these defects of character.

7   We humbly asked Him to remove our shortcomings.

8   We made a list of all persons we had harmed, and became willing to make amends to them all.

9   We made direct amends to such people wherever possible, except when to do so would injure them or others.

10 We continued to take personal inventory and when we were wrong promptly admitted it.

11 We sought through prayer and meditation to improve our conscious contact with God as we understood Him, praying only for knowledge of His will for us and the power to carry that out.

12 Having had a spiritual awakening as the result of these steps, we tried to carry this message to alcoholics, and to practice these principles in all our affairs.

Twelve-step programmes have been adopted by other groups dealing with addiction. Such programmes can be adapted to suit different personal, cultural and religious needs – although there is always a heavy emphasis on spirituality and a surrendering of free-will, first to the power of the addiction and secondly to the power of a sponsor and a notion of God. According to VandenBos (2007) they can be summarized thus:
- an acceptance that one cannot control one's addiction or compulsion
- a recognition of a greater power as a source of strength
- a need to examine past errors in one's history with the help of a supportive sponsor (experienced member)

Dual addictions are common – alcoholics may not be addicted to alcohol alone.

AA was established as a self-help group of addicts. It was seen by its founders as a benign anarchy with no top-down organization or hierarchy. That tradition continues today with each group being a self-contained independent entity with no membership fees. They depend on the goodwill of the members and volunteers to survive and are established internationally. By 2001, there were over 2 million members.

To learn more about Alcoholics Anonymous, go to www. pearsonhotlinks. com, enter the title or ISBN of this book and select weblink 7.7.

- an attempt to make amends for these errors
- an attempt to commit to a new life with a new code of behaviour
- a commitment to helping others who suffer from the same addictions or compulsions.

The key assumptions of powerlessness and the need to adopt a higher power on the road to recovery can be seen as controversial. If adopted professionally, it may mean an individual finding strength and support in a more experienced and former addict. However, this means care and addiction-expertise may be passed on by non-trained individuals who are not healthcare specialists. AA is an organization that believes in paying help forward, passing on expertise to others who need it. Healthcare professionals are not a key part of this paradigm and this has drawn both criticism and praise.

The unfortunate notion of 'thirteenth-stepping' has gained currency in recent years (Bogart, 2003) as male members can sometimes prey on vulnerable female members. AA has responded to these criticisms with clear guidelines suggesting men be sponsored by men, and women be sponsored by women except in the case of homosexual individuals who can be sponsored by members of the opposite sex.

Gaston et al. (2005) note the reliance on the notion of spiritualism in AA groups. They found a correlation between feelings of spirituality and the likelihood of AA being recommended to a friend. As far back as 1963, Cain was arguing that AA resembled a cult; it relied too heavily on dogmatic slogans and could become overly dependent on the group for therapy. However, group bonding and reliance are key aims of AA and companionship in this way is seen as supportive and therapeutic and many of Cain's criticism were seen as overblown. Honeymar (1997) notes how AA has many religious undertones which may infringe on an individual's cultural and personal identity.

The US Court of Appeals has ruled that individuals cannot be forced to attend an AA meeting as it may breach their First Amendment Rights guaranteed under the US constitution. This is despite many Hollywood depictions of judges ordering drunks to attend AA meetings.

'My name is John and I am an alcoholic.' An Alcoholics Anonymous meeting in progress.

To access Additional information 7.1 on Alcoholics Anonymous, please visit www.pearsonbacconline.com and follow the on-screen instructions.

Another criticism is the lack of subtlety in the meeting format. Shute (1997) argues that reliance on the medical model is too broad – not all AA attendees are full-blown alcoholics but they will be forced to see themselves as such in the context of the meetings. Moreover, alcohol is completely banned – sufferers are not advised to reduce drinking but to stop it completely. Shute argues that the disease approach and the definitive notion of abstinence

reduce the chances of all those in need receiving the appropriate help. Many drinkers drink too much but are not alcoholics; cutting out alcohol completely is not always an appropriate lifestyle choice, nor is it needed in all instances. Alcohol is a useful drug if used appropriately, although this view is not be shared by everyone.

Drug treatment

Disulfiram is often considered the most effective drug for dealing with alcoholism. Disulfiram blocks the enzyme acetaldehyde dehydrogenase from converting alcohol into the relatively harmless acetic acid. Alcohol is instead stored in the body as acetaldehyde and this is widely believed to be the cause of hangovers. Therefore, the effect of disulfiram is to cause an instant and intense 'hangover' in anyone who drinks alcohol while taking the drug. Symptoms such as shortness of breath, nausea, vomiting, throbbing headache, visual disturbance, mental confusion, postural fainting, and circulatory collapse can result. Krampe et al. (2006) conducted a 9-year study and found an abstinence rate of over 50%.

Naltrexone is a drug that reduces the craving for alcohol while the alcoholic consumes alcohol. In other words, the presence of naltrexone in the blood acts as negative reinforcer for alcohol consumption. It does this by reducing endorphin release. This approach is known as the Sinclair method and is an example of **pharmacological extinction**. It works on the principle that endorphins are part of the body's reward system for performing healthy behaviours (sex, eating, exercise, certain risk-taking behaviours). According to the principles of classical conditioning, the law of effect and social learning theory, the positive consequence for these behaviours provided by endorphins increases the likelihood of the behaviours being repeated.

EMPIRICAL RESEARCH

The Sinclair method (Sinclair 2001)

Alcoholics experience strong pro-alcohol conditioning which leads to an exaggerated argument for drinking and maintains drinking alcohol as a favourable option in their minds. The reward is thought to occur when neurons involved with drinking are saturated with endorphins which provide positive feelings. Therefore, if drinking occurs and the neurons are not saturated with the pleasurable endorphins, pro-alcohol conditioning is eventually undermined and extinguished.

Sinclair found 27% of naltrexone patients had no relapses to heavy drinking throughout 32 weeks, compared with only 3% of placebo patients. Sinclair argues that this clearly demonstrates the efficacy of naltrexone as long as it is used in conjunction with coping skills therapy. In addition, the data showed a detoxification period is not required and targeted medication taken only when craving occurs is effective in maintaining the reduction in heavy drinking. Together, these results make naltrexone a highly appropriate drug for alcoholics who experience highly pleasurable effects from drinking.

However, taking naltrexone before drinking will have to occur for the rest of the patient's life, otherwise the endorphin conditioning – the positive association with alcohol – will re-establish itself. Therefore, freedom from naltrexone would only result from complete abstinence from alcohol.

To access Additional information 7.2 on a possible new drug treatment for alcoholism, please visit www. pearsonbacconline.com and follow the on-screen instructions.

Drug treatments offer an effective way for alcoholics to control their corrosive habits but they are most effective if used in conjunction with other therapy and supported by motivation and a desire to control the behaviour on the part of the alcoholic. Drug treatments do not tackle the negative thought processes which may lead some people to drink, nor the underlying social issues which may have caused the alcoholic to drink excessively in the first place.

Biopsychosocial treatment (BPS)

This represents an eclectic approach to treatment. The approach assumes biological, psychological and social factors play a significant role in alcoholism and that they should be represented in treatment. Separating the illness into constituent elements allows the clinician to distinguish between volition (e.g. personal need, desire, motivation) and biologically deterministic elements (e.g. genetic predisposition and brain chemistry) which can often remove responsibility from the paradigm of understanding a person's illness.

Case formulations and the perspectives model

Tavakoli (2009) labels BPS as the dichotomizing of biology and psychology. He argues that this reductionism unintentionally promotes an artificial distinction between biology and psychology. In turn, this leads to unnecessary confusion in psychiatric assessments and treatment programmes. He suggests treatments should take place under the notion of a **case formulation**. This means a more personalized approach to patients and includes historical data, medical examination, and a variety of other relevant information to reach a diagnosis and treatment plan tailored for an individual patient.

Case formulations are also known as clinical formulations and are used extensively throughout the mental health profession. Psychiatric nurses can be particularly useful at helping construct a case formulation for a patient and then monitoring how it is implemented and the relative effects of treatment. They might consider: a problem list the patient may encounter in their day-to-day activity, origins of mental health problems, a working hypothesis for the treatment plan, and predicted obstacles to treatment while in the care of the hospital and beyond in the community.

Tavakoli also puts forward the **perspectives model** based on McHugh and Slavney's book *The Perspectives of Psychiatry* (1998).

Four perspectives are put forward:
- the disease perspective – what a patient has in terms of an identifiable illness
- the dimensional perspective – what a patient is in terms of their temperament and intellect
- the behavioural perspective – what a patient does in terms of the goal-directed, goal-driven features of their life
- the life story perspective – what a patient encounters in terms of their life story and the meaning they assign to events in their life.

McHugh and Slavney argue that the act of listening to patients is a therapeutic practice in itself and can offer some relief from whatever symptoms or grief the patients have. These researchers argue that any interest the clinician shows in the life-story of a patient promotes a deeper appreciation for the patient's innate temperament and the behavioural choices and tendencies they have demonstrated to date. This leads to an understanding of the unique set of circumstances that have combined to produce the patient who is susceptible to whatever currently ails them (cited in Tavakoli (2009)).

To access Revision notes 7.3 on Section 7.3, please visit www.pearsonbacconline.com and follow the on-screen instructions.

● **Examiner's hint**
You may wish to give a definition and a brief account of the causes of alcoholism before you examine the prevention strategies and treatments.
When you examine treatments, state the assumptions on which they rest. For example, biological treatments assume illness is caused by physiological mechanisms and so they aim to alter them or alleviate the symptoms.

EXERCISE

4   Produce an information document outlining prevention strategies or treatments for substance abuse.

7.4 Obesity

Learning outcomes
- Discuss factors related to overeating and the development of obesity.
- Discuss prevention strategies and treatments for overeating and obesity.

● **Examiner's hint**
The command term *discuss* means you should present a range of causes in a balanced and considered way. Do not dismiss entire theories, all have some merit and an eclectic approach is often the most appropriate way to address complex human phenomena.

What is obesity?

According to the World Health Organization, obesity is a medical condition in which excess body fat has accumulated to the extent that it may have an adverse effect on health. It is a major preventable cause of death worldwide.

The subject has become politicized and some campaigners see childhood obesity as an abuse issue. In this context, fast-food firms and societal norms are seen to have allowed children to be poorly educated about food, while obesity has been normalized by society and fat-acceptance groups.

Much of the following data in this section comes from studies conducted in the USA. This is because the USA has an advanced civil society with self-help groups, grass-roots organizations, and political debate as well as a generously funded research culture. While it is true that the USA has high levels of obesity, other Western nations also show increases in obesity rates. According to the US Centers for Disease Control and Prevention:
- between the periods 1971–74 and 1999–2002, the number of overweight teenagers soared from 6% to 16%
- between 2003 and 2006, 11.3% of children and adolescents were obese and 16.3% were overweight
- the obesity condition known as adult-onset diabetes was renamed type 2 diabetes, because the disease is increasingly seen in teenagers
- between the periods 1976–80 and 1999–2002, the rate of adult obesity more than doubled, rising from 15% to 31%
- the overall rate of obesity and being overweight in the USA were 47% in 1976–80 and 65% in 1999–2002.
- This overall rate has continued rising since 2002, although some studies show the recent rise has not been statistically significant.

 The overall rate of obesity and being overweight in the USA were 47% in 1976–80 and 65% in 1999–2002. It has continued rising since then, although some studies show the recent rise has not been statistically significant.

Like other Western countries with easy access to cheap processed food, the UK is experiencing an obesity crisis. According to Kessler (2010), three decades ago, fewer than 10% of Britons were obese, now it is 25%. It is projected that by 2050, obesity will be the norm in British society. Kessler also notes a disturbing trend: on average, people are getting heavier, but *the heaviest people are gaining disproportionately more weight than others*. The spread between those at the upper end of the weight curve and those at the lower end is widening. Simply put, people are getting fatter and overweight people are becoming more overweight.

The availability of fast food, processed food and a general lack of exercise have all contributed to this. However, not everyone is getting heavier and people are not forced to eat poor food and avoid exercise. Therefore, social scientists need to put forward theories as to why some people are becoming more obese whereas others are able to resist unhealthy temptations and remain healthy by eating good food and exercising regularly.

 Obesity is currently the largest single cause for the discharge of uniformed personnel from the US military (Basu, 2004).

In Western societies and those cultures that adopt fast-food habits, people are getting fatter and overweight people are becoming more overweight.

Sociocultural factors related to obesity

There are a number of political, cultural and economic reasons for the explosion of obesity in the West. The **sedentary lifestyle** is a major cause. In the past, work usually meant physical toil, now work is usually mechanized or at least involves very little physical energy expenditure.

The advent of cars, taxis and public transport means people do not spend as much energy travelling as they once did.

The social learning theory assumes people learn behaviour via processes present in the environment or culture (e.g. modelling and conditioning) via reward and punishment. Wilkinson (2005) reported on a British study that analysed 12 000 3-year-olds who were raised either by their grandparents or by their parents. The study suggests the risk for becoming overweight was 34% higher if grandparents cared for children full-time. It was further suggested that this was connected to grandparents using food as a reward for good behaviour as well as being less inclined to restrict children's urges.

 It is projected that by 2050, obesity will be the norm in UK society.

Secondhand obesity is the notion that children learn to be obese. It is also an example of how the Bandurian concept of modelling can lead to a corrosive behaviour being passed on to a child (children learn lifelong habits while in the presence of their parents) at the same time that obesity is normalized.

 The terms *obesity* and *obese* are seen as offensive by some fat activists and the term *fat* is preferred.

The fat-acceptance movement (sometimes known as the size-acceptance movement or the fat-liberation movement or just **fat power**) is a concerted effort to normalize obesity in society. Fat movements also aim to reduce prejudice and discrimination against fat people (particularly women) who are argued to be the subject of ridicule in the media and the workplace. Controversially, some fat-acceptance movements promote the notion that health is not linked to body size although this view is not universally shared by fat activists.

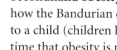 To learn more about fat-acceptance movements, go to www.pearsonhotlinks.com, enter the title or ISBN of this book and select weblink 7.8.

The movement can be seen as split into those people who are fat and want to lose weight and those who simply want civil rights for fat people and a wider acceptance of obesity.

The fast-food industry is an aggressive advertiser and targets children in particular by modelling product-consuming behaviour (e.g. celebrities endorsing the product) and providing positive associations with drinks and food. Hamburger and soft drink corporations have come under particular scrutiny after the recent explosion in childhood obesity.

Ludwig et al. (2001) conducted an observational study at the Children's Hospital in Boston on the relationship between soft drinks and obesity in children. The 19-month study involved 548 children whose average age was just under 12 years. It found that the chances of becoming obese increased significantly with each additional daily serving of sugar-sweetened drink (cited in Jacobson, 2005).

The following are all examples of how social learning theory is applied to selling processed-food products.

- In the USA in 2003, Coca-Cola spent $184 million on promotional activities including sponsoring sports events (*Advertising Age*, 2004). Associating their products with fashionable athletic events and people is a long-standing tradition for fast-food and soft-drinks manufacturers because it allows consumers to see healthy people associated with their product. Some sports stars advertise the products personally in return for lucrative deals.
- In 2004, Coca-Cola and its subsidiaries spent $2.2 billion on promotions worldwide and sold $22 billion worth of beverages (Coca-Cola Company, *Annual Report 2004*).
- Corporations understand the demographics of potential consumers and increasingly they are looking at young children who are easily influenced. In 1999, Dawn Hudson, Pepsi's chief of marketing, told the *New York Times* that marketing to the 8–12-year-old demographic was a priority: 'We're absolutely going to look at preteens', she said (Hays, 1999 cited in Jacobson, 2005).
- Schlosser (2001) outlines how soft-drinks manufacturers deliberately target school children as they are still developing their taste preferences and habits. Establishing brand loyalty at a young age increases the chances of a child becoming a consumer of the product throughout their lifetime.
- Companies pay US school districts for exclusive marketing rights. For example, Coca-Cola had a 10-year exclusive contract with Colorado Springs worth between $8 million and $11 million (Kaufman, 1999). Again, this demonstrates deliberate targeting of children.
- McDonald's operates more playgrounds designed specifically to attract children and their parents to its restaurants than any other private entity in the USA. The playgrounds, and high-sugar content of the products, provide positive associations with the industry and the corporation (Schlosser, 2001).
- Coca-Cola was the exclusive global marketing partner for *Harry Potter and the Sorcerer's Stone*, a film very popular with children. They were reported to be spending $150 million on marketing related to the film (Edwards, 2001). Similarly, Pepsi bought the rights to Yoda, the Star Wars creature (McCarthy, 2005). As noted above, Coca-Cola and Pepsi-Cola also regularly pay pop and sports stars to sell their products.
- In 2010, a UK consumer advice group, Which? found 38% of 8–11-year-olds listed McDonalds as their favourite restaurant because of the toys and 'happy meals' the company marketed to them. Which? expressed concern over the use of toys with fast-food, arguing they contributed to pester-power (the habit of children nagging parents for a particular consumer product).

There are also many positive role models who advocate a disciplined approach to food consumption, although perhaps their diet regime does not attract as much attention as those stars who are paid to advertise processed food. The Ultimate Fighting Championship

Volition, or pure will, is an underrated concept in psychology. Is this because it is difficult to measure? How do you measure will-power?

In 2004, Coca-Cola and its subsidiaries spent $2.2 billion on promotions worldwide and sold $22 billion worth of beverages (Coca-Cola Company, Annual Report, 2004).

(UFC) star Randy Couture is an advocate of a diet based on fresh fruit, vegetables, roots and tubers, nuts, and legumes, while avoiding meat and excess salt. This is done in order to adjust the acidity and alkalinity (pH balance) of his body and he argues it allows him to train for longer and recover faster.

Randy Couture is seen by many as the ultimate athlete. At 46 he was the oldest Ultimate Fighting Champion. He follows a strict diet with lots of fresh food – and he avoids junk food, naturally.

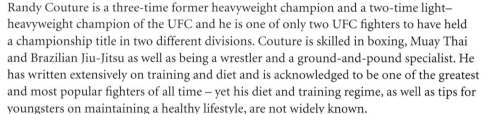

To learn more about mixed martial arts, go to www. pearsonhotlinks. com, enter the title or ISBN of this book and select weblink 7.9a. To learn more about Randy Couture, go to www. pearsonhotlinks. com, enter the title or ISBN of this book and select weblink 7.9b (you will then have to search on his name).

Many mixed martial artists and professional athletes either eat small amounts of red meat or abstain altogether.

Randy Couture is a three-time former heavyweight champion and a two-time light–heavyweight champion of the UFC and he is one of only two UFC fighters to have held a championship title in two different divisions. Couture is skilled in boxing, Muay Thai and Brazilian Jiu-Jitsu as well as being a wrestler and a ground-and-pound specialist. He has written extensively on training and diet and is acknowledged to be one of the greatest and most popular fighters of all time – yet his diet and training regime, as well as tips for youngsters on maintaining a healthy lifestyle, are not widely known.

In his 2001 book, *Fast Food Nation: The Dark Side of the All-American Meal*, Eric Schlosser investigated the US fast-food industry. He cites a study by the Center for Science in the Public Interest to outline the health consequences of the soft-drinks industry. The information following is from the same researcher (Jacobson, 2005).

- In 1978, the typical teenage male in the USA drank about seven ounces of soft drinks daily. Today, he drinks nearly three times that amount, deriving 9% of his daily caloric intake from soft drinks.

Many modern teens consume far more calories than their predecessors, they can be obese but have ailments associated with malnutrition such as calcium deficiency and an increased likelihood of bone fractures. This is because many of the consumed calories are empty – they have no nutritional value.

- Soft drinks contain large numbers of **empty calories** that have little nutritional benefit. Therefore, while many modern teens consume far more calories than their predecessors, they can be obese but have ailments associated with malnutrition such as calcium deficiency and an increased likelihood of bone fractures.

- Twenty years ago, US teenage males drank twice as much milk as soft drinks; now they drink twice as many soft drinks as milk.

As well as fast-food availability, there is also a crisis in the number of people eating healthy food. According to the US Department of Agriculture, in 1994:

- only 39% of boys and 31% of girls consumed the number of servings of vegetables recommended by USDA's food pyramid
- only 13% of boys and 15% of girls consumed the recommended amount of fruit
- only 29% of boys and 12% of girls consumed the recommended amount of dairy foods.

This suggests a lack of education as well as a lack of volition to eat healthily.

Biological factors related to obesity

The medical establishment accept that only a small minority of obesity cases are caused by physiological abnormalities. Most cases of obesity are caused by poor diet (characterized by cheap, highly processed food), lack of exercise and lack of self-discipline.

The following are some examples of physiological abnormalities that can cause obesity.

- **Hypothyroidism** is sometimes associated with weight gain. However, patients with an underactive thyroid generally show only a moderate weight increase of 5–10 pounds.
- Very rare genetic disorders including Froehlich's syndrome in boys, Laurence–Moon– Biedl syndrome and Prader–Willi syndrome, cause obesity.

Although most cases of obesity are caused by poor diet and lack of exercise, this does not mean that physiological factors have no part in shaping eating patterns. Genetic predisposition towards large or small appetite will have some influence. For example, the chances of a thin parent having an overweight child are only about 7% (Garn et al. 1981 cited in Crane and Hannibal, 2009). Having one obese parent increases the chances of the offspring being obese by 40%; having two obese parents increase the chances to 80%.

However, this can also be linked with secondhand obesity and learned lifestyles – healthy parents who eat healthily will pass that knowledge onto the child and vice versa. In this way, obesity is passed on via the cultural equivalent of the gene – the **meme**. Memes are ideas, symbols or behavioural practices which are transmitted from one mind to another through writing, speech, gestures, cultural or family rituals or other imitable phenomena. The term was first coined by Richard Dawkins in his book *The Selfish Gene* (1976). Memetic transmission of obesity is more likely than genetic transmission as the recent explosion in obese people points to an environmental change and a shift in how humans interact in their environment rather than an inherent genetic alteration.

Clearly, body type is inherited, but lifestyle choices are the key. Children who are fat stand more chance of being overweight as an adult (Srinivasan et al., 2005) because they will develop certain eating habits, though they will also be biologically primed to carry more fat cells into adulthood. It should be noted that children are not born with a predisposition to eat poor food and avoid exercise. There will always be biological variations in energy intake for individuals. Basal metabolic rate may well be under genetic influence (although definitive studies do not yet exist) and other bodily processes such as the rates of carbohydrate-to-fat oxidation and the degree of insulin sensitivity, which are closely involved in energy balance and therefore body weight (Ravussin, 1993) may also play a part. But these processes alone cannot account for the rapid growth of obesity in society nor the obesity within individuals. There have always been different body styles in human history but never has the human body been so overweight on such a scale before. The evidence is weak for innate predetermined factors in individuals to explain the obesity epidemic but that does not mean that food cannot be designed to influence physiological mechanisms to make us eat more.

To learn more about a healthy and active lifestyle, go to www. pearsonhotlinks.com, enter the title or ISBN of this book and select weblinks 7.10a, 7.10b and 7.10c.

How do you know you are hungry? Is it biological or psychological mechanisms that play a larger role?

Obesity in the media

David Kessler is a former commissioner of the FDA (Food and Drug Administration, USA). In an article for the *Guardian* newspaper (March, 2010) he argues that people are becoming **conditioned hypereaters**: 'conditioned' because food intake becomes an automatic response to widely available food, 'hyper' because the eating is excessive and hard to control. He made the following points.

Higher sugar, fat and salt intake actually make the individual want to eat more as they make the intake of food compelling for the brain. Neurons are stimulated and release dopamine, a chemical that has been linked with making people want to eat more. Food manufacturers understand this and deliberately engineer food to be 'compelling'.

People reach a **bliss point** with food; it is here they get the greatest pleasure from sugar, fat or salt. He interviewed industry insiders who detailed how corporations deliberately design food to create a bliss point, making a product indulgent or high in **hedonic value**, maximizing the chances of the consumer eating more as well as receiving positive rewards for eating the product.

Food itself has been deliberately changed in terms of its chemical composition: sugar, fat and salt are either **loaded** into a core ingredient (such as meat, vegetables, potato or bread), or **layered** on top of it, or both. Deep-fried tortilla chips are an example of loading – the fat is contained in the chip itself. When it is smothered in cheese, sour cream and sauce, it then becomes layered.

To what extent has this food been manufactured to make us eat more?

When this level of engineered complexity is built into food, the effect becomes more powerful. Sweetness is another example of food reward but it does not account for the full impact of a fizzy drink – its temperature and tingle, resulting from the stimulation of the trigeminal nerve by carbonation and acid, are essential in creating bliss points and hedonic value for money.

Food itself has changed in terms of its physical texture. Kessler interviewed an industry insider who argued that coleslaw composition has been altered to make it more palatable and therefore more desirable as a product. When its ingredients are chopped roughly, it requires time and energy to chew – less will be consumed and more nutritional benefit gained. However, Kessler argues, when cabbage and carrots are softened in a high-fat dressing, coleslaw becomes liquidized and will be guzzled by the consumer; the high fat content will make it more appealing to the brain.

Cognitive factors related to obesity

Maintaining a healthy lifestyle can be difficult, particularly in the face of corporate advertising, peer pressure, food bliss points and shifting societal norms with regard to weight gain. Eating healthily and exercising regularly takes self-discipline and motivation. It also requires people to educate themselves about the effects of food and their lifestyle. If an individual feels hopeless, then this can de-motivate them reducing and maintaining weight (Byrne, 2002).

However, individuals with high self-acceptance (i.e. people who are happy with their lifestyle choices) and extreme weight are unlikely to enact change. Although gaining weight can be seen as a problem, losing weight and maintaining a healthy lifestyle is a bigger obstacle. According to the Malaysian Association for the Study of Obesity (MASO, 2009) poor problem-solving skills usually lead to negative coping mechanisms that may involve behaviour that promotes weight gain as well as behaviour which prohibits it being shed.

Binge eating disorder (BED) affects approximately 2% of adults in the USA. Those who suffer from BED seek comfort in food and eat large amounts. Trigger points are usually emotional lows but the disorder has been linked to boredom and general impulsive behaviour. Research shows that binge eaters tend to have other psychiatric problems such as personality, anxiety and mood disorders, and more commonly depression (Marcus, 1995). BED is found in all ethno-cultural and racial populations although people who are obese and have BED often became overweight at a younger age.

EXERCISE

5 Design an information campaign to demonstrate the causes of obesity.

Prevention strategies for obesity

Clearly, the best way to deal with obesity is stop it developing in the first place. The following strategies are designed to remind people about maintaining a healthy lifestyle as well as to educate people about food: education, political intervention and the grass roots movement.

● **Examiner's hint**
Take an eclectic approach; rarely is one prevention strategy suitable on its own.

Education

Some health education programmes promote the notion 'No food is bad food if eaten in moderation'. However, many foods are not good for you as they contain high empty-calorie counts and large numbers of chemicals such as monosodium glutamate (MSG) to influence taste and texture. Such foods can influence habits and help establish routines for children that can easily become addictive – therefore, they *can* be labelled 'bad'. The no-food-is-bad approach can also give processed food the status of a treat by using it as a reward. Many healthcare professionals argue poor food should not be given to children at all, and at the very least it should not be promoted as desirable.

Education only works if people *want* to lose weight. The absence of volition can be a major barrier to weight reduction and groups such as the fat-acceptance movement are seen as an obstacle to convincing people that weight loss is in their best interest.

Many people remain ignorant about the food industry in terms of how food is produced and where it comes from. In 2002, the Royal Highland Education Trust (RHET) in Scotland interviewed 126 children aged 8 and 9. They found 30% did not know where eggs came from and over 50% thought oranges were grown in Scotland. The study was used to justify increased rural education for inner-city children, funding for farm visits, and general food

To what extent should childhood obesity be seen as a moral issue? Should different cultures be allowed different definitions of 'healthy' or is health a definitive notion?

education. Exercise and healthy eating are the best prevention for obesity but the Campaign to End Obesity in the USA states 52% of adults do not meet minimum physical activity recommendations and only 35.8% of high-school students are physically active for an hour or more every day. The campaign also notes that only 12% of adults and 2% of children eat a healthy diet consistent with federal nutrition recommendations.

Political intervention

In the USA, food labels are required by the FDA so consumers can make an informed choice about the food they eat. However, according to Obesity Action, foods sold in restaurants, hospital cafeterias and airplanes, or sold by food-service vendors (including vending machines) or food shipped in bulk (e.g. that which may be shipped to a restaurant for preparation) are exempt from labelling. However, labelling requires that people are active readers of the information and understand what impact the various chemicals and additives have. Otherwise, the labels are meaningless. In the UK, the Food Standards Agency (FSA) has clamped down on corporations who use misleading language on food packaging. They found 75% of consumers felt confused or misled. Some descriptions (e.g. heritage, classic, prime, full of country goodness, farmhouse and wholesome) were entirely meaningless. Corn-fed chickens were found to have been feed-injected with antibiotics to increase growth even though the label suggested they were a healthy alternative.

Fast food outlets are plentiful in poorer neighbourhoods. People are more reliant on public transport and are less likely to travel far to access healthier and more diverse food options.

Another area now under political regulation is commercial zoning: laws which govern where fast-food outlets can open are under the control of national and local governments. Mair et al. (2005) cite Ashe et al. (2003) who discuss how local communities can use zoning laws to create a retail market offering healthier foods. Currently, fast-food outlets are found in abundance in many predominantly poor areas and this has an impact on wider community health. Mair et al. state that wealthier neighbourhoods have more than three times as many supermarkets as the poorest neighbourhoods. Supermarkets have been linked with healthier diets as a greater range of food is available. However, the residents of poor neighbourhoods have less access to private transport thereby limiting their chances of visiting places with healthier food available. The Institute of Medicine of the National Acadamies (2005) report, *Preventing Childhood Obesity: Health in the Balance*, argues that local and state governments should work with communities to support partnerships and networks that expand the availability of and access to healthful foods.

Wealthier neighbourhoods in the USA have over three times as many supermarkets as the poorest neighbourhoods.

Grass roots movements

The USA comes in for criticism as a result of high levels of obesity but it is also a source of a significant number of community-based organizations which aim to benefit people – often overcoming political or corporate power in order to do so. Groups such as the Campaign to End Obesity, Two Angry Moms, Queen of Hearts Foundation, National Action Against Obesity (NAAO) and Obesity Action have made a significant contribution to the community landscape via media appearances, school visits and local organizing. According to Otto and Aratani (2006), many school districts in the USA have now banned soft drinks, junk foods and sweets from school vending machines and cafeterias in response to pressure from parents and anti-obesity groups.

To access Additional information 7.3 on obesity, please visit www.pearsonbacconline.com and follow the on-screen instructions.

Treatments for obesity

Dieting

A person should never engage in extreme weight-loss behaviour without first consulting a medical professional.

Geissler and Powers (2005) argue the key to weight loss is new habits associated with food and exercise. A healthy diet is not the same as **dieting**. Dieting is associated with a food programme designed to limit energy intake to a level below the rate of energy use. This results in weight loss because the body uses energy from stored fat. However, this cannot be maintained indefinitely. At some point, the individual has to balance their energy intake with energy use. This is achieved by a healthy diet with regular exercise in order to maintain the body weight at a constant level.

Many people who wish to lose weight find diets do not work for them. However, weight-loss trials with diets invariably work better in tightly controlled environments where clinicians can control what people eat. In less controlled environments, an individual's old eating habits are gradually reintroduced and weight loss is either slowed, halted or reversed. Geissler and Powers argue that high degrees of compliance and motivation, and a willingness to accept new diets and lifestyles are needed for the dieting process to be a success. These are often difficult to achieve and dieters can be dishonest about what they eat. To improve adherence, consideration should always be given to an individual's food preferences as well as their educational and socio-economic circumstances. Achieving behavioural as well as cognitive change – seeing food in a new way and understanding the challenges – is the key to success with such weight-loss programmes.

There are many types of diet.
- Very low-energy diets (VLEDs) aim to supply very little energy (in the form of calories) but provide all the essential nutrients. The calorie count is usually set at approximately 800 calories a day. However, reducing energy content so greatly requires increased nutritional density and this can be difficult to achieve with natural food. VLEDs should never be entered into without strict medical supervision.
- Low-energy diets (LEDs) set the calorie count at 800–1500 calories per day and thus allow for greater use of natural foods. Weight loss is less significant than with VLEDs but the long-term gains are greater as they introduce the individual to healthy, natural food and set habits and routines for greater long-term health.
- Low-fat diets (LFDs) reduce fat content but promote protein, complex carbohydrates and fibre. LFDs have been shown to be less effective than LEDs for obese patients (e.g. Geissler and Powers, 2005) but are still effective for overweight people
- Low-carbohydrate diets (LCDs) reduce carbohydrate intake but promote high levels of protein consumption. They have been shown to induce weight loss in obese patients but pose negative health risks for cardiovascular factors as well as showing poor long-term benefits.
- Alcohol abstinence has been shown to help weight loss. Alcohol suppresses fat oxidation which allows more fat to be stored. Consuming alcohol is also associated with weakening will-power which leads to individuals consuming foods not conducive to weight loss and a healthy lifestyle.

Self-help groups

Overeaters Anonymous (OA) is an organization similar in structure and intent to Alcoholics Anonymous. The same twelve-step programme is in force for people with problems related to food including, but not limited to, those with BED, anorexia,

To learn more about how grassroots movements are campaigning to end obesity, go to www.pearsonhotlinks.com, enter the title or ISBN of this book and select weblinks 7.11a, 7.11b and 7.11c.

Consuming alcohol with food means more fat will be stored.

compulsive overeating, and bulimia. OA's third tradition states that the only requirement for memberships is a desire to stop eating compulsively. A key internalization is for members to admit they are powerless over their desire for food and they embark on a spiritual journey to regain control of their compulsions. Another key element of OA is the notion that excessive weight gain or loss is a symptom of underlying problems and therefore, the aim of OA is to focus on these issues. Individuals do not report on weight gain or loss, instead members chart their personal, spiritual and emotional progress in the context of food and their wider lives.

Westphal and Smith (1996) report an average weight drop of 21 pounds but given the aims of the group, weight reduction cannot be the sole measure of success (not least because about 16% of members are not overweight but have either anorexia or bulimia). In a qualitative female-only study Ronel and Libman (2003) found a cognitive shift in world view (which is the true success for OA members) in four domains:

- experience of self
- universal order or God
- relationships with others
- perception of the problem.

The study has limited generalizability to men.

To learn more about Overeaters Anonymous, go to www.pearsonhotlinks.com, enter the title or ISBN of this book and select weblink 7.12.

Surgery

Gastric bypass procedures (GBP) are surgeries leading to a marked reduction in the functional volume of the stomach. They are accompanied by an altered physiological and psychological response to food. There are many variations designed to impact different areas of the digestive tract but most procedures involve reducing the size of the stomach pouch to limit food intake. The resulting weight loss is usually dramatic but such surgery is only considered for those patients who are morbidly obese (in danger of death as a result of their overeating). The surgery is a dramatic intervention and complications are common. It has been reported death occurs within a month in 2% of patients.

The aim of the surgery is to reduce the amount of food being consumed and to make the patient feel a level of fullness after ingesting only a small amount of food. However, the reduced size of the stomach pouch means a very disciplined approach to food is needed for the rest of the patient's life if they are to receive adequate nutritional demands.

Physiological change is dramatic. Adams et al. (2007) researched 43 post-operative patients and found that almost all of them tested positive for a hydrogen breath test. This suggests an overgrowth of bacteria in the small intestine. The overgrowth of bacteria will cause the gut ecology to change and will induce nausea and vomiting. Recurring nausea and vomiting will change the rate at which food is absorbed and this exacerbates the vitamin and nutrition deficiencies common in gastric bypass patients. These changes also prohibit adequate absorption of some essential minerals and nutrients and a carefully designed diet has to be followed as a result.

Psychological change occurs: most patients are able to actively enjoy participation in family and social activities. However, according to Elkins et al. (2005), many who have undergone the surgery suffer from depression in the following months as a result of a change in the role food plays in their emotional outlook. Severe limitations are placed on what the patient can eat and this can cause great emotional strain in individuals who have been used to a certain lifestyle and food choices. However, this should be set in an appropriate context: according to Adams et al. (2007) the long-term mortality rate of gastric bypass patients has been shown to be reduced by up to 40%. This suggests that although some people may be depressed following their operation, they might otherwise not be alive at all.

● Examiner's hint

Always avoid personal accounts of weight loss or gain. Psychology is an academic subject that demands you know how social scientists have addressed a particular problem.

To what extent is personal responsibility actually the responsibility of the person being held responsible? Discuss this in the light of research showing that food companies manipulate the chemical engineering of food and use sports stars to endorse poor food habits.

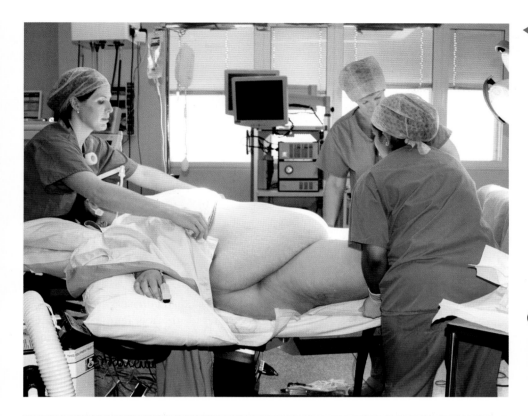

 Surgery is an extreme way to reduce obesity.

To access Revision notes 7.4 on Section 7.4, please visit www. pearsonbacconline.com and follow the on-screen instructions.

EXERCISE

6 Add prevention strategies and treatment to the information campaign you designed in exercise 5.

7.5 ## Health promotion

Learning outcomes
- Examine models and theories of health promotion.
- Discuss the effectiveness of health promotion strategies.

Psychologists have to consider how best to promote a message they believe to be in the best interest of the public. To do this, they have to consider how people think and why they choose to engage in the behaviours they do. For behaviour to change in any meaningful way, beliefs and thought processes also have to change. Therefore, social science researchers construct social cognition models to analyse why and how people behave in the way they do.

The health belief model (HBM)

This model was first developed by Rosenstock (1966) although it has been modified and improved over the years by different researchers. It rests on the assumption people will engage in healthy behaviour if they understand that a health problem will arise if they do not (Figure 7.1). For example: if people are made aware of the health dangers of eating too much (e.g. type 2 diabetes or reduced lifestyle choices), they will be motivated to eat less.

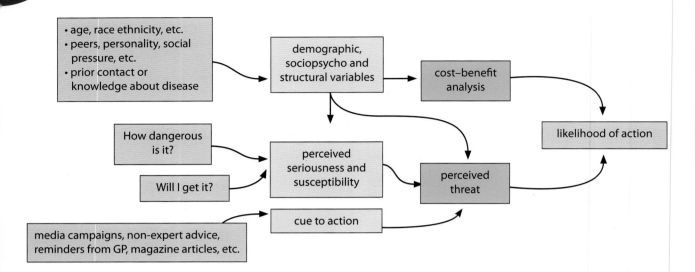

Figure 7.1

The key assumption of the HBM is that people are rational thinkers – that is, they are capable of making and following choices that are in their best interest.

People will first evaluate a threat to their health (e.g. fast food) and then engage in a cost–benefit analysis of what actions to follow to either counter the threat or ignore it. Evaluations and cost–benefit analyses of this kind are examples of cognitive processes which the model is trying to influence to cause a change in behaviour.

However, there are a number of key problems with this model.

1   The HBM assumes people are rational when the evidence is sometimes to the contrary. Consider the following accepted narratives in Western culture:

- processed fast food loaded with chemicals is unhealthy and leads to obesity
- smoking causes cancer
- binge-drinking poses health risks ranging from death and liver damage to injuries from falls and other risk-taking behaviour such as unprotected sex
- poor food served in schools contributes to bad behaviour and childhood obesity and negatively affects grades
- unprotected sex spreads STDs.

And yet people still eat cheap, highly processed food in increasing quantities, smoking is still relatively popular (although declining in the UK), binge-drinking is a major social concern, schools still serve poor food to students and people still engage in unprotected sex. In this way, the HBM fails to consider how people often ignore commonsense solutions to everyday problems and wilfully engage in behaviour that risks their health. This may be partly due to the notion of positive illusions (Taylor and Brown, 1988) whereby people tend to be more optimistic than pessimistic about the world. Positive illusions are an example of optimism bias and encourage people to be over-optimistic about the outcome of their health-risking behaviour.

2   The HBM assumes people care about their health or the health of those they care for. Health apathy can be defined as an absence or suppression of emotion, feeling or concern towards matters pertaining to personal health or to the personal health of people for whom individuals are responsible. This would explain why people still engage in unhealthy behaviour such as eating poor food when they are obese, and feeding poor food to others who are also obese.

3   The model ignores physiological determinism. Kessler (2010) argues that food is deliberately designed with the use of chemical enhancers to make it compelling and create a bliss point for the consumer. Therefore, positive rewards are artificially instilled in the food to encourage consumption above and beyond the need to eat for energy intake.

4   The HBM approach assumes people are active thinkers able to make choices within the realm of freewill. However, it ignores the levels of aggressive marketing that food corporations engage in, including establishing habits and tastes in young children so as to maintain their buying behaviour into adulthood. Alternative voices promoting a healthy, nuanced lifestyle (e.g. grass-roots campaigns) cannot match the advertising budgets of the multinationals aiming to promote a single product in a positive way. This is because a nuanced, healthy lifestyle cannot be tied to a single product whereas processed food is image-marketed with role models, movie tie-ins and other social learning theory techniques (e.g. playgrounds and free toys).

Ofcom is an independent telecommunications and competition regulator in the UK. Their research shows that TV advertising is one of a range of factors which influence food consumption by children. However, it had a 'modest direct effect' on children's food preferences, consumption and behaviour although it led to pester power as children tried to persuade parents to buy certain products (2003).

Healthier choices are less widely advertised. This dominance of the cultural landscape by food corporations renders people less inclined to make healthy choices. Otto and Aratani (2006) demonstrated how the banning of soft drinks, junk foods and sweets from school vending machines and cafeterias has improved the health of students in LA. However, this was achieved only in the face of determined resistance from food manufacturers.

5   The HBM considers only perceived obstacles to effective health regulation, not practical obstacles. Mair et al. (2005) cite Ashe et al. (2003) to show how fast-food outlets are often in abundance in poor neighbourhoods where people are less likely to have personal transport for ease of access to a wider range of food choices. The report of the Institute of Medicine of the National Academies (2005), *Preventing Childhood Obesity: Health in the Balance*, argues that local and state governments should work with communities to support partnerships and networks that expand the availability of and access to healthful foods removing real obstacles to healthy food and lifestyles.

 Does knowledge lead to empowerment? How do you force people to care about their health?

Theory of reasoned action (TRA)

Some of these criticisms are addressed by the theory developed by Fishbein and Ajzen (1975). The key assumption of this theory is people do not always indulge in behaviour that is in-line with their stated beliefs and intentions (Figure 7.2). Therefore, potential behavioural outcomes will resonate with different levels of intentional potency for each individual.

Figure 7.2
According to the TRA, intention is the best predictor of behaviour.

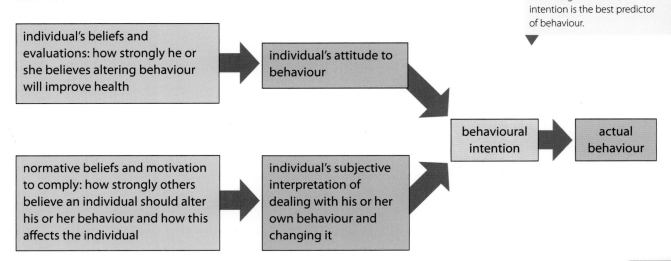

Theory of planned behaviour (TPB)

Ajzen (1985) modified the TRA into the Theory of planned behaviour when he added the concept of perceived behavioural control. Including self-perception in this way strengthens the original theory as it adds another layer of a person's own interpretation when assessing the likelihood of a planned behaviour being followed.

Self-efficacy theory (SET)

Another important influence was the concept of **self-efficacy**, originating from Self-efficacy theory (SET) put forward by Bandura (1977). Bandura argued that expectations such as motivation, performance and feelings of frustration associated with repeated failures influence how an individual approaches a problem. Bandura further divided expectations into two distinct areas:

- self-efficacy – the belief one can successfully engage in a behaviour to produce the desired outcomes (e.g. eat healthily and exercise regularly)
- outcome expectancy – a person's estimation that a given behaviour will actually lead to those desired outcomes.

Bandura notes people with a strong sense of self-efficacy:

- view challenging problems as tasks to be mastered
- develop deeper interest in the activities in which they participate
- form a stronger sense of commitment to their interests and activities
- recover quickly from setbacks and disappointments.

People with a weak sense of self-efficacy:

- avoid challenging tasks
- believe that difficult tasks and situations are beyond their capabilities
- focus on personal failings and negative outcomes
- quickly lose confidence in their personal abilities.

(cited Bandura, 1994).

According to Bandura, self-efficacy is the most important condition to enact behavioural change. TPB explains volitional behaviour, that is, behaviour we intend to engage in, as it maps out variables that influence our decision to perform. The TPB is useful as a tool to design psychological research into intention and action. For example, Conner et al. (2003) used it to help them construct questionnaires to uncover motivations for dietary behaviour because they found a disparity between nutrition and health needs and the use of dietary supplements. The model aided their deconstruction of social, psychological, knowledge and economic factors in investigating the phenomenon. They found health supplement users and non-users perceived the media (including books and magazines) to be a powerful influence on a person's decision to use additives to aid good health.

However, like the HBM, it does not address the effect of conditioning on behaviour. This is particularly pertinent to the food industry because it uses social learning theory techniques to sell food as well the deliberate engineering of the product to produce positive physiological associations and repeat buying.

The HBM is more descriptive in that it explains the forces in the environment which influence a person when they make a decision, whereas the TPB tries to explain why individuals make the choices they do on an individual level.

EXERCISE

7   Research a health promotion strategy for a health issue of your choice.

The effectiveness of health promotion strategies

Health promotion can be defined as the science and art of helping people change their lifestyle to move toward a state of optimal health (Minkler, 1989). It has always been associated with achieving greater health equity and eliminating health inequalities in society. The persistence of inequalities in health, despite overall improvements, continues to pose a major challenge to governments and policy makers. Particular groups in the community experience significantly poorer health and their overall life expectancy is lower than other groups (Hall, 2006).

Measurement of outcomes

Health promotion strategies have to be assessed in order to determine their success and to influence future policy. Health status should be measured before an intervention is carried out, the intervention itself should be measurable, and then health status should be measured again after the intervention. In this way, any possible change can be plausibly related to the intervention.

This approach is known as **measurement of outcomes** and is based on a scientific experimental paradigm – Does cause lead to an effect? Has the variable that has been manipulated (the health intervention) lead to a measurable effect in terms of the improvement of health?

Evidence-based treatment

The measurement of outcomes perspective uses an **evidence-based treatment (EBT)** approach and rests on the assumption that research into health campaigns has to produce statistically significant data to show an effect of the health strategy. It is an attempt to standardize the measurement of health and the effects of treatments or interventions. The EBT approach is very different from the subjective and highly personalized approach of some doctors who base their treatment on lore, experience or intuition passed on from generations of practitioners. This has little or no scientific basis. However, in practice healthcare is often a mixture of EBT (new research and drugs) and the subjective personalized experience between the patient and doctor.

The EBT approach considers the notions of efficacy and effectiveness.
- **Efficacy** – The relative improvement in health as the result of an intervention in a controlled randomized trial (essentially a scientifically based approach).
- **Effectiveness** – The relative improvement in health as the result of an intervention in a more realistic, everyday setting.

Often, controlled randomized trials produce different results to measures of effectiveness. Medical practitioners may also have individual experiences with a treatment or intervention that contradicts published findings.

The EBT approach has many advantages.
- Differences between efficacy and effectiveness can be identified.
- It can help identify hazardous interventions which may only show up in large datasets.
- It is used to monitor changes during treatment over time. Setting up a scientific approach to data collection negates the effects of subjective variables such as memory by an individual patient or medical practitioner.

However, there are some disadvantages.
- It requires a clearly defined population and a reasonable control of variables within it. This is often unrealistic.
- The heavy reliance on the underlying scientific principles is also unrealistic as many non-measureable variables (e.g. culture and self-belief) affect health outcomes.

 Health promotion can be defined as the science and art of helping people change their lifestyle to move toward a state of optimal health.

A measurement of outcomes approach is an attempt to standardize the measurement of health and the effects of treatments or interventions in a rigorous and scientifically defensible way.

 Efficacy refers to improvement in health as the result of an intervention in a controlled randomized trial. Effectiveness refers to improvement in health as the result of an intervention in a more realistic, everyday setting.

 To what extent is the science model flawed with regard to personal health? Does intuition or folklore have any place in modern medical practices? Is subjective experience less valid than an objective scientifically based approach?

- Appraisals of health should always consider the everyday and personalized variables that may influence susceptibility to campaigns and the will power to adopt healthier personal habits. These are difficult to quantify.

Population health approach

The most effective way to implement a health promotion strategy is often a population health approach (PHA). This can be defined as health promotion actions which are primarily targeted at the societal, community, structural or systems level. Using a PHA has many advantages as it requires the collaboration of multiple agencies: government, business and voluntary organizations. All need to work together in the field and in matters of environment, transport, education, corporate regulation and so on.

However, this macro method of tackling health issues has inherent disadvantages. According to Frohlich and Potvin (2008), PHA interventions may be compromised by inconsistencies between the social and cultural assumptions of public health practitioners and the targeted groups. Therefore, any PHA must take account of the various cultural and sub-cultural subtleties between groups in wider society. Such cultural groups may be defined by: gender, age, religion, sexual orientation, ethnic background, socio-economic background, dietary habits, and so on. For example, not everyone needs to be reminded about the dangers of eating too much processed food, and not all groups have access to exercise facilities such as a gym or a swimming pool, or be able to ride a bicycle to work.

Health fields

The Canadian government has long been associated with health promotion campaigns and is a world leader in this area. In 1974, health minister Marc Lalonde proposed a new **health field** concept. This notion promotes the idea that health should go beyond biology and be associated with four interdependent fields which together are responsible for determining an individual's health:

- environment
- lifestyle
- biomedical
- healthcare services.

Health inequalities

According to Minkler (1989) the Lalonde approach emphasized the role of the individual in improving their health as well as outlining the problem of health inequalities. **Health inequalities** or disparities refer to gaps in the quality of health and healthcare across racial, ethnic, sexual orientation and socio-economic groups. In the USA, for example, health inequalities are well documented in minority populations such as African Americans, Native Americans, Asian Americans, Latinos, and lesbian, gay, bisexual/pansexual and transgender people (LGBT). Therefore, health promotion strategies must consider the sub-cultural elements of society to be most effective.

Different sub-cultures may differ in the following ways.

- They may have different local health providers and resources. In the USA, this is a particular issue with the myriad of insurance schemes as well as the overall problem of the uninsured.
- They may have different attitudes to health and different behaviours stemming from cultural background and norms.
- They may have different education levels.
- They may have different transport needs.

Ernest Codman was a health practitioner pioneer who put forward 'the common sense notion that every hospital should follow every patient it treats, long enough to determine whether or not the treatment has been successful, and then to inquire "If not, why not?" with a view to preventing similar failures in the future.'

The Canadian government has long been a world leader in considering the health of their population and developing strategies to improve it. The USA spends more on healthcare per capita but many studies suggest Canadians are actually healthier than their American counterparts. The World Health Organization ranks Canada higher on healthcare performance overall.

- They may have different ways of consuming messages and have different views of government messages.
- They may have different incomes and this will affect how they take care of their health.
- They may have different experiences with healthcare professionals (e.g. homophobia, racism and sexism).

The Marmot Review (2010) is a major health promotion review study conducted in the UK. It stresses that tackling health inequalities is not simply a matter of social justice but also carries with it economic benefits and savings as people become healthier overall. It identifies key areas for future action across the social determinants of health. These include action on areas such as education, work, and promoting the notion of a healthy standard of living.

Increasing choice alone doesn't guarantee people will make healthy choices. They need to take onboard the notion of healthy living.

Health in the workplace

The workplace is a focused area for health promotion. This is an area where people spend a significant amount of time and it can influence mental, social and economic well-being. Workplace health promotion is also known as 'workplace health promotion programme' or 'worksite wellness programme' and other similar terms. The programmes promote activities such as exercise and stress management, and provide information on nutrition and how to stop smoking. In this way, employees can be taken out of their various sub-cultural groups (they are all in the group of employees) and health information can be delivered through a workplace paradigm. Workplace health promotion is, therefore, very effective at reaching large numbers of people from different cultural groups who would not otherwise gather in one place.

Chapman (2005) conducted a review of worksite health promotion and outlined a series of meta-analysis studies published between 1982 and 2005. He found worksite health promotion produced, on average, a decrease of 26.8% in sick-leave absenteeism, a decrease of 26.1% in health costs, and a decrease of 32% in workers' compensation costs. Another effective aspect of worksite health promotion is that it provides a large audience for health promotion messages.

 Workplace health promotion is a very effective way to reach large numbers of people from diverse cultural backgrounds.

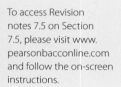

Health promotion has to produce cognitive dissonance to be effective. Cognitive dissonance is the uncomfortable feeling caused by holding two contradictory beliefs or ideas at the same time.

To access Revision notes 7.5 on Section 7.5, please visit www. pearsonbacconline.com and follow the on-screen instructions.

● **Examiner's hint**
The command term *discuss* means you should present a range of causes in a balanced and considered way

● **Examiner's hint**
When evaluating stress-reducing strategies, you can consider them in the context of each other, comparing their effectiveness with alternative strategies.

Cognitive dissonance

For health promotion to work, it must produce **cognitive dissonance**. This is the uncomfortable feeling caused by holding two contradictory beliefs or ideas at the same time (Festinger, 1957). The inherent assumption behind cognitive dissonance is that people are driven to reduce conflicting feelings or thoughts by changing their attitudes, beliefs, and behaviours, or by justifying or rationalizing them.

Causing cognitive conflict in this way forces people to reflect on their lifestyle choices and begin a process of changing or rationalizing them. For example, the effort to convince people to stop smoking: usually, people are aware that smoking is a major cause of cancer; reminding them of this should instigate cognitive dissonance, or at least re-activate existing cognitive dissonance and force either a change in behaviour or new ways to justify it.

However, people are capable of using **emotional dissonance** to regulate their lives. This phrase was coined by Hochschild (1983) and refers to when people can maintain a fake emotion (one they do not genuinely hold) for presenting in public. Hochschild was writing in the context of service employees summoning appropriate but unfelt emotions to serve customers. However, the principle can be applied here: for example, the person who says 'I know my diet makes me obese and I intend to change it,' but who does not agree with this view and tells themself they have 'fat genes.'

Public health campaigns have to take account of how people regulate their emotional inner worlds and recognize the mechanisms people employ to maintain their self-esteem and inner identity. Therefore, such campaigns have to tackle cognitive processes (what kind of information is presented) and emotional processes (how the information is presented). Information presented in a patronizing and demeaning way will be less effective than information which considers how people feel about themselves and their lifestyles.

EXERCISE
8   Discuss the effectiveness of health promotion strategies.

PRACTICE QUESTIONS
1   To what extent do biological factors influence one or more health-related behaviours?
2   Evaluate **one** psychological theory relevant to health psychology.
3   Discuss physiological social aspects of stress. Use empirical research to support your answer.
4   Evaluate **two** strategies for coping with stress. Use empirical research to support your answer.

To access Worksheet 7.1 with with a full example answer to question 1, please visit www.pearsonbacconline.com and follow the on-screen instructions

To access Worksheet 7.2 with additional practice questions and answer guidelines, please visit www.pearsonbacconline.com and follow the on-screen instructions.

 # 8 PSYCHOLOGY OF HUMAN RELATIONSHIPS

8.1 Introduction: What is the psychology of human relationships?

Learning outcomes
- To what extent do biological, cognitive and sociocultural factors influence human relationships?
- Evaluate psychological research (that is, theories and/or studies) relevant to the study of human relationships.

● **Examiner's hint**
The command term *to what extent* asks you to make a judgement about the influence of factors from each level of analysis in this area. You will find it helpful as you work through this chapter to keep a record of what factors appear to be involved and whether there is good evidence for the importance of their role. It would be a good idea to keep a note of studies that you can evaluate. Sometimes, an evaluation is provided for you but sometimes you will need to apply your own evaluation skills to judge the quality of studies in this area.

The psychology of human relationships looks at the nature and causes of relationships between people. This includes the origins of attraction and friendship, the nature of romantic relationships, and how these relationships change and end. The darker side of human nature is also considered, with a focus on why we occasionally fail to help others in need or are violent towards others in our own social group. The ultimate aim of this study is to understand our relationships with others and to improve the quality of these relationships.

As with other options topics, you are expected to pay attention to the relative contribution of the different levels of analysis to our understanding of human relationships. There is a significant contribution from evolutionary psychology in terms of why we engage in altruistic behaviour and why we are attracted to some people more than others. Cognitive models are used to describe the decision-making processes in bystander intervention, and in the origin and breakdown of relationships. There is a lot of research attempting to investigate the role of cultural factors in attraction and the formation of relationships. There is also a significant contribution from social and cultural norms to the occurrence of violence. Research supports most of the ideas covered in this chapter using a range of methods, including experiments, interviews, and questionnaires.

8.2 Social responsibility

Learning outcomes
- Distinguish between altruism and prosocial behaviour.
- Contrast two theories explaining altruism in humans.
- Using one or more research studies, explain cross-cultural differences in prosocial behaviour.
- Examine factors influencing bystanderism.

Prosocial behaviour and altruism

Prosocial behaviour refers to any behaviour that is intended to benefit others. The kind of behaviour typically studied by psychologists in this area includes many different variants of helping behaviour such as giving donations, rescuing someone in danger, sharing, volunteering for the fire service or a community building project, and carrying a bag or pushchair (baby buggy) for an overloaded mother. There are many acts that can be considered prosocial, and psychologists have been interested for some time in why people engage in them, and under what circumstances people tend *not* to help.

Sometimes the reason for engaging in prosocial behaviour is a selfish one. For example, if a person puts money in a charity box *in order to feel good*, **egoistic motivation** is behind the action. There is a strong argument that such egoism accounts for most prosocial behaviour. In contrast, **altruism** is the performance of prosocial actions *without expectation of benefit for oneself*. There has been significant argument over whether or not it is possible for any act to be truly altruistic. This is because it is often easy to identify possible benefits to the actor. Some people argue that the ultimate goal of all human behaviour is personal pleasure (this is known as psychological hedonism). However, others argue that **altruistic motivation** does exist, with personal benefit not the motive to act, but rather a concern for the welfare of others *despite the possible costs of acting*. Batson (1991) defines altruism as 'a motivational state with the ultimate goal of increasing another's welfare'. Note the clear difference in ultimate goals: in egoism, the ultimate goal is personal benefit, achieved in this context by helping others; in altruism, the ultimate goal is increasing another's welfare, regardless of personal cost or benefit.

Prosocial behaviour is behaviour that benefits others. Altruism is one type of prosocial behaviour; that which occurs without personal benefit as its ultimate goal.

Prosocial behaviour may be egoistic or altruistic.

EXERCISE

1 Discuss with classmates or family whether the following examples of prosocial behaviour are possible examples of altruism or not, and justify your opinion. Note that there are no correct answers here. You might like to try this exercise again after you have finished this chapter.

    a A woman walking in the centre of town sees a person standing on a corner with a map, looking lost. She stops and asks if he needs help finding something.

    b A teacher walking upstairs at school drops some books. Two students walking behind him pick them up and return them to him.

    c During a World Cup soccer game, a player knocks over one of his opponents and then offers a hand to help him up.

    d A whole class of students, on hearing about a family made homeless by an accidental fire, write letters to local businesses and ask them to make donations of money and household goods.

● **Examiner's hint**
The learning outcome for this section asks you to *distinguish* between altruism and prosocial behaviour. This means that you must be able to define both terms, give examples of them, and make the difference clear.

Theories and research into altruism

The empathy–altruism hypothesis

This approach to explaining altruism is based on the idea that an emotional response (empathy) is generated when another person *is perceived to be in need*. We are then motivated to help the person in need for their own sake. Empathy is notoriously difficult to define. However, in the context of this hypothesis it is taken to include a range of feelings that are focused on others rather than oneself, including sympathy, compassion, warmth and tenderness.

The leading figure behind this hypothesis is Daniel Batson. He suggests that the perception of need begins with the perception that the other person is experiencing a mismatch between their current state and their potential state – this could be in terms of mood, pain, hunger or safety. An observer must, therefore, be able to have knowledge about both the current and potential state of the other person. For example, consider encountering a person begging for money on the street. Although there might be many explanations for your decision to give money, it is quite likely that you would hesitate to do so if:

- you could not see the person and make a judgement about whether or not they were hungry
- you could see the person and did not think they looked in need.

Following the perception of need, Batson (1991) argues, a person is then likely to evaluate the situation in terms of possible rewards and costs for helping. Two different egoistic pathways to helping are possibly activated in the observer at this point:

- recognition of some potential reward for helping (e.g. a strong feeling of virtuousness, or recognition in the newspaper)
- recognition that seeing the person in need has triggered personal distress and that the observer can make the personal distress go away either by helping or by leaving the situation.

However, a third possibility – one that is altruistic rather than egoistic – is also possible: that the observer will adopt the perspective of the person in need. This is the empathy referred to in the name of the hypothesis. It requires in the observer the ability to imagine (correctly or incorrectly) how the person in need is feeling.

The strength of the observer's empathic response is then affected by how great the need is perceived to be and the strength of the observer's attachment to the person in need. This means that your empathic response should be greater if you feel that a close family member

 When there is an opportunity to help, we may see possible rewards for ourselves or feel empathy for the person in need.

or friend is having trouble, and the response will increase according to how severe you think their need is. However, an empathic response should not include a feeling of personal distress: this is a quite different emotional reaction that you might be motivated to reduce for your own benefit.

Does seeing two broken legs stimulate empathy in you?

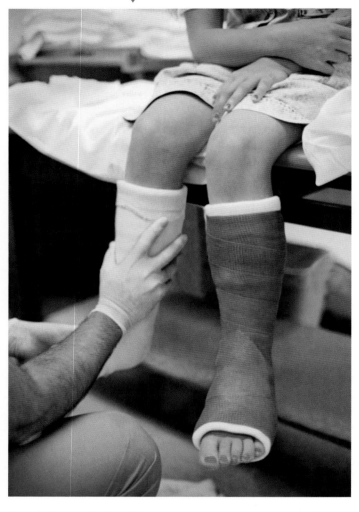

The empathy–altruism hypothesis has been empirically tested many times, partly to distinguish it clearly from the egoistic models that were favoured by mainstream psychology. The hypothesis has faced one particularly difficult problem: it is usually not possible to know from observed behaviour what the actor's true motivation is; indeed, the actor may also be unaware of their true motivation.

In an experiment by Toi and Batson (1982), female psychology students were played a recording of an interview purportedly with a fellow student named Carol, who had broken both her legs in a car accident. The researchers manipulated strength of empathy by asking participants to focus either on the information in the interview or on Carol's feelings about what had happened. They also manipulated 'ease of escape' by telling participants either that Carol was stuck at home or that she would be in the same tutorial group as the participant and was returning to university next week.

When given the opportunity to offer to help Carol by going through class notes with her, participants were far more likely to help if they had been listening with a focus on how Carol felt (i.e. with elevated empathy). Although the feeling that they would probably meet Carol next week did increase the likelihood that they would help, the researchers did not find this more social factor to be as important as participants' level of empathy.

If we assume that the empathy–altruism hypothesis is correct and that altruism truly does exist in humans, what significance does this have? Do charitable organizations already know this and manipulate the public to increase charitable donations? Is it morally acceptable if they do?

EXERCISE

2   List limitations of studies like this which try to manipulate empathy. Consider validity issues in particular; think about the concepts of ecological validity and artificiality.

Batson et al. (1983) overcame the problem of not knowing what level of empathy participants experience in this kind of experiment by running an experiment that measured empathy by self-report rather than trying to manipulate it. Participants were asked to report their emotional state after observing a same-sex stooge randomly receiving electric shocks while completing a task. The stooge showed extreme discomfort about receiving the shocks because of a childhood accident. The participants were then able to voluntarily take the place of the stooge, logically expecting that they would be able to tolerate the shocks better. Again, the researchers found that high levels of empathy predicted the decision to volunteer.

Modifications to this study including making the shock sound more painful – this lowered the rate of helping behaviour. This suggests that although the cost–benefit analysis that

people are assumed to carry out before deciding to help does indeed occur, the more powerful underlying motive preceding this is probably an empathic concern for the welfare of the other person.

The kin selection hypothesis

A very different approach to explaining altruism is taken by sociobiologists and evolutionary psychologists. According to theorists in these fields, altruistic behaviour certainly does occur, and it is likely to have been selected for during human evolution. This means that there is a survival advantage in displaying selfless helping behaviour. However, there is a troubling question for those working in this area. How it can be advantageous for individuals to risk their own survival, reduce their own access to resources, or increase another's likelihood of reproducing? All these forms of activity should reduce the frequency of a genetic tendency to help being passed on to descendants. A further troubling issue is raised by the observation that cooperative behaviour seems to occur very infrequently among non-human animals.

There is a common belief that meerkats are altruistic. They famously stand guard while others forage for food. Researchers have found, however, that the guards are the first to flee after sounding the alarm, so they have more time to escape than the others.

Meerkats standing guard: selflessly guarding others or selfishly watching out for themselves?

The idea of kin selection offers a fairly simple evolutionary explanation for altruistic behaviour in humans. The basic premise is that helping others in your family group, particularly direct descendants, will increase the chances of the genes that caused the helping behaviour being passed on. You may individually decrease your own chances of survival, but if you are helping a direct descendant, you are increasing the chances of your shared genes being passed on. Moreover, the set of genes that causes helping behaviour can be assumed to be present in other close members of the family as well.

One interesting piece of evidence that such behaviour really does exist among humans has been provided by Sime (1983). This researcher analysed accounts of how people fled from a burning building and found that when individuals were with unrelated group members before exit, they tended to become separated, while those with family members before exit tended to stay together. This would favour group survival.

Simpson and Kenrick (1997) suggest that our ingroup bias (pages 110–112) can be accounted for through kin selection, as it makes sense that a whole set of attitudes, opinions and behaviours should accompany an instinctive desire to help those who share many of the same genes. It is somewhat surprising, then, that we are not better able to identify those who share genes without clues like physical similarity. On the other hand, it should be no surprise that in situations where we are inclined to help, we tend to help people whom we perceive as more similar to us (page 261).

Kin selection theories suggest that we should favour close family in times of trouble.

Research done by Burnstein et al. (1994) is often considered to provide evidence for the kin selection hypothesis. They asked participants to report how likely it was that they would help people of varying degrees of relatedness, such as grandmother, first cousin or unrelated acquaintance. The situations in which participants could help ranged from basic favours to more extreme situations like the opportunity to rescue one person from a burning house. Not only did participants reveal that they were more likely to help closer relatives, this effect became more extreme as the possible cost to the participant increased. Other effects also fitted with an evolutionary explanation (e.g. younger people were more likely to be helped than older).

EMPIRICAL RESEARCH

Kin selection in UK and South African students (Madsen et al., 2007)

These researchers aimed to test the kin selection hypothesis experimentally using participants from two different cultures: UK students and South African students. One reason for using two different cultures is that the concepts 'kin' and 'family' are understood differently across the world, so if kin selection as an explanation for altruism did not seem to work in one of these groups, it may not be valid.

Participants were asked to perform a physical exercise that becomes increasingly painful: leaning against a wall with legs bent at the knee so that the thighs are parallel to the floor. Each participant had supplied a list of biological relatives but the list could not include relatives who shared a home with the participant. Before each trial, participants were told that one specific relative randomly selected from their list would receive payment according to the length of time they could stay in the 'seated' position against the wall.

The first version of this experiment, carried out in the UK, offered a rate of 40p per 20 seconds. Participants did, on average, spend more time in the uncomfortable position when the money was going to more closely related family members, although females were slightly more equitable than males. The experiment was revised and run again at a higher rate of pay.

Two separate groups of Zulu males in South Africa were then tested but with food items substituting for money. Again, participants made more effort to stay in the uncomfortable position for relatives who were biologically closer to them. There were some differences, particularly in that the Zulu participants did not seem to distinguish between cousins and biologically closer relatives such siblings, aunts and nephews.

Thus it appears that kin selection is indeed a powerful motivator to perform altruistic deeds.

EXERCISE

3   Find similarities and differences between the two theories in this section. As a guide, address the following questions for each of the two theories.

    a   Is the theory mostly focused on biological, cognitive, or sociocultural factors?

    b   Is the theory supported by valid empirical evidence? What kinds of method are used?

    c   What conclusions does the theory make about the existence and cause of altruism?

    d   Does the theory apply across genders and cultures?

Cross-cultural differences in prosocial behaviour

The empirical research on page 256 highlights some cross-cultural similarities and differences in altruism. There are many other studies that focus more generally on prosocial behaviour. After conducting a simple study into helping behaviour in the USA, Robert Levine began a wider study in major cities of 23 different countries to try and explore what the differences might be.

Among a great many other variables including population size, Levine et al. (2001) considered how the dimensions of individualism and collectivism in these cities might be connected with helping behaviour, and also the notion of simpatia or simpatico. This notion exists in several Spanish and Latin American cultures; it is a generally 'proactive socio-emotional orientation and concern with the social well-being of others' that provides a social impetus to help strangers.

Three helping situations were used:
- a pedestrian drops a pen on the street without noticing
- a pedestrian wearing a leg brace drops some magazines
- a blind pedestrian with a cane waits at a traffic light for assistance crossing the street.

◀ Who are you more likely to help?

From scores on these tests, an overall helping index was created. The top five cities were:
- Rio de Janeiro (Brazil)
- San Jose (Costa Rica)
- Lilongwe (Mali)
- Calcutta (India)
- Vienna (Austria).

The bottom five in the study were:

- Sofia (Bulgaria).
- Amsterdam (Netherlands)
- Singapore (Singapore)
- New York (USA)
- Kuala Lumpur (Malaysia)

There was a large difference between top and bottom, with Kuala Lumpur achieving less than half of Rio de Janeiro's overall score. Incidentally, it appears that the worst place to be a blind person crossing the street is Bangkok; the best in this study was Prague, but don't expect the Czechs to tell you you've dropped your pen.

None of the cultural variables the researchers measured were found to have a significant relationship with helping, but there was a relationship between greater purchasing power per capita and less helping behaviour. The researchers suggest this may be explained by more traditional value systems in countries that are less developed. However, this does not explain why Vienna was so high on the charts, or why Kuala Lumpur was bottom.

Another finding was that those countries high in simpatia were all above the mean in terms of helping behaviour. The researchers suggest that people living in these cultures are provided with a cultural script that tells them they should help. They note a possible confounding variable, however, in that the countries high in simpatia are also Roman Catholic. Whiting and Whiting (1975) also found that helping behaviour among children was more frequent in less industrialized countries.

The question remains then as to whether collectivism is a cause of increased prosocial behaviour or not. While it appears that individualistic cultures help slightly less often, the picture is more complicated than that. We are more likely to help members of ingroups than outgroups, and it seems that collectivist cultures have more clearly defined borders than individualistic cultures. Thus, there will be an interaction between the culture of the actor and his or her perception of the other's group membership. People within collectivist cultures may therefore be less likely to help a complete stranger, but more likely to help someone from their own cultural group who is not part of their immediate family. People in individualistic cultures, who prize independence, are likely to limit their kindness to members of their immediate family. This could be transmitted through child-rearing practices that reward or expect certain behaviours, such as sharing household chores (Whiting and Whiting, 1975).

However, it is important to remember that individualism and collectivism are on a dimension that *describes* cultures, rather than being dichotomous concepts; it is not clear that they *cause* differences in helping. It may be that other values which tend to thrive in these environments are responsible for differences in prosocial behaviour. It may even be because of the presence of such behaviour that the culture can be described as collectivistic or individualistic.

Other factors might be:

- the frequency with which we meet the people we might help, as evidenced by the tendency for cities with higher populations to be less helpful
- the encouragement or necessity to compete for resources, as described in Turnbull's controversial account of life with the extreme individualist Ik people of Uganda (1972)
- the norms of society that guide behaviour, such as whether it is appropriate to seek help from others or not.

Bystander intervention

One of the richest veins of social psychology literature relates to bystander intervention. It has long intrigued researchers as to how, why and under what circumstances a person who is not immediately involved in a situation either acts to intervene or decides not to. **Bystanderism** is the phenomenon of a person or people not intervening despite awareness of another person's need, the phenomenon of remaining a bystander. This covers a wide range of situations: for example, when a person is aware that their neighbour is physically abusive towards his family but ignores it, when students ignore the plight of a bullied child at school, when a silent majority take no action against a powerful minority engaging in war crimes, even to the extent of ignoring the escalation of such activity towards genocide.

Pioneers in this field of research were Bibb Latané and John Darley, who were inspired by the now well-known story of the murder of Kitty Genovese in New York in 1964. Kitty was repeatedly stabbed, and 38 people testified to having heard her screams, yet none of them intervened. The researchers' work led them to construct a cognitive model to explain the decision an individual makes to act or not. One of the key conclusions they drew was that the number of bystanders present has an enormous influence on the likelihood that one of them will help: the likelihood goes down as the number of bystanders increases. According to their 1970 model, people must first notice something is happening, then consider that someone is in need of help, then assume responsibility and also have some idea about what can be done to help. This means that the decision to help is not as simple as we might have thought: there are a set of cognitive antecedents to action, and it is perhaps a wonder that anyone ever intervenes.

 Many factors influence whether a bystander intervenes when a person is in need.

EMPIRICAL RESEARCH

Diffusion of responsibility, social influence and audience inhibition (Darley and Latané, 1968)

These researchers deceived university students into thinking they were actually participating in research about personal problems experienced by students. In all, there were 72 participants in the study; each in turn was led to one of many small rooms in a corridor and given instructions on the use of the microphone and headphones awaiting them.

They were told that others were participating at the same time, each kept anonymous in a separate room, with the researcher not listening. Each person, they were told, would disclose problems in turn and then take turns to comment on what had already been said. In fact, of course, the voices the participant would hear were recordings, and there were no other people present.

The first voice they heard was a male who described his troubles and mentioned that he experienced seizures sometimes, particularly when stressed. Other voices disclosed various problems intended to be irrelevant, with the real participant speaking last, to no real audience apart from the experimenter. Immediately afterwards, the first voice returned to comment and, of course, began to experience a seizure. He asked for help as the seizure came on, and eventually choked and became silent.

The researchers were measuring the amount of time taken from the beginning of the victim's plea for help to the participant standing up and leaving the room to notify the experimenter. The independent variable manipulated was the number of people the participant believed were also participating at the same time, and this was found to be extremely important. When participants thought they were alone with the victim, 85% acted within two minutes, compared with 31% of those who thought there were four other participants. After six minutes, 100% of the participants who believed they were the only one who could hear the problem reported the incident to the experimenter, whereas only 62% of those who thought there were four others did so.

The Darley and Latané (1968) study gives us one of the most important factors affecting bystanderism: **diffusion of responsibility**. When you are the only person who can deal with an emergency situation, you have 100% of the responsibility to do so (whether you actually choose to intervene or not). However, with more witnesses, each individual's share of the responsibility drops. It may be that in an ambiguous situation, we look to the actions of others for guidance (**social influence**); thus, inaction breeds inaction – if we see others not doing anything, we may not feel that it is necessary to do something. On the other hand, we may be afraid of appearing to overreact – sometimes known as a fear of social blunders or **audience inhibition**. In terms of Latané and Darley's model, this forms part of a person's judgement about whether intervention is necessary or appropriate. Imagine the embarrassment of offering to help someone who doesn't need help.

A study by Latané and Rodin (1969) asked male participants (in pairs, by themselves, or with a stooge who would not intervene) to fill in a questionnaire. The young woman who gave them the questionnaire went to an adjacent room, at which point a tape recording was started, beginning with a loud crash, the sound of a body hitting the floor and then painful moans. When alone, the participants went to help 70% of the time, compared with 40% when two naïve participants were together, and only 7% when there was a passive stooge.

A further study by Latané and Darley (1970) again had participants filling out a questionnaire in a room alone, with two other participants, or with two passive stooges. While they were there, smoke began to come into the room through a wall vent, continuing for six minutes, by which time the room would be filled with smoke. Of those who were alone, 75% left the room to report the smoke to the experimenter. Small groups of participants reported the smoke only 38% of the time, and the dampening influence of two passive stooges reduced the rate of reporting to just 10%.

Clearly there is a very powerful influence from others on our decision to help, although it is still not clear exactly which aspect is most important: diffusion of responsibility, audience inhibition or social influence.

Further research by Latané and Darley (1976) attempted to tease these factors apart by varying the conditions under which participants saw an experimenter experience a powerful electric shock through a closed-circuit television system. They concluded that simple diffusion of responsibility was important by itself, and that being able to communicate with others made help even less likely.

Arousal, costs and rewards

Piliavin et al. (1981) presented the arousal: cost–reward model to cover more factors involved in the decision to act or not.

Arousal

These researchers suggest that initially, when we observe another person in some sort of need or danger, we experience an orienting physiological response, one that actually slows down our heart rate, for example. This may then be followed by the fight-or-flight response, particularly when the situation is perceived as an emergency, so we are motivated to act in some way in order to return to a normal state. The greater the arousal is, the more likely it is that people will help.

The researchers' conclusion is supported by many studies, including Amato (1986). Amato interviewed participants after a bushfire near Melbourne and found that higher donations to help victims came from people who reported more feelings of shock or terror. This suggests that increased emotional arousal is followed by motivation to act to reduce that arousal.

Audience inhibition is the phenomenon of people not acting because they are inhibited by the knowledge that others are watching them.

Social influence in this respect refers to the influence of others on our ideas about what the most appropriate behaviour is in a particular situation.

Is it possible to conduct research that genuinely tests whether we will help others in need?

Experimental evidence is provided by Sterling and Gaertner (1983), who asked participants to do exercise to raise their heart rates. Although arousal increases the likelihood of a person acting, if the emergency they were then exposed to was ambiguous, they were less likely to help. This suggests that arousal is a kind of cue for us to act, but if we are not sure why we are aroused, we cannot be sure that acting will reduce the arousal. Thus both **arousal** and **ambiguity** are important factors affecting bystanderism.

Cost–reward

The second part of the arousal: cost–reward model is an evaluation of the consequences of intervening or not. Rewards are not easily identified, but their presence does increase the incentive to help. Costs will vary from situation to situation, but they might include danger, time and effort. There can also be costs to *not* intervening, such as a feeling of guilt or potential criticism by others, or even self-blame. These costs tend to increase with the perceived plight of the victim and when the expected costs of *not* intervening outweigh the expected costs of intervening, we are more likely to act. For example, we might not approach an adult who looks lost in a crowd and offer help, but we are more likely to help if we see a small child looking lost. The time and effort expended to help the child are smaller costs for many people than the guilt (or the negative judgement of accompanying friends) of not helping, so the child is more likely to receive an offer of help.

There are costs and rewards for intervening *and* not intervening.

Similarity, victim attributes and responsibility

One of the factors that seem to increase physiological arousal and feelings of empathy is **similarity**. Piliavin et al. (1981) are supported by a large body of literature which shows that people are more likely to act to help someone similar to them. The literature tends to focus on similarity in terms of race, nationality, age and gender.

One of the most famous studies into bystanderism is detailed in the empirical research box below. Dissatisfied with the tendency for research in this area to be conducted in contrived laboratory settings, the researchers carried out a field experiment to test the effect of race and the type of victim on helping behaviour on a subway train in New York.

EMPIRICAL RESEARCH

Subway emergencies (Piliavin et al., 1969)

The researchers staged emergencies on a subway train in New York, always between the same two stations. They estimate that 4450 people were included in their study, an average of 43 people in the carriage where the emergency took place, with an average of 8.5 people near the victim. They established four teams of experimenters, each team consisting of two female observers, a male victim and a male 'model' who would eventually help the victim if nobody else did. Each victim assumed two different roles, one as a drunken man smelling of alcohol and carrying a brown paper bag with a bottle in it, and the other as a man with a black cane. One of the male victims was black, and the other three were white. A further two independent variables were the proximity of the model to the victim and the amount of time he waited before intervening. At a specific time in the journey, the victim collapsed to the floor and lay without moving until people arrived to help. The model was given two specific set times to wait before helping, with the intention that the observers could record the effect of the model on the behaviour of others on the train.

The results showed that people were more helpful than the experimenters expected. The victim with the cane role received spontaneous help 62 out of 65 times, and even the drunken victim role elicited spontaneous help 19 out of 38 times. The helpers were 90% male and 64% white. The percentage of male helpers perhaps reflects the values of the time – female passengers commented, for example, that it was for a man to help in this situation. The percentage of white helpers is approximately the same as the distribution on the train, but it was noted that it was

continued

slightly more common for a white victim to be helped by a white person. The effects were more dramatic for the drunken victims. The researchers put this down to more empathy, sympathy and trust towards members of one's own racial group.

The four main conclusions from the study were as follows.

- Victims who appear sick are more likely to receive help than those who appear drunk. This is explained in terms of the higher costs of helping and lower costs of not helping a man seen as responsible for his own situation.

- In a mixed group, a male victim is more likely to be helped by men than women. The costs of helping are higher for women in terms of effort to move the victim, and there are low social costs to not helping as it was perceived at the time as not appropriate for a woman to be the first helper.

- In a mixed group, a victim is most likely to be helped by a same-race observer because of the low costs of not helping members of different race and, possibly, fear as a cost of helping.

- Diffusion of responsibility was not observed on trials with the cane, presumably because it was clearly identifiable as an emergency situation in which the victim needed help. There was, therefore, high risk of self-blame or guilt for not helping, and low cost – particularly in terms of the fear of social blunders mentioned above.

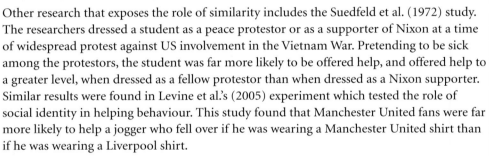

Levine et al. chose these two teams because of geographic proximity and a long rivalry between them. He proposed that social identity theory (page 110) could explain the results.

Other research that exposes the role of similarity includes the Suedfeld et al. (1972) study. The researchers dressed a student as a peace protestor or as a supporter of Nixon at a time of widespread protest against US involvement in the Vietnam War. Pretending to be sick among the protestors, the student was far more likely to be offered help, and offered help to a greater level, when dressed as a fellow protestor than when dressed as a Nixon supporter. Similar results were found in Levine et al.'s (2005) experiment which tested the role of social identity in helping behaviour. This study found that Manchester United fans were far more likely to help a jogger who fell over if he was wearing a Manchester United shirt than if he was wearing a Liverpool shirt.

An exception to the similarity rule can be observed in gender interactions. In general, men are more likely to help than women in the kind of situations that tend to be used in experiments. Women, on the other hand, are more likely to receive help. A curious study by Przybyla (1985) showed erotic and non-erotic films to male and female participants and then gave them an opportunity to help a male or female confederate who had knocked over some papers. The rate of helping was by far the highest among males who had seen an erotic film and had the opportunity to help a female confederate. This was possibly due to a misattribution of physiological arousal.

Mood

Another factor picked up by research into bystanderism is **mood**. Being in a good mood seems to encourage attraction towards strangers and more attention to positive features. Thus, the identification of possible costs to intervening is less likely to focus on risk when there is ambiguity. Being in a bad mood is a less powerful influence, perhaps only taking effect if it is the kind of mood that increases self-focus. This was noted by Berkowitz (1987), who found that effort on behalf of others was reduced when participants had higher self-awareness.

Competence and experience

A key component after recognizing that someone is in need of help, is knowing what can be done to help. Believing you have the competence to deliver the necessary help is a vital predictor of helping behaviour.

● **Examiner's hint**

The learning outcome for this section asks you to *examine* the factors that affect bystanderism. This means you need to be prepared to describe the factors, support them with research, and provide a balanced account. This will require a criticism of the methodology used in some of the studies and an identification of key strengths in the literature.

262

Although many researchers have looked for and found some differences in the personality of those who help and those who do not, Huston et al. (1981) interviewed 32 people who had intervened in criminal acts (including bank robberies and muggings) and compared their responses with those of people who had not intervened. They found that the major differences were physical: those who intervened were taller and heavier. They were more likely to have some kind of police or medical training. They also carried more self-belief and described themselves as aggressive and principled.

Pantin and Carver (1982) showed a first aid training video to female students and found that this increased their willingness to help a choking victim. It appears that knowing what to do in an emergency situation is not only helpful, it also increases one's sense of responsibility to act, perhaps by increasing the expected guilt of not helping.

To access Revision notes 8.1 on bystander intervention, please visit www.pearsonbacconline.com and follow the on-screen instructions.

EXERCISES

4   Construct a table and use it to record strengths and limitations of the major studies mentioned in this section. Consider in particular the ideas of ecological validity and mundane reality (revisit Chapter 2 for help with these). When you have finished, write a brief summary about the quality of research in this area of social psychology.

5   Review the material on social responsibility. Construct your own table as outlined below and complete it with brief notes. (You will add to this table as you work through this chapter.)

FACTORS AFFECTING HUMAN RELATIONSHIPS

	Biological	Cognitive	Sociocultural
Social responsibility			
Interpersonal relationships			
Violence			

● **Examiner's hint**
A general learning outcome for this option is to be able to discuss *to what extent* these factors influence human relationships in terms of the three areas on the left of your table. You should find there are several factors that can go in each cell of the table, and you should begin considering the relative importance of biological, cognitive and socio-cultural factors so that you can answer practice question 1 at the end of this chapter.

 ## Interpersonal relations

Learning outcomes

- Examine biological, psychological and social origins of attraction.
- Discuss the role of communication in maintaining relationships.
- Explain the role that culture plays in the formation and maintenance of relationships.
- Analyse why relationships may change or end.

The origins of attraction

The study of attraction can be enlightening, refreshing and frightening all at the same time, as we discover that, for example, biological factors we are not consciously aware of are very important in determining whether we are attracted to someone or not. On the other hand, one of the most reassuring factors involved in attraction is how much we already like a person. Researchers studying attraction have found, for example, that ratings of attractiveness are higher for photographs of people about whom participants have read a favourable story (Gross and Crofton, 1977). There is a large amount of research showing

that there are a number of biological, social, and cognitive factors that affect how much we are attracted to a person in the first place, whether as a friend or potential romantic or sexual partner.

Biological origins of attraction

Attraction to the opposite sex

A number of biological theories exist to explain attraction and one of the most fundamental is an evolutionary approach. Buss (1994) identifies two aspects of sexual selection that encourage the transmission of an individual's genes to the next generation:

- male ritual behaviour, frequently competitive, that marks an individual out as more dominant than his rivals and gives him better access to females
- characteristics of an individual that increase his attractiveness to females.

What makes men and women attractive? ▶

For humans, this means that males have to some extent evolved in such a way as to be sufficiently attractive to women for reproduction to be a possibility. The key principle of male attractiveness is that characteristics which will confer benefits to the female or her offspring are favoured. According to Buss, the key component is control over economic resources within the particular context the male lives in. This is likely to require territory and tools. This is particularly important for a human female because of the length of time required to carry and raise a child.

In order to recognize such control over resources, it seems that women in the vast majority of countries researched by Buss rate the social status of a man as a more important factor in mate choice than males do, even when the women have significant resources themselves. Other characteristics rated highly in Buss's surveys in the USA include:

- age a few years greater than the female's
- ambition
- dependability
- intelligence
- height
- good health as signalled by energy and lack of disfigurement.

According to Buss, social status is only attractive for women as a sign of economic well-being.

Acts of love and commitment, and signs of willingness to channel his resources to her (through gift-giving, for example) also contribute to a woman's mate choice. Kindness and sincerity feature highly, as evidenced by what women write in personal columns when advertising for a partner. Thus, the key features of males that women find attractive are passed on to descendants and those who do not possess the key attractive characteristics are less likely to be able to reproduce.

Men, on the other hand, are attracted to youth and health as they are the most transparent predictors of reproductive ability. Again, research in a variety of cultures supports this idea: men express a preference for a female partner at least two years younger, with more extreme preferences expressed in Nigeria and several other African countries. In the USA, Buss (1994) reports that at first marriage men are roughly three years older than their partner, at second marriage five years older, and by the third marriage, eight years older. Universally valued physical characteristics identified across cultures include clear smooth skin, full lips, lustrous hair, and the absence of facial scarring or acne. Facial and bodily symmetry is also universally valued, perhaps because it is another indicator of good health. Body shape appears to be important, but only in terms of its relationship with social status – men in cultures where food is scarcer report more interest in plumper women. Singh (1994) found that men tend to be interested in fat distribution as a sign of future reproductive capability rather than body mass. Thus, a thinner woman and a plumper one could be rated as equally beautiful if they had the apparently most prized waist to hip ratio of 0.7.

The female waist to hip ratio of 0.7 seems to be valued by men in most cultures.

Same sex attraction

While evolutionary explanations for homosexuality were addressed in Chapter 2 (page 62), it is interesting to note that research indicates that homosexual men are similar to heterosexual men in their focus on youth and health indicators. Homosexual women are similar to heterosexual women in the type of characteristics they favour, but display even less interest in physical characteristics than heterosexual women (Deaux and Hanna, 1984). Unfortunately this is still an under-researched area and suffers from the same definitional problems we met in Chapter 2 (page 62). Treating homosexual and heterosexual as dichotomous categories may not be a helpful foundation for such research.

As discussed in Chapter 2 (page 62), evolutionary psychology theories are difficult to evaluate because they are impossible to prove and very difficult to disprove. Researchers are working on establishing the mechanisms of attraction in the brain and this will give some support to the evolutionary explanation. It appears that the feeling of attraction, whether this is conscious or not, occurs when the hypothalamus triggers physiological arousal. Various factors are involved including cognitive and social factors. This is evidenced by the curious observation that humans can become aroused by thought alone – but being attracted by thought alone is generally not possible.

One of the most interesting discoveries in recent times has been of the role pheromones play in human attraction. It had been believed for some time that humans do not use pheromones in the same way that animals do. Wedekind et al. (1995) asked men to wear a clean t-shirt for two nights and then asked women to rate the smell of the shirts for attractiveness. Both men and women were tested for a particular set of genes implicated in the development of the immune system. The women's decisions on the attractiveness of the t-shirt smells were then correlated with the results of gene tests. The researchers found a relationship such that the greater the difference between the genes of the men and women, the higher the rating of attractiveness. This fits neatly with evolutionary theory, in that the offspring produced by parents with different immune systems will have a survival advantage. The possibility that we are unconsciously detecting genetic differences between ourselves and others is a curious one that we can expect to understand better in future.

If pheromones that we cannot consciously detect influence our attraction to others, how can we trust our conscious perception of the world, particularly in terms of our thoughts about why we find a person attractive?

Social and cognitive origins of attraction

There are a set of factors that we may be slightly more aware of, though we generally do not realize their role in attraction. These are discussed in turn.

Proximity

People we spend more time with because they live near us, work with us or go to school with us are more likely to become our friends and partners. A simple study by Festinger et al. (1950) found that 65% of pairs of university friends were living in the same building as each other, with 44% living next door to each other. As the distance between the pair increased, the number of friendships dropped accordingly.

Darley and Berscheid (1967) found that women reported more liking for a woman that they expected to talk to intimately than for a woman they were not expecting to talk to. This suggests that it is not just proximity and exposure that increase our attraction to someone, but also the expectation of interaction.

Familiarity

This applies not just to people but to many things in our lives, including animals, places, clothing and sounds. Jorgensen and Cervone (1978) found that participants rated photographs of strangers' faces as more attractive the more times they saw them. Zajonc (1968) referred to this as the 'mere exposure effect', as if it is sufficient for us simply to see a person several times for us to start to find them attractive. Much of Zajonc's work was based around the repetition of unfamiliar sounds such as words in Turkish or Chinese presented to native English speakers.

This idea is supported by Moreland and Beach (1992). They experimentally tested the idea by having student participants rate the attractiveness of female research assistants, some of whom had come to their class more often than others – those who had been seen more often were rated as more attractive.

Mita et al. (1977) found that we rate our own face and the faces of others less likeable when we see the mirror image of them. This is an interesting finding for those of us who find either a photograph or a mirror image of ourselves dissatisfying to look at. It follows that more time spent in front of the mirror should lead to increased self-liking, but perhaps more extreme distaste when viewing oneself in photos! Curiously, it appears that over-exposure is possible, and we do become bored and even disgusted by seeing or hearing the same stimulus over time.

We find a mirror image of faces less attractive – consider this next time you look at a photograph of people you know.

Reciprocity

This is a slightly more complicated factor. It seems that we are attracted quite powerfully to those who like us or are attracted to us. A study by Dittes and Kelley (1956) provided anonymous feedback to participants in a group discussion about the attitudes of the other participants towards them. Participants tended to report more attraction to group members if they believed those members liked them.

It appears, therefore, that our attraction is based on the recognition of familiarity, frequency and predictability of contact, *and* on the processing of other information available. This shows how fickle our attraction can be and gives strong evidence that biological factors alone do not account for attraction.

Similarity

This is another factor we seem to be swayed by. Although people often find themselves attracted to people who are similar in terms of ethnicity, social class or age, there are a number of people who find partners quite different in these respects. However, it seems that

we experience a more powerful attraction to people who are similar to us in terms of beliefs and attitudes.

Aronson and Cope (1968) ran an experiment that tested the effect of apparent similarity of attitude between a participant and the supervisor of an experimenter. They found that when the experimenter was less polite and likeable and the supervisor was then harsh towards the experimenter, the participant was more likely to offer help when the supervisor needed it as well as when the experimenter was polite and the supervisor was kind. It is debatable whether this help offer indicates attraction, but it is intuitively appealing.

A variation on the theme of similarity is the **matching phenomenon** which suggests that a cognitive process moderates our level of attraction by favouring those who somehow match us, whether this be in terms of perceived attractiveness, age or interests, etc.

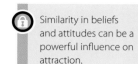
Similarity in beliefs and attitudes can be a powerful influence on attraction.

Social comparison

This occurs to moderate our ratings of attractiveness. A person will appear to be more attractive to us if we have been exposed to less attractive people beforehand. In the same way, an average-looking person will be perceived as less attractive if we have been exposed to more attractive stimuli. This was demonstrated in a study by Kenrick and Gutierres (1980). These researchers asked participants to rate the attractiveness of a woman after some of them had been watching *Charlie's Angels* (a television programme starring three attractive women). The average woman was rated as less attractive by those who had been watching the programme. Clearly this is a cognitive factor indicating that attraction cannot be understood in an isolated context: it is to some extent an individual experience.

Reward theory

A slightly different process is involved in the active pursuit of a relationship with a person we are attracted to, which is a kind of cost–benefit analysis. **Reward theory** can be detected frequently when you ask people why they are together. This is a question we often answer in terms of how others make us feel. We are often more inclined to spend time with people who make us feel good or offer some kind of social status or benefits. Both operant and classical conditioning seem to be involved here:

- operant conditioning in that if spending time with a person directly or indirectly offers us rewards, this is reinforcing and will increase the desired frequency of such interaction
- classical conditioning in that people we associate with positive emotions become a source of such emotions.
- Through higher order conditioning, we may find that a stranger reminds us of someone around whom we have already built positive emotions. This may perhaps explain why we often find ourselves attracted to people who are physically or emotionally similar to our parents.

Lewicki (1985) ran a study that asked participants to rate the friendliness of women in photographs. Participants who had previously spent time with a friendly experimenter who looked similar to one of the women in the photographs were more likely to choose this photograph. Participants in a similar study were exposed to a deliberately unfriendly experimenter and then asked to give their data from a fake experimental task to one of two females. They tended to avoid interacting with the woman who resembled the unfriendly experimenter.

The gain–loss hypothesis

This is a variation on reward theory. Aronson and Linder (1965) suggest that we are more likely to like someone if we initially dislike them but then change our minds. In their experiment, participants heard a confederate making either negative or positive comments about them to the experimenter. Participants' ratings of how much they liked the

To access Revision notes 8.2 on factors that influence attraction, please visit www.pearsonbacconline.com and follow the on-screen instructions.

Centrifugal means moving away from the centre; centripetal means moving towards the centre.

confederate were greatest when these evaluations moved from negative to positive. It might be an interesting exercise to consider how you felt about your closest friends when you first met them.

The role of communication in maintaining relationships

Another vein of psychological research focuses on how relationships are maintained after they are formed. This looks especially but not exclusively at romantic relationships. Some friendships last and others fade; some romantic relationships last a lifetime and others end quite quickly and dramatically. Communication is just one of many factors that have a significant role in keeping relationships together and tearing them apart.

Dindia and Canary (1993) defined four types of relationship maintenance:

- continuing a relationship or keeping it in existence
- keeping a relationship in a specified state, such as at a particular level of intimacy
- keeping a relationship in a satisfactory condition
- preventing or correcting relationship problems.

Canary and Dainton (2003) describe communication as a centripetal force that maintains relationships, suggesting that relationships are by nature destined to be pulled apart by centrifugal forces unless they are maintained. One of the simplest forms of communication for maintenance is routine conversation consisting of elements such as *How was your day?* and its rather mundane answer. The potential exchange of information in such conversation is likely to be small, especially over time, but any changes to this routine conversation are very noticeable. Canary and Dainton offer the example of responding to such a question with *Why do you ask?* This question is probably not part of a couple's script and would indicate some disturbance in the relationship.

Canary and Stafford (1994) identified five maintenance strategies that combat relationship decay:

- positivity – acting cheerfully, doing favours for your partner, trying to be spontaneous
- openness – talking about joint history, making disclosures about yourself
- assurances – offering comfort, affirming commitment to the relationship, asking if the partner is OK
- social networking – meeting friends or family for meals, asking mutual friends for relationship advice
- sharing tasks (completing joint responsibilities) – hanging the washing, cleaning the car, washing the dishes.

Weigel and Ballard–Reisch (1999) used this approach as the basis for an investigation into the relationship between the length of time a couple had been together and the amount of relational maintenance behaviour they engaged in. The researchers also considered satisfaction. Newer relationships tended to involve more explicit maintenance, but this appears to fade away as the relationship continues, returning in the later years of the relationship. Importantly, they also found that satisfaction was related to the use of maintenance behaviours.

John Gottman claims to be able to predict which marriages will end in divorce, partly through looking for a 'contempt' micro-expression in the partners' faces.

Gottman et al. (2003) famously claimed that positivity is a vitally important part of relationships, giving us the magic ratio of positivity to negativity in successful relationships of 5:1. They explain that this means that a negative statement or act in a relationship cannot be balanced with a single positive equivalent; at least five are needed. Research in this area can often be criticized because it relies so heavily on correlational research. We must ask whether successful relationships require such maintenance

behaviours in order to exist, or if the communication styles uncovered in research might stem from the quality of the relationship. This is a problem of bidirectional ambiguity as discussed in Chapter 1 (page 18).

A further problem is that when we rely heavily on self-report data, the research can be subject to bias. For example, when a person is satisfied with their relationship, they may be more likely to view interactions from their partner as positive, or to notice their attempts at openness or disclosure more than a person who is unhappy in their relationship and who focuses more on negative aspects. An interesting collection of findings indicates that women tend to engage in many of these maintenance behaviours more than men, especially in terms of sharing tasks and openness (Dindia and Canary, 2006). This raises the issue of whether research is adequately accounting for individual differences in maintenance strategy use across genders and cultures.

Weigel and Ballard–Reisch (1999) show that communication patterns differ across marital types. *Traditional* describes the type of marriage where the spouses view themselves as interdependent, and tend to communicate a lot but deny or avoid issues that might cause conflict. *Independent* types have more freedom and egalitarian roles and communicate with each other a lot to negotiate and renegotiate their relationship, and tend to confront issues rather than avoid them. *Separate* couples are less expressive in their communication than the other groups.

To learn more about John Gottman's work, go to www. pearsonhotlinks. com, enter the title or ISBN of this book and select weblink 8.1.

Self-report data is commonly gathered through questionnaires. Is it a good way to capture the truth?

EMPIRICAL RESEARCH

Marital type and maintenance behaviour (Weigel and Ballard–Reisch, 1999)

To test if there are differences in the type of maintenance behaviour used by different marital types, the researchers asked university students to distribute questionnaires to married couples they knew. The 141 heterosexual couples who returned the questionnaires were mostly Caucasian and their median length of marriage was 10 years. The questionnaire consisted of items from Canary and Stafford's (1992) Relational Maintenance Strategy Scale, which tests for positivity, openness, assurances, network use and sharing tasks, as well as scales to determine the type of marriage, their marital satisfaction and level of commitment.

Several differences were found. Traditional couples tended to use more maintenance behaviours than the other types, with separates using least. The cause of this difference is hypothesized to be related to their motivations for being in the relationship and their expectations regarding dependence. Of course, if two partners have little intention of being mutually dependent emotionally, it follows that they will not disclose as often or attempt to discuss issues that may cause conflict. Separates were also less likely to use openness and assurances than the other two types, while traditional couples were clearly different in their use of social networks and sharing tasks. Although previous research had found that traditional couples are most satisfied, this research failed to find any significant difference in satisfaction between the types, although several significant correlations were found within types between use of specific maintenance behaviours and satisfaction, commitment and love. For example, independents who engage in more assurance as a maintenance strategy report greater levels of love in their relationship, while the same strategy is associated more strongly with satisfaction for separates and traditionals.

EXERCISE

6   How easily could these research findings be applied? How useful are they?

To learn more about Tannen's work, go to www. pearsonhotlinks. com, enter the title or ISBN of this book and select weblink 8.2.

Deborah Tannen is a linguist and author of several books relating to communication in interpersonal relationships. She has studied communication differences between males and females in a general social context and in a work context. In *You Were Always Mom's Favorite* (2009) she focuses particularly on relationships between sisters. Her work has

John Gray, author of *Men are from Mars, Women are from Venus*, also argues that there are communication differences between men and women. For example, during a disagreement, a man tends to try to win rather than to understand his partner, while she tends to exaggerate events to demonstrate her emotion (e.g. Why are you *always* late?).

highlighted ways that men and women communicate within single sex groups and how the differences between them cause misunderstanding and conflict. Examples from her research include the tendency for women to say *Sorry* as a way to express empathy, while men use it and hear it as an apology. Both variants serve the purpose of maintaining same-sex relationships. Men who express a negative state of mood or feeling can be frustrated when a woman responds with her own experience of a similar feeling rather than acknowledging the importance of the man's. Men typically interrupt each other and expect to be interrupted in a rather competitive conversational style, while women tend to take turns more fairly. Thus there is a difficulty for women who might want to speak in a group of men but are unwilling to interrupt.

Although communication clearly has a role in maintaining relationships, it is important to note that it is only one of many strategic or routine devices we employ to keep ourselves together. The change and end of relationships is discussed on pages 272–274.

The role of culture in the formation and maintenance of relationships

A great deal of research has focused on relationships within individualistic societies such as are dominant in the Anglo-American world and western Europe. However, the growth of communities of ethnic minorities with different cultural values and the study of more collectivist cultures have allowed us to more clearly understand the various roles that culture plays in both the formation and maintenance of relationships.

Arranged marriages are common in some parts of the world.

One of the most important cultural differences is between those societies where young adults typically make their own choice about who their partner will be and societies where

marriages are arranged by the family. Although someone coming from a culture following the first of these norms might find it hard to believe, a large percentage of arranged marriages appear to be successful despite the absence of choice for the partners. Making such a choice for a relative can be an elaborate process and families often take great pride in attempting to find a good match. Perhaps it is no surprise that bypassing many of the distracting influences of passionate infatuation can have more successful long-term results.

There are certain universals to attraction in terms of mate preference (pages 204–205) but there are also cultural differences. In some countries, chastity and homemaking skills are more valued in women than other characteristics, particularly in more traditional societies with more clearly defined gender roles (Buss 1990). In these societies, what makes a good wife for a man is more easily determined by a man's family than it might be in more individualistic Western societies where high value is placed on romance and passion. Although there is evidence that this has little impact on marital satisfaction (Yelsma and Athappilly, 1988), it may be problematic that so much research in this area relies on questionnaire methods.

Cognitive dissonance could well affect the answers of respondents from both groups, with people unable to write that they are disatisfied. However, there may also be social norms affecting how appropriate it is to express dissatisfaction with a marriage. There are also different understandings across cultures about what is a good or a bad marriage. Affection, for example, may not be a big part of relationships for some cultures. Indo-Pakistani marriages tend to be satisfying when there is a strong religious component to the relationship, when there is financial security, and when there is relatively high status and parental acceptance by families with good reputations (Ahmad and Reid, 2008).

There is also significant evidence that expectations are changing in many traditional societies and more intimacy and romance is expected than previously, which can lead to difficulties.

Cognitive dissonance is also discussed on page 250. It is an uncomfortable feeling caused by holding two contradictory beliefs or ideas at the same time and a person is motivated to resolve this by changing one of them. Perhaps it is difficult for a person who is committed to a marriage to admit to being dissatisfied.

EMPIRICAL RESEARCH

Communication in South Asian Canadian relationships (Ahmad and Reid, 2008)

The researchers in this study attempted to investigate whether special communication styles were required to maintain arranged marriages. They focused specifically on listening styles in the relationship and constructed a survey to be completed without participants sharing their answers with their spouse. A snowball sample was obtained by asking the participants to give surveys to others they knew.

In particular, the researchers expected that their survey would show a strong relationship between marriage satisfaction and marriage type where levels of traditionalism are low and self-ratings of levels of listening to understand (as opposed to listening to respond) are high.

The researchers measured marital satisfaction using the Revised Relationship Adjustment Survey; this includes items such as 'My partner understands and sympathizes with me' as well as extra items relevant to the sample such as 'Our marriage has provided me with the financial and/or social security I want'. The degree of traditionalism in the marriage was measured on the Traditional Orientation to Marital Relationship Scale specifically constructed for this study. Listening styles were measured with the Listening Styles in Committed Relationship Scale, which includes items such as 'When my partner is explaining him/herself, I try to get a sense of what things must be like for him/her, so that I may better understand how he/she must be feeling' (listening to understand), and 'I don't find it necessary to pay close attention when my partner is talking, because I already know what my partner is going to say before he/she even says it'.

The researchers found significant correlations between scores on the scales as expected: there was less satisfaction among the more traditional relationships, and this was accompanied by a tendency to listen to respond rather than to understand. It is suggested that expectations of equality in the relationship increase effort to listen, which in turn increase satisfaction.

EXERCISE

7 This is a correlational study using self-report data from a survey. What kind of problems might this cause researchers when they interpret the results? What does the study show us about the role of culture in the formation and maintenance of relationships?

Canary and Dainton (2003) offer another example of how culture affects the maintenance of relationships. They show how Koreans tend to use less direct and explicit maintenance behaviours; for example, trying to appease their partners not by asking what they want but by anticipating – so they might, for instance, pour a second cup of coffee for a partner without asking. This links to the researchers' finding that Confucian concepts form the basis of Korean intimate relationships. So, for example, as long as a Korean person believes that their partner is engaging in eu-ri, a long-term obligatory association, they will remain in the relationship.

Why relationships change and end
Describing change in relationships

Knapp and Vangelisti (1996) proposed a model that describes the change of relationships through ten stages, the first five occurring in the growth of the relationship, and the last five occurring in the relationship's decline (Table 8.1).

TABLE 8.1 KNAPP AND VANGELISTI MODEL FOR CHANGE IN RELATIONSHIPS

Stage	Typical events and behaviour
Coming together – growth of the relationship	
initiation	• first meeting and brief interaction • first impressions are formed
experimenting	• small talk, testing the other person and searching for common ground
intensifying	• relationship becomes friendship • personal disclosures become common, especially regarding feelings about the relationship
integrating	• the two lives become more connected and partners consider each other in making plans • those outside the relationship become more aware of the couple • use of 'we' becomes more frequent.
bonding	• some form of commitment is made, often ritualized, like engagement, marriage, cohabitation or friendship rituals
Coming apart – decline of the relationship	
differentiating	• differences become more obvious and partners desire independence • some arguments over this may begin • more use of 'I' and 'my'
circumscribing	• partners avoid difficult topics in conversation as communication is restricted but public appearances are maintained
stagnating	• further restrictions in conversation; partners 'know' what the other will say and prefer not to start talking • may stay together in order to avoid greater pain of breaking up
avoiding	• one or both partners choose to avoid contact, through lateness or alternate commitments or direct expressions of disinterest
terminating	• physical distancing and dissociation as partners prepare to be individuals

Knapp and Vangelisti *describe* but do not *explain* changes in relationships.

There is a heavy emphasis on communication between the partners in this model, beginning with actively seeking out ways to communicate more with each other and closing with actively trying to find ways to avoid communicating until ready to separate. Although the model applies particularly well to romantic relationships, it can also apply to friendships and family relationships. It is not uncommon to notice avoiding behaviours in room-mates, siblings and parents as they prepare to move away for reasons other than dissatisfaction with the relationship (e.g. when a child first moves out of home). Researchers are presently particularly interested in how well this model applies given that technology such as social networking sites have made it easier for people to communicate despite distance.

The model does not offer analysis of *why* partners move from one stage to another but has become well known for its accuracy in describing *how* change tends to occur.

Psychologist Steve Duck has produced a large amount of research on relationships. One of his most important ideas is that we filter our relationships, based on sociological factors such as the locations where we allow ourselves to meet others, pre-interaction cues such as

information received about people before we meet them and stereotypes or prejudice, then interaction cues and cognitive cues based on what the other person says and the cognitive judgements we make about them (Duck, 1985).

Breakdown of relationships

Another vein of Duck's research has focused on the *reasons* for the breakdown of relationships. Reasons cited include predisposing personal factors and precipitating factors. Predisposing personal factors include personal habits and cultural differences, which can present background instability and resentment. However, in many relationships such tension can be tolerated or resolved. External precipitating factors are more often the immediate causes of breakdown. These include difficult work situations (e.g. one partner works in the morning and the other in the evening, one partner needs to travel for work) and infidelity (Duck, 1982).

Levinger (1980) suggests that the relationship will end if there appears to be no solution to a problem except a new life, if alternative partners are available, if there is an expectation that the relationship will fail, or if there is a lack of commitment to the relationship. Byrne and Clore (1970) suggest that learning theories can explain maintenance and break-up, particularly in terms of a classically conditioned association with difficult times and a lack of reinforcement for continued partnership.

Canary and Dainton (2003) suggest that relationships have a natural tendency to end. This means that we can begin to look at problems in relationships as catalysts for change rather than causes for change.

 A catalyst initiates or accelerates a process but doesn't necessarily cause it. Canary and Dainton suggest that problems don't cause a change but make it come faster.

Some sociological theories about the end of relationships focus on exchange and equity. When the relative rewards partners offer each other are perceived to be unbalanced, when costs begin to outweigh benefits, when alternative relationships are available and appear to offer better or more balanced rewards, and when there are few barriers to leaving the relationship, we are motivated to end it.

Two early theorists working in this framework were George Homans and Peter Blau. Their work has been very influential but it is clear that when applied to human relationships, it has significant flaws. Rational choice is a key part of relationships, but there is a range of situations that cannot always be accounted for in terms of rational choice, exchange and equity. Examples of such situations include the mother–son relationship, and the struggle faced by a woman to leave her abusive partner.

 People do not always move in to or out of relationships in apparently rational ways.

Thus it is necessary to look beyond an individual's cognitions and rationality to various factors that lead to the kind of dissatisfaction that leads to conflict and break-up. Duck (1988) suggested that differences in background and culture, and previous experience of relationship instability all contribute. It is not hard to imagine how differences in expectations and communication styles could lead to conflict.

EMPIRICAL RESEARCH

The dissolution of gay and lesbian relationships (Kurdek, 1991)

The break-up of heterosexual relationships has been difficult for researchers to study, and the relative infrequency of homosexual partnerships has made them even harder to study.

Kurdek was able to ask 13 couples (who were involved in a longitudinal study of gay and lesbian relationships, and who had broken up during the course of the study) to complete a survey that asked about the causes of their break-up.

continued

The answers given to open-ended questions were grouped into the following categories, presented in order of frequency:

- non-responsiveness (communication problems such as lack of assurance)
- partner problems (e.g. drug/alcohol abuse)
- sexual issues (e.g. partner had an affair)
- fusion (e.g. becoming too close and ignoring own needs)
- incompatibility (e.g. growing in opposite direction)
- control (e.g. one partner insisting things were done their way).

The participants were also asked to rate 11 common reasons for the break-up of heterosexual relationships on a scale from 1 to 5, where a high score indicated agreement that this was a factor in their break-up. Only three items achieved mean ratings above 3: frequent absence, sexual incompatibility and mental cruelty.

Kurdek was struck by the similarity of these results to research already completed on people who had been through the break-up of a heterosexual partnership. In particular, a breakdown in communication seems to play a major role in the dissolution of relationships.

● **Examiner's hint**
Consider what the implications are of the conclusion that the reasons for break-up are similar in heterosexual and homosexual couples.

EXERCISE

8   What strengths and limitations are there to this study?

8.4   Violence

● Examiner's hint
The command term *discuss* in relation to the effects of violence means you need to provide descriptions of both short-term and long-term effects and to address problems of research in this area, particularly focusing on methodological issues highlighted in the text. You should be sure to include reference to the studies in the empirical research boxes and remember to be critical about them too.

Learning outcomes
- Evaluate sociocultural explanations of the origins of violence.
- Discuss the effects of short-term and long-term exposure to violence.
- Discuss the relative effectiveness of two strategies for reducing violence.

Although there are many and varied explanations of the origins of violence, here we focus only on sociocultural explanations. Social learning theory appears to have a great deal of explanatory power across a number of situations.

Social learning theory explanations of violence

Bandura's experiments in the 1960s (page 122) gave clear evidence that children are more likely to engage in violent behaviour if they have previously been exposed to a violent model. A number of factors have been offered to explain how this might happen beyond the basic idea that children can learn through vicarious reinforcement. In particular, it seems that exposure to violence (whether via models that are similar or authoritative to the viewer, or observed via media like movies, television and video games) can lead to disinhibition and desensitization.

A longitudinal study of boys growing up in New York correlated a preference for violent television at age 8 with how aggressive their peers rated them at age 18, and later with the likeliness of them having committed a violent crime (Huesmann et al., 1984). This might be explained in terms of exposure to violent models over time causing the boys to lose the negative emotional reaction we initially have towards seeing violent acts (desensitization) and losing the urge to control aggressive impulses.

There are two key problems with this approach to explaining the origins of violence. One is that research to support the theory is very limited in what it can achieve. Ethical reasons clearly prevent researchers from experimentally inducing genuine violence in a realistic situation, leading to criticisms over the ecological validity of work such as Bandura's. The second key problem is that the approach cannot be taken to mean that all violence originates from observation or we would have a paradox – violence must occur in the first place to be observed. There are also a number of biological and cognitive factors involved in violence, including physiological arousal and the influence of hormones such as testosterone. In addition, there are other social and cultural conditions that might give rise to violence.

However, the theory does have significant strengths, mostly in terms of its usefulness in application. A large body of non-experimental research suggests that violence is affected by exposure to violent media; for example, the natural experiment tracking changes after the introduction of television in a small Canadian community (Williams, 1986), and the meta-analysis of studies conducted by Wood et al. (1991).

Other sociocultural explanations of violence make use of intergroup conflict theory (Sherif, 1966) and social identity theory (Chapter 2, page 110), suggesting that group membership plays a key role in developing the desire to act violently towards members of another group. However, these explanations are not as successful at clarifying why individuals actually perform violent acts or why an individual might act violently towards his or her own children or partner.

Social interaction explanation of violence

An alternative approach is offered by Tedeschi and Felson (1994) who suggest that interpersonal violence should be considered as a form of social interaction. This requires that it be seen in terms of a means to achieve a certain social or material outcome. This could be the respect of peers, it could be possession of a valuable item, it could be the reduction of frustration, an opportunity to have sex, or a sense of pride or vindication. This approach is particularly attractive when understood in conjunction with social identity theory, because it provides motives for both violence as a sign of group membership and violence as a way to compensate for loss of self-esteem.

It is also possible to consider reasons why violence is seen as an appropriate course of action to achieve these goals, and various factors associated with increased violence hint at a powerful role for culture and socialization, maintained through social norms (page 119). For example, a study by Fite et al. (2008) found that children of parents with a high level of conflict in their relationship are more likely to consider aggression as the appropriate course of action in a number of social situations.

Culture of honour

Moving to the wider culture, Cohen et al. (1996) describe the idea of a **culture of honour**, in which even small perceived insults *must* be met with violent retribution. They specifically argue that in the south of the USA, a past of lawlessness and instability has resulted in extreme self-reliance, which is reflected in loose gun-control laws today. Their previous research supports this idea in that they found a tendency for white males in this area to endorse statements of violence if the violence was used in the name of protection.

 To access Worksheet 8.1 on biological and cognitive factors in violence, please visit www.pearsonbacconline.com and follow the on-screen instructions.

 How can we best study the causes of violence? Should we focus more on psychology or biology?

Some consider violence to be simply a social interaction, like gift-giving or greeting.

 In a culture of honour, violence is accepted and expected in some circumstances.

 Gun ownership laws vary around the world: in many countries it is considered a right for a person to possess a gun to use to protect themselves or their property. In other places, this would be seen as inappropriate.

EMPIRICAL RESEARCH

The culture of honour (Cohen et al., 1996)

To test whether there was a difference in readiness to commit acts of violence between individuals from the north or south of the USA, these researchers set up an experimental situation for 83 university students, 42 northerners and 41 southerners.

The students were asked to fill out a questionnaire which they had to take to a table at the end of a long, narrow hallway. A confederate working at a filing cabinet part-way down the hallway had to push in the drawer of the filing cabinet as the participant walked past. When forced to do it again on the way back, the confederate did so with greater force, bumped into the participant, and called him an 'asshole'. A control condition ran without the bump or insult. Two observers in the corridor rated the participant's emotional reactions, particularly looking for anger and amusement. After the corridor incident, participants had to guess the emotions on pictures of faces and then do a story-completion exercise, containing scenarios such as the following.

> It had only been about 20 minutes since they had arrived at the party when Jill pulled Steve aside, obviously bothered about something.
>
> 'What's wrong?' asked Steve.
>
> 'It's Larry. I mean, he knows that you and I are engaged, but he's already made two passes at me tonight.'
>
> Jill walked back into the crowd, and Steve decided to keep his eye on Larry. Sure enough, within five minutes Larry was reaching over and trying to kiss Jill.

The researchers describe their debriefing as thorough, with a short questionnaire at the end revealing that the experimental group were more positive about the experiment than the control group.

Northerners were rated as more amused when they were bumped, but there was no significant difference in the tendency to project negative emotions onto the faces, although northerners were more likely to see happiness on the faces. However, insulted southerners were much more likely to end the above scenario in violence than northerners or southerners in the control group: 75% ended the scenario with injury or threat of injury to Larry. The researchers take this as evidence that northerners see the situation as a cause for amusement, while southerners see it as a spark to violence.

A second experiment used approximately the same procedure, but levels of cortisol and testosterone in participants' saliva were measured before and after the insult. Insulted southerners' cortisol levels rose far more than in any of the other conditions. In an addition to the experiment, the insulted southerners were willing to take a higher level of electric shock if others were watching. A third alteration had participants walking down the hallway again and being bumped and insulted. The effect of this was tested as another confederate walked down the hallway in a kind of 'chicken' game: the confederate would not stop walking forward, and the dependent variable was thus how close the confederate could get to the participant before the participant moved out of the way. Those from the south were far more affected by the insult: non-insulted participants stepped aside an average of 2.7m from the confederate, whereas those who were insulted averaged just 0.94m and perceived themselves as appearing less masculine to a witness.

The researchers suggest there are two reasons for these results. Southerners may have been more surprised by this rudeness than northerners, and have different scripts for dealing with being insulted. In a culture of honour, seemingly small insults become a matter of great importance as they are a threat to masculinity and must be addressed. When two members of such a culture engage each other, this leads to an escalation that can finish in homicide.

Story completion tasks allow participants to project their own values and personality onto the characters in the story.

To learn more about culture of honour research and some additional evolutionary perspectives on violence, go to www.pearsonhotlinks.com, enter the title or ISBN of this book and select weblink 8.3.
To learn more about crimes of honour involving violence against women, go to www.pearsonhotlinks.com, enter the title or ISBN of this book and select weblink 8.4.

9 This study contains several significant strengths compared to much of the research on violence. Provide a brief evaluation of the study, listing three strengths and three limitations. Do you think the conclusions are warranted?

Again, although the culture of honour is an important addition to our understanding of how violence may be encouraged, it is important not to ignore the role of other factors. Cognitions, particularly in terms of schemas and scripts for insult and retribution, clearly play an important role as not every member of a culture of honour engages in violent behaviour when threatened. Similarly, at a biological level of analysis, we might be able to see how such scripts for violence have evolved over time in particular environments. There are strong evolutionary arguments for intra-familial violence.

Feminist theory

A final perspective on violence must be considered because of its relevance to domestic violence. Feminist theory has been employed to explain the motivation of males to physically attack females. According to many theorists, the fact that it is so common for males to use physical violence in their homes is a symptom of male dominance in society. In order to assert their dominance and prevent any threat to their control over power and economic resources in the home, men resort to physical violence. In several countries in the world and in specific communities, there is something like a culture of honour among males, a script that instructs males to respond to threats to their power in this way and accepts or even rewards it when they do. Various cultural factors such as the need to 'save face' or 'keep the family together' tend to prevent anyone uncovering the abuse (Koverola and Murtaugh, 2006) and therefore support its continuation.

Earlier we considered the argument that altruism does not exist: that people do not perform prosocial behaviour without gaining some kind of personal profit. Compare this now with violence. Use the same logic to consider whether violence without motive occurs and how this affects your understanding about people.

The effects of exposure to violence

There is a wide range of forms of violence (e.g. persistent school bullying, violence among sports fans) and although many of the core effects of exposure are extremely similar, here we focus on exposure to domestic violence.

Domestic violence was increasingly the focus of research towards the second half of the 20th century because those working with victims and witnesses of this type of violence began to recognize its terrible psychological and social impact. It is of particular interest to investigate the effects of exposure on children because it has been estimated that 80% of children overhear violence between their parents, with almost as many seeing evidence of it, and between 30% and 60% of those children also suffering abuse at the hands of the perpetrator (Cahn, 2006).

Cahn (2006) describes the short-term effects that witnessing and experiencing violence can have on children:
- increased levels of anxiety and depression
- feelings of fear, anger, grief, shame, distrust and powerlessness
- increased risk of suicide
- increased risk-taking, school truancy, early sexual activity, substance abuse and delinquency
- diminished school performance
- increased risk of learning difficulties such as dyslexia
- obedience problems, more lying and more cheating at school
- problems maintaining relationships with others
- increased likeliness to respond to conflict aggressively.

Domestic violence has a profound effect on children, even when they are not the victims.

Although it can be extremely difficult to trace a causal connection between exposure to violence and potential long-term effects, Cahn cites the following:

- potential for boys to become abusers later
- increased likeliness that girls who enter violent relationships will tolerate the violence
- continuing depression for both males and females and low self-esteem in females.

A typical finding in domestic violence research is that male perpetrators are more likely to have come from homes where they witnessed or were victims of domestic violence (e.g. Rosenbaum and O'Leary, 1981). It is extremely important to remember that the majority of this information comes from correlational studies. Although it appears that many people who engage in violence in the home were once victims of violence themselves, it does not follow that victims of violence will become perpetrators in turn. Tavris and Aronson (2007) describe the terrible but not uncommon error made when children are separated from a parent because it is learned that the parent was previously a victim of domestic violence. A factor that compounds this problem is that a lot of data has been gathered from shelters – institutions established to provide a safe haven for victims of domestic violence. There may be quite significant differences in the amount and type of violence experienced or witnessed by those who enter a shelter as opposed to those who stay, and the removal from familiar surroundings may be an added trauma for children (Edleson, 1999).

Apart from the effects on children, there is also research into the effects on men and women. Post-traumatic stress disorder appears to be a very common effect, occurring in between 45% and 80% of women (Roberts, 2002).

If we cannot gather the necessary scientific evidence to support the notion that being the victim of violence causes a child to later become a perpetrator of domestic violence, what social implications might this have? Is it necessary to conduct experiments in this area?

EXERCISE

10   Consider what evidence would be required to establish a causal relationship between being the victim of domestic violence as a child and becoming a perpetrator later. Why is this unlikely to be found?

EMPIRICAL RESEARCH

Intimate partner violence and its possible effects on men's mental health (Rhodes et al., 2002)

This study aimed to find out what mental health problems are present in people involved in intimate partner violence (IPV). The participants in the study were a convenience sample of 1122 men, mostly African American, visiting the trauma centre of a public hospital for non-urgent treatment. They were asked to use a computer to complete a 20-minute health assessment questionnaire which contained items concerned with IPV, depression, traumatic stress, suicidality, substance use and general health. The researchers were then able to compare the scores of those who were involved in IPV (37%) with the scores of those who reported none (63%).

Their results suggest that mental health problems such as those measured are most common among those who are both victims and perpetrators of violence.

In particular, there seems to be a strong relationship between IPV perpetration and suicidal thoughts, particularly for those who are on both sides of the violence. While only 0.7% of those who didn't report IPV reported suicidal thoughts, 3.5% of the victim-only group reported them, 2.5% of the perpetrator-only group, and 23.4% of the group who were both victims and perpetrators. Depression showed a similar trend, with reports at 3.3%, 9.7%, 7.5% and 40.3% respectively.

In terms of behaviour such as smoking, use of other substances and not wearing seatbelts while driving, the men who were both victims and perpetrators seem to be more at risk.

11	What are the strengths and limitations of this study? The authors do not claim a causal link between violence and mental health. Do you think they should?

Battered woman syndrome – when victim becomes perpetrator

Referred to variously as battered person syndrome and battered spouse syndrome, this notorious condition was first described in the 1970s to explain the mystery of why a woman might stay with an abusive partner. While attempting to develop strategies to appease an abusive partner, women seemed to acquire passivity similar to the dogs in research by Seligman and Maier (1967) – characterized particularly by a lack of attempt to avoid punishment. With this explanation in place, lawyers started attempting to use the syndrome as a justification for a self-defence plea in cases where a woman had murdered her husband.

Saunders (1986) asked 52 battered women who had sought help from an agency or shelter to complete a lengthy questionnaire that assessed the frequency of different conflict tactics, their motivation for any violence in their relationship, and any social desirability bias in their responses. He found that the most frequent reason given for the violence which many of the women had carried out was self-defence (combined with fighting back). He suggests that much of the violence carried out by women is pre-emptory, to prevent an attack when the woman senses it is coming because of the partner's actions. He also points out that the kind of attacks most women engaged in were mildly harmful rather than seriously injuring. The study thus gives some support for the notion that violence begets violence and that one dangerous effect of domestic violence is the escalation of attacks to a sometimes deadly outcome.

 To learn about the story of Gaile Owens, who was sentenced to death for killing her partner, go to www. pearsonhotlinks. com, enter the title or ISBN of this book and select weblink 8.5. Be warned that some of the details are very disturbing.

Strategies for reducing violence

Group therapy and the Duluth model

One strategy for reducing violence is psychological treatment for the perpetrator. This can include individual therapy that tries to address the causes of violence or the increasingly common anger management courses that are run in groups. Here, we focus on group treatment for men who have been identified as perpetrators of domestic abuse.

 Group therapy for violent men usually includes lessons on anger management.

Robertson (1999) identifies three key problems that make the treatment of violent men difficult. All are centred on a lack of motivation to change their behaviour:
- culture and/or society may accept violent behaviour
- the violence is likely to have been effective in achieving particular goals and thus has been positively reinforced in the past
- a perpetrator of violence is seldom willing to submit to the power of therapists or facilitators and has not usually joined the programme out of choice.

To address these problems, group treatment can initially be a very favourable approach as it allows for the establishment of new group norms that do not accept sexism or violence. Thus, even within a culture that accepts violence, members of the group can be chastised for breaching the group's norms. A range of procedures can be carried out, including anger management training and cognitive–behavioural work focusing on developing insight into the costs and risks of violence relative to its rewards. Robertson (1999) describes

programmes running as intensive residential courses from as little as six week to as long as three years because it can take a long time for the violence to stop.

Although these programmes usually report a good success rate, there are a number of criticisms. First, it is very difficult to assess success. Rates of recidivism are one way, but as the majority of domestic violence goes unreported and unrecorded, this is not an easy statistic to use. Shepard (1992) examined recidivism rates five years after a Duluth intervention and found that 40% of the men on the programme were either convicted of assault or had received police attention for it. This, along with the findings of Dutton et al. (1997), suggests that rates of recidivism are higher than recorded statistics can tell us, and that certain personality characteristics plus, for example, a substance abuse problem, can also predict recidivism.

Scores on measures such as the Conflict Tactics Scale may change as a result of therapy, but as Robertson (1999) asks, are we enhancing the safety of battered women or producing better-educated batterers? That is, are we teaching participants what the correct answers to questions are rather than really changing behaviour? A further problem can be that reducing violence is not necessarily an appropriate target: how much difference does it make to a victim of domestic violence if the beatings are weekly or daily? This is not yet clear. In addition, there is a risk with any group treatment that members will share strategies for committing violence or hiding it.

One of the earliest approaches to group treatment was part of the Duluth model for preventing violence. This includes cognitive–behaviour therapy in groups along with multi-agency attention to the domestic situation (such as increased likelihood of arrest for violence). This has been adapted for use in a number of countries and has been the target of some quite vicious criticism because of its ideological focus on patriarchal violence – that in which a male perpetrator asserts power over a female victim through violence. It has been criticized for having too much – even an exclusive – focus on females as victims, even when they carry out more violence than the male. The Domestic Abuse Intervention Project Power and Control wheel (Figure 8.1) helps men identify the behaviours they use to control family members.

The model has also been criticized for its lack of focus on other issues that contribute to domestic violence, such as substance abuse. Despite the criticisms, the model is in widespread use and has been adapted to be less gender-biased and less culture-biased too. Robertson (1999) refers to its successful adaptation for use with Maori people in New Zealand, which makes better use of extended family and community support networks.

EXERCISE

12 **a** Make an information leaflet or brochure that details types of abuse or violence and possible effects on victims.

b Find out who people in your area can contact if they want help or advice about domestic violence and advertise this in your leaflet.

c Contact a local organization or psychologist to find out what kind of treatment or therapy is available and make a note of this on your leaflet.

PHYSICAL VIOLENCE SEXUAL

USING COERCION AND THREATS
Making and/or carrying out threats to do something to hurt her • threatening to leave her, to commit suicide, to report her to welfare • making her drop charges • making her do illegal things.

USING INTIMIDATION
Making her afraid by using looks, actions, gestures • smashing things • destroying her property • abusing pets • displaying weapons.

USING ECONOMIC ABUSE
Preventing her from getting or keeping a job • making her ask for money • giving her an allowance • taking her money • not letting her know about or have access to family income.

USING EMOTIONAL ABUSE
Putting her down • making her feel bad about herself • calling her names • making her think she's crazy • playing mind games • humiliating her • making her feel guilty.

POWER AND CONTROL

USING MALE PRIVILEGE
Treating her like a servant • making all the big decisions • acting like the "master of the castle" • being the one to define men's and women's roles

USING ISOLATION
Controlling what she does, who she sees and talks to, what she reads, where she goes • limiting her outside involvement • using jealousy to justify actions.

USING CHILDREN
Making her feel guilty about the children • using the children to relay messages • using visitation to harass her • threatening to take the children away.

MINIMIZING, DENYING AND BLAMING
Making light of the abuse and not taking her concerns about it seriously • saying the abuse didn't happen • shifting responsibility for abusive behavior • saying she caused it.

PHYSICAL VIOLENCE SEXUAL

 To learn more about a variation on the Duluth wheel for use with Muslim men, go to www. pearsonhotlinks.com, enter the title or ISBN of this book and select weblink 8.6.
To learn more about criticisms of the Duluth model, go to www. pearsonhotlinks.com, enter the title or ISBN of this book and select weblink 8.7.

Primary prevention strategies in schools

Primary prevention of violence attempts to stop the violence before it happens. Since so many aspects of mental and physical health are put at risk by violence, it is both economically wise and socially responsible for authorities to show an interest in programmes to reduce the level of violence in the community.

Education programmes have been devised to help males deal with norms about violence and to help females and children learn to recognize danger signs and develop coping and help-seeking strategies. One example of this is described by Brozo et al. (2002).

EMPIRICAL RESEARCH

'I know the difference between a real man and a TV man' (Brozo et al., 2002)

The authors of this research included two teachers of a group of 14 7th grade pupils in the USA. Pupils in this group studied a novel featuring young Hispanic and African Americans in New York and were expected to reflect on issues of masculinity and violence. They were in the middle of the exercise when the school shooting at Columbine High School occurred. As part of their studies, pupils were asked to complete a diary of their television viewing and consider portrayals of violence in other media, particularly in terms of the effect that the limited range of male types presented through media might have on behaviour.

At the conclusion of the period of activities and discussions, the students completed for a second time a survey about how much violence they had recently instigated. A significant reduction in self-reported violence was observed and responses to statements relating to the culture of honour concept (e.g. 'Real men protect their families by fighting') had changed. A student who initially wrote 'Yes ... Where I live you got to fight because people always messing with you,' afterwards wrote 'No ... you protect them better by having a good job and a good house.'

To access Worksheet 8.2 on domestic violence, please visit www.pearsonbacconline.com and follow the on-screen instructions.

EXERCISE

13   What issues are there with the validity of this study?

Programmes like the one described above are common enough in the USA these days. Smithey and Straus (2004) suggest that up to 67% of students are exposed to them and are becoming more knowledgeable about the nature and consequences of intimate violence. But it is very difficult to know if this has or can be translated into a reduction in violent behaviour. Similar conclusions were reached in 1998 by the National Research Council investigation into the effectiveness of strategies to prevent domestic violence: where there is quasi-experimental work comparing the effects of participation in schools that have run a programme and those that have not, the programme appears to have had an effect.

Edleson (2000) found that the longest follow-up study to investigate the effectiveness of school programmes was 16 months, which is clearly not long enough to observe the kind of sustained preventative effect that is intended by this kind of strategy.

Some police authorities keep a very close eye on people who are considered possible abusers, even using a criminal profile to identify those who are at risk of committing murder in the family, and intervene before it can happen. This may appear like the futuristic movie *Minority Report* in which telepaths warn agents about crimes before they happen.

Comparison of school-based prevention and group treatment strategies

EXERCISE

14 A basic framework to begin discussing the relative effectiveness of these two strategies is provided below. Copy the table below and complete it with brief notes and then construct a plan for a 22-mark essay.

	Group treatment	School-based prevention
Intended target of the intervention (which level of analysis?)		
How effectiveness is measured		
Evidence for effectiveness		
Problems with measurement of effectiveness		
Strengths of each intervention		
Limitations of each intervention		

PRACTICE QUESTIONS

1 Contrast **two** theories of altruism in humans. *[22 marks]*

● **Examiner's hint**
The command term *contrast* requires you to give an account of the differences between the two theories. Remember you can also be asked to *describe*, *explain* and *compare* the theories. For a 22-mark answer, it is often best not to start by describing first one theory and then the other, and then listing differences. A better strategy is to address both theories throughout the answer, comparing them in a number of ways such as their validity, usefulness, or the amount and quality of empirical research.

2 To what extent do biological factors influence prosocial behaviour? *[22 marks]*

3 Compare the role of sociocultural and cognitive factors in attraction. *[22 marks]*

4 Discuss the relative effectiveness of **two** strategies for reducing violence. *[22 marks]*

 To access Worksheet 8.3 with a full example answer to question 1, please visit www.pearsonbacconline.com and follow the on-screen instructions.

 To access Worksheet 8.4 with additional practice questions and answer guidelines, please visit www.pearsonbacconline.com and follow the on-screen instructions.

SPORT PSYCHOLOGY

9.1 Introduction: What is sport psychology?

Learning outcomes
- To what extent do biological, cognitive and sociocultural factors influence behaviour in sport?
- Evaluate psychological research (that is, theories and/or studies) relevant to the study of sport psychology.

Sport psychology is the scientific study of individual and group behaviour and mental processes in the context of sports. This field is concerned with how sporting performance can be improved with the application of psychological theory, and in developing an understanding of how participation in sport affects behaviour, thinking and emotion, in individuals and societies. Although there is much theory development in this field, many sport psychologists focus on applying theory, often from other contexts, to the sports context. This can include:

- assisting young sportspeople in their personal development with developmental theory
- minimizing the psychological effects of injury
- preventing addictions and supporting healthy lifestyles with knowledge gained from health psychology
- trying to prevent individual burnout and improve confidence
- helping sports organizations improve their management systems using organizational psychology theory
- helping community programmes to increase participation in physical activities.

Dr Martin Perry, a sport psychologist in the UK, keeps a blog relating to sport psychology. To learn more about the variety of contexts sport psychology can be applied to, go to www.pearsonhotlinks.com, enter the title or ISBN of this book and select weblink 9.1.

Sport psychologist Jos Vanstiphout chats with Ernie Els of South Africa on the putting green.

9.2 Biological, cognitive and sociocultural influences on behaviour in sport

Learning outcomes
- To what extent do biological, cognitive and sociocultural factors influence behaviour in sport?
- Evaluate psychological research (that is, theories and/or studies) relevant to the study of sport psychology.

● **Examiner's hint**
As with all the options chapters for the IB Psychology paper 2 exam, you are required to develop an understanding of how biological, cognitive and sociocultural factors influence behaviour in a particular context.
As you work through this chapter, keep your own record of useful studies and theories in the form of a reading diary; this will give you material that you can evaluate in the exam.

In the context of sport, the biological level of analysis focuses, for example, on the relationship between physiological arousal and sports performance. The cognitive level of analysis addresses information-processing styles of sportspeople and, for example, the positive and negative self-statements that accompany individual success and failure. At the sociocultural level of analysis, we can look at a variety of group dynamics and, for example, how team cohesion affects performance.

By the end of this chapter you should see how a variety of influences from all three levels of analysis can be integrated to provide a fuller explanation of sport psychology phenomena.

9.3 Emotion and motivation

Learning outcomes
- Evaluate theories of motivation in sport.

Cognitive evaluation theory

One of the key distinctions to understand in human motivation is the difference between intrinsic and extrinsic motivation.

Intrinsic motivation is motivation based on the task itself; for example, when a person finds reading books interesting or enjoyable, we can say that reading is intrinsically motivating for that person. Many people participate in sports because they enjoy the challenge; they may lose interest if playing against a weaker opponent – as the task becomes too easy, the incentive to put effort in seems to have decreased.

Extrinsic motivation is motivation based on the possible outcomes of engaging (or not engaging) in an activity; for example, success in tests at school or avoidance of the consequences of not engaging. Many children play sports that their parents or friends are interested in, and find it difficult to sustain attention. Their motivation is not enjoyment, but avoidance of the consequences (e.g. loneliness or disapproval) of not doing so.

Intrinsic motivation comes from the task; extrinsic motivation comes from knowledge or the consequences of engaging in the task.

Cognitive evaluation theory (CET) deals with interactions between these two types of motivation. According to CET, internal motivation is fundamentally based on the satisfaction of a psychological need for competence. Activities that meet this need are more intrinsically motivating for a person to participate in, as long as participation is accompanied by a sense of autonomy and control. In other words, the reason for participation is coming from inside the participant (Ryan and Deci, 2000).

External events that are rewarding or punishing in some way can shift a person's interpretation of the reasons for participation from internal to external or vice versa,

Sometimes, being obliged to do something reduces your interest in doing it.

resulting in significant changes in behaviour. For example, many students enjoy reading when they have free choice about what they read (autonomous choice); engaging in the activity is enjoyable in part because of a sense of competence. However, when they are asked to read books for school, their level of motivation might decrease because they did not make the choice autonomously and they sense that they are reading not because they want to, but because they have to.

Ryan (1982) explains that such external events have two functions:
- a controlling aspect
- an informational or feedback aspect.

The controlling aspect is some kind of perceived pressure to achieve a particular result – for example, when a young tennis player feels pressure from a parent to win a match. When a controlling aspect becomes important, it can lower a person's intrinsic motivation as they feel the reason for their participation no longer stems from their own needs.

Without such controlling aspects, informational aspects can play a role. Informational aspects are things like feedback from a coach or parent about performance, and can have a positive or negative impact on motivation. It is also possible for a person to provide their own informational feedback by such thoughts as: 'That was a really good shot; I'm better than my opponent' or 'I've missed my last three free throws: I'm having a bad game'.

Blanchard et al. (2009) asked a sample of 207 school-age basketball players to complete a questionnaire which included questions about the coach's interpersonal style. This was to test whether the perception of a controlling style affected their motivation to play basketball in terms of their feelings of competence and autonomy. The researchers found that there was a negative correlation between the degree of perceived controlling style and autonomy. Although no relationship was found with feelings of competence, researchers did find that feelings of autonomy and competence correlated strongly with positive emotions and satisfaction in sport.

Is it possible to measure a person's levels of motivation? Usually psychologists use self-reports but this approach does have limitations.

Kimball (2007) conducted interviews with 12 North American collegiate athletes to investigate the nature and role of autonomy in relation to their sport. She allowed herself to be interviewed first to check for any bias of her own and then needed to be careful to avoid constructing an interview that would invite participants to confirm the one bias she had: the expectation that athletes would feel controlled in their lives. Open-ended questions in a semi-structured format were asked and a thematic content analysis was carried out, resulting in three major themes:
- personal autonomy
- relational autonomy
- lack of autonomy.

She found that the sense of personal autonomy was strongly related to identity development and an increasing sense of maturity, and that it resulted in increased confidence and motivation. Relational autonomy is autonomy based on relationships with others such as God, parents or coaches. While this type of autonomy appeared to increase motivation, decisions based around relationships with others were more likely to be personally harmful. Lack of autonomy because of coach control or scholarships was found to be demotivating, but the athletes in the study described ways that they compensated for this. For example, they actively reframed information so that it appeared that their motivation was internal; thus they might remind themselves that it was their decision to sign up to be a collegiate athlete, and that continuing is rational because they enjoy the benefits of the healthy but restrictive lifestyle.

Quantitative investigations of this type of motivation have caused more controversy. On one hand is a vein of research which suggests that providing scholarships to players undermines motivation; for example, Kingston et al. (2006) found that scores on the Sport Motivation Scale could be used to discriminate between scholarship and non-scholarship athletes in the USA. On the other, is research which suggests that the athlete's perception of the behaviour of coaches may be more important as a mediating factor (Hollembeak and Amorose, 2005). Kimball's interviews (described above) may also support this idea.

Work by Cameron et al. (2005) suggests that the picture is more complicated than this. They found that the size of the reward is important – the kind of small reward used in experiments in laboratory settings is quite different from scholarships. Participants' perceptions of the controlling aspect of a reward are the result of an interaction between the nature of the task, individual factors and the reward itself. And Cameron has previously argued that intrinsic motivation is not, in fact, decreased by rewards (Cameron et al., 2001).

This demonstrates a typical criticism of explanations for behaviour at a cognitive level of analysis. Although laboratory studies can provide cause-and-effect relationships, they frequently lack ecological validity, as the tasks are often trivial, and the rewards are often small and inconsequential. It is ethically problematic to run an experiment on the effect of scholarships on levels of motivation, and thus questionnaires are frequently used to allow correlations to be obtained. Measurement of intrinsic motivation remains difficult, despite reasonably well-validated measures like the Sport Motivation Scale. This scale is successful in terms of the theory that was used to create it, but it is no surprise if an instrument designed to measure a theoretical construct like intrinsic motivation is capable of demonstrating the relationship between that construct and the factors that theoretically affect it.

Achievement goal theory

According to this theory, there are two different dimensions that account for how people interpret what success in sport means. These are referred to as goal orientations. Nicholls (1989) called them **task orientation** and **ego orientation**.

Task orientation is a focus on achieving particular goals based on improving skill or knowledge in a particular area and usually involves collaboration with others. Ego orientation is focused on the self in comparison with others, so that goals are based on establishing superiority over others.

Individuals can be measured on both dimensions, so that you could, for example, be stronger on one dimension than the other, or score similarly on both. Duda and Nicholls (1992) asked 207 high school students to complete a questionnaire assessing their goal orientations, satisfaction and interest and beliefs about the causes of success. Their findings led them to the conclusion that sport is a domain that allows individuals to demonstrate how good they are. Certainly, competitive sport is populated by individuals with a stronger ego orientation and, therefore, perceptions of ability are the best predictors of satisfaction in sport.

Hanrahan and Cerin (2009) gathered responses to a questionnaire from male and female Australian athletes involved in both team and individual sports. The females in the study had a stronger task orientation than the males at all levels of sport, from recreational involvement to international competition. The researchers found no differences between the sexes in ego orientation. Perhaps not surprisingly, those who played individual sports were found to have stronger ego orientation than those involved in team sports, suggesting that defining success as being better than others encourages a person to become involved in

People with task orientation are focused on carrying out a task to improve skill or knowledge.

People with ego orientation are focused on showing they are superior to others.

How would you tests the effects of a scholarship? Is it ethical to offer scholarships to sportspeople if it reduces their motivation?

To learn more about goal orientation and to work out your score on the task orientation and ego orientation, go to www. pearsonhotlinks.com, enter the title or ISBN of this book and select weblink 9.2.

individual sports. However, as is typical of much of the research into motivation in sport, the data here is correlational, and we cannot identify cause and effect.

Hanrahan and Cerin (2009) suggest that individual sports may appeal more to those with an ego orientation because they often involve ranking of individuals and facilitate comparison. However, some individual sports like track and field give better feedback about personal improvements than sports like squash and tennis, and therefore can attract people with high task orientation.

The usefulness of achievement goal theory in sport lies in its application to improve motivation in athletes. Individuals involved in team sports often need encouragement to increase their task orientation and take more pleasure from personal improvement and team spirit rather than maintaining a focus on demonstrating their particular skill. Hanrahan and Cerin (2009) suggest that such an increase in task orientation may be particularly important for males and individual sportspeople. A tennis player, for example, may find it difficult to measure improvements in his or her performance, as the goal of each match is to beat the opponent. There is little immediate feedback on whether or not beating the opponent reflects improvement in the player's game or merely demonstrates superiority on this occasion. Feedback from coaches becomes very important, as does setting targets like a reduction in the number of faults, or an increase in the number of times the player breaks his or her opponent's serve.

A tennis coach can provide helpful feedback in training.

Self-efficacy theory

Self-efficacy theory is a social-cognitive theory that focuses on the role of a person's expectations. Bandura (1977) distinguished between **outcome expectations**, which estimate the probability that a set of behaviours will lead to particular outcomes, and **efficacy expectations**, which are beliefs about one's ability to carry out the behaviours required. High self-efficacy is associated with motivation and success in many areas, including psychological therapy, education, and sports.

Bandura (1997) identified four sources of information about efficacy:
- previous successful performance (enactive mastery experience)
- vicarious experience (observing others' success)
- verbal persuasion
- emotional arousal.

Sport psychologists frequently provide interventions to improve self-efficacy using these four sources of information.

Enactive mastery experience is usually best provided through training and is naturally improved through experience of playing sport at a high level. However, coaches are often

hesitant to let skilled young sportspeople play at the highest level because they know that unsuccessful exposure to such experience early on can have damaging long-term effects on performance. This may be because of reduced self-efficacy which, in this context, is often recognized as a loss of confidence. In order for self-efficacy to be high, sportspeople need a healthy attitude towards failure, not interpreting it as evidence of incompetence.

Similarly, useful vicarious experience can be had by seeing others perform well, but it can be very demotivating to see fellow athletes failing. This tends to make a task seem more impossible.

Verbal persuasion from coaches, family, an audience, or even the commentary and predictions of self-talk have all been contributing factors to success; negative comments are a threat to success.

Interpretation of emotional arousal is also extremely important. A tendency to view the physical sensations as catastrophic or indicative of impending disaster can inhibit performance by lowering self-efficacy.

Bandura's work has been used to help people in all walks of life who fear that their feelings of distress are impairing their ability to function, and to reduce such distress by increasing self-efficacy. Similarly, in sport, the ability to perform optimally is inhibited by feelings of distress that can be linked to low self-efficacy, which may have resulted from negative self-talk or an unhealthy focus on a recent failure in performance.

Vicarious experience is gained when watching fellow athletes do well.

An example of a self-efficacy intervention is presented in Box 1. It uses several techniques that will be discussed later in this chapter.

EMPIRICAL RESEARCH

Positive interpretation of arousal-based imagery (Mellalieu et al., 2009)

These researchers wanted to examine the effect of training sportspeople to interpret motivational, general-arousal-based imagery in a more positive way. The five rugby players in the study were all trained to imagine a difficult situation in sport, such as when the game is tied and the player has the opportunity to kick a penalty that will win the game for his team. At the same time they imagined the physical sensations that would accompany the inevitable emotional arousal of the situation. They were taught to use self-talk to recognize that the physiological symptoms of emotional arousal (e.g. increased heart rate) were normal reactions to a stressful situation and to keep themselves focused on the task. Data were collected from participants immediately prior to competitive matches using several questionnaires such as the Positive–Negative Affects Questionnaire and the Sport Imagery Questionnaire.

The results indicated that by using this imagery technique during practice, players found that their anxiety levels were reduced and their confidence levels were much higher. The researchers quote from one of the participants:

continued

'Seeing yourself performing the kick successfully … even though you have all the same old nerves and worries … it builds your confidence so that you really believe you can do it no matter what you're feeling. So the usual worries I get beforehand aren't as destructive. I see them now as helpful as I'm confident I know I can make my kicks even with the pressure.'

The intervention was successful for all five participants and is therefore recommended as a way to improve efficacy and thereby enhance performance. However, the researchers warn that a reduction in competitive anxiety may not be desirable in all cases, particularly in contact sports like rugby, where relatively high levels of pre-competitive anxiety are thought to be needed.

Self-efficacy interventions can improve confidence for when a player prepares to take a penalty kick.

EXERCISE

1   This is an experiment with some important methodological limitations. Identify problems with the design and recommend modifications to improve our ability to infer a cause–effect relationship between the intervention offered and a reduction in anxiety.

Problems with measuring self-efficacy

To learn more about positive interpretations of failure, go to www.pearsonhotlinks.com, enter the title or ISBN of this book and select weblink 9.3.

Interventions based on self-efficacy have been very successful and there is a huge range of anecdotal evidence from professional sportspeople which suggests their success may be due to positive self-talk or positive interpretations of emotional arousal and performance failures. However, self-efficacy is a difficult variable to measure or manipulate, and most studies investigate individual components of it rather than the construct as a whole. In addition, more research is needed to help identify the differences between the kinds of self-efficacy that are useful in individual or team sports, for novice or experienced sportspeople, and for professionals or amateurs.

EXERCISES

2   You have looked at three theories of motivation in sport. Construct a table that lists strengths and limitations of each one.

3   What is the link between self-efficacy and physiological arousal?

9.4 The role of goal-setting in motivation

Learning outcomes
- Using one or more research studies, explain the role of goal-setting in the motivation of individuals.

Motivation is sometimes thought of in terms of goal-directed behaviour, so it is no surprise that a number of researchers have focused on the importance of goals. Cognitive evaluation theory, achievement goal theory and self-efficacy theory all place some importance on the type of goal or thoughts about the goal, but there is also research and theory relating specifically to goal-setting. Such research explains both how and why people set goals and, more importantly, shows how goal-setting can be used to improve all sorts of dependent variables like satisfaction and performance. Locke et al. (1981), pioneers in goal-setting theory, suggest that consciously chosen goals are behind most human behaviour.

Research into goal-setting has identified four conditions that are required in order for motivation and performance to be raised:
- goals must be clear and specific (a goal like 'winning' is too vague to be motivational; a goal to shave a few milliseconds off a personal time is far more likely to result in motivation and success)
- goals should be difficult
- the goal needs to be accepted (coaches and parents who set goals that are impossible will find them ineffective and possibly demotivating)
- feedback must be available, particularly about progress towards the goal rather than the achievement of the goal.

In addition, it seems that short-term goals are more likely to be motivating than long-term goals, although this may be a result of long-term goals tending to be vaguer and not offering feedback in the same way that short-term goals can.

Steinberg et al. (2000) suggest that another distinction in the type of goal set is important: mastery goals to do with improving skills tend to lead to more success.

 New Year's resolutions usually take the form of long-term goals and this may be why so few of them are successfully achieved.

Why is goal-setting so successful?

Latham and Locke (2006) explain that the reason goals are effective is that we are motivated to correct a discrepancy between a goal and knowledge of current performance. Without the goal, there is no discrepancy, and therefore no need for change. For example, a rugby player might know that he doesn't kick penalties successfully 100% of the time but not feel motivation to improve until he finds out exactly how low his percentage is. Believing that he should get at least 80% of his penalties over, he now faces the discrepancy and is motivated to correct it. Locke (1991) even suggests that this is such an automatic process when there is feedback that researchers need to be very careful in constructing control groups to compare with explicit goal-setting groups.

In addition, achievement of a goal is associated with feelings of satisfaction. This plays the part of a reward that will encourage the repetition of goal-directed behaviour. Further to this, interest in the activity increases as successful goal achievers tend to shift the perceived cause of their satisfaction from the achievement of the goal to the performance of the task. Thus, for example, a good golfer might perceive that what they enjoy about the sport is not the constant meeting of goals and self-improvement, but the activity itself.

Locke and Latham (2006) also suggest that self-efficacy and goal-setting are complementary theories in that self-efficacy is increased by the successful achievement of goals. It may be, therefore, that self-efficacy is still the motivational force underlying a person's willingness to engage in activity, but goal-setting describes one of the ways that self-efficacy can be increased.

EMPIRICAL RESEARCH

Can goal-setting prevent health problems? (Schofield et al., 2005)

This experimental study contributes to a body of literature relating to programmes that attempt to reduce the prevalence of adult health problems by increasing physical activity among young people. Although some teenagers are motivated to play sport, it appears to be harder to motivate those who are not interested to still engage in healthy levels of exercise.

This Australian study used 85 teenage girls who had been previously identified as 'low active' as participants. The girls were at three different schools, of which two were assigned a treatment, and one was kept as a control. One group of girls were each given a pedometer, a small device that can be attached to a person's belt to count the number of steps they take. This device can be used to set a goal of achieving a certain number of steps each day, and feedback is constantly available. Thus, the use of a pedometer allows for short-term, specific goals. The other treatment group were given time-based goals, which are also capable of giving feedback, but only about the passing of time.

Pedometers (here, worn on the waisteband) measure the number of steps taken.

The girls' physical activity was measured during and after the intervention, using the pedometers of girls who had been given them, and self-reporting for the other groups. The results indicated that after 6 weeks, the group using pedometers with daily step targets were showing the greatest increase in physical activity, while the other two groups showed no significant increase. However, after 12 weeks, the girls with time-based goals were also showing an increase. Thus it appears that setting goals, regardless of type, is effective in increasing motivation to engage in physical activity, and that in the short-term, the constant feedback of the pedometer effects this increase faster.

Pedometers are being used in programmes such as Girls Stepping Out and 10 000 steps in several countries, including Australia, New Zealand and Canada.

EXERCISE

4   What does this study show us about the role of goal-setting in motivation?

9.5 Arousal and anxiety and their influence on performance in sport

Learning outcomes
- Discuss theories relating arousal and anxiety to performance

● **Examiner's hint**
You can be asked to *discuss* theories of the effect of arousal and anxiety on performance. This means you need to be able to *describe* them, *evaluate* them and *compare* them with reference to research. It may help to plan an essay by constructing a table that compares the key points of each theory and also highlights strengths and limitations of each. Don't forget that self-efficacy theory can also be used to answer such a question.

Arousal is a physiological state that prepares the body for action, the fight or flight response (page 54). Through the release of hormones and activation of various parts of the brain, a person's alertness increases and their response times decrease. Although this sounds ideal for sports, arousal sometimes can manifest itself as anxiety and threaten performance. There are several theories that describe and explain this. Self-efficacy theory (page 288) is one theory that links cognition and physiological arousal. Other theories are presented here.

Drive theory

Several theorists have conceived of sports anxiety in terms of drive, including Hull (1943) and Spence (1956), and some interesting extensions were made by Zajonc (1965).

According to this theory, arousal (referred to as drive) is a non-specific increase in the activation level of the person that makes their dominant response more likely to occur and decreases the probability of other reactions. The dominant response is that which has priority, usually because it is well-learned. In the case of athletes, it is the response they have trained for in a particular situation. Where a person is not prepared for a situation, or has not practised enough for an action to be dominant, it can be expected that drive will cause the wrong response. Thus, when a penalty-taker in football is standing behind the ball looking at the waiting goalkeeper, the increase in drive will cause him to kick well (if he has practised enough for this to become the dominant response) or fail to score (if he does not have enough experience of this situation). In this theory, for a well-practised athlete, the degree of arousal has a direct effect on the quality of performance: more arousal means better performance. For inexperienced sportspeople, more arousal is likely to lead to increased errors.

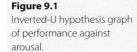

Drive is similar to arousal: physiological readiness to perform.

This theory is not very popular with sport psychologists these days as research and anecdotal evidence both provide a very simple refutation of the theory. Even for well-practised athletes, high levels of anxiety sometimes seem to inhibit performance.

The inverted-U hypothesis

This theory was developed to account for the inhibition of performance when a person has high levels of anxiety. It refers to the upside-down u-shape of the graph of performance against arousal (Figure 9.1). Performance increases with arousal at first, but after a certain point (which may vary between people, sports and skills) performance drops.

Figure 9.1
Inverted-U hypothesis graph of performance against arousal.

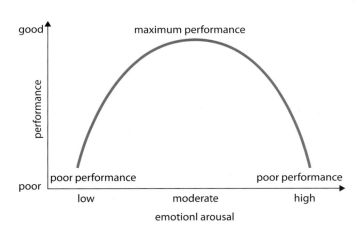

If we need to work out each individual's own optimum level of arousal, does this mean that research on groups is useless?

The key difference between this theory and drive theory is that in this case, *moderate* levels of arousal are associated with successful performance. Those sports that require fine movements and precision, such as shooting, bowls, or archery, are usually performed better with low arousal, while sports activities requiring more physical effort like throwing or tackling may be performed better with higher levels.

Sonstroem and Bernardo (1982) found support for this theory by studying female basketball players. They found that the optimum level of arousal is the median level experienced for any given athlete. This study was undertaken partly in response to criticism that the inverted-U hypothesis fails to account for individual differences in performance at different levels of arousal.

Other problems with the inverted-U hypothesis include a lack of empirical support (see the Raglin study opposite) a failure to distinguish between somatic anxiety and cognitive anxiety, and lack of clarity as to how performance might affect arousal. This last is because the relationship between arousal and performance has been established mostly through correlation. For example, an athlete might be increasingly aroused while engaging in their sport and then find their arousal drops because of a performance failure.

Cognitive anxiety is similar to worry.

Hardy and Fazey (1987) introduced a catastrophe model that tried to describe the relationship between arousal and cognitive anxiety. It suggested primarily that cognitive anxiety (referred to by Hardy (1999) as worry) has a mediating role in determining whether somatic arousal might lead to catastrophic effects. This would mean that when a person is highly aroused, being worried about performance at the same time would cause problems like choking. When a person has low physiological arousal, increasing cognitive anxiety can be beneficial.

Hardy et al. (1994) tested this by asking lawn bowlers to bowl under different conditions of physiological arousal and cognitive anxiety. They confirmed that performance suffered most when both were high. Baumeister (1984) suggests that cognitive anxiety in a high-pressure situation causes increased self-consciousness and a shift in attention to trying to control fine movements consciously, whereas a sportsperson normally performs the activity more automatically.

Studying the yips in a golfer.

A study by Smith et al. (2000) looked specifically at the physical symptoms of performance anxiety that can accompany choking, which are sometimes referred to as 'the yips'. Cricketers, tennis players, and particularly golfers, report that sometimes, in a high-pressure situation, they lose muscle control, which can lead to hitting the ball too hard or too softly. Smith et al. (2000) developed a questionnaire to distinguish between golfers who suffered from the yips and those who tended not to. They then asked the golfers to putt in different situations while heart rate, grip force and performance were measured. Those who said they had a tendency to get the yips showed worse performance and higher average heart rate than the others; they also gripped their putter more tightly. This suggests that there is a relationship between fine motor control and both cognitive and physiological anxiety that has still not been explained, only described.

Although it is clear that physiological and cognitive forms of anxiety play in a role in a sportsperson's failure to perform at their best, we don't yet understand why. It is worth noting

that a number of researchers have cited cognitive anxiety as a causal factor that interacts with self-confidence to affect performance, suggesting that self-efficacy may be reduced when levels of physiological arousal and cognitive anxiety are high. Again, however, we cannot be sure which comes first: a lack of confidence or increasing anxiety.

Optimal arousal theory

According to optimal arousal theory, every athlete has their own zone of optimal functioning (ZOF). As we have just seen, individual differences in arousal, and in performance while aroused and anxious are problems in this area of research. The work of Hanin (e.g. 1997) has been important in helping to account for these. This is not dissimilar to the inverted-U hypothesis, but focuses on the individual, suggesting that each person has a narrow range, somewhere between not anxious and extremely anxious, in which their performance will be best. This accounts for individual differences even when people are performing the same task, such as the golfers described by Smith et al. (2000) above.

Anxiety inventories like the State–Trait Anxiety Inventory (STAI) and the Competitive State Anxiety Inventory (CSAI) have been used to measure athletes' precompetitive anxiety so that it can be compared with performance to try to establish each individual's ZOF.

EMPIRICAL RESEARCH

Comparing ZOF with the inverted-U hypotheis (Raglin and Turner, 1993)

These researchers used two different theoretical approaches to try and account for the relationship between performance and arousal. Their participants were 68 male and female athletes from a North American University track and field team. The athletes were asked to recall their anxiety just prior to their best competition and to answer questions from the STAI in a classroom. Researchers used this as the basis to establish the range for each athlete's ZOF.

The researchers performed a correlational study prior to this research to establish that recall of anxiety is strongly related to actual anxiety, with a correlation of 0.80 between the tests at two different times.

After establishing the ZOF for each athlete, the researchers used a modified STAI to test predicted and actual precompetition anxiety. The researchers could then use this data to check whether the ZOF or an inverted-U hypothesis was a better way to account for the effects of anxiety on performance.

If the ZOF were better, wide individual variation would be seen within each event, but each individual's performance should be better within the ZOF identified for them. If the inverted-U hypothesis were more appropriate, performance should drop at higher levels of anxiety in each event with little variation across individuals (but the researchers allowed for some variation by also calculating athletes' median anxiety during the study as it was possible that this could correlate with performance).

Results clearly favoured the ZOF theory as each athlete's own performance was better when anxiety levels were within their own range as calculated by the researchers at the beginning of the study. The ZOF for most athletes was, interestingly, found to be at the extreme ends of the anxiety scale, further refuting the inverted-U hypothesis.

EXERCISES

5   Was this a valid test of the inverted-U hypothesis?

6   What implications does this research have for coaching strategies?

9.6 Skill development and performance

> **Learning outcomes**
> • Evaluate techniques for skill development used in sport

Mental imagery

Jonny Wilkinson is one of England's most successful rugby players. He famously kicked four penalties and then a drop-goal in the last minute of extra time to help England win the Rugby World Cup in 2003. How does he do it? He imagines a woman called Doris in the stands directly behind the goal posts and midway between them. And he kicks the ball to land it in Doris's arms. Strategies like this to improve skills are extremely common.

Jonny Wilkinson preparing to kick a penalty.

Two particular styles of imagery have been identified:
• internal imagery, in which the athlete imagines performing the activity
• external imagery, in which the athlete imagines from the perspective of an observer.

Moran (2009) suggests there is also a distinction between visual imagery and motor imagery, where the latter requires imagining the body actually moving, not just seeing it happen. Another way of categorizing imagery, as indicated by qualitative interviews with skydivers, is in terms of function. This can happen during training to learn simple or complex new skills, or to practise or improve new skills, or to reduce anxiety (Fournier et al., 2008). We also know that imagining carrying out an activity can be used as a means of enhancing performance, managing arousal and assisting rehabilitation after injury (Jones and Stuth, 1997).

We are going to focus on the use of mental imagery in performance enhancement. It is one of the most common techniques used by coaches in training for skills such as free-throw shooting in basketball, completing offensive plays in football, serving aces in tennis, bowling and catching in cricket, and for complex routines in gymnastics.

EMPIRICAL RESEARCH

Pre-performance rituals with mental imagery in water polo (Marlow et al., 1998)

Three experienced water polo team members with experience at taking penalties but who reported never having used mental imagery were interviewed and given personalized pre-performance rituals by a sport psychologist. Their rituals included relaxation breathing; concentration focus such as staring at the ball; and internal, external or both types of imagery to carry out the 'perfect shot' in a penalty situation: bouncing the ball off the water into the right corner of the goal.

They were asked to practise this mental imagery alone, and reported doing so for approximately half an hour a week. None of them were allowed to take penalties at training or in matches for the duration of the study. To prevent contamination, they were instructed not to communicate with other team members about the intervention.

After establishing a baseline performance by rating the penalties taken by the players on a scale of one to ten, the researchers asked the players to begin their mental practice. They continued to measure the players' performance regularly by asking them to take five penalties. This meant that their skill development in taking penalties could be tracked over time and compared with their baseline performance.

The three players all improved significantly – by 21%, 25% and 28%. Their improvements remained stable for the duration of the research.

EXERCISE

7 This was a single-subject research design as data was collected and analysed for individuals. With this in mind, list strengths and weaknesses of this study.

Problems identified by Jones and Stuth (1997) include an over-reliance on case study research and anecdotal evidence and, even where this has been replaced with more rigorous experimental approaches, a tendency to use small samples with poorly defined variables. It is extremely difficult to be certain that mental imagery is occurring in the minds of athletes in the same way and for the same duration.

Moran (2009) points out that many researchers instruct their participants not to think of something – a notoriously difficult thing to do. For example, when long-jumpers were instructed to imagine their jump with an internal perspective, they were told not to see that the jump was completed, but to feel it. Moreover, it is difficult to establish whether mental imagery is a cause or by-product of successful performance of skills as longitudinal research has seldom been carried out. Two further difficulties are that mental imagery appears usually to be accompanied by self-talk, and even if mental imagery is found to have a causal relationship with efficient skill development, it is difficult to establish how this happens.

 It is hard to control what participants think about in research.

One suggestion is that mental imagery creates a kind of programme for motor control that the brain can then carry out when the appropriate situation arises. Decety and Ingvar (1990) report that various parts of the frontal cortex are activated while a person is imagining carrying out a physical activity; thus, the more important timing and planning are in the performance of a skill, the more likely it is that having previously imagined performing the skill will help.

There is also evidence that the brain is activated when watching someone else performing the activity (Moran, 2009) and that high-level athletes (including basketballers and golfers) are better at predicting the outcome of another athlete's bodily actions than other experienced observers such as coaches and journalists (Aglioti et al., 2008). This may be because of the activation of networks of mirror neurons – a conclusion reached by Wright and Jackson (2007) after asking tennis players to watch serves and predict the direction of them while inside an fMRI machine. Considering the relationship between arousal and performance (page 293), it is worth noting that Deschaumes–Molinaro, Dittmar and Vernet–Maury (1991) found that physiological arousal during mental imagery was more like the actual physiological arousal that occurred while really competing for successful competitors than for weaker ones. This was a study of shooting competitors.

 Mirror neurons are networks of neurons activated in the brain when a person observes or thinks about an activity. Observing sports may actually allow a person to change their brain to improve future performance.

EXERCISE

8 These studies look at mental imagery at a biological level of analysis. Are there limitations to the methods used?

Self-talk

Another popular method suggested by coaches and sport psychologists to improve skills and enhance performance is the use of self-talk. Hardy (2006) defines self-talk as verbalizations or statements addressed to the self which serve at least two functions: instructional and motivational. In addition, there is a distinction between positive and negative self-talk; positive self-talk is that which facilitates performance and negative self-talk is that which is critical or pessimistic.

Instructional self-talk occurs when athletes gives themselves instructions or reminders about how to complete a task. For example, a tennis player might remind herself 'Get your feet planted', or a biathlete remind himself to hold his breath longer when he is shooting while tired. Motivational statements are encouragements a sportsperson uses, such as 'You can do it' or 'This is going in'. A further important distinction is whether the self-talk is overt or covert. Overt self-talk is often visible when we watch elite athletes, but we can only guess at what kind of covert self-talk is going on inside the person's head.

The effects of self-talk are fairly well documented in research. It appears to be a powerful motivational tool that can focus attention but in its negative form, it can reduce self-efficacy and contribute to choking. However, an obvious question is whether or not the effect is truly causal – does self-talk help athletes or are successful athletes more likely to engage in and respond to self-talk?

> Instructional self-talk is giving yourself verbal or mental instructions. Motivational self-talk is encouraging yourself verbally or mentally.

The Self-talk and Gestures Rating Scale (STAGRS) is used to measure the use of overt self-talk when researchers directly observe the sportsperson. It is clearly not possible, however, for an observer to record the internal thoughts of a player. This was illustrated by van Raalte et al. (1994). Using STAGRS, the researchers found that negative self-talk was used more by unsuccessful tennis players, but there was no difference in the amount of positive self-talk. They suggest that positive self-talk is more likely to be made silently than negative self-talk. This rather complicates the measurement process. Later research suggests that losing triggers negative self-talk, which illustrates the problem of causality. Verbalized negative self-talk may be observable following the loss of a point, but internalized negative self-talk cannot be observed and therefore cannot be cited as the cause of failures.

◀ Overt self-talk is observable in athletes.

To access Additional
information 9.1 on
hypnosis, please visit
www.pearsonbacconline.
com and follow the on-
screen instructions.

EMPIRICAL RESEARCH

Experimental self-talk in tennis (Hatzigeorgiadis et al., 2009)

In order to test the effectiveness of self-talk in tennis, the researchers randomly divided 72 young Greek tennis players into two groups. The experimental group were given a training session to introduce them to self-talk and were given self-talk cues such as 'shoulder' to focus their attention on how they moved their shoulder, and 'go' as a motivational cue to encourage themselves. To prevent Hawthorne effects, the researchers ensured the control group were also given a training session, but it was about technical aspects of the forehand.

The players were trained in an experimental task that involved completing a forehand shot that sent the ball over the net but under a rope placed above it. Each shot was given points according to how close to the baseline on the opposite side of the court it was. Two other dependent variables were measured: anxiety and self-confidence, using the Competitive State Anxiety Inventory.

Participants were asked to rate how often they used their self-talk. Two participants from the experimental group were removed from the data because they had not used any. Participants in the control group did use some self-talk but not consistently enough to be removed from the data.

The results showed that self-talk had a positive effect on performance and was associated with increased self-confidence and reduced cognitive anxiety. Changes in performance correlated with changes in self-confidence, suggesting that self-confidence is the mechanism by which self-talk improves performance. The researchers noted a concern that because the self-confidence measure was taken after the players completed the task, the results may not be valid.

● **Examiner's hint**
Two techniques for skill development have been discussed in this section, their strengths and weaknesses addressed. The key strength of both techniques is that they appear to be well supported by anecdotal and experimental evidence. To address the weaknesses, you should focus on the methodological problems such as the difficulty of observing mental activity.

EXERCISE

9   Why was the timing of the measurement of self-confidence a concern for the researchers? Do you think the research is valid?

 9.7
The influence of coaches on individuals and teams

Learning outcomes

*   To what extent does the role of the coach affect individual or team behaviour in sport?

In individual sports, the athletes often get the credit for their success, while in team sports, a coach can become quite famous in their own right. Sports teams at the highest level frequently pay a lot of money to bring in a top-quality coach, and high-profile failures commonly result in job loss. Clearly, the role of the coach is assumed to be an essential component of a team's success.

Consider the difficulties involved in trying to scientifically research the role of the coach. Can we ever be confident that we *know* the effects of a coach? Is it ethical to sack a coach when a team does badly?

EXERCISE

10   Review what you have covered so far in this chapter, making notes of what role a coach can play. Keep track of any relevant research.

Short and Short (2005) identify five key roles of a coach:

- teacher
- organizer
- competitor
- learner
- friend/mentor.

The competitor role is largely limited to coaches of team sports. These individuals often need to be active during the match, making substitutions and interacting with officials, for example. Therefore, their own anxiety, arousal, decision-making and performance should also be addressed. However, most research into the role of coaches focuses on their skills as teachers, and the context and nature of the relationship between coach and athlete.

One of the key influences of a coach is on motivational climate. Motivational climate has been described as the cues and expectations that contribute to a particular goal orientation. Goal orientation (page 287) can focus on improvement (creating a mastery climate) or comparative success (creating a performance climate). Where the coach is able to establish a mastery climate, higher levels of motivation, enjoyment, and performance can be found among younger athletes. Higher anxiety is associated with ego orientation, especially where there is the perception that the coach will penalize unsatisfactory performance (Vazou et al., 2005).

> Motivational climate is the term for the context in which sportspeople train and perform, and which could be for the aim of mastery or performance.

Balaguer et al. (2002) asked female handball players to complete a questionnaire and found that this type of motivational climate was also associated with feelings of competence and a sense of improvement in performance among players. A previous study of tennis players had found that task orientation was related only to a perception that their psychological competence was improving, not their performance. This highlights the notion that the type of feedback given to an individual sportsperson needs to be different when they are a member of a team.

Smith et al. (1979) described a training programme for coaches which emphasizes several of the key skills that might help establish this kind of climate, especially for children and young people to enhance enjoyment and maintain participation levels. This includes

- rewarding good plays immediately but also rewarding effort as much as results
- offering encouragement not punishment after mistakes, and giving instruction about how to correct the mistake
- maintaining order with clear instructions
- establishing expectations and the coach's role as instructor.

It seems apparent that young players in particular are more likely to persist with sports if they are satisfied with their coach. In a study by Fraser–Thomas et al. (2008), semi-structured interviews were conducted with teenage swimmers who had dropped out of the sport and their content compared with that of swimmers who were still engaged in the sport. While both groups of swimmers reported a range of coaching styles and behaviours, two things distinguished the two groups. These were having more than one coach, and experiencing a reciprocal, democratic relationship with the coach. Both features were described only by the group who had not dropped out.

The reciprocal relationship involved the coach sharing the swimmers' experience of considering dropping out and deciding not to. Interview research has indicated that parents and peers also play an important role in maintaining motivation to participate and perform in sport. This can happen through social bonds and friendships that contribute to the development of identity in teenagers; at the same time, competitive relationships inside a team might be particularly motivating, particularly for those with an ego-orientation in the goals they set themselves.

Parents can push children into a sport and insist that they continue to participate long after intrinsic motivation has gone for the child. On the other hand, parents are also able to provide extremely informative and supportive feedback that will increase self-efficacy. It is clear that a coach is not solely responsible for an individual athlete's motivation and performance.

Parents can provide positive motivation but often make children lose interest in playing sport.

Although a lot of research focuses on teenage involvement in sport, research with adult athletes indicates that the same relationship with the coach is important. Jowett and Cockerill (2003) found that closeness (trust and respect), co-orientation (shared goals and beliefs) and complementarity (cooperation and possession of different, complementary skills) with their coaches were all important to successful Olympic swimmers.

While a supportive environment appears to be a contributing factor to success, there are also specific coaching behaviours that seem to be important. A study by Keegan et al. (2009) summarized coach behaviour and its effects by running focus groups with 40 children between the ages of 7 and 11. Positive aspects included equal treatment, one-to-one coaching with instruction, evaluation and positive feedback, competitive tasks at the end of training, and varied and fun activities. Fault-finding in evaluation was seen as confusing and demotivating, as was the use of summative labelling comments such as, 'You're not good at that'. More effective were behaviour-specific comments with instruction about how to improve.

A review of tennis coaching literature leads Reid et al. (2007) to suggest that there are two key areas modern coaching should focus on:
- providing intrinsic feedback
- constructing player-centred training schedules that are less prescriptive and more varied.

The feedback that is most effective for novice players appears to be direct and immediate and to consist of both a description and prescriptive advice for correction. As players develop, they need to internalize the feedback process and become independent of the coach so that decision-making in competition does not cause anxiety. This requires delays in feedback, possibly using video, thus training the player to assess their own performance and provide their own feedback, and requiring them to come up with their own ideas about how to improve.

Baker et al. (2000) indicate that one of the coach's key influences is on anxiety. Clearly, the provision of positive and instructive feedback will help reduce a player's doubts about their own performance, and this will be an important mediating influence according to all theories relating to arousal or motivation. An important danger, however is that the coach can be a negative influence, particularly where there is negative rapport between player and coach.

The difficulty with this type of research, apart from a focus on young amateurs, is that it relies on subjective impressions of the coach's role. It is therefore quite possible that a more favourable opinion of the coach's effectiveness develops as a result of success. It is relatively rare for a coach to lose his or her job during successful times, even if the exact nature and effect of their influence is not clear. An intriguing possibility that explains differences in perceptions of coaching influence is the **self-fulfilling prophecy** phenomenon. The Fraser–Thomas et al. (2008) study of swimmers who didn't dropout possibly demonstrates this. The self-fulfilling prophecy effect occurs when the coach's perceptions of the athlete affect the way the coach treats the athlete, this encourages particular behaviours from the athlete that are consistent with the coach's initial perceptions.

A self-fulfilling prophecy is when having an expectation about the future causes the expected outcome to occur when it might otherwise not have done.

Short and Short (2005) describe this in terms of **expectancy theory**. The coach develops expectations of the athletes, which might be based on physical appearance or ethnic

Can coaches really know if a sportsperson is going to be successful?

To access Worksheet 9.1 on coaches' predictions about future success of athletes, please visit www.pearsonbacconline.com and follow the on-screen instructions.

Latrell Sprewell of the New York Knicks holds the record for most 3-pointers made in a row in a game. He hit nine shots in 2003 against the Los Angeles Clippers.

origin or gender, as well as on performance-related information such as the athlete's last race time or behaviour in practice. These expectations affect the way the coach treats the athlete in terms of time spent together and the type and frequency of feedback. In turn, this treatment affects the way the athlete responds, such that athletes of whom the coach has low-expectancy perform poorly, and those of whom expectancy is high, perform well. Either way, the coach's expectations are confirmed.

A review of biases involved in assessing sports performance by Plessner and Haar (2006) suggests coaches may need to be aware of:

- perception issues such as distorted visual input
- categorization issues such as the influence of stereotypes and reputation bias
- memory distortions such as constructive memory illusions whereby post-event information (e.g. who won) affects the coach's memory of how the athlete performed.

Thus we cannot clearly say, for example, whether the apparently crucial role of coach feedback during one-to-one instruction is a causal factor that determines athlete success, or if the coach differentially provides feedback, giving more to those expected to succeed. We cannot be sure if the coach's expectations about who will succeed are valid, because we know that a number of biases affect them. Research may need to more clearly study the causal relationship between the coach's role and performance by comparing the effect of equal training on athletes that coaches have high and low expectations of.

EMPIRICAL RESEARCH

The hot hand in basketball

A coach needs to guide strategy in a sport like basketball. A common belief in this sport features the hot hand, meaning that a player who has just scored two or three shots in a row is more likely to hit the next one. Gilovich et al. (1985) followed the Philadelphia 76'ers in the National Basketball Association (NBA) for one season and found that the probability of success of any given shot was independent of previous success. Many people are resistant to giving up the hot hand belief, although the research indicated that we should.

However, Burns (2004) distinguishes between the hot hand belief and hot hand behaviour – for example, a coach's decision to give the next shot to a player on a streak. An in-depth analysis of the phenomenon leads Burns to conclude that even if the belief is a fallacy, the behaviour of letting a player on a streak take the next shot is adaptive in that it leads to a team scoring more points.

In fact, a streak is information that correlates well with total field goal percentage for the season, which is a truer indication of how likely a player is to hit any given shot. The better a player is, the greater the chance of him achieving a streak. Thus, a coach's decision to give the next shot to a player on a streak is likely to be successful, but not because they have a hot hand; rather because a player on a streak is more likely to be good at hitting shots.

So we come to the curious conclusion that the hot hand doesn't exist, but acting on it works.

EXERCISES

11 What effect might a coach's decision to rely on one player have on the team?

12 Gather together advice for coaches about what their role is, what kind of relationship to establish with athletes, and summarize evidence for coaches influencing individual and team behaviour. You could present this as a brochure titled *Good practice for coaches*.

9.8 Team cohesion

Learning outcomes
- Explain relationships between team cohesion and performance.
- Describe aids and barriers to team cohesion.

● **Examiner's hint**
To write an essay on this topic, you need to describe examples of what coaches do and consider how effective coaches are. Concentrate on what research has shown coaches should focus to motivate and build the coach–athlete relationship, and promote team cohesion (see below). Be critical of research and theory, perhaps focusing on the difficulty of isolating the effect of the coach, and the difficulties presented by the self-fulfilling prophecy phenomenon.

Relationship with performance

One of the leading researchers in team cohesion, Albert Carron, defined team cohesion as 'a dynamic process that is reflected in the tendency for a group to stick together and remain united in the pursuit of its instrumental objectives and/or for the satisfaction of member affective needs' (Carron et al., 1998). Thus, he divides cohesion into two types: task cohesion and social cohesion. Task cohesion is the degree of working together to achieve common goals, while social cohesion is the degree to which members enjoy each other's company and like the other members of the team.

Typical of those who promote team cohesion as a key to success is Sven Göran Eriksson, a well-known Swedish football coach and manager who has enjoyed success with several high-profile teams. His key suggestions are that team members must learn to put the team's needs before their own, think in terms of 'we' more than 'I' and that the team must have clearly defined and understood roles and goals (Eriksson et al., 2002). The relationship is not just anecdotal; it is supported by a large body of research.

There is a relationship between team cohesion and performance, such that the more cohesive the team, the better their performance. It is not an extremely strong relationship, and most of the research in the area is correlational. This means that we cannot be sure that cohesion is a cause of good performance – it may be that successful teams are more likely to be cohesive. Researchers often describe the relationship as circular.

 Cohesion is associated with good performance but we don't know which is the cause and which is the effect.

Perhaps one reason for researchers finding only a moderate link is that individual and group sports are often mixed together in research. Carron's research indicates that in sports where individuals perform separately, the relationship between cohesion and performance is twice as strong (Carron et al., 2002). This is perhaps a curious finding when one might expect group pressures to be stronger in teams. Carron's research also indicates that the relationship is stronger among female teams.

Experimental work is very difficult to carry out in this area as it is usually lacking in ecological validity. It is not realistic to assign participants randomly to a group and instruct them in a way that leads to high cohesiveness and expect to observe differences quickly. Most teams develop cohesiveness over time and through shared experience. For example, Grieve et al. (2000) conducted an experiment that involved assigning participants to receive just such treatment before playing basketball but found that performance had a greater impact on cohesion than the reverse.

One important way that this relationship might be explained is through a team norm for productivity (Patterson et al., 2005). Gammage et al. (2001), for example, found that members of groups with strong productivity norms were more likely to say that they would train in the off-season. According to this idea, if the norm (an expected standard of behaviour) is to work hard and strive for group success, each individual member of the team will experience pressure to conform. Those who do not conform are likely to experience an urge to leave the team, which perhaps provides an alternative explanation for the cohesion–performance relationship: in teams with high cohesion, there may be more dropouts by underperforming players.

Many sports are now professional at the highest level, meaning that players with special talents can make a job out of their sport. This helps with team cohesion often because there are no barriers to attending practice. However, it may be demotivating if sporting interest becomes work.

Other norms relating to team cohesion include sacrifice behaviour, such as giving up personal social life in favour of socializing with team members and attending practice, as indicated by a study of top level New Zealand cricketers (Prapavessis and Carron, 1997). It is quite understandable that unwillingness to conform to this norm would lead sportspeople to abandon their involvement with the team as it represents a commitment many people are not prepared to make. Thus, a team comprised of members who have made the sacrifice seems to have increased team cohesion and, at the same time, it appears likely that those willing to make the commitment are also stronger performers.

Norms are understandably stronger in interdependent team sports than in individual sports, which means researchers need to be very precise in their selection of participants and description of variables. It is also quite important to consider what an appropriate measure of performance should be.

EMPIRICAL RESEARCH

Team pressure to work hard (Patterson et al., 2005)

The researchers wanted to explore the mediating role of norms in the relationship between team cohesion and performance. They recruited 298 adult athletes from a wide variety of sports teams, including interactive team sports (like soccer) and co-active team sports (like wrestling). The participants were asked to complete a Team Norm Questionnaire to establish perceptions of team norms for practice, competition and social situations. They also completed the Group Environment Questionnaire to measure perceptions of task and social cohesiveness.

Norms for teams were measured by comparing the ratings of individuals from the teams. Performance was measured using the Perceived Exertion Scale, which is a self-report of effort expended during competitions. The hypothesis was that teams with stronger norms and high cohesion would expend greater effort, and that task-related norms would be particularly important in cohesive teams.

The results gave mixed support for the hypotheses. The greatest effort was expended by teams with strong norms for social interaction and high team social cohesion. However, the lowest effort came from teams with strong norms for social interaction and low team social cohesion. There was no relationship between task-related norms and team cohesion.

EXERCISE

13   Briefly evaluate this study, with a focus on reliability and validity, especially relating to their performance measure.

Aids and barriers

The coaching style already discussed in terms of its ability to create a positive motivational climate, seems to be supportive of team cohesion. Thus, clear roles and guidance from the

coach, the encouragement of autonomy, feedback, equal distribution of one-to-one time, and a democratic approach all aid team cohesion.

Carron and Spink (1993) consider group cohesion to be the output and identify aids to team cohesion as inputs and throughputs. Inputs include team structure, role clarity, team norms and the nature of the team environment (e.g. team identity based on representing a small city). Throughputs include team goals and team sacrifices, elements that can moderate the effect of the inputs on creating team cohesion.

One particular aspect of the democratic approach to coaching that has been applied successfully in a range of sports is the joint setting of team goals. Goal-setting was discussed on page 291, where we saw how successful it is as a strategy to motivate, provide feedback and improve self-efficacy.

This can be more difficult to achieve in team sports as often the only easily visible outcome of effort is whether the team wins or loses a match. Individual feedback is often difficult to provide as it is difficult to assess the contribution of individuals to team performance. A goalkeeper in football might have an inflated sense of self-efficacy if he is able to keep a clean sheet, but conversely might feel an inappropriate level of responsibility if the opposing team score several goals. For this reason, in a team context, it is important to set team goals – these often take the form of process goals rather than outcome goals.

An outline of how this intervention can be carried out is summarized in Table 9.1. Its success in research is demonstrated in the Empirical research box on goal-setting. As with individuals, the acceptance and achievement of a challenging team goal increases feelings of efficacy and improves motivation, especially when good feedback is available. However, in a team context, researchers refer to **collective efficacy**, a shared belief in the team's ability to complete the tasks required to achieve the ultimate outcome of winning matches.

TABLE 9.1 OVERVIEW OF A TEAM GOAL-SETTING PROGRAMME (ADAPTED FROM SENECAL, LOUGHEAD AND BLOOM, 2008)

Principle	Strategy
selecting team goals	• athletes are provided with a list of performance indices (e.g. turnovers, steals, blocked shots, free throw shooting percentage) • from the list, each athlete independently identifies the four most important performance indices to establish for team goals • groups of five athletes agree on the four performance indices that will become team goals • the team as a whole agrees on the four performance indices that will become team goals
establish target for team goals	• each athlete independently identifies target levels for each of the four team goals • groups of five athletes agree on target levels • the team as a whole agrees on target levels
coaches remind players of team goals	• goals are posted in the team's locker room
evaluation, feedback, and re-evaluation are essential for team goal-setting effectiveness	• sport psychology consultant meets with team to review and discuss team goals after each block of three games • modifications to team goals or target levels are made if necessary

EMPIRICAL RESEARCH

Goal-setting as a means to team cohesion (Senecal et al., 2008)

A rare longitudinal, experimental intervention was used by these researchers to test the effectiveness of goal-setting as a means of team-building.

The researchers studied 86 female high-school basketball players aged between 14 and 18 from eight different teams for 5 months. Half of the teams were given a goal-setting intervention through the whole season, and the other four teams were used as a control with no psychological intervention at all.

continued

All goals on offer were process goals, and were specific and measurable (e.g. number of rebounds or turnovers) and were chosen according to the procedure outlined in Table 9.1.

Dependent variables in the study were group cohesion, measured by the Group Environment Questionnaire (GEQ) at the beginning and end of the season, and team performance, represented by the winning percentage at the end of the season.

The results showed that athletes were similar in their ratings of team cohesion at the beginning of the season (all quite high on cohesion), but the experimental group who had participated in goal-setting subsequently gave higher ratings of team cohesion than the control groups. However, contrary to expectations, this was not due to an increase in team cohesion among goal-setters, but rather a drop in team cohesion among the other teams. This suggests that goal-setting does more to maintain than to increase cohesion when cohesion is already high.

EXERCISE
14   Explain what modifications you would make to this study to address some of its limitations.

Attempts to build cohesion do not always work and often backfire, fragmenting a team.

Unfortunately, attempts to create team cohesion are not always easy or successful. A number of barriers to team cohesion are identified in Weinberg and Gould (2003):

- clash of personalities in the group
- conflict of task or social roles among members of the group
- breakdown in communication among group members or between the group leader and members
- one or more members struggling for power
- frequent turnover of group members
- disagreement on group goals and objectives.

While the experience of a personality clash is quite common and perhaps inevitable, especially as teams get larger, there is relatively little a coach can do to manage it once it has happened. Similarly, the other barriers identified above are hard to respond to, but they can be prevented, and the role of coaches and captains is very important in preventing these situations occurring.

Communication skills are probably the most vital ingredient here as difficulties with communication can lead to all of the other problems, and good communication skills can prevent them. A clear understanding of roles and an empathic understanding of the other people on the team are likely to prevent disagreement, and where there is disagreement, to prevent it becoming a problem. The democratic goal-setting process is a useful way to prevent struggles for power and disagreement on goals through encouraging the perception that everyone has participated. If a team member feels consistently ignored, it is likely that this is because he or she is somehow incompatible with the group or does not feel comfortable subscribing to group norms.

Interestingly, Spink et al. (2010) found that perceptions of team cohesion at the end of the season could predict the return of players after the off-season. In particular, those who felt there was low task cohesion were less likely to return to the team. This suggests that team cohesion involves another self-fulfilling prophecy. Those who do not believe the team is cohesive are more inclined to leave the team, which should result in a team with higher average perceptions of cohesion.

EXERCISE
15   Make a list of aids to cohesion and a list of barriers to cohesion
16   Review this section and construct a table that shows different ways to improve cohesion and indicate whether this has been shown to have an impact on performance.

9.9 Problems in sport

Learning outcomes
- Examine reasons for using drugs in sport.
- Discuss effects of drug use in sport.
- Discuss athlete response to stress and chronic injury.
- Compare models of causes and prevention of burnout.

Another role of psychologists working with athletes is to deal with a range of problems that come up during their careers. Three of the most dramatically damaging to an athlete's career are:

- problems with drugs (whether legal or illegal)
- stress and injury
- burnout.

Drugs in sport
Reasons for using drugs in sport

Many athletes and coaches seek to gain an advantage in their sports through performance-enhancing drugs. The use of drugs that enhance performance is called **doping**, probably in reference to dop, a stimulant drink used in South African ceremonies in the 18th century. The term was first used with reference to racehorses, and it appears that the practice is widespread whether the performer is horse, greyhound, sprinter or weightlifter.

A brief history of the use of drugs to enhance performance was reported by Sjöqvist et al. (2008) and this suggests that drug use has always accompanied sport. Ancient Olympic athletes, for example, used bread soaked in opium, mushrooms and strychnine. Anabolic steroids became popular in the 1950s, with their ability to enhance muscle growth and

Ben Johnson, winning the gold medal for the 100 metre sprint in 1988.

increase a user's power and speed. In 1959, studies demonstrated that amphetamines could improve performance in swimming and running. In 1960, amphetamines were found in the blood of a Danish cyclist who died at the Olympics. The use of both amphetamine and steroids increased during the 1960s and 1970s in a range of sports, despite the introduction of regulations against the use of drugs and new testing practices.

The majority of major sporting bodies have now banned performance-enhancing drugs, but there is an industry producing such drugs and helping coaches and athletes not to get caught. The International Olympic Committee, for example, began testing for banned drugs at the 1968 Olympics, and yet several high-profile cases have been reported in the media since then. Perhaps the most famous disgraced athlete is Ben Johnson, who won a gold medal in the 1988 Olympics but was later stripped of his medal.

According to the World Anti-doping Agency, approximately 1% of athletes tested are found positive for a banned substance. However, Striegel et al. (2010) suggest that the actual prevalence of use among elite athletes is more like 7% and use is probably much higher in some sports and for some substances. Use of amphetamines, for example, is more common in cycling, and use of steroids is more popular among bodybuilders and weightlifters. A 1995 US survey of elite athletes asked them if they would use a banned substance in two different scenarios:

- You will not be caught and you will win.
- You will win every competition you enter for the next 5 years but will then die from the side-effects.

Of the almost 200 respondents, 98% answered yes to the first question, and 52% to the second.

> Athletes, in general, are more concerned about health risks than moral reasons not to use drugs.

Many people consider that taking performance-enhancing substances is wrong, especially if they are banned, and it is tempting to blame the individual athlete for taking the drug. But there are a wide range of reasons why drugs are taken, apart from the simplistic notion of trying to improve performance. In the past, before substances were made illegal, performance-enhancement was not seen as quite so wrong, but nowadays there is a great deal of information about the dangers and unfairness of drug use. That alone makes it worthwhile to consider why individual athletes and coaches engage in such risky behaviour.

Ehrnborg and Rosen (2009) report that the primary motive is to maintain and improve physical performance, but that other reasons include coping with social and psychological pressures and striving to meet social and psychological goals. The pressure to perform at higher levels in sport probably accounts for differences in substance use between elite and amateur athletes. Verroken (2000) suggests that speculation about how widespread drug use is may be making it harder for young athletes to resist, even though a majority of athletes, coaches and doctors report believing that substance misuse is unacceptable. Coaches and fellow athletes can easily convince that 'everyone is doing it'. A study in Turkey by Özdemir et al. (2005) found that 79% of athletes believe their competitors are doping, while 14.5% of them admitted that they themselves were doping.

In addition, as there are financial gains to be made in sport, money becomes another motivator. Verroken (2000) summarizes the kind of relevant pressures athletes face as follows:

- pressure to win
- attitude that doping is necessary to succeed
- public expectations about national success
- financial rewards of winning
- desire to be the best in the world
- grants and fees to athletes from governments and sponsors, linked to performance
- coaching that focuses on winning as the only goal
- psychological belief that performance is assisted by a 'magic pill'
- expectations of the spectators, friends and family.

Another explanation is offered by the doping dilemma. This is a special form of the famous prisoners' dilemma – the model shows that the decision to take drugs is rational, because the athlete considers it likely that his competitors are taking drugs and therefore would perform at a different level. In order to be competitive and gain the maximum possible benefits, it is usually worth breaking the rules with a small chance of getting caught – after all if everyone breaks the rules, how can one person be morally chastised?

> How can we be sure that doping is wrong? If everyone had equal access to drugs, would it be fair to allow them in sport?

However, this must be balanced with an awareness of health risks (see below), the potential loss of honour, being banned from competition, and acquiring a negative reputation.

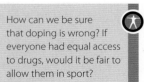

Ehrnborg and Rosen (2009) offer five reasons not to use performance-enhancing drugs:
- doping is cheating – it is not fair play
- doping has medical risks
- doping has brought lawyers into the sporting world – athletes may need legal help to prove innocence (even possession of doping agents is illegal in many countries)
- scientific studies in sport comparing different training methods will be invalidated if some athletes use doping agents during the study period
- doping destroys the image of sport.

Perhaps more education is needed for young people and coaches about all five of these areas if doping is to ever be controlled. Bloodworth and McNamee (2010) surveyed young British athletes and found that their attitudes reflect the values of recent anti-doping campaigns, with shame being the major motivator to not take performance-enhancing drugs. Their research also exposed some xenophobia about doping practices among athletes from other countries. Two examples of widespread doping have received a lot of attention in the media: East German athletes in the 1970s and 80s, and Chinese swimmers in the 1990s. Although evidence for the former is far more clear-cut, it seems likely that athletes have been instructed to take drugs in the form of steroids and growth hormones. This highlights an important problem in the literature relating to decision-making in terms of drug use in sport: sometimes it is not the athlete's decision; it may be a considered normal (even sometimes compulsory) in some social, cultural or national groups.

To learn more about proposals to transform cycling and eliminate doping, go to www.pearsonhotlinks.com, enter the title or ISBN of this book and select weblink 9.4.

● **Examiner's hint**
The learning outcome relevant to this section requires you to examine the reasons for drug use in sport. This means you need to address underlying assumptions of the reasons. When completing the exercise above, be aware of whether people think doping is right or wrong, and whether taking drugs is a rational, individual choice or if there are other influences.

EXERCISE
17 There are several reasons outlined above for athletes to use drugs in sport. What assumptions are made by each explanation?

Effects of drug use in sports

Stimulants, such as amphetamines and cocaine, are taken to increase alertness and competitiveness. They are often used in endurance events and explosive power activities, in particular to help athletes get through the 'pain barrier' that occurs in sports like cycling and marathon running and leads to many athletes giving up during competition. These drugs also tend to improve self-confidence, perhaps a short-cut to temporarily enhanced self-efficacy. Long-term use can lead athletes to develop a tremor and contributes to fatal heart damage. High doses can produce aggressive behaviour and psychosis.

Beta-blockers are sometimes used as hypertension medication because of their calming effect on the nervous system. In sport, they have the opposite effect to stimulants, calming an athlete down and helping improve their ability to control fine muscle movements. This makes these drugs useful in shooting and archery, for example. Possible problems with using these drugs include low blood pressure, light-headedness, and even depression in some instances.

Narcotics, including morphine and heroin, are used to help an athlete cope with pain. However, they carry an increased danger of injury as an athlete might be able to 'play through the pain' and exacerbate an existing injury or not notice the occurrence of a new injury.

Many young athletes begin using drugs because of peer pressure or encouragement from coaches. It is possible to develop addictions to some of these drugs and it can be very difficult for an athlete to contemplate stopping their drug use.

Anabolic agents include anabolic steroids and beta-2-agonists. These increase muscle size and strength. These drugs are popular in the form of water-soluble tablets which last for a shorter period of time in the body (so the athlete reduces their chances of getting caught) but are more dangerous in that the drug can contribute to liver disease. These substances are generally extremely popular among athletes, despite significant hormone-related side-

effects. Steroids are synthesized derivatives of the male hormone, testosterone. Men who take steroids may develop acne and/or breasts, their testicles may shrink, and there can be a reduction in sperm count; adolescent males may find their growth inhibited. Women tend to become masculinized, with a reduction in breast size, growth of facial hair and an irreversibly deepened voice. In all users, there is the possibility of liver and kidney cancer, interaction effects with other drugs and legal supplements, the possibility of stroke from high doses, and a likely weight gain from water retention.

Heidi Krieger as a shot-put athlete and her new identity – Andreas Krieger.

A dramatic example of the possible effects of steroid use is the case of Heidi Krieger, who won a gold medal for East Germany in the shot put in 1986. Her long-term steroid use as part of a training programme is said to have contributed to gender identity issues that ultimately resulted in her deciding to undergo a sex change. She is now called Andreas Krieger.

Peptide hormones include growth hormone (GH) and erythropoietin (EPO). GH is used particularly by younger athletes to increase size and strength, and EPO is used to maximize the oxygen capacity of blood, which is thought to improve endurance. Long-term use of EPO can lead to heart problems, blood clots, and stroke.

Diuretics are substances that encourage the excretion of urine. Common diuretics include tea and coffee, but other substances are used to help sportsmen to lose weight rapidly, to eliminate other drugs from their system faster, and to cope with the water-retention effects of steroids. Side-effects of this class of substance include dehydration, muscle cramps, nausea, headaches, and in the long-term, damage to the heart and kidney.

Athletes are less willing to take drugs if they think they will die younger because of them.

It is clear that there are significant dangers associated with drug use, even if, in the short-term, there might be the possibility of substantially improved performance. A great many amateur and professional athletes are taking performance-enhancing drugs. However, results from Bloodworth and McNamee's (2010) focus groups with young British athletes indicate that willingness to take banned substances dramatically drops when it is made clear that doping will result in a reduction in life expectancy of 10 years. Given that sportspeople often have a strong interest in their own health and well-being, an awareness of the potential dangers seems likely to be a powerful disincentive, certainly more powerful than either the shame or unfairness associated with doping.

Athlete response to stress and chronic injury

There are many high-profile examples of sportspeople who have been injured at the top of their game and never managed to return to form, as well as triumphant examples of athletes who suffered an injury and have returned to form. Of course, the threat and consequences of injury can be devastating whether an athlete is a top-level professional or for a young sportsperson for whom sports provide a framework for development and a sense of identity.

Similarly, stress affects athletes at all levels of performance. Although the type of stress can vary across sports and levels, support for sportspeople in dealing with stress is needed in many contexts. There are several psychological theories and models that explain different responses to stress and provide guidelines for managing it.

Stress in sport appears to be experienced in a similar way to the way it is experienced outside sport. Thatcher and Day (2008) confirm this using content analysis of semi-structured interviews with trampolinists to test whether eight factors contribute to sport as Lazarus and Folkman (1984) suggest they do in general. They confirmed the eight factors and found another two sport-specific factors:

- novelty (e.g. when an athlete enters a bigger competition than before)
- predictability (e.g. when a competition goes in an unexpected direction)
- event uncertainty (e.g. feelings about the likelihood of falling off a trampoline which may be encouraged by recent experiences of falling)
- imminence (e.g. the feeling of tension that grows as a competition approaches and doubts creep in)
- duration, particularly in terms of waiting time, which increases tension
- temporal uncertainty (e.g. competitions starting late or timings being changed) which interferes with pre-competitive preparation rituals and warm-ups
- ambiguity (e.g. lack of clarity about what judges want)
- timing in relation to the life cycle (e.g. when an athlete fears injury more because of events outside the sporting world, or pressures based on age and opportunities running out)
- self and other comparison (e.g. noting that a competitor is doing very well)
- inadequate preparation, in terms of sleep, food, training and warm-ups.

Although these factors all seem quite reasonably to increase stress, it is clear that not all athletes exposed to what *should* be stressful actually feel stressed or let it affect their performance. Studies into the concept of **mental toughness** suggest that it is a personality characteristic that can be used to explain response to both stress and injury. Kaiseler et al. (2009) found that although the stressors athletes consider important do not vary a great deal, the response to them does. Mental toughness, as measured by the Mental Toughness Questionnaire, seems to be associated with less stress intensity and more coping. Thus, when faced with the same problem, some athletes have a way to minimize its influence on them. This mental toughness manifests itself in characteristics like the ability to perceive challenges as opportunities rather than threats, and seems to share many characteristics with self-efficacy.

 Mental toughness can prevent athletes feeling stress.

Interestingly, the researchers found that different coping strategies are used by those with mental toughness; a tendency towards denial seemed to be a favourable coping strategy, while humour and self-blame were not. Ntoumanis and Biddle (1998) asked British athletes from universities to complete a questionnaire about coping strategies and found that the strategies themselves are not directly linked with outcome. For example, a number of athletes used disengagement as a coping strategy; those for whom it was a successful strategy experienced positive emotions and increased self-efficacy, while those who experienced negative emotions tended to conceptualize their disengagement as 'giving up'.

This raises an important issue in interpreting the role of stress for athletes. Most of the data is retrospective, obtained after the event, often by asking participants to recall stressful events. Stress is generally a term we reserve for negative experiences, and it seems likely that participants will show a bias towards remembering events that were associated with failure. Thus, when research shows a strong relationship between the experience of stress and poor performance or injury, we need to be very careful about interpreting the relationships as causal.

Cyclists face the threat of injury every time they race.

However, a vein of research into influences on motor behaviour found that anxiety levels affect visual processing and motor precision. For example, karate novices were more likely to be distracted by peripheral visual stimuli under a high-anxiety condition than experts (Williams and Elliott, 1999). Similarly, visual search patterns among drivers in an auto-racing simulation were found to be negatively influenced by anxiety. Bear in mind as well the research into the yips (page 294) where high anxiety, particularly among novices, resulted in loss of motor control. In some sports (e.g. shooting and golf) loss of visual and motor coordination might lead only to momentary failure, but the consequences of such distraction are more dramatic in sports where the body is moving at speed or faces obstacles. Ice skaters, rugby players, basketballers and cyclists all seem to face increased threat of injury due to loss of concentration, or over-aggressive behaviour resulting in injury. Although the number of people playing each sport in any given country varies, it is interesting to note that in the US in 1996, the National Electronic Injury Surveillance System documented over 500 000 injuries for basketball – only cycling and American football came close to this number (Table 9.2).

TABLE 9.2 TYPES OF INJURY AND THEIR FREQUENCY

Estimated injuries	Sport	Type of injury
529 837	basketball	cut hands, sprained ankles, broken legs, eye and forehead injuries
490 434	bicycling	feet caught in spokes, head injuries from falls, slipping while carrying bicycles, collisions with cars
460 210	American football	fractured wrists, chipped teeth, neck strains, head lacerations, dislocated hips and jammed fingers
275 123	ATVs mopeds minibikes	fractured wrists, dislocated hands, shoulder sprains, head cuts and lumbar strains, riders of ATVs frequently injured when thrown from vehicles
274 867	baseball softball	head injuries from bats and balls, ankle injuries from running bases or sliding into them
269 249	exercise exercise equipment	twisted ankles and cut chins from tripping on treadmills, head injuries from falling backward from exercise balls, ankle sprains from jumping rope (skipping)
186 544	soccer	twisted ankles or knees after falls, fractured arms during games
164 607	swimming	head injuries from hitting bottom of pools, leg injuries from falling into pools
96 119	skiing snowboarding	head injuries from falling, cut legs and faces, sprained knees or shoulders
85 580	lacrosse rugby ball games	head and facial cuts from getting hit by balls and sticks, injured ankles from falls

From scientificpsychic.com

While it is difficult to interpret the meaning of these statistics without the number of participants in each sport, it is clear that lapses in concentration and inadequate use of protective equipment are two major contributing factors to sports injuries. An interesting point is that, according to the statistics, the most dangerous sport for females in the US is cheerleading – it accounts for 70.5% of all catastrophic injuries for college-level female athletes and 62.5% of high school female catastrophic injuries.

Thus, sports injury is clearly a genuine threat for many sportspeople, but some deal with it and return to form, while others cannot. While some researchers have focused on the role of stress in causing injury, others focus on the role of injury in causing stress.

Grief–reaction–response model

In 1969, Elizabeth Kübler–Ross published a model outlining the stages through which a person goes as they cope with the news that they are going to die of a terminal illness. This has been widely applied in different fields of psychology, for example in coping with unemployment. Although the majority of sports injuries do not require that the athlete accepts the inevitability of dying, an injury, particularly a career-threatening one, has an enormous significance. Kübler–Ross's stages, as applied to a sports context, are as follows (Harris, 2003).

Many athletes are devastated when they suffer a serious injury as it may completely change their life.

1 Denial, for example when an athlete continues to play or returns to the sport early.

2 Anger, when the athlete realizes the significance of the injury, which could be a loss of identity, a loss of money, or the loss of an entire career.

3 Bargaining, which involves trying to find a way out of the situation the athlete finds themselves in.

4 Depression, which occurs as rehabilitation takes longer than expected, progress is slower than hoped for, or setbacks occur.

5 Acceptance and reorganization, which occurs if the athlete is mature enough and has strong social support.

Some have conceptualized this as a three-stage process, joining denial and anger together as a protest phase, followed by an acceptance phase and then a reorganization phase (e.g. Dawes and Roach, 1997). There is relatively little empirical support for the grief–response model, and it is clearly not possible to plan experimental work about phases of the injury process for ethical reasons. So researchers rely on qualitative methods to expose the lived experience of rehabilitation following injury.

EMPIRICAL RESEARCH

Experiences of athletes undergoing treatment for injury (Dawes and Roach, 1997)

In order to assess the emotional response of athletes to sporting injury and rehabilitation, these researchers used questionnaires to gather information about the emotions experienced by athletes undergoing rehabilitation. They noted that for ethical reasons it was not possible to establish a control group for comparison, as it would be strange to withhold treatment from athletes who needed it.

They used the Psychological Factors Affecting Sporting Injury (PFASI) questionnaire and an adapted Emotional Response of Athletes to Injury Questionnaire (ERAIQ) before and during physiotherapy for sports injuries. Using the questionnaires at five clinics, they were able to recruit 52 participants, including only 10 females, from a range of sporting activities.

Their results indicate that in general, negative emotions subside once treatment begins and positive emotions increase, but that the reverse occurs temporarily between the second and third treatments. Frustration and inconvenience are the major negative emotions

continued

experienced, and anger appears to vary more, probably in relation to how well rehabilitation is going. Excitement is the key rising positive emotion, and clearly leaves room for significant disappointment if athletes' optimism is not rewarded with good progress.

Beyond this, the researchers suggest that emotional responses vary a great deal between individuals, rather dismissing the idea that a stage theory such as grief–response can account for the process. Their major recommendation is that physiotherapists make an effort to discuss the athlete's emotional responses and help them stay realistic about the likely rate of recovery. Progress, for example, tends to slow as time goes on and athletes report rising rates of boredom that could threaten persistence with treatment. In addition, they note that athletes rate their injuries as more severe than the physiotherapists do, and this may be a useful target for psychological treatment near the beginning of their rehabilitation.

The study above indicates that a number of individual factors appear to be important in determining the nature of an athlete's psychological response to injury. This is a typical finding of research investigating grief models.

There are three main criticisms of the usefulness of this model in a sports context. The first is concerned with the validity of transferring the model from the study of emotional response to terminal illness to sports injury. The second is that there is considerable variation among athletes in type and seriousness of injury. The third is that although anecdotally the transfer of the model to sports appears to work nicely, empirical data are needed to be certain. None of the empirical data obtained, however, provide support for the prescriptive stage-by-stage process. Wortman and Silver (1989) found no evidence in a review of the literature, and specific studies of skiers by Udry et al. (1997) showed that while the stages *can* be used to describe the emotions of athletes recovering from injury, they do not always apply. Denial, for example, does not seem to apply to the majority of injured athletes.

Thus many researchers have turned to cognitive models to account for the experiences of athletes in rehabilitation.

Cognitive appraisal models of response to injury

Cognitive appraisal models take an information-processing approach to explaining the athlete's reaction to injury. A distinction can be made between primary appraisal and secondary appraisal. Primary appraisal consists of judgements about the threat (in this case probably relating to the severity of the injury). Secondary appraisal is the athlete's judgements about their ability to cope with the threat.

Wiese–Bjornstal and Smith (1993) and Wiese–Bjornstal et al. (1998) provided an explanation of the role of appraisals in the recovery process that addresses how appraisals affect behaviours like adherence to rehabilitation, and emotional responses including depression. Incorporating some of these ideas, a model of cognitive appraisal adapted for sports from Lazarus and Folkman (1984) by Udry et al. (1997) suggest that the response to injury occurs in five steps.

1 An injury occurs. It is important whether this is the first major injury an athlete has suffered, or is one of many. The degree of severity is also important.

2 Cognitive appraisal occurs. This involves the athlete's perceptions of how severe the injury is, which may bear no relation to the actual severity, and the perceived controllability of the situation. This appraisal will then affect the athlete's emotional response.

3 The emotional response occurs. For some athletes, it may be the grief response outlined above, but for others it may be far less significant.

4 The coping response occurs. In general, this involves changing the cause of the stress or changing the response to stress. For most athletes, it is not easy to alter the injury, except to work hard on correcting it, so the way they respond must be changed.

5 Adherence to the behavioural response. In effect, this means adherence to the treatment and rehabilitation programme. Setbacks can occur during this time and the athlete returns to the cognitive appraisal stage, so that their response to setbacks is mediated by their appraisal of the setback.

At two points in the model, social support is particularly necessary. At step 2, a person needs accurate information about their injury and needs to be encouraged to believe that the injury is no more serious than it really is. At step 4, they need support to find an appropriate response to their emotional state.

Vergeer (2006) carried out a case study of a 28-year-old rugby player who had dislocated his shoulder and been told that there was a 70% chance that he might never play rugby again. She used eight semi-structured interviews over 20 weeks to gather information about the way he was dealing with his injury psychologically, with a follow-up interview 3 years later. As regards his cognitive processing of the injury, it emerged that there were two sources of input: contact with medical personnel and his own bodily experiences, particularly pain and making errors of judgement about how much he could use his arm. For the first 5 or 6 weeks of rehabilitation, he was focused on establishing the extent of the damage and what effect this might have on his career. For example, he was told during this time that there might be nerve damage, which scared him, but consultation with another expert calmed him. After this period, he began to focus on progress, mostly in terms of a reduction in pain. Vergeer's interpretation of this case study emphasizes the importance of appraisals in determining emotional and behavioural responses. Positive emotions tended to come at times when progress was apparent, and negative emotions were stronger when he was fearful for his future, early on in his rehabilitation. She infers strong self-efficacy from his reports, particularly since a period of almost no progress during university examinations was not accompanied by negative emotions. He seemed to believe that the power to make progress rested in him, and as soon as he made the effort, he would see himself progressing again.

The more physical contact and threat of injury there is in a sport, the more important it is that the sportsperson is confident that their body is ready to return to action, as fear can prevent good performance.

The causes of burnout

Athletic burnout is often considered to be similar to the kind of burnout that occurs in other areas of life, such as work and study. Under the various pressures of involvement in an activity, individuals appear to lose energy, motivation and interest, and performance declines. In many cases, an athlete withdraws from the sport. Athletic burnout is described as an experience involving:

- emotional and physical exhaustion
- reduced accomplishment
- sport devaluation.

These factors describe the subjective experience of athletes. It is the athlete's feelings of tiredness, their perceived lack of achievement, and a decrease in the perceived benefits they get from their sport that are important in determining whether or not they suffer from burnout or are at risk of burnout.

Cresswell and Eklund (2006) suggest that burnout is a dynamic process and demonstrated this by asking rugby players to complete the Athlete Burnout Questionnaire (ABQ) several times during the season. This questionnaire is designed to measure the three key elements outlined above. They found that the components of burnout did change in intensity

To access Worksheet 9.2 on burnout, please visit www.pearsonbacconline.com and follow the on-screen instructions.

What is burnout? Does it really exist?

over the season, and perhaps more importantly, that rugby players in different positions experienced the components at a different rate. Forwards in rugby reached risky levels of physical exhaustion faster than backs, for example, and therefore are more likely to reach burnout faster. Although this provides an adequate description of what happens when an athlete is burning out, it does not explain what causes these perceptions and why some players are able to continue while others give up.

EXERCISE
18 Experiments tend not to feature in this area of sport psychology. Why might this be?

Cognitive–affective stress model

Smith (1986) conceptualizes the causes of burnout in terms of the interaction between situational and environmental demands and cognitive processes. He employs the cognitive processes of primary and secondary appraisal to explain the individual differences in response to the demands of sport. So, an athlete's primary appraisal of the intensity of demands combined with their secondary appraisal (the perception that they have the resources to cope) will determine whether they reach burnout or not. A cost–benefit analysis occurs, often resulting in the athlete leaving their sport as the costs have become too high. Rugby players, for example, might feel that the training programme is taking up a lot of time, and that this is more than they can cope with. If they are not professional players, they might feel that they do not have enough money and therefore cannot afford to be missing work to meet the demands of the team coach. Or they might find that travelling to away games is causing strain on relationships at home. Secondary appraisals will be made on the basis of an individual's understanding of financial stability and sporting ability, and also on knowledge of their social support networks.

Cresswell and Eklund (2004) found that perception of financial or sporting hassles was associated with the key characteristics of burnout outlined above. However, their research typically used questionnaires and took a cross-sectional approach that prevents any inference about the hassles causing burnout. Instead, it could be the case that athletes who are in a state of burnout are more likely to perceive their life as unreasonably challenging and their support as inadequate. Cresswell (2009) used a mid-season questionnaire to try to detect early signs of burnout and the results do indicate that the relationship is likely to be causal, a useful finding that allows coaches and managers to actively intervene to help prevent burnout.

We have still not identified, however, why some athletes' primary appraisal of hassles and secondary appraisal of coping resources are different from others. The concept of mental toughness was introduced on page 311. It appears that mental toughness is a personality characteristic of athletes that can, at high levels, prevent an athlete from making a catastrophic secondary appraisal – so that when faced with physical exhaustion, the athlete perceives it as an obstacle that can be overcome, possibly leading to more effort. It is difficult to say, however, whether mental toughness is really a cause of the difference between athletes because it is usually measured using questionnaires and correlated with the components of stress and burnout. Perhaps instead, 'mentally tough' is a way to describe athletes who regularly make favourable appraisals to survive impending burnout. If so, it would not be a personality trait, but a label given to those who successfully overcome physical and emotional stress.

Burnout in Swedish athletes (Gustafsson et al., 2008)

The researchers in this study used semi-structured interviews and inductive content analysis to identify the antecedents of burnout in elite athletes. A Swedish version of the ABQ was used to verify that the athletes had experienced burnout and 10 of the 12 highest scorers were interviewed. Because previous research had shown that burnout is a sensitive topic and athletes are often uncomfortable about possibly being seen as mentally weak, the researchers were careful to spend time building rapport and carried out the interview in a place of the athlete's choosing. The word 'burnout' was not mentioned.

Some of their findings are consistent with the cognitive–affective model. They show that some perceptions more commonly precede burnout than others; examples include:

- perceived lack of accomplishment
- exhaustion
- devaluation of sport participation
- an increasing lack of motivation
- having mainly ego-oriented goals
- avoidance strategies used as coping mechanisms
- feelings of depression and irritation.

Major contributing factors to burnout were identified as:

- lack of social support
- low autonomy in training
- too much training compared with the other aspects of life
- feeling overwhelmed by the expectations of others
- a sense of identity revolving only around sport
- a feeling of being trapped in sport
- a perfectionist personality.

From this, it appears clear that there is a significant role for appraisal and perception in the development of burnout. However, the research also suggests that motivation for involvement and personality play an important role.

Negative training stress model

This model comes from Silva (1990). It focuses more on physical factors involved in burnout than the thought processes. According to this model, athletes reaching increasingly higher levels in sport face increasing training loads. Athletes must adapt to these demands, and can do so positively or negatively. Thus, there is a risk involved of coaches, parents, or even athletes themselves creating too much of a coaching burden. This is because although positive adaptation is associated with better performance, negative adaptation results in burnout and can account for many young athletes giving up their sport. When training demands stretch beyond an individual's capabilities, the athlete begins a journey along a continuum of outcomes starting with staleness (the first failure of the body to cope with the stress of training) through overtraining (which occurs when the athlete attempts to train and perform while experiencing staleness) and ending in burnout (a physical state as well as a mental one). Silva's research has described athlete burnout symptoms as including loss of sleep, libido and appetite, and biochemical indicators of stress.

 The negative training stress model emphasises the risk of overtraining.

A study by another Silva, of Brazilian football players in training, gave clear indications of changes in blood composition as a result of training and associated this with a decline in performance (Silva et al., 2008). Lemyre et al. (2007) used questionnaires with a group of winter athletes at the beginning and end of the season and found that overtraining was indeed linked to burnout, independently of other factors measured in the study. However,

it is difficult to identify that overtraining has occurred using a questionnaire since it is theorized to be a step on a continuum that is both psychological and physiological. There is little research that has attempted to establish cause–effect relationships between the physical side of overtraining and the psycho-physiological phenomenon of burnout.

This model clearly emphasizes the role of physical overstretching, and does not see the psychological component of burnout as a cause in the same way that the cognitive–affective model does. It is a very individual approach to explaining the phenomenon of burnout, and fails to account for social and cultural factors that may contribute to burnout.

EXERCISE
19   What are the main similarities between the cognitive–affective stress model and the negative training stress model?

The commitment model

Raedeke (1997) attempted to create an explanation for burnout that accommodates the fact that stress does not lead to burnout for all athletes. Researchers included the concept of commitment as a contributing factor to burnout. Commitment can be seen as 'the desire and resolve to continue sports participation', and has three components:

- the attractiveness of the activity in question
- the attractiveness of alternative activities
- restrictions that mean the athlete cannot leave the sport.

As the study by Gustaffson et al. (2008) indicates, athletes who feel that their involvement in the sport continues because of barriers to leaving (e.g. parental expectations, a scholarship, a feeling of having invested a lot already) feel a sense of entrapment (page 317). Athletes who perceive that their involvement is because of the enjoyment they get from the activity compared to alternatives are less likely to burn out. Several cross-sectional studies have found positive correlations between burnout scores and sport entrapment. Raedeke (2004) applied this concept to understanding burnout in coaches, finding that coaches who experienced increased feelings of entrapment over the course of a year were more likely to experience increased exhaustion. The longitudinal nature of this research lends more support to the idea that entrapment is a possible cause of burnout.

Preventing burnout

Cognitive–affective stress management

This approach to preventing burnout focuses on teaching athletes how to better deal with the inevitable stress of sport. It focuses on identifying damaging cognitions, particularly in terms of reconstructing appraisals so they are less catastrophic.

Smith (1980) suggests that athletes should undergo pretreatment assessment to establish what situational and individual factors precede stress and what physiological and psychological symptoms of stress occur. Athletes are then instructed about the specific nature of their individual response to stress and are informed of the plan for their stress management training, with the requirement that they agree to participate fully in the programme. This phase is referred to as treatment rationale. In a final skill acquisition phase, the athlete undergoes training in physical relaxation, usually breathing exercises and muscle relaxation. This is carried out in conjunction with cognitive restructuring, whereby the athlete learns to ignore or change negative self-statements so they are more constructive; for example, 'The game's not over; remember the game plan and keep trying'. The final phase is skill rehearsal, requiring the athlete to imagine or recall stressful situations or watch films in order to enter a physiologically stressed state.

Stress management training may be beneficial for all athletes.

Other methods

There are clear implications for the prevention of burnout based on the negative training stress model and the commitment model. While instruction about dealing with stress is necessary, whether through cognitive–affective stress management or through hypnosis or stress inoculation training, there are other important ways to prevent burnout.

Athletes should be monitored carefully to detect the psychological signs of staleness before they reach the stage of overtraining. They may need to be given breaks from their training schedule and coaches should try to keep training varied so that fitness can be maintained without overworking specific muscle groups. Training diaries can assist with this, and can be used in conjunction with diet and rest advice.

The commitment model offers coaches and psychologists several ways to intervene. Again, it is necessary to pay attention to an athlete's emotional and physical status, and to provide relaxation training, but it is more important to identify individuals at risk by developing an understanding of their perceived reasons for being involved in the sport. A cognitive restructuring approach may be necessary for those who are already feeling a sense of entrapment. For others, intervention at earlier stages can focus on ensuring that sportspeople, particularly the younger ones, maintain a balanced lifestyle including activities other than sport. Parental and coaching pressures should not overwhelm the individual's intrinsic motivation for being involved and the athlete's sense of identity should not develop too narrowly (Raedeke et al., 2002).

Coaches and parents may not notice when an athlete begins to develop a sense of devaluation or a feeling that no progress is being made. They may not realize that if they continue to push, this will lead to the feelings of entrapment that frequently precede burnout. Raedeke et al. (2002) also suggest that building strong social support networks can both support an athlete who is feeling stressed and prevent an athlete from reaching a burnout stage.

Can we know whether an athlete will suffer burnout? Is it ethical to push athletes to always be better if it can result in loss of enjoyment and increasing stress?

PRACTICE QUESTIONS

1 Discuss how biological or cognitive or sociocultural factors influence behaviour in sport.

● **Examiner's hint**
If you kept a record of research and theories while working through this chapter, you should have a clear idea about how factors from each level of analysis influence behaviour in sport. You can focus on one area from this chapter (e.g. emotion and motivation, or burnout) or try to use several. Be sure that you describe the role of factors from the level of analysis you choose, support your description with research, and make conclusions with reference to the relative contribution of the other levels of analysis.

2 Define burnout. Compare **two** models of causes and prevention of burnout.

● **Examiner's hint**
Remember to describe the key elements of both models and to support your description with research where possible. *Comparison* should focus on similarities between the models rather than differences. Structure your answer so that you address the similarities of the models in order, rather than describe each and give a summary of similarities at the end. It is important to show evidence of critical thinking – for example, by addressing any relevant problems of reliability, validity or empirical testing shared by the models.

3 Evaluate **two** research studies investigating skill development in sport.

● **Examiner's hint**
You need to be able to briefly describe the aim, method and findings for both studies. However, the main focus of the essay must be on strengths and limitations of the studies. Strengths might include the possibility of establishing cause–effect relationships through experiments in this area, and ecological validity, but it is up to you to identify what these are for the specific studies you choose. Pages 296 and 299 include two good studies to consider for this question.

To access Worksheet 9.3 with a full example answer to question 3, please visit www.pearsonbacconline.com and follow the on-screen instructions.

To access Worksheet 9.4 with additional practice questions and answer guidelines, please visit www.pearsonbacconline.com and follow the on-screen instructions.

Theory of knowledge

In the group 3 subjects, IB students study individuals and societies. You should develop critical thinking skills and apply these in reflecting on the way that knowledge is accumulated in this discipline. There are a number of issues which the IBO suggests you can address while studying psychology to help you on your journey through the diploma. In this chapter we look at some of these in relation to research.

10.1 Natural sciences and psychological sciences

Consider these questions in relation to Research stimuli 1 and 2.

- To what extent are the methods of the natural sciences applicable in the human sciences?
- Are the findings of the natural sciences as reliable as those of the human sciences?
- Does psychological research ever prove anything? Why do we say that results only indicate or suggest?

As discussed in Chapter 1, psychology has tended to use the scientific method to acquire knowledge. Because the natural sciences follow an empirical approach, evidence must be acquired through observation to test hypotheses, and an unfalsifiable idea is an unscientific one. Some would argue that it is never possible for psychology to be as scientific as the natural sciences because, by definition, we are dealing with abstract concepts that are difficult to measure in a reliable and valid way.

Psychology researcher and natural scientist: whose work do you trust more?

- Consider the levels of analysis you study in this book. The biological level of analysis appears to be the most scientific. If a proper understanding of human behaviour is to be gained through scientific methods, all results from animal experiments must be generalized to humans. To what extent has this been done?

- There are a large number of case studies that provide empirical evidence of the biological influences on human behaviour. Is the case study method truly scientific? How satisfied are you that results gathered from individual cases can apply to all humans?

- In the natural sciences, experiments are replicated many times and many of the laws of natural science can be demonstrated in the classroom. What kind of factors prevent psychology from doing the same?

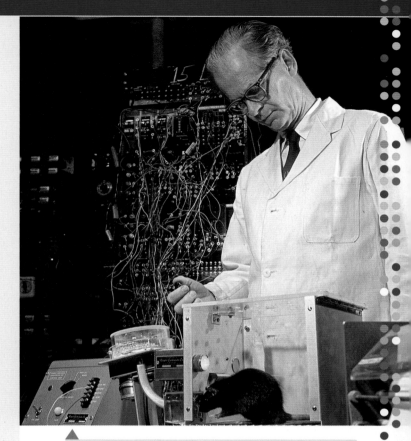

Can we generalize to humans from animal research?

Research stimulus 1

Time magazine describes recent research that attempted to find a cause for obsessive–compulsive disorder in mice. It claims that mice can show symptoms of the disorder, particularly in terms of repetitive grooming behaviour. The scientists interviewed had accidentally uncovered the possible role of a single gene which, when disabled, caused the rats to clean themselves so much that they developed facial sores. They gave the antidepressant Prozac to the rats and found that it eliminated the unusual behaviour.

Rats grooming: a form of obsessive–compulsive disorder?

 To learn more about research that has attempted to find a cause for obsessive–compulsive disorder in mice, go to www. pearsonhotlinks.com, enter the title or ISBN of this book and select weblink 10.1.

Research stimulus 2

It was claimed for some time that stress is a cause of various health problems like strokes and stomach ulcers. Researchers attempted to identify the mechanisms by which this might occur, looking for causal relationships between the perception of stress, the release of stress hormones, and the consequent effects on human physiology. More recent findings indicate that stress is *not* a key factor in strokes or stomach ulcers.

A Reuters report about the study (weblink 10.2) indicates that there is no difference in the number of stressful events experienced by people who have and have not had strokes. On the other hand, *Why zebras don't get ulcers* by Robert Sapolsky (2000) of Stanford University, explains that humans are exposed to stressful events in a way that most animals are not, and this is the reason, for example, that humans get stomach ulcers and zebras do not. However, two lines of argument create doubts about this idea. First, Australians Robin Warren and Barry Marshall discovered that bacteria were responsible for stomach ulcers, with the daring Marshall infecting himself with the bacteria to prove their argument. These two researchers were awarded the Nobel Prize for their work. Secondly, Professor Rob Briner of Birkbeck College, University of London, argues that stress has not been proven to cause any health problems because in a sense it does not even exist. There is no clear definition of stress, it does not map to any diagnosis, and although it has been studied a lot, we are not even sure if stress is a cause of health problems or a label given to a feeling associated with health problems. If the latter, it may be an emotional consequence rather than a cause. Do you feel frustrated *because of* stress, or is it the other way round?

 Whose life is most stressful?

To learn more about the relationship between stress and strokes, go to www. pearsonhotlinks.com, enter the title or ISBN of this book and select weblink 10.2.

To learn more about Robert Sapolsky's views, go to www. pearsonhotlinks.com, enter the title or ISBN of this book and select weblink 10.3. You can listen to Robert Sapolsky by downloading his podcasts through itunes for free.

To learn more about the Nobel prize awarded to Robin Warren and Barry Marshall, go to www. pearsonhotlinks.com, enter the title or ISBN of this book and select weblink 10.4.

To learn more about Rob Briner's argument and a response to it, go to www. pearsonhotlinks.com, enter the title or ISBN of this book and select weblink 10.5.

10.2 Limitations of psychology

Consider these questions in relation to Research stimuli 3 and 4.

- Are there human qualities or behaviours that will remain beyond the scope of the human sciences?
- To what extent can information in the human sciences be quantified?

There are a number of challenging human qualities and behaviours addressed in this book. Some of the research addressing these has been criticized because of artificiality or a lack of validity. The main reason we might doubt that research can adequately cover such topics as sexual desire, motivation for extreme aggression, empathy, and cognitive processes in early childhood is that it is difficult to obtain appropriate samples and define easily measurable target behaviours.

However, qualitative methodology is increasingly accepted as having scientific validity, and might offer more opportunities to study these challenging areas. One example is human grief. A model to describe grieving in response to imminent death was described in Chapter 9 (page 313) in relation to athletes' responses to injury. Quantifying grief seems like a formidable task, and yet it may be extremely important in relation to diagnosis of major depressive disorder, for example, as described in Chapter 5 (pages 165–166). Another facet of human experience that can be difficult to study is empathy. This is addressed in Chapter 8 (page 253), where we look at a theory about altruistic behaviour which suggests we do have an innate capacity for empathy. How can this empathy be defined and measured?

Is it possible to measure grief and empathy?

Research stimulus 4

In Chapter 2, looking at the biological level of analysis, we considered the role of the hormone oxytocin (page 57). Research suggests that empathy is increased by a nasal spray containing oxytocin: men who received either oxytocin spray or a control substance were asked to rate the depth of their emotional reaction to a set of emotionally charged pictures like a girl hugging her cat. Men who received the oxytocin tended to give answers showing more empathy, at levels described as being closer to women's. You can read an article about the study at weblink 10.7. The article also suggests that those who received the spray were more sensitive to feedback from human faces than others.

To learn more about whether or not oxytocin can improve your level of empathy, go to www.pearsonhotlinks.com, enter the title or ISBN of this book and select weblink 10.7.

Can a spray improve your empathy?

10.3 Ethical implications

Consider this question in relation to Research stimuli 5 and 6.

• Do knowledge claims in the human sciences imply ethical responsibilities?

Sometimes psychological research and theory have ethical implications. At the biological level of analysis, a lot of work has focused on the content of what we might call 'human nature', especially in terms of the influence of our genetic heritage and the evolutionary origins of our current behaviour.

At the sociocultural level of analysis, we have already discovered the powerful influence of social and cultural norms on behaviour. For example, research suggests that violence is supported by cultural values. Should governments intervene to ensure that media provide a balanced set of role models of behaviour, with more emphasis on positive models, so that young children do not learn to be violent and instead pick up more prosocial behaviour? When research indicates that there is a cycle of violence which means that children who are abused are at increased risk of later becoming abusive themselves, should social institutions be more active in ensuring that children develop anger management skills? At a more extreme level, when many key topics that interest psychologists (e.g. mental health problems and lower IQ score) are seen to be related to poverty, access to education and social support, is it appropriate not to take action to ensure that every human has the opportunity to flourish within their own environment?

Research stimulus 5

The American Psychological Association has published a brief interview with Chris E Stout of the University of Illinois at Chicago, who has specialized in the effects of globalization on people.

He says:

A lot of psychological research, in and of itself, is focused on avoiding conflict. When we consider what leads to wars, psychology is at the forefront – be it obedience to authority or simple passivity. Another well-supported theory is that of circumstance. This idea holds that war is less the result of malevolent dictators or the actions of inhumane ethnic or religious zealots, but rather disproportionate and unfair socio-economic circumstances, a generally dangerous or unsafe environment, and real or perceived risk of physical harm or loss to one's self, family, property or community.

Source: The American Psychological Association

Do we have a responsibility to limit their exposure to violence?

 To learn more about the interview with Chris E. Stout, go to www. pearsonhotlinks.com, enter the title or ISBN of this book and select weblink 10.8.

Research stimulus 6

Williams and Keating (2005) summarize of the effects of social inequality on mental health, covering those with advantages and those with disadvantages. Of particular interest are the range of individual and social effects of inequalities borne of class division, racism and sexism. Disadvantaged groups have less access to resources, more exposure to damaging experiences, and are more likely to receive medical treatment for mental health problems with little acknowledgement of social problems. The problem is not one-way, however. The burden of conforming to a social norm of silent power among white, middle-class men leads to an inability to acknowledge and discuss psychological problems. When social inequality has been shown to have a strong relationship with negative mental health outcomes such as increased levels of depression and schizophrenia, is it appropriate for society to adhere to policies that either ignore or accentuate social inequalities?

Social inequality.

10.4 History and culture

Consider this question in relation to Research stimuli 7 and 8.

- To what extent do the knowledge claims of the social sciences apply across different historical periods and cultures?

Modern psychology has attempted to address some of the cultural biases that were a feature of much of its earlier research. To some extent we must accept that the conclusions of psychology, particularly at the sociocultural level of analysis, might only ever apply to the context in which they were studied. If the conclusions made are valid for their context, the more important question is whether or not the methods used and the models or theoretical explanations that psychologists have established can be transferred to different historical and social contexts for confirmation.

Even the work of evolutionary psychologists must, by definition, be subject to eventual re-evaluation as the demands of the environment we live in change and certain characteristics become more or less adaptive for survival and reproduction. New technology has changed aspects of human behaviour such as communication. For example, the arrival of social networking websites and sms messaging have changed the frequency and depth of communication.

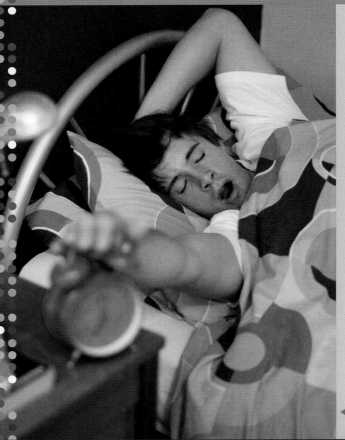

Research stimulus 7

An enormous amount of research has been done into teenage sleeping patterns. One key finding has been that many teenagers have something called delayed sleep phase syndrome (DSPS). This describes a pattern of sleepiness that is incompatible with the demands of life. Usually, this means a struggle to get up in the morning and go to school, tiredness during the morning, and alertness in the late evening. Recent research has suggested there may be a link with the use of technology (e.g. computers connected to the internet); other research suggests that a tendency to stay out late on Friday and Saturday nights may have contributed to this modern phenomenon.

 To learn more about sleep disorders, go to www.pearsonhotlinks.com, enter the title or ISBN of this book and select weblink 10.9.

Is this the best state for learning?

Research stimulus 8

Schizophrenia is a disorder involving a number of possible symptoms, including hallucinations and delusions. Its precise causes remain a mystery, and even its definition is somewhat problematic. John Read et al. (2004) give a description of the development of diagnosis for the disorder known as schizophrenia. They list the following as variables researchers have tried to associate with schizophrenia:

- handwriting
- blood type
- season of birth
- hip circumference of women
- ear shape
- size of gap between toes
- tattoos
- head circumference.

Some of these sound odd, but these findings have all been reported in research. Add to this the early descriptions of the disorder given by two key early theorists and it appears that some of the research is bound by historical and cultural norms – which means we must ask if some of our current thinking will later seem ridiculous.

Quotes from Kraepelin

'The loss of taste often makes itself felt in their choice of extraordinary combinations of colour and peculiar forms.'

'The want of a feeling of shame expresses itself in regardless uncovering of their persons, in making sexual experience public, in obscene talk, improper advances, and in shameless masturbation.'

'They conduct themselves in a free-and-easy way, laugh on serious occasions, are rude and impertinent towards their superiors, challenge them to duels, lose their deportment and personal dignity; they go about in untidy and dirty clothes, unwashed, unkempted, go with a lighted cigar into church.'

Quotes from Bleuler

'The patients sit about idle, trouble themselves about nothing, do not go to their work.'

'Patients are in love with a ward-mate with complete disregard of sex, ugliness or even repulsiveness.'

'Perversions like homosexuality and similar anomalies are often indicated in the whole behaviour and in the dress of the patient.'

- To what extent are these descriptions of schizophrenic behaviour likely to apply today and across cultures?

Does this picture show the madness of the patient or the doctor?

INTERNAL ASSESSMENT

Every IB psychology student must submit one simple experimental study as part of the requirements for the course. This is marked by your teacher and moderated externally. The mark for this piece of work makes up 25% of the standard level final grade and 20% of the higher level grade. It is up to you to plan and carry out this research, and there is a wide variety of possible experiments for you to engage in. The main purpose of this section is to help you choose and write up an appropriate study to earn good marks.

 Your experiment

The two most important things to bear in mind are:
- that your work is ethical
- that it is a genuine experiment.

Making sure your study is ethical

You should follow the ethical guidelines set out in Chapter 1 (pages 6–7), but there are also specific concerns for internal assessment projects:
- any psychological or physical discomfort is explicitly prohibited – this makes conformity and obedience experiments impossible
- studies involving ingestion are prohibited – this means that participants cannot be asked to eat, drink, smoke or chew any substance
- young children under 16 years old cannot be participants
- full informed consent must be obtained and recorded – this makes it unlikely that any deception or invasions of privacy will be possible
- as far as is practical, participants should be told exactly what is happening in the experiment and why
- anyone invited to participate in your experiment should be reminded of their rights to confidentiality and anonymity and their right to withdraw from the study at any time
- debriefing must occur, with evidence of this submitted as part of the report
- you should always be sensitive to any cultural or gender issues that might cause discomfort, and take action to prevent these occurring
- no animal studies can be carried out.

If you do not bear these ethical guidelines in mind and provide evidence that you have attempted to follow them, you could be awarded zero marks for the internal assessment component.

Making sure your study is a genuine experiment

Chapter 1 describes different types of experiment. You need to carry out an experiment that involves true manipulation of an independent variable. The biggest risk in this regard is that you try to use a quasi-experimental design which does not manipulate an independent variable but uses a pre-existing one like age, gender, culture or native language. It must be clear in your report that participants have been assigned *by you* to the different conditions of the experiment. Violation of this rule can also result in zero marks for the internal assessment component, so be sure that your independent variable does not already exist.

Choosing an experiment

If you are an SL student, you should replicate a study that has already been done. Well known and simple experiments are usually much easier to deal with. If you are an HL student, you need to do the same thing but you need to find more detail about the background to your study. And you have the freedom to make modifications to it. Many appropriate experiments come from the field of cognitive psychology, and you can find descriptions of these in Chapter 3.

Getting started: Planning
Defining your aim and identifying your variables

Every experiment has an intention to investigate the effect of the independent variable on a dependent variable. In the planning stages, you need to work out what effect you want to measure and how you can best do this scientifically. For example, your aim might be to investigate the effect of background music on recall of a list of words learned previously. You need to define your independent variable (background music) in a way that means you can clearly divide participants into two groups between which the only difference is whether they hear background music. Then you define your dependent variable (recall) in a way that is as reliable and valid as possible. Refer to Chapter 1 (pages 2–5) if you need to refresh your memory about reliability and validity. The most important consequence of your decision about the independent variable is that it informs your design of two groups: one group where the independent variable is manipulated (the experimental or treatment group), and another group (the control group) where everything is the same *except for* the independent variable. For the example above, you need to be clear *when* the background music is played – during learning or recall – and you need to be clear how the control group differed. You might choose to have the control group listen to nothing at all or you might choose to play some white noise so that they hear something but not music.

Levels of measurement

After you have decided what your variables are, you can consider what level of measurement you are using. This refers to how powerful and precise the measurement of your dependent variable is. There are four levels (Table 11.1). For your internal assessment, it is usually best to aim to measure at one of the higher levels as this allows for better analysis with statistics in the results section. It is best to make this decision before you collect your data.

TABLE 11.1 FOUR LEVELS FOR RECORDING DATA	
Nominal/ categorical	As you record data, you put it in categories (e.g. counting the number of Yes or No answers) where you cannot say that one category is bigger than the other, and it will not be meaningful to try and work out the average score.
Ordinal	The data can be put in order from smallest to biggest, but there is not necessarily an equal distance between the scores (e.g. when people are asked to rate their agreement on a Likert scale between 1 and 7, and we cannot be sure that the difference in agreement between 1 and 3 is the same as the difference between 3 and 5).
Interval	Data can be put in order and the intervals between the data points on the scale are equal (e.g. temperature). Temperature can be negative: although we can measure zero degrees Celsius, this does not mean there is *no* temperature, it is an arbitrary point on the scale labelled as zero.
Ratio	Data can be ranked and the intervals between data points are equal, and there is also a true zero point (e.g. weight – there is no negative weight; time taken to complete a task is also ratio level).

Confounding variables and controls

Once you have worked out what your independent and dependent variables are and how you are going to measure them, you need to think about what other variables could interfere with your results. For example, you might want to measure the effect of smell on memory recall and plan to ask participants to learn a list of words while there is a strong smell of orange and later try to remember the words with or without the same smell. You would therefore need to be very careful that there were no other strong smells in the place you do your experiment. You would want to be sure that the time of day does not affect people's memory as well. Although in psychology experiments it is unlikely that you will be able to identify and prevent every single possible confounding variable, it is important to try to do so. You could control for the effects of time of day, for example, by either testing all participants at the same time, or by splitting each of your groups in half and testing half the group in the morning and half the group in the afternoon.

Choice of design and the risk of expectancies and biases

The next planning consideration is whether you want to compare group averages across two different groups of people or compare differences in individuals who do two different tasks. For example, in the smell experiment referred to above, you could split all participants into two groups and have each participant recall the list of words *either* with the smell of orange *or* without it, and compare the average scores for each group (an **independent samples** design). Alternatively, you could ask each participant to complete the task twice, once with the smell *and* once without (a **repeated measures** design). Both approaches have advantages and disadvantages. The most obvious disadvantages of asking someone to do a task twice are that they may be better at it the second time (or even worse sometimes) especially if you use the same list of words, and they may notice the difference between the two tasks and therefore guess the aim of your experiment.

When the order affects performance, you have **order effects**. The simplest way to deal with this without changing to another design is to introduce **counter-balancing** – have half the participants do the two tasks in the order A then B, and the other half do the tasks in the order B then A. When participants guess the nature of the experiment, you may have **demand characteristics** as discussed in Chapter 1 (page 4).

The best design choice will be different for every experiment. Whatever design you choose, it is important to justify why you have chosen it or you will miss out on marks. To get the marks, make simple statements explaining your choice, for example: an independent samples design was used because it was clear that the tasks for the control group and experimental group were so similar that participants would recognize the difference and the experiment would become invalid because of demand characteristics.

Single- and double-blind

In single-blind designs, participants don't know which group they are in.

In double-blind designs, neither the participants nor the researchers know.

For your experiment to be valid, you will usually need to ensure that the participants don't know if they are in the control group or the experimental group. Review Chapter 1 to help you decide if you need to tell participants which group they are in, or even if it is best for you as the experimenter not to know which group they are in until after the experiment. In the smell experiment described above, using a control group that is presented with a different smell during recall might help to keep participants unaware of which group they are in.

HL only: How to write an operationalized hypothesis

The hypothesis is a statement that predicts what the outcome of your experiment will be. You need to have two of these in your introduction: the null hypothesis and the experimental hypothesis (also called the alternative hypothesis). The null hypothesis predicts that the independent variable will have no effect on the dependent variable, the experimental hypothesis predicts that there will be an effect. For your internal assessment, you should be able to clearly state what this effect will be, and indicate how it will be observed. Based on the results of your experiment, you will then reject one of the hypotheses. The hypothesis you create should follow logically from previous research you have found on your topic. Here are two examples of operationalized hypotheses.

Example 1

H1 (experimental hypothesis): The number of words recalled in a memory task will be significantly greater when participants learn and recall words while exposed to the same smell than when participants are exposed to different smells during learning and recall.

H0 (null hypothesis): Presence of same or different smells during learning and recall will have no significant effect on the number of words recalled.

Example 2

H1: Participants who hear background music while recalling a list of words will recall significantly more words than participants who hear white noise during recall.

H0: Presence of background music during recall will have no significant effect on number of words recalled.

Getting started: Sampling

What is representative sampling?

This was described in Chapter 1 (page 8). Ideally, your sample should be randomly selected from your target population so that we can assume your sample is representative (i.e. there is no systematic difference between your participants and the wider population). However, it is not easy for students to get a random sample, so it is important for you to explain how you obtained your participants and to explain enough about the characteristics of your sample to make it clear that your sample is appropriate for your research aim.

One of the most common methods used here is the opportunity or convenience sample. This is because it is easier to find participants this way, and they are more willing to agree to participate. This could mean, for example, that you ask students who are in a common area during a break, or you ask all the students in one of your classes, or perhaps members of your family. These approaches are all acceptable, but if you do not explain how you obtained your participants and give justification for using the method you chose, you will not get full marks.

The characteristics of your sample that are relevant to your experiment will be different for every internal assessment. Typically, you should describe the average age and the nationalities of your participants, native language (if language is used in one of the tasks participants complete) or musical abilities (if you are dealing with music). It is sufficient to have a sample of 20 people and it is not wise to have many more than this.

Allocation of subjects to groups

Although it may be difficult to obtain a random sample, it should not be difficult to randomly assign participants to the experimental and control groups. As far as possible, this should be done in a way that means every participant has an equal chance of being in both groups. You could toss a coin every time somebody agrees to participate to help make this decision, or you could list and number all participants and use a random number generator to choose which group they go in.

Sometimes this is not appropriate: for example, suppose you are using independent samples playing background music to one group while they recall a list of words, and playing white noise to a different group. Obviously, you can randomly choose which group gets which treatment, but there is a risk that one group may be quite different from the other in terms of memory or musical ability. What is important here is that you try to avoid any such bias, and describe clearly how and why you do this.

Getting started: Making a proposal

It is a good idea, if you are part of a class, to construct your research proposal and ask fellow students and your teacher to review it so that you can get feedback and make changes. At this point, the details do not need to be perfect, but feedback from others will help you to clarify where you need to be more precise in the final report. You should also be able to describe the studies your work is based on. Table 11.2 shows an example proposal.

TABLE 11.2 AN EXAMPLE RESEARCH PROPOSAL	
Research aim	To investigate the effect of background music on recall of a list of words
Independent variable	Presence of background music during recall
Dependent variable	Number of words recalled
Hypotheses (HL only)	H1: Participants who hear background music while recalling a list of words will recall significantly more words than participants who hear white noise during recall. H0: Presence of background music during recall will have no significant effect on number of words recalled.
How extraneous variables will be controlled for	The room needs to be very quiet so other noise does not interfere Students who play musical instruments should not participate
How the sample will be obtained	I will ask my friends to come to a classroom after school until 20 people have agreed; 10 people can choose to come on Tuesday and 10 on Thursday
How participants will be allocated to groups	I will let participants choose which day they can attend and then toss a coin to decide which day will be the treatment condition and which will be the control
Description of treatment group	Participants will learn a list of words for five minutes, wait for one minute while counting backwards, then I will play background music and ask them to write down as many words as they can remember
Description of control group	The same as the treatment group but I will play white noise while they write down the words.
Ethical issues	Informed consent form will be given at the beginning of the test Need to be careful with the volume of white noise as it can be quite uncomfortable to listen to
Questions and problems I have	Not sure if sample is random enough Don't know if I need different word lists for the two groups

Doing it: Issues to remember while collecting data

- Remember that every student needs to sign an informed consent form and that you need to keep the forms until you have finished the research and submitted your project.
- You need to construct standardized instructions and debriefing notes. Standardized instructions will make it easier for you to remember what to tell participants before and after the experiment. They will also make your experiment more reliable and prevent you inadvertently asking one group to do something slightly differently. They ensure that you are providing the participants with (a) enough information to make an informed decision about whether to participate or not and (b) a reminder that if they want to withdraw at any time, they can. Debriefing notes are important to fulfil the ethical guidelines and should explain the purpose of the experiment and what participants' results mean. The debriefing could occur immediately after the experiment, or it may be necessary to process individual participants' results and debrief them later. You need to put a copy of your instructions and debriefing notes in the appendices at the back of your report.

Writing the final report

Sections required for SL and HL are the same, but the content is slightly different (Table 11.3).

TABLE 11.3 BASIC FORMAT OF THE FINAL REPORT		
Section	**SL content**	**HL content**
Title page	• Title • Student name and number • Subject and level • Date, month and year of submission • Number of words	• Title • Student name and number • Subject and level • Date, month and year of submission • Number of words
Abstract	• Statement of aim • Summary of methods • Summary of results • Conclusion	• Statement of aim • Summary of methods • Summary of results • Conclusion
Introduction	• Aim of the study • Identification and explanation of study being replicated	• Aim of the study • Literature review • Operationalized experimental hypothesis • Operationalized null hypothesis
Method: Design	• Type and justification of experimental design and controls • Ethical considerations including informed consent • Independent and dependent variables	• Type and justification of experimental design and controls • Ethical considerations including informed consent • Independent and dependent variables
Method: Participants	• Characteristics of sample, sampling technique • Allocation of participants to conditions	• Characteristics of the sample, target population, sampling technique, • Allocation of participants to conditions
Method: Materials	• List of materials used, reference to copies in appendices	• List of materials used, reference to copies in appendices

continued

Section	SL content	HL content
Method: Procedures	• Describe in sufficient detail to allow full replication	• Describe in sufficient detail to allow full replication
Results	• Statement of the measure(s) of central tendency, as appropriate • Statement of the measure(s) of dispersion, as appropriate • Justification of choice of descriptive statistic • Appropriate use of fully explained graphs and tables	• Statement of the measure(s) of central tendency, as appropriate • Statement of the measure(s) of dispersion, as appropriate • Justification of choice of descriptive statistic • Reporting of inferential statistics and justification for their use • Statement of statistical significance • Appropriate use of fully explained graphs and tables
Discussion	• Interpretation of descriptive statistics • Comparison of findings to the study being replicated • Identification of limitations of the student's research • Suggestions for modification to address limitations of the student's research • Conclusion	• Interpretation of descriptive and inferential statistics • Comparison of findings to studies and theories reviewed in the introduction • Identification of limitations of the student's research • Suggestions for modification to address limitations of the student's research • Conclusion
References	• Works cited within the report listed in a standard format	• Works cited within the report listed in a standard format
Appendices	• Raw data tables and calculations • Supplementary information • One copy of instrument(s) used • Copy of standardized instructions and debriefing notes • Copy of blank, informed consent form (participant and/or parent)	• Raw data tables and calculations • Supplementary information • One copy of instrument(s) used • Copy of standardized instructions and debriefing notes • Copy of blank, informed consent form (participant and/or parent)
Words	1000–1500	1500–2000
Total marks	20	28

11.2 Notes and advice on assessment criteria

Assessment criteria and requirements from the IB Psychology Guide © International Baccalaureate Organization 2009.

A Introduction

SL requirements for maximum 2 marks

The study replicated is clearly identified and relevant details of the study are explained. The aim of the student's study is clearly stated.

HL requirements for maximum 5 marks

Background theories and/or studies are adequately explained and highly relevant to the hypotheses. The aim of the study is clearly stated. The experimental and null hypotheses are appropriately stated and operationalized. The prediction made in the experimental hypothesis is justified by the background studies and/or theories.

Notes and advice

Whether you are an SL student or an HL student, you need to make reference to studies that are relevant and include enough detail to show their relevance. Detail should focus on the aim, method and findings of these studies. At SL, you only need to describe the study you are replicating, but at HL you need to do more. The studies selected should be handled in such a way as to logically lead to a rationale for your own hypothesis. At HL, you should therefore give an explanation of the general area of investigation, summarize at least three key studies that are relevant, and use those findings to construct logical experimental and null hypotheses, explaining the link between the experiment you are carrying out and the background studies.

B Method: Design
SL and HL requirements for maximum 2 marks

The independent variable and dependent variable are accurately identified and operationalized. The experimental design is appropriate to the aim and its use is appropriately justified. There is clear indication and documentation of how ethical guidelines were followed.

Notes and advice

Clarity is extremely important in this section and you may need to rewrite your work several times before it is clear enough. Remember that operationalization means that it is clear exactly how the independent variable will be manipulated and how the dependent variable will be measured. Remember also that you need justification for the design you chose when planning your research (i.e. repeated measures or independent samples). This requires knowledge of the strengths and limitations of the designs. Remember to explain how you used your consent form and to state that you have included a sample in an appendix.

C Method: Participants
SL and HL requirements for maximum 2 marks

Relevant characteristics of the participants are identified. The sample is selected using an appropriate method and the use of this method is explained. HL only: The target population has been identified and is appropriate.

Notes and advice

If you are an HL student, you must ensure that you identify your target population. This is the group of people to whom you think your results apply, so your sample must be representative of the target population. The most important thing is for you to provide enough detail about the characteristics of both your sample and the target population for the reader to make a judgement about how appropriate your decision is.

D Method: Procedure
SL and HL requirements for maximum 2 marks

The procedural information is relevant and clearly described, so that the study is easily replicable. Details of how the ethical guidelines were applied are included. Necessary materials have been included and referenced in the appendices.

Notes and advice

What you need here is enough information for someone else to repeat what you have done. Many candidates find it effective to do this in bullet-points.

E Results: Descriptive
SL and HL requirements for maximum 2 marks

Results are clearly stated and accurate and reflect the aim/hypotheses of the research. Appropriate descriptive statistics (one measure of central tendency and one measure of dispersion) are applied to the data and their use is explained. The graph of results is accurate, clear and directly relevant to the aim/hypotheses of the study. Results are presented in both words and tabular form.

F (HL only) Results: Inferential
HL requirements for maximum 3 marks

An appropriate inferential statistical test has been chosen and explicitly justified. Results of the inferential statistical test are accurately stated. The null hypothesis has been accepted or rejected appropriately according to the results of the statistical test. A statement of statistical significance is appropriate and clear.

Notes and advice for criteria E and F

You need to present your results in a way that other people can understand. This means you need to use graphs and tables to show your results, and also describe the results in words. The information you have obtained from participants takes the form of raw data, usually scores or ratings from each participant. This information should go in an appendix, and you should use your results to calculate descriptive statistics appropriate to your data. You will need one measure of central tendency and one measure of dispersion. Measures of central tendency are used to describe where the middle of your data is, and include the mode (most frequent score), the median (the middle score when scores are placed in order), and the mean (the average score, obtained by adding all scores together and dividing by the number of participants). Measures of dispersion are used to describe how spread out your data are, and include the range, quartiles, and the standard deviation.

Which measures you choose depends on what level of data you obtained (Table 11.4) – interval and ratio level are usually the best for you to work with. For example, if you only asked participants Yes/No questions, you will only be able to present the mode as a measure of central tendency. In addition you will not be able to get full marks because you cannot calculate a measure of dispersion. If you have a choice of measure, you need to justify it. For example, the mode is a simple reflection of what was the most common answer, but it is not necessarily in the middle of the data set, and is quite possible to have several modes. The mean is a good rough estimate of where the middle is, but when there are extreme scores (outliers), the mean is affected by these and may therefore not be very precise.

TABLE 11.4 LEVELS OF MEASUREMENT AND APPROPRIATE MEASURES		
Level of measurement	**Appropriate measure of central tendency**	**Appropriate measure of dispersion**
nominal	mode	none
ordinal	mode or median	range
interval	mode, median and mean	range, quartiles, standard deviation
ratio	mode, median and mean	range, quartiles, standard deviation

This will affect your decision about what kind of graphs and tables to use. It is quite acceptable to present percentages on a table, and in many cases, pie charts and bar charts are acceptable. The important thing to remember in constructing your graph is that you must not put raw data on it; you should be presenting frequency of responses in a way that shows you have processed your data. Remember that graphs and tables all need to have titles and units of measurement, and graphs should be clearly labelled. It is also important that you do not produce graphs of irrelevant information. For example, it is unlikely to be worthwhile presenting findings for males and females separately, as this could not have been relevant to your research aim.

You should use your processed data to make a decision about whether or not your results are what you expected. If you are an SL student, it is sufficient to compare your results to what was explained in your introduction, and to make a statement that explains how the results are relevant to your research aim.

If you are an HL student, you need to do the same thing *and* you also need to establish whether any differences obtained are big enough, in light of the number of participants in the study, for you to reject the null hypothesis. In order to do this, you need to carry out an inferential statistical test. The purpose of these tests is to compare your results with what could be expected to occur simply by chance. If it is possible to get your results just by chance (usually anything more than a 5% probability, written as $P = 0.05$), then you do not have a significant difference, and you must reject your experimental hypothesis. If the chance of getting your results randomly is very small, then you can assume that there is a systematic effect and that this is due to the manipulation of the independent variable, and you can therefore reject the null hypothesis.

The test you choose is dependent on the level of measurement of your data and whether you used independent samples or repeated measures (Table 11.5). You should use a textbook dedicated to research methods and statistics or search on the internet for the appropriate test and instructions on how to conduct it.

TABLE 11.5 LEVELS OF MEASUREMENT AND APPROPRIATE INFERENTIAL STATISTICAL TESTS

Level of measurement	Appropriate test for independent samples	Appropriate test for repeated measures
nominal	chi-squared (χ^2 test)	
ordinal, interval or ratio	Mann–Whitney U test	Wilcoxon signed ranks test

For interval and ratio data it is also possible to use *t*-tests, but sometimes it is hard to justify their use, so it is often safer to aim to use one of the tests in Table 11.5. Regardless of which test you choose, you need to justify it by explaining that you chose it based on the design and the level of measurement. In the case of the *t*-test, you would need to explain that you chose it on the basis that it is more powerful even though it assumes your sample come from a normally distributed population, which is not usually the case for the samples used in internal assessments.

Once you have carried out the test, you will need to make a statement that explains what you have done. This statement should state which test you used and why, give the value obtained in the test (e.g. for the chi-squared test, the appropriate level of probability) and then state whether, on this basis, you can reject the null or the experimental hypothesis.

Example

A chi-squared test was carried out because the data were nominal and two independent samples were being compared. A significant difference was found ($\chi^2 = 4.78$, $p<0.05$) and we can therefore reject the null hypothesis.

F (SL) / G (HL) Discussion

SL requirements for maximum 6 marks

Discussion of results is well developed (for example, differences in the results of calculations of central tendency and/or dispersion are explained). The findings of the student's experimental study are discussed with reference to the study being replicated. Limitations of the design and procedure are highly relevant and have been rigorously analysed. Modifications are suggested and ideas for further research are mentioned. The conclusion is appropriate.

HL requirements for maximum 8 marks

Discussion of results is well developed and complete (for example, descriptive and inferential statistics are discussed). The findings of the student's experimental study are discussed with reference to relevant background studies and/or theories. Limitations of the design and procedure are highly relevant and have been rigorously analysed. Modifications are suggested and ideas for further research are mentioned. The conclusion is appropriate.

Notes and advice

This is the section where you bring everything together. You should first refer to what you wrote in the introduction as you need to explain what your results mean in relation to that. SL students need to note whether or not their results are the same as the original study, and explain why. HL students need to explain whether or not they got the results they expected on the basis of the background studies they described in the introduction and why. Identification of limitations should follow. Note that obtaining the results you expected is not a strength of the study. Often the richest discussion comes from trying to find reasons why there was no difference between treatment and control groups. Typical limitations are in terms of order effects, demand characteristics, and extraneous variables like noise which might have been prevented with better design. Modifications should be thoughtful rather than simplistic, and your ideas for further research should try to extend the topic of study beyond what you have done to add further to our understanding of the topic area under investigation.

To learn more about scholarly writing and referencing, go to www.pearsonhotlinks.com, enter the title or ISBN of this book and select weblink 11.1.

G (SL only) Presentation

Requirements for maximum 2 marks

The report is within the word limit of 1000–1500 words. The report is complete and in the required format. The reference for the study being replicated is cited using a standard method of listing references. Appendices are labelled appropriately and are referenced in the body of the report. The abstract is clearly written and includes a summary overview of the student's experimental study, including the results.

H (HL only) Citation of sources

HL requirements for maximum 2 marks

All in-text citations and references are provided. A standard citation method is used consistently throughout the body of the report and in the references section.

I (HL only) Report format

HL Requirements for maximum 2 marks

The report is within the word limit of 1500–2000 words. The report is complete and in the required format. Appendices are labelled appropriately and are referenced in the body of the report. The abstract is clearly written and includes a summary overview of the student's experimental study, including the results.

Notes and advice for criteria G, H and I

Be very careful with the word limit. It is easy to write too much, and the ability to be concise (e.g. when describing independent and dependent variables) is valuable.

Referencing is an important skill and helps you demonstrate that you have not plagiarized someone else's work. In your reference list you need to include any research that you have referred to in the text *but no more*, regardless of any further reading. The format of your in-text referencing may be done in any formal style, and your school may have a policy on this.

Many students struggle with the abstract and try to put in too much information in. Don't write more than 200 words, and follow the advice in Table 11.3.

When you refer to an item that is in your appendix, you should write, for example, (see Appendix 1: Sample consent form); be sure that the numbered appendices correspond with your text.

 To access Additional information 11.1 to 11.4 – internal assessments for both SL and HL, a sample consent form and a guide to working out descriptive and inferential statistics relevant to your internal assessment – please visit www.pearsonbacconline.com and follow the on-screen instructions.

12 ADVICE ON THE PSYCHOLOGY EXTENDED ESSAY (EE)

Do not attempt to do your EE in psychology unless you are studying this subject as part of your IB programme. The material needed is extremely technical and very difficult for non-psychology students to master.

Unlike EEs in some other subjects, the psychology EE does not require you to collect any data. It is based on literature review – that is, the discussion of studies and relevant theories that have already been published. In fact, you are *not allowed* to carry out empirical research of your own or in any way collect your own data.

What we are talking about here is an essay which is more extended than a usual essay in both scope and length, and is written in psychology. Although all this sounds self-evident, it is nevertheless a fact that students often misunderstand these basic tenets. Consequently, they submit EEs that lack appropriate organization and content; are 'extended', if at all, in the wrong way, and do not relate to the right kind of psychology. However, with due care, writing an EE in psychology can be interesting, enjoyable and attract the highest marks. Like EEs in other subjects, EEs in psychology present you with an opportunity and a challenge.

The EE as an opportunity

What can I write my EE about?

The EE gives you the chance to deepen your knowledge in an area of psychology you are interested in. Psychology is a very diverse field; it offers the student an impressive level of choice when it comes to selecting an appropriate topic for the EE. You can choose a topic from the core material, the options, or indeed move beyond the syllabus entirely.

The core

Are you equally interested in all levels of analysis? Do you find the topics covered in the cognitive level of analysis as interesting and exciting as those covered in the sociocultural level of analysis? Within the cognitive level of analysis, are you equally impressed by discussions of memory models and studies of flashbulb memory? In the sociocultural level of analysis are you equally attracted to general theories of stereotype formation or to more specific phenomena such as stereotype threat? What about topics from the biological level of analysis? Are you impressed by modern cognitive neuroscience with its colourful fMRI scans? Precisely what do studies based on such scans tell us about cognition that cannot be investigated by behavioural techniques? Do you find fascinating the fact that several phenomena are being addressed at more than one level of analysis? fMRI studies of conformity, social and cultural factors in flashbulb memory, and the role of brain damage underlying amnesia are only three of the many relevant examples here.

EXERCISE
1   List at least two topics you find most interesting for each of the three levels of analysis.

Options

Perhaps, your interests lie more in the specialist areas represented by the options. Are you interested in abnormal psychology or you are more intrigued by sports psychology, health psychology, developmental psychology or the psychology of human relationships? And which precise phenomena or topics within these broad areas of psychological inquiry appeal to you most? Of all therapeutic approaches, for instance, which ones raise the most profound questions for you? Is there a particular mental disorder you feel like researching in detail? You may be interested in stress and, in particular, stress at work or the relationship between stress and personality. Or, perhaps you are most interested in the role culture may play in the formation and maintenance of relationships. Research on the psychology of adolescents may be something you always found useful and appealing.

EXERCISE
2 List at least two topics you find most interesting from each of the two options you are covering in class.

Going beyond the IB syllabus

You can choose to do your EE on a psychological issue or phenomenon not covered in the syllabus. If you are doing business and management in addition to psychology, for example, you may wish to do your EE on work motivation or leadership. However, if you were to do this, your approach should be properly psychological and your essay should be based on sources coming from the well-established field of organizational psychology. Or you may have an interest in criminal profiling and would not mind reading extensively in the field of forensic psychology in order to get all the knowledge you would need to write an EE in this field. That would be fine.

EXERCISE
3 List at least two topics in psychology that interest you but are not covered in the syllabus. Do they sound promising as EE topics?

Pop psychology and self-help topics

Not everything with psychology on the title is appropriate material for your EE, even if it has been written by a psychologist. You *cannot* write an EE based on what is often called pop psychology or rely on self-help books for inspiration and content for your EE. These types of psychological writing owe very little to the methodological rigour and theoretical foundations of modern academic psychology. While often handling the same topics as academic books, they do so in a different manner. Thus, there are several hundred titles about how to overcome stress, or shyness or indeed how to become successful in relationships or at work. The better among them can be of some value to those seeking to address personal problems. But in the vast majority of cases, they are written with non-academic audiences in mind and they tend to make exaggerated claims about how well their suggestions are based on scientific evidence.

Your essay should be based on academic psychology – psychology developed in universities around the world and taught, as part of their main programme of studies, to psychology students at both university and pre-university levels. Big bookshops always have separate sections for academic psychology and pop psychology. You material should be drawn from mainstream academic research in psychology. If in doubt, ask your teacher.

So, the range of topics you can choose from is really huge. But, as we discuss below, and as it also happens in other walks of life, freedom comes at a price.

 ## 12.2 The EE as a challenge

How can I write a successful EE?

Your EE is not a general essay about some interesting topic in psychology. It has a very specific aim: to address the **research question**. Selecting an appropriate research question is absolutely crucial to writing a good EE. Essentially, your EE will be good to the extent to which it really answers this question.

What is an appropriate EE research question?

To write a good EE, you need a good research question. One you can answer within the word limit of 4000 words at the right level of detail and depth. You may think that this word limit is generous. You may even wonder how on Earth you will be able to write so much. If you do it properly though, it is likely that exactly the opposite will soon be your problem: too few words, and so much to write.

Some research questions are too broad for an EE
- Does stress relate to illness?
- Are there any effective treatments for depression?
- Are modern theories of work motivation useful in applied settings?
- What determines whether flashbulb memories of an event will form?
- Explanations of the déjà-vu phenomenon.

EXERCISES

4 Try to justify the view, which you may find strange at this stage, that these research questions are not focused enough and, therefore, in their current form should be avoided.

5 Look at your answers to Exercises 1 and 2. Are the topics unacceptably broad?

Some research questions are well focused for an EE
- To what extent is stress involved in coronary heart disease?
- To what extent are medicines used in the treatment of depression better than placebos?
- What valid statements can be made about the use of Locke and Latham's goal-setting theory to increase motivation in work settings?
- What is the current evidence about the role of social sharing of memories in the formation and maintenance of flashbulb memories?
- Is it possible to explain the occurrence of the déjà-vu phenomenon using Kusumi's theory on the role metacognition plays in this phenomenon?

EXERCISES

6 In what sense are these questions more focused?

7 In what ways are well-focused questions more likely to result in better EEs?

8 Write well-focused questions for the topic areas you identified in Exercises 1 and 2.

Even well-focused research questions are not easy to answer. They require a lot of specialist information. Finding such specialist material is a task that cannot be completed in a matter of days or even weeks. You should let your EE 'grow' over a number of months. Never commit yourself to a research question for which you have not already established that you can find the relevant theories and studies.

What is an appropriate treatment of my well-focused research hypothesis?

For your EE to address your research question successfully, it should involve:
- specialist knowledge
- systematic analysis and evaluation
- logical progression.

Specialist knowledge

When theories or experiments are described in class, term assignments and tests one can often get away with very little detail. Yet these theories and studies may occupy dozens of pages in more specialist books and scientific journals. Your internal assessment, involving anything up to 2000 words, gives you some idea of what it takes to describe and discuss an experimental study in a systematic manner. Entire books sometimes are being written to fully explain and discuss a single psychological theory.

You do not have to study all that has been written in the area relevant to your EE. That would be impossible. You do not even have to come close to it. But you will need to go beyond the types of source you use on a daily basis for your IB psychology course.

You may wish to start with general accounts of the relevant phenomena in your textbooks. The next step up would be to go to a more specialist textbook. Thus, if you are interested in flashbulb memory you can start with the coverage of the topic of memory in a general textbook like this one. Then look for access to some specialist book on memory. See if it has a whole section on flashbulb memory. At around this time, you will know that you cannot hope to write your EE on flashbulb memory in general. You need to make your research question specific, for example: What is the current evidence about the role of social sharing of memories in the formation and maintenance of flashbulb memories? Table 12.1 below shows different types of source material in order of specialization.

Source material	Order of access	Example
TABLE 12.1 HIERARCHY OF SOURCE TYPES FOR FLASHBULB MEMORY REVIEW		
general textbooks	1	this textbook other textbooks with a sizeable section on flashbulb memory
specialist textbooks	2	Baddeley A, Eysenck MW and Anderson MC. (2009). *Memory*. Psychology Press
specialist books	3	Luminet O and Curci A. (Eds). *Flashbulb Memories: New Issues and New Perspectives*. Psychology Press. Select relevant chapters according to research question
scientific journal papers	4	Talarico M and Rubin D. (2003). Confidence, not consistency, characterizes flashbulb memories. *Psychological Science* 4(5): 455–61.

How can you find all these materials?

Your library will have some general textbooks and may have some more specialist books in the area of your interest. Local libraries can also be of help. If you live in a university city, ask your librarian whether your school can get you access to the university library.

What about journal papers? To start with, you can use Google Scholar to identify papers relevant to your EE. Realistically, you will probably have free internet access to the abstract of any article you are interested in on the internet. This can provide you with precious relevant information for your EE. However, in most cases, the full paper will be accessible only to paying customers and university libraries. Check whether your library subscribes to any journals that may be relevant, or if you can get access through your library to a university library. Occasionally, the entire article may be available free online, as is the case with the Talarico and Rubin paper. Your supervisor can give you additional advice on how to find relevant sources.

Of course, the internet is useful for all sorts of material. Whatever your chosen research question, there will be a lot of relevant material on the internet. By all means make use of it but always treat such material carefully. Everybody and anybody can contribute material to the internet and site quality varies. Be guided by good judgement and help from your supervisor.

Table 12.1 is an ideal progression; you should not get dispirited if your resources are not as complete. Do your best with whatever sources you can secure. What matters, in addition to finding relevant material, is how you orchestrate your sources in such a way as to address your research question in a reflective, evaluative and methodical fashion. But you need to be realistic. If you cannot, early in the process, find enough technical material for your favourite topic, *choose something else.*

You may wish to work backwards from establishing which areas of psychology are well-represented in the sources available to you and then try to find a research question that interests you and could be answered adequately. There is no need to feel unduly frustrated if your resources let you down in your favourite area in psychology – the process of researching and writing up an EE often proves more exciting and useful than the actual research question it addresses.

Although academic books and journals should be your main sources, you can also use information from newspapers, other magazines, TV programmes. But be careful: treat such sources with care and always apply the necessary evaluation to any material you use from them. Such sources can give you ideas to explore further using appropriate technical material of the type described above. *Never* use non-academic material on its own. It may be appropriate to use when you simply need to illustrate a phenomenon. For example, an interview somebody provides to the media about his or her memory of a disaster may serve well as an illustration of flashbulb memory – but it is in no way a substitute for the technical material to be found in the sources in Table 12.1.

Systematic analysis and evaluation

You need to engage seriously with analysis and evaluation when discussing theories and studies.

Regarding theories, the issues you should be addressing include the following.
- What are the essential claims made by the theories I am discussing and how do they relate to one another and to other theories?
- Do I approach my research question from a number of different perspectives?
- Are some perspectives better suited to tackle some aspects of the phenomena under discussion than others?

To find the Talarico and Rubin paper, go to www.pearsonhotlinks.com, enter the title or ISBN of this book and select weblink 12.1.

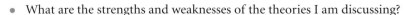

- What are the strengths and weaknesses of the theories I am discussing?
- Are the theories well-supported by the empirical evidence I cite?
- Is there evidence of extensive theory triangulation in the area of interest?
- Have the relevant theories proved useful in generating valuable research?

Relevant questions to keep in mind when discussing empirical studies include the following.

- What are the strengths and weaknesses of the empirical studies I involve in my EE?
- What is their internal and external (including ecological) validity?
- Am I justifying in some depth the critical remarks I am making about validity issues? A laboratory experiment is not necessarily ecologically invalid and a field experiment may happen to be well-controlled to detect with confidence causal relationships between the variables investigated.
- To the extent I use non-experimental evidence, am I discussing the limitations of such research and in particular the fact that it does not lead to confident statements about cause and effect?
- Am I aware of the need for method triangulation and discuss, if possible, several methods relying on different research methods?
- Are there other empirical studies which have findings that contradict the findings of the studies discussed?

As you can see there is no place for superficial criticisms in the EE. All criticisms should be properly justified.

Make sure you raise relevant ethical and cultural issues throughout your EE. Do the studies you discuss raise ethical issues? Do the theories you discuss raise such issues? Do they, for example, make claims that can prove damaging to sections of society (e.g. minority or disadvantaged groups)? Are you aware of cross-cultural studies addressing the topic you are investigating? Could it be that the research you are discussing is culturally biased?

The IB *Psychology guide* has a section on how best you can be critical in psychology. It is called 'Critical thinking in psychology: A framework for evaluation'. If you do not already have access to the guide, ask your supervisor to make this section available to you.

Logical progression

Your EE should culminate in a number of conclusions about your research question. It is your responsibility to convince your reader about the validity of these conclusions. Never lose sight of the research question. Scrutinize each paragraph and ask yourself questions like the following.

- Precisely what that is relevant to my research question am I trying to accomplish in this paragraph?
- How did the need for this paragraph arise given what I have been discussing before it (i.e. in the previous paragraph or two)?
- To what extent is this paragraph advancing the arguments I have been developing?
- How does this paragraph contribute towards the conclusions I will reach in my EE?

Everything in your EE should follow logically and systematically from what has gone before and it should pave the way towards what is forthcoming (i.e. the next paragraph or so). Make sure you relate logically different points of view, and that you establish a close logical link between the theories you explore and the empirical studies you relate to them. Your essay will be based on a number of claims. Make sure that you:

- state these claims precisely
- justify every claim by providing appropriate evidence
- support theoretical claims with evidence from empirical studies
- accompany studies with proper methodological critiques
- consider, when appropriate, counterclaims.

There are no simple answers in psychology. As a psychology student, you already know that. Relay the same impression to your reader. There will be shortcomings in the theories and studies you discuss and the issues will not be all settled by the end of your essay. Give the impression that you are contributing to an ongoing and complex discussion, not that you have solved all the riddles surrounding your research question.

How should I structure my EE?

Title page

The title should be brief, informative and precise. Often, stating the research question (especially if it does not sound very technical), or rephrasing it, should be enough.

Abstract

The abstract presents an overview of your entire EE. The word limit for the abstract is 300 words. The abstract should state your research question, give a brief idea of how the EE addresses it, and offer a summary of the major conclusions. You should write this section at the very end.

Contents page

The contents page provides a list of all the sections and subsections of your EE with the page number on which each can be found.

Introduction

Why did you go into the trouble of writing an EE on your research question? Why did you choose it? What are the strengths and weaknesses of existing contributions to the issues addressed by your research question? How does your essay contribute towards a better understanding of the question you are addressing?

Although you need to refer to relevant theories and studies in the introduction, this will be at a very general level and in the service of providing an appropriate rationale for your choice of research question. Your views and conclusions should not be mentioned in the introduction. Whatever else you do, make sure that your introduction contains a clear statement of your research question. Do not just throw it in, tell your reader explicitly: *This is my research question.*

Body

This is the main part of your EE. This is where all that was explained above happens. With appropriate specialist material, expressed by using proper technical terminology, you state your claims and you justify them; you describe theories and studies and relate them to one another; you apply critical analysis and you show your analytical skills. You can use subheadings to signpost the development of your arguments.

Conclusion

This is not a rough paragraph, full of generalities, written at the last moment before submission. It is a summary of your major claims and what conclusions can be reached

with respect to the research question. You made some promises in your introduction. Tell your reader about the extent to which you feel you have honoured them. You had mentioned that you felt certain issues needed further attention. Well, have you paid enough attention to them and what are your conclusions? What else remains to be done in the research area defined by your research question? What types of progress would you want to see? What types of progress seem realistic?

Bibliography/references

A bibliography is list of all the sources you have cited in your EE. You can mention any sources you have used but do not directly refer to in the essay in the introduction or as an acknowledgement. But the bibliography should list *only* sources explicitly cited in your essay. Use references throughout to indicate to the reader where you got the information you use and to credit any views you express which are not your own. The formal references in your bibliography should provide all the information your reader needs to find the material as it appeared in the original sources.

Appendices, footnotes and endnotes

You should not need to include appendices, footnotes and endnotes. Note that examiners are not obliged to read such material. So don't try to evade the word limit by including important material in notes or appendices as this is likely to be penalised by mark loss.

 ## 12.3 Notes and advice on assesment criteria

Your EE will be assessed on the basis of the following assessment criteria from the IB Online Curriculum Centre © International Bacalaureate Organization. Read this material repeatedly while preparing your essay and always ask yourself and your supervisor if what you write scores high on these criteria.

Assessment criteria
Criterion A: The research question (2 marks)
The research question is clearly stated in the introduction and sharply focused, making effective treatment possible within the word limit.

Notes and advice
Of course, the 2 marks relate to how clearly you have expressed your research question and how well you justified it in the introduction. As emphasized throughout this chapter, without an appropriate and well-focused research question you will be scoring very low on most of the rest of the criteria as well.

Criterion B: Introduction (2 marks)
The context of the research question is clearly demonstrated. The introduction clearly explains the significance of the topic and why it is worthy of investigation.

Notes and advice
See the discussion on page 346 for what goes into the introduction.

Criterion C: Investigation (4 marks)

An imaginative range of appropriate sources has been consulted and relevant material has been carefully selected. The investigation has been well planned.

Notes and advice

See the discussion on page 344 about how best to secure the relevant material for your EE.

Criterion D: Knowledge and understanding of the topic studied (4 marks)

The essay demonstrates very good knowledge and understanding of the topics studied. Where appropriate, the essay clearly and precisely locates the investigation in an academic context.

Notes and advice

See the discussion on page 343 for the types of source that would be proper for your EE. Note again that although technical books and scientific papers are ideal sources, what matters are finding appropriate studies and theories and discussing them in a way that directly addresses your question. Whatever you do, be sure to make extensive use of existing psychological theories and psychological empirical studies.

Criterion E: Reasoned argument (4 marks)

Ideas are presented clearly and in a logical manner. The essay succeeds in developing a reasoned and convincing argument in relation to the research question.

Notes and advice

See the discussion on page 345 about logical progression.

Criterion F: Application of analytical and evaluative skills appropriate to the subject (4 marks)

The essay shows effective and sophisticated application of appropriate analytical and evaluative skills.

Notes and advice

See the discussion on pages 344–345 about systematic analysis and evaluation.

Criterion G: Use of language appropriate to psychology (4 marks)

The language used communicates clearly and precisely. Terminology appropriate to psychology is used accurately, with skill and understanding.

Notes and advice

Throughout your essay, you should be using the terminology used by academic psychologists to discuss their theories and studies. You should provide clear technical definitions of the main key concepts mentioned in your essay.

Criterion H: Conclusion (2 marks)

An effective conclusion is clearly stated; it is relevant to the research question and consistent with the evidence presented in the essay. It should include unresolved questions where appropriate to psychology.

Notes and advice
See the discussion on page 346 about the conclusion.

Criterion I: Formal presentation (4 marks)
The formal presentation is excellent.

To learn more about scholarly writing and referencing, go to www. pearsonhotlinks.com, enter the title or ISBN of this book and select weblink 12.2.

Notes and advice
You need to have a title page, a table of contents and page numbers. You also need to provide an appropriate bibliography and references. And you must stay within the word limit, otherwise your EE will score 0 on this criterion. Seek further advice from your supervisor on referencing and the formal layout of your EE.

Criterion J: Abstract (2 marks)
The abstract clearly states the research question, how the investigation was undertaken, and the conclusion(s) of the essay.

Notes and advice
You need to be careful with the abstract. You must include all three of the features noted in order to get any points. If you omit any of these you will score 0. You will also score 0 if your abstract exceeds 300 words.

Criterion K: Holistic judgement (4 marks)
The essay shows considerable evidence of intellectual initiative, breadth and depth of understanding, and insight.

Notes and advice
It is easier to demonstrate this criterion by outlining what would *not* score highly on it. There is very little initiative involved in writing an EE on flashbulb memory, based on material drawn from a couple of introductory textbooks and a few visits to the net. The research question can be made more interesting and reflect intellectual initiative by making it more specific. Examples here could include the following.

- To what extent is flashbulb memory different from other forms of autobiographical memory?
- To what extent is flashbulb memory different from event memory?
- Precisely how is emotionality involved in the formation and maintenance of flashbulb memory?

How would your examiner know that you are exhibiting intellectual initiative here? Basic accounts of flashbulb memory may not even use terms like autobiographical memory or event memory and certainly do not go into the details of precisely how emotionality may be involved in the formation and maintenance of flashbulb memory. Without intellectual curiosity and initiative, you would not even have considered such research questions.

Similarly, the way you handle your evidence, the extent to which you are critical and reflective about what you are writing, will give ample information about how confident your understanding of the relevant technical material is.

And finally, unless you worked hard on a variety of sources and thought deeply about what you were reading, you would not be able to develop a personal voice on what you are writing. You would not be in a position to develop and articulate your own informed views on the issues your EE addresses.

ANSWER GUIDELINES

Research methods

This chapter deals with material that is examinable only for HL students in Paper 3.

In the markscheme below, we interpret 'low' as 1–3, 'mid' as 4–7 and 'high' as 8–10.

Marks	Level descriptor
A Knowledge and comprehension	
0	The answer does not reach a standard described by the descriptors below.
Low	There is an attempt to answer the question but knowledge and understanding is limited, often inaccurate or of marginal relevance to the question. The response makes no direct reference to the stimulus material or relies too heavily on quotations from the text.
Mid	The question is partially answered. Knowledge and understanding is accurate but limited. Either the command term is not effectively addressed or the response is not sufficiently explicit in answering the question. The response makes limited use of the stimulus material.
High	The question is answered in a focused and effective manner and meets the demands of the command term. The answer is supported by appropriate and accurate knowledge and understanding of qualitative research methodology. The response demonstrates a critical understanding of qualitative research methodology applied to the stimulus material.

From IB Psychology Guide © International Baccalaureate Organization 2009

1 The command term *explain* asks you to give a detailed account including reasons or causes.

You should start by explaining what credibility is. As it is impossible to remove all ambiguity from the research process, it is important instead to consider the breadth and depth of information gathered and how well the researcher appears to have analysed it. In short, how believable are the researcher's conclusions? This can only be judged if the researcher has given very detailed descriptions of context and methods, and has acknowledged potential sources of bias.

In giving reasons why credibility is important, you can compare it with the need to establish validity in quantitative research. In quantitative research, we are interested in how well the researcher has isolated the variables of interest so that the conclusions made are the only logical possibilities. Qualitative research is more ambiguous; the reader is taken on a journey by the researcher, with the researcher's conclusions as the endpoint. If the researcher has not given enough information about how and why decisions were made in designing and conducting the research, then the reader cannot comfortably believe the conclusions. In addition, if the researcher has not been reflexive enough, we may suspect that bias in their methodology or in the gathering of data has affected their results without them realizing it. It is always likely that a researcher has expectations and it is only when they acknowledge them and attempt to account for them that their conclusions have credibility.

In relation to the research stimulus provided:
- Is it likely that the researcher was biased?
- Were any steps taken to prevent or account for this?
- Did the method chosen, a participant observation, suitably achieve the researcher's aim?

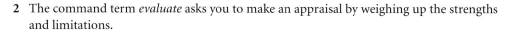

2   The command term *evaluate* asks you to make an appraisal by weighing up the strengths and limitations.

This question asks you to reach a conclusion about how good the method used in this study was in terms of achieving the aims of the researcher. There is no correct conclusion to make, and it is therefore very important that you justify your conclusion using your own knowledge and evidence from the stimulus.

To access Worksheet 1.2 with a full example answer to question 2, please visit pearsonbacconline.com and follow the onscreen instructions.

State the aim of the study and identify the type of observation used. Here we have an overt participant observation with data recorded by a naïve observer unaware of the aims of the research but who had a checklist of contexts and behaviours to look at.

Typical strengths of overt, qualitative participant observations include:
- observer is able to obtain rich data by becoming part of the group and by not restricting or prescribing specific target behaviours to be observed
- data gathered may be less affected by demand characteristics than other overt observations because the participants have the opportunity to get more comfortable with the observer
- observation is more ethical than covert observations and involves minimal deception.

Typical limitations include:
- risk of the observer 'going native' and losing the neutral perspective
- risk of demand characteristics and very artificial behaviour
- introduction of new behaviour that would not have occurred if the researcher were not there (e.g. arguments or romance)
- inability to make cause–effect conclusions.

Consider whether these strengths and limitations apply in the context of the research stimulus. The aim of the research is not to establish the cause of behaviour, it is to obtain a rich description of behaviour, and it seems that this has been achieved. But is it a credible description of behaviour? Consider the likelihood that the observer's presence has changed the behaviour of the individuals concerned. Is it possible the participants were on their best behaviour for their guest?

Consider also other criteria for the evaluation of qualitative research (page 12). Although transferability can only be established with an understanding of some other context you want to apply the results to, we can consider whether the research is transferable to one- or two-person living situations. Would participant observations work in that context and would we find similar activity happening? Confirmability and dependability could also be considered. In a research stimulus like this, it is not likely that you will have full information about what biases the researcher has identified and tried to eliminate, but you do have some indications here, so you should make reference to them.

Remember to end with a clear statement indicating your conclusion about how appropriate the use of participant observation was in this context.

Note: the research stimulus uses the expression 'mental handicap'. This term is not used any more. It is more politically correct to refer to the participants as having learning difficulties.

3   This study used a checklist to guide the observer in making detailed notes about behaviour she observed. Distinguish between qualitative and quantitative data that could be obtained in a study such as this.

The command term *distinguish* asks you to make clear the differences between two or more concepts or items.

The differences between qualitative and quantitative methodology in general were addressed on pages 10, 11 and 12. The different types of data obtained in quantitative and qualitative observations are addressed on pages 21 and 22.

The key difference is that the tendency to use a grid and count prescribed behaviours in quantitative research results in numerical data that can be processed in terms of descriptive statistics like the mean and mode. Although this might be easy to process and compare with other research contexts, it does not give a very detailed description of the situation observed. Qualitative data such as was obtained here, however, is very detailed and tends to be less obviously affected by the prescriptive nature of grid-based research. This is because in the act of constructing a grid the researcher imposes his or her expectations on the research. Thus, the qualitative data is rich and possibly more credible. The downside of this is the difficulty in processing qualitative data such as the excerpt provided in the research stimulus, Analysis of this data would be time-consuming, possibly relying on content analysis.

Make sure you refer to the research stimulus, not just to research in general. In addition, remember to stay focused on the question, which asks you to make the differences clear, not simply to describe one and then the other.

Core chapters

Chapters 2–4 deal with Core material examinable in Paper 1.

Short answer questions

In the markscheme below, we interpret 'low' as 1–3, 'mid' as 4–6 and 'high' as 7–8.

Marks	Level descriptor
A Knowledge and comprehension	
0	The answer does not reach a standard described by the descriptors below.
Low	There is an attempt to answer the question but knowledge and understanding is limited, often inaccurate or of marginal relevance to the question. The response makes no direct reference to the stimulus material or relies too heavily on quotations from the text.
Mid	The question is partially answered. Knowledge and understanding is accurate but limited. Either the command term is not effectively addressed or the response is not sufficiently explicit in answering the question. The response makes limited use of the stimulus material.
High	The question is answered in a focused and effective manner and meets the demands of the command term. The answer is supported by appropriate and accurate knowledge and understanding of qualitative research methodology. The response demonstrates a critical understanding of qualitative research methodology applied to the stimulus material.

From IB Psychology Guide © International Baccalaureate Organization 2009

Essay questions

Each answer is marked out of 22 and the markscheme below is applicable to all questions.

Marks	Level descriptor
A Knowledge and comprehension	
0	The answer does not reach a standard described by the descriptors below.
1–3	The answer demonstrates limited knowledge and understanding that is marginal to the question. Little or no psychological research is used in the response.
4–6	The answer demonstrates limited knowledge and understanding relevant to the question or uses relevant psychological research to limited effect in the response.
7–9	The answer demonstrates detailed, accurate knowledge and understanding relevant to the question and uses relevant psychological research effectively in support of the response.

B	Evidence of critical thinking:
0	The answer does not reach a standard described by the descriptors below.
1–3	The answer goes beyond description but evidence of critical thinking is not linked to the requirements of the question.
4–6	The answer offers appropriate but limited evidence of critical thinking or offers evidence of critical thinking that is only implicitly linked to the requirements of the question.
7–9	The answer relevant and explicit evidence of critical thinking in response to the question.
C	Organization
0	The answer does not reach a standard described by the descriptors below.
1–2	The answer is organized or focused on the question. However, this is not sustained throughout the response.
3–4	The answer is well organized, well developed and focused on the question.

From IB Psychology Guide © International Baccalaureate Organization 2009

 # Biological level of analysis

Short answer questions

1 The command term *explain* asks you to give a detailed account and explain the underlying rationale.

For short answer questions, you need to get straight to the point. There is no need for an introduction. Begin by identifying the two hormones you are going to write about. Three were discussed in this chapter (adrenalin, melatonin and oxytocin); others are discussed in Chapters 5–9.

You need to be sure to do two things for each hormone. First, describe what the hormone is believed to do and, where possible, explain how this happens. For example, melatonin is secreted in darkness and the hormone signals the pituitary gland to 'turn off' many functions in the brain and body. Secondly, use specific examples. For melatonin, you can explain its possible role in SAD and jet lag, with reference to research such as Avery et al. (2001). You do not need to describe the research in great detail or evaluate it for a short answer question; it is sufficient to briefly describe the aim, procedure and findings, remembering always to make it clear how the example shows the function of melatonin in behaviour.

2 The command term *describe* asks for a detailed account.

You need to get straight to the point. Identify the explanation you are going to describe. There are many offered in this book, including explanations for homosexuality and homicide in this chapter, and for altruism and attraction in Chapter 8. If you can name the researchers who have contributed to the explanation, it will make a better impression, but it is not required.

An example from this chapter is Homicide Adaptation Theory. A description needs only to cover the basic ideas of the theory: that we are genetically predisposed to kill other humans in specific situations because it increases the chances of our own survival until we can reproduce; in some cases, by killing those who are competing with our own children for resources, we increase the chance of our genes being passed on through our children.

A competent description of this particular theory will need to go a little bit further than this: include a brief description of the concept of the cost–benefit analysis that indicates that there are significant costs to homicide that make the theory less likely to be valid.

3 The command term *explain* asks you to give a detailed account and explain the underlying rationale.

Many interactions between cognition and physiology are covered in this book: the interactions between hormones and stress in Chapter 7; the use of mental imagery in sports in Chapter 9; the effect of neuronal degeneration on memory in Chapter 3. In this chapter, an excellent example is the Schachter and Singer (1962) study addressing the role of adrenalin and cognition in emotion. Be sure to explain that their two-factor theory of emotion considers the arousal provided by adrenalin and the mental processing of context. Specifically, in their study they found that it was possible to affect the type of emotion experienced by their participants by (a) providing physiological arousal through an injection of adrenalin and (b) putting them in a room where they were given contextual cues to experience the physiological arousal in terms of either happiness or anger. Thus, according to these researchers, a specific emotion is the result of an interaction between physiological arousal and cognitive processing of context.

4 The command term *explain* asks you to give a detailed account and explain the underlying rationale.

To access Worksheet 2.3 with a full example answer to question 4, please visit pearsonbacconline.com and follow the onscreen instructions.

There are many studies in this book that address the role of specific parts of the brain in human behaviour. For example, the role of the hippocampus in memory (this chapter and Chapter 3; the role of the amygdala in phobias in Chapter 5). In this chapter, the case studies of Janet, HM, and Phineas Gage are relevant. The focus of the question must be on the study, and it is essential to address the aim, procedure and findings of the study. For example, the primary aim of the study of HM was to determine the effects of the complications in his brain surgery; secondarily, the study aimed to clarify what parts of his brain were damaged or removed so as to understand the relationship between the damage to his brain and the effects on his memory. Several methods were used in this case study that lasted around 50 years, including interviews, memory tests, and miniature experiments comparing HM's performance on tests with 'normal' participants. The key findings were that there was significant damage to his hippocampus on both sides of his brain, and although he appeared to have a short-term memory and could hold a conversation with those interviewing him, he could not retain explicit memories of these occasions such as names, dates or facts. This suggests, but does not prove, that the hippocampus plays a role in the formation of long-term memories.

Essay questions

1 The command term *discuss* asks you to present a considered and balanced review that includes a range of arguments, factors or hypotheses. Opinions or conclusions should be presented clearly and supported by appropriate evidence.

The focus of this question is on how and why brain-imaging technologies are used, with examples and evaluation of the use of these technologies.

You could begin by describing the technologies from this chapter (EEG, CT, PET, MRI, and fMRI) and then give examples and evaluation. However, a better answer would focus on the *use of* technologies rather than the technologies themselves. Thus, you should begin by addressing researcher and medical practitioner interest in investigating the structure of brains for research (e.g. Maguire et al., 2000 and Draganski et al., 2004) or diagnosis; and to determine the possible cause of behavioural changes (e.g. the case studies of Janet and HM). This can be done with CT scans and MRI scans. Explain the

difference between these two technologies and the strengths and limitations of each, and give some examples of research that uses them. The strengths and limitations of the technologies should be reflected in the examples you choose.

Next, address interest in investigating the function of the brain, using functional imaging technologies: the fMRI and PET scans. Again, this can be used in diagnosis or research. PET was used to investigate function in MA's brain while he spoke and used sign language, and fMRI was used in Brefczynski–Lewis et al. (2007) to investigate the difference in function between experienced and novice meditators. Again, you should focus on strengths and limitations of the technologies for the purposes intended, and these should be reflected in the studies you describe.

There are many other examples of the use of technologies throughout the book and you can use these to add depth to your answer. Remember that in order to get credit for organization, if you reach a conclusion, it should logically follow from the entire structure of your essay and be supported by the evidence you have presented.

To access Worksheet 2.4 with a full example answer to question 2, please visit pearsonbacconline.com and follow the onscreen instructions.

2 Discuss ethical considerations related to research studies at the biological level of analysis.

The command term *discuss* asks you to present a considered and balanced review that includes a range of arguments, factors or hypotheses. Opinions or conclusions should be presented clearly and supported by appropriate evidence.

This learning outcome is one that you need to address for all three levels of analysis. Be very clear about the considerations relevant specifically to research in the biological level of analysis; it is not sufficient to give a general description of ethical considerations for all research.

You should identify the major considerations in an introduction. The key ideas to cover are:
- the impossibility of conducting true experiments that would cause psychological or physical harm
- the reliance, therefore, on case studies and natural experiments
- the use of animal experiments, which is controversial.

You will need to include several examples of research for each of these three points. Try to identify studies in this book that are true experiments involving human participants that investigate behaviour at the biological level of analysis and are ethical. The experiments investigating the roles of oxytocin (Morhenn et al., 2008) and melatonin (Avery et al., 2001) are both ethical experiments but in both cases our knowledge of cause and effect is limited because of ethical considerations in their design.

Show how case studies and natural experiments are the only way to investigate the effect of damage to the brain, using examples of research in this chapter (e.g. HM and Janet) to show that such studies are usually free from ethical problems but also suffer from the same reduction in our ability to make causal conclusions.

Explain the controversy of animal experiments: give examples of research and refer to the ethical guidelines for research using animals from Chapter 1; consider whether the animals suffered unreasonably. Remember that when animals are expected to suffer permanent disability or incapacity after research, the ethical thing is to euthanize them; but many people believe that this is disrespectful to life, so even though it is ethical within the paradigm of biological research, many people have a philosophical objection to this.

3 Cognitive level of analysis

Short answer questions

1   The command term *outline* asks for a brief account or summary.

There are several examples of cognitive processes to choose from including memory, perception, decision-making and language. Given the detailed coverage of memory in this chapter, it would be best if you chose memory as the relevant cognitive process. Two models of memory were discussed in detail – the multistore model and levels of processing. Any would do, but the multistore model may be easier to summarize. You can use an information-processing flowchart to aid your description of Atkinson and Shiffrin's (1968) model but be aware that you must also describe it in words.

2   The command term *describe* asks for a detailed account.

Based on the material presented in this chapter, you can answer this question by giving a detailed account of Brown and Kulik's (1977) theory of flashbulb memory. Note that the question does not ask for an evaluation, simply a description of the theory.

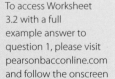

To access Worksheet 3.1 with a full example answer to question 3, please visit pearsonbacconline.com and follow the onscreen instructions.

3   The command term *explain* asks you to give a detailed account and explain the underlying rationale.

Here you need to describe the relevant material and explain the rationale underlying the use of technology. You must, in addition to giving a detailed discussion, explain why and how we rely on the technologies used in the investigation of cognitive processes. In this chapter, you could choose examples from the discussion of fMRI studies of decision making and cognitive reappraisal, or the MRI studies. From Chapter 2, you could choose to discuss the role of the hippocampus in memory.

4   The command term *analyse* asks you to break down what you are discussing in order to bring out the essential elements or structure of what you are addressing.

Analysis of how individualism–collectivism may affect flashbulb memory would involve a detailed account of precisely how this cultural dimension can affect a process like flashbulb memory. Discussion of the mediating role of emotional expression and social sharing should figure extensively in your answer.

Essay questions

To access Worksheet 3.2 with a full example answer to question 1, please visit pearsonbacconline.com and follow the onscreen instructions.

1   The command term *evaluate* asks you to make an appraisal by weighing up strengths and limitations.

Schema theory is discussed in some detail in this chapter and Chapter 4. You should use material from both chapters to answer the question.

The relevant studies should be clearly outlined before they are used to evaluate schema theory. Choose your studies in a way that allows you to evaluate major claims of schema theory. The emphasis throughout should be on the strengths and the weaknesses of schema theory. Obviously, the quality of the empirical studies used to evaluate the theory is also very relevant. Use the material presented in this book and your general knowledge of methodology to address issues relevant to the internal and external

(including ecological) validity of the studies you discuss. Always remember to relate the studies to the theory. It is the theory that is being evaluated.

2   The command term *discuss* asks you to present a considered and balanced review that includes a range of arguments, factors or hypotheses. Opinions or conclusions should be presented clearly and supported by appropriate evidence.

The interaction of cognitive and biological factors was addressed through (a) discussion of Schachter and Singer's two-factor theory and (b) Lazarus's appraisal theory of emotion. Either, or both, of these theories can be used to answer the question. If you refer to both, then you can afford to provide less detailed accounts of them. The interaction is very simple to demonstrate in the case of the two-factor theory. You can start with it and then refer to Lazarus's theory to elaborate further on the exact nature of the cognitive processes (appraisals) involved in emotion. The fMRI studies of cognitive reappraisal on pages 98–99 are useful as they relate Lazarus's theory to biology. Your conclusions should reflect the way you develop your arguments. Does your discussion lead to the conclusion that cognitive and biological factors are closely related in emotion? Remember, you must address explicitly *the extent to which* cognitive and biological factors interact in emotion.

 4   Sociocultural level of analysis

Short answer questions

1   The command term *outline* asks for a brief account or summary.

The two principles outlined in this chapter were: (a) that the social and cultural environment influences individual behaviour and (b) that we construct our conceptions of the individual and social self. Briefly describe these two principles and give a couple of examples drawn for the material covered in this chapter. Remember to relate just about everything you learn in this chapter to these two principles. Make sure you only refer to *two* principles; not *one* and not *three* or more.

2   The command term *explain* asks you to give a detailed account and explain the underlying rationale.

Based on the material covered in this chapter, you can choose to explain either the fundamental attribution error (FAE) or self-serving bias. You have to explain what psychologists believe about how the attributional bias comes about, or what functions it serves. All the statements made should be properly argued for and relevant empirical studies should also be discussed.

3   The command term *describe* asks for a detailed account.

You have plenty of choice here. You could discuss group polarization or groupthink. If you do, be careful to identify them as relevant *factors*. What they have in common is that they refer to group decision-making in settings requiring that a consensus is reached. Or, you may wish to address more specific factors such as the role of cohesiveness in groupthink phenomena. The question can also be answered by referring to culture as a factor influencing conformity.

 To access Worksheet 4.1 with a full example answer to question 3, please visit pearsonbacconline.com and follow the onscreen instructions.

4   The command term *explain* asks you to give a detailed account and explain the underlying rationale.

After defining the two terms, you need to give some examples that illustrate the definitions as well as explain the necessity of both etic and emic approaches to research.

Essay questions

1 The command term *evaluate* asks you to make an appraisal by weighing up strengths and limitations.

You should do so by referring to relevant empirical studies. After an outline of the theory, you should relate it to the minimal group paradigm as well as to additional studies testing the theory in the areas of stereotyping and conformity. The studies should, of course, be evaluated but the emphasis is on the extent to which, taken as a set, they support the theory's central claims.

To access Worksheet 4.2 with a full example answer to question 1, please visit pearsonbacconline.com and follow the onscreen instructions.

2 The command term *discuss* asks you to present a considered and balanced review that includes a range of arguments, factors or hypotheses. Opinions or conclusions should be presented clearly and supported by appropriate evidence.

Note that *research* refers both to theories and empirical studies. In this chapter, conformity research is discussed in some detail. Theoretical ideas included the dual-process model and explanations based on social identity theory. Make an appropriate selection of studies that you can summarize easily and which you can evaluate. Refer to evaluative comments made in this chapter but also evaluations you can articulate on the basis of your knowledge of methodology.

Options chapters

Chapters 5–9 deal with Options material, which is examined in Paper 2.

Each answer is marked out of 22 and the markscheme for essay questions on pages 352–353 is applicable to all questions on Paper 2.

5 Abnormal psychology

To access Worksheet 5.3 with a full example answer to question 1, please visit pearsonbacconline.com and follow the onscreen instructions.

1 The command term *discuss* asks you to present a considered and balanced review that includes a range of arguments, factors or hypotheses. Opinions or conclusions should be presented clearly and supported by appropriate evidence.

You need to decide which disorder you are going to write about. It may be tempting to include things you know about other disorders but you are clearly asked to focus on **one**. The three disorders you looked at in this chapter were phobias, depression, and anorexia nervosa. You are free to make your own choice but the widest range of possible biological factors can be found for phobias and depression.

Briefly outline your chosen disorder. Ensure that the symptoms of the disorder have been covered as this will probably be important in your answer later. Explain how you are going to answer the question by briefly outlining the biological factors you will discuss and how you will discuss them. For example, we looked at evolutionary explanations for phobias, genetic explanations and brain activity.

The body of your essay needs to demonstrate knowledge and comprehension by explaining the factors you have chosen with reference to research. For example, if you are writing about biological preparedness, you need to explain the idea with reference to Öhman et al. (1975). But remember that you also need to show critical thinking. If discussing biological preparedness, for example, you could criticize the methods used in

Öhman et al.'s study and the general problems of trying to gain experimental evidence for evolutionary psychology theories.

By covering at least two biological factors in this way, you will be able to reach a conclusion that is supported by your arguments. It should be clear from your answer that although biological factors have been identified and studied in numerous ways, like much research at the biological level of analysis, experiments in this area are often artificial and therefore much of our knowledge is based on correlation rather than causation.

2 The command term *evaluate* asks you to make an appraisal by weighing up strengths and limitations.

You should choose two studies that you know in sufficient detail to provide a meaningful evaluation. Studies that might be good for this include Caetono (1973), Rosenhan et al. (1973), Åhs et al. (2009) and Öhman et al. (1975) but there is a range of other possibilities. The studies do not need to be related to each other, but you may find it easier to evaluate them if your are able to compare and contrast their strengths and limitations.

Begin with a description of the first study. Do not go into too much detail but provide enough information that the aim, procedure and findings are clear. The procedure is likely to be particularly important as that is where many of the strengths and limitations can be found.

Follow the description by evaluating the study: explain strengths and limitations. In Chapter 1 we looked at how you can best evaluate studies. Consider (where appropriate) how the sample was obtained; if there were ethical problems with the study or if, in avoiding ethical problems, the study has low ecological validity; if participant or researcher expectancies may have altered the results; and so on. Bear in mind that it is not sufficient, for example, to state that a study lacks ecological validity: you need to make clear *how* the study is lacking and show that you understand why it is important. Using correct terminology is a good start, but by itself is not enough.

Repeat this for your second study. You need to make a conclusion as the definition of the command term suggests you make an appraisal. Make sure you provide this after evaluating each of the studies: a few sentences to explain what your judgement is about the quality of the study and the validity of the conclusions will be sufficient.

3 The command term *evaluate* asks you to make an appraisal by weighing up strengths and limitations.

Begin by choosing your disorder: phobias, depression or anorexia nervosa. Then decide which mode of treatment to focus on. Exercise 7 in this chapter will have given you the information you need to construct an answer to this question.

A good example would be individual treatment for phobias. Begin by explaining what a phobia is, particularly in terms of symptoms. Follow this with an explanation of available treatments: for phobias, we looked at systematic desensitization, in vivo exposure and cognitive restructuring.

Remember to complete your evaluation by explaining strengths and limitations of each treatment and referring to studies that help you draw your conclusions. You may find it useful to evaluate by referring to *other* types of treatment. For example, in the section on depression, we looked at interpersonal therapy as an alternative to some of the more theoretically based individual treatments and considered research that compared its effectiveness with other forms of therapy.

Your final appraisal can be expressed in a brief conclusion that clearly summarizes the argument you have made about how valid, accurate or effective the treatment is.

4 The command term *examine* asks you to consider an argument or concept in a way that uncovers the assumptions and interrelationships of the issue.

You need to explain the basis of different approaches to explaining normality and abnormality with reference to research and theory.

Consider the idea, for example, that deviation from social norms constitutes abnormality and is, therefore, a symptom we might be interested in treating. It is a good idea to use examples of behaviour connected with the disorders you have studied. For example, if a person refuses to eat with other people or plays with their food a lot, these might be signs of an eating disorder. Address the problems with defining abnormality this way and, where possible, make reference to research. Any research that addresses cultural differences in abnormality will be extremely useful to you to make your point.

Don't forget that you need to consider normality as well, so you will want to make reference to Jahoda's (1958) explanation of ideal mental health. You could link this to symptoms of the phobia, depression and anorexia nervosa to make your explanation clear.

6 Developmental psychology

1 The command term *to what extent* asks you to present a consideration of the merits of an argument or concept. Usually, you need to come to a supported conclusion. Opinions or conclusions should be presented clearly and supported by appropriate evidence.

You need to come to a general conclusion such as: Environmental and cognitive factors influence human development to a significant extent. But biological factors, as evidenced by the work carried out with gender development, are a potent influence on human development.

Cognitive factors
You may wish to restate the Piagetian belief that intelligence is under genetic control and develops in the form of predisposed stages; also the notion that children do not passively receive their knowledge but are curious, self-motivated and seek out information to construct their own understanding of the environment. You may wish to discuss the notion of schemas and the two types of adaptation.

Sociocultural factors
You may wish to discuss the effect diet and/or parenting has on development. You may wish to discuss diet as a biological factor. You might also wish to discuss Schoon and Bartley's notion of resilience as it contains sociocultural elements (academic competence, an effective and supportive family life, an effective social environment, employment).

Biological factors
You may wish to discuss the notion of gender as a biological drive as evidence by the cross-species phenomenon of rough and tumble (R&T) play. It is prevalent in the males of most mammals, in particular in chimpanzees, orang-utans and humans (Braggio et al., 1978) and even squirrels (Biben, 1998). It is widely accepted that R&T play is the result of hormonal changes in males – influxes of testosterone in early infanthood (the priming or organizing effect) and again at puberty (the activating effect). Jarvis states most research carried out into R&T play of young human and non-human primates

indicates such play creates valuable practice for the complex social interactions creatures need to undertake in order to become competent, socially mature adults.

Beach (1974) found female dogs which were exposed to male hormones were more likely to urinate like male dogs. Young et al. (1964) found female monkeys which were exposed to male hormones were more likely to engage in R&T play.

2 The command term *evaluate* asks you to make an appraisal by weighing up strengths and limitations.

You need to outline the strengths and limitations of the work of either Piaget or Vygotsky. Piaget offers the most detail and his ideas can be evaluated in the context of Vygotsky. You would need to introduce Piaget's ideas but the question emphasis is on evaluation.

To access Worksheet 6.1 with a full example answer to question 2, please visit pearsonbacconline.com and follow the onscreen instructions.

Positive evaluations

- Piaget produced the first comprehensive theory of child cognitive development; it has generated debate and stimulated research.
- Piaget modified theory to take account of criticisms and envisaged it constantly changing as new evidence came to light.
- Much criticism has been levelled at the 'ages and stages' but it is important to remember the theory is biologically based and demonstrates the child as a dynamic thinker, anxious to achieve coherence and test theories.
- Piaget was the first to investigate if biological maturation drove cognitive development. His vision of childhood cognitive changes regulated by biology is now widely accepted and supported by cross-cultural research.
- Piaget developed the notion of constructivism. He argued children are active in constructing their knowledge of the world rather than passive receivers of information. This is also now widely accepted. It changed notions of childhood and significantly influenced education.

Negative criticisms

- Piaget's methods have been criticized as too formal for children. When the methods are changed to show 'human sense', children often understand what is being asked and show cognitive ability outside their age-appropriate stage. Small sample sizes mean caution should be used when generalizing to large groups and cultures.
- Piaget failed to distinguish between competence (what a child is capable of) and performance (what a child can show when given a particular task). When tasks were altered, performance (and therefore competence) was affected.
- The notion of biological readiness has been questioned. If a child's cognitive development is solely driven by innate factors, training should not be able to propel the child onto the next stage.
- Piaget has been criticized for under-estimating the role of language in cognitive development.
- Piaget has been criticized for under-estimating the role of social development in cognitive development. The three-mountain experiment presents a social scene but Piaget focused on it as an abstract mental problem.
- The theory is very descriptive but does not provide detailed explanations for the stages. Piaget's supporters would counter, given his broad genetic explanations, that the technology did not exist for him to research his assumptions in depth.
- The model can be seen as too rigid and inflexible. However, supporters argue Piaget never intended it to be seen in such a light, and it should be seen as a metaphor and a guiding principle for teaching and learning.

3 The command term *discuss* asks you to present a considered and balanced review that includes a range of arguments, factors or hypotheses. Opinions or conclusions should be presented clearly and supported by appropriate evidence.

You need to clearly outline the effects on cognitive development of each of the variables (factors) you wish to use. Some may be more potent than others. Some will have knock-on effects (e.g. poverty may impact parenting availability, schooling and diet). You may develop these under an umbrella argument of socio-economic variables. You may wish to take each variable in isolation and dedicate one or two paragraphs to each. You need to present clear empirical evidence in this answer. The concept of variables is plural: you need to do more than one. Take one from social (e.g. parenting) and one from environmental (e.g. diet). It is unlikely the examiner will penalize you for failing to identify which are social and which are environmental as they are presented together in the syllabus.

4 The command term *examine* asks you to consider an argument or concept in a way that uncovers the assumptions and interrelationships of the issue.

You need to clearly demonstrate you understand what attachment is by defining it and then presenting a theory – Bowlby. You may also wish to briefly mention 'a strange situation' as an example of how attachment has been researched. For subsequent formation of relationships, you need to mention Hazan and Shaver (1987) who studied parent/child interactions as well as romantic couplings. You may also wish to mention Miyake et al. (1985), who studied Japanese mothers who place great value on developing close relationships with young infants and are rarely separated from them. As a result, American children show greater avoidant attachment than Japanese children (which can be interpreted as showing greater independence) whereas Japanese children show higher rates of secure attachment (leading to greater sensitivity to group needs as adults).

7 Health psychology

To access Worksheet 7.1 with a full example answer to question 1, please visit pearsonbacconline.com and follow the onscreen instructions.

1 The command term *to what extent* asks you to present a consideration of the merits of an argument or concept. Usually, you need to come to a supported conclusion. Opinions or conclusions should be presented clearly and supported by appropriate evidence.

You need to discuss the biological aspects of one or more health-related behaviours in a *balanced* way which means making an appraisal of each *in the context of* each other.

You may wish to discuss the influence of biological factors in the context of alcohol abuse or obesity or both. Whichever you choose, you should clearly identify the area(s) for the examiner.

2 The command term *evaluate* asks you to make an appraisal by weighing up strengths and limitations.

You need to outline the assumptions of one of the two models we looked at: the Health belief model (HBM) or the Theory of reasoned action (TRA). You should then discuss the strengths and problems associated with them. These guidelines consider the HBM.

The HBM rests on the assumption people will engage in healthy behaviour if they understand a negative health problem will arise if they do not. The key assumption is that people are rational thinkers – that is, they are capable of making and following choices that are in their best interest. Therefore, the HBM offers an optimistic view of the human condition and promotes the idea that people are responsible members of society with a keen interest in their own health.

People first evaluate a threat to their health (e.g. fast food) and then engage in a cost–benefit analysis of actions to either counter the threat or ignore it. Evaluations and cost benefit–analyses of this kind are examples of cognitive processes which the HBM is trying to influence to cause a change in behaviour.

There are a number of key problems with the HBM.
- It assumes people are rational when the evidence is sometimes to the contrary.
- It assumes people care about their health or the health of those they care for.
- It ignores physiological determinism.
- It assumes people are active thinkers able to make choices within the realm of freewill.
- It does not consider practical obstacles to effective health regulation, it only considers perceived obstacles.

You may wish to discuss some of these criticisms in the context of Theory of Reasoned Action (TRA), although you should make that clear to the examiner and your answer should remain focused on the HBM.

3 The command term *discuss* asks you to present a considered and balanced review that includes a range of arguments, factors or hypotheses. Opinions or conclusions should be presented clearly and supported by appropriate evidence.

You need to discuss physiological, psychological and social aspects of stress in a balanced way which means making an appraisal of each in the context of each other. Your answer should be in two parts – physiological and social aspects of stress.

Physiological aspects of stress
- Gender – Frankenhauser et al. (1976) reported boys have adrenaline rushes in exams that take longer to return to normal, whereas girls had a gentler, lower increase and returned to normal much quicker.
- Hormones – Children who had been exposed to significant stress in their home life (such as marital discord, alcoholism and child abuse) had impaired growth due to a lowering of the production of growth hormone in the pituitary gland (Powell et al. 1967).
- Immune system – Stone et al. (1987) report a correlation between a change in mood and a change in antibody concentration in bodily fluids – suggesting good moods contribute to a healthy immune system. Gross (1996) argues people often catch colds soon after periods of high stress (such as exams) and cites Goetsch and Fuller (1995) who refer to studies that show decreases in the activity of lymphocytes (white blood cells that fight viruses) among medical students during their final exams.

Social aspects of stress
- Change – Holmes and Rahe (1967) suggest a major cause of stress is some form of *change* and they compiled the Social Readjustment Rating Scale (SRRS) to rate potential social events out of 100 for their potential to lead to stress (e.g. death of a spouse was given a rating of 100, change of school was given 20).
- Workplace stress – According to The National Institute for Occupational Safety and Health (NIOSH), workplace stress can be defined as the harmful physical and emotional responses that occur when there is a poor match between job demands and the skills and resources, or personal needs of the worker (1999). You may wish to discuss Hochschild's ideas (1983). She argued the pressure of needing to conform to work expectations can lead to negative effects such as emotional dissonance (where the person feels false and hypocritical) and this leads to stress and anxiety. Rutter and Fielding (1988) positively correlated the suppression of emotions in the workplace with stress and negatively correlated the suppression with job satisfaction.

Job autonomy, in a managerial sense, can also affect stress levels – workers with less job autonomy and therefore less ability to make decisions about their own lives have been shown to experience greater levels of stress. Marmot et al. (1997) found clerical and office support employees in the civil service were four times more likely to die of a heart attack than those in the most senior grades. Theorell et al. (1985) found greater blood pressure in high demand–low control occupations such as waiters and cooks.

4 The command term *evaluate* asks you to make an appraisal by weighing up strengths and limitations.

You need to outline the strengths and limitations of stress inoculation training (SIT) and yoga.

SIT

SIT was developed by Meichenbaum in the 1970s and takes a cognitive approach to treatment with the underlying aim of changing thought processes to combat the effects of stress. According to Meichenbaum, to be most effective, the training should come before the onset of extreme anxiety not after a stressful event (he saw the therapy in the same way as a medical inoculation). SIT is designed to be individually tailored to the needs of the person suffering stress and comes under the banner of cognitive-behavioural therapy as it changes thought and behaviour.

Evaluation – positives

- SIT accepts the stress an individual can experience is often unavoidable (e.g. in the workplace).
- SIT tailors the therapy to the needs of the client with the active cooperation of the client.
- The client-centred approach promotes equality between client and therapist and empowers the client to take control of their stress management.
- SIT posits emotional and cognitive awareness at the forefront of the therapeutic environment thereby increasing the chances of long-term success.

Evaluation – negatives

- Individuals vary in how they respond to treatment and some may not be able to cope with the stressors present in their environment regardless of the training they undertake.
- SIT takes time and money and is not suited to the lifestyles of everyone.
- SIT is a rigorous programme requiring high levels of commitment and motivation.
- SIT requires a discussion of feelings and personal thoughts, thus it is more suitable for some cultures than others.

Yoga

Yoga represents a holistic approach to stress reduction and incorporates physical, cognitive and spiritual concepts with the aim of making the individual more self-aware and more aware of the universe around them. This cosmic awareness is thought to reduce stress and promote physical and mental well being. Yoga is an expansive term and so it is difficult to give precise evaluations for the whole practice. However, some generalizations can be made.

Evaluation – positives

- Yoga improves quality of life in a very broad sense (Cohen, 2006). It provides exercise, relaxation and self-awareness; it puts the individual in touch with like-minded people with regular social interaction.
- Most yoga classes consist of a combination of physical exercises, breathing routines, and meditation. These activities make yoga beneficial for people with certain health conditions such as hypertension, asthma, and back problems.

Evaluation – negatives

- Stress often has a very specific source relative to the individual (e.g. marital, occupational) that may need specialist counselling or therapy.
- Yoga is often a holistic lifestyle choice for its practitioners; it incorporates many sensible ways to take control of one's life and live a more peaceful and healthy existence (e.g. new food habits). It cannot, therefore, be said to produce exacting health benefits.
- The physical exertions are not suitable for everyone.

8 Psychology of human relationships

1 The command term *contrast* asks you to give an account of the differences between two (or more) items or situations, referring to both (all) of them throughout.

 To access Worksheet 8.3 with a full example answer to question 1, please visit pearsonbacconline.com and follow the onscreen instructions.

The two relevant theories in this chapter are kin selection and the empathy–altruism hypothesis. Do not attempt to answer the question by simply *describing* the two theories: be explicit in showing that you understand the differences between them.

If you completed exercise 2, you will have a summary of similarities and differences between the theories and you can use this to help you plan your answer.
- Briefly explain the two theories.
- Highlight that although both emphasize biological factors, the empathy–altruism hypothesis is also concerned with cognitive factors. Explain these.
- Address the empirical evidence for the theories. Kin selection is an evolutionary theory, so it is virtually impossible to test experimentally; its validity is questionable. Although experiments test the validity of empathy–altruism, we may find them artificial. Give details of problems in research with both theories in order to get marks for critical thinking. Consider also what ideal tests of these theories would look like.
- Gender and culture are possibly very important in altruism. Explain how these factors are, or are not, accounted for by the two theories.
- Make a brief conclusion. You are not asked to choose one of the theories and justify it as being better, so your conclusion can be brief.

2 The command term *to what extent* asks you to present a consideration of the merits of an argument or concept. Usually, you need to come to a supported conclusion. Opinions or conclusions should be presented clearly and supported by appropriate evidence.

You need to provide an explanation of what the biological factors that influence prosocial behaviour are, and you need to contrast this with the importance of non-biological factors in order to inform a conclusion.

Address the biological factors by explaining the importance of emotional arousal (empathy–altruism hypothesis) and the evolutionary theory of kin selection. Given that there are cross-cultural differences in prosocial behaviour, we cannot say for certain that biology plays an exclusive role. Justify how important you feel culture is by referring to the quality of research in these areas.

There is a lot of research about the various sociocultural and cognitive factors that influence bystander intervention. You can use this to build an argument against the importance of biological factors. As you plan the essay, you may find that building a table to balance biological and non-biological factors against each other will help to clarify your conclusion.

3   The command term *compare* asks you to give an account of the similarities between two (or more) items or situations, referring to both (all) of them throughout.

This question asks only about sociocultural and cognitive factors. Biological factors are not required. Remember you need to include research and evaluation.

Address proximity, familiarity, reciprocity, familiarity, the matching phenomenon, social comparison, reward theory and the gain–loss hypothesis, mentioning research where appropriate and consider how these factors contribute to attraction. To gain marks for critical thinking, your answer could focus on similarities in terms of their power in determining attraction, the amount of research that supports them and the quality of that research.

4   The command term *discuss* asks you to present a considered and balanced review that includes a range of arguments, factors or hypotheses. Opinions or conclusions should be presented clearly and supported by appropriate evidence.

You need to clearly outline two strategies: group therapy to reduce domestic violence and primary prevention strategies in schools. Describe these strategies and highlight any similarities and differences you observe. Your answer to exercise 10 will help you here.

The focus of your discussion should *not* be on how well one strategy has been proven to be effective, as it is very difficult to establish good measures of the phenomenon under investigation. Consider why available research methods have not been able to provide more than a vague idea of how effective each strategy is. Consider the way that their effectiveness is measured and what their effect is supposed to be. A final section of your essay could consider how applicable each approach is likely to be across cultures.

More advanced students may consider the causes of domestic violence and note how well the two strategies address biological, cognitive and sociocultural factors that influence violence. How well could a primary prevention programme work, for example, if the cause of violence is mostly biological?

It is not essential for you to reach a conclusion, but you may find that the balance of your argument is weighted towards the effectiveness of one strategy rather than the other. If you state this in your conclusion, be sure that you have supported your statement with a justification based on the evidence you have presented in the body of your answer.

 ## 9   Sport psychology

1   The command term *discuss* asks you to present a considered and balanced review that includes a range of arguments, factors or hypotheses. Opinions or conclusions should be presented clearly and supported by appropriate evidence.

If you kept a record of research and theories while working through this chapter, you should have a clear idea about how factors from each level of analysis influence behaviour in sport. You can focus on one area (e.g. emotion and motivation or burnout) or try to use several. However, don't try to cover too much breadth or you risk being only descriptive and not having time for critical thinking.

If you choose the cognitive level of analysis, you could begin by outlining cognitive evaluation theory with appropriate research to support your description. Provide a critical appraisal of the theory by outlining strengths and limitations of research that support it. Repeat this process with achievement goal theory and goal setting in general, and self-efficacy. This gives you a substantial discussion of the role of cognitive factors.

In addition, you can consider the role of cognitive appraisal in anxiety and arousal, and response to injury.

To ensure you gain good marks for critical thinking and organization, note whether there are any limitations or strengths that are common to research into cognitive processes in sports psychology. For example, the heavy emphasis on questionnaires may be a problem that invalidates much of what we know about cognitive processes in sport. Addressing methodological problems throughout your essay will allow you to make a good summary in your conclusion that is supported by appropriate evidence.

2   The command terms *define* asks you to give the precise meaning of a word, phrase, concept or physical quantity. The command term *compare* asks you to give an account of the similarities between two (or more) items or situations, referring to both (all) of them throughout.

Define burnout: a phenomenon involving a variety of symptoms (name them). You could mention that burnout can be measured using questionnaires such as the Athletic Burnout Questionnaire.

There are three models you could choose from: the Cognitive affective stress model, the Negative training model, and the Commitment model. More information is given in this chapter about the first two of these.

Explain similarities between the two models. Remember to describe the key elements of both models and to support your description with research where possible.

If you completed exercise 12, you should already have a record of the main similarities between these two models. Similarities are often more difficult to find than differences. Both models are focused on burnout occurring in the individual, even if they approach it in different ways. There are similarities in the methods used to research the models, particularly in terms of the use of questionnaires, and this exposes similar limitations of the models: there is limited evidence to suggest that either explanation of burnout is correct because ethical concerns prevent the kind of experiment that would help inform our understanding better. A further similarity is that they are theories that have practical applications: both models provide guidance for coaches and parents to help prevent burnout. In both models, the prevention of burnout may involve similar steps.

3   The command term *evaluate* asks you to make an appraisal by weighing up strengths and limitations.

To access Worksheet 9.3 with a full example answer to question 3. please visit pearsonbacconline.com and follow the onscreen instructions.

You should begin by choosing two studies that you know in sufficient detail to provide a meaningful evaluation. Useful studies here include Mellalieu, Hanton and Thomas (2007) relating to the use of imagery and self talk to moderate arousal; Schofield et al.'s study about goal-setting with pedometers (2007); Raglin and Turner (1993) relating to the inverted-U hypothesis; Marlow et al.'s water polo study (1998); and Hatzigeorgiadis et al.'s self-talk study (2009). There are other possibilities. The studies do not need to be related to each other, but you may find it easier to evaluate them if you are able to compare and contrast their strengths and limitations.

Begin with a description of the first study. Do not go into too much detail but provide enough information that the aim, procedure and findings are clear. The procedure is likely to be particularly important as that is where many of the strengths and limitations can be found.

Follow the description by evaluating the study: explain strengths and limitations. In the Chapter 1 we looked at how you can best evaluate studies. Consider (where appropriate) how the sample was obtained; if there were ethical problems with the study or if, in avoiding ethical problems, the study has low ecological validity; if participant

or researcher expectancies may have altered the results; and so on. Bear in mind that it is not sufficient, for example, to state that a study lacks ecological validity: you need to make clear *how* the study is lacking and show that you understand why it is important. Using correct terminology is a good start, but by itself is not enough.

Repeat this for your second study. You need to make a conclusion as the definition of the command term suggests you make an appraisal. Make sure you provide this after evaluating each of the studies: a few sentences to explain what your judgement is about the quality of the study and the validity of the conclusions will be sufficient.

4   The command term *to what extent* asks you to present a consideration of the merits of an argument or concept. Usually, you need to come to a supported conclusion. Opinions or conclusions should be presented clearly and supported by appropriate evidence.

If you completed exercises 7 and 8 in this chapter, you will have identified a number of ways that the coach can have an impact:
- reducing anxiety through self-talk training
- contributing to or preventing burnout and dropout
- giving feedback that increases or decreases self-efficacy
- creating a positive motivational climate.

There is theory and research relating to all of these and you must support your explanation of the effects of a coach on behaviour with relevant research. However, you need to do more than simply explain the possible effects: you should provide a judgement on how important the coach's role is. From the material in this chapter, you will find it very difficult to argue that the role of the coach is a small one: while athletes do a lot of work themselves, most of them are guided and affected by a coach. The Fraser–Thomas et al. (2008) study comparing those who dropped out of swimming and those who did not is one example of research supporting the importance of the coach's role.

However, there is the possibility that a coach's biases lead to self-fulfilling prophecies, and it is not so much the coach's work as the coach's perceptions that are important. Consider also that a causal link has not been established because of the typical methods used in sports psychology (i.e. a heavy focus on questionnaire data). Questionnaire data is usually unable to provide causal information, and in addition is very prone to response biases. With a lot of research based on youth samples, it is not difficult to imagine how participants may overstate the importance of their coach. These evaluative points should be clearly made when you address the research supporting your conclusion.

REFERENCE LIST

1 Research methodology

Bales RF. (1950). *Interaction process analysis: A method for the study of small groups.* Reading, MA: Addison–Wesley

Buchanan D. (2001). The role of photography in organization research: A re-engineering case illustration. *J Manage Inquiry* 47:151–64

Burnell K, Coleman PG, Hunt N. (2009). *Coping with traumatic memories: Second World War veterans' experiences of social support in relation to the narrative coherence of war memories.* Ageing and Society (online) 30: 7–78

Eisner EW. (1991). *The enlightened eye: Qualitative inquiry and the enhancement of educational practice.* New York, NY: Macmillan Publishing Company

Hussey J, Hussey R. (1997). *Business research: A practical guide for undergraduate and postgraduate students.* London: Macmillan

Lincoln YS, Guba EG. (1985). *Naturalistic inquiry.* California: Sage Publications

McCray JA, Bailly MD, King AR. (2005). **Personality and individual differences.** *J Gen Psychol* 38(5):1097–105

Middlemist RD, Matter ES. (1976). Personal space invasions in the lavatory: Suggestive evidence for arousal. *J Pers Soc Psychol* 33(5):541–46

Rosenthal R. (1966). *Experimenter effects in behavioural research.* New York: Appleton–Century–Crofts

Spradley J. (1979). *The ethnographic interview.* New York: Holt Rinehart and Winston

Stake RE. (1994). Case studies. In: NK Denzin, YS Lincoln (eds). *Handbook of qualitative research* (pp236–247). Thousand Oaks, CA: Sage Publications

Vervoort T, Goubert L, Eccleston C, et al. (2008) The effects of parental presence upon the facial expression of pain: The moderating role of child pain catastrophizing. *Pain* 138:2277–85

Walker L. (2005). Men behaving differently: South African men since 1994. *Cult Health Sex* 7(3):225–38

Weiner E. (2005). No (wo)man's land: The post-socialist purgatory of Czech female factory workers. *Soc Probl* 52(4):572–92

Yin R. (1989). *Case study research: Design and methods* (rev. edn). Beverly Hills, CA: Sage Publishing

Yin R. (1994). *Case study research: Design and methods* (2nd edn). Beverly Hills, CA: Sage Publishing

2 The biological level of analysis

Avery DH, Eder DN, Bolte MA, et al. (2001). Dawn simulation and bright light in the treatment of SAD: A controlled study. *Biol Psychiat* 50(3):205–16

Bailey JM, Pillard RC. (1991). A genetic study of male sexual orientation. *Arch Gen Psychiat* 48(12):1089–96

Bonson KR, Murphy DL. (1996). Alterations in responses to LSD in humans associated with chronic administration of tricyclic antidepressants, monoamine oxidase inhibitors or lithium. *Behavioural Brain Research* 73:229–33

Brefczynski–Lewis JA, Lutz A, Schaefer HS, et al. (2007) Neural correlates of attentional expertise in long-term meditation practitioners. *Proc Natl Acad Sci USA* 104:11483–88

Clausen J, Keck DD, Heisey WM. (1948). Experimental studies on the nature of species: III Environmental responses of climatic races of *Achillea. Carnegie I Wash* Publication 581

Damasio H, Grabowski T, Frank R, et al. (1994). The return of Phineas Gage: The skull of a famous patient yields clues about the brain. *Science* 264:1102–05

Draganski B, Gaser C, Busch V, et al. (2004). Changes in grey matter induced by training. *Nature* 427:311–12

Durrant R. (2009). Born to kill? A critical evaluation of homicide adaptation theory. *Aggress Violent Beh* 14(5):374–81

Herrnstein RJ, Murray C. (1994). *The Bell Curve: Intelligence and Class Structure in American Life.* New York: Free Press

Heston LL. (1966). Psychiatric disorders in foster home reared children of schizophrenic mothers. *Brit J Psychiat* 112(489):819–25

Holt–Lunstad J, Birmingham WA, Light KC. (2008). Influence of a 'warm touch' support enhancement intervention among married couples on ambulatory blood pressure oxytocin alpha amylase and cortisol. *Psychosom Med* 70:976–85

Lewy AJ, Emens J, Jackman A, et al. (2006). Circadian uses of melatonin in humans. *Chronobiol Int* 23(1&2):403–412

Maguire EA, Gadian DG, Johnsrude IS, et al. (2000). Navigation-related structural change in the hippocampi of taxi drivers. *Proc Natl Acad Sci USA* 97:4398–403

Morhenn VB, Park JW, Piper E, et al. (2008) Monetary sacrifice among strangers is mediated by endogenous oxytocin release after physical contact. *Evol Hum Behav* 29(6):375–83

Myers RE, Sperry RW. (1953). Interocular transfer of a visual form discrimination habit in cats after section of the optic chiasm and corpus callosum. *Anat Rec* 115:351

Ogden JA. (2005). *Fractured minds: A case–study approach to clinical neuropsychology*. Oxford: Oxford University Press

Pedersen CA, Boccia ML. (2003). Oxytocin antagonism alters rat dams' oral grooming and upright posturing over pups. *Physiol Behav* 80(2–3):233–41

Read J, Mosher L, Bentall R. (2004). Models of madness: Psychological social and biological approaches to schizophrenia. Hove UK: Brunner–Routledge

Santtila P, Sandnabba NK, Harlaar N, et al. (2008) Potential for homosexual response is prevalent and genetic. *Biol Psychol* 77:102–05

Schachter S, Singer JE. (1962). Cognitive social and physiological determinants of emotional state. *Psychol Rev* 69:379–99

Sperry R. (1968). Hemisphere deconnection and unity in conscious awareness. *Am psychol* 23(10):723–33

Tierney MC, Varga M, Hosey L, et al. (2001). PET evaluation of bilingual language compensation following early childhood brain damage. *Neuropsychologia*. 39(2):114–21

Turner RA, Alternos M, Enos T, et al. (1999). Preliminary research on plasma oxytocin in normal cycling women: Investigating emotional and interpersonal distress. *Psychiatry* 62:97–113

Zietsch BP, Morley KI, Shekar SN, et al. (2008). Genetic factors predisposing to homosexuality may increase mating success in heterosexuals. *Evol Hum Behav* 29:424–33

③ The cognitive level of analysis

Anderson JR, Reder LM. (1979). An elaboration processing explanation of depth of processing. In: L Cermak and F Craik (eds). *Levels of processing in human memory*. Hillsdale, NJ: Erlbaum

Atkinson RC, Shiffrin RM. (1968). Human memory: A proposed system and its control processes. In: KW Spence and JT Spence (eds). *The psychology of learning and motivation* (Vol. 2). London: Academic Press

Baddeley A, Hitch G. (1974). Working memory. In: GH Bower (ed.). *Recent advances in learning and motivation 8*. New York: Academic Press

Baddeley A. (2009). What is memory? In: Baddeley A, Eysenck MW, Anderson CA. *Memory*. Hove and New York: Psychology Press

Bandura A. (1977). *Social learning theory* (2nd edn). Englewood Cliffs, NJ: Prentice–Hall

Barrett LF. (2006). Solving the emotion paradox: Categorisation and the experience of emotion. *Pers Soc Psychol Rev* 10:20–46

Bartlett FC. (1932). *Remembering*. Cambridge University Press

Basabe N, Ros M. (2005). Cultural dimensions and social behaviour correlates: Individualism–collectivism and power distance. *Rev Int Psychol Soc* 1:189–225

Bothwell RK, Brigham JC, Pigott MA. (1987). An exploratory study of personality differences in eyewitness memory. *J Soc Behav Pers* 2:335–43

Bower GH, Black JB, Turner TJ. (1979). Scripts in memory for text. *Cognitive Psychol* 11:177–220

Bransford JD, Johnson MK. (1972). Contextual prerequisites for understanding: Some investigators of comprehension and recall. *J Verb Learn Verb Be* 11:717–726

Broadbent DE. (1958). *Perception and communication*. Oxford: Pergamon

Brown R, Kulik J. (1977). Flashbulb memories. *Cognition* 5:73–99

Cannon WB. (1929). *Bodily changes in pain hunger fear and range*. New York: Appleton

Chomsky N. (1959). Review of Skinner's verbal behaviour. *Language* 35:26–58

Colby MAE, Weaver CA, III. (2006). Comparing eyewitness memory and confidence for actors and observers in product identification situations: Extending findings and methodology from criminal justice. *App Psychol Crim Just* 2:145–62

Conway MA, Anderson SJ, Larsen SF, et al. (1994). The formation of flashbulb memories. *Mem Cognition* 22:326–43

Craik FIM, Lockhart R. (1972). Levels of processing. *J Verbal Learn Verbal Be* 11:671–84

Craik FIM, Tulving E. (1975). Depth of processing and the retention of words in episodic memory. *J Exp Psychol Gen* 104:268–94

Craik FIM, Watkins MJ. (1973). The role of rehearsal in short-term memory. *J Verbal Learn Verbal Be* 12:599–607

Davelaar EJ, Goshen–Gottstein Y, Ashkenazi A, et al. (2005). The demise of short-term memory revisited: Empirical and computational investigations of recency effects. *Psychol Rev* 112:3–42

Deffenbacher KA, Bornstein BH, Penrod SD, et al. (2004). A meta-analytic review of the effects of high stress on eyewitness memory. *Law Human Behav* 28:687–706

Eakin DK, Schreiber TA, Sergent–Marshall S. (2003). The presence and absence of memory impairment as a function of warning and misinformation accessibility. *J Exp Psychol Learn* 5:813–25

Eichenbaum H. (2000). A cortical-hippocampal system for declarative memory. *Nat Rev Neurosci* 1:41–50

Eysenck MW. (1978). Levels of processing – critique. *Brit J Psychol* 69:157–69

Eysenck MW. (2009). Eyewitness testimony. In: Baddeley A, Eysenck MW, Anderson CA. *Memory*. Hove and New York: Psychology Press

Eysenck MW, Keane MT. (2010). *Cognitive psychology: A student's handbook*. (6th edn). Hove and New York: Psychology Press

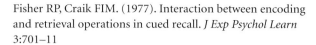

Fisher RP, Craik FIM. (1977). Interaction between encoding and retrieval operations in cued recall. *J Exp Psychol Learn* 3:701–11

Fiske ST. (2004). *Social Beings: A Core Motives Approach to Social Psychology*. Wiley.

Gauld A, Stephenson GM. (1967). Some experiments relating to Bartlett's theory of remembering. *Brit J Psychol* 58:39–50

Glanzer M, Cunitz AR. (1966). Two storage mechanisms in free recall. *J Verb Learn Verb Be* 5:928–935

Glanzer M. (1972). Storage mechanisms in recall. In: GH Bower (ed.). *The psychology of learning and motivation: Advances in research and theory* (Vol. 5) (pp129–93). San Diego, CA: Academic Press

Herrald MM, Tomaka J. (2002). Patterns of emotion-specific appraisals coping and physiological reactivity during an ongoing emotional episode. *J Pers Soc Psychol* 83:425–33

Hodges JR, Patterson K, Tyler L. (1994). Loss of semantic memory: Implications for the modularity of mind. *Cognitive Neuropsych* 11:505–42

Huettel SA, Stowe CJ, Gordon EM, et al. (2006). Neural signatures of economic preferences for risk and ambiguity. *Neuron* 49:765–75

Ihlebaek C, Love T, Eilertsen DE, et al. (2003). Memory for a staged criminal event witnessed live and on video. *Memory* 11:319

Ilse ADA, van Halteren–van Scherder T, Hulstijn W. (2007). Motor-skill learning in Alzheimer's disease: A review with an eye to clinical practice. *Neuropsychology Review* 17:203–12

James W. (1890). *The principles of psychology*. New York: Henry Holt & Co

Julian M, Bohannon JN, Aue W. (2009). Measures of flashbulb memory: Are elaborate memories consistently accurate? In: O Luminet and A Curci (eds). *Flashbulb memories: New issues and new perspectives* (pp. 99–122). Hove and New York: Psychology Press.

Kensinger EA, Corkin S. (2003). Neural changes in aging. In: L. Nadel (ed.). *Encyclopedia of cognitive science.* London: Macmillan

Kuppens P, van Mechelen I, Smits DJM, et al. (2003). The appraisal basis of anger: Specificity necessity and sufficiency of components. *Emotion* 3:254–69

Lazarus RS. (1982). Thoughts on the relation between emotion and cognition. *Am Psychol.* 37:1019–24

Lazarus RS. (1991). *Emotion and adaptation.* New York: Oxford University Press

Levenson RW. (1992). Autonomic nervous system differences among emotions. *Psychol Sci* 3:23–27

Lockhart RS, Craik FIM. (1990). Levels of processing: A retrospective commentary on a framework for memory research. *Can J Psychology* 44:87–112

Loftus EF. (1979). *Eyewitness testimony*. Cambridge, MA: Harvard University Press

Loftus EF, Palmer JC. (1974) Reconstruction of automobile destruction: An example of the interaction between language and memory. *J Verb Learn Verb Be* 13:585–589

Loftus EF, Loftus GR, Messo J. (1987). Some facts about weapon focus. *Law Human Behav* 11:55–62

Lorenzo A, Yuan M, Zhang Z, et al. (2000). Amyloid beta interacts with the amyloid precursor protein: A potential toxic mechanism in Alzheimer's disease. *Nat Neurosci* 3:460–64

Luminet O, Bouts B, Delie F, et al. (2000). Social sharing of emotion following exposure to a negatively valenced situation. *Cognition Emotion* 14:661–88

Luminet O. (2009). Models for the formation of flashbulb memories. In: O Luminet and A Curci (eds). *Flashbulb memories: New issues and new perspectives.* Taylor & Francis Group, Psychology Press

Macrae CN, Milne AB, Bodenhausen GV. (1994). Stereotypes as energy–saving devices: A peek inside the cognitive toolbox. *J Pers Soc Psychol* 66:37–47

Marshall G, Zimbardo P. (1979). Affective consequences of inadequately explaining physiological arousal. *J Pers Soc Psychol* 37:970–88

Mezzacappa ES, Kelsey RM, Katlin ES. (1999). The effects of epinephrine administration on impedance cardiographic measures of cardiovascular function. *Int J Psychophysiol* 31:189–96

Miller GA. (1956). The magical number seven. *Psychol Rev* 63: 81–97

Murdock BB. (1962). The serial position effect in free recall. *J Exp Psychol* 64:482–88

Neisser U, Harsch N. (1992). Phantom flashbulbs: False recollections of hearing the news about *Challenger*. In: E Winograd and U Neisser (eds). *Affect and accuracy in recall: Studies of 'flashbulb' memories* (Vol. 4). New York: Cambridge University Press

Ochsner KN, Gross JJ. (2008). Cognitive emotion regulation: Insights from social cognitive and affective neuroscience. *Curr Dir Psychol Sci* 17:153–58

Ohman A. (2000). Fear and anxiety: Evolutionary cognitive and clinical perspectives. In: M Lewis, JM Haviland (eds). *Handbook of emotions* (2nd edn). New York: Guildford Press

Otani H, Kusumi T, Kato K, et al. (2005). Remembering a nuclear accident in Japan: Did it trigger flashbulb memories? *Memory* 13:6–20

Paez D, Bellelli G, Rime B. (2009). Flashbulb memories culture and collective memories: Psychosocial processes related to rituals emotions and memories. In: O Luminet and A Curci (eds). *Flashbulb memories: New issues and new perspectives.* Taylor & Francis Group, Psychology Press

Parrott AC. (2000). Human research on MDMA (3,4-methylenedioxymethamphetamine) neurotoxicity: cognitive and behavioural indices of change. *Neuropsychobiology* 42:17–24

Pasupathi M. (2001). The social construction of the personal past and its implcations for adult development. *Psychol Bull* 127:651–72

Paulus MP, Hozack N, Zauscher B, et al. (2001). Prefrontal parietal and temporal cortex networks underlie decision-making in the presence of uncertainty. *Neuroimage* 13:91–100

Pavlov I. (1928). *Lectures on conditioned reflexes.* New York: International Publishers

Peterson LR, Peterson MJ. (1959). Short-term retention of individual verbal items. *J Expl Psychol* 58:193–98

Platt ML. (2002). Neural correlates of decisions. *Curr Opin Neurobiol* 12:141–48

Purves D, Brannon E, Cabeza R, et al. (2008). *Principles of Cognitive Neuroscience.* Sunderland, MA: Sinauer Associates

Reisenzein R. (1983). The Schachter theory of emotion: Two decades later. *Psychological Bulletin* 94:239–64

Riniolo TC, Koledin M, Drakulic GM, et al. (2003). An archival study of eyewitness memory of the *Titanic's* final plunge. *J Gen Psychol* 130:89–95

Robinson MD. (1998). Running from William James' bear: A review of preattentive mechanisms and their contributions to emotional experience. *Cognition Emotion* 12:667–96

Rumelhart DE. (1975). Notes on a schema for stories. In: DG Bobrow and A Collins (eds). *Representation and understanding: Studies in cognitive science.* New York: Academic Press

Salthouse TA, Becker JT. (1998). Independent effects of Alzheimer's disease on neuropsychological functioning. *Neuropsychology* 12:242–52

Schacter S, Singer JE. (1962). Cognitive social and physiological determinants of emotional states. *Psychol Rev* 69:379–99

Schank RC, Abelson RP. (1977). *Scripts plans goals and understanding: An inquiry into human knowledge structures.* Hillsdale, NJ: Lawrence Erlbaum

Schwindt GC, Black SE. (2009). Functional imaging studies of episodic memory in Alzheimer's disease: A qualitative meta-analysis. *Neuroimage* 45:181–90

Selco DJ. (1990). Deciphering Alzheimer's disease: The amyloid precursor protein yields new clues. *Science* 248:1058–60

Skinner BF. (1938). *The behaviour of organisms.* New York: Appleton–Century–Crofts

Skinner BF. (1957). *Verbal behaviour.* New York: Appleton–Century–Crofts

Smith CA, Lazarus RS. (1993). Appraisal components core relational themes and the emotions. *Cognition Emotion* 7:233–69

Speisman JC, Lazarus RS, Mordkoff AM, et al. (1964). The experimental reduction of stress based on ego defence theory. *J Abnorm Soc Psych* 68:397–98

Squire LR. (1987). *Memory and brain.* New York: Oxford University Press

Talarico JM, Rubin DC. (2003). Confidence not consistency characterises flashbulb memories. *Psychol Sci* 14:455–61

Wager D, Davidson ML, Hughes BL, et al. (2008). Prefrontal–subcortical pathways mediating successful emotion regulation. *Neuron* 59:1037–50

Wang Q, Aydin C. (2009). Cultural issues in flashbulb memory. In: O Luminet and A Curci (eds). *Flashbulb memories: New issues and new perspectives.* Taylor & Francis Group, Psychology Press

Watson JB. (1913). Psychology as the behaviorist views it. *Psychol Rev* 20:158–77

Whalen PJ, Rauch SL, Etcoff NL, et al. (1998). Masked presentations of emotional facial expressions modulate amygdala activity without explicit knowledge. *J Neurosci* 18:411–18

Williams HL, Conway MA, Cohen G. (2008). Autobiographical memory. In: G Cohen, MA Conway (eds). *Memory in the real world* (3rd edn). Hove, UK: Psychology Press

Winograd E, Killinger WA, Jr. (1983). Relating age at encoding in early childhood to adult recall: Development of flashbulb memories. *J Exp Psychol Gen* 112:413–22

Winograd E, Neisser U. (eds). (1992). *Affect and accuracy in recall: Studies of 'flashbulb' memories* (Vol. 4). New York: Cambridge University Press

Yuille JC, Cutshall JL. (1986). A case study of eyewitness memory of a crime. *J Appl Psychol* 71:291–301

Zajonc RB. (1980). Feeling and thinking: Preferences need no inferences. *Am Psychol* 39:117–23

 # The sociocultural level of analysis

Abrams D, Hogg MA, Marques JM. (2005) *The social psychology of inclusion and exclusion.* UK: Psychology Press

Abrams D, Wetherell M, Cochrane S, et al. (1990). Knowing what to think by knowing who you are: Self-categorisation and the nature of norm formation conformity and group polarization. *Brit J Soc Psychol* 29:97–119

Abramson LY, Metalsky GI, Alloy LB. (1989). Hopelessness depression: A theory-based subtype of depression. *Psychol Rev* 96:358–72

Almagor M, Tellegen A, Waller, NG. (1995). The big seven model: A crosscultural replication and further exploration of the basic dimensions of natural language trait descriptors. *J Pers Soc Psychol* 69:300–07

Aronson E, Wilson TD, Akert RM. (2007). *Social psychology* (7th edn). The Upper Saddle River, NJ: Prentice–Hall

Asch SE. (1951). Effects of group pressure on the modification and distortion of judgments. In: H Guetzkow (ed.). *Groups, leadership and men.* Pittsburgh, PA: Carnegie

Asch SE. (1956). Studies of independence and conformity: A minority of one against a unanimous majority. *Psychol Monogr* 70: (Whole No. 416)

Augoustinos M, Walker I, Donaghue N. (2006). *Social cognition: An integrated introduction.* (2nd edn). London: Sage

Ayoun B, Moreo P. (2009). Impact of time orientation on the strategic behaviour of Thai and American hotel managers. *J Hosp Marketing Manage* 18:676–91

Bandura A. (1965). Influences of model's reinforcement contingencies on the acquisition of imitative responses. *J Pers Soc Psychol* 1:589–93

Bandura A. (1977). Social learning theory (2nd edn). Englewood Cliffs, NJ: Prentice–Hall

Bandura A. (1986). *Social foundations of thought and action: A social cognitive theory.* Englewood Cliffs, NJ: Prentice–Hall

Bandura A. (1997). *Self-efficacy: The exercise of control.* New York: WH Freeman and Co

Bandura A. (2006). Social cognitive theory. In: S. Rogelberg (ed.) *Encyclopedia of industrial/organisational psychology.* Beverly Hills: Sage Publications

Bargh JA, Chen M, Burrows L. (1996). Automaticity of social behaviour: Direct effects of trait construct and stereotype activation on action. *J Pers Soc Psychol* 37:230–44

Baron RA, Branscombe NR, Byrne D. (2008). *Social psychology* (12th edn). Boston, MA: Allyn and Bacon

Baron RS. (2005). So right, it's wrong: Groupthink and the ubiquitous nature of polarized group decision making. In: Zanna MP (ed.) *Advances in experimental social psychology 37* (pp219–53). San Diego: Elsevier Academic Press

Bem SL. (1985). Androgyny and gender schema theory. A conceptual and empirical integration. In: TB Sonderegger (ed.). *Nebraska symposium on motivation 1984: The psychology of gender.* Lincoln: University of Nebraska Press

Benjamin LT, Simpson JA. (2009). The power of the situation: The impact of Milgram's obedience studies on personality and social psychology. *Am Psychol* 64:12–19

Berns GS, Chappelow J, Zink CF, et al. (2005). Neurobiological correlates of social conformity and independence during mental rotation. *Biol Psychiat* 58:245–53

Bernstein WM, Stephan WG, Davis MH. (1979). Explaining attributions for achievement: A path analytic approach. *J Pers Soc Psychol* 37:1810–21

Berry JW. (1969). On cross-cultural comparability. *Int J Psychol* 4:119–28

Billig M, Tajfel H. (1973). Social categorization and similarity in intergroup behavior. *Eur J Soc Psychol* 3:27–52

Blass T. (1991). Understanding behavior in the Milgram obedience experiment. *J Pers Soc Psychol* 60:398–413

Bond R, Smith PB. (1996). Culture and conformity: A meta-analysis of studies using Asch's (1952, 1956) line judgment task. *Psychol Bull* 119:11–137

Brewer MB, Chen Y–R. (2007). Where (who) are collectives in collectivism? Toward a conceptual clarification of individualism and collectivism. *Psychol Rev* 114:133–51

Brown RJ. (1978). Divided we fall: An analysis of relations between sections of a factory workforce. In: H Tajfel (ed.). *Differentiation between social groups: Studies in the social psychology of intergroup relations.* London: Academic Press

Burger JM, Cornelius T. (2003). Raising the price of agreement: Public commitment and the lowball compliance procedure. *J Basic App Soc Psychol* 33:923–34

Burger JM. (1999). The foot-in-the-door compliance technique: A multiple-process analysis and review. *Pers Soc Psychol Rev* 3:303–25

Chamorro–Premuzic T. (2007). *Personality and individual differences.* Oxford: Blackwell

Chartrand T, Pinckert S, Burger JM. (1999). The effects of delay and requester on the foot-in-the-door technique. *J Abnorm Psychol* 29:211–21

Chen H, Sharon N, Rao AR. (2005). Cultural influences in consumer impatience. *J Marketing Res* 42:291–301

Cialdini R, Wosinka W, Barrett D, et al. (1999). Compliance with a request in two cultures: The differential influence of social proof and commitment/consistency on collectivists and individualists. *Pers Soc Psychol B* 25:1242–53

Cialdini RB. (2009). *Influence: Science and practice* (5th edn). Boston: Allyn and Bacon

Cohen CE. (1981). Personal categories and social perception: Testing some boundaries of the processing effects of prior knowledge. *J Pers Soc Psychol* 40:441–52

Costa PT, McCrae RR. (1992). *NEO-PI-R professional manual.* Odessa, FL: Psychological Assessment Resources

David B, Turner JC. (1996). Studies in self-categorisation and minority conversion: Is being a member of the outgroup an advantage? *Brit J Soc Psychol* 35:179–99

Deutsch M, Gerard HB. (1955). A study of normative and informational social influence upon individual judgment. *J Abnorm Soc Psychol* 51:629–36

di Pellegrino G, Fadiga L, Fogassi L, et al. (1992). Understanding motor events: A neurophysiological study. *Exp Brain Res* 91:176–80

Dobbs M, Crano WD. (2001). Outgroup accountability in the minimal group paradigm: Implications for aversive discrimination and social identity theory. *Pers Soc Psychol Bull* 27:355–64

Dolin D, Booth–Butterfield S. (1995). Foot-in-the-door and cancer prevention. *Health Commun* 7:55–56

Draguns JG, Tanaka–Matsumi J. (2003). Assessment of psychopathology across and within cultures: Issues and findings. *Behav Res Ther* 41:755–76

Durkin K. (1995). *Developmental social psychology: From infancy to old age.* Malden: Blackwell

Duval TS, Silvia PJ. (2002). Self-awareness probability of improvement and the self-serving bias. *J Pers Soc Psychol* 82:49–61

Earley PC. (1993). East meets west meets mideast: Further explorations of collectivistic and individualistic work groups. *Acad Manage J* 36:319–48

Epstein S. (1983). A research paradigm for the study of personality and emotions. In: MM Page (ed.). *Personality: Current theory and research.* Lincoln: University of Nebraska Press

Esser JK, Lindoerfer JS. (1989). Groupthink and the space shuttle *Challenger* disaster: Toward a quantitative case analysis. *J Behav Decis Making* 2:167–77

Eysenck HJ. (1992). Four ways five factors are not basic. *Pers Indiv Differ* 13:667–73

Eysenck MW. (1992). *Anxiety: The cognitive perspective.* Hove, UK: Lawrence Erlbaum Associates Ltd

Fein S, Hilton JL, Miller DT. (1990). Suspicion of ulterior motivation and the correspondence bias. *J Pers Soc Psychol* 58:753–64

Fein S. (2001). Beyond the fundamental attribution era. *Psychol Inq* 12:16–21

Fiske ST. (1998). Prejudice stereotyping and discrimination. In: DT Gilbert, ST Fiske and G Lindzey (eds). *The handbook of social psychology* (4th edn). New York: McGraw–Hill

Fiske ST, Dyer LM. (1985). Structure and development of social schemata: Evidence from positive and negative transfer effects. *J Pers Soc Psychol* 19:381–400

Fiske ST, Neuberg SL. (1990). A continuum of impression formation, from category-based to individuating processes: Influences of information and motivation on attention and interpretation. In: MP Zanna (ed.). *Advances in experimental social psychology* Vol. 23 (pp1–74). New York: Academic Press

Fiske ST, Taylor SE. (2008). *Social cognition: From brains to culture.* McGraw–Hill

Freeman JR, Fraser SC. (1966). Compliance without pressure: The foot-in-the-door technique. *J Pers Soc Psychol* 4:195–203

Gergely G, Bekkering H, Kiraly I. (2002). Rational imitation in preverbal infants. *Nature* 415:755

Gilbert DT, Jones EE. (1986). Perceiver-induced constraint: Interpretations of self-generated reality. *J Pers Soc Psychol* 50:269–80

Gilbert DT, Malone PS. (1995). The correspondence bias. *Psychol Bull* 117:21–38

Girandola F. (2002). Sequential requests and organ donation. *J Soc Psychol* 142:171–78

Goethals GR, Zanna MP. (1979). The role of social comparison in choice shifts. *J Pers Soc Psychol* 37:1469–76

Grieve P, Hogg MA. (1999). Subjective uncertainty and intergroup discrimination in the minimal group situation. *Pers Soc Psychol Bull* 25:926–40

Gosling SD. (2008). *Snoop: What your stuff says about you.* New York: Basic books

Hall ET. (1959). *The silent language.* Greenwich, CT: Fawcett

Hamilton DL, Gifford RK. (1976). Illusory correlation in interpersonal perception: A cognitive basis of stereotypic judgments. *J Expl Soc Psychol* 12:392–407

Hartshorne H, May MA. (1928). *Studies in the nature of character: Studies of deceit.* New York: Macmillan

Haslam SA, Turner JC. (1992). Context-dependent variation in social stereotyping 2: The relationship between frame of reference self-categorisation and accentuation. *Eur J Soc Psychol* 22:251–78

Heine SJ, Lehman DR, Markus HR, et al. (1999). Is there a universal need for self–regard? *Psycholl Rev* 106:766–94

Heine SJ, Lehman DR. (1997). Culture dissonance and self-affirmation. *Pers Soc Psychol Bull* 23:389–400

Hewstone M, Martin R. (2008). Social influence. In: M Hewstone, W Stroebe, K. Jonas (eds). *Introduction to social psychology: A European perspective* (4th edn). BPS Blackwell

Hodges BH, Geyer AL. (2006). A nonconformist account of the Asch experiments: Values pragmatics and moral dilemmas. *Pers Soc Psychol Rev* 10:2–19

Hofstede G. (1984). *Culture's consequences: International differences in work-related values.* Beverly Hills, CA: Sage

Hofstede G. (2001). *Culture's consequences: Comparing values behaviours institutions and organizations across nations.* Thousand Oaks, CA: Sage

Hofstede G, Bond M. (1988). Confucius and economic growth: New trends in culture's consequences. *Organ Dyn* 16:4–21

Hogg MA. (2010). Influence and leadership. In: ST Fiske, DT Gilbert, G Linzey (eds). *Handbook of social psychology* (Vol. 2). Hoboken, NJ: John Wiley & Sons Inc

Hogg MA, Hains SC. (1998). Friendship and group identification: A new look at the role of cohesiveness in groupthink. *Eur J Soc Psychol* 28:323–41

Hogg MA, Vaughan GM. (2008). *Social psychology* (5th edn). London: Prentice–Hall

Hogg MA, Turner JC, Davidson B. (1990). Polarised norms and social frames of reference: A test of the self–categorisation theory of group polarization. *J Basic App Soc Psychol* 11:77–100

Hornick J, Zaig T, Shadmon D, et al. (1990). Comparison of three inducement techniques to improve compliance in a health survey conducted by telephone. *Public Health Rep* 105:524–29

Janis IL. (1972). *Victims of groupthink.* Boston, MA: Houghton Mifflin Co

Jellison J, Arkin R. (1977). Social comparison of abilities: A self-presentation approach to decision-making in groups. In: J Suls, R. Miller (eds). *Social comparison processes: Theoretical and empirical perspectives.* Washington, DC: Hemisphere Press

Johnson TJ, Feigenbaum R, Weiby M. (1964). Some determinants of consequences of the teacher's perception of causality. *J Educ Psychol* 55:237–46

Jones EE, Harris VA. (1967). The attribution of attitudes. *J Exp Soc Psychol* 3:1–24

Jones EE. (1979). The rocky road from acts to dispositions. *Am Psychol* 34:107–17

Jost JT, Banaji MR. (1994). The role of stereotyping in system-justification and the production of false consciousness. *Brit J Soc Psychol* 33:1–27

Keitner GI, Fodor J, Ryan CE, et al. (1991). A cross-cultural study of major depression and family functioning. *Can J Psychiat* 36: 254–59

Kleinman A. (1988). *Rethinking psychiatry: From cultural category to personal experience.* New York: Free Press

Lau RR, Russell D. (1980). Attribution in the sports pages. *J Pers Soc Psychol* 39:29–38

Levine RV, Norenzayan A. (1999). The pace of life in 31 countries. *J Cross Cult Psychol* 30:178–205

Lipsitz A, Kallmeyer F, Abas A. (1989). Counting on blood donors: Increasing the impact of reminder calls. *J App Soc Psychol* 66:871–74

Manson SM, Shore JH, Bloom JD. (1985). The depressive experience in American Indian communities: A challenge for psychiatric theory and diagnosis. In: A Kleinman, B Good (eds). *Culture and depression.* Berkeley: University of California Press

Marsella AJ, Kaplan A, Suarez E. (2002). Cultural considerations for understanding assessing and treating depressive experience and disorder. In: M Reinecke, M Davason (eds). *Comparative treatments of depression.* New York: Springer

Marsella AJ, Sartorius N, Jablensky A, et al. (1985). Cross-cultural studies of depressive disorders. In: A Kleinman and B Good (eds). *Culture and depression.* Berkeley: University of California Press

Matsumoto D, Juang L. (2008). *Culture and psychology* (4th edn). Thomson: Wadsworth

McCrae RR, Costa PT. (1999). A five-factor model theory of personality. In: LA Pervin, OP John (eds). *Handbook of personality: Theory and research.* New York: Guilford

McCrae RR, Costa PT. (2003). *Personality in adulthood: A five-factor theory perspective.* New York: The Guildford Press

Meineri S, Gueguen N. (2008). An application of the foot-in-the-door strategy in the environmental field. *Eur J Soc Sci* 7:71–4

Milgram S. (1963). Behavioural study of obedience. *J Abnorm Soc Psychol* 67:371–78

Milgram S. (1974). *Obedience to authority: An experimental view.* New York: Harper & Row

Miller DT, Ross M. (1975). Self-serving biases in the attribution of causality: Fact or fiction? *Psychol Bull* 82:213–25

Mischel W. (1968). *Personality and assessment.* New York: Wiley

Mischel W. (1973). Toward a cognitive social learning reconceptualisation of personality. *Psychol Rev* 80:252–83

Moscovici S. (1984). The phenomenon of social representations. In: RM Farr and S Moscovici (eds). *Social representations.* Cambridge/Paris: Cambridge University Press/ Maison des Sciences de l'Homme

Moskowitz DS. (1986). Comparison of self-reports reports by knowledgeable informants and behavioural observation data. *J Pers* 54:294–312

Mummendey A, Otten S. (1998). Positive–negative asymmetry in social discrimination. In: W Stroeber, M Hewstone (eds). *European Review of Social Psychology 9* (pp107–43). Chichester: Wiley

Myers DG, Bishop GD. (1970). Discussion effects on racial attitudes. *Science* 20:97–98

Oakes PJ, Haslam SA. (2001). Distortion and meaning: Categorisation on trial for inciting intergroup hatred. In: M Augoustinos and KJ Reynolds (eds). *Understanding the psychology of prejudice racism and social conflict.* London: Sage

Osborne JW. (2001). Testing stereotype threat: Does anxiety explain race and sex differences in achievement? *Contemp Educ Psychol* 26:291–310

Ozer D, Benet–Martinez V. (2006). Personality and the prediction of consequential outcomes. *Annu Rev Psychol* 57:401–21

Palak MS, Cook DA, Sullivan JJ. (1980). Commitment and energy conservation. *App Soc Psychol Annu* 1:235–53

Pervin LA. (2003). *The Science of Personality* (2nd edn). New York/Oxford: Oxford University Press

Petrova PK, Cialdini RB, Sills SJ. (2007). Consistency-based compliance across cultures. *J Exp Soc Psychol* 43:104–11

Pike KL. (1954*). Language in relation to a unified theory of the structure of human behaviour* (Pt. 1) (preliminary edn). Glendale, CA: Summer Institute of Linguistics

Platow MJ, McClintock CG, Liebrand WBG. (1990). Predicting intergroup fairness and ingroup bias in the minimal group paradigm. *Eur J Soc Psychol* 20:221–39

Rizzolatti G, Craighero L. (2004). The mirror-neuron system. *Annu Rev Neurosci* 27:169–92

Roberts BW, DelVecchio WF. (2000). The rank–order consistency of personality traits from childhood to old age: A quantitative review of longitudinal studies. *Psychol Bull* 126:3–25

Rubin M, Hewstone M. (1998). Social identity theory's self-esteem hypothesis. A review and some suggestions for clarification. *Pers Soc Psychol Rev* 2:40–62

Sabibi J, Siepmann M, Stein J. (2001). The really fundamental attribution error is social psychological research. *Psychol Inq* 12:1–15

Salganik MJ, Dodds PS, Watts DJ. (2006). Experimental study of inequality and unpredictability in an artificial cultural market. *Science* 311(5762):854–56

Schwier C, van Maanen C, Carpenter M, et al. (2006). Rational imitation in 12-month-old infants. *Infancy* 10:303–11

Sherif M. (1935). A study of some social factors in perception. *Arch Psychol* 27:1–60

Sherman JW, Kruschke JK, Sherman SJ, et al. (2009). Attentional processes in stereotype formation: A common model in stereotype formation. *J Pers Soc Psychol* 96:305–23

Sherman SJ. (1980). On the self-erasing nature of errors of prediction. *J Pers Soc Psychol* 39:211–21

Shiraev E, Levy D. (2004). *Cross-cultural psychology: Critical thinking and contemporary applications*. Boston: Allyn and Bacon

Smith ER, Mackie DM. (2007). *Social Psychology*. (3rd edn). New York: Psychology Press

Smith ER, Semin GR. (2004). Socially situated cognition: Cognition in its social context. *Adv Exp Soc Psychol* 36:53–117

Spencer SJ, Steele CM, Quinn DM. (1999). Stereotype threat and women's math performance. *J Exp Soc Psychol* 35:4–28

Steele CM, Aronson J. (1995). Stereotype threat and the intellectual test performance of African Americans. *J Pers Soc Psychol* 69:797–811

Stroessner SJ, Plaks JE. (2001). Illusory correlation and stereotype formation: Tracing the arc of research over a quarter century. In GB Moskowitz (ed.). *Cognitive social psychology: The Princeton Symposium on the legacy and future of social cognition.* Mahwah, NJ: Erlbaum

Tajfel H, Turner C. (1979). An integrative theory of intergroup conflict. In: WG Austin, Worchel S (eds). *The social psychology of intergroup relations.* Monterey, CA: Books/Cole

Tajfel H, Billig M, Bundy RP, et al. (1971). Social categorization and intergroup behavior. *Eur J Soc Psychol* 1:149–78

Takano Y, Sogon S. (2008). Are Japanese more collectivistic than Americans? Examining conformity in in-groups and the reference-group effect. *J Cross Cult Psychol* 39:237–50

Tanaka–Matsumi J. (2001). Abnormal psychology and culture. In: D Matsumoto (ed.). *The handbook of culture and psychology.* New York: Oxford University Press

Triandis H. (2002). Odysseus wondered for 10 I wondered for 50 years. In: Lonner W, Dinnel D, Hayes S, et al. (eds). *Online readings in psychology and culture.* Bellingham, WA: Centre for Cross-Cultural Research, Western Washington University

Turner JC. (1981). The experimental social psychology of intergroup behaviour. In: JC Turner, H Giles (eds). *Intergroup behaviour.* Oxford, UK: Blackwell

Turner JC. (1982). Towards a cognitive redefinition of the social group. In: H Tajfel (ed.). *Social identity and intergroup relations.* Cambridge: Cambridge University Press

Turner JC, Oakes PJ. (1989). Self-categorisation and social influence. In: PB Paulus (ed.). *The psychology of group influence* (2nd edn). Hillslade, NJ: Erlbaum

Turner JC, Pratkanis AR, Probasco P, et al. (1992). Threat cohesion and group effectiveness: Testing a social identity maintenance perspective on groupthink. *J Pers Soc Psychol* 63:781–96

Wallach MA, Kogan N, Bem DJ. (1962). Group influences on individual risk taking. *J Abnorm Soc Psychol* 65:78–86

WHO. (1983). *Depressive disorders in different cultures: report of the WHO collaborative study of standardized assessment of depressive disorders.* Geneva: World Health Organization

Williams EF, Sogon S. (1984). Group composition and conforming behaviour in Japanese students. *Jpn Psychol Res* 26:231–34

Williams JE, Best DL. (1982). *Measuring sex stereotypes: A thirty nation study.* Berkeley, CA: Sage Publications

Yamamoto K, Soliman A, Parsons J, et al. (1987). Voices in unison: Stressful events in the lives of children in six countries. *Child Psychol Psychiat* 28:855–64

Zuckerman M. (1979). Attribution of success and failure revisited or: The motivational bias is alive and well in attribution theory. *J Pers* 47:245–87

 ## 5 Abnormal psychology

Åhs F, Pissiota A, Michelgård A, et al. (2009). Disentangling the web of fear: amygdala reactivity and functional connectivity in spider and snake phobia. *Psychiat Res.* 172:103–08

Armfield JM. (2006) Cognitive vulnerability: a model of the etiology of fear. *Clin Psychol Rev* 26:746–68

Arntz A, Lavy E, van den Berg G, et al. (1993). Negative beliefs of spider phobics: a psychometric evaluation of the spider phobia beliefs questionnaire. *Adv Behav Res Ther* 15:257–77

Arrindell W, Eisemann M, Richter J, et al. (2003). Masculinity–femininity as a national characteristic and its relationship with 68 national agoraphobic fear levels: Fodor's sex role hypothesis revitalized. *Behav Res Ther* 41(7):795–807

Arroll B, Goodyear–Smith F, Lloyd T. (2002). Depression in patients in an Auckland general practice. *New Zeal Med J* 115(2):176–78

Bandura A. (1982). Self-efficacy mechanism in human agency. *Am Psychol* 37:122–47

Beck AT. (1976). *Cognitive therapy and the emotional disorders.* New York: New American Library

Bennett–Levy J, Marteau T. (1984). Fear of animals: what is prepared? *Brit J Psychol* 75:37–42

Benjamin J, Ben–Zion IZ, Karbofsky E, et al. (2000) Double-blind placebo-controlled pilot study of paroxetine for specific phobia. *Psychopharmacology (Berl)* 149:194–96

Best Practice Advocacy Centre. (2008). Cultural Competency Series: Maori Mental Health. *Best Practice Journal.* 14:31–35

Beutler LE, Engle D, Mohr D, et al. (1991). Predictors of differential response to cognitive experiential and self-directed psychotherapeutic procedures. *J Consult Clin Psychol* 59:333–40

Binitie A. (1975) A factor-analytical study of depression across cultures (African and European). *Brit J Psychiat* 127:559–63

Bowers WA. (2002). Cognitive therapy for anorexia nervosa. *Cogn Behav Pract* 9:247–53

Broich K. (2009). Committee for Medicinal Products for Human Use (CHMP) assessment on efficacy of antidepressants. *Eur Neuropsychopharm* 19(5):305–08

Brown GW, and Harris T. (1978). *Social origins of depression.* London: Tavistock

Bruch H. (1962). Perceptual and conceptual disturbances in anorexia nervosa. *Psychosom Med* 24:187–94

Bulik C, Sullivan PF, Tozzi F, et al. (2006). Prevalence heritability and prospective risk factors for anorexia nervosa. *Arch Gen Psychiat* 63(3):305–12

Burke HM, Davis MC, Otte C, et al. (2005). Depression and cortisol responses to psychological stress: a meta-analysis. *Psychoneuroendocrino* 30:846–56

Butler AC, Chapman JE, Forman EM, et al. (2006). The empirical status of cognitive-behavioral therapy: A review of meta-analyses. *Clin Psychol Rev* 26:17–31

Caetano DF. (1973) Labelling theory and the presumption of mental illness: An experimental design. *J Health Soc Behav* 15:253–60

Chapman LK, Kertz SJ. Zurlage MM, et al. (2008). A confirmatory factor analysis of specific phobia domains in African American and Caucasian American young adults. *J Anxiety Disord* 22:763–71

Chiao J, Blizinsky K. (2010). Culture–gene coevolution of individualism–collectivism and the serotonin transporter gene. *P Roy Soc B* 277(1681):529–37

Choy Y, Fyer AJ, Lipsitz JD. (2007). Treatment of specific phobia in adults. *Clin Psychol Rev* 27:266–86

Cohen CI. (2002) Social inequality and health: Will psychiatry assume center stage? *Psychiat Servs* 53:937–39

Cosgrove L, Krimsky S, Vijayaraghaven M, et al. (2006). Financial ties between DSM–IV panel members and the pharmaceutical industry. *Psychother Psychosom* 75(3):154–60

Cryan JF, Kaupmann K. (2005). Don't worry 'B' happy! A role for GABA$_B$ receptors in anxiety and depression. *Trends Pharmacol Sci* 26:36–43

Cuijpers P, van Straten A, Warmerdam L, et al. (2009) Psychotherapy versus the combination of psychotherapy and pharmacotherapy in the treatment of depression: a meta-analysis. *Depress Anxiety* 26(3):279–88

Cutuli JJ, Wiik KL, Herbers JE, et al. (2010). Cortisol function among early school-aged homeless children. *Psychoneuroendocrino* 35(6):833–45

Davey GCL, McDonald AS, Hirisave U, et al. (1998). A cross-cultural study of animal fears. *Behav Res Ther* 36:735–50

Ellis A. (1962). *Reason and emotion in psychotherapy.* New York: Lyle Stewart

Fairburn CG, Shafran R, Cooper Z. (1999). Invited essay: a cognitive behavioural theory of anorexia nervosa. *Behav Res Ther* 37:1–13

Fallon AE, Rozin P. (1988). Body image, attitudes to weight and misperceptions of figure preferences of the opposite sex: A comparison of men and women in two generations. *J Abnorm Psychol* 97:342–45

Faravelli C, Degl'Innocenti BG, Aiazzi L, et al. (1989). Epidemiology of anxiety disorder in Florence. *J Affect Disorders* 19:1–5

Fernald LC, Gunnar MR. (2009). Poverty-alleviation program participation and salivary cortisol in very low-income children. *Soc Sci Med* 68:2180–89

Gabilondo A, Rojas–Farreras S, Vilagut G, et al. (2010) Epidemiology of major depressive episode in a southern European country: Results from the ESEMeD–Spain project. *J Affect Disord* 120:76–85

Hagen EH, Watson PJ, Thomson JA. (In preparation: April 2004). Love's labour's lost: Depression as an evolutionary adaptation to obtain help from those with whom one is in conflict. Resubmission; rejected without review *J Amer Med Assoc, Lancet, New Engl J Med*

Hankin BL, Abramson LY. (2001). Development of gender differences in depression: an elaborated Cognitive Vulnerability–Transactional Stress Theory. *Psychol Bull* 127(6): 773–96

Harris DJ, Kuba SA. (1997). Ethnocultural identity and eating disorders in women of color. *Profl Psychol-Res Pr* 28:341–47

Hermann A, Schäfer A, Walter B, et al. (2009). Emotion regulation in spider phobia: role of the medial prefrontal cortex. *Soc Cogn Affect Neurosci* 4:257–67

Hodges J, Oei TPS. (2007). Would Confucius benefit from psychotherapy? The compatibility of cognitive behaviour therapy and Chinese values. *Behav Resh Ther* 45:901–14

Holtkamp K, Konrad K, Kaiser N, et al. (2005). A retrospective study of SSRI treatment in adolescent anorexia nervosa: insufficient evidence for efficacy *J Psychiatr Res* 39:303–10

Hyun MS, Chung HI, Lee YJ. (2005). The effect of cognitive-behavioral group therapy on the self-esteem depression and self-efficacy of runaway adolescents in a shelter in South Korea. *Appl Nurs Res* 18(3):160–66

Iancu I, Levin J, Dannon PN, et al. (2007). Prevalence of self-reported specific phobia symptoms in an Israeli sample of young conscripts. *J Anxiety Disord* 21:762–69

Jahoda M. (1958). *Current concepts of positive mental health.* New York: Basic Books

Kaye WH, Nagata T, Weltzin TE, et al. (2001). Double-blind placebo-controlled administration of fluoxetine in restricting- and restricting-purging-type anorexia nervosa. *Biol Psychiat* 49:644–52

Kendler KS, Gatz M, Gardner CO, et al. (2006). A Swedish national twin study of lifetime major depression. *Am J Psychiat* 163(1):109–14

Kessler RC, Merikangas KR. (2004). The national comorbidity survey replication (NCS–R): background and aims. *Int J Meth Psych Res* 13:60–68

Kirov G, Murray RM. (1999 Ethnic differences in the presentation of bipolar affective disorder. *Eur Psychiat* 14:199–204

Kirsch I, Deacon BJ, Huedo–Medina TB, et al. (2008). Initial severity and anti-depressant benefits: a meta-analysis of data submitted to the Food and Drug Administration. *PLoS Med* 5:e45

Lacasse JR, Leo J. (2005). Serotonin and depression: A disconnect between the advertisements and the scientific literature. *PLoS Medicine.* 2(12):1211

Lee S, Leung T, Lee AM, et al. (1996). Body dissatisfaction among Chinese undergraduates and its implications for eating disorders in Hong Kong. *Int J Eat Disorder* 20:77–84

Levav I, Kohn R, Golding JM, et al. (1997). Vulnerability of Jews to affective disorders. *Am J Psychiat* 154:941–47

Levinson DF. (2005) The genetics of depression: a review. *Biol Psychiat* 2005.08.024 [epub ahead of print]

Lumpkin PW, Silverman WK, Weems CF, et al. (2002). Treating a heterogeneous set of anxiety disorders in youths with group cognitive behavioral therapy: A partially nonconcurrent multiple-baseline evaluation. *Behav Ther* 33:163–77

McDermut W, Miller IW, Brown RA. (2001). The efficacy of group psychotherapy for depression: A meta-analysis and review of the empirical research. *Clin Psychol-Sci Pr* 8:98–116

Merckelbach H, de Jong PJ, Muris P, et al. (1996). The etiology of specific phobias: A review. *Clin Psychol Rev* 16:337–61

Mezzich JE. (2002). *Culture and psychiatric diagnosis: A DSM–IV perspective.* Washington DC: American Psychiatric Press

Morgan C, Dazzan P, Morgan K, et al. (2006). First episode psychosis and ethnicity: Initial findings from the AESOP study. *World Psychiatry* 5(1):40–46

Nicholls D, Chater R, Lask B. (2000). Children into DSM don't go: A comparison of classification systems for eating disorders in childhood and early adolescence. *Int J Eat Disorder* 28:317–24

Nicholson A, Pikhart H, Pajak A, et al. (2008) Socio-economic status over the life-course and depressive symptoms in men and women in Eastern Europe. *J Affect Disord* 105:125–36

Norton KI, Olds TS, Olive S, et al. (1996). Ken and Barbie at life size. *Sex Roles* 34:287–94

Öhman A, Erixon G, Lofberg I. (1975). Phobias and preparedness: Phobic versus neutral pictures as conditioned stimuli for human autonomic responses. *J Abnorm Psychol* 84:41–45

Okulate GT, Olayinka MO, Jones OBE. (2004) Somatic symptoms in depression: evaluation of their diagnostic weight in an African setting. *Brit J Psychiat* 184:422–27

Öst L, Stridh B, Wolf M. (1998). A clinical study of spider phobia: Prediction of outcome after self-help and therapist-directed treatments. *Behav Res Ther* 36:17–35

Palmer D, Ward K. (2006). *Unheard voices: Listening to refuges and asylum-seekers in the planning and delivery of mental health service provision in London. A research audit on mental health needs and mental health provision for refugees and asylum seekers.* London: Commission for Public Patient Involvement in Health

Parker G, Parker I, Brotchie H, et al. (2006). Interpersonal psychotherapy for depression? The need to define its ecological niche. *J Affect Disord* 95:1–11

Peters L, Slade T, Andrews G. (1999). A comparison of ICD10 and DSM–IV criteria for posttraumatic stress disorder. *J Traumatic Stress* 12:335–43

Polivy J. (1981). Group therapy as an adjunctive treatment for anorexia nervosa. *J Psychiat Treat Eval* 3:279–83

Read J, Mosher L, Bentall R. (2004). *Models of madness: psychological social and biological approaches to schizophrenia.* Hove, UK: Brunner–Routledge

Read J. (2007). Why promoting biological ideology increases prejudice against people labelled 'schizophrenic'. *Aust Psychol* 42(2): 118–28

Rentz TO, Powers MB, Smits JAJ, et al. (2003). Active imaginal exposure: Examination of a new behavioral treatment for cynophobia (dog phobia). *Behav Res Ther* 41:1337–53

Riordan S, Donaldson S, Humphreys M. (2004) The imposition of restricted hospital orders: potential effects of ethnic origin. *Int J Law Psychiat* 27:171–77

Rivas–Vazquez RA, Blais MA. (1997). Selective serotonin reuptake inhibitors and atypical antidepressants: a review and update for psychologists. *Prof Psychol-Res Pr* 28:526–36

Robins CJ, Block P. (1989). Cognitive theories of depression viewed from a diathesis–stress perspective: evaluations of the models of Beck and of Abramson, Seligman and Teasdale. *Cognitive Ther Res* 13:297–313

Roland C. (1970). Anorexia nervosa: A survey of the literature and review of 30 cases. In: C Roland (ed.). *Anorexia and obesity.* Boston: Little Brown

Rosenhan DL. (1973). On being sane in insane places. *Science* 179:250–57

Sarek M. (2006). Evident exception in clinical practice not sufficient to break traditional hypothesis. *PLoS Medicine* 3(2):267

Sartory G, Daum I. (1992). Effects of instrumental controllability on the phasic cardiac response and subjective fear of phobic stimulation. *J Psychophysiol* 6:131–39

Sato M. (2006). Renaming schizophrenia. A Japanese perspective. *World Psychiatry* 5(1):53–55

Seeman M. (2007). All psychosis is not schizophrenia especially not in women. *Clinical Schizophrenia and Related Psychoses* 1(3):277–82

Shafran R, Booth R, Rachman S. (1993). The reduction of claustrophobia II: Cognitive analyses. *Behav Res Ther* 31:75–85

Skre I, Onstad S, Torgersen S, et al. (2000). The heritability of common phobic fear: a twin study of a clinical sample. *J Anxiety Disord* 14:549–62

Strahan EJ, Spencer SJ, Zanna MP. (2007). Don't take another bite: How sociocultural norms for appearance affect women's eating behavior. *Body Image* 4:331–42

Striegel–Moore RH, Bulik CM. (2007). Risk factors for eating disorders. *Am Psychol* 62(3):181–98

Surbey M. (1987). Anorexia nervosa amenorrhea and adaptation. *Ethol Sociobiol* 8:475–615

Sypeck MF, Gray JJ, Etu SF, et al. (2006). Cultural representations of thinness in women redux: Playboy magazine's depiction of beauty from 1979 to 1999. *Body Image* 3(3):229–35

Tapsell R, Mellsop G. (2007). The contributions of culture and ethnicity to New Zealand mental health research findings. *Int J Soc Psychiatr* 53(4):317–24

Taylor SE, Brown JD. (1988). Illusion and well–being: A social psychological perspective on mental health. *Psychol Bull* 103:193–210

Thorpe SJ, Salkovskis PM. (1995). Phobic beliefs: Do cognitive factors play a role in specific phobia? *Behav Res Ther* 33:805–16

Toseland RW, Siporin M. (1986). When to recommend group treatment: A review of the clinical and the research literature. *Int J Group Psychoth* 36:171–201

Truax P. (2001). Review: group psychotherapy is effective for depression. *Evidence-based Mental Health* 4:82

van Kuyck K, Gerard N, Laere KV, et al. (2009). Towards a neurocircuitry in anorexia nervosa: Evidence from functional neuroimaging studies. *J Psychiat Res* 43(14):1133–45

Wakefield JC, Schmitz MF, First MB, et al. (2007). Extending the bereavement exclusion for major depression to other losses: evidence from the National Comorbidity Survey. *Arch Gen Psychiat* 64:433–40

Wilhelm FH, Trabert W, Roth WT. (2001). Physiological instability in panic disorder and generalized anxiety disorder. *Biol Psychiat* 49:596–605

Woodside DB, Kaplan AS. (1994). Day hospital treatment in males with eating disorders – response and comparison to females. *J Psychosom Res* 38:471–75

Wu LT, Anthony JC. (2000). The estimated rate of depressed mood in US adults: Recent evidence for a peak in later life. *J Affect Disord* 60:159–71

Yasuhara D, Homan N, Nagai N, et al. (2002). A significant increase in the prevalence of eating disorders in Japan: 1998-year survey. *International Congress Series: Psycho-neuro-endocrino-immunology: A common language for the whole human body* 1241:297–301

Zandian M, Ioakimidis I, Bergh C, et al. (2007). Cause and treatment of anorexia nervosa. *Physiol Behav* 92(2):283–90

 ## Developmental psychology

Ackerman BJ. (1997). Effects of divorce on children: Traits of resiliency and school intervention. Center for Positive Practices. www.eric.ed.gov

Ainsworth M, Blehar M, Waters E, et al. (1978). *Patterns of attachment.* Hillsdale, NJ: Erlbaum

Archer J. and Lloyd B. (2002). *Sex and gender.* Cambridge University Press

Archer S. (1982). The lower age boundaries of identity development. *Child Dev* 53:1551–56

Beach E. (1974). Effects of gonadal hormones on urinary behaviour in dogs. *Physiol Behav* 12:1005–13

Bee H. (1995). *The developing child.* New York: HarperCollins

Behrend DA, Rosengren KS, Perlmutter M. (1992). The relation between private speech and parental interactive style. In: RM Diaz, LE Berk (eds). *Private speech: from social interaction to self-regulation.* Hillsdale, NJ: Erlbaum

Bem SL. (1974). The measurement of psychological androgyny. *J Consult Clin Psychol* 42:155–62

Berenbaum S, Snyder E. (1995). Early hormonal influences on childhood sex-typed activity and playmate preferences. *Dev Psychol* 31:31–42

Biben M. (1998). Squirrel monkey play fighting: making the case for a cognitive training function for play. In: M Bekoff and J Byers (eds). *Animal play* (pp161–82). Cambridge: Cambridge University Press

Blum D. (2002). *Love at Goon Park: Harry Harlow and the science of affection.* Perseus Publishing

Bower TGR. (1982). *Development in infancy* (2nd edn). San Francisco: WH Freeman. Cited in Moore M, Meltzoff A. (1999). New findings on object permanence. *Brit J Dev Psychol* 17:563–84

Bowlby J. (1951). *Maternal care and mental health.* New York: Schocken

Braggio JT, Nadler RD, Lance J, et al. (1978). Sex differences in apes and children. *Recent Advances in Primatology* 1:529–32

Britner J, Reppucci N. (1997). Prevention of child maltreatment: Evaluation of a parent education program for teen mothers. *Journal of Child and Family Studies* 6:165–75

Britton P. (1997). *The jigsaw man.* UK: Bantam Press

Brownell KD, Napolitano MA. (1995). Distorting reality for children: body size proportions of Barbie and Ken dolls. *Int J Eat Disorder* 18(3):295–98. Cited in Croll J. (2005)

Bussey K, Bandura A. (1992). Self-regulatory mechanisms governing gender development. *Child Dev* 63:1236–50

Carter DB, Patterson CJ. (1982). Sex roles as social conventions: The development of sex role stereotypes. *Dev Psychol* 18:812–25

Caspi A, McClay J, Moffit T, et al. (2002). Role of genotype in the cycle of violence in maltreated children. *Science* 297:865

Condon R. (1988). Innuit growth: Growth and change in the Canadian Arctic (Paper ISBN 0-8135-1364-2). NJ: Rutgers University Press

Conner D, Knight D, Cross D. (1997). Mother's and father's scaffolding of their two year olds during problem solving and literary interactions. *Brit J Dev Psychol* 15:323–338

Cook JT, Ohri–Vachaspati P, Kelly GL. (1996). Evaluation of a Universally Free School Breakfast Program Demonstration Project; Central Falls, RI. Medford, MA: Center on Hunger Poverty and Nutrition Policy, Tufts University

Croll J. (2005) Body image and adolescents. In: J Stang, M Story (eds). (2005) *Guidelines for Adolescent Nutrition Services.* Minneapolis: school of Public Health, University of Minnesota

Dobbs D. (2009). *The Science of Success.* The Atlantic online. www.theatlantic.com

Elder GH, Conger D. (2000). *Children of the land: Adversity and success in rural America.* Chicago: University of Chicago Press

Ellis BJ, and Boyce WT. (2005). Biological sensitivity to context. *Curr Dir Psychol Sci* 17(3)

Erikson E. (1950). *Childhood and Society.* New York: WW Norton & Co

Erikson E. (1969). *Gandhi's truth: On the origin of militant violence.* New York: Norton

Eysenck M. (2000). *Psychology: A student's Handbook.* UK: Psychology Press

Fagot BI. (1985). A cautionary note: Parents' socialization of boys and girls. *Sex Roles* 12:471–76

Felliti VJ, Anda RF, Nordenberg D, et al. (1998). Relationship of childhood abuse and household dysfunction to many of the leading causes of death in adults: the Adverse Childhood Experiences (ACE) Study. *Am J Prev Med* 14:245–58

Field TM, de Stefano L, Koewler JHI. (1982a) Fantasy play of toddlers and preschoolers. *Dev Psychol* 18:503–08

Food Research Action Centre (2010). Breakfast for learning. www.frac.org/pdf/breakfastforlearning.pdf

Fraley RC, Shaver PR. (2000). Adult romantic attachment: Theoretical developments emerging controversies and unanswered questions. *Rev Gen Psychol* 4:132–54

Harlow HF, Suomi SJ. (1971). Social recovery by isolation-reared monkeys. *P Natl Acad Sci USA* 68(7):1534–38

Hazan C, Shaver P. (1987). Romantic love conceptualized as an attachment process. *J Pers Soc Psychol* 52:511–24

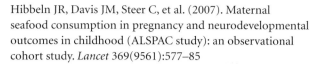

Hibbeln JR, Davis JM, Steer C, et al. (2007). Maternal seafood consumption in pregnancy and neurodevelopmental outcomes in childhood (ALSPAC study): an observational cohort study. *Lancet* 369(9561):577–85

Howes C, Matheson CC. (1992) Sequences in the development of competent play with peers. Social and social pretend play. *Dev Psychol* 28:961–74

Hughes M. (1975). *Egocentrism in pre-school children*. Edinburgh University: unpublished doctoral dissertation. Reported in Donaldson M. (1978). *Children's Minds*. London: Fontana

Huston AC. (1983). Sex typing. In: EM Hetherington (ed.). *Handbook of child psychology* Vol. 4: *Socialization personality and social development*. New York: John Wiley & Sons Inc

Jarvis P. (2006) 'Rough and tumble' play: Lessons in life. Evolutionary Psychology 4:330–46. www.human-nature.com/ep

Kagan J. (1982). *Psychological research on the human infant: An evaluative summary*. New York: WT Grant Foundation

Killgore WD, Yurgelun–Todd DA. (2004). Sex-related developmental differences in the lateralized activation of the prefrontal cortex and amygdala during perception of facial affect. *Percept Motor Skill* 99(2):371–91

Kohlberg L. (1966). A cognitive-developmental analysis of children's sex-role concepts and attitudes. In: EE Maccoby (ed.). *The development of sex differences* (pp82–173). Stanford, CA: Stanford University Press

Lamb ME, Roopnarine JL. (1979). Peer influences on sex role development in preschoolers. *Child Dev* 50:1219–22

Leary M, Greer D, Huston A. (1982) *The relation between TV viewing and gender roles*. Paper presented at Southwestern Society For Research in Human Development, Galveston, Texas

Lenroot R, et al. (2007) *Sexual dimorphism of brain developmental trajectories during childhood and adolescence*. Montreal, Canada: NIMH/CHP McGill University

Lewis M. (1972). State as an infant–environment interaction: An analysis of mother–infant interaction as a function of sex. *Merrill–Palmer Quarterly* 18:95–121

Liben L. and Signorella M. (1993). Gender-schematic processing in children: the role of initial interpretations of stimuli. *Dev Psychol* 29:141–49

Lorber J. (1994). *Paradoxes of gender*. Yale: Yale University Press

Love J, Kisker E, Constantine J, et al. (2005). The effectiveness of Early Head Start for 3-year-old children and their parents: Lessons for policy and programs. *Dev Psychol* 41:885–901

Luthar SS, Cicchetti D, Becker B. (2000). The construct of resilience: A critical evaluation and guidelines for future work. *Child Dev* 71(3):543–62

Mahoney J, Lord H, Carryl E. (2005). An ecological analysis of after-school program participation and the development of academic performance and motivational attributes for disadvantaged children. *Child Dev* 76:811–25

Main M, Solomon J. (1990). Procedures for identifying infants as disorganised/disoriented during the Ainsworth Strange Situation. In: MT Greenberg, D Cicchetti, and EM Cummings (eds). *Attachment in the preschool years* (pp121–60). Chicago: University of Chicago Press.

Marcia JE. (1966). Development and validation of ego identity status. *J Pers Soc Psychol* 3:551–558

Marcus DE, Overton WF. (1978). The development of cognitive gender constancy and sex role preferences. *Child Dev* 49:434–44

Marsh HW. (1989). Age and sex effects in multiple dimensions of self-concept: A replication and extension. *Aust J Psychol* 37:197–204

McGarrigle J, Donaldson M. (1974). Conservation accidents. *Cognition: International Journal of Cognitive Psychology* 3:341–50

McLaughlin JE, Bernstein LS, Crepinsek MK, et al. (2002). *Evaluation of the School Breakfast Program Pilot Project: Findings from the First Year of Implementation*. US Department of Agriculture Food and Nutrition Service. Report No. CN-02-SBP

Meilman PW. (1979). Cross sectional age changes in ego identity status during adolescence. *Dev Psychol* 15:230–31

Michigan Department of Education (MDE). (2002). *What research says about parent involvement in children's education in relation to academic achievement*. www.michigan.gov/documents/Final_Parent_Involvement_Fact_Sheet_14732_7.pdf

Miyake K, Chen S, Campos JJ. (1985). Infant temperament mother's mode of interaction and attachment. In: Japan: an interim report. *Monogr Soc Res Child* 50:276–97

Moscovici S. (1993) The invention of society: psychological explanations of psychological phenomena. In: Jovchelovitch S. (2007). *Knowledge in context: Representations community and culture*. Hove: Routledge

New York Center for Children. (2004). Prevent Child Abuse New York, Fact Sheet. http://preventchildabuseny.org/pdf/2004CANFactSheet.pdf

O'Donnell M, Sharpe S. (2004). The social construction of youthful masculinities: Peer group sub-cultures. In: S Ball (ed.). *RoutledgeFalmer Reader in Sociology of Education* (pp89–127) London: RoutledgeFalmer

Piaget J, Inhelder B. (1956). *The child's conception of space*. London: Routledge

Raloff J. (1989). In-school breakfasts improve test scores. *Sci News* 14 October

Sagor R. (1996). Building resiliency in students. *Educ Leadership* 54(1):38–41

Schoon I, Bartley M. (2008). The role of human capability and resilience. *Psychologist* 21:24–27

Segal J, Jaffre J. (2007). Attachment and adult relationships: How the attachment bond shapes adult relationships. Helpguide. www.helpguide.org

Slaby RG, Frey KS. (1975). Development of gender constancy and selective attention to same-sex models. *Child Dev* 46:849–56

Suomi S. (2005). Cited in 'Tackling aggression in men'. *Sydney Morning Herald* 29 June 2006

Taylor M, Cartwright BS, Carlson SM. (1993a). A developmental investigation of children's imaginary companions. *Dev Psychol* 29:276–85

Thompson M. (2000). *Raising Cain: Protecting the emotional life of boys*. Ballantine Books

Tizard J, Schofield WN, Hewison J. (1982). Collaboration between teachers and parents in assisting children's reading. *Brit J Educ Psychol* 52(1):1–11

TV-Turnoff Network. (2005). Facts and figures about our TV habits. www.tvturnoff.org. Cited in Croll J. (2005).

Wang M, Haertel G, and Walberg H. (1995). Educational resilience in inner cities. In: M Wang and E Gordon (eds). *Educational Resilience in Inner-City America.* Hillsdale, NJ: Lawrence Erlbaum Associates

Waterman CK, Waterman AS. (1975). Fathers and sons: A study of ego-identity across two generations. *J Youth Adolescence* 4:331–38

Williams JE, Best DL. (1990). *Measuring sex stereotypes: A multi-nation study*. Newbury Park, CA: Sage

Wood D, Bruner JS, Ross, G. (1976). The role of tutoring in problem solving. *J Child Psychol Psyc* 17:89–100

Young W, Goy R, Pheonix C. (1964). Hormones and sexual behaviour. *Science* 143:212–18

7 Health psychology

Advertising Age (2004). 100 leading national advertisers. Cited in Jacobson M. (2005)

Adams T, Avelar E, Cloward TR, et al. (2007). A study to assess morbidity following gastric bypass surgery. *Contemp Clin Trials* 26:534–51

Adams TD, Gress RE, Smith SC, et al. (August 2007). Long-term mortality after gastric bypass surgery. *N Engl J Med* 357(8):753–61

Ajzen I. (1985). From intentions to actions: A theory of planned behavior. In: J Kuhl, J Beckmann (eds). *Action control: From cognition to behavior*. Berlin/ Heidelberg/New York: Springer–Verlag

Alcoholics Anonymous (2001). Chapter 5: How it works. *Alcoholics Anonymous* (4th edn). Alcoholics Anonymous World Services. www.aa.org/bigbookonline/en_bigbook_chapt5.pdf

Ashe M, Jernigan D, Kline R, et al. (2003). Land use planning and the control of alcohol, tobacco, firearms and fast food restaurants. *Am J Public Health* 93(9):1404–08

Bandura A. (1977). Self-efficacy: Toward a unifying theory of behavioral change. *Psychol rev* 84:191–215

Bandura A. (1994). Self-efficacy. In: VS Ramachaudran (ed.). *Encyclopedia of human behavior* (Vol. 4). pp71–81. New York: Academic Press

Basu S. (2004). Military not immune from obesity epidemic. US Medicine. www.usmedicine.com/dailyNews.cfm?dailyID=187

Bogart CJ. (2003). '13th-stepping:' Why Alcoholics Anonymous is not always a safe place for women. *J Addict Nurs* 14(1):43–47

Byrne SM. (2002). Psychological aspects of weight maintenance and relapse in obesity. *J Psychosom Res* 53:1029–36. Cited at Malaysian Association for the Study of Obesity: Scientific Conference on Obesity (MASO 2009) 2–13 August 2009, Kuala Lumpur

Chapman L. (2005). Meta-evaluation of worksite health promotion economic return studies: 2005 update. *The Art of Health Promotion*. www.awcnet.org

Chen M, et al. (2005). Alcohol advertising: What makes it attractive to youth? *J Health Commun* 10. Cited in: Institute of Alcohol Studies fact sheet. Institute of Alcohol Studies. www.ias.org.uk

Coca–Cola Company. *Annual Report 2004*. (pp. 2, 41). www2.coca–cola.com/investors/annualandotherreports/2004/pdf/koar_04_10k.pdf

Cohen L. (2006). Participating in yoga during treatment for breast cancer improves quality of life. *News Release*. MD Anderson Cancer Center, The University of Texas

Cohen S, Tyrell DA, Smith AP. (1991). Psychological stress and the common cold. *New Engl J Med* 325:606–12

Cole A, Kmietowicz Z. (2007). BMA calls for action on 'epidemic' of alcohol related problems. *BMJ* 334(7608):1343

Conner M, Kirk S, Cade J, et al. (2003). Environmental influences: Factors influencing a woman's decision to use dietary supplements. *J Nutr* 133:1978S–82S

Crane J, Hannibal J. (2009). *IB Course Companion: Psychology: Psychology Course Companion (IB Diploma Programme)*. Oxford: Oxford University Press

Cross C. (2004). *Genes and alcoholism*. Wellcome Trust. http://genome.wellcome.ac.uk

Dawkins R. (1976). *The Selfish Gene*. UK: Oxford Paperbacks

Day E, Gaston RL, Furlong E, et al. (2005). United Kingdom substance misuse treatment workers' attitudes toward 12-step self-help groups. *J Subst Abuse Treat* 29(4): 21–27

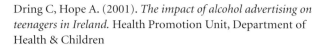

Dring C, Hope A. (2001). *The impact of alcohol advertising on teenagers in Ireland.* Health Promotion Unit, Department of Health & Children

Edwards E. (2001). A Harry issue for Coke. *Washington Post.* Nov. 13 2001. P. C14

Elkins G, Whitfield P Marcus J, et al. (2005). Noncompliance with behavioral recommendations following bariatric surgery. *Obes Surg* 15(4):546–51

Festinger L. (1957). *A theory of cognitive dissonance.* Stanford, CA: Stanford University Press

Fishbein M, Ajzen I. (1975). *Belief attitude intention and behavior: An introduction to theory and research.* Reading, MA: Addison–Wesley

Foegen JH. (1988). Hypocrisy pay. *Employee Responsibilities and Rights Journal* 1:85–87

Food Surveys Research Group, Agricultural Research Service, US Department of Agriculture (1997). *Pyramid Servings Data: Results from USDA's 1995 and 1996 Continuing Survey of Food Intakes by Individuals.* (1996 Pyramid servings tables 2B 3B 4B). www.barc.usda.gov/bhnrc/foodsurvey/home.htm

Frankenhauser M, Dunne E, Lundberg U. (1976). Sex differences in sympathetic–adrenal medullary reactions induced by different stressors. *Psychopharamacology* 47:1–5

Frohlich K, Potvin L. (2008). Transcending the known in public health practice: the inequality paradox: the population approach and vulnerable populations. *Am J Public Health* 98(2):216–21

Garn et al. (1981). Cited in Crane J, Hannibal J. (2009)

Gaston RL, Day E, Furlong E, et al. (2005). United Kingdom substance misuse treatment: workers' attitudes toward 12-step self-help groups. *J Subs Abuse Treat* 29(4): 321–27

Geissler C, Powers H. (2005). *Human Nutrition* (11th edn). Churchill Livingstone

Goetsch V, Fuller MG. (1995). Stress and stress management. In: D Wedding (ed.). *Behaviour and Medicine.* St. Louis, MO: Mosby-Year Book

Grandey A. (2000). Emotion regulation in the workplace: A new way to conceptualize emotional labor. *J Occup Health Psych* 5(1):95–110

Gross R. (1996). *Introduction to psychology: The science of mind and behaviour.* Bath, UK: Hodder and Stoughton

Hall R. (2006). A focus on equity and health inequalities (editorial). *Health promotion strategies* 6(1)

Hartfiel N, Havenhand J, Khalsa SB, et al. (2010). The effectiveness of yoga for the improvement of well-being and resilience to stress in the workplace. *Scand J Work Env Hea* 2010 Apr 6 [Epub ahead of print]

Hays C. (1999). Private sector; bridging a 'generation next' gap. *New York Times* 31 January p2

Hill L, Casswell S. (2001). Alcohol advertising and sponsorship: Commercial freedom and control in the public interest. In: N Heather, JS Peters, T Stockwell (eds). *International handbook of alcohol dependence and problems.* Hoboken, NJ: John Wiley & Sons 2001

Hochschild AR. (1983). *The managed heart: The commercialization of human feeling.* Berkeley, CA: University of California Press

Holmes TH, Rahe RH. (1967). The social readjustment rating scale. *J Psychosom Res* 11(2): 213–18

Honeymar M. (1997). Alcoholics Anonymous as a condition of drunk driving probation: when does it amount to establishment of religion. *Columbia Law Rev* 97(2):437

Institute of Medicine of the National Academies. (2005). *Preventing childhood obesity: health in the balance.* Food and Nutrition Board (FNB), Board on Health Promotion and Disease. www.iom.edu

Jacobson M. (2005). *Liquid candy: How soft drinks are harming Americans' health.* Washington, DC: Center for Science in the Public Interest

Johnson C, Drgon T, Liu QR, et al. (2006). Pooled association genome scanning for alcohol dependence using 104 268 SNPs: validation and use to identify alcoholism vulnerability loci in unrelated individuals from the collaborative study on the genetics of alcoholism. *Am J Med Genet B* 141(8):844–53

Kagan J. (2007). *What is emotion: History measures and meanings* London: Yale University Press

Kaplan H, Sadock B. (1998) *Synopsis of psychiatry* (8th edn). Baltimore: Williams and Wilkins

Kaufman M. (1999). Fighting the cola wars in schools. *Washington Post.* Mar. 23 1999. P. Z12

Kessler D. (2010). Obesity: The killer combination of salt, fat and sugar. *Guardian* 13 March

KidsAndAdvertising www.kidsandadvertising.co.uk, accessed October 2010

Krampe H, Stawicki S, Wagner T, et al. (2006). Follow-up of 180 alcoholic patients for up to 7 years after outpatient treatment: impact of alcohol deterrents on outcome. *Alcohol Clin Exp Res* 30(1):86–95

Lasater J. (1995). *Relax and renew: Restful yoga for stressful times.* Berkely, CA: Rodmell Press

Lazarus RS. (1966). *Psychological stress and the coping process.* New York: McGraw–Hill

Lister S. (2009). The price of alcohol: an extra 6000 early deaths a year. *The Times.* 19 October 2009

Ludwig DS, Peterson KE, Gortmaker SL. (2001). Relationship between consumption of sugar sweetened drinks and childhood obesity: a prospective observational analysis. *Lancet* 357:505–08

Mair J, et al. (2005). The use of zoning to restrict fast food outlets: A potential strategy to combat obesity. PublicHealthLaw.net

Marcus MD. (1995). Binge-eating and obesity. In: KD Brownell, CG Fairburn (eds). *Eating disorders and obesity: a comprehensive handbook*. New York: Guilford Press

Marmot Review. (2010). Fair Society, Healthy Lives: A Strategic Review of Health Inequalities in England Post-2010. www.marmot–review.org.uk

Marmot MGH, Bosma H, Hemingway E, et al. (1997). Contribution of job control and other risk factors to social variations in coronary heart disease incidence. *Lancet* 350(9073):235–39

MASO. (2009). Obesity and our environment. In: Malaysian Association for the Study of Obesity: Scientific Conference on Obesity (MASO 2009) 2–13 August 2009, Kuala Lumpur: pp441–44

McCarthy M. (2005). 'Star Wars' goes utterly commercial. *USA Today*. Apr. 25 2005. P. 2B

McHugh PR, Slavney PR. (1998). *The Perspectives of Psychiatry*. (2nd edn). Baltimore, MD: JHU Press

Mead M. (1935). *Sex and Temperament in Three Primitive Societies*. Harper Perennial, (republished 2001)

Meichenbaum D. (1996). Stress inoculation training for coping with stressors. *The Clinical Psychologist* 49:4–7

Menzies I. (1975). A case study in the functioning of social systems as a defence against anxiety. In: A Coleman, W Bexton (eds). *Group relations reader*. California: GREX

Minkler M. (1989). Health education, health promotion and the open society: an historical perspective. *Health Educ Behav* 16(1):17–30

NIOSH. (1999). *Stress at work*. US National Institute for Occupational Safety and Health DHHS (NIOSH). Publication Number 99–101

Nutt D, King LA, Saulsbury W, et al. (2007). Development of a rational scale to assess the harm of drugs of potential misuse. *Lancet* 369(9566):1047–53

Ofcom. (2003). Television advertising of food and drink products to children – Impact Assessment. www.ofcom.org.uk

Otto M, Aratani L. (2006). Soda ban means change at schools. *Washington Post*, retrieved 17 April 2010

Overstreet D. (2000). Twin study suggests genetic link between craving alcohol, sweets. University Of North Carolina At Chapel Hill. Cited in *Science Daily*, retrieved April 6 2010. www.sciencedaily.com/releases/2000/11/001107070216.htm

Ovisignkina MR. (1976). The redemption of interrupted activities. In: J de Rivera (ed.). *Field theory as human science: Contributions of Lewin's Berlin group*. New York: Garden Press

Perrow C. (1984). *The normal accident*. New York: Basic Books

Pinel J. (1993). *Biopsychology*. USA: Allyn & Bacon

Poulos CX, Zack M, (2004). Low-dose diazepam primes motivation for alcohol and alcohol-related semantic networks in problem drinkers. *Behav Pharmacol* 15(7):503–12

Powell GF, Brasel JA, Blizzard RM. (1967). Emotional deprivation and growth retardation simulating idiopathic hypopituitarism. Clinical evaluation of the syndrome. *N Engl J Med*. 276(23):1271–78

Prescott CA, Caldwell CB, Carey G, et al. (2005) The Washington University twin study of alcoholism. *Am J Med Genet B* 134B:48–55

Ravussin E. (1993). Energy-metabolism in obesity – studies in the Pima Indians. *Diabetes Care*. 16(1):232–38

Reed G. (1999). *Optimism protects bereaved HIV–positive men*. Cited in The American News Service

RHET (2002). BBC News. Bid to crack egg ignorance

Ronel N, Libman G. (2003). Eating disorders and recovery: Lessons from Overeaters Anonymous. *Clin Soc Work J* 31(2):155–71

Rosenstock IM. (1966). Why people use health services. *Milbank Meml Fund Q* 44(3):94–127

Rutter DR, Fielding PJ. (1988). Sources of occupational stress: an examination of British prison officers. *Work Stress* 2:291–99

Saffer H, Dave D. (2003). *Alcohol advertising and alcohol consumption by adolescents*. NBER Working Paper No. 9676. Cited in the Institute of Alcohol Studies fact sheet. www.ias.org.uk

Samia J, Pierce M, Teret S. (2005). *The use of zoning to restrict fast-food outlets*. The Center for Law and the Public's Health at Johns Hopkins & Georgetown Universities

Schlosser E. (2001). *Fast Food Nation*. New York: Houghton Mifflin Co

Selye H. (1956) *The Stress of Life*. New York: McGraw–Hill

Shute N. (1997). The drinking dilemma: by calling abstinence the only cure, we ensure that the nation's $100 billion alcohol problem won't be solved. *US News & World Report* 123(9):54–64. http://silkworth.net

Sinclair JD. (2001). Targeted use of naltrexone without prior detoxification in the treatment of alcohol dependence: A factorial double-blind placebo-controlled trial. *J Clin Pharmacol* 21(3):287–92. http://journals.lww.com

Snyder LB, Milici FF, Slater M, et al. (2006). Effects of alcohol advertising exposure on drinking among youth. *Arch Pediat Adol Med* 160:18–24. Cited in the Institute of Alcohol Studies fact sheet. www.ias.org.uk

Srinivasan R, Berenson G, Freedman D, et al. (2005). The relation of childhood BMI to adult adiposity: The Bogalusa heart study. *Pediatrics* 115(1): 22-27 (doi:10.1542/peds.2004-0220)

Stone A, Reed B, Neale J. (1987). Changes in daily event frequency precede episodes of physical symptoms. *J Hum Stress* 13:70–74

Tache J, Selye H, Day S. (1979). *Cancer Stress and Death.* New York: Plenum Press

Tavakoli HA. (2009). A closer evaluation of current methods in psychiatric assessments: a challenge for the biopsychosocial model. *Psychiatry (Edgmont)* 6(2):25–30. www.ncbi.nlm.nih.gov

Taylor SE, Brown J. (1988). Illusion and well–being: A social psychological perspective on mental health. *Psychol Bull* 103:193–210

Theorell T, Knox S, Svensson J, et al. (1985). Blood pressure variations during a working day at age 28: Effects of different types of work and blood pressure level at age 18. *J Hum Stress* 11:36–41

VandenBos GR. (2007). *APA dictionary of psychology* (1st edn). Washington, DC: American Psychological Association

Westphal VK, Smith JE. (1996). Overeaters Anonymous: Who goes and who succeeds? *Eating Disorders* 4(2):160–70

Which? (2010). www.which.co.uk/advice/marketing-fast-food-to-kids/fast-food-chains-investigated/index.jsp

Wilkinson E. (2005). Grandparents who care for children 'boost obesity risk'. www.news.bbc.co.uk/2/hi/health/8513112.stm

 Psychology of human relationships

Ahmad S, Reid DW. (2008). Relationship satisfaction among South Asian Canadians: The role of 'complementary–equality' and listening to understand. *Special Issue: Relationship Research in India and South Asia – Interpersona* 2(2):131–50

Amato PR. (1986). Emotional arousal and helping in a real-life emergency. *J Appl Soc Psychol* 16:633–41

Aronson E, Cope V. (1968). My enemy's enemy is my friend. *J Pers Soc Psychol* 8:8–12

Aronson E, Linder D. (1965). Gain and loss of esteem as determinants of interpersonal attractiveness. *J Exp Soc Psychol* 1:156–71

Batson CD, O'Quin K, Fultz J, et al. (1983). Influence of self-reported distress and empathy on egoistic versus altruistic motivation to help. *J Pers Soc Psychol* 45(3):706–18

Batson CD. (1991). *The altruism question: Toward a social psychological answer*. Hillsdale, NJ: Lawrence Erlbaum Associates

Berkowitz L. (1987). Mood self-awareness and willingness to help. *J Pers Soc Psychol* 52:721–29

Brozo WG, Walter P, Placker T. (2002). 'I know the difference between a real man and a TV man': A critical exploration of violence and masculinity through literature in a junior high school in the 'hood. *J Adolesc Adult Lit* 45(6):530–38

Burnstein E, Crandall C, Kitayama S. (1994). Some neo–Darwinian decision rules for altruism: Weighing cues for inclusive fitness as a function of the biological importance of the decision. *J Pers Soc Psychol*. 67(5):773–78

Buss DM. (1990). Evolutionary social psychology: prospects and pitfalls. *Motiv Emot* 14:265–86

Buss DM. (1994). *The evolution of desire: Strategies of human mating.* : New York: Basic Books

Byrne D, Clore GL. (1970). A reinforcement model of evaluative processes. *Personality: an International Journal* 1:103–28

Cahn N. (2006). Child witnessing of domestic violence. *Handbook of children culture and violence*. Sage Publications

Canary DJ, Dainton M. (2003). *Maintaining relationships through communication: Relational contextual and cultural variations*. Hillsdale, NJ: Lawrence Erlbaum

Canary DJ, Stafford L. (1992). Relational maintenance strategies and equity in marriage. *Commun Monogr* 59:239–267

Canary DJ, Stafford L. (1994). *Communication and relational maintenance.* New York: Academic Press

Cohen D, Nisbett RE, Bowdle F, et al. (1996). Insult, aggression and the southern culture of honor: an 'experimental ethnography'. *J Pers Soc Psychol* 70(5):945–60

Darley J, Latané B. (1968). When will people help in a crisis? *Psychol Today* 2:54–57,70–71

Darley JME, Berscheid E. (1967). Increased liking caused by the anticipation of personal contact. *Hum Relat* 20:29–40

Deaux K, Hanna R. (1984). Courtship in the personals column: The influence of gender and sexual orientation. *Sex Roles* 11:363–75

Dindia K, Canary D (eds). (2006). *Sex differences and similarities in communication* (2nd edn). Mahwah, NJ: Erlbaum

Dindia K, Canary DJ. (1993). Definitions and theoretical perspectives on maintaining relationships. *J Pers Soc Psychol* 10:163–73

Dittes JE, Kelley HH. (1956). Effects of different conditions of acceptance upon conformity to group norms. *J Abnorm Soc Psychol* 56:100–07

Duck S. (1985). Social and personal relationships. In: ML Knapp and GR Miller (eds). *Handbook of Interpersonal Communication*. (pp665–86). Beverly Hills, CA: Sage

Duck SW. (1982). A topography of relationship disengagement and dissolution. In: SW Duck (ed.). *Personal Relationships 4: Dissolving Personal Relationships*. (pp1–30). London: Academic Press

Duck SW. (1988). *Relating to others*. Chicago: Dorsey

Dutton DG, Ogloff JRP, Hart SD, et al. (1997). Wife assault treatment and criminal recidivism: An eleven-year follow up. *Int J Offender Ther* 41(1):9–23

Edleson EL. (1999). Children's witnessing of adult domestic violence. *J Pers Soc Psychol*. 14(8):839–70

Edleson J. (2000). *Primary prevention and domestic violence*. Paper presented at National Collaborative Violence Prevention Initiative Meeting hosted by Family Violence Prevention Fund, 15 February 2000

Festinger L, Schachter S, Back I. (1950). *Social pressures in informal groups: A study of human factors in housing*. Stanford, CA: Stanford University Press

Fite JE, Bates JE, Holtzworth–Munroe A, et al. (2008). Social information processing mediates the intergenerational transmission of aggressiveness in romantic relationships. *J Fam Psychol* 22(3):367–76

Gottman JM, Murray JD, Swanson C, et al. (2003). *The mathematics of marriage: Dynamic nonlinear models*. MIT Press

Gross AE, Crofton C. (1977). What is good is beautiful. *Sociometry* 40:85–90

Huesmann LR, Eron LD, Lefkowitz MM, et al. (1984). Stability of aggression over time and generations. *Dev Psychol* 20(6):1120–34

Huston TL, Ruggiero M, Conne R, et al. (1981). Bystander intervention into a crime: A study based on naturally occurring episodes. *Soc Psychol Quart* 44:14–23

Jorgensen BW, Cervone JC. (1978). Affect enhancement in the pseudorecognition task. *Pers Soc Psychol Bull* 4(2):285

Kenrick DT, Gutierres SE. (1980). Contrast effect and judgements of physical attractiveness. *J Pers Soc Psychol* 38:131–40

Knapp ML, Vangelisti AL. (1996). *Interpersonal communication and human relationships* (3rd edn). Boston: Allyn &Bacon

Koverola C, Murtaugh C. (2006). Domestic violence. In: Y Jackson (ed.). *Encyclopedia of multicultural psychology*. Sage

Kurdek LA. (1991). The dissolution of gay and lesbian couples. *J Soc Pers Relat* 8:265–78

Latané B, Darley JM. (1970). *The unresponsive bystander: Why doesn't he help?* New York: Appleton–Century–Crofts

Latané B, Darley JM. (1976). *Help in a crisis: Bystander response to an emergency*. Morristown, NJ: General Learning Press

Latané B, Rodin J. (1969). A lady in distress: Inhibiting effects of friends and strangers on bystander intervention. *J Exp Soc Psychol* 5:189–202

Levine RM, Prosser A, Evans D, et al. (2005). Identity and emergency intervention: How social group membership and inclusiveness of group boundaries shape helping behavior. *Pers Soc Psychol Bull* 31: 443–53

Levine RV, Norenzayan A, Philbrick K. (2001). Cross-cultural differences in helping strangers. *J Cross Cult Psychol* 32:543–560

Levinger G. (1980). Toward the analysis of close relationships. *J Expl Soc Psychol* 16:510–44

Lewicki P. (1985). Nonconscious biasing effects of single instances on subsequent judgments. *J Pers Soc Psychol* 48(3):563–74

Madsen EA, Tunney RJ, Fieldman G, et al. (2007). Kinship and altruism: A cross-cultural experimental study. *Brit J Psychol* 98(2):339–59

Mita TH, Dermer M, Lmogjt J. (1977). Reversed facial images and the mere-exposure hypothesis. *J Pers Soc Psychol* 35:597–01

Moreland RL, R Beach. (1992). Exposure effects in the classroom: The development of affinity among students. *J Exp Soc Psychol* 28:255–76

National Research Council. (1998). R Chalk and R King (eds). *Violence in families: Assessing Prevention and Treatment Programs*. Washington, DC: National Academy Press

Pantin HM, Carver CS. (1982). Induced competence and the bystander effect. *J Appl Soc Psychol* 12(2:100–11

Piliavin IM, Rodin J, Piliavin JA. (1969). Good Samaritanism: An underground phenomenon? *J Exp Soc Psychol* 13:289–99

Piliavin JA, Dovidio JF, Gaertner SL, et al. (1981). *Emergency intervention*. New York: Academic Press

Przybyla DPJ. (1985). *The facilitating effects of exposure to erotica on male pro-social behavior*. Unpublished doctoral dissertation. University of NY at Albany

Rhodes KV, Lauderdale DS, He T, et al. (2002). 'Between me and the computer': Increased detection of intimate partner violence using a computer questionnaire. *Ann Emerg Med* 40(5):476–84

Roberts AR. (2002). *Handbook of domestic violence intervention strategies: policies programs and legal remedies*. New York: OUP

Robertson N. (1999). Stopping Violence programmes: enhancing the safety of battered women or producing better-educated batterers? *New Zeal J Psychol* 28(2):68–78

Rosenbaum A, O'Leary KD. (1981). Marital violence: Characteristics of abusive couples. *J Consult Clin Psychol* 49:63–71

Saunders DG. (1986). When battered women use violence: husband-abuse or self-defense? *Violence and Victims* 1(1): 47–60

Seligman ME, Maier SF. (1967). Failure to escape traumatic shock. *J Exp Psychol* 74(1):1–9

Shepard M. (1992). Predicting batterer recidivism five years after community intervention. *J Fam Violence* 7(3):167–78

Sherif M. (1966). *In common predicament: Social psychology of intergroup conflict and cooperation.* Boston: Houghton Mifflin

Sime JD. (1983). Affiliative behavior during escape to building exits. *J Environ Psychol* 3:21–41

Simpson JA, Kenrick DT. (1997). *Evolutionary social psychology.* Mahwah, NJ: Erlbaum

Singh D. (1994). Is thin really beautiful and good? Relationship between waist-to-hip ratio (WHR) and female attractiveness. *Pers Indiv Differ* 16(1):123–32

Smithey M, Straus A. (2004). Primary prevention of intimate partner violence. In: H Kury and J Obergfell–Fuchs (eds). *Crime prevention – New approaches.* Mainz, Germany: Weisser Ring Gemeinnutzige Verlags-GmbH

Sterling B. S, Gaertner S. L. (1983). The effects of anger on helping behavior. *Acad Psychol B* 5:221–27

Suedfeld P, Bochner S, Wnek D. (1972). Helper–sufferer similarity and a specific request for help: Bystander intervention during a peace demonstration. *J Appl Soc Psychol* 2:17–23

Tannen D. (2009). *You were always Mom's favourite.* NY: Random House

Tavris C, Aronson E. (2007). *Mistakes were made (but not by me): Why we justify foolish beliefs, bad decisions and hurtful acts.* Orlando, FL: Harcourt

Tedeschi JT, Felson RB. (1994). *Violence aggression and coercive actions.* Washington, DC: American Psychological Association

Toi M, Batson CD. (1982). More evidence that empathy is a source of altruistic motivation. *J Pers Soc Psychol* 43(2):281–92

Turnbull CM. (1972). *The mountain people.* New York: Simon & Schuster

Wedekind C, et al. (1995). MHC-dependent preferences in humans. *P R Soc London* 260:245–49

Weigel DJ, Ballard–Reisch DS. (1999). The influence of marital duration on the use of relationship maintenance behaviours. *Communication Reports* 12(2):59–70

Whiting BB, Whiting JWM. (1975). Children of six cultures: A psycho-cultural analysis. Cambridge, MA: Harvard University Press

Williams TM (ed.). (1986). *The impact of television: A natural experiment in three communities.* New York: Academic Press

Wood W, Wong FY, Chachere JG. (1991). Effects of media violence on viewers' aggression in unconstrained social interaction. *Psycholl Bull* 109(3):371–83

Yelsma P, Athappilly K. (1988). Marital satisfaction and communication practices: Comparisons among Indian and American couples. *J Comp Fam Stud* 19(1):37–54

Zajonc RB. (1968). The attitudinal effects of mere exposure. *J Pers Soc Psychol* 9(2):1–27

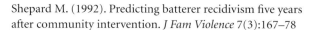

9 Sport psychology

Aglioti SM, Cesari P, Romani M, et al. (2008). Action anticipation and motor resonance in elite basketball players. *Nat Neurosci* 11:1109–16

Baker J, Cote J, Hawes R. (2000). The relationship between coaching behaviours and sport anxiety in athletes. *J Sci Med Sport* 3(2):100–19

Balaguer I, Duda JL, Atienza FL, et al. (2002). Situational and dispositional goals as predictors of perceptions of individual and team improvement satisfaction and coach ratings among elite female handball teams. *Psychol Sport Exerc* 3:293–08

Bandura A. (1977). Self-efficacy: Toward a unifying theory of behavioral change *Psychol Rev* 84:191–215

Bandura A. (1997). *Self-efficacy: The exercise of control.* New York: Freeman

Baumeister RF. (1984). Choking under pressure: Self-consciousness and paradoxical effects of incentives on skillful performance. *J Pers Soc Psychol* 46:610–20

Blanchard CM, Amiot EE, Perreault RJ, et al. (2009). Cohesiveness coach's interpersonal style and psychological needs: Their effects on self-determination and athletes' subjective well-being. *Psychol Sport Exerc* 10(5):545–51

Bloodworth A, McNamee M. (2010). Clean Olympians? Doping and anti–doping: The views of talented young British athletes. *Int J Drug Policy* 21(4):276–82

Burns BD, Corpus B. (2004). Randomness and inductions from streaks: 'Gambler's Fallacy' versus 'Hot Hand'. *Psychonom B Rev* 11(1):179–84

Cameron J, Banko KM, Pierce WD. (2001). Pervasive negative effects of rewards on intrinsic motivation: The myth continues. *Behav Analyst* 24:1–44

Cameron J, Pierce WD, Banko KM, et al. (2005). Achievement-based rewards and instinsic motivation: A test of cognitive mediators. *J Educ Psychol* 97(4):641–55

Carron AV, Brawley LR, Widmeyer WN. (1998). Measurement of cohesion in sport and exercise. In: JL Duda (ed.) *Advances in sport and exercise psychology measurement* (pp213–26). Morgantown, WV: Fitness Information Technology

Carron AV, Colma MM, Wheeler J, et al. (2002). Cohesion and performance in sport: A meta-analysis. *J Sport Exerc Psychol* 24(2):169–88

Carron AV, Spink KS. (1993). Team building in an exercise setting. *Sport Psychol* 7(1):8

Cresswell SL, Eklund RC. (2004). The athlete burnout syndrome: possible early signs. *J Sci Med Sport* 7(4):481–87

Cresswell SL, Eklund RC. (2006). Changes in athlete burnout over a thirty-week 'rugby year'. *J Sci Med Sport* 9(1):125–34

Cresswell SL. (2009). Possible early signs of athlete burnout. *J Sci Med Sport* 12(3):393–98

Dawes H, Roach NK. (1997). Emotional responses of athletes to injury and treatment. *Physiotherapy.* 83(5):243–48

Decety J, Ingvar DH. (1990). Brain structures participating in mental simulation of motor behavior: a neuropsychological interpretation. *Acta Psychol* 73:13–34

Deschaumes–Molinaro C, Dittmar A, Vernet–Maury E. (1991). Relationship between mental imagery and sporting performance. *Behav Brain Res* 45:29–36

Duda JL, Nicholls JG. (1992). Dimensions of achievement motivation in schoolwork and sport. *Journal of Educational Psychology* 84:290–99

Ehrnborg C, Rosen T. (2009). The psychology behind doping in sport. *Growth Horm IGF Res* 19(4):285–87

Eriksson S, Railo W, Matson H. (2002). *Sven–Goran Eriksson on management: the inner game – improving performance.* London: Carlton

Fournier JF, Deremaux S, Bernier M. (2008) Content characteristics and function of mental images. *Psychol Sport Exerc* 9:734–748

Fraser–Thomas J, Côté J, Deakin J. (2008). Understanding dropout and prolonged engagement in adolescent competitive sport. *Psychol Sport Exerc* 9:645–62

Gammage KL, Carron AV, Estabrooks PA. (2001). Team cohesion and individual productivity: the influence of the norm for productivity and the identifiability of individual effort. *Small Gr Res* 32(1):3–18

Gilovich T, Vallone R, Tversky A. (1985). The hot hand in basketball: On the misperception of random sequences. *Cognitive Psychol* 17:295–314

Grieve FG, Whelan JP, Meyers AW. (2000). An experimental examination of the cohesion–performance relationship in an interactive team sport. *J Appl Sport Psychol* 12(2):219–35

Gustafsson H, Hassimen P, Kenttä G, et al. (2008). A qualitative analysis of burnout in elite Swedish athletes. *Psychol Sport Exerc* 9(6):800–16

Hanin YL. (1997). Emotions and athletic performance: Individual zones of optimal functioning model. *European Yearbook of Sport Psychology* 1:29–72

Hanrahan SJ, Cerin E. (2009). Gender level of participation and type of sport: Differences in achievement goal orientation and attributional style. *J Sci Med Sport* 12:508–12

Hardy L, Fazey J. (1987). The inverted–U hypothesis: a catastrophe for sport psychology? Communication to the Annual Conference of the North American Society for the Psychology of Sport and Physical Activity, Vancouver BC Canada

Hardy L, Parfitt CG, Pates J. (1994). Performance catastrophes in sport: A test of the hysteresis hypothesis. *J Sports Sci* 12:327–34

Hardy L. (1999). Stress anxiety and performance. *J Sci Med Sport* 2:227–33

Hardy L. (2006). Speaking clearly: A critical review of the self-talk literature. *Psychol Sport Exerc* 7(1):81–97

Harris LL. (2003). Integrating and analyzing psychosocial and stage theories to challenge the development of the injured collegiate athlete. *J Athl Training* 38(1):75–82

Hatzigeorgiadis A, Zourbanos N, Mpoumpaki S, et al. (2009). Mechanisms underlying the self-talk–performance relationship: The effects of motivational self-talk on self-confidence and anxiety. *Psychol Sport Exerc* 10:186–92

Hollembeak J, Amorose AJ. (2005). Perceived coaching behaviors and college athletes' intrinsic motivation: A test of self-determination theory. *J Appl Sport Psychol* 17:20–36

Hull CL. (1943). *Principles of behavior.* New York: Appleton–Century

Jones L, Stuth G. (1997). The uses of mental imagery in athletics: an overview. *Applied and Preventative Psychology.* 6(2):101–15

Jowett S, Cockerill IM. (2003). Olympic medallists' perspective of the athlete–coach relationship. *Psychol Sport Exerc* 4:313–31

Kaiseler M, Polman R, Nicholls A. (2009). Mental toughness, stress, stress appraisal, coping and coping effectiveness in sport. *Pers Indiv Differ* 47(7):728–33

Keegan RJ, Harwood CG, Spray CM, et al. (2009). A qualitative investigation exploring the motivational climate in early career sports participants: Coach parent and peer influences on sport motivation. *Psychol Sport Exerc* 10:361–72

Kimball A. (2007). 'You signed the line'. Collegiate student athletes' perception of autonomy. *Psychol Sport Exerc* 8(5):818–35

Kingston KM, Horrocks CM, Hanton S. (2006). Do multidimensional intrinsic and extrinsic motivational profiles discriminate between athletic scholarship status and gender? *Eur J Sport Sci* 6:53–63

Kubler–Ross E. (1969). *On Death and Dying: What the Dying Have to Teach Doctors, Nurses, Clergy, and Their Own Families.* New York: Macmillan

Latham GP, Locke EA. (2006). Enhancing the benefits and overcoming the pitfalls of goal setting. *Organ Dyn* 35:332–40

Lazarus RS, Folkman S. (1984). *Stress appraisal and coping.* New York: Springer

Lemyre PN, Robers GC, Stray–Gundersen J. (2007). Motivation overtraining and burnout: Can self-determined motivation predict overtraining and burnout in elite athletes? *Eur J Sport Sci* 7(2):115–26

Locke EA. (1991). The motivation sequence, the motivation hub and the motivation core. *Organ Behav Hum Dec* 50:288–99

Locke EA, Latham GP. (2006). New directions in goal-setting theory. Current directions in psychological science *Curr Dir Psychol Sci* 15(5):265–68

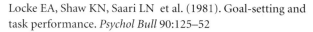

Locke EA, Shaw KN, Saari LN et al. (1981). Goal-setting and task performance. *Psychol Bull* 90:125–52

Marlow C, Bull SJ, Heath B, et al. (1998). The use of a single case design to investigate the effect of a pre–performance routine on the waterpolo penalty shot. *J Sci Med Sport* 1(3):143–55

Mellalieu SD, Hanton S, Thomas O. (2009). The effects of a motivational general-arousal imagery intervention upon preperformance symptoms in male rugby union players. *Psychol Sport Exerc* 10(1):175–85

Moran A. (2009). Attention concentration and thought management. In: B Brewer B (eds). *The Olympic handbook of sports medicine and science: sport psychology*. Oxford: Wiley–Blackwell

Nicholls J. G. (1989). *The competitive ethos and democratic education*. Cambridge MA: Harvard University Press

Ntoumanis N, Biddle SJH. (1998). The relationship between competitive anxiety achievement goals and motivational climates. *Res Q Exercise Sport* 69:176–87

Özdemir L, Nur N, Bagcivan I, et al. (2005). Doping and performance enhancing drug use in athletes living in Sivas mid-Anatolia: A brief report. *J Spors Sci Med* 4:248–52

Patterson M, Carron A, Loughead T. (2005). The influence of team norms on the cohesion–self-reported performance relationship: A multi–level analysis. *Psychol Sport Exerc* 6:479–93

Plessner H, Haar T. (2006). Sports performance judgments from a social cognitive perspective. *Psychol Sport Exerc* 7:555–75

Prapavessis H, Carron AV. (1997). Sacrifice cohesion and conformity to norms in sport teams. *Group Dynamics* 1(3):231–40

Raedeke TD. (1997). Is athlete burnout more than just stress? A sport commitment perspective. *J Sport Exercise Psy* 19(4):396–417

Raedeke TD. (2004). Coach commitment and burnout: A one-year follow-up. *J Appl Sport Psychol* 16(4):333–49

Raedeke TD, Lunney K, Venables K. (2002). Understanding athlete burnout: Coach perspectives. *Journal of Sport Behaviour* 25(2):181–206

Raglin JS, Turner PE. (1993). Anxiety and performance in track and field athletes: A comparison of the inverted-U hypothesis with zone of optimal function theory. *Pers Indiv Differ* 14:163–71

Reid M, Crespo M, Lay B, et al. (2007). Skill acquisition in tennis: Research and current practice. *J Sci Med Sport* 10:1–10

Ryan RM, Deci EL. (2000). The darker and brighter sides of human existence: basic psychological needs as a unifying concept. *Psychol Inq* 11(4):319–38

Ryan RM. (1982). Control and information in the intrapersonal sphere: An extension of cognitive evaluation theory. *J Pers Soc Psychol* 43:450–61

Schofield L, Mummery WK, Schofield G. (2005). Effects of a controlled pedometer-intervention trial for low-active adolescent girls. *Med Sci Sport Exer* 37(8):1414–20

Senecal J, Loughead TM, Bloom GA. (2008). A season-long team-building intervention: examining the effect of team goal setting on cohesion. *J Sport Exercise Psy* 30(2):186–99

Short SE, Short MW. (2005). Essay role of the coach in the coach–athlete relationship. *Lancet* 366:529–30

Silva ASR, Santhiago V, Papoti M, et al. (2008). Psychological biochemical and physiological responses of Brazilian soccer players during a training program. *Sci Sport* 23:66–72

Silva JM. (1990). An analysis of the training stress syndrome in competitive athletics. *J Appl Sport Psychol* 2(1):5–20

Sjoqvist F, Garle M, Rane A. (2008) Use of doping agents particularly anabolic steroids in sports and society. *Lancet* 371:1872–82

Smith AM, Malo SA, Laskowski ER, et al. (2000). A multidisciplinary study of the 'yips' phenomenon in golf: an exploratory analysis. *Sports Med* 30:423–37

Smith RE, Smoll EL, Curtis B. (1979). Coach effectiveness training: A cognitive–behavioral approach to enhancing relationship skills in youth sport coaches. *J Sport Psychol* 1:59–75

Smith RE. (1980). A cognitive–affective approach to stress management training for athletes. In: CH Nadeau, WR Halliwell, KM Newell, et al. (eds). *Psychology of motor behavior and sport*. Champaign, IL: Human Kinetics

Smith RE. (1986). Towards a cognitive–affective model of athletic burn-out. *J Sport Psychol* 8:36–50

Sonstroem RJ, Bernardo P. (1982). Intraindividual pregame state anxiety and basketball performance: a reexamination of the inverted–U curve. *J Sport Psychol* 4:235–45

Spence KW. (1956). *Behavior theory and conditioning*. New Haven, Conn: Yale University Press

Spink KS, Wilson KS, Odnokon P. (2010). Examining the relationship between cohesion and return to team in elite athletes. *Psychol Sport Exerc* 11(1):6–11

Steinberg G, Singer R, Murphey M. (2000). The benefits to sport achievement when a multiple goal orientation is emphasised. *Journal of Sport Behaviour* 23(4):407–22

Striegel H, Ulrich R, Simon P. (2010) Randomised response estimates for doping and illicit drug use in elite athletes. *Drug Alcohol Depen* 106(2–3):230–32

Thatcher J, Day MC. (2008). Re-appraising stress appraisals: The underlying properties of stress in sport. *Psychol Sport Exerc* 9(3):318–35

Udry E, Gould D, Bridges D, et al. (1997). Down but not out: Athlete response to season-ending injuries. *J Sport Exercise Psy* 19(3):229–48

van Raalte JL, Brewer BW, Rivera PM, et al. (1994). The relationship between observable self-talk and competitive junior tennis players' match performances. *J Sport Exercise Psy*. 16(4):400

Vazou S, Ntoumanis N, Duda JL. (2005). Peer motivational climate in youth sport: A qualitative inquiry. *Psychol Sport Exerc* 6:497–516

Vergeer I. (2006). Exploring the mental representation of athletic injury: A longitudinal case study. *Psychol Sport Exercise* 7(1):99–114

Verroken M. (2000). Drug use and abuse in sport. *Clinical Endocrinology and Metabolism* 14(1):1–24

Weinberg RS, Gould D. (2003). *Foundations of sport and exercise psychology* (3rd edn). Champaign, IL: Human Kinetics

Wiese–Bjomstal D, Smith A. (1993). Counseling strategies for enhanced recovery of injured athletes within a team approach. In: D Pargman (ed.). *Psychological bases of sport injuries.* (pp149–82). Morgantown, WV: Fitness Information Technology

Wiese–Bjornstal DM, Smith AM., Shaffer SM, et al. (1998). An integrated model of response to sport injury: Psychological and sociological dynamics. *J Appl Sport Psychol* 10:46–69

Williams AM, Elliott D. (1999). Anxiety expertise and visual search in karate. *J Sport Exercise Psy* 21:361–74

Wortman CB, Silver RC. (1989). The myths of coping with loss. *J Consult Clin Psychol* 57:349–57

Wright MJ, Jackson RC. (2007). Brain regions concerned with perceptual skills in tennis: An fMRI study. *Int J Psychophysiol* 63:214–20

Zajonc RB. (1965). Social facilitation. *Science* 149:269–74

 # Theory of knowledge

American Psychological Association. (2009). The psychological impact of globalization. www.newswise.com/articles/view/550991/

Read J, Mosher LR, Bentall RP. (2004). *Models of madness – psychological social and biological approaches to schizophrenia.* London: Routledge

Sapolsky RM. (2000). *Why zebras don't get ulcers.* New York: Freeman and Co

Williams J, Keating F. (2005). Social inequalities and mental health. In: A Bell, P Lindley (eds). *Beyond the water towers: the unfinished revolution in mental health services 1985–2005.* London: Sainsbury Centre for Mental Health

RESEARCHERS' INDEX

GENERAL INDEX

A

abnormal psychology
  answer guidelines 358–60
  definition 144
  ethical issues 149
abnormality 145–8
  diathesis–stress model of abnormal behaviour 36, 61
absenteeism 26
abstract modelling 120
accomodation 184
acetylcholine 51, 53, 85–6
achievement goal theory 287–8, 291
active listening skills 31
adaptation 183–4
adenosine 52
adolescence 211–16
  biological approach 212–13
  cognitive approach 211
  identity crises 214–16
  sociocultural approach 211–12
adrenaline 54–5
Advertising Standards Authority (ASA) 228
affective disorders 165–74
aggression: social learning of 121–2
agoraphobia 162
Alcoholics Anonymous (AA) 229–31
alcoholism 146, 225–31
  biopsychosocial treatment (BPS) 232
  case formulations 232
  cognitive/sociocultural factors 226–8
  drug treatment 231
  perspectives model 232
  physiological factors 225–6
  social learning theory and 226, 227
alienation 220
altruism 252–6
  empathy–altruism hypothesis 253–5
  kin selection hypothesis 255–6
altruistic motivation 252
Alzheimer's disease (AD) 42, 43, 61, 84–7, 148
  amyloid plaques 86
  neurofibrillary tangles 86
American Association of University Women 213
American Psychiatric Association 148
American Psychological Association (APA) 325
  research guidelines 6–7
amnesia 44
amphetamines 307, 308, 309
amygdala 91
anabolic steroids 307, 308, 309–10
androgyny 206
animal research 36–7
anorexia nervosa 146, 151, 174–9
  diagnosis 174–5
  etiology: biological level of analysis 175–6
  etiology: cognitive level of analysis 176
  etiology: sociocultural level of analysis 176–7
  treatment 177–9
anterograde amnesia 44
antisocial behaviour 61
anxiety disorders 156–65
aphasia 40
appraisal 160–1
  conscious/unconscious 90–1
  emotion and 88–9
arousal 260–1
  autonomic 87, 90
  and bystanderism 260–1
  and emotion 55, 87–8, 89
  emotional 288, 289
  physiological 55, 87–8, 89
  in sport 293–5
arranged marriages 270–1
Asch paradigm 127
assessment *x*
  extended essays *xii*, 340–9
  internal *xii*, 328–39
assimilation 184
associative learning 67
attachment 194–9
attention 78
attention-deficit-hyperactivity-disorder (ADHD) 148
attraction 263–8
  biological origins 264–5
  social/cognitive origins 266–8
attribution errors 107–9
audience effects 21
audience inhibition 260
autonomic arousal 87, 90
autonomy
  emotional 220
  job autonomy 221
  and motivation 285–6
  personal 286
  relational 286

B

Barbie/Ken dolls 213
battered woman syndrome 279
behaviour
  culture and 134–9, 154–5
  genetics and 58–61
  influence of social/cultural environment 103
  and mental representations 69
  patterns of 36
  physiology and 50–8
  situational/dispositional factors in explanation of 104–7
behaviourism 67–8
benzodiazepines 163, 229
Berger, Hans 40
beta-blockers 309
binge eating disorder (BED) 239
biological level of analysis *ix*
  anorexia nervosa 175-6
  answer guidelines 353–5
  depression 167–8
  ethical issues 36–8, 64–5
  historical/cultural development 34
  phobias 158–60
  principles of 35–7
  research methods 37–8
biological sex 205
biomedical therapy
  for depression 171–2
  for phobias 163–4
biopsychosocial treatment (BPS) 232
Blau, Peter 273
Bleuler, Eugen 327
body image 212–13
Bowlby, John 195–6
brain function
  and environment 49
  localization of 39–41
  split-brain patients 45–6
brain-imaging technology 5
brain structure 48, 85
  amygdala 91
  corpus callosum 43, 45
  hippocampus 43, 44, 48, 80, 85
Briner, Rob 322
British Psychological Society (BPS): research guidelines 6–7
Broca, Paul 40, 45
Broca's aphasia 40
Bulger, Jamie 200